Piercing the Fog

Intelligence and Army Air Forces Operations in World War II

John F. Kreis
General Editor

with contributions by
Alexander S. Cochran, Jr.
Robert C. Ehrhart
Thomas A. Fabyanic
Robert F. Futrell
John F. Kreis
Williamson Murray

Air Force History and Museums Program
Bolling Air Force Base
Washington, D.C., 1996

FOREWORD

WHEN JAPAN ATTACKED PEARL HARBOR on December 7, 1941, and Germany and Italy joined Japan four days later in declaring war against the United States, intelligence essential for the Army Air Forces to conduct effective warfare in the European and Pacific theaters did not exist. *Piercing the Fog* tells the intriguing story of how airmen built intelligence organizations to collect and process information about the enemy and to produce and disseminate intelligence to decisionmakers and warfighters in the bloody, horrific crucible of war. Because the problems confronting and confounding air intelligence officers, planners, and operators fifty years ago still resonate, *Piercing the Fog* is particularly valuable for intelligence officers, planners, and operators today and for anyone concerned with acquiring and exploiting intelligence for successful air warfare. More than organizational history, this book reveals the indispensable and necessarily secret role intelligence plays in effectively waging war. It examines how World War II was a watershed period for Air Force Intelligence and for the acquisition and use of signals intelligence, photo reconnaissance intelligence, human resources intelligence, and scientific and technical intelligence.

Piercing the Fog discusses the development of new sources and methods of intelligence collection; requirements for intelligence at the strategic, operational, and tactical levels of warfare; intelligence to support missions for air superiority, interdiction, strategic bombardment, and air defense; the sharing of intelligence in a coalition and joint service environment; the acquisition of intelligence to assess bomb damage on a target-by-target basis and to measure progress in achieving campaign and war objectives; and the ability of military leaders to understand the intentions and capabilities of the enemy and to appreciate the pressures on intelligence officers to sometimes tell commanders what they think the commanders *want* to hear instead of what the intelligence *discloses*. The complex problems associated with intelligence to support strategic bombardment in the 1940s will strike some readers as uncannily prescient to global Air Force operations in the 1990s.

A half century ago, accurate, timely intelligence contributed significantly to victory and hastened the end of World War II. Such a legacy is worth reading and thinking about by all those responsible for building, maintaining, and employing air power. How well intelligence is integrated with air operations is

Foreword

even more important today than it was in the past. It will continue to prove as critical in the next century as it has been in this one.

RICHARD P. HALLION
Air Force Historian

PREFACE

THE MILITARY CALAMITY IN EUROPE in mid-1940 called into serious question the ability of Great Britain to survive before the German onslaught. The near collapse of the Soviet Union in late 1941 after Germany's invasion prompted President Franklin D. Roosevelt to conclude he would eventually have no choice but to take up active, declared participation in the conflict. Japan's attack on Pearl Harbor on December 7, followed by Hitler's declaration of war on the United States, decided the how and when. The Japanese attack not only plunged America into the war; the surprise of that attack underscored the woeful state of American military intelligence. Unable to meet the demands of field commanders and planners, military intelligence deficiencies imperiled efforts of the Army and Navy to defeat the enemies ranged against them worldwide.

The Army Air Forces (AAF) were particularly deficient in information about enemy air forces and targets, a situation prompted by the AAF's subsidiary position within the Army and by the limited understanding of the new art of air warfare. Improvements in that understanding and in the relationships between intelligence analysis and the use of its product in preparing first-rate offensive and defensive air and joint air-land-sea operations are the subject of this history.

This volume treats the wartime period between 1941 and 1945, although preliminary discussion explores the interwar era, a time when the U.S. Army Air Corps developed an air doctrine that would place such strenuous demands on air intelligence during World War II. For the wartime period, the study weighs the impact of air intelligence on doctrine, planning, strategy, tactics, resources, and joint and combined operations. This history addresses the various tools of intelligence including ULTRA, MAGIC, photointelligence, and Y intelligence. Human intelligence, the information from agents knowledgeable about enemy areas, is addressed in those geographical regions where it influenced air operations. In recounting events of the Pacific war, place names are spelled as they were at the time, and Japanese personal names are presented with the family name preceding the given name.

Works of this nature and magnitude are possible only with the generous assistance of a variety of institutions and individuals. The authors are indebted to the Yale University Library for permission to cite and quote from the Henry L. Stimson Diaries and to the helpful staffs at the Library of Congress,

Preface

Manuscript Division; the National Archives, Military Reference Branch, and the Washington National Records Center; The U.S. Army Military History Institute; the Air Force Historical Research Center; Air University Library; and the Reference Branch at the Air Force History Support Office. A special thanks is offered to those historians at the Air Force History Support Office who diligently read and critiqued the numerous early drafts and the publication division for turning draft work into final form.

Eagle Aviation Services and Technology, Inc. (EAST, Inc.), of Chantilly, Virginia, researched and wrote this book while under contract to the U.S. Air Force. The Office of the Assistant Chief of Staff, Intelligence, Headquarters, USAF, provided the funding, while the Air Force History and Museums Program served as executive agent for project oversight.

Special thanks are owed Maj. Gen. James C. Pfautz (USAF, Ret.), who sponsored and fully supported this project while serving as Assistant Chief of Air Staff, Intelligence, and to Richard H. Kohn, former Air Force Historian, who saw the work undertaken. It fell to the members of the final review panel to read the manuscript in its entirety, and to these people the authors owe special appreciation for their insights and advice. Richard G. Davis, Diane T. Putney, Herman Wolk, R. Cargill Hall, Eduard Mark, and Col. David Tretler represented the Office of Air Force History on the panel, while Richard Wolf participated from the Air Force Intelligence Agency. The panel's outside scholars included General Pfautz, who long believed that a historical analysis of this nature would be of interest to the informed public, B. Franklin Cooling of the Department of Energy, Ray Cline, formerly of the Office of Strategic Services and the Central Intelligence Agency, Capt. Roger Pineau (USN, Ret.), who served as an intelligence officer in the Pacific during World War II, Kenneth McDonald of the Central Intelligence Agency, and Edward J. Drea of the U.S. Army Center for Military History. The suggestions and perspective offered by the outside scholars were especially helpful.

The authors are indebted to Frank W. Anderson, former NASA deputy historian and an Air Force intelligence officer during World War II, for the substantive editorial support he brought to this project and to Barbara Wittig, project editor for this volume.

AUTHORS

ALEXANDER S. COCHRAN, Jr., teaches military history and strategy as a Professor of Military History at the Air War College, Maxwell Air Force Base, Alabama. He received a B.A. in history from Yale University and a Ph.D. in history from the University of Kansas. His publications include *The MAGIC Diplomatic Summaries* and *Lemnitzer: His Life and Times,* as well as numerous book chapters and articles on World War II strategy and intelligence.

Professor ROBERT C. EHRHART is editor and principal author of *Modern Warfare and Society,* coeditor of *Air Power and Warfare,* and author of several articles on military history and airpower doctrine. A twenty-year veteran of the U.S. Air Force, he holds a Ph.D. in history from the University of Texas at Austin and an M.S. in Forestry/Range Management from the University of Montana. He serves as a Visiting Assistant Professor at the University of Montana's School of Forestry.

THOMAS A. FABYANIC is President of Eagle Aviation Services and Technology (EAST), Inc. He is the author of *Strategic Air Attack in the United States Air Force: A Case Study* and of various chapters and articles on war, air doctrine, and military professionalism. He earned an M.A. and a Ph.D. in history at St. Louis University.

ROBERT FRANK FUTRELL holds a B.A. and an M.A. from the University of Mississippi and a Ph.D. from Vanderbilt University. During World War II, he served as a historian with the U.S. Army Air Forces at the AAF Tactical School and with the Far East Air Forces in the Philippines. He is the author of *The United States Air Force in Korea, 1950–1953; The United States Air Force in Southeast Asia, The Advisory Years to 1965;* and *Ideas, Concepts, Doctrine: A History of Basic Thinking in the United States Air Force.* He is also the author of numerous articles related to air power history. Before retirement, Futrell served for many years as a professor of military history at the Air University, Maxwell AFB, Alabama.

JOHN F. KREIS, a retired U.S. Air Force officer, is a historian and military and defense analyst as well as a Senior Fellow of the Air Force Historical Foundation. He holds a B.A. in economics from Willamette University, Salem, Oregon, and an M.A. in medieval history from the University of Delaware. He is the author of *Air Warfare and Air Base Air Defense, 1914–1973,* as well as numerous articles on air power history and operations.

Authors

WILLIAMSON MURRAY is Professor of History at The Ohio State University and an Intelligence Officer in the U.S. Air Force Reserve. Among his publications are *Military Effectiveness* (which he coauthored in three volumes); *Strategy for Defeat: The Luftwaffe, 1933–1945,* and the previous edition, *Luft-waffe*; and *The Change in the European Balance of Power, 1938–1939: The Path to Ruin.* He holds a B.A., an M.A., and a Ph.D. in history from Yale University.

TABLE OF CONTENTS

Page

FOREWORD iii
PREFACE v
AUTHORS vii

                    Introduction
                          John F. Kreis 1

Chapter 1   **Early Intelligence Organization in the Army Air Corps**
                          Thomas A. Fabyanic and Robert F. Futrell 11
                American Air Intelligence in World War I 12
                Air Intelligence in the 1920s 17
                Air Intelligence in the Early 1930s 20
                The Air Corps Tactical School and Air Intelligence 24
                Acquisition and Evaluation of Air Intelligence:
                      Developments in Europe and Asia 28
                The Approach of War 39
                AWPD-1: Planning an Air War 46
                Air Intelligence on the Eve of Pearl Harbor 51
                A Tentative Assessment 54

Chapter 2   **The Tools of Air Intelligence: ULTRA, MAGIC,**
               Photographic Assessment, and the Y-Service
                        Alexander S. Cochran, Jr., Robert C. Ehrhart, and
                          John F. Kreis 57
                ULTRA 59
                The Importance of ULTRA in the European Theater 74
                Photointelligence 80
                Y Intelligence 94
                ULTRA and MAGIC in the Pacific and CBI 99
                B Section 105
                Operational SIGINT and the Far East 106

Contents

Chapter 3	**Building an Air Intelligence Organization and the European Theater** *Robert C. Ehrhart, Thomas A. Fabyanic, and Robert F. Futrell* .... 111 Pearl Harbor and Implications for Air Intelligence .... 113 Creating the Office of the Assistant Chief of Air Staff, Intelligence .... 116 Air Intelligence Training .... 126 The Air War in Europe: Organizing Eighth Air Force's Intelligence .... 132 Eighth Air Force: Early Operations .... 140 Countering the German Air Force .... 146 Intelligence Implications for the Strategic Air Campaign in Europe .... 150 TORCH and Northwest Africa 157
Chapter 4	**The European Theater of Operations, 1943–1945** *Robert C. Ehrhart* .... 171 Mediterranean Theater: 1943–1945 .... 173 Strategic Air Operations in Europe: Spring 1943 to Spring 1944 .... 190 OVERLORD and Tactical Air Operations in Western Europe: 1944–1945 .... 224 Strategic Air Operations: Summer 1944 to Spring 1945 237
Chapter 5	**The Pacific and Far East, 1942–1945** *John F. Kreis* .... 247 The South and Southwest Pacific .... 249 Assessing the Watchers: The Allied View of Japanese Air Intelligence 292
Chapter 6	**Taking the Offensive: From China-Burma-India to the B–29 Campaign** *John F. Kreis* .... 297 China and the Fourteenth Air Force .... 312 The Central Pacific .... 324 B–29 Operations Against Japan 329

Contents

Chapter 7 **Planning the Defeat of Japan: The A–2 in Washington, 1943–1945**
John F. Kreis 349
Organization and Interservice Relationships 355
Army Air Forces' Y-Service 361
Far East Target Analysis 364
German and Japanese Interchanges and Implications
  for the War on Japan 371
Army Air Forces Intelligence and the Atomic Bomb .. 380
The Reorganization of 1945 389

Chapter 8 **Retrospection**
Williamson Murray 393
Doctrine, Intelligence, and Air Power: The Prewar
  Preparations 395
Intelligence and the Air War in Europe 401
Intelligence and the War in the Pacific 413
Conclusion 421

NOTES 425
GLOSSARY 465
BIBLIOGRAPHIC NOTE 469
SELECT BIBLIOGRAPHY 476
INDEX 483

PHOTOGRAPHS

Maj. Gen. Mason M. Patrick, Brig. Gen. William Mitchell 19
Brig. Gen. Haywood Hansell, Jr., Col. Grover C. Brown 49
Maj. Gen. Henry H. "Hap" Arnold 50
An Enigma machine 62
Lt. Gen. Elwood R. Quesada, Brig. Gen. Orvil A. Anderson, Maj. Gen.
  Frederick L. Anderson, Lt. Gen. O. P. Weyland 71
Maj. Gen. Hoyt S. Vandenberg, Maj. Gen. James H. Doolittle 72
Medmenham 86
Wing Commander Douglas Kendall, Lt. Col. William J. O'Connor;
  Aerial photo plotting 88

Contents

Brig. Gen. Ira C. Eaker, Capt. Elliot Roosevelt 91
Maj. Gen. Carl A. Spaatz 92
Brig. Gen. George C. McDonald 93
Maj. Gen. Muir S. Fairchild, Brig. Gen. Edgar P. Sorenson, Maj. Gen.
    Walter R. Weaver, Maj. Gen. George E. Stratemeyer 123
Col. Harris B. Hull 144
Lt. Gen. John K. Cannon, Col. Karl L. Polifka 179
Operation STRANGLE 186
Lt. Gen. Earle E. Partridge 187
The Combined Bomber Offensive 196–197
Oil campaign in Romania 210–211
Bombing offensive against the German rail system 214–215
The German V–1—V–2 effort 218–219
Operation OVERLORD 225
Lt. Gen. George C. Kenney, General Nathan F. Twining 254
Lt. Gen. Millard F. Harmon, Lieutenant Ennis C. Whitehead 258
Battle of the Bismarck Sea 266
Air attacks on Rabaul 273
Maj. Gen. Victor Bertrandais 282
Maj. Gen. Clayton L. Bissell 302
Air attacks on Japanese supply lines 316
Brig. Gen. Clinton D. Vincent; Bombing in China 319
Maj. Gen. Claire Chennault, Lt. Gen. Albert C. Wedemeyer 321
Maj. Gen. Willis H. Hale, Maj. Gen. Robert W. Douglass, Jr. 327
Maj. Gen. Laurence S. Kuter 330
Maj. Gen. Kenneth B. Wolfe, Brig. Gen. Curtis E. LeMay 336
Brig. Gen. Lauris Norstad 341
Tokyo fire-bomb raid 343
Col. Paul W. Tibbetts and the crew of the *Enola Gay* 345
Nagasaki mushroom cloud 347
General Thomas D. White, Maj. Gen. James P. Hodges 351
Maj. Gen. Howard C. Davidson 362
Maj. Gen. Richard C. Lindsay 379
P–38, F–13 419

MAPS

Western Mediterranean 159
Italy 185
German Air Industry Targets 193
P–47 Escort Ranges 198

Contents

P–38 and P–51 Escort Ranges 199
German Synthetic Oil Plants 200
CROSSBOW 217
Normandy 227
Pacific Ocean Areas 255
Southwest Pacific Battle Area 264
China–Burma–India 299
B–29 Bases 337

CHARTS

G–2, Southwest Pacific Area 260
Directorate of Intelligence, Fifth Air Force 262
Comparative Air Intelligence Functions in China–Burma–India 303
Relationship of Combined Photographic Interpretation Units to Eastern
    Air Command 309
A–2, U.S. Army Air Forces 356

INTRODUCTION

CREATING THE ARMY AIR FORCES' (AAF's) intelligence organization in World War II proved a complicated undertaking, requiring new skills and technologies to meet a host of demands. Fashioned and completed within four years, the novel enterprise helped shape the conduct and outcome of that conflict. Beginning the war with a handful of people pursuing information in Washington, air intelligence ended the war with thousands of men and women processing enormous amounts of data and analyzing millions of photographs for what would soon become America's newest and most technically oriented armed service.

Finding that his service had an inadequate understanding of potential enemy air forces, in May 1939 Maj. Gen. Henry H. "Hap" Arnold, Chief of the U.S. Army Air Corps,* began establishing personal contacts with those who might help provide it. That month Arnold met unobtrusively at West Point with Charles A. Lindbergh, the first man to fly solo across the Atlantic and recently returned from a celebrated tour of Germany. During the meeting, Arnold later noted, Lindbergh provided more information about the German Air Force's "equipment, apparent plans, leaders, training methods and present defects" than Arnold had as yet received from any other source.[1] The Army Air Corps began studying its intelligence requirements that summer, but it had hardly defined them before America entered World War II. Once in the conflict, in conjunction with other services and in different regions of the world, the AAF greatly increased its ability to collect, analyze, and disseminate the information and material that came to be called air intelligence.

Defining intelligence as it affected air operations was one of the first steps in creating an intelligence system. Air intelligence included all the information about an opponent and his military, air, and naval forces that could reduce risk or uncertainty in planning and conducting air combat operations. Commanders have always sought such information, but for the AAF the demands of intelligence gathering and analysis in World War II were beyond the ken of most of the officers who had served between the wars. When America formally

---

*The Army Air Corps became the AAF with an Air Staff in June 1941. With reorganization of the Army on March 9, 1942, the AAF became coequal with the Army Ground Forces and Army Services of Supply (later the Army Service Forces).

entered the war, air intelligence was needed for two types of air warfare: tactical and strategic. Tactical, or operational, air intelligence analysts working in the war theaters had to locate opposing enemy forces and attempt to define their size, combat capability, technology, and tactics. Analysts had to locate targets for the tactical air units that would support the plans of the joint air-ground or air-sea operations commander.

Strategic intelligence, similar in principle to its tactical counterpart, also required seeking, analyzing, and disseminating information beyond that needed to support the direct clash of opposing forces. In pursuing the Allies' World War II military aims, strategic air intelligence analysts attempted to identify German, Italian, and Japanese national war-making resources that could most effectively be attacked by a limited strategic bomber force. These intelligence studies also attempted to establish priorities to guide destruction of target groups as diverse as petroleum refining and distribution, transportation, aircraft assembly, and steel production. Despite the substantial and growing effort that airmen applied to this problem, target categories and priorities could not always be clearly defined, or agreed upon; uncertainty over what was critical to the enemy's wartime economy could never be completely eliminated.

Once the analytical process was reasonably complete, the information had to be imparted to commanding officers so that they might decide how best to concentrate and use the available air power. Air commanders, for a variety of reasons, might or might not be willing to accept an intelligence assessment. The intelligence officers identified the targets they believed should and could be attacked. But the capabilities of opposing air defenses could not always be determined precisely, and evidence to support any assessment had to be convincing. Many commanders exhibited a natural reluctance to accept another's suggestions or recommendations because a decision that proved wrong in combat could be disastrous to their command and career. Ego sometimes intervened, making it difficult for a commander to accept ideas counter to his preconceived notions. For intelligence officers, whether stationed in Washington, Europe, or the Far East, the first important task usually involved gaining the trust of the senior officer they served. Only then could their work begin to influence planning and operations.

To be effective, intelligence analysts had to produce information that was timely and useful to a commander. No matter how perceptively drawn the intelligence officers' observations might be, delay in preparation or dissemination could mean that an operations planning staff received the information too late. Adjusting to new demands for intelligence and learning to use intelligence products to best advantage did not always come quickly or easily to the AAF's officer corps.

Adding to the challenge, on December 7, 1941, the United States armed forces had no effective central intelligence organization responsible for collecting, analyzing, and disseminating data about enemies or potential

Introduction

enemies. The Army (War Department) and Navy (Navy Department) each provided for its own intelligence needs; the War Department's General Staff G–2, or Army Intelligence, also fulfilled AAF intelligence needs. The G–2 office had expanded from 22 people in 1939 to 500 in December 1941. With such rapid growth, few on the G–2 staff were proficient in intelligence work.[2] Before the war, the Air Staff had but a small office, the Information Division, only a part of which attempted to establish contacts with federal agencies able to provide facts and reports about foreign air power. Fewer than a dozen people formed this rudimentary air intelligence office.[3]

A good example of the inadequacy of the ramshackle prewar intelligence structure of the AAF can be seen in the preparation of the air requirements annex to the War Department's Victory Program, generally called AWPD–1. That air plan, drawn up by a small group of officers during the summer of 1941, was the initial AAF blueprint for air warfare during World War II. AWPD–1's basic premise was to secure victory in Europe by the application of enough high-altitude aerial bombardment to break down the industrial and economic structure of Germany while holding the Japanese at bay in the Far East. The plan envisioned destroying Germany's electric power production, her transportation system, and her ability to process petroleum and manufacture synthetic oil products. AWPD–1 was not an operations plan that laid out such things as logistics, command arrangements, and base assignments; rather, it stated the overall purposes of the air offensive and estimated the numbers and types of aircraft, the amount of bombs needed, the trained people and the overall time required, and the general target categories and numbers of installations to be attacked. After the war, Haywood S. Hansell, Jr., one of the plan's authors and an officer who had worked in Arnold's prewar air intelligence office, noted that not only was strategic intelligence sparse, but the planners had not realized what immense demands their air plan would make upon the wholly inexperienced air intelligence office. AWPD–1 itself made no provision for gathering target information, organizing photointerpretation to support the reconnaissance aircraft, or determining whether targets selected were the correct ones and whether attacks on them had actually achieved the hoped-for results.[4] In tactical air warfare, air intelligence specialists had to deal with a wide range of tactical problems.

The absence of a central, coordinated intelligence operation doubtless contributed to the disaster at Pearl Harbor and in the Philippine Islands, where in one day the Japanese destroyed virtually the whole of the AAF's strategic and tactical air capability in the Far East. Throughout the war, no central intelligence activity served either the armed forces or national policy. Prewar creation of the office of the Coordinator of Information (later called the Office of Strategic Services [OSS]) and the Joint Intelligence Committee of the Joint Army-Navy Board (later the Joint Chiefs of Staff [JCS]) were too little and far too late to solve the problem in the early years of fighting. The OSS was itself prevented from developing to its full potential. At no time during the war did any OSS office, including that of the director, receive deciphered code (ULTRA) material, except for a small amount from British sources. The full effects of the disparate and for the most part uncoordinated intelligence efforts varied greatly. Sometimes the services acted together, as in early 1944 when the U.S. Army, Navy, and AAF, in conjunction with the Royal Air Force (RAF), divided worldwide responsibilities for combined air intelligence. This division of labor essentially recognized existing activities and, by reducing duplication of effort and increasing the speed of work, partially solved a number of problems. Although the respective services gained the intelligence tasks they most preferred, the agreement did not address the core issue of central control of the collective work, nor did it solve the interservice or organizational problems faced by the air intelligence specialists in the various war theaters. Perhaps the extraordinary pressures of total war, the personalities of the leaders involved, and the conduct of certain sensitive activities—such as the highly secret cryptanalytical projects of the Army, Navy, Federal Bureau of Investigation, and Coast Guard—precluded any overarching, centrally controlled intelligence organization.

After the attack on Pearl Harbor and the Philippines, the need for adequate, reliable information about the enemy became at times desperate. Between December 1941 and May 1942, Japanese forces swept throughout Southeast Asia and threatened Australia and New Zealand. Having occupied the continent of Europe, German forces advanced on Moscow, while U-boats savaged Allied shipping in the Atlantic. Allied leaders clamored for an immediate air offensive against Germany. Responding to these conditions, the AAF's wartime intelligence effort, like the air arm itself, grew rapidly.

Early wartime conditions, to be sure, multiplied pressures on the young air intelligence officers, most of whom had no previous experience in this arcane business. They had to respond to demands for intelligence about combat conditions in almost a dozen theaters of war. Responses to the demands for intelligence in each region of conflict, as one might imagine, varied greatly. No theater air force was the equivalent of any other in terms of its size, mission, organization, personnel, fighting experience, or in its allocation of aircraft and weapons. So no air intelligence office in any theater working for a major air commander was quite like any other.

The Assistant Chief of Air Staff (AC/AS), Intelligence, or A–2, supervised all of the field intelligence operations, though exercising no direct control over units in the field. This office did have specific duties in support of General Arnold, of the Twentieth Air Force, and of other Air Staff offices.[5] For the field, the A–2 provided such things as target folders, area studies, maps, and related materials. The A–2 also coordinated the assignments of trained intelligence specialists, directed the operation of stateside intelligence training programs,

Introduction

and dealt with the other services or agencies that supported air intelligence around the world.

Two numbered air forces far removed from one another illustrate the differences that far-flung air intelligence officers experienced. Facing the *Luftwaffe,* the Eighth Air Force in Great Britain could draw on the RAF's years of air intelligence experience and on the products of ULTRA's penetration of the German Enigma encryption device. From the earliest days of American air operations in Europe, the Eighth's intelligence office (and then that of the U.S. Strategic Air Forces in Europe [USSTAF]) possessed advantages unknown to airmen in the same line of work in other theaters. Across the Pacific Ocean, facing Japan's army and naval air forces, the Fifth Air Force in Australia and New Guinea had built its air intelligence on the slim base of trained Australian specialists and the experience of some American airmen who had escaped from the Philippines and the Netherlands East Indies. The Japanese encryption methods, particularly those of the Japanese Army, proved extremely difficult to penetrate, and ULTRA sources in that region were for many months limited to extracts from the MAGIC diplomatic summaries and to the fruits of U.S. Navy intelligence efforts in Honolulu, where direction finding, traffic analysis, and entry into some of the Japanese Navy's encryption systems shed light on some of the enemy's important capabilities and intentions. The size and tasks of air intelligence in Alaska, China, India, Egypt, or the Central Pacific had to be tailored to fit the needs of the local Allied command structure and the enemy situation.

Nor did the number of people assigned in one locale reflect the extent of the problems addressed or accomplishments made by air intelligence elsewhere. Differences in enemy forces, climate and terrain, commander's priorities, chain of command, availability of information, and the application of new technology—all created different circumstances that affected the local A–2's involvement in planning, strategy, and tactics. For example, the RAF's practical experience in aerial photography operations, its excellent cameras and reconnaissance aircraft, and, above all, the skilled photointerpreters at RAF Medmenham (the main British photoreconnaissance center) strongly influenced creation of a similar and highly productive AAF effort in the British Isles. Interwar American photographic experimentation had resulted in development of the wide-angle strip camera excellent for terrain mapping, the long-distance oblique camera, and high-altitude cameras plus a wide variety of film. The RAF and the AAF were ideally suited in the advantages each brought to the Alliance.[6] Photoreconnaissance and photointerpretation became extremely important tools for air and ground intelligence everywhere, but, until 1944, in no other theater were its practitioners as proficient as the American and British Allies in the United Kingdom.

When American air officers in Great Britain realized the importance of photointelligence to tactical and strategic bombardment, they were convinced that no modern air force could operate without it. That meant the AAF needed its own photoreconnaissance organization, if for no other reason than to avoid dependence on another service or country for this critical intelligence. That conviction grew among Eighth Air Force leaders, a conviction later conveyed to Washington: the service had to develop its own photointelligence resources to support an eventual, separate air force.

In Washington, the air intelligence function had its first reorganization in March 1943. To focus and concentrate intelligence under a single officer, the AAF disbanded the Air Staff intelligence operations unit—the Air Forces Intelligence Service—subsuming much of their work in an expanded A–2. General Arnold soon changed the direction of air operations intelligence studies and air operations planning when he created the Committee of Operations Analysts (COA). The COA, as it became known, drew on intelligence information from many sources, including A–2, to determine target priorities for Germany and, later, for Japan. That these priorities, in hindsight, were not always the most appropriate ones does not gainsay the times when they were correct nor the importance of a focused attempt to seek the most effective answers to the most difficult questions involving the employment of strategic air power.

The COA, although independent of A–2, became one of the primary users of air intelligence material as it drew up target category recommendations aimed at destroying German industry and Hitler's military. Despite the efforts of the COA and the OSS's Enemy Objectives Unit (EOU) in London, unforeseen technical difficulties associated with high-altitude precision daylight bombardment and German air defenses forced changes in the strategic bombardment planning. In 1944 the COA turned its attention to a similar effort directed at Japan. In the Orient, persistently inclement weather and high winds aloft (i.e., the jet stream) over the Japanese home islands likewise prompted changes in strategic bombing tactics.[7] These unanticipated problems only intensified air intelligence efforts; among many AAF leaders, strategic bombing doctrine remained virtually an article of faith.

General Arnold's decision to organize the COA marked a significant change in the AAF's recognition and acceptance of air intelligence. The AAF's commanding general realized the importance of a target plan that would ensure the best use of American strategic bombers to destroy an enemy's capacity to wage war. Creation of the strategic bombardment forces had, after all, rivaled or exceeded the investment in the Manhattan Project. Arnold drove his people relentlessly throughout the war; he knew that the fortunes of a postwar air force rested on how well he and his service met the war's demands, and on demonstrating air power's importance in ending the war as rapidly as possible.

Enlisting experts from outside the AAF—using businessmen, scholars, and engineers to analyze prospective target systems—was typical of Arnold. He did much the same thing for AAF scientific research, enlisting scientists first under

Introduction

the direction of Edward L. Bowles, head of the communications division of the department of electrical engineering at the Massachusetts Institute of Technology, and later the aerodynamics expert, Theodore von Kármán, of the California Institute of Technology.[8] But the existence of COA, independent of the Air Staff, was to many air intelligence officers an indictment of their work, showing that Arnold did not trust his own A–2 to undertake the targeting assignment—at least that was the impression of Brig. Gen. Edgar Sorenson, chief of A–2 at that time.

If the hesitancy of the commanding general to place full faith and trust in his intelligence specialists meant that he judged the young air force to be short of all the skills needed for independence, it surely implied that A–2 lacked public and professional stature. Perhaps this accounted for the frequent changes in the wartime officers assigned as AC/AS, Intelligence. It may also have kept A–2 from competing effectively with the other service intelligence chiefs for the resources available, thus leaving the AAF at an operational and political disadvantage.

Air intelligence within the AAF did compete with other service intelligence agencies. Turf scraps over roles, missions, and prerogatives continued throughout World War II and into the postwar period. The most prominent among the A–2's rivals, and the organization most reluctant to give the Air Staff's intelligence office an unfettered hand, was the War Department General Staff, G–2. The G–2 served as the main intelligence agency for the U.S. Army,[9] setting policy and controlling subordinate offices' activities and relationships with other agencies. Since the AAF was a branch of the Army, one or another of the G–2's components could be quick to perceive a future diminution of its own operation and, in classic bureaucratic fashion, refuse to affirm the need for an independent A–2, or even the need of the A–2 to conduct what easily might be recognized as pressing air intelligence duties. The enormous undertaking of the war eventually forced some bureaucratic moderation and increased autonomy for the A–2; the Army's main intelligence office, even with its own internal air intelligence unit, simply could not meet all of the demands for intelligence information.

Although G–2 staff offices gave up some of their control and allowed increased latitude of action for A–2 during the war, they always did so informally. The G–2 chief retained formal authority and responsibility for all Army intelligence matters, including those of the AAF. By war's end, the A–2 still existed rather ambiguously as a temporary wartime expedient. The frustrations of those who worked for air intelligence around the world, but most especially in Washington, reflected the general frustrations of many in the AAF who sought recognition as a separate and equal service.

Some in the AAF (and its A–2 office) unquestionably viewed the Army's ground officers (and its G–2) as a malevolent force intent on suppressing the air arm (and its intelligence function), but that perception was unfair. In some areas, the G–2 had good reason for refusing the A–2 freedom of action. The G–2's Military Intelligence Service never divulged to more than a few of A–2's most senior people (who were themselves prohibited from disclosing their knowledge) the nature and extent of the ULTRA interception and decryption system. That effort, pursued in conjunction with the British Government Code and Cypher School, was too important to risk compromising. Unfortunately for all concerned, the G–2's refusal to be open about its activities left feelings of uneasiness, deep frustration, and confusion among A–2 officers throughout the war.[10]

Such conflicts were not limited to the Army; serious interservice difficulties existed as well. For much of the war's early years, the rival Navy and Army cryptographers took potshots at one another. In March 1943, E. E. Stone of Naval Intelligence (OP–20–G, the Navy decrypting agency) wrote to the Director of Naval Communications, opposing the Army G–2's suggestion to merge Army and Navy radio intelligence. Stone remarked on the Army's frequent complaints that the Navy was not disclosing vital information by pointing out that it was information from Navy decrypts of Japanese messages that made possible the devastating success of General MacArthur's Fifth Air Force B–25s and Seventh Fleet PT boats at the battle of the Bismarck Sea. Stone went on to state, "As for General Strong's [Maj. Gen. George V. Strong, G–2] remarks concerning the fact that allocation agreement prevents the Army from working on material which is vital to it, the fact is the Army has accomplished practically nothing whatsoever in obtaining operational radio intelligence." To support his case, Stone claimed that the Navy had just taken over from the Army responsibility for a Japanese Army–Navy liaison cryptographic system used in the Southwest Pacific that the Army had been unable to solve in a year. Within a week, Stone said, "we made more advance than the Army [had] in twelve months."[11]

Making matters the more sensitive, soon after Pearl Harbor and the Battle of Midway, British officials had become uneasy; they did not believe Americans could be trusted with full knowledge of the ULTRA effort and the information it produced. The U.S. services were just too lax with security, the British believed. British distress increased when the U.S. Navy staged the "Yamamoto Mission" in April 1943; Great Britain temporarily broke off negotiations with American officials for sharing ULTRA and MAGIC information.[12] Not until the late spring of 1943 did a G–2 representative travel to London to be initiated into the closed world of the operational use of ULTRA. It was months later, perhaps not until early 1944, before General Arnold and his A–2 gained access to British ULTRA information sent to the G–2 from England.

Arnold learned about the *MAGIC Diplomatic Summaries* shortly after the attack on Pearl Harbor, but his formal knowledge of both the European and Far East versions of ULTRA, the Allies' most valuable World War II secret, came much later. In England, the staff of the Eighth Air Force, which planned and

Introduction

conducted the daylight strategic bombardment of Germany and occupied Europe, received information from the British cipher accomplishments at a much earlier date. Sworn to secrecy, those in the Eighth who knew could discuss the information with very few others engaged in the same tasks. In Washington, the Air Staff could claim no such need to know and it remained largely isolated from ULTRA information. Arnold seems to have learned about the secret independently, probably from a number of sources, including Maj. Gen. George C. Kenney home from the Southwest Pacific in March 1943, and from some of his Eighth Air Force officers in London. Many years after the war, General George C. Marshall's biographer recalled that Marshall told him that he never gave Arnold access ". . . to any of that [ULTRA] material. He found out on his own."[13] Ever the shrewd politician, Arnold knew that the information from ULTRA could advance the success of combat operations, and he used it to the advantage of his service.

At other times, U.S. Navy leaders conducting military operations in the Pacific sometimes seemed reluctant to release intelligence information to the AAF. But the Navy-dominated Joint Intelligence Center, Pacific Ocean Area, headquartered with the Commander-in-Chief Pacific, at Pearl Harbor, normally maintained harmonious relations with the largely U.S. Army–staffed Southwest Pacific Area Central Bureau in Brisbane, Australia. In early 1944, Great Britain and the United States divided air intelligence responsibilities between London (for the Axis powers in Europe) and Washington (for Japan). The American military services, in turn, subdivided responsibility for differing aspects of intelligence operations among the Navy, Army, and the AAF. Although still a combat arm of the Army, the AAF had considerable autonomy because of Arnold's status as a member of the JCS. The AAF became a recognized junior partner in the worldwide intelligence analysis enterprise.

The division of responsibilities in Washington worked to the AAF's long-term advantage, especially when the JCS created the Joint Target Group (JTG) in September 1944. Directing its attention primarily to target systems in Japan, but with a continuing side interest in Germany, the JTG functioned as a joint-service office within and under the auspices of the A–2. Having a predominant influence in the JTG gave the AAF an advantage after the war, when the B–29 bomber force became the nucleus of a Strategic Air Command. The position of the AAF as executive agent for joint strategic target planning matched well the postwar responsibilities that devolved to strategic air power.

By the time of Japan's surrender in September 1945, the various intelligence organizations of the AAF worldwide exhibited a breadth of abilities and competence surprising for the short period in which they had existed. That achievement resulted from appointing well-qualified people from civilian life to key assignments; associating closely with British and Commonwealth intelligence agencies; and receiving unstinting support from the nation's colleges, universities, and businesses. Many intelligence issues remained to be

Piercing the Fog

addressed at war's end, and others would soon surface in the postwar era, when the United States faced an increasingly truculent and most-secretive former wartime ally, the Soviet Union.

CHAPTER 1

Early Intelligence Organization in the Army Air Corps

INSTITUTIONALIZING MILITARY INTELLIGENCE in the United States began only in the last years of the nineteenth century, and air intelligence has been a distinctly twentieth-century phenomenon. The evolution of American air intelligence in the decades preceding World War II was marked by contention. Compounding the problems of establishing and then of implementing the new air intelligence organizations and functions was the relationship between these issues of air intelligence and the broader questions of the role and position of the American air forces.

An air force intended primarily to provide direct support to ground forces would require intelligence different from that required by an air force that had expanded, "independent" missions. Determining the most effective organization for the collection, evaluation, and dissemination of air intelligence depended on both the purpose of the air arm and its position within the military establishment. Given the lack of consensus throughout this period on either the role or the position of American air forces, the Army's uncertainty regarding air intelligence was inevitable.

As late as one month before its entry into World War I, the U.S. Army lacked any form of air intelligence organization. In the course of that war, the development of the U.S. Army's Air Service spawned several organizations, both in Washington and with the American Expeditionary Force (AEF) in France, concerned with air intelligence or air information, as it was variously called. Despite the broad application of air power during that conflict, most American Army officers came away convinced the Air Service would remain subordinate to the dominant ground forces. To the extent they thought about it, air intelligence (by whatever title) involved primarily the use of airplanes and balloons to obtain information regarding enemy military forces to support an Army commander's decisions. At times, it also included the collection and evaluation of information regarding the air forces of real or potential enemies; on this information British, French, and, later, American flyers planned their earliest counterair missions in attacks on German airfields.

Events in the war and visions of future aviation developments convinced some airmen that air power had a role beyond immediate support for ground forces. If so, air intelligence had to include a much wider scope and had to be the responsibility of individuals and agencies able to understand and best use it.

In the years between the world wars, issues of air intelligence in the United States were closely linked with the more fundamental questions of the role of air power and its place in the military establishment. The air intelligence struggles of this period centered on two axes, organizational and functional. Organizational disputes involved questions of the importance of air intelligence and the determination of which offices within the War Department should be responsible for the relevant information. Initially addressed within the context of the War Department General Staff (WDGS) structure, enactment of the Air Corps Act of 1926 initiated debates among elements of the Air Corps as well.

Functional arguments involved more conceptual questions of what *constituted* air intelligence. In the 1920s airmen agreed that the collection and evaluation of data necessary to compile the air order of battle (OB) and the gathering of other data relevant to foreign air forces were the main tasks of air intelligence. By the mid-1930s, airmen were developing the concept of strategic air warfare; they argued it was no longer sufficient to know the enemy's immediate military capability either in the air or on the ground. Despite their efforts to promote the doctrine of strategic bombardment, even they failed to fully grasp the true extent of the collection and analysis tasks such a doctrine implied.

The revolutionary nature of the strategic bombing doctrine developed at the Air Corps Tactical School (ACTS) at Maxwell Field, Alabama, required a comprehensive understanding of an enemy's economic system, with special emphasis on war production and its underlying support factors. No American air war theorist fully understood this, although some like Muir S. Fairchild developed an early appreciation for the task. The failure, perhaps inevitable, to resolve basic issues regarding American air power before World War II made the development of an adequate air intelligence capability almost impossible. Moreover, the neglect the Army and the Army Air Corps as institutions demonstrated toward intelligence compounded these inherent problems. When Japanese bombs fell on Pearl Harbor and Clark Field, the U.S. Army and its AAF still lacked a complete grasp of what air intelligence entailed, what it was supposed to accomplish, and how it should be organized.

American Air Intelligence in World War I

When the United States declared war on the Central Powers in April 1917, military intelligence reflected the general state of unpreparedness in which the

Early Intelligence Organization

Army found itself. Maj. Gen. Peyton C. March, wartime Chief of Staff, recalled that when the United States went to war, the Army intelligence organization consisted of two officers and two clerks. On May 23, 1917, in the General Staff's War College Division, a Military Intelligence Section opened, and in February 1918, a separate Military Intelligence Division (MID) replaced the section. Finally, on August 26, 1918, the Army indicated its appreciation of military intelligence by elevating it to one of the four coordinate divisions of the General Staff, under the Assistant Chief of Staff, Intelligence, or G–2. The MID became the operating agency supporting the policy-making G–2; by the end of the war, the MID consisted of 282 officers, 29 noncommissioned officers, and 948 civilian employees.[1] With the wartime growth of the Army's intelligence service, a specialized study of similar needs of air commanders became clear.

The genesis of American air intelligence occurred with the reorganization of the Army's air arm, the Signal Corps' Aeronautical Division, on March 19, 1917. This reorganization created an Air Intelligence Section in Washington to collect and file foreign aeronautical data (primarily of a technical nature, e.g., engine performance, aircraft characteristics, armament developments). This office, which was soon renamed the Information Section, would distribute this information as digests to Army aviation units.[2]

The American declaration of war made the work of the Intelligence Section markedly easier. As long as the United States was a nonbelligerent, military observers found it difficult to obtain information on the European air forces. When the United States joined the Allies in April 1917, British, French, Italian, and Russian missions hurried to Washington, bringing technical information on friendly and enemy air forces and seeking American material assistance.* When President Woodrow Wilson transferred aviation from the Signal Corps to the new Air Service in May 1918, this section became the Air Service's Aeronautical Information Branch. For the most part, the branch received its information through the MID, but in August 1918 the General Staff authorized the Air Service to send about twenty officers to Europe to keep it informed of activities and developments of the Air Service, AEF.[3]

In organizing his intelligence function within the AEF after his arrival in June 1917, General John J. Pershing adhered to the existing doctrine that a theater army commander was responsible for combat intelligence in his area of operations. Pershing established an Intelligence Section and classified it as the Second Section (G–2) General Headquarters (GHQ) AEF.[4] The GHQ Intelligence Section (G–2) included the MID (G–2–A), whose subfunctions included Air Intelligence (G–2–A–7). At HQ AEF in Paris, different sections of G–2–A–7 worked on interrogation of captured airmen, enemy air OB, bombing targets, technical information, and enemy air activity.

---

*For a time in the summer of 1917, Maj Henry H. Arnold, later Commanding General of the AAF, was the officer in charge of this section.

Piercing the Fog

The G–2-A–7 people also supervised branch intelligence officers (BIOs) attached to each army headquarters and each army observation and bombing group at a ratio of one per corps observation group and one per observation or bombing squadron operating independently at the front lines. The BIOs were neither pilots nor aerial observers; they were frequently strangers to the flying units for which they were expected to perform briefing and interrogation work. The BIOs were attached rather than assigned to the flying units because G–2 GHQ AEF insisted on having an integrated intelligence organization.[5] The importance of the G–2-A–7 organization stemmed from the command relationships between air and ground forces within the AEF. In France, the Air Service AEF did not have operational control over flying units. It existed to provide logistical, administrative, training, and personnel support for the conduct of air combat operations. Operational air units were attached to and were under the control of divisions, corps, and armies. Information relating to air operations largely flowed through ground army channels.[6]

Its supporting role did not prevent the Air Service AEF from developing its own internal air intelligence capability. Inspired by the Air Information Section in Washington, Lt. Col. Thomas D. Milling succeeded in establishing an Intelligence Section, Training Department, Air Service AEF under the guise of the Air Service's responsibility to train American aviation personnel and units. When it opened in December 1917, the unit's initial purpose was to serve as an acquisition and distribution point for aeronautical information useful for training. The section soon moved to Tours, France, and was redesignated the Information Section, Air Service (ISAS), AEF.[7]

The G–2 of Pershing's GHQ AEF assumed responsibility for acquiring and distributing intelligence information about the enemy's intentions. The ISAS was to collect and pass on information needed for education in the latest developments in aerial activity. In March 1918, the Information Section, together with radio, photography, and balloon activities, became a group headed by Col. Charles DeForest Chandler. The scope of the Information Section's mission broadened to encompass the collecting, filing, editing, compiling, and distributing of all military and technical aeronautical information received from any source. Additional responsibilities were the collection and publishing of instructional material on airplanes and engines. The functions of the Information Section complemented those of G–2-A–7 in that the latter concentrated primarily on current intelligence, while the former addressed information less immediately critical.[8]

During the war, the ISAS AEF issued over 300 bulletins relative to American, Allied, and enemy aviation, including, by directive, "Tactical and strategical lessons learned at the front . . . [and] technical information of enemy inventions and enemy usages of their air service." After the war, the Air Service retyped many of these bulletins on its own stencils in Washington, issuing them as circulars to influence tactical thinking. In the last months of hostilities, the

Early Intelligence Organization

Information Section received the additional task of preparing an elaborate Air Service AEF history, a function thought necessary to capture all the lessons learned during the war.[9]

"Before our entry into the war," General Pershing wrote, "European experience had shown that military operations can be carried out successfully and without unnecessary loss only in the light of complete and reliable information of the enemy."[10] The invention of the aeroplane provided another means by which to obtain this information. In preparing for war, European armies had expected to use observation balloons, dirigibles, and airplanes for aerial scouting. The conflict was only weeks old when events proved the value of the new machine in this capacity.

Reconnaissance by the British Royal Flying Corps in August 1914 provided timely and accurate reports of German dispositions. These, according to the British field commander, "proved of great value" and helped "to avert danger and disaster" in the Battle of Mons.[11] In September, the Royal Flying Corps' discovery of a gap between German armies and the exposed right flank of the advancing forces set the stage for the Battle of the Marne, which prevented an early German victory. According to the official British historian of World War I, the senior Allied commander, Marshal J. J. Joffre, owed British aviators "the certainty which had enabled him to make his plans in good time."[12]

Nor were French or German aviators less active. French flyers flew more than 10,000 reconnaissance missions in the first months of the war, especially to provide aerial fire adjustment for the mobile French 75-mm field guns. Aerial observation became a specialty of the French Air Force. According to Field Marshal Erich Ludendorff, German artillery also achieved "better shooting by means of aerial observation."[13]

During the period of trench warfare between the winter of 1914 and the German spring offensive of 1918, aerial observation became increasingly sophisticated, to include aerial photography of enemy trench systems and troop concentrations. To blind the enemy's reconnaissance while preventing him from doing the same to one's own capability led to the rapid evolution of aerial combat. In the last phase of the war Allied aviation again provided timely information on German troop dispositions and movements as they retreated. It also supported ground offensives, including tank operations, with fire support and immediate reconnaissance. Recalling this experience in a lecture in 1930, the future commander of the Allied Expeditionary Air Force (AEAF) during the Normandy invasion, Air Marshal (then Wing Commander) Trafford L. Leigh-Mallory, observed, "The vital importance to an armored force commander of air information cannot be emphasized too highly. . . ."[14]

Senior U.S. Army leaders recognized the vital role aerial observation had played in the war. Referring to intelligence in his posthostilities report, General Pershing noted that "warfare with battle lines separated by short distances only, makes possible the early acquirement of information. . . ." While there were many means to obtain this information, he went on, "With us the simple methods, such as *observation from the air* [emphasis added] and ground and the exploitation of prisoners and documents, have proved more effective than the less direct means."[15]

For ground commanders, the World War I experience contributed to a perspective that defined air intelligence largely as the use of aircraft to collect information usable by ground commanders. This stemmed from the fact that most of the activity of Air Service units (which were in combat only seven months) was directly tied to ground operations, either in observation or artillery spotting or in direct combat support through strafing and bombing of enemy positions. World War I, including the limited Air Service AEF experience, showed that aviation had more than one role and therefore required more than one form of air intelligence.

The report of the Chief of G–2–A–7 (Office of Air Intelligence) at GHQ AEF illustrated clearly that most of the work done by his office involved information not immediately related to either observation or direct support. Rather, it dealt with the collection, evaluation, and dissemination of information necessary to conduct air operations apart from support. The Air Order of Battle Section obtained and kept current information on "enemy air and balloon units, enemy airdromes, and the organization of the enemy's Air Service" for inclusion in the daily Summary of Air Information. Recognizing the effects that individual leaders can have on an air unit, G–2–A–7 kept a file on "prominent German airmen . . . with a view to determining what might be expected of any new unit to which these flyers were assigned . . . and to determine which German air units were the most prominent. . . ." Each month the G–2–A–7 office distributed a map and list of airdromes showing the location, size in hangars, sheds, estimated capacity, and units present. Much of this information came from photographs, and reports always distinguished between visual reportage and photographic confirmation. Changes in enemy dispositions were relayed in the daily Summary of Air Information.[16]

The Enemy Activity Section concentrated on air rather than on ground forces. The office sought to determine where the enemy was most active (seeking thereby to ascertain his intentions), to monitor developments in enemy tactics, and to understand the German system of training as a means of evaluating strengths and weaknesses. Information came from observers at antiaircraft (AA) batteries, postmission interviews (in modern terminology, debriefings), prisoners, and captured documents. The report referred, for example, to "two captured German documents, showing how pursuit and battle planes were to operate over the lines, [which] proved to be of great value to Allied airmen." Officers from G–2–A–7 met weekly with Allied counterparts to exchange information.[17]

Even less immediately related to the support of ground forces were the duties of the Bomb Target Section. Although the war ended before plans for

Early Intelligence Organization

extensive offensive air strikes could be implemented, by November 1918 the AEF had developed target folders on such systems as railroad stations and switching yards, manufacturing plants, and billeting areas and supply dumps in Germany. Compilation and distribution of this information was primarily the responsibility of the Bomb Target Section, which also monitored the results of Allied and American bombing attacks and the location of enemy barrage balloons, AA batteries, and searchlights. Some of the section's work was quite sophisticated. Referring to an analysis of railroad systems behind enemy lines, for example, its report noted: "Narrow-gauge roads, main lines and railway centers were observed, to determine at which points [the] most damage could be done. Photographs were taken, maps made and statistics compiled on the amount and importance of traffic going through various centers. When complete, this information was sent to operations officers . . . and after they had made their decisions, maps and photographs of the targets decided upon were sent to the bombing squadrons which were to carry out the raids."[18] In sum, by the end of the war airmen could see a requirement for intelligence to contribute to the effective preparation and conduct of air operations that might or might not be immediately tied to ground force activities.

Air Intelligence in the 1920s

For the postwar Air Service, the organizational struggles over responsibility for air intelligence began with the Army Reorganization Act of 1920. This legislation generally reflected the desire of General Pershing, who had become Chief of Staff in 1919, to organize U.S. Army headquarters in Washington along the lines of the wartime AEF. The WDGS now included five divisions: Personnel (G–1), Military Intelligence (G–2), Operations and Training (G–3), Supply (G–4), and War Plans. Theoretically coequal, the chiefs of all the offices were brigadier generals, except for the G–2 who was generally a colonel.

The duties of the Assistant Chief of Staff, Intelligence (G–2), included the requirement to support the War Plans Division (WPD) in strategic planning and to provide War Department intelligence to field commanders at the outbreak of hostilities. In postwar reductions, the MID of G–2 was cut to 25 officers and 52 civilians by 1924, where it would remain until modestly increased in 1940. The number of military and assistant military attachés dropped drastically from a high of 94 in November 1918. In spite of the rapid expansion and growth of aviation, the War Department usually authorized Air Service officers as assistant military attachés only in London, Paris, and Rome.[19]

The Air Corps Act of 1926 provided additional representation for air matters on the WDGS. A new G–2 Air Section (shortly elevated to the more important status of a branch) was responsible for policy matters and questions pertaining to the use of Air Corps personnel in combat intelligence, aerial photography and mapping, codes and communications between air and ground, and advice on special studies. The first head of the Air Section was an experienced Air Corps officer, Maj. Joseph T. McNarney. As specified by the Air Corps Act, in 1930 the G–2 Intelligence Branch absorbed the separate Air Branch.[20]

Within the Air Service, air intelligence organizations and functions also changed in the immediate postwar years. In January 1919, Maj. Gen. Mason M. Patrick, Chief of the Air Service, approved a plan to phase out the Information Section, Air Service, AEF, and transfer its key personnel and printing equipment to Washington to join a new Information Group, the Office of Director of Air Service. In May 1919, Air Service orders specified the principal function of this Information Group as "the gathering and dissemination of all information of value to the Air Service." The Air Service reorganization required that the new Information Group maintain a library, and the Air Service declared it "essential that copies of all reports, manuals, pamphlets, and publications of a tactical, technical, or engineering nature received in the Air Service be furnished that Group in order that its library may be kept up to date."[21]

Maj. Horace Hickam, the first Information Group Chief, divided his office into collection, dissemination, and library divisions, plus a special division charged with responsibility for preparing congressional correspondence and distributing information to the public press. Hickam also believed the Information Group should be "the central publishing office of the Air Service, whether the output be rigging charts, handbooks, folders, tactical bulletins, curricula, technical reports, organizational diagrams, or the like." Such freewheeling notions drew protests from others within the Air Service. One charge stated the Information Group was "attempting altogether too much and a good part of the work being undertaken is of little or no value to the service in general."[22]

The Information Group also specified that all assistant military attachés for air (in Paris, London, Rome, and The Hague) should be conversant with new aeronautical developments in the United States and the countries to which they were accredited. Toward this end, the Air Service Engineering Division in January 1920 prepared a questionnaire for London and Paris specifying technical information wanted in the fields of electrical equipment, instruments, parachutes, radios, and aerial photography. From London, the air attaché remonstrated that it was no simple matter to secure technical information (the individual had to be versed in aviation developmental programs). Regardless that the British Air Ministry was quite reluctant to release technical information, the questionnaire technique persisted nevertheless.[23]

Despite the activities of the attachés, in 1920 Brig. Gen. Billy Mitchell complained about a lack of aeronautical information from overseas. Allegedly to get the flamboyant Mitchell off the scene while the Washington Naval

Early Intelligence Organization

Two of the early leaders of the air component of the U.S. Army, Maj. Gen. Mason M. Patrick *(left),* Chief of the Air Service in the 1920s, and, standing beside him, his gifted and troublesome subordinate, Brig. Gen. William Mitchell. General Mitchell's court martial in 1925 became a national showcase for the new, progressive ideas of the Army's air arm. As Col. Carl A. Spaatz said of his own testimony at the trial, "They can't do anything to you when you're under oath and tell them answers to their question."

Disarmament negotiations were in progress, General Patrick sent Mitchell, with his aide, Lt. Clayton Bissell, and aeronautical engineer Alfred Verville, on an inspection trip to France, Italy, Germany, Holland, and England during the winter of 1921–1922. Mitchell was apparently pleasantly received on his trip, but soon after his visit to Paris and London, the British and French governments began to pose demands for technical information in exchange for what they had given him. Some of the questions went beyond limited technical matters. The French, for example, wanted to know American military opinion regarding "giant or very powerful" military aircraft and multiengine planes.[24]

By 1925 the duty tours of the Air Service air attachés assigned to postwar European capitals at the end of the war were close to completion. At this juncture, the Air Service Engineering Division recommended that all air attachés be graduates of the Air Service Engineering School and that they be brought back to the United States at least once a year to remain current on aeronautical developments in progress. This proposition had merit, but the Air Service did not think its appropriations would stand the expense of so much foreign travel. The Engineering Division dismissed a countersuggestion that it send development engineers on temporary duty to European capitals, perhaps on a yearly basis. Too few commissioned air engineering officers were left in the postwar Air Service to allow such a dispersion of effort.[25] The Air Service and its successor, the Air Corps, nevertheless looked with favor upon overseas travel by air officers on leave time. In 1928, for example, one active-duty engineering officer, Lt. Victor E. Bertrandais, visited Great Britain and France and filed a very astute report on aviation factories he had visited. Bertrandais concluded that "the United States surpasses England and France in production methods and as a whole our workmanship and aircraft practices are far superior to anything observed in England and France."[26] (In World War II, Bertrandais would be an effective chief of supply and maintenance for General Kenney in the Southwest Pacific.)

The creation of the Air Corps in 1926 had little immediate impact on air intelligence in a functional sense, although it did result in the inevitable restructuring in Washington. An Air Corps Information Division, Office of the Chief of Air Corps (OCAC), replaced the Air Service Information Group. Divided into four sections—air intelligence, photography, publications, and press relations—the Information Division was charged to collect "essential aeronautical information from all possible sources." This information would include "the uses of aircraft in war, including the organization of the various air forces of the world, tactical doctrines, types of aircraft used, and organization of the personnel operating and maintaining aircraft."[27] Except for the responsibility of the intelligence section to support War Department strategic planning, the Information Division of OCAC remained a collection agency. The intelligence section routinely received foreign intelligence through the MID and maintained liaison with the Air Branch. A magazine and book library was begun. The intelligence section also tried to compile digests of foreign aviation information and compare foreign air forces. This potential workload far exceeded the Intelligence Section's capabilities, since for many years it was manned by only one officer and two to five civilians.[28]

Air Intelligence in the Early 1930s

While the assistant military attachés in the major European capitals remained the principal source of information on foreign aviation developments, the Air Corps detailed an officer once each year to visit Japan and compile a report on aircraft developments there. These efforts notwithstanding, the Air Corps by no means considered itself fully informed about aircraft development overseas, primarily because foreign nations now imposed restrictions on information of potential military value. Italy, France, and England all had far more stringent secrecy measures than did the United States. The Japanese imposed particularly severe constraints on the acquisition of military and naval information, and they limited access strictly to what they wanted foreign representatives to see. One reason for this militant secrecy may have been their knowledge that in the 1920s the United States had been intercepting and translating Japanese messages to their negotiators at the Washington Naval Disarmament Conference. In 1929, when the new Secretary of State, Henry L. Stimson, learned of this accomplishment, he reputedly reacted strongly. Such interceptions of foreign governmental communications, he was said to have decried, were "highly unethical." In reaction to the secretary's order that such activity cease, Herbert O. Yardley, former head of the War-State Cipher Bureau, published a book in 1931 that revealed the extent of U.S. code breaking. The Japanese quickly changed their cipher system and reacted coldly to American requests for air information.[29]

While the State Department no longer participated in cryptanalysis, the War and Navy Departments continued to do so, each on its own. In the War Department, however, code interception was handled as a communications function within the Signal Intelligence Service of the Chief Signal Officer, and was thus outside the purview of the MID and other military intelligence channels.[30]

Developments concerning accessibility to military information from other nations occurred at the same time other modifications of relevance to air intelligence were happening within the United States itself. One of the most important of these was a shift in thinking about strategic war plans, the results of which had clear implications for air planning and intelligence. When the United States began to prepare strategic war plans in 1904, they were color coded by nation: RED for Great Britain, BLACK for Germany, GREEN for Mexico, and ORANGE for Japan. The development of Japanese militancy in the 1920s engendered an ongoing review of ORANGE plans and a continuing estimate that Japan was the most likely future adversary for the United States. Although a combined British-Japanese (RED-ORANGE) attack on the United States was not likely, it did assume an important role in American war planning in the 1930s as a worst-case situation.

The Army Reorganization Act of 1920 had confirmed the U.S. Army's traditional mission of defense of the coasts and sea frontiers of the United States. Several years later the Air Corps Act made a distinction between air service aviation (observation) and a GHQ Air Force that would probably be committed against an enemy before the surface forces engaged. Responsibility for coastal defense and the potential requirement for GHQ Air Force to strike before ground forces were employed assumed additional significance in 1922. In that year the Washington Naval Treaty imposed a quota upon American, British, and Japanese capital ships that would have given the latter two nations naval superiority over the U.S. Navy in the rather unlikely event of a RED-ORANGE attack.

It was under these circumstances that Army Chief of Staff General Douglas MacArthur and the Chief of Naval Operations, Admiral W. V. Pratt, reached an agreement concerning coastal defense. As described by MacArthur, "Under it the Naval air forces will be based on the fleet and move with it as an important element in performing the essential missions of the fleet afloat. The Army air forces will be land based and employed as an element of the Army in carrying out its missions of defending the coasts, both in the homeland and in overseas possessions."[31] The Army Air Corps took seriously its responsibility to defend the United States and its territories from naval or air attack. One of the considerations in its efforts to develop a long-range bomber (the B–17 and later the B–29) was the militarily sound principle of locating and defeating an enemy as far from one's shores as possible. The issue of the air forces' strategic defensive role would become entangled in doctrinal and bureaucratic struggles with the U.S. Navy and in debates over strategic offensive operations. In March 1938 the Air Corps identified its primary task as defense of the United States against air attack, to be achieved by "destruction of enemy aviation at its bases."[32]

The strategic focus of RED-ORANGE planning marked a change from earlier War Department emphasis on intelligence training for field combat to training and preparation for hemispheric defense. In 1926, War Department Training Regulation (TR) 210–5 had focused wholly on intelligence support for Army surface combat. By 1932, the Command and General Staff School (C&GSS) at Fort Leavenworth, Kansas, responsible for the Army's principal intelligence training, began to advance a tentative doctrine more suited to strategic intelligence. This approach argued intelligence estimates had to be determined by enemy capabilities existing at a given time and projected into the future.[33] Such an approach called for an analysis of the enemy's potential as well as his current capability; this, in turn, required greater insight into his industrial structure. The requirement for air forces to strike the enemy at a distance from the United States called for a more detailed knowledge of areas at least within the Western Hemisphere and, as technology progressed, perhaps even farther afield. At any rate, the 1938 objective of achieving air defense of the United States by destroying the enemy at his bases clearly called for a broader scope of intelligence requirements than was needed simply to support ground forces.

The thrust of strategic thinking toward hemispheric defense also caused subtle changes in the status of the Information Division, OCAC, even though no changes were made in its official charter. According to War Department regulation, the OCAC Plans Division provided information for the General Staff's strategic planning. The office could not meet the demands placed on it, so others moved to fill the void. In July 1933, Lt. Col. Walter R. Weaver, chief of the Information Division, complained to the acting executive officer of the

Early Intelligence Organization

OCAC that the Plans Division was exceeding its authority by collecting and evaluating intelligence on foreign military forces. Plans Division responded by pointing out that the Information Division had failed to provide the necessary data. Weaver then used the ensuing dispute to urge that his division be manned adequately to accomplish its data-collection tasks.[34]

Maj. Gen. Benjamin D. Foulois, Chief of the Air Corps, supported the argument that the Information Division was, in Weaver's words, "G–2 for the Air Corps."[35] In the depths of the depression, the division could not be enlarged, and it continued to perform this function with the insufficient manpower then available.[36] This controversy between Plans and Information in mid-1933 was to a certain extent only a small paper storm, but it reflected the buffeting institutional air intelligence would take in debates that would arise later in the decade as a result of strategic air planning.

A more significant problem arose with the creation of the GHQ Air Force in March 1935. Because the GHQ Air Force was a mobilization day (M-day) force (i.e., it had to be prepared to conduct combat operations at the outset of hostilities), it was directly responsible to the Chief of Staff. In terms of intelligence, airmen recognized this requirement would preclude the WDGS from making information available to an operational commander on the outbreak of hostilities. GHQ Air Force argued that its status demanded additional autonomy in air intelligence, both for following foreign technical developments and for planning air operations beyond the lines of, and before the employment of, Army surface forces. The WDGS G–2 rebutted that such a duplication of intelligence systems was an unnecessary expense hardly likely to be funded by an economy-minded Congress. GHQ Air Force was authorized an intelligence section, and in August 1935 a GHQ Air Force memorandum declared, "This headquarters, in cooperation with the Office of the Chief of the Air Corps and the WDGS, is responsible for duties pertaining to War Department Intelligence."[37]

While the Army MID fretted that the activation of the GHQ Air Force would threaten its status as the hub of military intelligence, more immediate problems arose within the Air Corps itself from uncertain and somewhat contentious relations between the OCAC Information Division and GHQ Air Force Intelligence. The OCAC wanted to handle all air intelligence functions except those applicable to GHQ Air Force maneuvers and exercises or specifically required as contributions to U.S. war plans in which GHQ Air Force might be involved. The OCAC argued the general mission of collecting, evaluating, and disseminating air intelligence was an OCAC information function. GHQ Air Force wished to have the Information Division transfer material from the MID and to develop and supply maps. The GHQ staff maintained that all combat air intelligence in war and intelligence training within assigned units in peacetime were inherent functions of its commanding general. When a joint Army-Navy war plan was approved, for example, the

Piercing the Fog

GHQ Air Force commander would be required to submit his detailed plan of operations, whether the plan was for independent air action or operations in connection with surface force warfare.[38]

The GHQ Air Force had clear jurisdiction over the instruction, training, and tactical employment of its combat units and personnel, including intelligence personnel. Not enough Air Corps intelligence officers were available to perform the required intelligence activities in the operating units. Since such people were thought to be chiefly useful in times of combat, intelligence sections (called S–2 in lower-level units) in each of the three GHQ Air Force combat wings were usually first to experience staff reductions. S–2 sections were called upon to give most of their time to public relations, considered an intelligence function because it involved release of military information to the public, counterpropaganda, and, in time of war, censorship.[39] Some time was required to work out these contentious issues, and remnants of disputes among combat air forces, the central air establishment, and the G–2 would linger throughout World War II.

The Air Corps Tactical School and Air Intelligence

The different interpretations regarding responsibility for air intelligence that existed within the Air Corps in the 1930s would shortly be overshadowed by even more serious disagreements between soldiers and airmen. At the center of these disputes were the fundamental issues of the role of air power and an air force's position in the national defense establishment. These larger issues affected basic questions of air intelligence, including what constituted air intelligence, and which groups were best able to obtain, evaluate, and disseminate this material. These questions would not be resolved before the United States entered the next world war, but the center for much of the Air Corps' prewar air warfare thinking was the ACTS at Maxwell Field. Most of the AAF's World War II combat leaders spent one or more assignments at ACTS, and its influence on plans, doctrine, and the personal relationships of these men should not be overlooked.

Differences regarding the employment of air power were clearly evident in 1934 when General MacArthur called upon the WPD, WDGS, to prepare an Army position on air warfare to be published as TR 440–15, *Employment of the Air Forces of the Army*. The initial draft by WPD asserted that the "land campaign" was "the decisive factor in war." While air operations would be intensive at the beginning of a war, the advantages of "'alluring' air mission at such a time should be weighed against the requirement to keep superior air forces in being to support operations which would take place after the ground armies made contact. The greatest part of the [draft] paper dealt with the employment of air forces in continental defense."[40]

In a strongly worded critique of the WPD draft, the ACTS proclaimed that the regulation was too narrowly predicated on the geographic isolation of the United States and focused too tightly on ground operations. In reality, the ACTS paper rejoined, "The principal and all important missions of air power, when its equipment permits, is the attack of those vital objectives in a *nation's economic structure* [emphasis added] which will tend to paralyze that nation's ability to wage war and thus contribute to the attainment of the ultimate objective of war, namely, the disintegration of the will to resist." Very little of the thought in the ACTS critique appeared in the regulation as officially published on October 15, 1935. The regulation recognized "that a phase of air operations would probably precede the contact of the surface forces and that the outcome of this phase would exert a potent influence upon subsequent operations. . . . [T]he effect which air forces were capable of producing and the extent to which they would influence warfare [were] still undetermined."[41] Despite its limited impact on TR 440–15, the ACTS's critique was of great significance, for it expounded clearly and forcefully the fundamental differences in soldiers' and airmen's concepts on the employment of air power. While not ignoring the role of air power in support of the land campaign and continental and hemispheric air defense, the ACTS developed and taught what can be described most accurately as revolutionary concepts about the employment of air power in strategic offensive—concepts that had broad implications for air intelligence, but implications that were not fully recognized, even by airmen.

Broadly defined, officers at the ACTS argued that strategic air power, as manifested primarily by the B–17 aircraft, could be decisive by bringing about the collapse of both the means and the will of an adversary to conduct war. The ACTS maintained that identification and destruction of so-called vital targets within an industrial nation's economic structure would be decisive, i.e., would win the war. It does not appear that the school's proponents of this concept for strategic bombardment fully grasped the significance of the interrelationship between strategic targeting of an industrial state and the need, let alone the difficulties, of acquiring and then analyzing vast amounts of economic data. Indeed, a central figure in all air planning in the 1930s, and for much of World War II as well, Maj. Gen. Haywood S. Hansell, Jr., admitted that to the best of his knowledge nobody seems to have recognized, as late as 1939, the critical need to conduct industrial analysis if the concept of strategic air attack was to be translated into practice.[42] This lack of understanding by proponents of strategic air attack led to conditions wherein civilian analysts assumed responsibility for key intelligence tasks. In the area of economic analysis and industrial targeting, civilians eventually took the lead from the uniformed military in World War II.

Although the ACTS people recognized that U.S. military policy was defensive, they reasoned that only offensive actions could win a war. The same group also rationalized that in a war against a major adversary in Europe, allied bases would be available for land-based U.S. aviation.[43] In the school year 1933–1934, Maj. Donald Wilson was instructor in charge of the Air Force course. In this course, Wilson visualized future wars for survival between industrial nations that depended upon a closely knit and interdependent industrial fabric to support their war efforts. He maintained that precision air attacks against essential elements could collapse the industrial fabric of a nation; as few as three main systems—e.g., transportation, electric power, and steel manufacture—would suffice.[44] As air power thinkers struggled with defining the role of an air force, they began to glimpse the implications of intelligence for expanded air operations. In planning the school year 1935–1936, Lt. Col. H. A. Dargue, the school's assistant commandant, stated that military intelligence had always been approached from a ground warfare point of view; at best, air intelligence had been considered to involve the enemy's air combat forces. The ACTS, he now declared, must pay more attention to an expanded view of air intelligence, which included studies of each of the major powers, their military and economic policies, economic and political structures, raw materials, geography, and known and potential air bases.[45]

In 1935–1936, intelligence data of major nations provided by the MID did not include the depth of information required by Dargue's view of air operations against an opponent's industrial fabric. The War Department went so far as to forbid independent school examination of the economies of foreign countries, arguing that such was the responsibility of the MID.[46] Almost immediately, the ACTS staff sought a way around the restriction that they saw as hampering their analysis of air power. One method of addressing such issues as the identification of appropriate economic target systems and how best to destroy or cripple them through air operations without violating War Department prohibitions was to study the industrial fabric of the United States as a concomitant of a defensive military policy.

In the spring of 1936, a group of ACTS students, including Majors Byron E. Gates and Robert M. Webster, launched a study of potential attack against the northeastern United States. The scenario called for a RED (British) offensive to take the form of a sustained strategic air offensive, surprise raids against vital points in the U.S. industrial system, or establishment and defense of advanced naval and air bases in Canada. The study concluded that little prospect existed for RED to invade and establish bases in Canada because of the tremendous shipping tonnage required to move it into the area in the face of determined U.S. opposition. Without forward bases, a sustained land-based strategic air offensive with relatively short-range aircraft would be impossible. But RED had aircraft carriers, and the committee warned that surprise air attacks or sabotage could disrupt "certain key points" in the northeastern United States "upon which the capacity of the United States to produce the munitions of war depends."[47]

Out of this initial study, the ACTS officers continued an analysis of the organic economic systems that, if neutralized, would paralyze a modern state.

The RED attack scenario identified the U.S. electric power system as the heart of its industrial system, followed, in order of priority, by transportation (chiefly railroads), fuel refining and distribution, food distribution and preservation, and steel manufacturing. Destruction of a number of highly concentrated factories would add a crippling blow; these included electric generator, transformer, switch gear, and motor manufacturing plants; locomotive manufacturing; and aluminum and magnesium producers. To strike these targets effectively would mean defeating the air defense forces. The best method of defeating the air defense would entail attack on air bases, aircraft and engine factories, sources of aviation fuel, and attrition through air combat attendant to these missions.[48]

On the basis of these preliminary studies, the ACTS study concluded that the ideal objective for air attack would be an undefended vital element of an enemy's national structure that consisted of only a few individual targets concentrated within a relatively small area. Since G–2 was responsible for War Department intelligence, the ACTS wanted G–2 to determine the three most important vital elements in foreign countries against which war plans were being prepared. This effort would be followed by the collection of detailed information on the individual targets within each of the vital elements. The detailed information then would be used to prepare objective folders that would permit air commanders to plan and execute aerial attacks on the various targets comprising each of the three vital elements. The school staff further asked that all intelligence work be coordinated in terms of the most likely operations to be undertaken on M-day.

In accordance with the projected strategic air concept, ACTS officers considered the priority of operations, and hence of intelligence collection, to be defense of the continental U.S.; defense of the Western Hemisphere; and offensive operations against Japan, Germany, Italy, Great Britain, France, or Russia.[49] However valuable such a study might have been as an educational tool, or however potentially useful it might be in the event of war, in the middle to late 1930s the work far exceeded the limited analytical capability of the MID. In addition, neither the G–2 nor the War Department as a whole was committed to the *projected offensive* employment of aviation envisioned at ACTS.

Even with their collective efforts, it is doubtful that the attachés, G–2, and the War Department could have satisfied the intelligence demands generated by the concept of strategic air attack developed at the ACTS. To move from the conceptual to the planning phase required a comprehensive yet detailed analysis of the economic infrastructure of a potential adversary. Targets were, as always, the central issue. Determining them first required identification and analysis of the crucial target systems representing the adversary's economic structure. Specific targets within the broader target system categories then could be identified. Selection of targets for attack would require further analysis to determine their degree of residual capability or cushion, their recuperative capability, a country's dispersal potential, and a host of other factors. In short, target determination would require the skills of thoroughly competent intelligence officers aided by economists, statisticians, and technical experts.

Acquisition and Evaluation of Air Intelligence: Developments in Europe and Asia

As the world moved toward war in the late 1930s, the number of officers serving abroad as military attachés or assistant military attachés increased to thirty-two as the realization of air warfare potential grew. Reports from these men continued to be the principal sources of intelligence data available to G–2. When assigned, each military attaché received a copy of the *Index Guide for Procurement of Military Intelligence*. This booklet contained 1,000 or more subject headings, called topics or subtopics that were leads to their enquiries, and also a coding system used by the G–2 office in the War Department to assemble and file information. In addition to numbered reports, the attachés were responsible to submit annual summary reports (largely statistical) on subjects such as the host nation's aviation industry. If the Army in the United States needed particular information, the G–2 undertook to get it from the military attachés in the field. When G–2 received information, they classified and evaluated it before drawing deductions and conclusions. The information was then said to have been "digested" and ready for dissemination.[50]

Although G–2 recognized the value of disseminating intelligence immediately, personnel limitations frequently resulted in delays. Nor did G–2 always receive new data expeditiously. For example, reports from the U.S. military attaché in Tokyo required three weeks to reach G–2. In the dissemination of intelligence information in the United States, OCAC Information Division published the less sensitive items in a serial monograph for official use only entitled "G–2 Information Prepared by Information Division, 1934–1938." The MID circulated some items of classified information with time limits on user retention and a provision prohibiting their reproduction. This procedure caused GHQ Air Force to complain that air groups and squadrons received only a small number of intelligence summaries which were often to be kept for short periods, the supposed security of classified information considered more important than the instruction of recipient units. In 1938, not even General Arnold, Chief of the Air Corps, was on distribution for G–2 information believed to be very sensitive. Such information, Arnold learned from Brig. Gen. Sherman Miles, Acting G–2 WDGS, was restricted to members of the General Staff.[51] Arnold was irritated, but for the moment, he could do little.

Throughout much of the 1930s, U.S. Army and Army Air Corps intelligence focused on developments in Europe rather than in the Far East. Military planners believed a war in the Pacific would be primarily a Navy affair and would not require a major Army commitment. They also considered Japan too dependent on trade with the United States to risk a war that would jeopardize her gains in Manchuria. The reports that did come from Japan in the early years of the decade tended to reinforce the widely held opinion that Japan lacked a real military capability. The July 1935 annual aviation report for Japan filed by the U.S. military attaché in Tokyo described Japan's Army Air Force as being filled with large numbers of obsolete aircraft: "The unwise policy of some years ago of storing up an immense amount of spare planes in depots and the apparent failure to note the rapid changes which occur in aeronautical developments has been impressed upon the Japanese, but it is doubtful if they will deliberately scrap planes which have some use, even if obsolete."[52]

Maj. James F. Phillips, a graduate of the Air Corps Engineering School, made the annual U.S. military inspection of Japanese Army aviation in May 1936. Phillips filed both an official report through the Military Attaché in Tokyo and an informal letter to the Air Matériel Division at Wright Field. "Superficial treatment," he wrote, "was very courteous—including much bowing, hissing, and gallons of tea being drunk—but verbal information was often exaggerated or misleading." Phillips was an early, though not sole, practitioner of an error that came to be common prior to World War II: underestimating or belittling Japanese ability. In that year's report, Phillips noted that the morale of Japanese air personnel was extremely high, but that practically all Japanese Army air matériel was copied from American or English standard types, and was therefore about four to six years out of date. Phillips saw, he noted, "no really modern airplanes."[53] He was seeing only what the Japanese wanted him to see.

In November 1936, Japan signed the Anti-Comintern Pact with Germany and Italy, and in July 1937 Japanese military forces marched into northern China. Upon the passage of a military secrets act, the task of U.S. military and naval attachés in Japan became almost fruitless. Discussions of service aircraft or of the aviation industry were drastically curtailed. Even the attachés of powers ostensibly associated with Japan complained that their connections were inadequate to ensure a reasonable exchange of information.[54] In view of the extreme difficulty in obtaining information in Japan itself, Lt. Cmdr. Ralph A. Ofstie, who became Assistant U.S. Naval Attaché for Air in Tokyo in 1935, thought Japan's attack in China provided "a golden opportunity to see how and with what material Japan carries on a war." After a visit to Shanghai, Ofstie came away unimpressed with the aerial prowess of either the Chinese or Japanese. Capt. Harold M. Bemis, the U.S. Navy attaché, reported the substance of Ofstie's observations: "The Japanese have been bold and courageous, but they have exhibited a mediocrity in operations and in material which mark them as distinctly inferior to other major powers in this vitally important element of war."[55] In a briefing conducted later in Washington, Ofstie doubted that Japan would use her fleet at any considerable distance from her own waters, even though Japanese aviation in China was principally naval, since the bulk of

Piercing the Fog

Japanese Army aviation remained in Manchuria as a counter to the ever-present Soviet threat.

"Originality," Ofstie went on, "is certainly not a trait of the Japanese and this quite evidently applies to their aviation equipment. Everything is basically of foreign origin—planes, engines, and instruments. They do build well, however, and the results are creditable, but being copied from foreign developments their equipment must necessarily be at least a couple of years behind that of the leading occidental powers." Ofstie concluded: "I believe that there is no doubt that we are markedly superior to the Japanese in the air—in piloting skills, in material, and in ability to employ our aircraft effectively on the offense and the defense."[56] In reviewing reports from China, Air Corps Capt. Patrick W. Timberlake noted inadequate armament on bombers, a general lack of bombing accuracy, and lack of serious damage to bomber targets caused in part by instantaneous fuzes and light case bombs. "There is no question concerning the courage of either Chinese or Japanese pilots," he added, "but it is felt . . . so far as operations have progressed, the personnel, the individual tactics, and the operations are distinctly inferior to those of major powers in this vitally important element of war."[57]

The early intelligence reports that emphasized the obsolescence of Japanese aircraft appear to have been correct, at least to the extent that the true facts were kept hidden from prying foreign eyes. By 1938, however, more ominous assessments arrived in Washington. In China as a civilian advisor to the Chinese Air Force, Claire Chennault considered it to be his duty as a retired Air Corps officer to send intelligence back to Washington. In January 1938, he sent the U.S. Army Adjutant General a confidential report on a Japanese single-seater pursuit plane, type I–96, which he described as "the most maneuverable monoplane which has appeared in China." It was also employed regularly to support bomber penetrations as deep as 250 miles. Chennault originally thought that this plane was a copy of a French fighter, but by May 1938 he reported that it was an original Japanese design. It would later be identified as the Type 96 Mitsubishi fighter nicknamed "Claude." Chennault wrote: "Japan is self-supporting and independent of foreign supplies in building airplanes."[58]

In the first year after the Japanese invasion of China, the MID and the Office of Naval Intelligence (ONI) harbored the view that "the economic and material structure of Japan would collapse."[59] By September 1938, there were few indications that such a collapse was in the offing. As a student at the ACTS in 1938, Capt. Thomas D. White—later to distinguish himself as an air intelligence officer, air commander, and chief of staff, United States Air Force—prepared a thesis on "Japan as an Objective for Air Attack, 1937–1938." He noted that the U.S. war objective against Japan would be to force "political acquiescence; and that this would not necessarily require occupation of enemy territory." According to his thesis, Japan's economic structure was so highly integrated that the destruction of one vital link might bring "a succession of collapses in allied spheres of industry or finance until the entire nation is prostrate or a disheartened population forces its government to sue for peace." White recommended that railroad destruction, blockade of sea lanes, and air attack against hydroelectric installations deserved highest priority as objectives of attack in Japan.[60]

The major problem in planning such an air strategy, White observed, was a lack of intelligence information for air targeting. Reporting forms used by attachés in making aeronautical assessments emphasized military matters, such as OBs, numbers and types of aircraft, and aircraft specifications. White recommended that U.S. military attachés abroad be required to submit reports including data needed for targeting for an air bombardment strategy. He wanted more active cooperation in peacetime to establish relations between U.S. intelligence agencies and such international corporations as Standard Oil, General Electric, and General Motors. Company representatives residing abroad could possibly obtain detailed information on vital elements of hostile societies. White also recommended that Air Corps officers who understood air strategy should be assigned to G–2 to begin analyses of all major nations.[61]

In 1939 the Chinese captured intact a Japanese Nakajima Type 97 (Nate) fighter and brought it to Chengtu where Chennault flew it in extensive service and combat tests. Chennault brought a dossier on this plane to Washington later in 1939. Of this visit, he recalled that most of the staff officers in the Munitions Building were "flying swivel chairs and puttering with war plans.... The plans were all for Europe." When Arnold asked Chennault to lecture his staff on the Sino-Japanese war, Chennault recalled that it was only with great difficulty that someone finally managed to find a map of China, and then it had very little detail on it. (Chennault claimed in his memoirs that the Air Corps never got a copy of his dossier on the Nate, but later search of files in Washington revealed that the report received a usual distribution, including a copy to the MID.) After returning to China, Chennault recalled getting a letter from the War Department thanking him for his data, which had been turned over to "aeronautical experts" who had stated that it was impossible to build an aircraft with the performance Chennault had submitted in his specifications.[62]

Substantial technical data did become available for evaluation at Air Matériel Division, Wright Field, Ohio, but the Intelligence Branch of the Information Division, OCAC, did not always make full use of it. General Hansell, who for a time held responsibility for foreign air force matters within the Intelligence Branch, admitted after the war, "We maintained a close liaison with Wright Field, where there was a section called 'Technical Air Intelligence' ... that did make engineering analyses of foreign aircraft. We used their estimates fairly extensively ... but the distance between the two offices was considerable, and we didn't make as much use of that technical intelligence as we might have."[63]

Piercing the Fog

On the other side of the globe, military attachés reported diligently, if not always accurately, aviation developments in Europe. Over the course of two tours as an assistant military attaché, Brig. Gen. Martin F. Scanlon, Air Corps, spent most of the 1930s in London. His personal diaries were replete with an active social life, and his dispatches revealed an initial British aloofness that warmed to friendship and confidentiality with the rise of the German *Luftwaffe*. In response to a G–2 letter requesting information about the RAF, the military attaché in London replied in April 1929 that all efforts to obtain official information on air tactics, war plans, operations, and so on had been "practically fruitless."[64] In November 1930, then-Major Scanlon informed G–2 that "the Air Ministry declines to give any information on the Air Defenses of London as it considers that the defensive measures are too vital and confidential to disclose."[65] As the RAF expanded after 1935, the U.S. military attaché, Col. Raymond E. Lee, reported that "bits of information picked up in odd conversations, here and there, or from newspaper cuttings, are not sufficiently complete or accurate to give more than a very sketchy and inaccurate skeleton" of the scope of the expansion program. In September 1938, Lee nevertheless forwarded some data that he had obtained from the Air Ministry with the understanding that it must be treated as "completely confidential." About this same time, Scanlon, now a lieutenant colonel, pointed out that if the United States intended to get information from the Air Ministry, it would be necessary to exchange equivalent U.S. data on both Army and Navy aviation.[66]

Perhaps because of increased tensions in Europe during 1938–1939, the British began to demonstrate greater openness. In 1939, when G–2 asked for a description of British air defense systems, Washington received complete details about the RAF, along with relevant concepts for its employment. In the event of war with Germany, the report stated, London and other cities would be defended by day fighters held on the ground until the ground observer corps, ships at sea, and general reconnaissance aircraft provided warning of an approaching attack. In view of the experiences gained in Spain and China, the attaché remarked, the British gave "considerable thought" to furnishing fighter escort for bombers, thus permitting bomber crews to perform their duties more efficiently, without having to devote all their time to their own protection. Bomber units would probably be sent abroad, not for the purpose of supporting field forces but simply for the reason that bases in France would increase their effective range. The primary objectives of these units would be enemy munitions factories, aircraft factories, air bases, foundries, supply dumps for ammunition and petrol, important railroads, bridges, and other lines of communication.[67]

In his endorsement to Scanlon's report, Colonel Lee noted that Great Britain was extremely vulnerable to attack by air. Until the United Kingdom could be made reasonably secure against air attack, Lee wrote, the government would sacrifice the initiative, both diplomatically and militarily. The increase

Early Intelligence Organization

in fighter squadrons over the number of bomber squadrons, as well as the emphasis placed on AA artillery, offered evidence of the concern for defense against aerial bombardment. Lee added that most of those principally concerned with defense believed Great Britain would undergo a severe ordeal, with much damage and many casualties, for two to six months, after which initial enemy efforts toward paralyzing the country would have been successfully withstood, and the military and air initiatives would begin to pass to Britain.[68]

British concern rightly focused upon the newly recreated German Air Force (GAF). By the late 1920s, even though German pilots were secretly training in the Soviet Union, the Germans were apprehensive of the air disarmament enforced upon their country by the Versailles treaty and by the fact that they were surrounded by other nations with air forces. When Adolf Hitler came to power in Berlin, the *Luftwaffe* commenced a remarkable rebuilding effort. Quite soon, fifteen modern factories were reportedly devoting all their time to building aircraft, and eight factories were said to be concentrating on aircraft engines. At a social dinner given in his honor by the Foreign Press Union on May 2, 1935, General of Aviators Herman Goering, Reich Minister of Aviation, surprised the world with a supposedly frank report on Germany's aviation program. Goering said that Germany had had no aerial weapons at the time Hitler took over the government; a completely new and modern air force had been built almost overnight by developing "technical and industrial possibilities to their utmost." "I am not telling you anything surprising," Goering said, "when I emphasize that the German aerial forces are so strong that whoever attacks Germany will have a very difficult stand in the air. For the German fighting forces do not include a single old motor. What is possessed today by the aerial fighting forces in the way of airplanes and motors is the most modern product in existence."[69]

During the crucial years of Hitler's aggregation of power, then-Major Truman Smith served as U.S. military attaché in Berlin. One of his two assistants was an Air Corps officer, Capt. Theodore Koenig. Koenig an able pilot, but he lacked a technical and an intelligence background. On May 6, 1935, Koenig forwarded to Washington a report of Goering's remarks with the conclusion that the Minister's statements were apparently correct. "It is not believed, however," Koenig continued, "that the air fighting force which he referred to is now organized and equipped for immediate action but it is believed that the organization and equipment is well underway and that upon the completion of the construction of airdromes and necessary quarters and hangars, the picture of the German air force as painted by General Goering will be a reality. It is further believed that this force will be equal to that of France."[70]

In the autumn of 1935, Captain Koenig's reports of information regarding the GAF were prefaced with a caveat: "Events are changing very rapidly in Germany and what may be considered good information today may be completely changed tomorrow." Koenig expressed an inability to provide an index report because of a lack of definite details. He could not understand why the Air Ministry was manufacturing Ju 52 aircraft in such large numbers.* He considered these planes to be excellent commercial transport aircraft, but they were in no way first-class bombers. He expected "to soon witness the production of very modern types of military aircraft which had either been secretly designed and tested, or possibly manufactured."[71] Although Major Smith asked that Captain Koenig be replaced by a technically qualified officer early in 1936, Maj. Arthur W. Vanaman, Air Corps, did not arrive in Berlin until July 1937.

In May 1937, when Charles Lindbergh traveled to Europe, it occurred to Smith that a Lindbergh visit to Germany might open contacts beyond Koenig's reach. Lindbergh and his wife began a ten-day visit to Germany on July 22, when they were warmly received by Goering and other high-ranking *Luftwaffe* officials. On a tour of *Luftwaffe* stations and aircraft factories, Lindbergh missed seeing new Messerschmitt fighters still in prototype, but he was told of their operational specifications. At the Heinkel factories, Lindbergh and Smith saw the new He 111 bomber; at Dessau they had a preview of the Ju 87 Stuka dive bomber. Lindbergh was not greatly impressed by the quality of most of the German aircraft types he saw, but he was tremendously impressed by the vitality that infused the German aviation effort. In September and October 1937, Lindbergh again visited Germany, and in these months he and Major Vanaman saw most of the aircraft that the *Luftwaffe* would use in World War II.

Later in October, Lindbergh worked with the military attachés preparing a "General Estimate as of November 1, 1937," which Major Smith transmitted to Washington over his signature, admitting the views he expressed were influenced by Lindbergh. Smith later said the report was deliberately written in dramatic style to attract high-level attention. The report noted the "astounding growth" of German air power from a zero level in just four years. "It is difficult to express in a few words the literally amazing size of the German air industry. . . . Behind this industry stands a formidable group of air scientists, with large and well equipped laboratories and test fields, constantly pushing forward the German scientific advance. . . . The actual November 1st strength of the G Air Force is probably from 175 to 225 squadrons."[72]

In March 1938, Major Vanaman used equally overblown language in describing the use of the GAF in the *Anschluss* between Germany and Austria: "Each cog and wheel functioned efficiently. Heavy bombers and swift fighters accomplished their mission by demonstration, troops were landed by airplane to initiate the attack, and the motorized troops arrived to complete the task and annihilate any resistance. . . . Thus the Air Force has made history as an instrument adapted to quick decisive movements so necessary in modern

---

*Although widely used by the Germans as a transport, the Ju 52 was originally viewed as a bomber.

Early Intelligence Organization

warfare."[73] In August and early September 1938, Lindbergh visited Russia and Czechoslovakia. In his return through Paris on September 9, he expressed pessimism in an interview with Col. H. H. Fuller, the U.S. military and air attaché. Fuller reported: "Col. Lindbergh believes that Germany has the outstanding air force of the world today and that it exceeds in power those of Russia, France, and England combined. German equipment, machinery and factories he considered the best in the world."[74]

Well after the Second World War Col. Truman Smith prepared a memoir on his air intelligence activities in Berlin during the 1930s which generally revealed that he had taken upon himself the task of awakening America to the danger of the Nazi menace. Although in retrospect he believed that the conclusion of the general air estimate of November 1, 1937, had stood up extremely well, Smith noted some important lacunae. "The most significant omission is the report's failure to state that the *Luftwaffe* was not a long-range air force, built around heavy bombers with the primary mission of destroying cities and factories far behind the enemy's lines, but rather an air force designed to operate in close support of Germany's ground armies." Another shortcoming dealt with personnel of the GAF: "While the report took note of the great personnel difficulties which the *Luftwaffe* was encountering, it failed to mention the inexperience and inefficiency of many generals of the *Luftwaffe*. . . . Most of these were infantry and artillery generals transferred into the *Luftwaffe* at the commencement of the rearmament in 1933. This lack of able and experienced air generals was to become a more appreciable factor in causing the *Luftwaffe*'s destruction when the Second World War drew to its conclusion."[75] For all his technical expertise, Lindbergh, the Lone Eagle, apparently had missed a crucial point about the GAF: by organization, training, and aircraft selection it was not an instrument for conducting independent strategic air warfare by heavy bombardment. "This failure to grasp the essential character of the *Luftwaffe*," wrote General Telford Taylor, "goes far to explain the exaggerated predictions of destruction which Lindbergh was soon spreading far and wide."[76]

On July 24, 1936—two days after Lindbergh's first visit to Berlin—emissaries of General Francisco Franco arrived in Germany to request Hitler's assistance in a fascist overthrow of Spain's republican government. In the dock at the Allied war crimes trial at Nuremberg, Goering remembered the buildup of the *Luftwaffe* and the Spanish Civil War. When Franco asked the Fuhrer for support, particularly in the air, Goering recalled, "I urged him to give support under all circumstances, firstly, to prevent the further spread of Communism; secondly, to test my young *Luftwaffe* in this or that technical respect."[77] In Spain, the German *Condor Legion* tested new equipment and perfected the tactics and techniques of air-ground support to be used in Europe. Aided by German and Italian air units, nationalist forces under General Franco were victorious against Spanish government forces until November 1936. At that point, the republicans, aided by an International Brigade and Russian aircraft, successfully defended Madrid.[78] The Spanish Civil War would drag on for three more years.

Six months into the war, the U.S. military attaché in Spain, Col. Stephen D. Fuqua, Infantry, and his assistant for air, Capt. Townsend Griffiss, Air Corps, submitted a summary report on lessons of the air war based on sources in the Spanish Air Ministry and official and unofficial personal contacts. The report, sent in February 1937, stated bluntly: "The flying fortress [concept] died in Spain." It then continued:

> The peacetime theory of the complete invulnerability of the modern type bombardment airplane no longer holds. The increased speeds and modern armament of both the bombardment and pursuit plane have worked in favor of the pursuit.... Pursuit must be employed to protect bombardment or, it is better to say bombardment must rely upon pursuit for its protection. Bombardment must consist of two types of airplanes; the large, heavy weight-lifter for night and the very fast plane for day. The day bombardment must sacrifice all for speed and a reasonable bomb load, but first of all it must be fast.... The old formula of high altitude bombing is exploded. Pursuit with its tactics of attack operates better at high altitudes. It is easier for friendly pursuit to protect a bombardment formation when that formation is at low altitude.... The day bombardment of the future will be done at an extremely low altitude—say 500 feet—using delayed fuzed bombs.... The proportion of pursuit planes to bombardment should be in the ratio of two for one.[79]

Subsequent reports from Captain Griffiss took a more judicious theme that air strength on both sides was so small that aviation could be used only for battlefield support, but Griffiss's report had badly damaged U.S. Air Corps positions by the middle of 1937.

A course in the Army War College conducted during September 1937 used a text entitled "Air Forces and War," which argued that air power had limited value when employed independently and was chiefly useful in support of surface troops. The text cited the air attachés' report from Spain, repeating that "high-altitude bombing was ineffectual, that the 'Flying Fortress' concept had 'died in Spain,' and that small bombers and fighters, which could operate from cow-pasture facilities, were of the utmost utility." Adding to the force of the text, Col. Bryon Q. Jones, a senior Air Corps officer serving on the staff of the Army War College, completely endorsed it in a lecture on September 9, 1937. Jones, who was so astute that he transferred to the Cavalry in 1939, stated that "the Spanish Civil War had demonstrated that ... air power had not progressed markedly from ... World War I." He advocated the "employment of GHQ aviation in close support of ground forces," with "attachment of attack and bombardment [units] to lower echelons ... in the same manner as artillery."[80]

Seeking to counteract the reports from Spain, Maj. Gen. James Fechet, the retired Chief of Air Corps, put out a pamphlet saying air operations in Spain were "sporadic attempts by light bombers and other types dropping light bombs and firing machine guns. . . . These not by the wildest stretches of the imagination are air force operations."[81] Rebutting the Jones lecture, two Air Corps officers assigned to the G–3 WDGS prepared a paper pointing out that Jones was inconsistent with approved Army doctrine laid out in TR 440–15. Maj. Gen. Stanley D. Embick, the G–3, refused the finding. "Aviation," Embick wrote in October 1937, "is a new arm. Our present War Department doctrine has had to be based necessarily on theory and assumption rather than on factual evidence. *Now* we are getting evidence of that character. No doctrine is sacrosanct, and of all military doctrines that of our Air Corps should be the last to be so regarded."[82]

General Arnold became Chief of the Army Air Corps in late 1938, and he later recalled that the U.S. military attaché reports from Spain "were not only weak but unimaginative."[83] In 1938, however, Maj. Gen. Malin Craig, Army Chief of Staff, accepted the arguments of those who believed that operations in Spain and China illustrated the fact that new defensive weapons—particularly AA armaments and antitank weapons—had met the challenge of the notable innovations in offensive weapons—the airplane and the tank. The greatly increased power of the new defensive weapons, Craig noted, had "restored to the defense the superiority it seemed to lose with the advent of the new offensive arms. . . . It is largely because of these new defensive weapons that we find current operations confirming anew the testimony of history that the Infantry is the core and the essential substance of an army. It alone of all the arms approximates a military entity. It alone can win a decision. Each of the other arms is but an auxiliary—its utility measured by the aid that it can bring to the Infantry."[84] In the summer of 1938, General Craig indicated that he wanted to turn over the coastal defense role for long-range bombers to the Navy by refusing to authorize the purchase of additional B–17s. On August 6, 1938, the Chief of Air Corps was informed that developmental expenditures for fiscal years 1939 and 1940 would be "restricted to that class of aviation designed for the close support of ground troops and the protection of that type of aircraft."[85]

Despite the intelligence indications that Germany was building a tactical air force, both the U.S. Army Air Corps and the RAF appeared reluctant to accept the fact that any emerging air force would deviate from the strategic bombing doctrine of Giulio Douhet. In the case of Great Britain, Maj. Gen. Kenneth Strong, who would later become General Dwight D. Eisenhower's A–2 at Supreme Headquarters, Allied Expeditionary Force, would remember that in Imperial Defense College lectures he had described the GAF as "basically ancillary arms" to the operations of the German Army. It seemed to him this description did not suit those who were concerned with strategic air operations and an independent mission for the RAF. In any event, he was forbidden to include in his lectures any comments on the employment of the *Luftwaffe* in war.[86]

Piercing the Fog

During 1934–1935, the British government accepted the theory that in a future war Germany might try to score a quick victory by a large-scale devastating air attack. The Air Staff estimated that casualties on the order of 20,000 might be expected in London within the first 24 hours of aerial bombardment; within a week these might rise to 150,000. A seeming British fear of aerial bombing had been apparent to authorities in Nazi Germany as early as 1934, and it became the substance for a diplomacy that might be characterized as *Luftpolitik*. Paralyzed by the prospect of German war, Great Britain and France abandoned Czechoslovakia to Adolf Hitler in the Munich appeasement pact on September 30, 1938.[87] In General Arnold's words, "Without firing a shot, dropping a bomb, or even starting an engine, Hitler's *Luftwaffe* and his armored forces won for him his first major victory of World War II."[88]

Some historians have believed that the Munich agreement saved Great Britain by providing a year in which to prepare for the *Luftwaffe*. More recent scholars argue that British military intelligence failed the government at a critical juncture. The *Luftwaffe*, they stress, was grossly unprepared for a two-front war in September 1938, and preparations for an air offensive against Great Britain were "totally inadequate" because the GAF had "tied its plans for both 1938 and 1939 closely to the operations of the army" rather than planning for strategic operations.[89]

In the United States, President Franklin D. Roosevelt had listened to men, such as Ambassadors Hugh Wilson in Berlin and William C. Bullitt in Paris, who agreed that Hitler's power rested on an already large air force capable of rapid expansion from existing airplane factories. Ruminating on the inadequate reports from Wilson and Bullitt, Roosevelt reached a conclusion that immediately benefited the Air Corps. At a meeting on November 14, 1938, the President "issued instructions which General Arnold described as the 'Magna Carta' of the Air Force. Roosevelt announced that airplanes—not ground forces—were the implements of war which would have an influence on Hitler's actions." He wanted vastly increased U.S. aircraft production and preparations "to resist [an Axis] assault on the Western Hemisphere 'from the North to the South Pole.'"[90]

Increased support for the Air Corps within the War Department found manifestation in many ways, not the least of which was the appointment of Brig. Gen. George C. Marshall as Deputy Chief of Staff in the summer of 1938. Subsequently, Marshall, who became Acting Chief of Staff in July of 1939 and Chief of Staff the following September, foresaw a much broader use for air power than his predecessor did. When the question of the Army Air Corps' mission was raised again, it was resolved in a definitive statement approved on September 15, 1939. This War Department Air Board report declared, "Air Power is indispensable to our national defense, especially in the early stages of war. Our aviation in peacetime, both its organization and its equipment, must

Early Intelligence Organization

be designed primarily for the application of Air Power in the early days of war. The basis of Air Power is the bombardment plane."[91]

The Approach of War

The Air Board's conclusion marked an important step in the evolution of American air forces. Having gained recognition for a role independent of ground operations, the Army's airmen now had to acquire an air intelligence capability to plan for and execute such operations.

Capt. Robert C. Oliver graduated from the Army C&GSS in the mid-1930s and became instructor in military intelligence at the ACTS. His lectures revealed the deficiencies of existing intelligence organizations to support an air power strategy predicated on neutralizing the basic vital elements of an enemy nation. Oliver explained the two schools of thought in regard to intelligence: one the method of "intentions," the other the method of "capabilities." The method of intentions had long been used in the American Army; it involved a knowledge of hostile dispositions to project an enemy's intentions. The method of capabilities had been used, among others, by Napoleon; it involved determinating an enemy's ability to perform any number of actions. These abilities would dictate which actions were more likely to be used than others, while some actions would be seen as highly unlikely.[92]

The air power strategy, Oliver argued, required a close scrutiny of aspects of an enemy's capabilities not traditionally included in the scope of military intelligence. The prevailing surface strategy, on the other hand, involved a normal intelligence collection of the mere strength, dispositions, and fighting efficiency of an enemy's armed forces. Three types of intelligence estimates were commonly made by the G–2 section and used by the WPD: combat, political, and economic appraisals. Oliver urged that a fourth estimate—the study of an enemy nation from the standpoint of its vulnerability to air attack—was required to permit the WPD to revise existing war plans to include the application of air power. In April 1939, Captain Oliver noted that the old *Index Guide* for attachés did not contain instructions for collecting information required for this fourth estimate. He recommended that the *Guide* be amended and that G–2 provide three to six weeks of instruction on intelligence collection to all new military attachés. This instruction would focus on identification of possible air force objectives. After identifying vital areas and gathering data on them through military attachés, the G–2 could then prepare objective folders on targets in the countries under consideration.[93]

In the spring of 1939, Captain Oliver, with the C&GSS's assistance, prepared a study to be forwarded to the Chief of Air Corps and thence to the Chief of Staff, U.S. Army, recommending changes in the military intelligence procedure. To assist the G–2 in making intelligence estimates for offensive air operations, the study recommended that several Air Corps officers recently graduated from ACTS should be detailed to G–2 for the sole purpose of initiating and carrying out air estimate studies. The study recommended that data from the G–2 information collection agencies (military attachés, foreign missions, and other nonpublicized agencies) should be arranged and compiled into objective folders by the OCAC, with the OCAC Plans Section required to initiate, build, and serve as custodian of these files. Since a need to gather detailed information concerning hostile air forces was present in peace and war, the study also recommended that the Air Corps establish an effective intelligence section to obtain information from new sources. This section would provide information to operational Air Corps units in an appropriate form.[94]

The Air Corps was not represented on the Joint Army-Navy Board which began in 1939 to draw up the series of RAINBOW war plans, and the joint planners in the WPD rarely called for Air Corps assistance. The result was a tendency to create plans that called for air force employment only in direct support of ground arms. Moreover, wrote Lt. Col. Carl A. Spaatz, Chief of the OCAC Plans Division, to General Arnold in August 1939, air intelligence required to support air operations under any of the several U.S. strategic plans was not being maintained ready for use.[95] Arnold convened on August 23 a board of officers under the presidency of Maj. James P. Hodges which included Maj. Thomas D. White, Capt. Robert C. Oliver, and Capt. Gordon P. Saville.[96]

After six days of meetings, the board filed the most comprehensive analysis of Air Corps intelligence requirements to that time. It concluded that the expansion of the Air Corps and the War Department's acceptance of the concept of possible strategic employment of Army air power necessitated a consideration of the effects of air power in all war planning. This, in turn, imposed on information collection and processing agencies an additional, and perhaps major, task. The Air Corps needed intelligence that would permit the Chief of Air Corps to make recommendations relative to strategic planning and other defense projects and would permit technical planning in aircraft development. The report agreed that War Department intelligence responsibilities should be located where means and facilities were available. G–2 could continue to maintain general, nontechnical information about foreign air forces. The Chief of Air Corps should be responsible for gathering technical information on foreign aviation and for processing all information on the use of aircraft for AA defense. The OCAC already processed information on potential landing fields, airdromes, and air bases, and this should remain an Air Corps function.[97]

The Air Corps Intelligence Board's report was not formally submitted to the General Staff; instead, Brig. Gen. George V. Strong, Assistant Chief of Staff, WPD, a member of the earlier War Department Air Board, handled it. In a memo to Arnold on October 5, 1939, Strong completely accepted all the requirements specified as necessary for intelligence support for air matters. Observing that the G–2 was reestablishing a separate Air Section to coordinate all aviation intelligence activities in G–2, Strong believed that the Assistant Chief of Staff G–2 should continue to obtain and assimilate all War Department air intelligence and maintain a current summary of air operations in the European war that had begun with Germany's attack on Poland on September 1, 1939. The Air Corps would prepare airway (route) and objective (target) cards as information became available, and would process information of a technical nature pertaining to foreign aviation.[98]

Coming so soon after the outbreak of war in Europe, the Air Corps Intelligence Board's findings generated interest in the activities of G–2. Even President Roosevelt became involved in military observation abroad, asking General Marshall on September 9, 1939, "[W]hat are we doing about it?"[99] In the OCAC, the Information Division's Intelligence Section maintained connection with G–2 on matters of foreign intelligence. On December 1, 1939, the OCAC directed the Information Division to implement the recommendations of the Air Corps Intelligence Board and to organize and operate the Intelligence Section accordingly. This instruction was to remain in effect until Air Corps intelligence procedures had been "exhaustively studied."[100] Under this mandate, the OCAC Information Division started to collect information outside MID channels when it considered intelligence produced by MID to be inadequate. In May 1940, a representative of the G–2 orally and informally consented to this practice, with the proviso that MID remain the official contact with the Navy and State Departments. G–2 could hardly do otherwise, inasmuch as General Miles lacked the staff to carry out all that was expected of his people. The practice of informal approval with express reservations came to be used more and more as the war progressed and the bureaucratic competition became more complex.

In part because of attention focused on technical intelligence by the Air Corps Intelligence Board, the War Department on September 6, 1940, officially directed the chiefs of all arms and services to establish and maintain intelligence sections as part of their respective organizations.[101] On October 23, Arnold further directed the OCAC Information Division to establish an Evaluation Section that would assess foreign information received from all sources and prepare an air bulletin each week summarizing foreign trends and developments of interest to senior Air Corps commanders and staffs.[102]

In November 1940, the Air Corps changed the name of its Information Division to the Intelligence Division. At this time, the Intelligence Division's Foreign Intelligence Section consisted of a Current Intelligence Branch (Capt. J. F. Olive, Jr.), Operations Planning Branch (Capt. Haywood S. Hansell), and Foreign Liaison Branch (Capt. Elwood R. Quesada). For the expansion of Air Corps intelligence, additional Air Corps Reserve officers and some civilian experts were available. Two notable civilians turned military were Dr. James T. Lowe, a specialist in diplomatic history and international relations, and Capt. Malcolm W. Moss, a man broadly experienced in international business who headed an Air Estimates and Objective Folders Unit under the Operations Planning Branch.[103]

The OCAC Intelligence Division assumed a broad interpretation of what was meant by technical evaluation. Air intelligence considered General Strong's October 5, 1939, memo a War Department directive; the G–2 regarded it as only a suggestion. Early in 1941, Brig. Gen. Sherman Miles, the G–2, objected to a ten-page paper that Hansell had written, "Basis for Intelligence for an Air Estimate of the Situation—Europe." Miles claimed that the MID was responsible for evaluating comprehensive intelligence information; the intelligence section of an arm or service was authorized only to make technical evaluations of information pertinent to that arm or service. Refereeing the difference, the head of the WPD, Brig. Gen. Joseph T. McNarney, himself an air officer, ruled that the Air Corps study was a technical evaluation. He added that air objective folders prepared by Air Corps intelligence were also technical evaluations, even though they might be filled with considerations of the economic or political value of a target.[104] McNarney's opinion favoring the Air Corps' intelligence office seems to have been a very broadly based decision. It may have been rendered out of loyalty to his colleagues, but it certainly pointed out the wide rift between air intelligence in the Air Corps and the G–2.

When the G–2 asked the Chief of Staff to overturn McNarney's ruling, the Air Corps rebuttal demanded that "not only should all information possessed by the MID be made available, but that no hindrance should exist to the collection of additional information by the personnel of the Intelligence Division, Office, Chief of Air Corps, from sources within the United States." Upon seeing these demands signed by Maj. Gen. George H. Brett, Acting Chief of Air Corps, General Miles notified the Chief of Staff on June 12, 1941, that serious duplication existed in practically all phases of military intelligence and that the Air Corps' actions would continue such duplication unless intelligence responsibilities were promptly delineated. A quick decision was necessary because a major reorganization of the Air Corps was in process and specific intelligence functions ought to be cleared up before a new HQ AAF was established.[105]

As Chief of Air Corps and Acting Deputy Chief of Staff for Air after October 1940, Arnold was already aware of the muddle in air intelligence when he became commanding general of the newly established AAF on June 20, 1941. According to Hansell, Truman Smith, after his return from Germany in 1940, informed Arnold of many details regarding the *Luftwaffe* and German aircraft production, information about which Arnold was unaware but which the G–2 already knew. Arnold, surprised and unhappy with news that he considered important to Air Corps planning and operations, went to see General Miles. Miles informed him that since the Chief of Air Corps was not a member of the WDGS, he was not eligible to see such sensitive information. That was too much for Hap Arnold, who went to see General Marshall to get added authority

Early Intelligence Organization

for air intelligence information gathering by the air staff. Marshall seems to have seen the lack of logic in having an air force that did not understand its potential enemies; he approved an expanded air attaché role with limited participation by Captain Hansell and Major White, who laid out the information gathering requirements.[106]

Hansell also recalled Arnold's earlier involvement in the complex bureaucratic wrangling over intelligence responsibilities that arose from a paper Hansell had prepared in 1940 proposing U.S. Army engineers be sent to survey the Burma Road leading into China. When the paper got into the hands of General Miles, he sent it to the Deputy Chief of Staff, Maj. Gen. William Bryden, with the complaint that the OCAC had no business intruding in such matters. The Deputy Chief passed the complaint to Arnold, noting stiffly that if the officers of the OCAC Information Division had no more useful occupation than this, he was prepared to disband the division and transfer its personnel to G–2, where their talents could be directed to some useful purpose. General Arnold was miffed, most probably because he had not known about Hansell's original paper. He sent the correspondence back to the Information Division with the laconic comment, "I am inclined to agree with Gen. Bryden."[107]

The staff officers in the OCAC, and then in the new AAF, pushed hard for greater autonomy from G–2. Two weeks before establishment of the AAF, the Chief of the Intelligence Division, Col. Robert C. Candee, prepared a critique of his division's relations with G–2 for General Brett. He recalled the G–2's resentment about the informal Burma Road proposal and said that Arnold's chief of staff had refused to pay for Air Corps proposals to send air observers abroad and to collect technical intelligence information from New York industrial concerns. A week before General Arnold assumed his new position as head of the AAF, Brett told him that if all intelligence for air force operations had to come from G–2, the Air Corps Intelligence Division would be practically eliminated and air force operations would be at a standstill. A month later, on July 5, 1941, Colonel Candee made a detailed comparison of intelligence functions of MID and the AAF for Arnold. His report concluded, "The AAF desperately needs freedom to prepare for war. Therefore, its intelligence functions should not be restricted by the views and routine channels and practices of the MID."[108]

With the establishment of the AAF, Arnold brought Brig. Gen. Martin Scanlon back from his post as military air attaché in London to become the first AC/AS, Intelligence (A–2). Both Scanlon, and Lt. Col. Harold L. George, AC/AS, WPD, considered the AAF to be virtually autonomous. George argued that the Air War Plans Division (AWPD) was the proper agency to formulate all plans for employment of air power. General Scanlon believed A–2 should provide all the air intelligence upon which to base the plans. "It is apparent," he wrote, "that all restrictions which tend to limit the reliability and efficiency of the Air Intelligence Division should be removed." According to Scanlon, air intelligence comprised evaluated information necessary for the effective conduct of air operations beyond the sphere of influence of surface forces, or in lieu of surface forces, or in support of ground or sea forces, or in AA defense. Preparation of such evaluations required information upon which strategic and tactical objectives could be selected for air offensives, to include air route guides, target analyses, objective folders, navigation charts, enemy OBs, and performance characteristics of enemy aircraft.[109]

General Arnold wanted a quick solution to the delineation of responsibilities; at the end of July 1941 he sent Scanlon to discuss the matter informally with General Miles. As in the past, Miles vigorously and unequivocally declared that the function of collecting intelligence information was the exclusive responsibility of MID, and he denied A–2 the privilege of establishing channels outside of MID. On July 28, 1941, Arnold decided to place the entire problem before General Marshall, sending him a memo on the subject of responsibility for air intelligence. After noting recommendations and justifications he had made previously as Chief of Air Corps, Arnold put forward new arguments based on his new responsibilities as Commanding General of the AAF, charged by Army regulations with control of both the OCAC and the former GHQ Air Force, now designated the Air Force Combat Command. He wrote that in his new job he had to have nearly complete freedom of action from G–2 in intelligence matters. To prevent unnecessary duplication, and no doubt to try to make the suggestion more palatable to the G–2, he suggested that G–2 and A–2 coordinate and cooperate by exchanging available intelligence and checking with each other to see whether information newly desired had not already been collected. He also suggested that G–2's air section remain in MID to handle requirements for air intelligence in the employment of ground or combined forces.[110]

In the same July 28 memorandum to General Marshall, Arnold put in a bid for responsibility over the burgeoning number of Air Corps officers being sent on missions overseas or assigned as assistant military attachés. In November 1940, the Joint Army-Navy Board had taken note of threatened German aerial penetration into Latin America and had declared that the War and Navy Departments would support establishment of U.S. missions in all republics of the Western Hemisphere, with priorities to countries north of Brazil and Ecuador. A number of Air Corps officers had already been sent to Latin American capitals.[111]

Less than a week after the declaration of war by England and France in September 1939, the U.S. War Department had asked those governments if temporary-duty U.S. Army observers could accompany their armies in the field. Approval led to a steady stream of observer reports to the War Department. From Paris, Lt. Col. George C. Kenney reported that captive balloons were completely impractical for observation, as were slow and vulnerable observation planes. Serving in London as a special observer from May to September

Early Intelligence Organization

1940, Carl Spaatz, now a full colonel, had a first-hand view of some of the heaviest fighting of the *Luftwaffe* blitz against England. He quickly concluded "that the Germans had developed 'a mass of air geared to the Army' which was not going to . . . prevail against the 'real air power' developed by the British." Unfortunately, Spaatz noted, the British had committed themselves to short-range planes only to find they needed long-range bombers.[112] By December 1940, the number of U.S. Army special observers sent abroad on various tasks had reached twenty officers, half of them from the Air Corps.[113] More followed the next year.

In the face of these extensive activities, Arnold proposed in July 1941 that Air Corps officers on attaché or mission duty be designated military air attachés, to be appointed through G–2 but to act as collectors of air intelligence. Special intelligence missions were to be assigned only after it was ascertained whether G–2 might have the desired intelligence. In cases of military necessity, the commander of the AAF would have the right to collect necessary air intelligence without consulting G–2. Arnold also requested that A–2 maintain direct liaison with foreign air attachés in the United States and that all cables concerning air matters be forwarded by G–2 to AAF Headquarters as soon as decoded and before being processed.[114]

In response to General Arnold's paper, General Miles complained to the Chief of Staff that work being done by A–2 was contrary to Army regulations. Miles's memo of August 11, 1941, said that Arnold's contentions presented "a perfect picture of dual intelligence, a picture of two offices, largely duplicating each other's work and yet independent as to the results obtained—a picture of parallel lines, meeting nowhere." In rebuttal, Arnold denied that duplication and divergent studies and estimates would result from his proposals, which were not intended to take away G–2's prerogatives, but were meant to speed up obtaining timely and adequate information necessary for technical, tactical, and strategic planning in the AAF. Early in September, General Scanlon had studied applicable Army regulations and pointed out that while MID was charged with general intelligence duties and supervision of intelligence, nothing appeared to prevent other agencies performing the same duties under MID supervision.[115]

The War Department issued its command decision delineating intelligence responsibilities on September 10, 1941. The decision stated that the responsibility imposed on MID for collecting, evaluating, and disseminating military information pertained to the AAF as well as to other arms. The MID was charged with compiling information for comprehensive military studies and with preparing such studies and estimates. AAF intelligence agencies were to compile and evaluate technical and tactical information received from MID and other sources, plus collect technical air intelligence from sources abroad through cooperation with MID. All of these types of information were required by the AAF for their development and for such operations as they might be directed to perform.[116] The War Department delineation disappointed Scanlon, as it left the AAF with too little authority for what he saw as its needs. A few days after the War Department decision was issued, and hoping to fight the decision, Scanlon sent Arnold evidence of an unsound MID evaluation relative to the *Luftwaffe*'s attacks on vital points in Britain's national structure. Arnold decided he could not then press the issue any further. He sent Scanlon's paper back with a cryptic remark: "We are getting what we want and we will simply try out the whole scheme."[117]

Scanlon, at an air staff meeting on September 11, 1941, put the best possible face on the problem, stating "that G–2 had agreed to practically everything we had asked for. Much of it will not be written but is understood." According to the agreement, A–2 had to check with G–2 for availability of information on a given topic. If none were available, A–2 officers, working through G–2 organizations, could obtain it. In addition, G–2 agreed to provide complete reports from their sources so the Air Staff could prepare their own studies. Finally, A–2 was authorized direct contact with other government departments as well as with foreign military attachés on duty in this country.[118] The jurisdictional paper contained a *modus vivendi* that more or less settled the political wrangling and set a pattern for continuing G–2/A–2 relations. It appeared that as long as *the* G–2 was *officially* responsible for intelligence collection and dissemination, Miles would be willing to delegate much of the air intelligence operation to the A–2, the organization most vitally concerned and having the qualified people and desire to do the work. The A–2 continued to be chafed by MID restraints, and the AAF would periodically request severance of its A–2 from G–2's control.

AWPD–1: Planning an Air War

Early in 1941, Anglo-American military staff conferences in Washington began to consider "principles of cooperation 'should the United States be compelled to resort to war.'" The three aviation experts involved were Air Vice Marshal John C. Slessor, RAF; Col. J. T. McNarney, the Air Corps officer assigned to WPD; and Capt. DeWitt C. Ramsey, U.S. Navy. On March 27 the Anglo-American representatives issued a document to be known as American-British Conversations–1 (or ABC–1). Since Germany was the most powerful Axis partner, the main Allied effort would be conducted in Europe, and the democracies would depend largely on the U.S. Pacific Fleet to maintain a defense against Japan. "The Allied offensive in Europe was to include economic pressure through blockade, a 'sustained air offensive' against German military power, early defeat of Italy, and the buildup of forces for an eventual land offensive against Germany. As rapidly as possible, the Allies would achieve 'superiority of air strength over that of the enemy, particularly in long-range striking forces.'"[119]

Early Intelligence Organization

McNarney doubtless knew Air Corps viewpoints, but he represented the WPD. The U.S. Army Air Corps as such had no representation at the American-British Conversations. On March 22, 1941, however, Colonel Candee (OCAC, Intelligence) and Brig. Gen. Carl A. Spaatz (OCAC, Plans) jointly signed an air estimate of the situation. The two concluded:

> While heavy air attacks on England will continue, there will be no serious attempt at a land invasion. The Axis can strangle Britain—slowly, methodically. Time is in favor of the Axis for the next year. It must be expected that the Axis will obtain complete domination over Continental Europe this summer, including the Balkans and possibly Turkey and Asia Minor. . . . Britain must hold until aid from America can bring her air forces to a parity with the Axis. Until then she cannot hope to take the offensive. The war must be fought on a basis of attrition of items critical to the Axis—oil, steel, and foodstuffs, of which we have a superiority. Any active participation by the United States in the European war will probably result in swift, aggressive action by the Japanese against the East Indies and Malaya. If it becomes apparent that the U.S. will become an active belligerent, the Axis powers will seek to have us commit our efforts simultaneously in Europe and in the Far East. This is the worst situation in which we could possibly place ourselves.[120]

In the aftermath of ABC–1, the U.S. War and Navy Departments established closer relations with Great Britain. The Navy sent an observer group to London under Rear Adm. Robert L. Ghormley, and on May 8, 1941, Maj. Gen. James E. Chaney, Air Corps, was ordered to England as a special army observer to carry out secret instructions of the Secretary of War. His real mission was to "work out joint plans of operation and, in the event of war, to assume command functions for such forces as may be employed." The secretary had authorized for Chaney a complete general staff, including a G–2. Establishment of this Special Observers Group in London raised the question of its relationship to Brig. Gen. Raymond E. Lee, the military attaché to Great Britain. From Washington, General Miles informed General Lee that he and the Special Observers Group were mutually independent. Lee was under the supervision of MID, but he was to provide the observers with copies of all his reports.[121]

The Candee-Spaatz estimate of the situation prepared on March 22, 1941, had posed many intelligence questions relative to the work RAF intelligence might have accomplished against Germany. It had recommended that one or more U.S. Army Air Corps officers be attached to the RAF intelligence directorate with free access to gather intelligence required for employment of American air forces if the United States went to war. In the summer of 1941 Haywood Hansell, now a major, arrived in England and received a generous welcome from RAF intelligence. In regard to air target materials, Hansell found on balance that the AAF was better informed on German electric power, petroleum, and synthetic product resources. The RAF knew more about German aircraft and engine production, the GAF, and German transportation. By the end of his visit he had acquired nearly a ton of documents, mostly classified target folders. It was with some relief that he got the cargo hauled back to Washington in a bomber.[122]

On July 9, 1941, some two weeks after Hitler attacked Russia, President Roosevelt asked the Secretaries of War and Navy to prepare an estimate of the overall production requirements required to defeat America's potential enemies. After some delay, the AWPD, headed by Colonel George, was brought into the problem to determine the maximum number of air squadrons the AAF would ultimately require to garrison a great number of geographic sites and to hold what the officers termed reserves of opportunity. George assigned this task to Lt. Col. Kenneth Walker, head of the War Plans Group of the AWPD. Walker brought together a small task force including Hansell, now back from Great Britain and assigned to the War Plans Group, Lt. Col. Max F. Schneider, an able logistician, Lt. Col. Arthur W. Vanaman from A–2, and Lt. Col. Laurence S. Kuter from G–3. The group conceived their task as being to determine air requirements to accomplish the strategy laid out in ABC–1, which had been incorporated into the U.S. strategic war plan RAINBOW 5. A thick study known as AWPD–1, "Munitions Requirements of the AAF," was bound on August 12, 1941, after only seven working days.[123]

The air mission outlined in AWPD–1 followed that defined in the earlier ABC–1. It called for a sustained air offensive against Germany pending a land offensive if an invasion of the continent became necessary. The air planners thought it improbable that a surface invasion could be mounted against Germany for at least three years. If the air offensive was successful, a land offensive might not even be necessary. Three lines of air action were open against a German economy and society supposedly already strained to support the military campaign in Russia. The first, which would accomplish the broad air mission in Europe, required disruption of Germany's electric power and transportation systems, destruction of her oil and petroleum resources, and the undermining of the morale of her people by air attack against civilian concentrations. The second possible line of air action, representing intermediate objectives that might be essential to accomplishing the principal effort, required neutralizing German air power by attacks against air bases, aircraft factories, and aluminum and magnesium production centers. A third line of action, which might be necessary to protect the operating base in England, included attacks against submarine bases, surface seacraft, and possible invasion ports.[124]

AWPD–1 called for neutralizing the following target systems and targets: electric power, 50 generating plants and switching systems; transportation, 47 marshaling yards, bridges, and canal locks; and synthetic petroleum, 27 production plants. The GAF targets included 18 airplane assembly plants, 6 aluminum plants, and 6 magnesium plants. The air offensive against Germany would precede any operations against Japan. Destruction of the GAF thus became the intermediate objective in the European war. The plan envisioned B–17 and B–24 strikes from England and the use of bases in Egypt and

Early Intelligence Organization

Brig. Gen. Haywood Hansell, Jr.   Col. Grover C. Brown

Northern Ireland to accommodate B–29 and B–32 bombers that would be built. Still larger B–36 bombers would have to be designed and built to fly from Newfoundland across Europe, to the Middle East. This contingency would be needed if the British Isles were lost. Based upon the plan of operations they outlined, planners made what would prove to be a very accurate determination of the force requirements of the AAF for World War II.[125]

Although AWPD–1 became a landmark American air force document, its authors strayed from intelligence doctrinal procedures expressed in *U.S. Army Basic Field Manual, Military Intelligence* (printed in 1938 as the revision to TR 210–5, *Military Intelligence,* 1926). Looking back years later, General Hansell noted that he and his associates were never fully abreast of air technical intelligence from abroad. The basic intelligence doctrine explicitly provided that operational command decisions were to be based upon the desired mission objective as affected by the enemy, the means available, and the environment. In retrospect, an experienced air intelligence officer, Col. Grover Brown, would point out in 1951 that the U.S. air strategy for Europe did not properly consider the effect of enemy capabilities. The air planners had not intended to consider enemy capability; as entering arguments, they projected maximum acceptable attrition and the range limitations of Axis bombing aircraft.[126] The lack of sufficiently detailed data about German industry left U.S. planners ignorant of the excess capacity that existed during the early war years.

During the completion of AWPD–1, Major Hansell prepared and mailed to Chaney and Arnold a memo entitled "An Air Estimate of the Situation for the Employment of the Air Striking Force in Europe (ABC–1)." The estimate, which doubled as Hansell's report of his trip to the United Kingdom, was quite similar to AWPD–1, but it was more candid. In contrast to the British belief that

Piercing the Fog

Maj. Gen. Henry H. "Hap" Arnold

air bombardment would break the morale of the German people, Hansell argued for precision attacks, at least initially. Then, "as German morale begins to crack, area bombing of civil concentrations may be effective." Which of the preferred AWPD–1 target systems might be attacked would depend upon the size of the available striking force. Bomber attacks would have to penetrate into Germany for great distances, and escort fighters—as yet undeveloped—would need to accompany the heavily armed bombers. Finally, Hansell argued against piecemeal force employment, urging that an air force of significant size be organized and trained in the United States before deploying to England.[127] Hansell apparently assumed that adequate intelligence existed for the AWPD–1 targets and that precise target intelligence would not be necessary for attacks against what he had termed "civil concentrations."

The completed AWPD–1 reached the WPD of the WDGS before Arnold returned from Argentia, Newfoundland, where he had gone with Marshall for the conversations between President Roosevelt and Prime Minister Winston Churchill. The plan had been checked and tacitly approved by Robert A. Lovett, Assistant Secretary of War for Air. By September 1, both Marshall and Secretary of War Henry L. Stimson had been told of the plan. They liked its concept.

The development of AWPD–1, and its almost immediate acceptance by the Secretary of War and chief of staff of the Army, finally presented air intelligence with the challenge that had been unfolding since the mid-1930s when the ACTS began to articulate its belief in the decisiveness of strategic air attack when employed against the industrial web of an adversary. What previously had been conceptual and notional about targeting now became operational and specific. To execute AWPD–1, AAF leaders had to determine which targets in Germany were both vital to her industrial war machine and vulnerable to strategic air attack. The answers would come from air intelligence, which

Early Intelligence Organization

existed only superficially. A great shortcoming existed in RAF intelligence: The target folders contained little analysis of the targets as elements within the German industrial fabric.[128] The earliest strategic air plan, AWPD–1, suffered from the same shortcomings that affected earlier conceptual thinking and which would later plague early U.S. air operations in Europe: the lack of information on enemy economic and industrial systems sufficiently comprehensive and detailed to permit accurate determination of the vital systems and selection of critical nodes within any one system. Only the experience of war would reveal the full ramifications of the relation between strategic bombing doctrine and the collection and evaluation of intelligence—and would prove just how difficult were the collection and assessment of such information in the midst of conflict.

Air Intelligence on the Eve of Pearl Harbor

The gaps in strategic air intelligence notwithstanding, U.S. military intelligence was, in general, better prepared to support a war in Europe than to serve the defense of the Pacific theater of operations. The anomaly of this situation is particularly striking in view of long-standing American interests in the Pacific and the fact that the Army's Signal Intelligence Service was reading lower-grade Japanese codes and ciphers by early 1939, while Navy code breakers had tapped into the Japanese secret diplomatic code that they called MAGIC.

When the Japanese attacked China in 1938, the U.S. Joint Army-Navy Board called for a revised ORANGE plan based upon a new international situation, but still providing for a position of readiness in the strategic triangle of Alaska-Hawaii-Panama. The recognition by late 1939 that the United States was much likelier to become involved against several powers rather than against Japan alone led to the development of a series of RAINBOW plans to replace the old single-color plans. RAINBOW 4, which was approved by the Secretaries of War and Navy and tacitly accepted by Roosevelt in June 1941, assumed the United States would be allied with Great Britain and France against Germany, Italy, and Japan. RAINBOW 5 called for the adoption of a strategic defensive position in the Pacific until victory over the European Axis would allow transfer of resources adequate for an offensive against Japan.

Even before the adoption of RAINBOW 5 in the summer of 1941, the AAF had started to build up strength in the Pacific. In mid-February 1941, the AAF began to send more modern fighters to Hawaii. In early April, General Arnold committed twenty-one B–17 bombers to Honolulu, the delivery flight being completed the next month. With the transfer of part of the U.S. Pacific Fleet to the Atlantic in the summer of 1941, War Department planners suggested sending four additional groups of B–17s to the Pacific—two each to Hawaii and the Philippines—where their presence might act as a threat to keep the Japanese at bay. Even though the AAF had a total of only 109 B–17s, and with bombers already promised to Great Britain, Arnold agreed to this recommendation. Arnold hoped, perhaps wished, that enough new, heavy bombers would block any Japanese plan to attack the Philippines.[129] This decision, as well as all others regarding the Pacific, had to be made on the basis of very limited knowledge about the potential enemy. A veil of nearly complete secrecy had all but negated normal functions of Army and Navy attachés in the collection of military intelligence in Japan.

In the Central Pacific, the Japanese held a marked advantage in maintaining secrecy. Establishing absolute control over the islands mandated to her by the League of Nations, the Japanese were able to build important naval bases in the Marianas, Carolines, and Marshalls and to conduct naval maneuvers in this vast area, unseen by Western eyes. This area was known to Americans as the Vacant Sea because few commercial vessels and no U.S. naval vessels moved through the area. These seas lay between the great southern trade routes that went from Hawaii to the coasts of Japan and China and the great northern circle routes that skirted the Aleutians. General Mitchell had toured the perimeters of the mandates in the fall of 1923, gathering as much information as possible, and in 1924 he predicted the Japanese would probably use the islands eventually as a springboard for an attack on Pearl Harbor, the Hawaiian Islands, and the United States.[130]

There are those who argue the disappearance of Amelia Earhart was related to Japanese efforts to cover up their activities. In July 1937, during their transworld flight, Earhart and her navigator Fred Noonan disappeared at sea after a flight from Lae, New Guinea, on a 2,556-mile flight to Howland Island. No one has ever found their bodies or plane, and it has been alleged, but never substantiated, that they were on a spy mission for the United States. According to this supposition, they went down, were picked up by the Japanese somewhere off the Marshall Islands, and were taken to Saipan, where they eventually died.*
U.S. researchers and writers who have examined the Earhart disappearance have split opinions on the issue, but those who suggest Japanese involvement have offered little substantive evidence to support their allegations.[131]

Japanese sources deny both the spying charge and the existence of any rationale for spying. As recently as February 1987, Comdr. Chihaya Masataka, a Japanese naval officer who served during World War II, disputed the spy assertion and, moreover, claimed that the Japanese engaged in no abnormal buildup of defensive fortifications on the mandated islands.[132] His views are consistent with those offered at the Eleven Nation Military Tribunal in 1946

---

*In March 1992, The International Group for Historic Aircraft Recovery claimed to have found evidence that Earhart and Noonan landed on Nikumaroro Island (formerly Gardiner Island) about two hours' flying time from Howland. Nikumaroro is one of the Phoenix Islands, at that time controlled by the United States and Great Britain.

when 310 Japanese witnesses also denied charges that Japan had rearmed the mandated islands before the war, although Japan did deepen the harbors and built airfields and roads there.[133] Amelia Earhart aside, the mandated islands remained a blind spot in American military and naval intelligence prior to Pearl Harbor. Intercepted radio traffic, however, alerted the Pacific Fleet to extensive activities there, and the United States eventually determined that Japan's Fourth Fleet and part of the Sixth Fleet's submarines were based at Truk and Kwajalein.[134]

In the summer of 1941, General Arnold found Adm. Harold R. Stark, the Chief of Naval Operations, very much worried about what the Japanese were doing at Truk and Rabaul. Arnold arranged for some of the B–17s going to the Philippines to fly off course and take photographs of the two islands. In the confusion that attended the Japanese attack on the Philippines in December, the photographs were lost without having contributed to war preparations.[135] In late November the AAF ordered B–24 bombers equipped with photographic capability and fully armed to be sent over Truk and Rabaul to take pictures from high altitude. The first such B–24 arrived in theater without guns, and it was not possible to switch armament from the B–17s already there. Before the proper weapons could be sent, the Japanese attack on Clark Field had destroyed the B–24s.[136]

Explaining the inadequacy of the estimates of likely Japanese actions in late 1941, Miles pointed out that at the time MID had been heavily concerned with Europe. "We were still primarily concerned, up to November 1941," he said, "with the European war, the outcome of that war. We were still feverishly preparing for what we called hemispheric defense. The success of German arms was the most obvious threat to the Western Hemisphere." In early December, General Miles thought that a Japanese line of action against the south was "very probable" and that southern expansion would involve the Philippines. If the United States went to war with Japan, Hawaii and Panama might very well be attacked, but not immediately. Miles knew that the Japanese were capable of making an attack on Hawaii. "I did not believe, up to a very late date, that it was probable that they would make that attack at the outbreak of war, for the reason that . . . such an attack . . . had to result from two separate decisions of the Japanese: one to take on a war with a great naval power, and presumably with two great naval powers. . . and second, to start that war, or at least make this attack on a great fortress and fleet, which inherently jeopardized the Japanese ships making the attack to some extent, and which rested almost solely for success on the unpredictable circumstances that they would find that fortress and that fleet unprepared to meet that attack."[137]

Arnold offered a similar estimate, although with less elaborate explanations: "Looking back on it, I am convinced now that we all assumed that the Japs would attack the Philippines. We were fairly sure that they would cut our air line, because they had to cut our line to stop our heavy bombers from getting to the Philippines. We were pretty sure that they would attack Wake and Midway when they did attack. . . . So I think that there was a general acceptance of the possibilities of Japanese aggression, certainly against the Philippines and against Wake and Midway, and possibly, against Hawaii."[138]

Evaluations of the intelligence failure at Pearl Harbor would reveal deficiencies not only in organization but also in interpretation. Miles himself stated: "In estimating the situation . . . there are two principles that should be followed: One is never to lose sight of or ignore anything that the enemy may do that is within its capabilities whether you think it is wise for him to do that or not . . . . The second is to concede to your enemy the highest form of good sense and good judgment."[139] There are those who argue that the U.S. government somehow had advance warning of the Pearl Harbor attack which it chose to ignore. The most exacting examination of the story of Pearl Harbor, however, concludes that the United States was genuinely surprised.[140] That surprise resulted in no small way from the intelligence analysis failure that accepted estimates of probable enemy intentions rather than accepting broad-range assessments of enemy capability for alternate actions.

A Tentative Assessment

Had Pearl Harbor represented an isolated failure of prewar intelligence, it would have been difficult enough to explain. As the United States found itself at war, the attacks on Pearl Harbor and the Philippines were examples of what Arnold later referred to as "one of the most wasteful weaknesses in our whole setup . . . our lack of a proper Air Intelligence Organization."[141]

To a large extent, the problems with air intelligence in the years before 1942 reflected the broader issues of the role of air power and its place in the national defense establishment. In an era when honest differences of opinion and inevitable bureaucratic infighting were exaggerated by tight budgets and crippling manpower limitations, struggles over where to place air intelligence functions within the War Department and the Air Corps were inevitable. The uncertain and often confusing responsibilities of General Staff and Air Corps/Air Forces intelligence organizations reflected a search for organizational identity in the development of the Air Corps. As with any evolutionary process, progress proceeded by fits and starts, with false offshoots and inappropriate adaptations occurring along the way.

Compounding organizational issues were the broader, and ultimately more critical, conceptual ones of defining what constituted air intelligence and determining how it should be acquired, interpreted, and disseminated. Those airmen who developed the theory of strategic bombing at the ACTS in the 1930s recognized that it demanded far more than traditional intelligence information such as enemy OBs and combat capabilities. Their grasp did not include the breadth and depth of information required, nor the ramifications of obtaining and evaluating it; this became obvious once strategic bombing operations began in 1942.

At the very least, the prewar American military intelligence apparatus was clearly inadequate. The intelligence structure could not acquire the type of information required for the theories of strategic air operations that airmen had advanced and planned for in such key documents as AWPD–1. Obtaining relevant data became even more difficult once hostilities commenced. Moreover, as the war years would demonstrate, the question of who was best qualified to evaluate that information, and thus be in a position to affect both planning and operations, was not nearly so simple as airmen had believed in the 1930s.

Finally, any assessment of the American Army's air intelligence prior to Pearl Harbor, and the effect of that intelligence on plans and preparations, must confront obvious flaws in the assessment of soon-to-be enemies. Because they assumed that potential foes would develop forces for the same purposes and employ them in the same manner as they themselves, military and civilian observers misread capabilities and intentions of both the Japanese and the German Air Forces. How successfully and how quickly these problems in intelligence—whether organizational, procedural, or interpretive—could be corrected would directly affect the ability of the AAF to conduct the air war after Pearl Harbor.

CHAPTER 2

The Tools of Air Intelligence:
ULTRA, MAGIC, Photographic Assessment and the Y-service

THE REVELATION IN 1974 that the western Allies had been reading the most secret German messages throughout the Second World War has led to a new interest in the relationship of intelligence to the planning and conduct of operations in that conflict. Unfortunately, the tendency in some quarters has been to overemphasize the role of what has come to be called ULTRA—information from high-grade signals intercepts—while neglecting other elements of intelligence. American air leaders and their staffs drew upon a full range of intelligence sources and methods of collection and analysis to gain the most complete picture of the enemy, including his tactics and technology, his strengths and weaknesses, and his capabilities and objectives. These methods included photointelligence, economic studies based on prewar statistics and extrapolated wartime production levels, elaborate networks of informants, well-placed observers, resistance groups, and analyses of aircraft components and designs by aviation technicians thousands of miles from a combat theater. Although signals intelligence (SIGINT) in Europe and the Far East eventually became a primary source of air intelligence, it attained this position only gradually, and it succeeded then because SIGINT could reach into the most sensitive of the enemies' activities. For much of the war, more of the intelligence that went into the planning and execution of strategic and tactical air operations came from other sources.

ULTRA and diplomatic cryptography (MAGIC) were not the only elements within the field of SIGINT. SIGINT included interception, deciphering, translation, and analysis of enemy low-grade ciphers; interception of unencoded enemy radio transmissions; analysis of radio and wireless traffic patterns (traffic analysis); and efforts to locate and catalog enemy electronic emissions. Direction finding (DF), the process of determining the location of enemy transmitters through a process of triangulation based on the angle at which transmission signals were received by two or more receivers, was primarily of tactical value and generally had greater applicability to ground and naval operations. This was so because enemy army headquarters were more likely than air corps headquarters to relocate frequently, and fleets at sea were often moving or preparing to move. For airmen, DF also came to be used to determine the location and signal characteristics of radar, which allowed commanders to judge AA defenses and fighter control capabilities and then to adapt mission planning. The primary purpose of traffic analysis (TA) was to secure at least some information about the enemy's presence and possible organization when deciphering the messages was not possible. This method of intelligence involved analyses of communications frequencies and message patterns (length, volume, and direction), and it could provide information on the location and size of an enemy headquarters and the level of potential activity by forces under its command. SIGINT was the method for tracking and analyzing enemy aircraft navigational beams and for analyzing enemy radar development and employment.

SIGINT reflected a modern adaptation to a traditional objective of military intelligence—trying to intercept the enemy's communications. In the same sense, aerial photography represented a modern application of the traditional intelligence role of the cavalry, marking as it did the effort to find a higher hill from which to observe the enemy. More precisely, photographic intelligence consisted of two distinct but intimately related tasks, each requiring unique skills, equipment, and organization. The first—photoreconnaissance—consisted of the operational missions to take the photographs. The second—photointerpretation—involved making military sense from the photos' content.[1] Despite the lack of emphasis placed on this method of intelligence collection in the U.S. Army between the wars, photointelligence would prove essential to the planning, conduct, and evaluation of nearly all aspects of air combat operations. In the strategic air war in Europe, accurate and current photographs were so essential for target folders that, for much of the war, missions were not flown unless they were available.[2]

The most closely guarded secret of the war was ULTRA. Despite the number of individuals who dealt with or knew about this intelligence tool, not until almost three decades after Germany's surrender did it become public knowledge. The breaking of the Enigma encryption machine and the use of intelligence thus acquired represented one of the greatest coups in the history of military intelligence. A certain irony lies in the fact that the supposedly naïve and soft democracies of the West were the most successful in one of the most subtle but most difficult aspects of the war—cryptanalysis.

Yet this success did not come overnight, nor was its impact uniform in time or place. Not until mid-1943 did it begin to influence the strategic air war against Germany, and almost another year passed before it made a major impact on strategic planning decisions in that campaign. In the tactical air arenas, ULTRA would be useful in North Africa and subsequent operations in Sicily and

Italy, but it reached its zenith in the battle for Northwest Europe, two and a half years after the United States entered the war. During the same period, the Japanese messages the American cryptanalysts had been reading since 1941 contained both diplomatic and military information. Although the Navy began its Japanese code-breaking efforts as early as 1927, and it had a fairly good grounding in the analysis of Japanese naval message traffic, regular breaking of the Japanese Navy and Army ciphers continued to be a long and laborious process. The most valuable Japanese Army codes would not begin to be broken until early in 1943.

The methodologies and characteristics of ULTRA, photointelligence, MAGIC, and the form of tactical SIGINT known as Y intelligence collectively became the major fundamental components of air intelligence. An understanding of what they were, how they operated, and how they were incorporated into the AAF's planning and operations is essential for understanding the role of intelligence in air operations.

ULTRA

Secretary of State Henry L. Stimson's perhaps apocryphal admonition that "gentlemen do not read other gentlemen's mail" notwithstanding, nations traditionally have done so, and World War II was no exception. As impressive as the American effort was against the Japanese diplomatic and military high-grade ciphers in the Pacific, the British had made even greater strides against the European Axis. Assisted initially by the Poles and the French, they had succeeded in breaking many of the German and Italian top-secret military ciphers long before the United States became a belligerent. By the time American forces began combat operations, the British had established extensive facilities in England and throughout the Mediterranean to intercept German and Italian radio signals. The nerve center of this far-flung effort was the innocuously named Government Code and Cypher School located at Bletchley Park (BP), a former country estate some fifty miles northwest of London.*[3]

Intercepting electronically transmitted signals is a simple process. For this reason those who do not wish their signals to be read resort to ciphers—the use of numbers, symbols, and letters to represent other symbols and letters. It was BP's role to decipher the enemy's messages, then to translate them, and finally

---

*The Germans were, of course, doing the same thing, often very effectively. During early operations in the Western Desert, for example, they routinely read messages describing British intentions and capabilities sent by the American military attaché in Cairo. Similarly, the German Navy's *B-Dienst* radio intelligence unit intercepted and skillfully used Allied naval messages to attack convoys until the summer of 1943.

to assess their potential intelligence value and pass this information to appropriate government sections and commanders.

By far the most difficult of these tasks was the first. Given the complexity of the ciphering device the German military used for most high-grade messages—the Enigma machine—deciphering was a daunting job. Each of the German services used Enigma machines, but with differing keys. The British and later the Allied teams at BP worked on all of the varied keys, only some of which they succeeded in breaking. Not all keys that were read could be read consistently. The German Army's signals were most difficult for the Allied code breakers, and those of the *Luftwaffe,* the most lucrative. Ironically, it was the seeming impossibility of breaking into the Enigma that made it such a unique and unprecedented source of intelligence. Convinced that the system was impenetrable, the Germans made extensive use of Enigma machines throughout the war, relying almost exclusively on them for the overwhelming majority of their high-grade enciphering. Even had the Germans wanted to do so, replacing Enigma with new machines would have been very difficult, given the large number in use.[4]

The Enigma was indeed a formidable machine. Originally adapted by the German armed forces from a commercial machine in the late 1920s and modified several times thereafter, it operated somewhat along the lines of a typewriter. The keys were attached to a complex system of wires, rotary wheels (initially numbering three, with more added later), electric lights, and plugboard connectors. As each letter was typed on the keyboard, it sent an impulse through the machine which set rotary wheels into motion and, based on a predetermined setting, caused a different letter to light up. To decipher the message, the recipient had to have an identical machine, set to the proper master setting, on which an operator would type the enciphered message in groups of five letters. The machine would reverse the process and light up, letter by letter, with the original message.

Although Polish cryptanalysts had begun to read Enigma messages as early as 1933, subsequent German modifications and the variety of possible settings meant that, as one American historian has summarized, "The breaking of the Enigma was not a one-time feat, but an extraordinary, continuous process."[5] Because of the number of interchangeable wheels, the potential settings for each one, the possible plug connections, and the variety of master settings, it has been estimated the number of possible settings on an Enigma could have been as high as 2.69×10^{23} for each key.[6] During the war, different elements of the German military used more than 50 separate master keys or ciphers (e.g., Red was the general-purpose GAF code, while Garlic was the GAF weather key).[7]

The first decipherments were carried out painstakingly by hand with the assistance of cribs—clues that might be revealed by the repetitious use of certain words or phrases, or even by the style of specific operators. This approach meant extensive delays between transmission of the original German

Tools of Air Intelligence

message and its decipherment and subsequent translation by BP. In the summer of 1939, the Poles offered the British an Enigma they had themselves built, and which they had used to read German traffic for some years.[8] The following spring, the British developed the Bombe, an electromechanical calculating machine that could determine daily Enigma settings much more quickly than could manual analysis. With the production of additional Bombes, the speed with which Enigma messages could be deciphered improved significantly.[9]

In February 1944, the British introduced an even more sophisticated machine, the Colossus, capable of handling up to 25,000 bits per second. Ten of these were in operation by the spring of 1945. Colossus was aimed not at the Enigma but at an even more complex machine, the *Geheimschreiber* (literally, secret writer), an on-line teleprinter, penetration of whose signals required the construction of an early programmable electronic digital computer. *Geheimschreiber*, called Fish by the Allied analysts, transmitted messages of the highest command. Enigma encrypted for transmission the more operationally and tactically oriented military traffic. Fish decryption was rarely current, from three to seven days behind, once the machine's design was understood and its signals were broken in 1943.[10] The lack of quick transcription of Fish traffic was not necessarily a drawback; the nature of the information transmitted was not as perishable as that sent by Enigma.

Deciphering of Enigma messages took place in Hut 6, one of several temporary buildings that soon dotted the grounds at BP. From there, German Army and Air Force messages went to Hut 3, while naval messages were handled in Hut 8. At Hut 3, watch officers were responsible for translating the messages and establishing an initial priority for handling before passing them to Army (3–M) or Air (3–A) intelligence sections. Army and Air Force officers evaluated and analyzed each message, determined which operational command had a need to know, and prepared a signal for transmission to the appropriate headquarters (including agencies such as the Air Ministry), sometimes with annotations from previous ULTRA intercepts to assist the recipients in their evaluation. Between January 1944 and the end of the war, BP sent almost 50,000 messages with intercepted signals information to Supreme Headquarters, the Air Ministry, and other addressees.

The outgoing traffic, however, represented but a small part of the total volume of intercepted German military and civil messages. Most messages contained annotated comments from other ULTRA decrypts intended to help the recipient put the data into reasonable context.[11] To aid in this process, Hut 3 maintained an air index which consisted of hundreds of thousands of cards on which was recorded information on everything relating to the GAF, from unit designations and locations, to weapons and equipment, to scientific terms, and even including phrases or words whose meaning had not yet been determined.[12]

The special communications channels established to provide this supersensitive material to operational field headquarters consisted of a special

An Enigma machine captured from the German Army in France in August 1944.

communications unit (SCU), which operated the radio equipment for receiving and sending signals, and a special liaison unit (SLU) responsible for deciphering, physically controlling, and destroying ULTRA material. SCU and SLU members served with every senior field commander who received ULTRA information. Dissemination of Enigma-generated intelligence—and especially its source—was tightly restricted, particularly in the early years, to a very small number of senior commanders and staff officers. Accordingly, a new security classification designator was created: TOP SECRET ULTRA. Over time, the designation ULTRA came to be applied to that intelligence derived from the German Enigma machine traffic and to decrypted Japanese traffic as well.

Early in 1941, a small delegation of experts working for the U.S. Army's Signal Intelligence Service went to London for conferences with the British on cryptographic technology. The meetings were an outgrowth of the October 1940 visit to the United States by Sir Henry Tizard, one of the guiding mentors of the British radar defense system, and several others. The Tizard Mission brought to America a number of new scientific-military developments including the cavity magnetron, essential to generating microwave radar signals. Following the American visit to London, the British received copies of the American PURPLE and RED machines for use in decrypting Japanese diplomatic and naval radio traffic. In return, although after some delay, the British sent one of their copies of the German Enigma machines to Washington.[13]

American involvement in the operational aspects of Great Britain's ULTRA system evolved only slowly after December 1941. This growth was in marked contrast to the previously concluded extensive Anglo-American exchanges of cryptographic technology in early 1941 and to the rapid development of otherwise remarkably integrated Anglo-American intelligence operations and organizations. During the first eighteen months, American military commanders in Europe and their superiors in Washington received only limited distribution of decrypted ULTRA and did not understand, except for a very few technical experts like the cryptologist William F. Friedman* of the Army's Signal Intelligence Service, how the British handled the deciphering, distribution, or analysis of this intelligence.[14] For strategic air operations over Europe as well as during Operation TORCH and the subsequent struggle for North Africa, the British maintained complete control over the interception, decryption, evaluation, and distribution of Enigma-generated intelligence.

By the spring of 1943 the United States sought a greater role in SIGINT activities in Europe. The British remained extremely reluctant to relinquish their monopoly over the Axis codes and ciphers, in part because the United States already had a blemished record when it came to keeping military secrets. Just days before Pearl Harbor the isolationist *Chicago Herald Tribune* had published the text of the War Department's so-called Victory Program for the development of American military capabilities necessary to defeat the Axis in the event of war. The *Tribune*'s source for this document was almost certainly an officer within the War Department. In addition, from the fall of 1941 to the summer of 1942 the Germans had broken the code used by the American military attaché in Cairo, and they used the information thus gained in operations against the British in the Western Desert. By 1943, however, the Americans could offer an important bargaining chip, after recently breaking several of the major Japanese high-level military ciphers.[15]

Despite an obvious wariness on both sides, the two governments signed an agreement on sharing information on May 17, 1943. According to this document, the British would continue their efforts against the German and Italian high-grade ciphers (ULTRA) as well as lower-grade signals and radio traffic sent in the clear (unencoded).† The Americans would continue their assault against Japanese military, air, naval, and diplomatic ciphers.[16] The partners agreed to continue exchanging intelligence so gained and to establish special procedures to ensure its secure handling and to prevent it from being inadvertently commingled with intelligence from other sources. These

---

*William F. Friedman (1891–1969), a cryptanalyst of great ability, began to appear prominently in Army SIGINT during World War I. After the war, Friedman worked as the Army's chief cryptanalyst in a very small office directed more to developing new codes and ciphers than to penetrating those of foreign powers. He was instrumental in training Army officers in cryptography and cryptanalysis and in leading the team that broke the PURPLE cipher.

†Low-grade and high-grade in this context refer to the complexity of encipherment, not to the inherent value of the intelligence that might be derived from intercepted signals.

procedures basically followed those the British were already practicing. Signals containing ULTRA material could be sent over only the most secure communications channels and handled solely by the SCUs with secure, mostly one-time, cipher pads. Access to raw (undisguised) ULTRA would be restricted to individuals who had been indoctrinated in its special value and who had a definite need to know. Finally, the agreement provided for liaison officers who would handle ULTRA to be assigned to all major Allied air and land commanders.[17]

While these negotiations were underway in Washington, Col. Alfred McCormack,* Deputy Chief of Special Branch, Military Intelligence Service (MIS); Maj. Telford Taylor,† General Counsel of the Federal Communication Commission, recently brought into the MIS Special Branch; and William Freidman, who had been instrumental in breaking the Japanese diplomatic codes, were in the United Kingdom to study the SIGINT organization and procedures at BP. With the formal agreement between the two nations, Taylor, promoted to lieutenant colonel, remained in the United Kingdom to serve as the senior American MIS representative for ULTRA.[18]

---

*Col. Alfred McCormack (1901–1956) was Deputy Chief of the Special Branch of the MIS from May 1942 to June 1944 before becoming Chief of the Directorate of Intelligence, MIS. In January 1942, Secretary of War Henry L. Stimson appointed McCormack as his special assistant, assigning him to study the way the War Department handled SIGINT and to recommend improvements. McCormack, a lawyer in civilian life, entered the Army commissioned as a lieutenant colonel. He eventually attained the rank of colonel. It was his recommendation that led to the establishment of the Special Branch within MIS in May 1942. Special Branch was a unit staffed, in part, by lawyers and highly educated civilians who received commissions as Army officers and whose job it was to analyze, evaluate, interpret, process, and disseminate SIGINT systematically for the War Department. Upon his discharge from the Army in 1945, McCormack worked with the State Department on intelligence matters until April 1946, when he returned to his private law practice. For an account of Colonel McCormack's wartime experiences and for his personal War Department files see SRH–185 and SRH–141, pts 1, 2, NA, RG 457.

†Col. Telford Taylor (1908–) was in charge of the London Branch of MIS, headquartered at the American Embassy at Grosvenor Square. He entered the Army as a major in 1942 after attending Harvard Law School and serving as a lawyer from 1933 to 1942 for federal agencies and congressional committees. From 1945 to 1955 he served as a prosecutor in the Nuremberg war crimes trials. He was promoted to brigadier general in 1946 and remained with the Army for three more years. He later practiced law in New York City and became a professor of law at Columbia University. Among his books are *Sword and Swastika: Generals and Nazis in the Third Reich* (New York, 1952), *Nuremberg and Vietnam: An American Tragedy* (New York, 1970), and *Courts of Terror: Soviet Criminal Justice and Jewish Emigration* (New York, 1976). His most important book was *Munich: The Price of Peace* (New York, 1979).

Tools of Air Intelligence

Despite the signed agreement, according to the official history of MIS activities in London, the early months of this new relationship were marked by "a lack of confidence on both sides." Not until September did the British permit Taylor rather than their own officers to determine what to forward to Washington. It would take another year before virtually all signals went across the Atlantic without having to be cleared through London.[19] Until January 1944, the bulk of the material Washington received through Taylor's office dealt with the German Army rather than the *Luftwaffe*. With the arrival at BP of an AAF officer in January 1944, the amount of air intelligence increased significantly. By June 1944, ULTRA material, which expanded considerably from January to June, was sent to the United States by air three times weekly, in addition to material deemed sufficiently time-sensitive to be transmitted by radio.[20] In the late summer of 1943, Colonel Taylor had moved his office from London to BP. That fall, the first American cryptanalysts and translators began to work in Hut 6 and perform as watch officers in Hut 3. By spring 1944, some fifty American officers and enlisted men were serving as cryptanalysts and translators at BP.[21] By June 1944, two USAAF officers were functioning with the air intelligence section of Hut 3 as well.

In January 1944, Taylor established an organization known as 3–US to handle the analysis and dissemination aspects of ULTRA intelligence. The members of 3–US selected messages and summaries to be sent to Washington. Its officers were also incorporated into the existing Hut 3 Army and Air Force intelligence sections that evaluated decrypted messages and sent appropriate signals to field commands throughout Europe and the Mediterranean. In addition, Taylor's organization served as the parent headquarters for the American liaison officers assigned to operational commanders—designated special security officers (SSOs) and special security representatives.* At its peak, 3–US contained sixty-eight people. Ten performed liaison duties between BP and Washington; twelve served as intelligence officers in Hut 3, and three handled various administrative duties in London. Nineteen American technicians had been incorporated into the British SCU/SLU communication system, and twenty-four officers served as special security liaison officers at operational headquarters.[22]

The SSOs were the conduits through which American commanders received ULTRA. For air forces in Europe and the Mediterranean, tactical air commands were the lowest headquarters to which SSOs were sent. (For a variety of reasons, the situation was more complicated in the Pacific theaters; that is addressed later in this chapter.) These individuals, only twenty-eight of whom served in Europe during the war, were all personally selected by Colonel

---

*The term "Special Security Representative" was the designation for the senior liaison officers. Since most American air headquarters had only one liaison officer, the term "Special Security Officer," or SSO, will be used throughout this study.

65

McCormack. They remained MIS representatives under the command of Colonel Taylor and were attached rather than permanently assigned to operational headquarters.[23]

In March 1944, the U.S. Army Chief of Staff personally delineated the responsibilities of these officers, whose ranks ranged from lieutenants to lieutenant colonels. In a letter to General Eisenhower, the senior American officer in Europe, General Marshall wrote of the SSOs, "Their primary responsibilities will be to evaluate ULTRA intelligence, present it in useable form to the commanding officer and to such of his senior staff officers as are authorized ULTRA recipients, assist in fusing ULTRA intelligence with intelligence derived from other sources, and give advice in connection with making operational use of ULTRA intelligence in such fashion that the security of the source is not endangered."[24] This was a heavy burden. In the words of one junior officer, it was a great compliment that his commanding general entrusted him to evaluate signals rather than reading them himself, but it was also one that "produced gray hairs."[25]

The SSOs were not the only individuals indoctrinated into or authorized to handle ULTRA. By the fall of 1944, in fact, the number of indoctrinated officers had expanded well beyond commanders and senior staff officers. General Spaatz's personal intelligence officer at HQ USSTAF (Adv.) handled ULTRA along with other intelligence sources. At least four USSTAF officers on duty in the Air Ministry had access to ULTRA.[26] By the end of the war, some twenty-five to thirty officers in HQ Eighth Air Force were cleared to receive ULTRA.[27]

The circle of indoctrinated individuals remained quite small. At HQ Ninth Air Force, it included only the commanding general, the director of intelligence, and a few others, including the director of operations, but none of his subordinates.[28] In the Southwest Pacific, the Fifth Air Force director of operations was not cleared for ULTRA until late in 1944, and his deputy Lt. Col. Francis C. Gideon knew only that Capt. Phil Graham, who was serving as the SSO, "was in that kind [special intelligence] of business."*[29] The Chief of Staff of XIX Tactical Air Command (TAC), which supported Third Army in Europe, was not cleared for ULTRA until October 1944, more than four months after D-day.[30]

Regardless of the scope of his clientele, it remained the SSO's responsibility to shepherd ULTRA, ensure its secure handling, and prevent operational decisions that might jeopardize its continuance. The delicate situations in which this placed junior officers somewhat explains their special status outside the normal headquarters command structure. Their position allowed them greater freedom to remind senior officers of the restrictions on the handling, discussion,

---

*Gideon, later the Fifth's deputy for operations and subsequently a lieutenant general, also noted he could not "recall a single instance when Phil Graham's information was particularly valuable to me." Intvw, Dr. Robert C. Ehrhart with Lt Gen Francis Gideon, May 18, 1988, p. 22.

and use of ULTRA. Since not everyone within a headquarters was indoctrinated for ULTRA, even within intelligence sections this detached position also made it easier, though it was still delicate, to bypass such individuals.

This approach also could be used to circumvent those few individuals who, although indoctrinated, did not accept the importance of ULTRA. For example, for a period of time at Ninth Air Force, the director of intelligence ordered the SSO not to discuss ULTRA with his nominal superior, the chief of operations intelligence, because the latter refused to integrate it into the intelligence process. The SSO instead dealt directly with the directors of intelligence and operations.[31] The Eighth Air Force SSO reported "suspicion and apparent jealousy existed," and noted the chief of target section was "outspoken" in his distrust of ULTRA and preference for photointelligence and prisoner of war (POW) interrogations.[32]

To explain their presence, their special insights, and their access to the commanding general, SSOs had to invent appropriate titles. These included titles such as GAF expert, Russian liaison officer, evaluations and appreciations officer, air OB expert, and general liaison and special reports officer.[33] Maintenance of this cover often required a great deal of time and effort. For example, as the "GAF expert" at XXIX TAC, Capt. Langdon Van Norden also received all non-ULTRA intelligence on OB, airfields, and aircraft, and he prepared reports in addition to handling all ULTRA traffic.[34] Despite a certain degree of curiosity among nonindoctrinated intelligence officers, none of the SSOs assigned to air headquarters identified the issue of suitable cover as a major problem. These officers agreed they had little trouble keeping separate in their own minds what was ULTRA and what had come from other sources.[35]

Rigid compartmentalization also necessitated physically separating ULTRA from other intelligence material, sometimes creating administrative and logistics difficulties. The SSO with IX TAC reported that when he landed on "the Far Shore" after D-day, his first "office" was a log in an apple orchard, and his only support material, a portable map case.[36] Another SSO noted sharing a trailer with the director of intelligence had the advantage of constant access, but the many nonindoctrinated visitors made it difficult to work with ULTRA materials.[37] More demanding on the individuals involved were limitations on the number of SSOs, which placed heavy demands on these individuals and sometimes reduced the availability of ULTRA, particularly among tactical air forces. This was especially evident at air headquarters, probably due to their smaller size compared to their ground counterparts. At most air headquarters the single SSO was on call twenty-four hours a day. When a tactical air command headquarters was physically separated from its army coheadquarters—as happened during fast-moving operations in the summer of 1944—the appropriate special communications unit went with the army headquarters. During these periods, some SSOs spent up to nine hours daily traveling between headquarters and the SCU. Not surprisingly, service during these periods was limited.[38]

The most serious limitation caused by the compartmentalization of ULTRA was that it made more difficult the primary task of the SSOs—the interpretation of ULTRA and its fusion with other sources. To do these tasks properly required the SSO not only to keep abreast of all ULTRA intelligence, but also to read, digest, and correlate other sources as well. The interpretation of intelligence from other sources and the use of ULTRA-derived insights to guide interpretations of this other material were complicated and delicate processes which often had to be accomplished indirectly. One ULTRA liaison officer commented not only on the time and effort required to deal with ULTRA and non-ULTRA sources, but also on the loneliness of having no one at his level with whom he could discuss possible interpretations and ideas.[39]

The reluctance to clear individuals in key intelligence positions contributed to the difficulties of using ULTRA most effectively. At Ninth Air Force (Adv.), for example, the chief of the operational target intelligence branch was not indoctrinated until late in the winter of 1944–1945, despite ULTRA's primary role in the targeting process. Until that individual was cleared, the integration of ULTRA into the selection and evaluation of Ninth Air Force bomber targets was done primarily by Capt. Charles Kindleberger, who was actually assigned to the adjacent 12th Army Group.[40] An immediate postwar study by MIS on the handling of ULTRA noted that burdening a single individual with sole responsibility for ULTRA sometimes resulted in that officer's becoming so busy handling and caring for signals that he had little time left for reflection and analysis. Cautioning against the tendency to turn intelligence officers into administrative clerks, the report observed, "The heart of intelligence is not busy work."[41]

To most effectively use the insights ULTRA offered, which often came in seemingly disjointed fragments, SSOs developed organizational and presentational techniques which contributed to their grasp of the intelligence picture and enabled commanders and staff officers to integrate this intelligence into their decisions. Almost all kept files of some type arranged into categories. The extensiveness of these files varied with the amount of information received, its relevance to a unit's operations, and the extent of friendly and enemy activity. At Ninth Air Force the SSO records included air OB files on enemy units—location, personnel and equipment strengths, state of training, and prospective movements—as well as information on the status and operational use of enemy airfields by aircraft type.[42] The XIX TAC SSO divided his files into GAF intentions, capabilities, and operations; potential targets and damage reports; air OB; special information, e.g., jet developments; and enemy ground force information.[43] Less systematized was the arrangement of the XII TAC SSO in Italy, who kept an annotated notebook while returning messages to the SCU for destruction.[44]

Most officers tried to maintain maps and charts to present ULTRA intelligence in an easily understood manner. The burden of segregating ULTRA was illustrated by the comment of one SSO that he kept two sets of maps: one

Tools of Air Intelligence

that included ULTRA intelligence for briefing the commander and indoctrinated staff officers; the other, without ULTRA information, was for "visitors."[45] At the other extreme was the A–2 at XII Tactical Air Force in Italy. According to one cleared officer, "Maj. Corning operates out of his shirt pocket, merges all sources in his mind and is not given to pat statements about what part of his total knowledge is supplied by special intelligence."[46]

Few American air commanders read the signals from BP on a regular basis, preferring to rely on the SSO or senior intelligence officer. Maj. Gen. Elwood R. Quesada, commander of the IX TAC, for example, expected his SSO to compare ULTRA with other sources and to evaluate it in the light of their mission at the commander's evening intelligence briefing.[47] Similarly, while the commander of XXIX TAC and his directors of operations and intelligence readily accepted and used ULTRA, they rarely read the raw signals.[48] The commander of Eighth Air Force, Maj. Gen. James H. Doolittle, and his deputy for operations, Brig. Gen. Orvil A. Anderson, were such avid adherents of ULTRA that they insisted on maintaining an SLU at headquarters. The SSO presented ULTRA at the morning briefing, and he attended the evening targeting meeting as well. Both Doolittle and Anderson frequently asked what ULTRA had to offer on subjects under discussion.[49]

The SSO's most frequent contact was not always with the commanding general. As SSO at HQ USSTAF, Lt. Col. (later Colonel) Lewis F. Powell, Jr., saw Spaatz only occasionally, but he discussed ULTRA daily with the deputy commander for operations, Maj. Gen. Frederick Anderson.[50] While the SSO of XIX TAC maintained an excellent relationship with Maj. Gen. O. P. Weyland, he briefed the general only periodically. His routine contacts were with the A–2, who fused ULTRA with other sources and briefed Weyland and Third Army commander Lt. Gen. George Patton.[51] Even within a single headquarters, procedures differed over time. At Ninth Air Force, one director of intelligence instructed the SSO to prepare written summaries and appreciations. His successor, Col. Richard Hughes, preferred that the SSO annotate the signals and then discuss them personally with him. Both directors of intelligence briefed Maj. Gen. Hoyt Vandenberg, the Ninth Air Force commander.[52]

At most headquarters, SSOs presented ULTRA at a daily briefing to the commanding general and indoctrinated officers, most often in the morning. These daily briefings generally lasted fifteen to thirty minutes and covered the past twenty-four hours' activities and signals, as well as offered reports on special topics such as jet aircraft development.[53] At HQ USSTAF, the chief of operational intelligence blended ULTRA into his overall intelligence situation briefing without indicating the source of any piece of information.[54] At the TACs, the daily briefing was often conducted jointly with the commander and staff of the supported army, and included both air- and ground-oriented ULTRA. An SSO briefed Weyland and Patton together almost every morning.[55]

To supplement these formal briefings, many SSOs prepared frequent written reports on special topics such as V-weapons, jet fighter developments, and enemy ground reinforcements.[56] All routinely delivered priority incoming signals or discussed their contents with the commanding general or other senior officers several times a day. No standard operating procedure existed overall. The Fifteenth Air Force ULTRA representative, for example, annotated signals he deemed significant, and he hand carried them to the senior officers, but he did not prepare written summaries or reports.[57]

At most headquarters, indoctrinated officers stopped by the SSO's office at least daily, often several times a day, to read signals or review appropriate maps and charts.[58] The Ninth Air Force director of operations routinely reviewed ULTRA-based charts on enemy airfields and bridges while considering missions for the 9th Bombardment Division's tactical bombers.[59] In southern France the A–2 and A–3 consulted the XII TAC SSO before preparing intelligence summaries or operations orders.[60]

In their decision to identify and segregate a single SSO to handle ULTRA material, the American forces differed from their British allies. By the summer of 1943, the latter had adopted a more integrated system in which selected members of the regular intelligence staff processed ULTRA signals. In contrast to the American SSOs, these individuals did not receive special training at BP but were indoctrinated in place, as deemed necessary for the effective performance of their intelligence responsibilities.[61] The greater willingness of the British to indoctrinate intelligence officers was reflected in joint intelligence organizations such as the various headquarters under Mediterranean Allied Air Command, most of which included several ULTRA-cleared RAF officers but no, or at best one or two, indoctrinated Americans.[62]

One benefit of the British procedure was that it integrated ULTRA into the larger intelligence picture at a lower level, a step several American SSOs strongly recommended in their postwar reports.[63] As evaluated by one American SSO, such an arrangement allowed ULTRA to assume "its proper dimension of another source of intelligence . . . rather than the conjuring act seen in some subordinate American headquarters." On the other hand, this individual also observed that in the area of providing "special training in use and interpretation of ULTRA [at BP] . . . the American system is superior."[64] Through the fall of 1944, in fact, the American system evolved into a modified version of this as-needed arrangement, with subsequent improvements in ULTRA's immediate operational value. The Ninth Air Force SSO, for example, commented that the indoctrination of the chief of the targets branch significantly enhanced ULTRA's usefulness in the targeting process. Unfortunately, this step did not occur until March 1945.[65]

Tools of Air Intelligence

Lt. Gen. Elwood R. Quesada

Brig. Gen. Orvil A. Anderson

Maj. Gen. Frederick L. Anderson

Lt. Gen. O. P. Weyland

A problem of particular significance to air headquarters was the strict prohibition laid down against placing indoctrinated officers in positions that might result in their capture. Since for airmen this meant no combat missions, it was certainly a reason to limit access among operations staffs. Even so, this rigid rule was violated on several occasions, including once by an AAF general who bailed out of a crippled aircraft and became a prisoner of the *Luftwaffe* in June 1944. Fortunately, the Germans never interrogated him to the point of his revealing the unique information.[66]

Maintaining the absolute secrecy of this unique source was not the only problem SSOs and their superiors faced. Determining the significance of any given message required ingenuity and the ability to extrapolate from often incomplete clues. For one thing, ULTRA was only as good as the information the

Piercing the Fog

Maj. Gen. Hoyt S. Vandenberg   Maj. Gen. James H. Doolittle

original German sender put into an Enigma message. If the latter was inaccurate or incomplete, so too was ULTRA. Sometimes originators were deliberately inaccurate; more often intercepted messages were incomplete either in their content or in their assessment of a situation.[67]

ULTRA was incomplete in the sense that BP, for all its excellence, could not intercept every German Enigma signal, and many of the signals that it did intercept were incomplete or could be only partially deciphered. While the number of signals BP sent to the field rose significantly between 1943 and 1944, what it presented often resembled a jigsaw puzzle with at least some pieces missing. Sometimes the available pieces were sufficient by themselves to recreate the total picture. More often, the blanks could be filled in only by other sources or extrapolated on the basis of what was available. Increasing the difficulty of this exploitation, particularly with regard to the enemy's intentions, was the fact that BP only rarely intercepted communications between senior enemy headquarters and among senior commanders. Most Enigma signals contained information that related to activities or orders representing only portions of an overall operation or reorganization.

The role of the intelligence officers in Hut 3 was crucial, for they determined the initial value of a given message and prepared the signals to operational commands. Not every message was forwarded to all headquarters. The typical message leaving Hut 3 contained the English translation of the German text (with emendations explaining missing words or sections) for a field commander's consideration. Also on the message would be, whenever possible, notations putting the text into the context of previous intercepts, such as the state of the known German command organization, supply arrangement, or the like. Not all of the SSOs assigned to air headquarters agreed about the sufficiency of what their headquarters received. Some SSOs appear to have believed they should have been sent more than they got, either more signals or at least more frequent and annotated summaries from a more fully informed higher headquarters. At least one SSO argued that BP or at least someone above his level should have provided more extensive interpretations, rather than their simply forwarding raw messages.[68] BP's intelligence officers argued that they were not in a position to provide such commentary because they deliberately knew nothing about friendly dispositions or intentions, and thus lacked the broad context that the SSOs supposed.[69] On the other hand, at least one SSO recalled that "higher headquarters" (which he did not identify) had done a good job of summarizing material that, while not necessary in an immediate operational sense, provided useful background.[70] Analysts at BP's Hut 3 added only comments derived from other ULTRA material. This segregation of information served both to keep other Allied plans and intentions secure and to avoid any incorrect interpretations of policy from creeping into BP's prime product: intelligence data. Field commanders bore the responsibility for using the special intelligence; it would not have been fair or militarily wise to lay upon them extraneous information or possibly spurious suggestions.

The question of how much material was received seemed most critical at the tactical air commands, which appear to have gotten relatively little intelligence of events and developments outside their immediate area of operations. The SSO for XXIX TAC noted after the war that his commanding general constantly sought a broader perspective than was provided, believing the flexibility of air power meant his force's mission or even location might be changed quickly under the press of combat.[71]

The issue of context was crucial. Despite its uniqueness, ULTRA material was like any other piece of intelligence in that it was less apt to be misinterpreted if placed in the larger picture; it was more effective when fused with other intelligence. Virtually to a man, the SSOs, despite their privileged positions as the keepers of this unique asset, reiterated both the necessity for integrating ULTRA with other sources and the related danger of relying solely on what they referred to as Source. Recognizing the struggle of intelligence officers to meet the incessant demands of commanders for information while maintaining the security of ULTRA, the SSO at IX TAC spoke for many when he admitted, "The two easy errors, isolation from other sources and the conviction that ULTRA will provide all the needed intelligence, are indeed the Scylla and Charybdis of the representative. ULTRA must be looked on as one of a number of sources."[72]

Finally, even after it became nearly comprehensive in its presentation of quantifiable data such as OB, fuel shortages, and unit locations, ULTRA did not relieve intelligence officers or their commanders from maintaining an open mind in drawing conclusions from this plethora of data. Even the most famous surprise of the war in Europe—the German offensive in the Ardennes in

December 1944—resulted not from a lack of evidence, but from a failure to interpret that evidence correctly.

The Importance of ULTRA in the European Theater

The importance of ULTRA in the air war against the European Axis became very complex. In the first place, there were several air wars in Europe and the Mediterranean, some of which occurred simultaneously, each having its own character. ULTRA's role differed at least slightly among all. ULTRA's influence changed significantly through the course of the war. Not until the spring and summer of 1943, for example, did it affect strategic air planning and operations to any important degree.[73] Finally, the very procedures established to shield its existence increased the normal problems of establishing direct linkages among intelligence, planning, and operations.

ULTRA's influence in American strategic air operations against Germany fell into three broad categories: target selection, damage assessment, and information about the primary opponent: the *Luftwaffe*. Until 1944 ULTRA provided only limited assistance to the selection of target systems or individual targets. None of the strategic air plans prepared through 1943—AWPD–1, AWPD–42, the Casablanca Directive, the Eaker Plan, or even Operation ARGUMENT (the concentrated campaign against the German aircraft industry and GAF)—was based primarily on ULTRA. The USSTAF recommendation of March 1944 that the GAF was sufficiently weakened to permit a refocusing of effort was supported in large part by ULTRA. At the same time, the targets recommended for next attention, the German oil industry, had long been considered a critical objective which awaited only the capability for the mass attacks that Eighth Air Force finally acquired that winter.

Because information regarding industrial capacity and conditions only occasionally went through German military communications channels, Enigma transmissions rarely provided the kind of information upon which strategic planners depended. The basis for selection of broad target systems was the economic analysis developed by such groups as the COA and the EOU, interpreted and adjusted by operational considerations such as distance, weather, and size of the available bomber force. A USSTAF study on the use of ULTRA material and the strategic air war concluded in 1945 that "on the whole it seems fair to say the major decisions on the employment of strategic air power would have been the same had ULTRA not been available."[74] This assessment was supported by others intimately connected with intelligence and the planning of strategic air operations. Looking back thirty years later, Lewis Powell came to a similar assessment: "I think even if there had been no ULTRA, that with aerial reconnaissance, primarily, plus the work of scholars and economists, we would have identified the target systems in Germany. It may have taken us longer—in fact, I know it would have taken us much longer—but in the end we would have destroyed the German economy."[75]

In the area of targeting, ULTRA's contribution lay not in the initial selection of target systems but in the "absolutely un-arguable proof" it provided that the policies and target systems American airmen had selected were indeed correct.[76] This unique insight largely overrode the normal tendency in the face of the unknown to hedge one's bets by spreading resources across a spectrum of targets in the hope of getting parts of many, if it was not possible to get them all. It enabled American airmen to press the strategic bombing offensive against selected targets—first the *Luftwaffe* and aircraft industry, and then oil—with a degree of assurance they otherwise would have lacked. Perhaps more importantly, it enabled them to convince others of the validity of their arguments.

A second responsibility of intelligence in the strategic air war was to assess the damage inflicted on targets, its impact on the enemy's industrial production, and, ultimately, its effect on his military capability. Here, too, Enigma provided only occasional glimpses, since much of this information did not ordinarily flow through military channels. According to the USSTAF analysis, throughout most of 1943 many ULTRA reports were "too vague and general to be of importance operationally." They were, for much of this period, too sporadic or incomplete to provide the basis for evaluation or, more importantly, future targeting decisions. Aerial photography remained the best way to assess bomb damage.[77] Even in this period, ULTRA reports that identified specific structural damage enhanced photointerpretation by enabling interpreters to correlate visual evidence with German reports of structural damage. The result was an improved method for estimating impact and blast damage.[78]

During 1944 the volume and accuracy of damage reportage carried by Enigma increased to the point that the enemy provided "a considerable amount of information on [bombing] results."[79] By that fall, USSTAF received ULTRA signals of target damage the day after a raid, which were followed up the next day with aerial reconnaissance to confirm and clarify the Enigma intelligence.[80] Since 1944 was also the year the American strategic bomber force grew to significant size and possessed at least a limited capability to engage in radar bombing, the impact of this more detailed intelligence was magnified beyond what it would have been in previous years.

While photointerpretation remained a fundamental part of the process of assessing the damage to a facility's productive capability, ULTRA provided a special perspective. As skilled as the Allied photointerpreters at Medmenham had become, only ULTRA could advise intelligence officers and operational planners that a damaged facility expected "resumption of production in approximately 8 days." Reports indicating no interruption to production provided an invaluable counterbalance to the tendency to assume that physical damage to a plant automatically reduced or halted production.[81] By the last year of the war, ULTRA was not only providing a better glimpse of the enemy's industrial condition, it was also influencing operational decisions on when to bomb and toward what targets to shift bombing's focus.

When the Allied landing at Normandy compounded the pressures the German military already faced on the eastern front, in Italy, and in the skies over Germany, Enigma increasingly began to reveal shortages of supplies, equipment, and personnel. This information influenced operational decisions in the land war in western Europe. It also affected strategic air operations. Such intelligence, particularly as it related to oil and fuel, confirmed the direction of the strategic air campaign. By the fall of 1944, such insights had an even more direct impact on that campaign. To a large extent, it was ULTRA that provided the basis for several changes in target system priorities and the addition and elimination of different target systems from strategic bombing priority lists.

ULTRA most fully encompassed the numerous aspects of the air war in Europe through the insight it provided into the GAF. While stressing the interrelated nature of air intelligence, the Eighth Air Force SSO added that the reports ULTRA provided "of the strength, dispositions, composition, production, wastage, reserves, and serviceability of the GAF . . . were the raw materials of knowledge that produced most of our picture of the institution . . . [which] was our major strategic target until April of 1944."[82] Through 1943, ULTRA monitored the buildup of the German fighter defenses and the decision to concentrate resources on the air defense of the Reich. While the aircrews who engaged this expanding force could have offered some cogent observations along these lines, ULTRA provided a more accurate monitoring of this buildup as well as the command structure under which it was organized. It enabled the Allies to trace at least some of the steps the enemy was prepared to take to prevent Allied air attack, and it offered some insight into the enemy's perspective of the struggle for the skies over Germany.

It is not true that ULTRA enabled Allied intelligence to eavesdrop on every decision of the German high command, for the *Geheimschreiber* remained a difficult system to penetrate, and many reports and decisions went out in ways other than radio messages. It must have been reassuring in the fall of 1943, as the Eighth and Fifteenth Air Forces were suffering heavy casualties, to read the following admission of the Air Officer for Fighters in Berlin: "The fighter and heavy fighter formations have not been able to secure decisive success in our defense against American four-engine formations."[83] By the spring of 1944 it was both ULTRA and photographic evidence that gave Spaatz an understanding of the damage wrought by the AAF's campaign against the German fighter force. This Allied campaign, code named ARGUMENT, had been repeatedly postponed since November 1943 because of poor weather. ARGUMENT's objective was a series of aerial assaults on German fighter production (from ball-bearing manufacture to engine and airframe assembly) and on airfields and aircraft storage areas. The Allied air commanders hoped to break German air defenses to relieve pressure on the Combined Bomber Offensive (CBO) and to cripple the *Luftwaffe* before the planned Allied landings in France. For six days in February (the 20th to the 25th), Allied bombers struck repeatedly in what has since been labeled "Big Week." But it was only with an understanding of the German losses in the air battles and from bombardment that Spaatz could recommend with confidence a shift away from the German aircraft industry and a focus on strategic air power's ultimate objective: destruction of the enemy's capability to conduct military operations through the dislocation of his industrial capability and economic resources.[84]

In establishing this picture, Allied air intelligence received invaluable assistance from the GAF. From the beginning of the war, the *Luftwaffe* was notoriously lax in communications security.[85] The British broke the primary GAF ULTRA key early in the war, and the *Luftwaffe*'s message traffic continued to be one of the most prolific sources of intelligence. Most helpful in this regard was the *Luftwaffe*'s daily report. As Lewis Powell recalled, "Literally almost every day, every combat unit of the German Air Force would report on the number of airplanes that were serviceable, on the number of crews who were ready and fit to fly, and, if there had been combat the day before, on the casualties, and the wins claimed."[86] Moreover, because German air liaison officers assigned to Army commands used certain GAF keys on their Enigma machines, BP routinely used their knowledge of the GAF keys as cribs or clues for breaking into the more difficult German Army ciphers.

The information Enigma provided on the *Luftwaffe* could be almost encyclopedic in its scope. Without exhausting the full range, it included orders establishing commands, including chain of command structures, areas of responsibility, missions, functions, and commanders; unit strengths, training programs, and status; locations and impending moves; airfield status, support requirements, supply status, and status and movements of ground support elements; number of serviceable aircraft, losses, requirements for replacements, and allocations of new aircraft; and operations orders, missions scheduled and flown, and results.[87]

Even without intercepting every GAF message, using the air index at BP and the more mission–specific files the SSOs maintained at air headquarters, it was possible to develop over time a nearly complete picture of the *Luftwaffe*. This flow of intelligence was so great that, according to Lewis Powell, "The intelligence officers in Hut 3 probably knew more about it [the *Luftwaffe*] than [did] high-ranking German officers."[88] Within the context of the overall war, the real value of ULTRA regarding the GAF may not have lain so much in the information it offered on enemy operations as in what it revealed about the GAF's deteriorating logistical base. It was this look into the German supply system that revealed long-term trends and thus allowed for the application of the most effective pressure on all elements of the *Luftwaffe* as well as other segments of the *Wehrmacht*.[89]

Piercing the Fog

ULTRA's relationship to Allied tactical air operations in Europe and the Mediterranean differed in several respects from its influence on the strategic air war. In contrast to the perspective of American strategic air forces, the *Luftwaffe*'s fighter force was not the Allied tactical air forces' primary opponent in either Italy or western Europe after the autumn of 1943. The primary contribution of ULTRA was in the targeting process. Most of the ULTRA signals relevant to tactical air operations contained information on German land rather than air forces. While ULTRA was distributed only down to the strategic numbered air forces, in the tactical air chain of command it went one level lower, to the tactical air commands.

The decline of the *Luftwaffe* as a threat to Allied tactical air operations was strikingly evident. Despite preinvasion concerns by airmen in the United Kingdom and in Washington, the *Luftwaffe* put up insignificant resistance to Operation OVERLORD. Enigma did provide information that contributed directly to successful Allied air operations in the weeks immediately after D-day. Looking back on the war, however, General Robert M. Lee, who became director of operations for Ninth Air Force in September, 1944, maintained he did not "recall getting an awful lot on . . . [enemy] air operations, because it didn't have much of an impact on us."[90] Special security officers properly maintained files and charts on the status and condition of GAF units, but they and their superiors recognized, as the SSO with the First Tactical Air Force (Prov.) recorded, that "Allied air superiority was too overwhelming to be affected by anything the GAF might do."[91]

More than one SSO complained that BP continued to overemphasize the GAF long after it had ceased to be a dominant factor. The special advisor on targeting for Ninth Air Force, Maj. Lucius Buck, referred to a "Battle of Britain" mentality in the RAF and the resultant emphasis on air OB at the expense of targeting intelligence as "inconsistent with American concepts of offensive air power."[92] Lt. Col. Leslie L. Rood, at XII TAC, also commented on BP's concern with the *Luftwaffe,* noting his command's staff "were completely uninterested in its [GAF's] grandiose plans and ineffective operations."[93]

ULTRA's contribution to tactical air planning and operations depended to a large extent on the level of command. At the numbered air forces and above, its value was the background information it provided which became the backdrop on which policy and broad operational decisions were made. From the perspective of the Ninth Air Force director of operations, it was "the accumulation of information" rather than specific target intelligence that constituted ULTRA's greatest contribution.[94] Similarly, for Twelfth Air Force's tactical bombers, ULTRA's contribution was assessed not in terms of providing targeting (which came from a variety of sources) but in the cumulative evidence that the interdiction campaign in Italy was adversely affecting the enemy's supply channels.[95]

Tools of Air Intelligence

At the tactical air command level, ULTRA did offer frequent inputs for mission planning. This proved especially valuable because higher headquarters generally provided only broad guidance, while leaving the TACs to determine, plan, and execute their own missions in conjunction with the appropriate Army headquarters. Some of this intelligence pertained to the GAF. Enigma messages enabled Allied night fighters to conduct very effective intercepts against German transports attempting to resupply the beleaguered fortresses along the Atlantic coast in the summer of 1944.[96] ULTRA provided extensive intelligence on the primary target of tactical air forces—the German Army. This information ranged from the specific—the location of enemy units, fuel and supply depots, and movements—to more general insights into losses and shortages of equipment and manpower. Close coordination between army and tactical air command staffs frequently allowed such intelligence to provide the basis for air interdiction missions.

In contrast to strategic air operations, ULTRA provided the tactical forces with greater assistance in target selection than in damage assessment. For XII TAC in Italy the SSO reported, "The occasional damage reports on specific targets are of doubtful value because [XII] TAC attacks vast numbers of small targets every day."[97] According to one postwar report on ULTRA's use, in general there was "a scarcity of immediate intelligence" on fighter-bomber damage in western Europe.[98] The SSO at Ninth Air Force noted that photoreconnaissance and interpretation were generally more useful in damage assessment than was ULTRA. The same individual added, however, that ULTRA's damage assessment contribution was particularly important in the winter of 1944 when weather often prevented effective aerial reconnaissance.[99]

ULTRA's overriding contribution for both tactical and strategic air operations was the guidance it provided in evaluating other sources, in interpreting otherwise unclear information, and in directing more effective employment of other intelligence capabilities and resources. Certainly the SSOs who were responsible for ULTRA and for blending it with other sources of intelligence clearly viewed this as its primary contribution: "The greatest value which the special intelligence officer can be to the headquarters which he is serving is to be constantly developing and exploiting in a legitimate manner [i.e., with proper cover] the general intelligence which he knows has been confirmed by source . . . [and] in guiding the employment of other intelligence sources in order to build up the general intelligence picture. . . ."[100] In short, ULTRA substantiated intelligence from other sources. It also suggested where to look and for what to search in other sources. Lt. Col. James Fellers expressed the objective toward which all SSOs strove in this regard: "The ultimate aim of every intelligence section is to build the ordinary intelligence picture up to the level of the very special intelligence picture."[101] At Fifteenth Air Force, for example, the ULTRA SSO contributed his "superior wisdom" to the interpretation of aerial photographs for the targets branch.[102] According to the Y intelligence officer at Ninth Air Force, "During the past year few days passed during which ULTRA did not insert itself into the estimates and opinions of the 'Y' staff. . . . ULTRA is the guide and censor for 'Y,' and at the same time the latter is a secure vehicle by which ULTRA may be disseminated under cover."[103]

Equally important, ULTRA acted as a censor, weeding out incorrect intelligence interpretations, assessments, and assumptions. At Fifteenth Air Force, for example, ULTRA's primary role was assessed as one of negative influence: "Special intelligence tells Murphy [the SSO] and his superiors what *not* to rely on [from other sources]. Rarely does he get anything of pure operational value, something which causes him to rush in to A–3 demanding that a mission be laid on."[104] At every headquarters where they were attached, SSOs ensured that intelligence documents such as weekly air intelligence summaries and daily intelligence bulletins were based on ULTRA or at least contained no incorrect information.[105] In his discussion of the relative merits of the different sources of intelligence, one SSO cautioned against leaving "out of the weighing the very important guiding influence" ULTRA exerted through appreciations sent from higher to subordinate headquarters, based on ULTRA material of which the recipients were unaware.[106]

Photointelligence

To a large extent photointelligence—photoreconnaissance and photointerpretation collectively—was the backbone of air intelligence in World War II, especially in strategic air operations. In the air war against Japan, for example, Maj. Gen. Haywood Hansell considered the first B–29 photoreconnaissance flight over Japan on November 1, 1944, "probably the greatest . . . single contribution . . . in the air war with Japan."[107] In its after-action report on the air war over Germany, the EOU in London expressed a similar view by noting that, because of the shifting nature of the German aircraft industry, "only photographic interpretation could confirm precisely many important changes."[108] Even officers who dealt extensively with ULTRA were emphatic in their evaluation of photoreconnaissance and interpretation. An ULTRA-indoctrinated observer in the Mediterranean theater in 1944, for example, noted that with the decline of the GAF and the subsequently greater importance of targeting as intelligence's primary function, "Probably the most valuable source [of intelligence] is photography."[109] In January 1945, while serving as both SSO at HQ USSTAF and chief of operational intelligence with responsibility for the integration of *all* intelligence, Col. Lewis Powell stated that "perhaps the most important . . . [intelligence source] is Photo Reconnaissance."[110] Powell could not then [1945] reveal his knowledge of ULTRA, but he knew that without photoreconnaissance the AAF would have lacked not only maps but a wide

Tools of Air Intelligence

variety of methods to pinpoint specific targets. The same situation obtained in the Far East.

That photointelligence played such a critical role reflected tremendous progress in the development and employment of this analytical tool by the AAF after December 1941. Although the American Air Service had done a great deal of aerial photography in the last year of the Great War, this function and training for the skills it demanded were reduced drastically in the financially bleak interwar years. The Air Corps established an aerial photography school at Lowry Field, Colorado, in 1938, but it taught only the mechanics of aerial photography rather than its uses. Despite the technical work of several individuals on camera developments, most notably Lt. (later Brig. Gen.) Robert Goddard, the Army Air Corps did not have separate photoreconnaissance units; the Corps incorporated this function into its bombardment groups. Not until the spring of 1942 would the AAF establish separate photoreconnaissance units using F–7s (B–24s) and F–9s (B–17s).[111]

None of the eventual belligerents in World War II could be considered advanced in using aerial photography for intelligence by the late 1930s. When the Americans got into the war, the British had had more than two years to work out many of the technical and organizational problems. The United States drew heavily on this experience even before December 1941. American observers in the United Kingdom between the spring of 1940 and the winter of 1941 noted the importance of photoreconnaissance in their reports to Washington. One of them, Capt. Harold Brown, was instrumental in determining the emphasis that the Harrisburg Intelligence School (located in Harrisburg, Pennsylvania) placed on photointelligence. Although it would continue to make great strides in the development of equipment—including lenses, mounting techniques, and film development processes—during the war, the AAF did not develop an aircraft designed specifically for reconnaissance. Squadrons used existing aircraft types converted in various degrees for photoreconnaissance, depending on the characteristics of each theater and the stage of the war.

Early experiences in North Africa quickly demonstrated the unsuitability of the slow and unmaneuverable F–7s and F–9s when matched against German air defenses. Some 25 percent of the original force sent to support TORCH were shot down in the first three months of operations.[112] As a result, in the Mediterranean and European theaters—where speed, maneuverability, and constant vigilance were the reconnaissance pilot's best defenses—the F–4 (P–38E) and variations of the F–5 (P–38G/H) became the primary American reconnaissance aircraft. Despite improvements made in later versions of the F–5, they remained less capable than the British Mosquito or Spitfires IX and XII, the latter being the premier reconnaissance craft of this theater. Although American airmen considered using the Mosquito and actually operated Spitfire IXs in 1943, in early 1944 the commander of the 8th Photo Reconnaissance

Wing (Prov.), Col. Elliot Roosevelt, son of the American president, decided to stick with American-made F–5s supplemented by F–6s (P–51s).

In the Pacific, aerial photography of enemy-held areas routinely required aircraft with greater range than any converted fighter could provide. On the night of March 26/27, 1944, two F–7s flew a 20-hour, 2,500-mile night mission to photograph Japanese installations in the Palau Islands.[113] The F–7 and F–10 (B–25) dominated aerial photography in the Southwest Pacific and were used extensively in the China-Burma-India (CBI) Theater to reach into southern Burma and to overfly the east China coast and islands to the south. Because these planes could not rely on speed and maneuverability and because distances were too great for fighter escort, long-range reconnaissance aircraft were almost always armed. American forces did use field-modified fighters where appropriate, including P–40s, P–39s, P–38s, and eventually P–51s.

Another difference between the European and Pacific theaters was that most of the enemy-held territory in western and central Europe was accessible to some degree of aerial photography relatively early in the war, whereas the Japanese home islands remained out of reach much longer. Early B–29 missions flown against Japan from China lacked current photographs of their targets. Not until November 1, 1944, did the AAF fly the first reconnaissance mission over Tokyo and Nagoya from Saipan. Each of the seventeen photomissions flown between November 1 and the first B–29 attack of November 24, 1944, as well as those that followed, involved a 1,500-mile flight to the target area, a one-hour run (period of active photography), and a 1,500-mile return leg. Initially flown with field-modified B–29s, these missions were later conducted by factory-converted F–13s (B–29s) which carried an exceptional array of different cameras.[114]

Photoreconnaissance missions were flown for various reasons, which can be grouped into a few categories: area (overview) coverage, point (static) objectives, coverage of enemy activities (movements), damage assessment, and photographic support for land operations. Each required specific equipment, mission profiles, and photographic coverage. Overview coverage of an area provided a basic knowledge of what targets, activities, or other intelligence clues might be available in a designated area. In the Pacific and CBI theaters, where maps were often outdated or nonexistent, many of the early missions involved photomapping. In all theaters, broad-sweep coverage provided the background upon which to build more detailed pictures when necessary. In the fall of 1943, Col. George C. McDonald, then chief intelligence officer for Northwest African Air Forces (NAAF), ordered coverage of some 60,000 square miles in southern Germany, Hungary, and the Balkans when it appeared the Germans were beginning to shift or develop industry in these regions.[115] Photointerpreters would review the initial overviews to identify the existence and location of a broad range of possible targets or key facilities including airfields, transportation centers, troop concentrations, supply dumps, gun emplacements, and factories. Area coverage might provide the basis for searches for very specific targets. This was the approach used in the search for the German V–1 and V–2 launching sites in northern France, Belgium, and Holland in 1943 and 1944.

Point missions flown against specific, and usually static, objectives almost always resulted in large-scale photography for detailed analysis of specific targets. Such missions provided the photographic basis for target selection for strategic air operations, including identification of aiming points, location and nature of defensive systems, and changes and modifications of installations over time. It was the photointerpreters' analysis of the region around Marienburg that elicited the strong suspicion that the airfield was a factory producing Focke-Wulf fighters. Once technical analysis of the maker's plates of several crashed FW 190s established Marienburg as a good target, the Eighth Air Force launched a highly successful attack on the aircraft manufacturing complex in early October 1943.[116] The results of these types of missions provided the framework and core of strategic, and sometimes tactical, mission target folders in all theaters. Coverage of specific targets also provided the basis for the bomb damage assessments (BDAs) essential not only to understand the accuracy of an attack but also to evaluate the impact of the damage on a facility's productivity. Evaluation played a critical role in decisions regarding the need for and timing of reattacks. Photointerpretation was an art that demanded great skill in assessing photographs and an ability to reason and deduce facts from images. The presence of camouflage indicated some enemy interest in preventing observation; it caught an evaluator's eye. Photointerpretation depended upon aerial photography's producing good-quality images, something not always possible in the European weather. Serendipity also mattered. If the reconnaissance pilot chanced to see an interesting sight, he might turn on his camera, as in May 1942 when a British pilot photographed Peenemunde's airfield and new construction.

Just how important air commanders considered this information to be was reflected in a February 8, 1944, message from Spaatz to Lt. Gen. Ira C. Eaker, while the latter was commanding the Mediterranean Allied Air Forces (MAAF). It was, declared Spaatz, "of utmost importance" that first-phase interpretation reports (based on recce missions flown within two hours of a strike) of a projected Fifteenth Air Force raid on February 9 be furnished to him immediately. Because the "determination of [follow-up] operations depends on PRU [Photographic Reconnaissance Unit] reports," the acquisition and interpretation of the necessary photographs were "of the highest priority, over all other activity."[117]

Where land force operations were planned or underway, a great deal of aerial photography as well as visual reconnaissance supported such activity. In Italy, close air support to the U.S. Fifth Army was based on "extensive use of annotated photographs...."[118] Between May 6 and 20, 1944, the American 10th

Piercing the Fog

Reconnaissance Group flew 232 missions along the Channel coast to record the German defenses. Some of these missions were flown as low as 15 feet above the sea.[119] Nor was this support limited to the European Theater. When AAF aerial photos revealed the size and shape of the proposed landing zones on Bougainville to be considerably different from those on existing charts, the amphibious assault at Empress Augusta Bay was redirected in November 1943.[120] Just as photo and tactical (visual) reconnaissance groups supported Allied ground advances in Europe, the 71st Reconnaissance Group operated over the Philippine Islands in 1945, providing intelligence on enemy troop deployments and dispositions, movements and bivouac areas, road and bridge construction, and even the weather that was developing behind enemy lines.[121] A basic characteristic of photographic reconnaissance was its repetitive nature. On certain occasions one-time coverage was adequate. For the most part, however, a fundamental element of the interpretation process was the comparison of activity over time: repairs to plants, the buildup of flak* units, new road construction, or changes in the numbers or types of aircraft at an airfield.

Analysis of the results of aerial reconnaissance flights—photointerpretation—occurred at three levels. First-phase interpretation was carried out at the recovery base of flying units to provide operational commanders and their staffs a quick initial evaluation, especially in assessing the results of air strikes. In the first months of Eighth Air Force operations, the development and analysis of aerial photographs took two days, with both steps occurring at Medmenham. In March 1943, Eaker directed that a photographic processing facility be established at the American reconnaissance base at Mount Farm near RAF Benson and that photointerpretation officers be assigned to his headquarters to provide immediate prints so he could more quickly judge the results of a given strike.[122]

With the growing requirements for tactical air forces to support land operations in all theaters and the subsequent emphasis on targets more fleeting than those subjected to strategic air bombardment, the demands made on rapid first-phase interpretation increased. By the middle of 1943, first-phase interpretation was accomplished within two to three hours after a reconnaissance plane landed. To increase still further the availability of first-phase interpretation during the effort against the German V–1 flying bomb sites in 1944, the HQ USSTAF Directorate of Intelligence established special procedures under the so-called Dilly Project, whereby a courier hand carried photos from the AAF's photointerpretation center at Mount Farm to General Spaatz.[123]

---

*Flak, short for the German *Fliegerabwehrkanone*, became the commonly used term for AA gunfire.

Second-phase interpretation, often accomplished by the same individuals, or at least the same units, as those responsible for the first-phase work, consisted of a more detailed analysis of photographs to find anything that might have immediate operational value. This still rapid but more detailed assessment allowed photointerpreters to look for and determine links between what might at first glance be overlooked or be thought to be unconnected activities, if seen in isolation. This phase lasted approximately 24 hours, until the next day's batch of material arrived.[124]

While photointerpreters assigned to the operational units usually conducted the first and second phases, personnel assigned to specific subjects or areas of expertise did third-phase interpretations at a central facility. Thus the Central Interpretation Unit (CIU) at Medmenham contained one section that concentrated on airfields, another that focused on aircraft, and a third that dealt with aircraft factories. These central facilities performed the detailed and often long-term analyses that influenced not so much daily operations, but longer term strategic and policy decisions. Even before the American strategic bombers began to concentrate on Axis oil production, Medmenham had seven photointerpreters focusing on this industry.[125] Concentration of resources (both human and matériel) at central locations provided the capability to review old photographs in the light of new clues, to concentrate assets on high-priority projects, and to have sections interact for new perspectives.

The organization of both photoreconnaissance and photointerpretation assets underwent several changes as the war progressed. Early in the war, limited resources necessitated centralizing the control of British reconnaissance and interpretation functions. By the time the United States began air operations in England, RAF photointerpretation had been largely concentrated at the CIU at Medmenham, while reconnaissance units flew from RAF Benson. Eighth Air Force assigned American photointerpreters to the CIU and established its flying organizations (eventually evolving into the 7th Photo Reconnaissance Group, and later into the 8th Reconnaissance Wing) at Mount Farm. At Medmenham, the RAF had an extensive photointerpretation operation divided into several sections. Film from regular reconnaissance flights over established enemy facilities came to the CIU, where interpreters examined it in detail to discern significant changes or other indications of suspicious enemy intent. For example, one section at the CIU used reconnaissance photography to prepare target folders, and another analyzed AA facilities. Each section prepared special reports on its area of specialization. As another example, the AA analysts' work led to flak studies that allowed attacking aircraft to avoid some dangerous areas on their runs to and from targets. In contrast, the AAF's photointerpretation capability was very limited early in the war. Photographic specialists who had trained at the AAF's Harrisburg Intelligence School worked at Medmenham for some time before the Eighth Air Force established its own photographic interpretation capability.[126]

Piercing the Fog

Medmenham. The RAF Central Interpretation Unit (later the Allied Central Interpretation Unit) was located on a commandeered estate called Danesfield, high on a wooded bluff overlooking the Thames River some 30 miles north of London and three miles upstream from Henley-on-Thames (of Regatta fame). Most of the offices were in the main house, whose crenelated towers show in the center of the photo. On the back and far sides of the house, the long, low extensions were Nissen huts containing the large photo-processing labs and the enlisted quarters. The officers mess and quarters were off the top edge of the photo in the woods across the Henley-to-Marlow road. For a landing field, Medmenham used RAF Benson, some seven miles away. A training center as well as an operational unit, at one time or another the cast of characters at Medmenham included officers from all British and American services plus officers from the far corners of the British Empire as well as Free French, Danes, Norwegians, Czechs, Poles, Belgians, and Dutch. Women outnumbered men. An adjunct activity was the modeling section, which used aerial photos to make remarkably accurate, detailed three-dimensional models of vital targets. With few regular officers and a three-shift schedule, the monthly "parades" that straggled past the reviewing stand brought a look of pure horror to the face of the regular RAF Group Captain who had to take the salute.

During Operation TORCH, American and British photoreconnaissance and photointerpretation units were not located near each other, nor, in the case of the Americans, were the intelligence units located near their strike units, and initially, little coordination took place among them. Because U.S. reconnaissance units were located too far to the rear, it took as much as forty-eight hours to get mission results to the attack units. Geographic and electronic communica-

Tools of Air Intelligence

tions difficulties were resolved with the gradual advance of Allied armies eastward and by the development of additional fields. Centralization of direction for both photoreconnaissance and photointelligence came with the creation of the Northwest African Photographic Reconnaissance Wing (NAPRW) under Lt. Col. Elliot Roosevelt. This arrangement allowed more effective assignment of priorities to the innumerable requests for support, reduced overlap of reconnaissance units on the basis of requests from different ground units, and allowed third-phase interpretation at a CIU established in Algiers. When NAAF became MAAF in December 1943, the NAPRW became the Mediterranean Allied Photographic Reconnaissance Wing (MAPRW).[127]

When war came to the Pacific in December 1941, the United States had no designated or properly equipped reconnaissance aircraft, no field laboratory capability, and no qualified U.S. photointerpreter in the entire region.[128] In the Southwest Pacific and South Pacific theaters, this scarcity of assets forced the evolution, largely on an *ad hoc* basis, of joint photoreconnaissance and photointerpretation organizations. Such amalgamations as Navy cameras, Marine photography technicians, and AAF aircraft were common through many of the early island campaigns.[129] In contrast to Europe, the vast size of these Pacific theaters and the limited facilities at any one location resulted in a more decentralized structure of command and control and allocation of photointelligence units. At one time, the 17th Reconnaissance Squadron (AAF) headquartered at Guadalcanal maintained detachments at Bougainville, Munda (New Georgia), and Green Island in the northern Solomons to provide immediate response to Allied forces operating in these widely separated areas.[130]

The situation in the remote CBI regions was even more elementary. The first American photoreconnaissance units did not begin operations in either the China or India-Burma regions until the closing months of 1942—nearly a year after air operations had begun. Until that time General Chennault's American Volunteer Group and China Air Task Force had to rely on jury-rigged equipment. The India Air Task Force operating in Burma at least had the advantage of RAF capabilities in India, and American photointerpreters received training at the RAF school in Karachi.[131] A true combined organization in India came with the creation of the Eastern Air Command's Photo Reconnaissance Force in December 1943. This organization, commanded in its first year by the veteran RAF Group Capt. S. C. Wise, served the same role as Roosevelt's NAPRW. The Combined Photographic Interpretation Centre at Calcutta performed third-phase interpretation and photographic production.[132]

As the war progressed, the initial trend toward centralization of photoreconnaissance and interpretation assets and units was, to an extent, reversed. In large part, this shift stemmed from the need to provide timely support for tactical air and land operations as well as the increasing number of units available by the spring of 1944. In Europe and the Mediterranean it reflected two other factors. The first was a difference in American and British philosophies, with the former

Wing Commander Douglas Kendall, RAF *(above left)*, was in overall charge of intelligence activities at Medmenham and the only person there cleared for ULTRA information. To his right is his U.S. Air Force counterpart, Lt. Col. William J. O'Connor. As aerial photos arrived, they were roughly plotted by the map area covered *(below)* and sent to the appropriate section for more precise location and detailed analysis.

more inclined to allocate reconnaissance units to operational subcommands than the latter was. The second involved the concern of American airmen to establish an independent capability, not just in photoreconnaissance and photointelligence, but in all aspects of air intelligence as well.

Decentralization occurred particularly in the assignment of photoreconnaissance units and the execution of second-phase interpretation. In the Mediterranean, HQ MAAF established reconnaissance policy and retained control of the MAPRW and Mediterranean Photo Interpretation Centre (which continued third-phase interpretation). In the spring of 1944, HQ Mediterranean Allied Tactical Air Force and Twelfth Air Force acquired their own photoreconnaissance and interpretation capability.[133] Mediterranean Allied Strategic Air Force and Fifteenth Air Force did the same that fall.[134]

The most dramatic effort to decentralize photointelligence occurred in the early months of 1944. Throughout 1943, the American 7th Photo Reconnaissance Group at Mount Farm had been under the operational control of the Air Ministry's assistant director of intelligence for photography, while American photointerpreters had been integrated into the CIU at Medmenham. Neither Spaatz nor his director of intelligence in the new USSTAF, McDonald, fully approved of this arrangement. They took steps in early 1944 to establish "direct control of a fully-functioning [American] reconnaissance and intelligence organization. . . ."[135]

Spaatz's chief concern was clearly focused on the future and predicated on the potential requirement to uncouple American photoreconnaissance and interpretation capabilities in the event elements of USSTAF were sent to another theater (i.e., the Pacific). Spaatz was also concerned with the development of an American air intelligence organization able to continue after the war, and the close alliance with the British, was over.[136] Evidence is strong also that Colonels McDonald and Roosevelt, the latter serving as Spaatz's reconnaissance advisor, sought a complete break from the existing Anglo-American organization and the establishment of a wholly American capability and organization under HQ USSTAF. They intended to pull American personnel out of Medmenham and to establish a full interpretation capability at HQ USSTAF.[137]

The initial outcome of this American effort—which the British vehemently opposed—was the creation in February 1944 of the 8th Photo Reconnaissance Wing (Prov.) to ensure continued reconnaissance support for strategic air operations preceding and subsequent to Operation OVERLORD.[138] After months of memoranda, proposals, counterproposals, and meetings (including at least one chaired by Spaatz), first- and second-phase photointerpretation for daylight bombing missions were shifted in May 1944 to HQ USSTAF. British and American interpreters at Medmenham, redesignated as the Allied CIU, continued to perform third-phase interpretation. For more effective coordination and to reduce duplication of effort, the Allies established a Joint Photo

Piercing the Fog

Reconnaissance Committee with American and British Army, Air Force, and Navy representatives.[139] In August 1944, the 8th Photographic Reconnaissance Wing (Prov.) was redesignated the 325th Reconnaissance Wing. Roosevelt retained his dual responsibilities as commander, 325th Reconnaissance Wing, and photoreconnaissance advisor to Spaatz.[140]

Photographic interpretation was a fundamental element of air intelligence, but, like the other tools of air intelligence, it was not without problems. While the limited number of photoreconnaissance units was most obvious in the first eighteen months of the war, especially in the Pacific theaters, the constant expansion of air operations always placed correspondingly increasing demands on new photoreconnaissance and interpretation units. As late as January 1945, at the HQ USSTAF–hosted American air intelligence officers' conference, Elliot Roosevelt noted that requests for reconnaissance support continued to exceed resources despite the presence of twenty-nine American and fifteen RAF squadrons in western Europe and Italy.[141]

In a more directly operational sense, timing of photographic missions caused problems, particularly in strategic poststrike damage assessment. To provide the almost immediate review air commanders sought, a portion of every American bomber force carried cameras to record strikes in progress. The resulting pictures were often unduly gratifying. With fires blazing, buildings collapsing, and smoke obscuring the target, they often suggested greater than actual damage. Throughout the war, those immediately involved in photoreconnaissance and photointelligence processes, including Roosevelt, argued against putting too much stock in these first pictures. They were equally emphatic in their opposition to sending reconnaissance aircraft over a target within hours of an attack because the results, again due to obstructions, were still not worth the effort or the danger.[142] One of the leading British photointerpreters noted it often took several weeks to obtain truly accurate photographs for analyzing bomb damage since the enemy first had to raze damaged buildings and clear away debris.[143]

Even more difficult than assessing physical destruction to the exterior of a target were accurate assessments of the interior damage and the impact of such damage on a facility's output. Postwar analysis by the United States Strategic Bombing Survey (USSBS) would reveal that destruction of essential machinery at aircraft production and repair facilities was almost always much less than even the most conservative photointerpreters, let alone the operators, judged. For other industries, damage assessment could be better. Photointerpretation of damage at the synthetic oil production facility at Leuna, for example, showed fewer discrepancies in the USSBS's postwar analysis. This was owing to the nature of the plant that had more areas exposed to overhead observation and to direct bomb damage. The USSBS specialists made their assessments by comparing wartime photography and interpretation reports with on-the-spot surveys and interviews of managers and employees. The ability of factory

Tools of Air Intelligence

Brig. Gen. Ira C. Eaker

Capt. Elliot Roosevelt

personnel to make repairs locally, and often unobserved, complicated the task of damage assessment.[144]

Reflective of the mental framework that predominated during the war was the observation of Col. Guido Perera of the COA. In a memorandum to Maj. Gen. Laurence S. Kuter, HQ USAAF AC/AS, Plans on the effects of strategic air operations against the German aircraft industry, Perera accurately pointed out the difficulties of damage evaluations based on "high altitude photographs varying widely in quality." But he arrived at the wrong conclusion when he stressed, "The industrial damage just listed [in the memorandum] is the absolute minimum statement of accomplishment. Greater damage is a practical certainty."[145]

Just finding the target in an aerial photograph could be extremely difficult. Unless the photointerpreters knew what to look for, even the best among them might overlook crucial evidence. A structure that proved to be a launching pad for the early tests of the German V–2 rocket at Peenemunde had been dismissed for several months as merely part of a group of unknown, mysterious rings before additional clues led interpreters to pull out their old photographs and take another look.[146] Misled by scientific intelligence into concentrating their attention along rail lines, photointerpreters missed the construction of buzz-bomb launch sites in northern France until a report from a French underground agent suggested they broaden their search. Photographs previously taken of the area around Bois Carré were then reexamined by an Anglo-American team which located a total of ninety-six suspected V–1 launch sites.[147]

Piercing the Fog

Maj. Gen. Carl A. Spaatz

As the Germans increased the dispersal of their production facilities throughout 1944, the task of photointerpretation demanded increasing ingenuity. Constance Babington-Smith, one of the most skilled British photointerpreters, wrote after the war that by 1944 she and her colleagues found themselves searching out "the most unimaginable hiding places: to lunatic asylums and chocolate factories, to vast fantastic underground workshops, to firebreaks in pine forests and tunnels on autobahns." In fact, she summarized, "one's usual standards of what was possible or impossible had to go by the board."[148]

As with all the tools of intelligence, photoreconnaissance and photointerpretation were most effective when employed in conjunction with one or more of the other forms. The guidance provided by a POW interrogation, the clue passed under cover by SIGINT, or the comments offered by an agent on the ground were often indispensable. Such clues suggested where to concentrate reconnaissance efforts, or they might focus the attention of interpreters on given photographs as well as providing suggestions on how to make sense of what they saw. Such guidance might come from almost any source. Advertisements appearing in German technical journals in 1942 for oil engineers provided the first clues that led eventually to the reconnaissance mission that revealed the nearly complete construction of the first part of a huge refinery at Brux, Czechoslovakia. When completed in 1944, Brux would be one of Germany's largest oil complexes.[149]

Both the British Secret Intelligence Service and the American OSS maintained close contacts with photointelligence agencies. Agent reports often provided initial tips on German activity in occupied territories. This proved to

Tools of Air Intelligence

Brig. Gen. George C. McDonald *(Courtesy, National Archives)*

be especially the case in the development of the German V–1 and V–2 weapons. Conversely, aerial photographs served as an effective means of evaluating the reliability of agent reports. Although few photointerpreters were aware of activities at BP, a close link always existed between it and the CIU at Medmenham.[150]

Links with less directly operational organizations were also important. Economic analysis agencies such as the COA and the EOU were extremely useful to photointerpreters as they tried to understand where they might look for factories and industrial installations in Europe and to interpret the degree of damage inflicted by an attack. The chief of Medmenham's enemy airfields section credited the American EOU with providing a clearer focus and direction to the photographic reconnaissance and analysis of aircraft factories. As a result of the American analysts' insistence on greater emphasis in this area and their suggestions on what to look for, in 1943 CIU added some fifty aircraft production facilities to their reconnaissance program.[151] Information derived from this expansion played a role in targeting for the February 20–25, 1944, campaign against the German aircraft industry.

Even when other sources identified a potential target, air planners and operators relied on photointelligence in the preparation and execution of air operations. Aerial photography contributed to the setting of target priorities by providing evidence of the status of newly built or repaired factories. It also formed the basis of target folders and was used for determining approaches and egress routes, aiming points, anticipated flak locations, and even types of bombs. Accurate interpretation of photographs also prevented unnecessary attacks, freeing resources for more important targets. Based on ground reports in 1943 that indicated that a Junkers factory at Schonebeck was producing aircraft engines, Eighth Air Force scheduled an attack with what were still scarce resources. The astute observations of CIU photointerpreters of the absence of test beds in any photographs of this facility led to a reevaluation and subsequent cancellation of what would have been a wasted mission.[152]

Y Intelligence

In Europe and North Africa the greatest role of SIGINT after ULTRA was the interception and application of low-grade signals traffic and transmissions made in the clear (i.e., unencrypted). The latter occurred mainly between aircraft or between aircraft and ground control stations. While precise terminology and technical definitions changed during the course of the war, British and American airmen in both operations and intelligence commonly used the term "Y intelligence" to refer to the interception and handling of low-grade Axis codes as well as plain-language radio traffic.* The British organization responsible for radio interception of both low- and high-grade enemy ciphers, the "Yorker Service," was commonly referred to as Y-Service.[153] In addition to monitoring tactical and strategic radio message and voice traffic, the British Y-Service recorded radar, navigation, and other enemy electronic transmissions. All of the recorded information became intelligence data when forwarded to the appropriate commanders.

In these other SIGINT areas, as in ULTRA, the British had both extensive experience and an elaborate organization in place when the initial Eighth Air Force cadre arrived in Great Britain in early 1942. The American air forces in Europe developed some capability to handle German low-grade cipher traffic and to translate uncoded radio messages, but they relied heavily on their ally in all aspects of SIGINT. American understanding of the British interception, evaluation, and dissemination of enemy information grew slowly. Only after the April 1943 visit of Colonels McCormack and Taylor and William Friedman did Americans provide substantial staffing of various parts of BP's operation. The British system for transmitting special intelligence to the field remained the one in use in Europe and the Mediterranean throughout the war. Additionally, several American army and air signals units received training from British forces.[154] Although the British dominated Allied SIGINT in Europe and the Mediterranean throughout the war, their exclusive role was modified as the war

---

*Technically, the American term for these activities was "Radio Intelligence," but because most documents prepared at AAF headquarters within the European theaters commonly used the term "Y intelligence," we will adhere to this convention as well.

continued. American SIGINT units operated in North Africa and during Allied operations in Sicily and Italy. As the strategic air war evolved, American airborne Y intercept operations began in the fall of 1943 to give long-range bomber formation commanders in the Mediterranean the benefit of immediate intercepts of fighter pilots' and controllers' transmissions. By the winter of 1943–1944, under the press of the intensified Allied bombing campaign, a large portion of German air defense operations occurred beyond the range of U.K.-based signals intercept stations. In January 1944 Eighth Air Force began experiments with airborne radio intercept operations conducted by British-trained American aircrew members. (American bomber forces striking German targets from bases in the Mediterranean had begun limited airborne signals interception the previous fall.) When American tactical air forces moved to the continent in June 1944, they established mobile intercept facilities that were linked to American fighter control centers.[155]

Although ULTRA did not play a significant role in the planning and conduct of American air operations over Europe proper until the late spring of 1943, Y intelligence had immediate operational application from the very beginning of Eighth Air Force operations. Strategic air operations relied on Y intelligence in three areas: employment of fighter escorts, postmission analysis, and planning for future missions. In the actual conduct of operational missions, SIGINT was more important in the employment of escorting fighters than of the bomber forces. Y intelligence enabled Eighth Air Force and VIII Bomber and Fighter Command headquarters to monitor enemy reactions to bomber raids. Since the attacking bombers maintained radio silence, commanders could follow their forces by listening to the transmissions of the enemy's air defense network. The RAF's Y-Service, responsible for collating all plain-language transmissions intercepted by a fan of receiver sites located along the coast, passed pertinent enemy voice radio traffic and call sign data to the American headquarters over secure telephone lines. Stations at RAF Cheadle intercepted German Morse code transmissions, decoded them, and forwarded information pertaining to GAF intentions and actual interceptions of bomber formations. This information often included enemy alert notices and takeoff orders. Intelligence from these sources was usually received at AJAX—VIII Fighter Command—within five to twenty minutes of the original enemy transmission.[156] While the bomber force was out of escort range (which occurred frequently until the arrival of the P–51s in January 1944), little could be done with this situational intelligence during the inbound portion of a raid. When limited navigational skills often caused significant deviations from planned flight routes, the information gained from the enemy via Y enabled more effective and accurate escort rendezvous with the returning bombers. During late 1942 and 1943, when German fighters could harass the bomber force all the way to the Channel coast, a successful rendezvous could significantly reduce bomber losses.

Piercing the Fog

Y intelligence contributed as well to the detailed enemy reaction reports Eighth Air Force A–2 and A–3 prepared jointly after each mission. The purposes of these studies were to determine what aspects of an operation had been conducted smoothly, identify problem areas, spot trends in enemy defenses, analyze enemy tactics, and assess the probable benefits of different defensive formations. To assist in report preparation, RAF Canterbury forwarded to Eighth Air Force a detailed analysis, known as the Canterbury Digest, of SIGINT acquired during each mission. In addition, Air Ministry Intelligence (A.I.4) prepared and forwarded to the Americans longer term studies on the GAF's OB, tactics, and radio identification methods and procedures.[157]

Y intercepts contributed to the enemy reaction studies in several ways. By monitoring aircraft transmissions, they provided comments on the enemy's running assessment of the course of the air battle and, more importantly, offered insight into German aerial tactics. By identifying the German fighter control locations, Y contributed to the picture of the enemy's air defense organization and areas of responsibilities. By linking call signs with the times and places that the enemy aircraft checked in with ground fighter controllers, SIGINT enabled Allied intelligence to determine more accurately the most likely locations of primary fighter bases and the probable zones of concentrated attack.

By listening to initial German warnings of incoming American raids, SIGINT operators could determine the range of enemy radar equipment, especially since ground controllers often indicated which site provided information. Occasionally, SIGINT could pick up intelligence on the results of American strikes against enemy airdromes. When a ground controller advised a fighter he could not return to his normal base because of damage, Allied intelligence knew they had damaged that field; it also confirmed which units were stationed there. Directives to defensive interceptors low on fuel to land at secondary recovery bases sometimes allowed operators to identify previously unknown fields. The enemy also revealed flak locations in his transmissions. Such revelations came either in the form of the identification of specific locations to fighters or, more frequently, instructions to break off attacks at a certain point. Radio interceptions helped to confirm the downing of enemy fighters by aerial gunners and sometimes revealed the fate of friendly bombers that had dropped behind the main force.[158]

The information thus provided influenced both bomber and fighter operations. With regard to bomber operations, Y intelligence was more valuable in operational planning than in targeting. The insights it provided rarely affected decisions on which targets to attack. Brig. Gen. Harris B. Hull, Eaker's A–2 in Eighth Air Force, recalled that they basically knew where the targets were in those days. If the weather and available force permitted, Hull remarked that "you were gonna go" regardless of the locations of defensive fighter forces.[159] Y intelligence's role was to assist the operational mission planners to determine

Tools of Air Intelligence

the most effective approaches and tactics. By identifying the most likely locations of defensive fighter units, Y information affected the selection of optimum ingress and egress routes.[160]

A second critical contribution of Y intelligence to mission planning was information on rendezvous points for enemy interceptors and the locations where enemy mass attacks were most likely to occur. This information allowed American planners to select optimum rendezvous points for friendly escorts. During the period when the heavy bombers had to rely on relays of fighters even to escort them as far as the German border, this reduced the possibility that one set of escorts would depart before replacements arrived or, worse, that this would happen right where the Germans were massing.[161]

Finally, the ability, depending on meteorological and technological conditions, to intercept enemy weather reports from as far east as the Balkans and Russia enabled Y-Service to contribute to strategic mission planning a better, if still incomplete, picture of weather systems likely to develop over projected target areas. Given the American reliance on visual bombing, this knowledge was important for selecting primary and secondary targets for specific missions. On the other hand, atmospheric conditions could themselves handicap Y intelligence by reducing the range of the original German transmissions or by affecting the intelligibility of messages received.[162]

Efforts to extend the range and value of Y intelligence by including airborne operators in bomber formations proved of limited tactical value in both Eighth and Fifteenth Air Forces, but they contributed information for postmission analysis. Limited airborne operations began in the Mediterranean theater in October 1943. By March 1944, the Americans had trained eleven operators and allocated them to Fifteenth Air Force units. The results remained modest by the end of that year. Operators were present on only a few bombers. They could provide immediate warning information only to their own crew, since radio silence precluded broadcasting over radio frequencies. To have done so would have revealed their presence to the enemy and made their aircraft immediate priority targets.[163]

According to a report prepared by the HQ AAF Air Communications Office, many combat groups failed to grasp the potential value of this airborne Y-Service. Some even refused to install British-loaned equipment in unit aircraft. The personnel system's failure to allocate slots to this task compounded the commanders' reluctance to withdraw men from other positions within their organizations. An additional limiting factor in Italy was the lack of airborne tape recorders through the fall of 1944. This meant operators could monitor only one frequency at a time and simultaneously had to take detailed notes. Not surprisingly, only five of the eleven trained individuals developed "a working method of gaining valuable information."[164]

In a meeting of senior air intelligence officers in Europe in January 1945, an extended discussion on Y intelligence concluded, while ground-based Y intelligence used by tactical air forces was in good shape, "Airborne 'Y' problems have been long and painful." Problems included lack of equipment rugged enough for air operations, limited numbers of qualified individuals, and conflicts between signals and intelligence over organizational responsibilities for maintenance and operations. Despite an Air Ministry report that indicated Eighth Air Force's use of airborne operators rose from six per mission in July 1944 to twelve per mission in October of that year, the Eighth Air Force Director of Intelligence reported in January 1945 that the Eighth was sometimes lucky to get two Y operators airborne per mission.[165]

Even with these problems, airborne Y operators contributed in both Europe and the Mediterranean to the accumulation of intelligence for postmission analysis, particularly before ULTRA became prolific. In fact, an Eighth Air Force report stated the airborne input, which was incorporated into the RAF's Canterbury Digests, was "the only basic source material of signals air intelligence originated by Eighth Air Force."[166] In Italy, the role of the airborne Y interceptors in postmission analysis was further enhanced because the mountainous terrain in northern Italy took offensive bombers beyond effective Allied radar and radio range much more quickly than the terrain in western Europe did.

Y intelligence for American tactical air operations began in North Africa and continued through the course of the war. In contrast to strategic air operations from the United Kingdom, American tactical air forces developed independent SIGINT service units. The first of these arrived in the United Kingdom in the fall of 1942 to participate in Operation TORCH. During the North African campaign, American SIGINT detachments remained under British tutelage, with RAF Y-Service maintaining overall responsibility for all SIGINT in the theater. Detachments of the American 849th SIGINT Company supported the Allied invasions of Sicily and the Italian mainland. According to the senior American intelligence officer in the theater, even in this period the Americans continued to "rely on R.A.F. channels for information and general directions."[167] By early 1944, the decline of the GAF in Italy resulted in a corresponding decrease in useful tactical air intelligence from radio interception.[168]

During preinvasion tactical air operations against Occupied Europe in the spring of 1944, British Y-Service passed SIGINT to the Control Centre at RAF 11 Group, which acted as the operations center for the RAF units and IX Fighter Command. The IX Fighter Command SIGINT officer was an integral member of the Y staff at the center. In June, the advanced echelon of Detachment 3, 3d Radio Squadron (Mobile), began radio intercept operations with IX TAC on the continent only three days after the initial landings at Normandy.[169] While this detachment and follow-on units assigned to the other tactical air commands maintained operational links with their British counterparts, their primary ties

Tools of Air Intelligence

were into the American fighter control centers. At each fighter control center, the Y officer sat beside the chief controller. This arrangement allowed for the immediate operational application of time-sensitive Y information, since the chief controller was in direct contact with airborne aircraft as well as with the appropriate tactical air control headquarters.[170]

Y intelligence's contributions to tactical air operations were particularly important during the campaign in North Africa, the invasions of Sicily and Italy, and the period surrounding the landing at Normandy. In North Africa, it provided initial warning of incoming air raids before Allied radar was operational or while the enemy was still beyond radar range.[171] Correlating radio intercepts with sources such as radar and ULTRA, SIGINT also collected information on enemy tactics and the disposition of his forces. By linking enemy call signs with locations, Y intercepts often yielded clues on enemy operating bases and provided the initial basis for attack planning. As with strategic air operations, Y intercepts were essential to Allied efforts to determine the location, organization, capabilities, and structure of the enemy's air defense networks in these tactical campaigns. Y intercepts provided Allied forces with timely intelligence on what enemy units were airborne and often what their objectives were and what the specific rendezvous points were for units coming from different bases.[172] Y intelligence was particularly effective when properly fused with ULTRA. Decrypted German messages might indicate the time and location of projected enemy missions, but Y intercepts provided real-time, concrete information which confirmed German activities. It was, in that sense, the most accurate and current intelligence available.

ULTRA and MAGIC in the Pacific and CBI

SIGINT in the war against Japan had an origin and prosecution unlike that found in Europe. While European ULTRA began as a joint Polish-French-British effort in the late 1930s, it became wholly British after the June 1940 fall of France. The reading of German signals then became a bilateral Anglo-American operation when the Americans joined as full partners in mid-1943. SIGINT that concentrated on Japan began prewar as a largely American endeavor, and it remained so throughout the war except for the CBI and Australian participation in the Southwest Pacific. Both its development as a tool of air intelligence and its use in strategic and tactical operations in the Pacific war were peculiarly American. The term MAGIC has come to be applied indiscriminately to this American scrutiny of Japanese radio traffic. In fact, MAGIC was a very specific subdivision, correctly applied to the decryption of Japanese diplomatic messages. Such information circulated through the hands of very few senior civilian officials and military and naval commanders in Washington, D.C. Only at times did it have a direct military application. In all theaters of the Pacific and

Piercing the Fog

CBI, ULTRA intercepts, done in Washington, Honolulu, India, or Brisbane, Australia, came to play a significant role in the AAF's planning and operations. The specific importance of this source in the war against Japan varied greatly from theater to theater and from numbered air force to numbered air force.[173]

The American effort against Japan began in the 1920s, continuing at various levels up to and throughout the war. Initially, its focus was unlike that of the Allies in Europe. During the late 1930s, the bulk of German message traffic intercepted and decrypted by the British dealt with military topics, in part because of the covert German efforts to conceal their own remilitarization efforts which were specifically prohibited by the Versailles treaty.[174] Fearing German military efforts most, the British directed decrypting efforts toward these areas; inasmuch as the Americans were most concerned with Japanese economic expansionism, their priorities concentrated on this threat.[175] The bulk of Japanese message traffic intercepted and decrypted by the Americans in the 1930s concerned Japanese naval operations and diplomatic and political matters directly related to Japan's expansionist foreign policy.

With respect to encrypting messages, the Japanese during the 1930s relied on a system similar to the Germans': machine-enciphered messages. The Japanese systems were more formidable than those of the Third Reich, for the Japanese language is extremely difficult for Westerners to master. To Americans, the logic of the German language (its sentence structure and thought progression) came relatively easily because of common cultural and linguistic traditions. Asian conceptualization in both thought process and sentence structure was dramatically different for all but those few Americans who had studied and understood Asian culture. The shortage of American linguists comfortable in the Japanese language and perceptive to Japanese culture limited Pacific ULTRA operations from their inception during the 1930s until well into the war.[176]

American code breakers during the 1930s focused their efforts on Japanese naval and diplomatic traffic because they had been able to break those encryptions, whereas they could not penetrate the Japanese Army's cipher system. The Japanese were in the process of establishing an overseas empire and understandably had to rely upon wireless communications rather than land lines for diplomatic discussions. Although most Americans were unfamiliar with the internal functioning of Japanese society, Washington's analysts felt more comfortable with Japanese diplomatic efforts because these tended to follow Western logic. As a consequence, American code breaking efforts against the Japanese were better developed in a diplomatic rather than in a military context.

There existed a limited American appreciation of Japanese military affairs in general and air operations in particular. Most analysis of Japanese military and aviation matters in the 1930s was secondhand. It came from Japanese diplomatic appreciations of the military situation sent between the Tokyo

Tools of Air Intelligence

foreign office and its overseas embassies or from military reports sent by overseas Japanese military attachés on diplomatic situations. The result was an imperfect reading from a military standpoint. For example, whatever military warnings concerning Japanese planning for the attacks on Pearl Harbor and the Philippines that American intelligence analysts might have gleaned from MAGIC intercepts in November and early December 1941, they were funneled through a diplomatic prism. Little wonder they were badly interpreted, for diplomatic noise overrode military intention.[177]

Although the Japanese cipher and code systems, particularly the diplomatic system embodied in the PURPLE machine, had weaknesses, and although the Japanese were aware that their communications were under attack, they remained confident in the overall security of their systems. The Japanese military instituted several improvements intended to defeat attempts to decipher messages, to discourage direction finding, and to make more difficult long-term traffic analysis. Immediately before the attack on Pearl Harbor, naval ciphers changed (more than one month before they would normally have done so). In late May 1942, naval ciphers changed again as the battle of Midway drew near, but American naval communication specialists had already learned enough to give Admiral Chester W. Nimitz the insight he so badly needed. In August 1942, with the furor in America that accompanied disclosure in the *Chicago Tribune* of the Midway knowledge (and as disclosed by radio commentator Walter Winchell at about the same time), Japanese naval authorities devised a new cipher that began a different key each day at midnight. The Japanese apparently did not understand what the Americans had done, but their change meant that the Navy's experts had to begin the process of learning and cracking the new cipher every twenty-four hours. Their change slowed, but did not stop, the success of American cryptanalysis.[178]

Responsibility for SIGINT support to the AAF rested in Washington with the U.S. Army Signal Corps' SIGINT Service (SIS, later called the Signal Security Agency). SIS listening-post operators copied Japanese Army transmissions and forwarded them to Washington where they were decrypted and translated at Arlington Hall Station. During the war, the AAF organized several radio squadrons that also intercepted and transcribed Japanese message traffic, sending much of the material to Arlington Hall for decryption. The messages were then passed to the MIS. Special Branch of the MIS analyzed the material, preparing from it useful data to be made available to War Department planners. The secretary of war had established Special Branch in 1942 to resolve the problem of inadequate analysis of radio intercepts made apparent in the Pearl Harbor attack. In fact, Special Branch was a direct descendant of the Army-Navy intelligence sections established to handle Japanese radio traffic analysis in the 1920s. In the early 1930s, Secretary of State Stimson had ended State Department funding of the code breaking effort against the Japanese diplomatic traffic; that effort subsequently fell to the military departments.

Piercing the Fog

Given the overall shortage of funds within both the Navy and War Departments during the middle and late 1930s, it is not surprising that precious few dollars and resources were made available to support the code breakers' efforts to attack the Japanese codes and ciphers. That the effort survived as it did until 1941 was most fortunate.[179]

The two military departments insisted upon operating their own collection and decryption efforts. In an apparent prewar economy effort, they alternated submitting their analyses and reportage to Washington's senior decision makers. Given the compartmentalization inherent in all SIGINT, this splintering of analytical resources complicated a difficult situation. The geography and environment of the Pacific area further aggravated the situation in the years before Pearl Harbor. Given the maritime character of the Pacific region, the Navy Department viewed this area as its own. The Office of Naval Intelligence (ONI) concentrated on diplomatic traffic with naval implications. The MIS of the War Department concerned itself primarily with the Army's lonely fortress in the Philippines as well as the forces in Hawaii. The Army's interests lay in the land war in China and potential Japanese ground operations elsewhere. Air intelligence tended to get lost between these two elements.

Also important in understanding the working of Special Branch were intraservice bureaucratic interests. Within the War and Navy Departments, responsibilities for SIGINT were divided. The signal departments of each service became responsible for interception and decryption of enemy messages. Detailed analysis and subsequent dissemination was the responsibility of the services' intelligence chiefs—the War Department's G–2 and the Navy's ONI. Presumably, the two individuals heading these specific organizations were to prescribe priorities for interception and decryption; left unresolved was overall responsibility. The Pearl Harbor disaster served as mute evidence of unsettled priorities and divided responsibilities.

Shortly after Pearl Harbor, Henry L. Stimson, now Secretary of War, and probably with the support of President Roosevelt, concluded that Japanese diplomatic traffic was not being given sufficiently close attention. Stimson set about finding a better method, and in doing so he decided that the problem could best be solved by a person with an executive background and experienced in handling and presenting large cases involving complicated facts.[180] The Secretary of War turned to a New York lawyer and former colleague, Alfred McCormack, and charged him with recommending overall improvements to the signals analysis task. McCormack, commissioned for the purpose, joined Col. Carter W. Clarke in Washington. The two soon formed what would become Special Branch, responsible within the War Department for analysis and dissemination of intercepted SIGINT. An agreement with the Navy Department and the Federal Bureau of Investigation consolidated the diplomatic effort in Special Branch. Special Branch also handled review and interpretation of Japanese Army signals while the Navy concentrated on Japanese naval traffic.[181]

Tools of Air Intelligence

Part of this arrangement was the implicit agreement that, at least in the early days of fighting, the Department of the Navy would be concerned with the Pacific.

McCormack quickly realized that he needed to get important SIGINT in a usable format and in a timely fashion to Washington's decision makers. He decided to use a periodic intelligence summary based upon the latest MAGIC intercepts integrated with previous MAGIC information. Started in March 1942 and initially called The MAGIC Summary, these reports quickly proved a distinct improvement over the pre–Pearl Harbor practice, whereby the services merely forwarded portions of intercepted messages with little or no analysis. By the end of 1942, these summaries, having been redesignated The *MAGIC Diplomatic Summaries,* were issued daily, integrating both diplomatic and military analysis gleaned from other intelligence sources. The Secretaries of War and the Navy; the Chief of Staff, U.S. Army; the Commander-in-Chief, U.S. Fleet; and the Chief of Naval Operations and key staff officers of the service departments saw the daily synopses. Although Arnold and his AC/AS, Intelligence saw the MAGIC summaries, not until late 1943 or early 1944 did they receive ULTRA access. A copy of the MAGIC summaries reached the White House map room, and by late 1942 the President's naval aide was reading the digest to Roosevelt during his daily physical therapy sessions. Presidential confidant Harry Hopkins and senior military advisor Admiral William Leahy checked the summaries each morning. During presidential absences from Washington, Roosevelt received daily MAGIC information in the form of disguised intelligence briefings. At least at the highest level, SIGINT based upon MAGIC was having an impact.[182]

The degree and significance of the impact of MAGIC on national war policy remains difficult to assess, primarily because all copies of the MAGIC Summaries, except the record copy, were destroyed by the recipient after reading, and few of the key participants referred to them in diaries or correspondence. Wartime security measures strictly forbade mentioning any linkage of signals decryption and the source.[183] It is likewise difficult to link the specifics of high-level decisions on strategic use of airpower in the Pacific to MAGIC. Most of these decisions resulted from deliberations of the JCS or the war strategy of the president and his advisors. Again, strict security provisions prohibited explicit mention of MAGIC or ULTRA and its relationship to such decisions that appeared in the JCS papers. MAGIC regularly provided Japanese attaché reports from places such as Hanoi and occupied China on the specific results of AAF bombing attacks as well as long-term analysis of economic problems. To these MAGIC assessments, air intelligence experts often added other SIGINT data and their own analyses that stressed what impact the air campaign was having upon future Japanese war-waging capabilities.[184] Such firsthand bomb damage assessments bolstered the AAF's demands for operations targeted on the seizure of forward air bases. As these MAGIC reports were going directly to major decision makers, one must assume a degree of influence. During the last twelve months of the war in the Pacific, analyses in the MAGIC Summaries on the economic impact of the AAF's strategic bombing campaign increased, attesting to the devastating impact that the American air attacks were having upon both the civilian economy and domestic opinion.[185]

Such influence by air intelligence specialists grew slowly until late 1943. MAGIC analysts themselves recognized that much of the intelligence with air implications derived from diplomatic sources was, in fact, secondhand. Examples of such information that became available to the Allies were the delicate Japanese-Russian negotiations over neutrality, the sporadic and unsuccessful attempts by the Axis to break the Allied sea blockade with the use of German and Japanese submarines, the shifting diplomatic and political situations in Indochina and Thailand, the anti-British activities of the Indian and Burmese puppet governments, and the Japanese attempts at peace negotiations with Chungking. In mid-1943, the MAGIC summaries included several major studies on Japanese military budget expenditures in Thailand and Indochina which provided evidence of military initiative there as well as detailed analyses on various aspects of the Japanese war economy, including rice, pig iron, and aluminum production and rail transportation. But these had little immediate tactical application in the Pacific air war.[186]

Another reason for the lack of high-level air intelligence in 1943 lay in the periodic inability of American code breakers to decrypt Japanese Army or Navy codes.* Unlike the Japanese MAGIC diplomatic messages, which were enciphered by an Enigma-type machine and could be deciphered by the American PURPLE device, the Japanese Army and Navy high-level codes were enciphered by use of conventional but very difficult code books. The U.S. Navy broke the Japanese JN–25 naval code first, in part because there were more navy than army messages available for study. The Japanese Navy codes could be deciphered by early 1942, although portions of many messages were often unclear. For a time after January 1943, when a submarine loaded with code books was captured, most naval codes could be deciphered. Japanese Army codes began to yield in the spring of 1943, but they could not be broken consistently until early 1944, when Allied forces captured a truckload of code books. Even when coded messages could not be read, however, SIGINT gained valuable information from traffic analysis by establishing locations of enemy transmitters with radio direction finders and noting their signals activity. Because the Japanese naval air forces were more security minded, American SIGINT was more successful against army air units, gradually establishing air OBs, patterns of flight, types of aircraft, airfields in use, and eventually tracking tail numbers of aircraft moving in and out of the forward area.[187]

---

*The Japanese had no independent air force; the Japanese Army and the Japanese Navy maintained their own air forces.

Tools of Air Intelligence

The results of the Navy's efforts to penetrate Japanese naval ciphers were the information on Japanese intentions that led to the standoff in the Coral Sea, blocking Japan's advance on Port Moresby and ensuring the victory at Midway, which crippled Japan's carrier operations. In March 1943, the Army opened the Wireless Experimental Center in New Delhi—a cooperative effort with the British ULTRA operation. Code breakers there soon broke a Japanese military code—the water transport code.[188] As a result, throughout the remainder of the war SIGINT contributed to attacks on critical Japanese shipping, initially through monitoring of actual shipping schedules and eventually through directing specific attacks by American submarines.[189] An example of this occurred in April 1944 when analysts learned of a major Japanese resupply convoy of 9 merchant vessels and 12 escorts moving from Chinese ports to Hollandia bases with over 20,000 troops and supplies. American naval submarines sank at least 4 of these vessels with a loss of over 4,000 troops.[190]

B Section

By mid-1943, determined that SIS continue in breaking a fairly representative flow of Japanese military ciphers and having obtained sufficient manpower to conduct a comprehensive analytical program, Colonel McCormack established a section dedicated to studying Japanese military messages and disseminating the results—the B Section.[191] Initial efforts by the new organization proved frustrating as the code breakers encountered a bewildering array of codes being used by the Japanese services, often with only fragmentary intercepts. They lacked background data; as the official history notes, there were "difficulties of translation and possibilities of erroneous interpretation. . . . It had become evident that the potential of intelligence to be derived from Japanese military traffic could be derived only by employing a very large number of personnel of the highest quality." Addressing the need for qualified analysts, in early January 1944 McCormack agreed to an authorized strength in B Section of 280 officers and 120 enlisted members. Recruiting proved difficult, and by the middle of that year the Army had assigned only 79 officers and 65 enlisted.[192]

Though few in number, the air members of the new section began from its inception to accumulate information about the Japanese Army Air Force. Using AAF officers trained at the AAF's air intelligence school as well as other flying officers, this OB section became the primary source of intelligence on the organization of the Japanese Army Air Force by March 1944.[193] From message intercepts, B Section constructed a detailed air OB as well as unit dispositions and strength estimates. In April 1944, section members began to prepare weekly estimates of Japanese air strength that were issued separately from the *MAGIC Diplomatic Summaries* and other analytical products. These reports were part of the larger *Japanese Order of Battle Bulletins* that also began to appear in weekly format for use both in Washington and the Far East.[194] By July, the analysts had amassed sufficient data to organize a Pacific OB conference. Such conferences met on an irregular basis until August 1945.[195]

Air members of B Section also cooperated with air members of F–22, the ONI branch responsible for signal intelligence, which also produced estimates on the Japanese Naval Air Force. The B Section and F–22 consultation eventually led to a joint estimate of Japanese air strength. The formation and evolution of B Section thus represented a critical step in the operational use of SIGINT for AAF operations in the Pacific. By the end of the war, the Americans shared this information with the British Air Ministry.[196]

Operational SIGINT and the Far East

As B Section began to produce operational intelligence concerning the Pacific, Col. McCormack now faced the same dissemination problem there as he had in Europe: how to transmit this analysis securely and then how to monitor its use to ensure that the priceless source was not compromised. As with the Germans in Europe, the Japanese still appeared unaware that some of the keys to their cryptography had been broken. Operational exploitation had to be measured against possible compromise. This required tough measures.

A complicating factor for Special Branch in implementing such measures was the relationship of the American Navy and Army SIGINT organizations in the Pacific. These units provided Pacific commanders with operational intelligence that they had intercepted, decrypted, and analyzed; in some instances they contributed to major operational successes, among which were the battles of the Coral Sea, Midway, and the Bismarck Sea.[197] Hardened by these operational successes, neither service was about to be told by Washington how to use or even how to handle locally derived SIGINT.

The Navy and Army SIGINT organizations in the Pacific in early 1942 grew from the field operations set up in the pre–Pearl Harbor days. Both services, mirroring Washington, had attempted to maintain their own intercept and translation capabilities while sharing the information they obtained. Evidence suggests that this split responsibility at MacArthur's Far East headquarters contributed in December 1941 to the destruction on the ground at Clark and Iba Air Fields of the B–17s and P–40s that constituted the air force which the general had counted on so heavily for the defense of the Philippines. In a 1945 memoir, the Army commander of the SIGINT unit in the Philippines later claimed that the Navy decoders were not working on weekends, so critical information in the Navy's possession did not reach MacArthur and his key staff.[198]

By early 1942, the Army and Navy had established separate SIGINT operations in the Pacific. Each group was producing, without consultating with

Washington or Special Branch, SIGINT that had immediate operational use. From a technological point of view, each organization possessed the same ability as Washington for rapidly decrypting the intercepted messages once the ciphers had been broken. In Brisbane and especially in Honolulu, intelligence operations were integrated into the planning process. Each Pacific headquarters saw itself as fully operational and largely self-sufficient with regard to SIGINT. The March 1942 decision by the JCS to split the Pacific Theater into two areas—the Navy-oriented Pacific Ocean Area (POA) under the command of Admiral Chester W. Nimitz, and MacArthur's Army-oriented Southwest Pacific Area (SWPA)—served to complement the two services' emerging regional signal intelligence organizations. Moreover, SIGINT in the CBI region was entirely separate from the other two Pacific war theaters.

The POA (Navy) SIGINT operation centered on Fleet Radio Unit, Pacific (FRUPac), which functioned as the radio intelligence section of the Intelligence Center, Pacific Ocean Area.[199] Critical to the operational influence of FRUPac had been its ability in early 1942 to intercept, decrypt, analyze, and disseminate the critical SIGINT that facilitated the naval standoff in the battle of the Coral Sea, and then to provide the key analyses that led to the dramatic victory at the Battle of Midway.[200] These experiences validated the operational use of SIGINT. Furthermore, both battles showed the new role of carrier-based aviation in the war. Although not recognized at the time, the loss of Japanese carriers at Midway would limit the employment of Japanese airpower largely to land-based assets. The air superiority mission in the theaters became more focused than it would have been had Japan retained a strong carrier arm.

The SWPA organization providing SIGINT for operational use in 1942 grew from roots transplanted from Corregidor along with MacArthur in March of that year. During those desperate days in the Philippines, the U.S. Army detachment responsible for intercept and decryption of Japanese signals—the 2d Signal Company—had functioned under the direction of MacArthur's signal officer, Col. Spencer B. Akin.[201] These specialists were among the few evacuated from the Philippines to Australia by submarine. After arrival in Melbourne, the 2d Signal Company was reinforced by the 837th Signal Service Detachment to form the American nucleus of the SWPA SIGINT organization—what became known as Central Bureau (CB).[202]

MacArthur's operational concern in early 1942 was to blunt the Japanese offensive and the anticipated invasion of Australia; he was allocated precious few resources for this task. Until the war assumed a more stable character, concern for the use of intercept intelligence was not one of the general's highest priorities.[203] Thus it was his land deputy, Australian General Thomas Blamey, who provided the genesis for CB. In mid-1942, Blamey asked the SWPA commander to form "a combined bureau . . . [responsible for] the receipt, collation, examination, and distribution of information obtained by intercept organization." MacArthur approved this suggestion, noting the potential benefits to the bureau from the "recent receipt from the War Department of labor saving machinery [punch-card tabulating equipment]." To this the Australians added ULTRA experience in the form of the Australian Special Wireless Group, which had seen considerable experience against the Germans in North Africa and the Near East. The group included some British personnel who had escaped from Singapore. Thus from its inception, CB was multinational.[204]

The personnel in CB greatly outnumbered those in Special Branch; CB grew from 1,000 in 1943 to more than 4,000 by war's end. Special Branch never exceeded more than a few hundred. Americans comprised 50 percent of CB's personnel. At MacArthur's insistence, the U.S. Navy was excluded from the regular work. The presence of a U.S. Navy Liaison Officer with SWPA, Captain Arthur H. McCollum, allowed the regular interchange of information between FRUPac and CB, intelligence that went directly to MacArthur and his G–2.[205] Given the Allies' rather desperate and chaotic state in the SWPA in 1942, it is not surprising that CB at first operated without a formal charter. Its code breakers initially produced data from low-level message traffic. From this and rudimentary traffic analysis came what was known at SWPA as RABID intelligence. In light of the essentially defensive SWPA mission during 1942, RABID offered little tactical information for MacArthur. The general did, however, become concerned with its casual handling by the Australians, warning his Australian land commander that "the Australian agencies normally disseminate information to echelons that have no immediate use thereof."[206] Concerned at a possible compromise of RABID, and therefore of CB, MacArthur placed the organization and the function under the supervision of his G–2, Maj. Gen. Charles A. Willoughby, and charged him with future control and content of the intelligence gleaned from Akin's effort. This arrangement remained in force throughout the war. What the SWPA commander had done, of course, was to take the same steps that were being taken in Washington with the establishment of Special Branch under Col. McCormack.

To control this form of intelligence, MacArthur's G–2 decided initially to use a special daily report based upon CB-generated intelligence known at SWPA as the BJ Report. Given his own passion for centralization, Willoughby soon replaced this with a daily *Special Intelligence Bulletin* which became known in SWPA as the *Willoughby Bulletin*.[207] He severely limited distribution within SWPA to MacArthur, Sutherland, and the G–3. Initially excluded from regular review of the Willoughby Bulletin was MacArthur's SWPA air deputy and Fifth Air Force commander, Maj. Gen. George C. Kenney.

Willoughby could not ignore SIGINT for the simple reason that he lacked other conventional intelligence sources. In 1942 and through 1943, most of the Allies' other data on the enemy came from the Allied Intelligence Bureau, which oversaw the coast-watching activities, and the Allied Translator and Interpreter Section, which sought to exploit captured documents and POW

Tools of Air Intelligence

interrogations and such photointelligence as became available. As the official histories for these activities make clear, these sources did not produce sufficient intelligence by themselves. Coast watching was hampered because combat intelligence staffs distrusted, as one war history put it, the "cloak and dagger" type of agent, which produced reluctant coordination, while a dearth of qualified linguists hampered the interpreters.[208] Photographic and visual aerial intelligence depended upon good weather (notably hard to find in some parts of the SWPA) and having aircraft in the right place at the right time. If MacArthur and his subordinates were to rely upon intelligence sources for operational planning, much of it would have to be from radio intercepts and traffic analysis. At approximately the same time as Kenney prepared his Allied Air Force for a campaign against the Japanese, the SIGINT Service at Arlington Hall and the B Section of MIS began to break the Japanese military codes. McCormack's desire to integrate all signals-derived intelligence entailed closer coordination with all field interception operations and the passage of SIGINT data through a special and highly secure, centrally controlled system of SSOs.

It also meant establishment of policy. As General Marshall stated to General MacArthur in a letter of May 1943, "a uniform policy . . . with respect to the handling and use of Japanese ULTRA in theaters of operation" is necessary. Apparently, MacArthur interpreted this as Washington's interfering in the SWPA SIGINT operation. The SWPA commander balked and did not answer his superior for two months. At issue was B Section's insistence upon direct communications between Washington and their SSOs. What McCormack wanted in the SWPA was an arrangement similar to that already in place in Europe for the handling of ULTRA. MacArthur saw this as an unwarranted intrusion and told Washington that it was "a violation of all sound military organization. . . . If this view [that the theater commander must retain control of *all* forces in his theater] is not accepted," he announced, "I would prefer not having the organization proposed established in this theater." It took a personal visit by Colonel McCormack's assistant two months later to convince the SWPA commander otherwise; even then MacArthur insisted that SSOs "be under my control for administration and discipline."[209] MacArthur's attitude long influenced his use of Washington-derived SIGINT.

The SWPA commander, and some of his senior staff, continued to view the SSOs from Washington with great suspicion throughout the war. MacArthur directed that Willoughby exclude them from the CB, and his G–2 consciously snubbed them.[210] It is tempting to conclude that MacArthur's apparent dismissal of SIGINT from Washington lay in his egotism. It was more likely based on his perception that he was already well served by his own SIGINT, and additional material would not be worth the price of interference that might come with it.

CHAPTER 3

Building an Intelligence Organization

THE JAPANESE ATTACKS ON AMERICAN FORCES and Hitler's subsequent declaration of war thrust the United States into a conflict she had long hoped to avoid. Nevertheless, within three weeks, President Roosevelt, Prime Minister Churchill, and their military advisors met in Washington to lay the framework that would underlie their plans and actions for the next three years.

The most important decision of that conference (designated "ARCADIA") was that the two nations would fight the war as allies in the fullest sense of that word. Unlike the previous world war, the United States would be a full partner, not merely an associated power. While the Grand Alliance eventually consisted of a host of nations including the Soviet Union, the fundamental cement of that alliance was the Anglo-American union. Despite the blows the Japanese were inflicting on both the United States and Great Britain in the Pacific and Far East, ARCADIA reaffirmed the Europe-first strategy laid down the previous year in the ABC–1 Agreement that came from the Anglo-American connections. The British, at war with Germany and Italy for more than two years, would, at least for the near term, be the senior partner in that theater. The United States, with interests throughout the western Pacific and having greater resources, would predominate in the Pacific.

For American airmen, the second major decision at ARCADIA was the commitment to a major strategic role for air power. Within the American military, the question of air power had been, and would be, vigorously debated. Within the Alliance, discussions over air power's contribution to the defeat of the Axis in Europe, or at least how best to make that contribution, continued until the summer of 1944. The earlier British commitment to strategic air operations and the inability in the immediate future to strike Germany with any other means led to an agreement to build up American air forces toward this end. Regarding the related issue of maintaining a defensive position in the Pacific pending the defeat of Germany, the press of events would weaken this decision.

By the spring of 1943 American air forces were conducting a full range of air operations around the world. From the United Kingdom, Eighth Air Force slowly and with several diversions began the air campaign that would ultimately contribute decisively to the defeat of Germany. In North Africa, from November 1942 to May 1943, American air forces not only supported Allied armies directly through close air support, but they engaged in counterair, interdiction, and air transport operations. In the Southwest Pacific, General Kenney's Fifth Air Force pioneered innovative employment of land-based air power in support of both land and sea forces. At the end of a logistics train more than halfway around the globe, Maj. Gen. Claire Chennault's Fourteenth Air Force and its predecessors would constitute almost the entire American force in China, while Tenth Air Force operated from India against the Japanese in remote Burma.

As the AAF prepared for and then went into combat, it had to build, train, equip, and employ units simultaneously. In the case of air intelligence, the AAF lacked not only resources and experience but also clear ideas of what intelligence was supposed to do and how best to do it. The months from January 1942 through the spring of 1943 marked the real birth of American AAF air intelligence. During this period, the development of intelligence organizations occurred at all levels, from HQ AAF in Washington to the combat squadrons in the field, and it saw the introduction of the first air intelligence training program. As in other aspects of the air war, U.S. airmen benefited from the experience and guidance of their British counterparts in air intelligence. Circumstances precluded simply adopting RAF organizations and procedures as such, even in Europe. The variety of demands and conditions confronted in the global war meant that all aspects of intelligence had to be adapted to the unique circumstances of each theater. The requirements as well as the resources Generals Spaatz and Eaker found in Europe were in many respects quite different from those Generals Nathan Twining, Kenney, Chennault, or Clayton Bissell faced in the Pacific and in Asia.

The evolution and use of intelligence reflected the strains and potential benefits of joint and combined operations. Not surprisingly, debate over force structure, resource allocation, and operational responsibilities among the U.S. services did not cease with the declaration of war. Often, coordination and agreement on issues was easier between similar services within the Anglo-American alliance than it was among the services of a single nation, particularly the United States. This was as true with respect to intelligence as it was to the allocation of resources or to the conduct of operations.

Under the constant pressures of planning, executing, and evaluating air operations, the weaknesses of prewar air intelligence within the AAF quickly became obvious. In its opening phase, for example, the daylight, precision bombing campaign over occupied Europe revealed the enormity of the demands this doctrine would make on intelligence. A greater awareness of the importance of intelligence drove the development of new organizations, new approaches, and new capabilities. Indicative of the revolution in air intelligence was the increase in the types of sources, including those such as ULTRA, unknown to

American airmen before their entry into the war, and those like aerial photoreconnaissance, whose operational applications had received little attention before the war. New uses for standard peacetime procedures found application in technical analysis of downed enemy aircraft or captured equipment.

Pearl Harbor and Implications for Air Intelligence

Perhaps no single event in American history has been the subject of as much analysis and hindsight judgment than has the Japanese attack on Pearl Harbor. The apparent failure to interpret the content of Japanese diplomatic messages (MAGIC) seems to make Pearl Harbor a classic case of the failure of intelligence. But to focus exclusively on MAGIC is to ignore other factors equal to, if not more important than, the events that led to December 7th. For at its core, Pearl Harbor was not a failure of intelligence so much as it was a failure of command. The circumstances surrounding the surprise attack on American forces at Hawaii and the Philippines offer an almost endless detailing of how not to prepare for war. In implications for air intelligence, and for planning and operations, these insights can be considered within two broad categories: organization (including the structure of intelligence agencies and the collection and dissemination of intelligence) and evaluation.

Neither the War nor the Navy Department was organized to take advantage of the information MAGIC and other sources provided. By tradition and practice, intelligence was a junior, and neglected, branch of the services. Neither service had a central organization for evaluating such intelligence as was available. Within the WDGS, the chief of the MID, Brig. Gen. (then Col.) Hayes A. Kroner, admitted that development of a central evaluation capability was still in "the planning stage" in 1941.[1] Any coordination that did occur was at best informal. Although a Joint Intelligence Board had been created in the fall, it had met only once by December 7, and that was late in November. The lack of a central analysis capability meant that no group had the responsibility or the time to reflect on bits of intelligence nor to ponder the possible links among seemingly disparate fragments of information. Consequently, the several critical and potentially decisive signals that flowed into infant intelligence analysis channels were subjected only to fragmented, often isolated, review.

The most obvious instance of this fragmentation was the excessive control imposed on access to intercepted high-level Japanese message traffic. Rightly concerned with the consequences of losing this unique look into Japanese decision making, senior American military leaders imposed rigid controls not only on the source, but on the information itself. This well-intentioned restraint was achieved at the expense of exploiting what that information might offer. A number of people in key positions did not have access to this essential information and the clues it provided. As an astonishing example, the chief of the Intelligence Branch of MID, responsible for intelligence estimates for the G–2 and the Chief of Staff, did not have access to Japanese intercepts.[2]

Reflecting both the excessive security surrounding signals intelligence and the perceived value of intelligence was the decision to withhold such information from senior commanders in Hawaii. Whether any of them would have acted differently is open to debate. The Commander, Pacific Fleet, Admiral Husband Kimmel, did get the gist of critical information in long, personal letters from the Chief of Naval Operations, while Lt. Gen. Walter C. Short, Commanding General of the Army's Hawaiian Department, demonstrated a general apathy toward intelligence. His narrowly focused interpretation of the war-warning message he received on November 27 as referring strictly to sabotage suggests that direct access would not have had any significant effect. The failure to implement a secure means of passing appropriate information to commanders likely to be in the line of fire was both an organizational failure and a reflection of the lack of appreciation of the potential role of intelligence in the preparation and conduct of military operations.

Even without SIGINT, it did not take much imagination to recognize the general deterioration of Japanese-American relations. Daily receipt of decrypted messages in Honolulu could have provided no stronger warning than the War Department's message of November 27: "Negotiations with Japan appear to be terminated to all practical purposes. . . . Japanese future action unpredictable but hostile action possible at any moment." The Navy message sent the same day was even more explicit: "This dispatch is to be considered a war warning."[3]

After the event, individuals would point to qualifiers in these messages to explain why neither the Pacific Fleet nor the Hawaiian Department was prepared for the attack that occurred ten days later. The very fact that so much attention was paid to the supposed qualifiers highlights the fundamental failure of the commanders at Oahu: they simply did not believe an attack would happen there.[4] During one of the Army's investigations, Brig. Gen. Sherman Miles, WDGS G–2 in December 1941, stated, "The primary responsibility of military intelligence [is] . . . to advise the Command what the enemy may do and possibly do or more probably do."[5] It was in the execution of this responsibility that the collective American intelligence community most signally let down. The fundamental intelligence failures leading to Pearl Harbor lay neither in process nor organization; they lay in attitudes and outlooks.

Not only did the intelligence agencies not question the implicit assumption that a serious attack on Hawaii was not a possibility, they contributed to its happening. Colonel Kroner, Chief of the Intelligence Branch of MID, testified he did not recall any MID estimates prepared for the G–2 and the Chief of Staff that addressed this as a probability.[6] Asked why the final estimate preceding the attack had focused solely on Europe, General Miles explained he had wanted to counter the "defeatist attitude" about Nazi Germany he saw within the

General Staff. Moreover, he continued, there was no need to address an attack on Hawaii because, having been studied for twenty years, "it was so obvious."[7] In contrast, Col. Rufus Bratton, Chief, Far East Section, MID, recalled they had not included a possible Japanese attack on Hawaii because they believed the Navy to be on the alert, and "we therefore relegated such an attack to the realm of remote possibility."[8] While MID apparently considered the possibility of a covering raid somewhere in the Pacific, it saw this as the Navy's concern, despite the fact the Army's purpose for being in Hawaii was to defend the islands and the fleet.[9]

MID estimates on the Far East in the year leading up to the attack focused almost exclusively on possible Japanese moves into Southeast Asia and the Netherlands East Indies (NEI). Even an ONI report that the Japanese had apparently created a new task force did not influence this emphasis. Only in the estimate of January 1941—eleven months before the attack—was there a reference to the possibility of "raids and surprise attacks against Pacific ports on the mainland as well as against Alaska."[10] Naval officials were no more perceptive. No ONI estimate addressed the Japanese capability of air attack against Pearl Harbor.[11] In the Navy Department's November 27th message, the impact of the arresting first sentence was lessened by the explicit assessment that "the number and equipment of Japanese troops and the organization of naval task forces indicates [sic] an amphibious expedition against either the Philippines [,] Thai or Kra Peninsula [sic] or possibly Borneo." While "Continental districts [,] Guam [,] Samoa [are] directed [to] take appropriate measures against sabotage," Oahu was not even mentioned.[12]

In the months before December 1941, American intelligence officers and their superiors focused on what they saw as Japanese intentions at the expense of understanding their capabilities.[13] Intelligence officers fell into the trap of assessing Japan's intentions within the framework of American logic and interpretation of what the Japanese should do, rather than what the Japanese might think they should do. This tendency to discount Japanese decision making was to return to dog American air commanders at other times, but not with such catastrophic results as it did in December 1941.

As General Miles admitted, "We underestimated Japanese military power." According to Miles, authorities had evaluated the opponent on his "past record," which they believed was "not impressive."[14] The difficulty of obtaining accurate intelligence made assessment difficult, but evidence of Japan's strengths as well as weaknesses was available. By overlooking or ignoring this evidence, authorities assumed a level of capability that encouraged an incorrect assessment of intentions. Admiral Kimmel spoke for many when he admitted off the record, "I never thought those little sons-of-bitches could pull off such an attack, so far from Japan."[15]

Creating the Office of the Assistant Chief of Air Staff, Intelligence

In the years preceding World War II, the U.S. Army Air Corps and then the AAF had undergone a series of reorganizations as the nation searched for the proper roles for air power and the means to accomplish them. As an essential element in the planning and execution of air operations, air intelligence within the Air Corps and AAF had been affected each time a change occurred. The onset of war did not eliminate organizational issues or questions of responsibility regarding air intelligence functions; if anything, the crises the United States now faced exacerbated the dilemma while underscoring the urgency of a resolution. One of the major themes in the evolution of air intelligence and its impact on planning and operations in the first part of the war was the ongoing effort to develop the most effective air intelligence structure within AAF headquarters in Washington and to determine its relationships with its Army and Navy counterparts.

Pearl Harbor demonstrated the ineffectiveness of American military and naval intelligence and revealed that at least part of the problem stemmed from the lack of Army-Navy cooperation regarding intelligence. To secure cooperation and coordination on all matters involving joint action of the U.S. Army and Navy, on January 23, 1942, the Secretaries of War and Navy directed a reorganization of the Joint Army-Navy Board plus the creation of a Joint Army-Navy Planning Committee and Joint Strategic Committee to supplement the Joint Intelligence Committee (JIC). The duties of the JIC were to prepare daily joint summaries of military and other directly related intelligence for the president and other high officials, and such other special information and intelligence studies as the joint board required. The JIC was to have full access to MID and Naval Intelligence Division files. When the JCS organization replaced the Joint Army-Navy Board in February 1942, the committees established to support the joint board continued under the JCS. Like other JCS committees, the JIC prepared papers concerning agenda items for the JCS's meetings.[16]

In March 1942, a War Department reorganization created three autonomous and coordinate commands under the Chief of Staff: Army Ground Forces, AAF, and Services of Supply (later the Army Service Forces). The implementing directive reaffirmed the overall planning, coordination, and supervisory role of the WDGS, but it prohibited the General Staff from involvement in administrative details and operating activities of these commands. Although the directive authorized Air Corps officers to comprise 50 percent of the General Staff, that goal would not be reached because of the scarcity of qualified Air Corps officers. With respect to intelligence, the reorganization authorized G–2 to enlarge his Air Section, and it buttressed his responsibility for collecting all intelligence, both air and ground.[17] The March 1942 reorganization amalgamated the old OCAC and the Air Force Combat Command into HQ AAF. Accordingly, the intelligence functions of both these groups were transferred to the office of the AC/AS, Intelligence, also referred to as A–2.*[18] To perform his responsibilities to collect, evaluate, and disseminate air intelligence, the AC/AS was provided an A–2 staff and a subordinate Air Intelligence Service (AIS) which reported to the AC/AS through its director. The A–2 staff was to establish policy and provide overall guidance on air intelligence functions within the AAF. AIS would serve as the operating agency to collect, evaluate, and disseminate tactical and other air intelligence, develop training programs for air intelligence people, and operate air security services. By June 1942, 210 officers were assigned to air intelligence duties under the AC/AS, Intelligence.[19]

Despite pressures on all agencies to reduce the number of people in the Washington area, AC/AS, Intelligence continued to expand. Upon his assignment as the A–2 in June 1942, Col. Edgar P. Sorenson argued for an additional 58 people. It was not enough, he explained, for his organization to depend upon intelligence sent to it; his staff also had to seek out information from the many agencies in Washington that had useful data. In the summer of 1942, A–2 officers made a weekly average of 437 contacts with 25 different Washington agencies. In the Informational Intelligence Division, for example, only 25 percent of the products it prepared came from information automatically sent to it. At the same time, Sorenson noted, manpower shortages prevented the accomplishment of tasks vital to the operating commands. The Operational Intelligence Division had completed only half of a schedule calling for 361 objective folders for all theaters. Under the threat of a severe impairment in targeting at a critical juncture, Sorenson got the 58 additional officers (including 4 officers for an AAF Historical Section added to A–2 in June 1942).[20]

The division of responsibilities between the A–2 staff and AIS reflected the then-current AAF approach of separating policy and operating functions. This philosophy proved more appropriate in theory than in practice, and shortly the decentralized structure evolved into a much more centralized one. The division proved especially burdensome for air intelligence; the A–2's office was with the Air Staff in the Munitions Building, and the AIS was at Gravelly Point, near the Washington, D.C., municipal airport. As part of yet another AAF reorganization, in March 1943 all air intelligence functions were telescoped into the office of the AC/AS, Intelligence, where they fell into five principal divisions: Operational Intelligence, Informational Intelligence, Counter Intelligence, Combat Training and Liaison, and Historical.[21] The March 1943 reorganization also established a Special Projects section supposedly to focus on the development of a more professional and realistic intelligence staff operation. Under the

---

*During the four years of war there would be eight different Assistant Chiefs of Air Staff for Intelligence.

press of daily activities, however, the special staff became a catchall for unrelated activities not properly chargeable to any of the other divisions.[22]

Parallel to AAF efforts to clarify the responsibilities of intelligence within its own organizations was the continuing effort to establish the proper relationship between the Air Staff A–2 and the WDGS G–2. Airmen were convinced the former had to control the whole cycle of collection, analysis, and dissemination of air intelligence because the entire process was necessary to prepare target folders, enemy air OBs, air route guides, pilot manuals, and other materials required to support air forces in contemplated theaters of operations. Moreover, as a member of the JCS and the Combined Chiefs of Staff (CCS) and as de facto Army air advisor to the President of the United States, the Commanding General AAF required a completely integrated and uninhibited intelligence staff supporting him.[23]

In fact, for more than a year A–2's relations with G–2 continued to be defined primarily by the War Department letter of September 10, 1941. A–2 had no primary collection agents and received practically all its information secondhand from G–2, the ONI, and such agencies as the OSS and the Foreign Economic Administration (FEA).[24] Some air intelligence officers were at least slightly bitter that they received rather than collected intelligence. One remarked, "It is up to us to take the information we get and to holler like stuck pigs for more when we feel short-changed. . . . By request to MIS [Military Intelligence Service, G–2] for information on a particular subject, cables to MAs [Military Attachés] and theater commanders are sent out, and in the course of time it returns to us." Still, the time required to get desired information through channels resulted in "considerable delay," and information was often "summarized or evaluated in transit so that the original picture is not presented in detail to Headquarters, Army Air Forces."[25]

Both the MIS Air Group and the A–2 Intelligence Service often examined the same problems, with unnecessary duplication and the danger of expressing confusing divergences. In March 1942, a British Air Ministry delegation pointed out that the two American and one British intelligence evaluation groups were having difficulty arriving at the same estimate of the enemy's air OB.[26] In view of these British criticisms and reports of delays in getting information from the United Kingdom, the War Department authorized General Arnold to detail officers through the Commanding General, European Theater, to temporary duty with the British Air Ministry to facilitate procurement of bombardment target information, technical aviation data, and other theater combat intelligence.[27]

Because control of all forces in a theater of operations remained under each theater commander, responsible to the JCS, HQ AAF initially could not even deal directly with air units outside the continental United States. One incident, however, especially raised the ire of General Arnold and resulted in a modification to this restriction. On September 18, 1942, Arnold requested Brig. Gen.

Building an Air Intelligence Organization

William D. Butler, Commanding General, Eleventh Air Force, Alaska, to send a comprehensive story immediately by airmail on the September 14 action at Kiska. On September 20th, Butler responded: "Am required by existing agreement Chief of Staff and Cinch [Commander-in-Chief, U.S. Navy] to submit to Comtask [Commander Task] Force Eight for approval prior to send msg. Will try to get it through."[28]

Two weeks later the Chief of the Air Staff, Maj. Gen. George E. Stratemeyer, forwarded directly to General Marshall a very strong memorandum stressing the necessity for the Commanding General, AAF, to receive promptly full and accurate information of the needs and requirements for training and equipment of Air Forces units so these experiences could be assimilated and disseminated to other commands throughout the world as quickly as possible. "Lessons learned from combat experience with Japanese forces in Alaska today might save pilots and planes in Australia tomorrow," the memorandum intoned, and "the most appropriate medium for evaluating and disseminating this vital information . . . is the Headquarters of the Army Air Forces in Washington." In response to the Air Forces' concerns, the War Department authorized overseas Air Force units to send copies of technical and tactical information, operational reports, and intelligence data directly to HQ AAF, in addition to sending the same material upward through command channels.[29]

In July 1943 the AC/AS, Intelligence formally requested the creation of an A–2/G–2 committee to study the relations of the two in air matters. Col. T. J. Betts, Deputy G–2, and Col. W. M. Burgess, Chief, Informational Intelligence in A–2, headed the joint committee. In its report, the committee pointed out that while the MID had overall responsibility for the collection, evaluation, and dissemination of military information, including that pertaining to the AAF, in practice something of a division of labor had developed. While the G–2's air unit accomplished the detailed preliminary work for estimating enemy and neutral air orders of battle, A–2 performed the detailed work on tactical and technical air intelligence, airdromes, and related information. The committee concluded that while there appeared to be "an appreciable duplication of work," it was in fact the minimum possible since the two units reported to different masters, either to the Army G–2 and through him the Chief of Staff, or to the Commanding General, AAF.[30]

In the midst of these ongoing organizational struggles, the officers and men of AC/AS, Intelligence strove to fulfill the dual functions of that office: service to the Commanding General, AAF, and support to the combat commands. In executing these responsibilities, the Informational and Operational Intelligence Divisions played the critical roles.

The Informational Intelligence Division's general functions included collecting, evaluating, and disseminating information about both enemy and friendly air activities. It furnished the commanding general with situation reports, prepared special studies on probable developments in tactical and technical intelligence, published bulletins, maintained the Air Intelligence Library, and operated the Air Room.[31] Management studies of this division in 1942 and 1943 were often critical, noting that form was emphasized too much over substance. Instead of innocuous briefings and glossy magazine-style publications, the management surveys stressed the need for timely, decision-oriented presentations to the commanding general and his senior staff and bulletins to provide useful information to operational commands.[32] Given Arnold's insatiable demands for information on every aspect of the AAF, it is not surprising that significant improvements were made in the Air Room presentations. To support air forces worldwide, MID eventually produced and distributed the Air Force General Information Bulletin, disseminating technical and tactical intelligence much as Stratemeyer had argued for in his memorandum to Marshall.

The primary burden for providing operational intelligence to combat commands resided with the Operational Intelligence Division. Under the direction of Lt. Col. Malcolm Moss, the target information portion of this division was charged to prepare air estimates for strategic planning, assemble information relative to actual and potential objectives for air attack (especially industrial and economic targets), and develop air objective folders and target charts for operational use.*[33] Despite initial efforts in the late 1930s and analyses prepared in the development of AWPD-1, this office faced a formidable task. An example is Lt. Gen. Ira C. Eaker's final report as Commanding General, Eighth Air Force, when he reflected that, on arriving in the United Kingdom in early 1942, "Almost no information regarding targets in Germany, strength and disposition of G.A.F., etc. or target material, pictures, maps, etc. was available in the United States. In effect, we had no intelligence information and material about Germany and her occupied territories."[34] Accurate and detailed information regarding the Japanese Empire was even sparser.

In Europe, rather than starting from scratch, American airmen agreed to rely primarily on British intelligence resources and organizations. By tacit agreement, Eighth Air Force, working through the British Air Ministry, assumed primary responsibility for intelligence regarding Germany, while AAF A-2 concentrated on other theaters, including the Mediterranean and Pacific.

---

*Air estimates were broad studies of the nature and vulnerabilities of economic and industrial systems important to an enemy's potential to sustain military operations. Objective folders were compilations of factual data, including aerial photographs and maps when available, on actual and potential industrial-military targets within specific geographical areas. Folders were intended for use by commanders and operations and intelligence officers for mission planning and air crew briefings. Target charts, for use by individual bomber crews, showed specific information regarding the exact location of enemy objectives and highlighted terrain features and other landmarks to aid pilots and bombardiers in locating their targets.

Building an Air Intelligence Organization

Moss's target section did undertake a series of air intelligence estimates of western Axis industries in late 1942 which were incorporated into the later Report of the COA.[35]

While Eighth Air Force could rely on major British assistance, AAF forces in North Africa depended more on A–2. Of 364 target charts completed by the end of October 1942, 213 addressed potential targets in Africa or Spain, while 113 more in final preparation covered targets in Italy.[36] Special studies completed in 1942 in support of pending operations in North Africa included "Airfield and Topographic Information" on Spain, North Africa, and the Casablanca area (February 1942); "Information for TORCH" (September 1942); "Target Information on Italy, Sardinia, and Balearic Islands" (September 1942); and "RR Targets: Italy, Sicily, and Sardinia" (June 1943).[37] References to Spain were based upon the uncertain reaction of that country to the Northwest African landings. Should Spain join the Axis alliance, knowledge of that country would prove essential.

Colonel McDonald—an old-line Air Corps intelligence officer and A–2 of Twelfth Air Force, NAAF and MAAF, in 1942 and 1943—judged HQ AAF A–2 estimates of enemy industries and transportation systems in North Africa definitely useful for combat planning. He was more critical of the time and expense spent in Washington to make the folders attractive. "The most useful contribution from Washington could have been simple folders on individual targets, including mimeographed and photographic and photostat material . . . sent forward promptly as soon as the information could have been prepared." Charts and folders for Italy that came from Washington were of little help because they were based on outdated information.[38] By early 1943 the NAAF had facilities in Algiers to provide all charts needed for the Mediterranean. The NAAF, like the Eighth and Twelfth Air Forces, indicated it no longer needed HQ AAF charts.[39]

At the same time, A–2 sections were addressing items of interest in the Pacific as well. Even before the outbreak of war, A–2 had undertaken the preliminary "Survey of Japanese Iron and Steel Industry." In 1942 special studies included those on flying conditions in Japan; Japanese aircraft, copper, and steel industries, air defenses, and shipping; and target priorities. Of the 105 objective folders published between October 1942 and May 1943, 69 focused on targets under Japanese control.[40] Because of the scarcity of current information on conditions in Japan (the result of Japanese efforts to prevent intelligence collection in the 1930s) much of this material would prove of limited value. Nevertheless, it was illustrative of ongoing efforts in the early months of the war.

Technical air intelligence in the early 1940s experienced the same fluctuations and evolutions as those affecting other aspects of air intelligence. The U.S. Army Air Corps had gathered some technical data in China in the late 1930s regarding the Japanese Army Air Force. Although not revealed at the time, the U.S.S. *Panay* had been loaded with remnants of Japanese equipment when the Japanese sank her in the Yangtze River. The emphasis of Air Matériel Command's Technical Data Laboratory on testing and improving American designs provided little time or experience for analyzing captured material. On the other hand, since 1939 the British had acquired considerable expertise in this area. The Air Ministry included a technical intelligence section that contained both a technical staff and crash officers, the latter being individually responsible for a given area of the British Isles. When an enemy plane crashed, the crash officer went immediately to the scene, assessed what technical aspects he could, and immediately questioned any downed enemy airmen.

In October 1942, Maj. Gen. Muir S. Fairchild, AAF Director of Military Requirements, had asked intelligence to focus on likely German counterstrikes to allow the AAF to change equipment and tactics before such enemy actions could take their toll. "It appears obvious," Fairchild said, "that the success or failure of our European offensive may depend to a large degree upon the ability of our intelligence services, both in Great Britain and in the United States to anticipate well in advance any changes in the German strategy, tactics, and equipment."[41] To assist in implementing a program to address Fairchild's concerns, Squadron Leader A. W. Colley, an experienced RAF technical intelligence officer on detached duty to HQ AAF, arrived in 1942 at Air Matériel Command at Wright Field to help organize an air technical intelligence (ATI) course. This course taught candidates how to prepare initial *pro forma* evaluation reports and how to determine what captured material should be forwarded for more detailed analysis within the theater or at Wright Field. By the end of March 1943, thirty-three Air Forces officers and ten Navy officers had graduated from the ATI course. Upon graduation, the officers went to Washington for ten days of indoctrination in A–2 before going to overseas theaters. Meanwhile, the British continued to carry the burden of crash intelligence in both the European and Pacific theaters.[42]

In the Southwest Pacific, AAFSWPA initiated active crash intelligence in Australia, although few Japanese aircraft were available for study because most had fallen into the ocean. The *pro forma* report worked out by the Allied Air Forces was eventually adopted by AC/AS, Intelligence for standard use throughout the AAF. One Royal Australian Air Force (RAAF) officer with practical engineering experience maintained a roving crash inspection headquarters in New Guinea. On one occasion, three Type 99 Val fighters located after the Japanese abandoned them were dismantled and shipped to Brisbane for examination. The Fifth Air Force also tried to obtain intelligence from nameplates on equipment, but since initially no American air officer or enlisted man was capable of translating Japanese, RAAF and British Army personnel had to perform this function.[43]

To improve both the value of technical intelligence and the attention paid to it, in June 1943 Sorenson wrote to the commanding general of each USAAF

Maj. Gen. Muir S. Fairchild Brig. Gen. Edgar P. Sorenson
Maj. Gen. Walter R. Weaver Maj. Gen. George E. Stratemeyer

numbered air force. He emphasized the importance of technical intelligence but noted the mission was not being handled well. ATI was not coming in from Alaska, Hawaii, India, or China. Although a workable system of technical intelligence was in effect in the SWPA, only a fraction of captured Japanese equipment was available for scrutiny there. To alleviate the lack of capability to provide acceptable analysis of matériel, the A–2 recommended that Sorenson be authorized to establish a captured air equipment center at a location where most required facilities were available or easily procurable.[44]

While the AAF attempted to improve crash intelligence, the U.S. Navy conducted a similar activity at a captured enemy equipment unit set up in early 1943 at the Anacostia Naval Aircraft Factory outside Washington D.C. The JIC proposed a joint technical air intelligence activity in which the Anacostia unit would handle a major portion of the work. The proposal was shelved because neither service was prepared to work with the other. In June 1943 the Navy resurrected the proposal, suggesting the Army be in charge of a "test section" at Nashville, Tennessee, while the Navy supervised a "development section" in Washington to produce and disseminate timely technical aviation data.[45] At this point, another matter impinged upon the proposal for joint crash intelligence. In North Africa, General Eisenhower had sponsored a Joint Intelligence Collection Agency (JICA) under his G–2. Sorenson initially thought the JICA would merely collect information and forward it to the United States. When the JICA requested assignment of an experienced air technical officer, however, Sorenson provided Lt. Col. Byron R. Switzer from his own staff.[46]

Soon afterward, AAF Intelligence requested information from JICA on the use of laminated methyl methacrylate in the canopy of the German FW 190. From North Africa, McDonald rebuked Sorenson for going to an "outside ground agency" with his request for the Focke-Wulf canopy. McDonald informed Sorenson that he was sending a Messerschmitt 109G and a FW 190, both flyable, to Wright Field for testing. "In closing," he wrote, "I may add that the type of Intelligence which has contributed most to the air, sea, and ground operational successes in the Libyan and Tunisian Campaigns is Air Intelligence developed and applied by personnel who have an appreciation of air values. . . . It therefore behooves the Air Force to maintain a high degree of control over all matters pertinent to air intelligence and not pass it on to personnel who are not particularly qualified to do justice to it." Sorenson defended himself by explaining that JICA had a courier aircraft to and from the United States and therefore was thought best able to get a canopy to Wright Field quickly. "I agree with you," Sorenson wrote, "that Air Intelligence is the most important intelligence yet developed in North Africa. Further, that the old conventional G–2–ONI [organization] is out of date. However, since we are not going to be able to do away with the latter in one fell swoop, the best solution is to impregnate it with those who are Air Intelligence minded."[47]

When Maj. Gen. O. P. Echols, the AC/AS, Matériel, Maintenance, and Distribution, was asked to comment on Sorenson's proposal that AC/AS, Intelligence have its own technical engineering evaluation capability, he did not agree that this was needed or that it would necessarily be advantageous. Divided responsibilities between engineering and intelligence agencies had little to do with the problems involved in crash intelligence, he insisted. The Air Matériel Command at Wright Field had never had facilities or requisite personnel to handle crash intelligence. If adequate facilities and people could be obtained, the status quo in crash intelligence ought not be changed.[48] Within AC/AS, Intelligence, Colonel Burgess, chief of Informational Division, continued to press the importance of field technical intelligence, but he admitted that the difficulties of obtaining enemy equipment could be attributed largely to shipping congestion, the press of other activities, and souvenir hunters who often looted crash sites. In the summer of 1943 two Japanese fighters and a Bf 109 arrived in the United States, received minor repairs at Wright Field, and were turned over to the AAF Proving Ground Command at Eglin Field, Florida, for flight testing.[49]

In the autumn of 1943 Squadron Leader Colley was asked to comment on AAF technical intelligence. He reported that the AAF's Air Intelligence Section at Wright Field was, in effect, "buried," while the Navy's Air Technical Section at Anacostia was well set up. Combining or more closely coordinating AAF and Navy ATI functions, he suggested, would eliminate duplication and enhance overall technical intelligence.[50] Colonel Burgess was inclined to believe the best solution was to place all technical intelligence pertaining to air, whether from Army or Navy sources, under one coordinating head. In a memo dated November 10, 1943, he noted that assignment of responsibility for Japanese air intelligence was under consideration by the JCS. He recommended that the existing arrangement for technical air intelligence continue until the major decision of how to handle Japanese air intelligence in the aggregate was made.[51]

Two years into the war, it was obvious that questions on the role and structure of air intelligence organizations, at least at the HQ AAF level, had not been fully resolved. A detailed study of HQ AAF Air Intelligence by AAF Management Control in September 1943 observed that "the Intelligence Office tends to become an end in itself, rather than a means to an end which is really the intelligence role." The survey team argued for a creative intelligence structure to procure, produce, and distribute early and advance intelligence rather one that overzealously guarded and withheld information. Intelligence, they concluded, was really a service (i.e., support) activity with many customers for its products.[52]

Air Intelligence Training

One of the most serious obstacles to the development of effective air intelligence in the AAF when war came was an almost total absence of qualified officers and the lack of even a basic training program. In the 1930s, a few Air Corps officers had secured some intelligence orientation in the course at the C&GSS at Fort Leavenworth, and there was a quota for Air Corps officers in the photographic interpreter course at the Engineer School at Fort Belvoir, Virginia. The ACTS at Maxwell Field had also included a block of intelligence instruction. The Leavenworth intelligence course emphasized ground warfare, and, after the ACTS closed in June 1940, no instruction was available for air intelligence. In July 1941, Maj. Gen. George H. Brett, Chief of Air Corps— now that Arnold had become Chief, AAF— pointed out that the Air Force Combat Command did not have more than twenty-five officers assigned to intelligence duties who could be considered even partially qualified for their jobs. Brett urged that the AAF proceed with plans to establish a basic intelligence school.[53]

In reviewing proposals for air intelligence instruction in September 1941, the War Department G–2's office stated all arms and services had the same intelligence requirements: to determine the location, strength, composition, and probable lines of enemy action. Therefore, "all instruction along military intelligence lines should be unified and presented in one school only."[54] To buttress this argument, the MID referred to the War Department letter of September 10, 1941, to assert that G–2's responsibilities for all military intelligence operations also applied to intelligence instruction. Interestingly, Brig. Gen. Harry L. Twaddle, WDGS G–3 (Operations) agreed with the AAF's position that independent air missions and operations required a special type of air intelligence instruction that was essentially a study of the economic and industrial systems of potentially hostile nations.[55] Despite the MID argument, the AAF requested, and the Army Chief of Staff approved, a budget item to expand facilities at Bolling Field, Washington, D.C., for an air intelligence school. Congress quickly voted necessary funds in December 1941.

AAF planning for air intelligence had been strongly influenced by the amount of information the British were reportedly obtaining from interpretation of aerial photographs. General Brett's memorandum of July had noted, "One of the more prolific sources of intelligence is that secured by photographic means. The value cannot be overemphasized."[56] In the United States the Air Corps was developing aerial photographic equipment but had made no provision for either operating units or photographic analysts. Capt. Harvey C. Brown, a key figure in the development of American wartime photo intelligence, completed an RAF photointerpretation course in August 1941 and received practical training at the RAF CIU. In recalling his experience in Britain, Brown remembered the "British had developed their photointerpretation organizations to an amazing degree.... It was generally accepted that CIU provided at least 80 percent of the total information on German activities and installations." Brown returned to Washington in December 1941 to organize the AAF photointelligence program. He also advised on the selection of personnel for training in the new Air Intelligence School, favoring the British philosophy that people with backgrounds in science and research were best suited for photointerpretation.[57]

Formal AAF air intelligence training began quite precipitously. On December 8, 1941, a ten-day photointerpreter course began in makeshift facilities at Bolling Field. Many of the students, newly commissioned AAF Combat Command officers, had been pilots in World War I. The AAF Air Intelligence School was formally established at Bolling on January 13, 1942, with the first class scheduled to arrive two weeks later. Fortunately, the president of the University of Maryland in College Park offered the necessary facilities for the first class. The acceptance of this offer delayed the school's opening until February 16, 1942.[58]

Air Force leaders recognized that the facilities at College Park would not be adequate for the expansion due to come. Even before the first class of 33 officers had graduated from the college course, the AAF paid $300,000 to purchase the Harrisburg Academy in Harrisburg, Pennsylvania, for the new site of air intelligence training. Officially designated the Army Air Forces Air Intelligence School, the Harrisburg school was better known as the photointerpretation school, since that was two-thirds of its original curriculum; the additional one-third was combat intelligence training. At first, photointerpretation training was considered the responsibility of the OCAC Intelligence Division, but in the evolving AAF, training became the responsibility of the newly created AAF Technical Training Command.[59]

The evolution of the Air Intelligence School reflected the confusion and often conflicting demands characteristic of all aspects of the American war effort in these months. Its first commandant, Col. Egmont F. Koenig, was the only Regular Army officer assigned to the school, and the only officers who had any military experience were former national guardsmen with some flying background or officers drawn into military service from civilian life before America entered the war. Koenig originally intended to copy the RAF system in which older, successful businessmen were selected for intelligence duties at the squadron, group, and command levels. The first class of sixty-eight students which began training in April 1942 were "all men of affairs, intensely patriotic, and unfailing in their devotion to duty." They included lawyers, bankers, businessmen, and even mayors. All were commissioned directly from civilian life and required some military indoctrination during their six-week course. Most of the 183 students in the second Harrisburg class also came straight from civil life, but the AAF then decided future intelligence officers had to be graduates of the AAF Officer Candidate School (OCS). Most of the 293 officers in the third class, which began in August, had received indoctrination at OCS.

The average age of the men in the third class was about forty, and Koenig described this class as "outstanding in every possible way."[60] In England, the Assistant A–2, VIII Bomber Command, Lt. Col. Carl H. Norcross, observed that the reputation of graduates of the first three Harrisburg classes was excellent. The men were surprisingly well trained by a faculty that recognizably had no opportunity for work or experience in the field.[61]

The dearth of experienced officers and the urgent need to staff operational commands with these scarce individuals affected the composition of the Harrisburg faculty and, to some extent, its curriculum as well. Except for the officers who opened the school, practically all faculty incumbents during 1942 came from the school's graduates. Colonel Koenig recognized that this policy necessarily led to an increasingly parochial instruction—many faculty members had fewer than three months' service and had never been in an airplane, making them questionable as instructors for the combat intelligence course expected to qualify group and squadron intelligence officers who would work closely with combat airmen. Additionally, the more energetic and valuable an instructor, the more anxious he was to leave Harrisburg for combat service. To maintain morale, Koenig tried to reward effective service at the school with transfer to an operational assignment after completion of six months or more as an instructor. In his end-of-tour report in September 1942, Koenig recommended instructors be "restricted largely to disabled front line fighters and men with actual combat experience and that less than half of the new instructors should be taken from the student body."[62] Months would pass before fluctuations in the AAF personnel system would permit such discrimination.

The rapid expansion of the AAF in the summer of 1942 resulted in significant changes in the composition and caliber of the intelligence school's student body. The Koenig approach of selecting only men of exceptional backgrounds became impossible to maintain. Even before his departure, Koenig noted that the 277 students of the fourth class reflected more quantity than quality. "Many students," he observed, "turned in blank papers as solutions to their problems, others plainly indicated that they were neither interested nor cared about subjects which had little relation to the practicalities of their next assignment." Ten percent of this class failed to graduate and were sent to a replacement center for other assignments.[63] In October 1942, the new commandant, Col. Harvey N. Holland, confronted a whirlwind as enrollment leaped from fewer than 300 to more than 900 students per class. Many students in the expanded classes were poorly qualified for intelligence work and had poor attitudes, as reflected in a lack of interest, tardiness, poor work, cheating, and sleeping in class. Norcross, who visited the school in January 1942, observed, "The quality of the students is the poorest in history. They are younger—in many cases too young to serve satisfactorily in the field as intelligence officers."[64]

Norcross reported that the faculty was in near revolt, with very low morale. The faculty particularly resented the fact that the school was under the Technical Training Command. "They all feel," wrote Norcross, "that T.T.C. knows nothing about intelligence, cares nothing about it, and actually is doing them much harm. . . . They feel that the School is declining rapidly and inevitably." Norcross recommended that the commandant be an intelligence officer (Holland was not), that the school be placed directly under A–2 in Washington, and that faculty morale be built up by more rapid promotions, a promise of assignment to combat duties after at most nine months, and other recognitions. Everything possible should be done as well to improve the selection of students and give them incentives for good work.[65]

In the aftermath of Norcross's visit, the air inspector of the First District, Technical Training Command, spent a month at Harrisburg before filing a report in March 1943. He concluded that the Norcross report was exaggerated, although he agreed that morale was low, the quality of students in the seventh class the lowest ever, and the instructional staff not of the highest caliber. While selection of faculty members from the school's graduates had provided for excellent specialized instruction from an academic perspective, "it has resulted . . . in producing a faculty with very little military training, experience, or background." The result was "a rather in-bred, closely knit organization resentful of any imposition of supervision or restraint from outside their immediate circle." In spite of these observations, the inspector could not agree with Norcross's views that the school was on a decline.[66]

The faculty were not alone in expressing dissatisfaction with subordination to the AAF Technical Training Command. In October 1942, Colonel Sorenson had expressed his opposition, even though this arrangement satisfied the AAF's efforts to separate policy and operating functions. Sorenson objected to the prohibition against direct communication between the school and his A–2 staff and the inability of the school commander to get undesirable students transferred elsewhere. "It has not been shown," he said, "that the Technical Training Command has performed any extensive essential function for the Air Intelligence School, nor that it has given that school any material assistance." Maj. Gen. Walter R. Weaver, commanding Technical Training Command, not unnaturally objected to any change thar would violate AAF policies on organization and decentralization. At the time, the Air Staff agreed with Weaver.[67] Within five months, however, the A–2 would assume responsibility for the Harrisburg program.

When the AAF reorganization in March 1943 modified the principle of separating planning and operating agencies, the air intelligence school moved from the Technical Training Command to the immediate supervision and jurisdiction of AC/AS, Intelligence. This reorganization ensured closer contact between the school and agencies responsible for air intelligence, provided a direct channel for getting action on school problems, and made the school more responsive to changes in combat theaters. It also allowed for the strengthening of the types and methods of air intelligence training and made easier the elimination of officers unsuited for intelligence duties. The assignment of Col. Lewis A. Dayton, a former Texas Ranger, as commandant at Harrisburg contributed to a restoration of school spirit. The school history noted that at his first staff meeting Dayton had "immediately won the wholehearted cooperation of the staff" with his forthright and engaging willingness to meet head-on the problems everyone knew existed.[68] During 1943 the school benefited from an increased flow from overseas of combat intelligence material useful for teaching purposes. An influx of instructors with overseas experience, reflecting Colonel Koenig's recommendation of the previous fall, added realism to the curriculum as well.[69]

Just as the AAF was working out the organizational and administrative bugs affecting the intelligence school, another shift in AAF personnel planning raised new challenges. After greatly expanded classes in the winter of 1942, OCS quotas were reduced tenfold in January 1943, from 3,000 to 300 candidates monthly. This reduced the number of potential new officers available to go to Harrisburg to a more manageable level, but it also meant the school did not receive the 350 to 400 students needed every six weeks to meet overseas manning requirements. The VIII Bomber Command, for example, was expanding combat operations early in 1943 and made frequent calls for intelligence officers, even if untrained. In the same period, Fifth Air Force in the SWPA sought Harrisburg graduates to staff their expanding intelligence functions.[70] To help meet these demands, the AAF selected newly commissioned officers with apparent intelligence qualifications and shipped them directly to the theaters for training at the unit level. In addition, officers identified for or already with continental air forces, commands, and other activities were reassigned.[71] Finally, senior intelligence officers urged operational commands to ensure that trained intelligence officers were not wasted. Colonel Koenig was not the only individual to note that "too many of our graduates finished as mess officers, counterintelligence officers, or simple clerks in the Headquarters to which they were assigned."[72]

Over the course of the war, the air intelligence school graduated slightly more than 9,000 officers. This figure includes individuals who attended the school after it moved to Orlando, Florida, in the spring of 1944, when it became the Intelligence Division of the School of Applied Tactics. More than half the graduates received specialized training in combat intelligence. This course, which focused on the group and squadron levels, addressed briefing preparation, debriefing of combat crews, aircraft recognition training, preparation and use of objective folders, target charts and maps, report preparation for higher headquarters, and use of intelligence data such as enemy air OB, tactics, and targets.

Another 28 percent took the photointerpretation course, while the rest were assigned to base intelligence (economic analysis), POW interrogation (language training), or, in Orlando only, radar mapping and analysis. Until March 1943, all students began with three weeks of general air intelligence. Specialist training then consisted of three additional weeks for combat intelligence and photointerpretation, six for POW interrogation, and four for base intelligence. Beginning with the ninth class in March 1943 the combat and photointerpretation courses were extended two weeks. When the school moved to Florida in 1944, the radar mapping and analysis course ran six weeks, while language preparation (by this time only in Japanese) was reduced to three.[73]

Even with the training they had received, graduates of the AAF Air Intelligence School were qualified only as basic intelligence officers. Whenever possible, the operational commands to which they were assigned provided theater-specific qualification training. In Europe, where AAF units performing daylight operations needed more combat intelligence and photointerpretation officers than their RAF counterparts operating at night, the VIII Bomber Command intelligence school gave a capsule introduction to American and RAF intelligence organizations and procedures. This program, initiated in May 1942 under the direction of the VIII Bomber Command A–2, Maj. Harris B. Hull, included a visit to an RAF or AAF airdrome for two to three weeks and concluded with such specialized training as might be required.

In the South Pacific Area (SPA) and the SWPA, environmental factors imposed additional requirements for intelligence officers. The A–2 of the advanced echelon of Fifth Air Force on New Guinea concluded that many of the early Harrisburg graduates were too old for work in a difficult climate. He admitted that a great deal depended upon the individuals themselves: If they had energy, brains, and a good personality, they could sell themselves to the aircrews and their commanding officers. Another old hand in the Southwest Pacific theater reported, even "Harrisburg-trained combat intelligence officers are not worth their salt until they have at least a month's experience in the combat zone."[74]

Obviously, trained intelligence officers were better than ones untrained, and had an air intelligence training program been organized before 1941, it would have functioned more effectively once war broke out. The Harrisburg Air Intelligence School—begun with little advance planning, staffed with instructors with no combat experience, enrolled with students unaccustomed to military affairs, and subject to the whims of a personnel system straining to respond to a host of demands—did surprisingly well. In December 1943, the Commanding General of Eighth Air Force, Ira Eaker, stated in his report at the conclusion of his assignment, "Graduates of the Intelligence School at Harrisburg, Pennsylvania, had received excellent basic training."[75]

The Air War in Europe: Organizing Eighth Air Force's Intelligence

At the Washington Conference of January 1941, American and British military leaders had agreed that in the event of a wartime alliance, success would depend on the close collaboration of intelligence agencies.[76] Despite differences in operational doctrine, experience, and requirements, the integration achieved during the war was unique in the history of military intelligence. Immediately after Pearl Harbor, the RAF's Assistant Chief of Air Staff, Intelligence (ACAS [I]), Air Vice Marshal C. E. H. Medhurst, flew to the United States to lay the groundwork for this cooperation.

Integration of air intelligence functions in the United Kingdom began with the arrival of Brig. Gen. Ira Eaker and the advance contingent of Eighth Air Force in February 1942. Eaker decreed that in establishing its intelligence structure, Eighth Air Force would complement rather than compete with existing RAF and Air Ministry intelligence agencies.[77] As an initial step, the RAF invited Major Hull and one of the five men who accompanied Eaker to the United Kingdom, to attend the RAF Intelligence School.[78] In May, ACAS (I) agreed that RAF Bomber Command would supply its American counterparts with "all requisite intelligence . . . on a parallel with R.A.F. Commanders" until the U.S. intelligence functions were fully established.[79] The Air Ministry even established a new section specifically to link its air intelligence with the American Air Forces.[80] The thread of RAF support ran throughout the early period of activation and establishment. Looking back, General Charles Cabell, who held critical positions both at HQ AAF and in Eighth Air Force, reflected, "Their contributions to us . . . have been tremendous in giving us an intelligence organization which we were entirely lacking."[81]

The crude state of American military intelligence prior to 1942 was reflected in the tables of organization (TOs) of the initial air units to arrive in the United Kingdom. They contained no full-time intelligence positions below the level of VIII Bomber and Fighter Commands. Consequently, in March 1942 Eaker followed up a personal letter to Maj. Gen. Carl "Tooey" Spaatz, Commanding General, Eighth Air Force, still in the United States, with a message requesting fifty intelligence officers "as soon as possible." So great was the need that Eaker suggested commissioning selected individuals directly from civilian life and sending them overseas.[82] Several of these individuals were personally selected either by Major Hull or by highly placed Air Staff officers and were "taught how to salute and put on to a plane."[83] More formally, fifty new officers went directly to the United Kingdom from Officer Training School. Nine graduates of the Harrisburg Intelligence School and one experienced Air Staff officer also arrived in the fall.[84] In spite of this influx, Eighth Air Force requested an additional ninety intelligence officers in April 1943.[85]

Building an Air Intelligence Organization

As American intelligence personnel arrived in the United Kingdom, some took positions with either the RAF or Air Ministry intelligence organizations; others attended training programs within British units.[86] RAF officers joined A–2 sections within HQ Eighth Air Force and VIII Bomber and Fighter Commands. The original intent of this exchange had been to allow the newcomers to learn British procedures, but it quickly developed into a true combined (allied) arrangement. So effectively did this integration evolve that, according to the official British history of wartime intelligence, several sections within the Air Ministry's Air Intelligence, including groups responsible for OB, operational intelligence, and tactical and technical intelligence, were "virtually Anglo-American organizations."[87]

Nor was this integration confined to staff levels. Recognizing the elaborateness of signals intelligence and the sophistication the British had already achieved, Eighth Air Force did not establish an equivalent to their ally's radio intercept branch, the famous Y-Service, but it received signals intelligence from that organization.*[88] Similarly, rather than build a photointerpretation capability from scratch, American officers and enlisted men were assigned to the existing British organization at Medmenham, the CIU. In fact, as early as June 1941, before the United States had entered the war, Americans had begun photointerpretation training with the British, with eleven officers completing the course by October of that year.[89] By June 1943, thirty personnel from the AAF would be at Medmenham as well as thirty from the U.S. Army and eleven from the U.S. Navy.[90]

American airmen had already recognized the value of aerial photography through their observations of British air operations. Although they had largely ignored aerial photography in the 1930s, when it had threatened to divert aviation resources to civilian mapping projects, they knew, in the words of a member of the original Eighth Air Force contingent, that photoreconnaissance and interpretation were "essential to the preparation of target material and for briefing combat crews; the maintenance of systematic checks on enemy airfield activity, shipping and troop movements; the acquisition of information on enemy aircraft production; the location of enemy ground defense installations; and for the assessment of damage from Allied bombing of enemy targets."[91] While Eighth Air Force eventually established its own photoreconnaissance units, the war in North Africa siphoned away two of them before they could begin operations from the United Kingdom. Until March 1943, the Eighth depended on RAF support; as of the end of that month, RAF photorecce aircraft had flown 117 sorties specifically for Eighth Air Force requirements.[92] Even after American photographic flying units became established, all photographic interpretation in the United Kingdom remained the province of CIU (eventually redesignated the Allied CIU).

---

*See Chapter 2 for discussion of the organization of signals intelligence.

Piercing the Fog

The exception to the integration of Anglo-American intelligence involved the handling of ULTRA. Until May 1943, the interception, translation, evaluation, and dissemination of ULTRA remained solely a British responsibility, and at that, it occurred only in England and North Africa. Even at American headquarters such as WIDE WING (Eighth Air Force) and PINE TREE (VIII Bomber Command), British-manned special liaison units controlled ULTRA material. Knowledge that ULTRA even existed was limited to a mere handful of individuals consisting of senior commanders and key staff officers.*

While Eighth Air Force and the RAF worked closely in the acquisition and evaluation of intelligence, differences in operational objectives and methods precluded the mere imitation of British information, analysis, procedures, or organizations. These differences, the requirements which arose from them, and the responses by American commanders and their staffs reflected the intimate relationship among strategic objectives, intelligence, and operational planning and execution.

As originally configured, the office of the Eighth Air Force A–2 was an umbrella agency whose responsibilities included intelligence about enemy OB, capabilities, and potential targets. To eliminate an overlap in the targeting process between A–2 and A–5 (the Assistant Chief of Staff for Plans), in December 1942, Lt. Col. Richard Hughes and his Target Branch were moved from A–2 to A–5.[93] With this reorganization, Eighth Air Force A–2 retained two primary responsibilities. The first was to keep the commanding general and operations officer up to date through the collection and collation of intelligence regarding the enemy. This included OB and technical data on enemy aircraft, matériel, tactics, and vulnerabilities. The A–2 evaluated this intelligence to assess its accuracy and significance in explaining enemy capabilities and the relative importance of enemy activities and objectives.

A–2's second principal task was to disseminate appropriate intelligence material throughout the staff and to higher, adjacent, and lower air units through estimates of the situation, map updates, periodic and special intelligence reports, and regular intelligence summaries. A–2 also prepared and distributed maps, aircraft and ship recognition material, and weather data.[94] Sources for this information included the British Army, Royal Navy, and Air Ministry Intelligence and various War Department agencies in Washington, the OSS, Office of Naval Intelligence, G–2 of the U.S. Army's European Theater of Operations, intelligence agencies of other Allied nations (including the Free French and the Polish government-in-exile), photointerpretation reports, POW interrogation reports, and combat crew observations.[95] In the fall of 1942,

---

*Chapter 2 contains a more detailed discussion of the organizational structures, technical aspects, and handling of ULTRA penetration of German and later Japanese cryptology, as well as the MAGIC intelligence derived from American intercepts of Japanese high-level diplomatic codes.

Building an Air Intelligence Organization

intelligence officers flew on both British and American bomber missions to study better ways to identify targets and to determine what combat intelligence aircrews needed to reach their targets and to return in the face of enemy defenses.[96] Their experiences contributed to the development of operationally oriented maps and charts, and modifications to mission briefings and debriefings.

One area in which British experience and support proved inadequate was that of mapping. The reason for this gap lay in fundamental differences in doctrine for the employment of strategic air power.[97] Because RAF Bomber Command operated at night against area targets, detailed maps of flight routes and target areas and accurate photographs of targets were unnecessary. The daylight, precision bombing that lay at the heart of American strategic air doctrine required a much higher degree of exactness of position as well as a detailed knowledge of the target and the approaches to it. Eighth Air Force intelligence responded to these needs with a series of innovative measures in the fall of 1942.

One of the most significant innovations was the development of perspective target maps, called Geerlings maps, named for Captain Gerald K. Geerlings, the skilled architect and draftsman turned intelligence officer who devised them. Early missions had demonstrated that standard flat maps offering only a straight-down view did not provide the ever-changing perspective aircrews experienced as they approached the target. Existing maps and photographs tended to be so cluttered with detail as to mask critical landmarks that might provide the proper sense of position in the midst of an ongoing air battle. As described in the Eighth Air Force history,

> *The perspective target map* is printed in four colors on a sheet 32" square. In the center there is a circular map of the target area including only such details and features as can be recognized from the air, covering a radius of seven miles around the target itself, with a scale just under one inch to the mile. The center map is surrounded by perspective drawings of the target area as seen from six different approaches. Two drawings are devoted to each approach. The outer drawing which is intended for the navigator shows the target as it appears from a distance of 15 miles at an altitude of 26,000 feet. The inner drawing, for the bombardier, shows the target in larger scale as it appears from seven miles and at an altitude of 26,000 feet.[98]

Printed so they could be folded and taken in the air, Geerlings maps greatly improved situation awareness and bombing accuracy. In the spirit of Anglo-American cooperation, both American and British draftsmen helped prepare these maps, which eventually covered all priority targets. The British Army Ordnance center did the printing and made distribution to all VIII Bomber Command and RAF stations.[99]

Complementing the Geerlings maps were landfall identification maps, also developed by Eighth Air Force A–2. By providing aviators an accurate perspective of where they reached the coast as they turned east from the North Sea toward the continent, these maps significantly reduced the tendency to stray far from the intended route due to weather, enemy action, or simply inexperience in navigation. As German defenses became more complex in response to the bombing campaign, Eighth's A–2 worked closely with other agencies, including the British War Office's Anti–Aircraft Artillery Department, to produce flak maps.* These maps provided the known locations of AA artillery batteries, searchlights, balloons, smoke screens, decoys, and search and control radars.[100]

So valuable were these products, especially the perspective target and landfall identification maps, that General Arnold not only congratulated the Eighth, but asked Eaker's opinion on the feasibility of London or Washington's preparing similar maps for other theaters, where units could then impose the most current local data. A draft response prepared for the commanding general suggested theater differences were such that it was neither feasible nor desirable to undertake such a project. It was, in fact, never done, but airmen elsewhere made similar devices, particularly in the CBI region.[101]

Another critical area in which differences in American and British operational procedures directly affected intelligence requirements lay in the realm of target development and analysis of specific target data. Here also the contrasting strategies of night area bombing and daylight precision bombing necessitated the development of American air intelligence and planning capabilities oriented differently from those of the British. Because the British emphasized night bombing of large industrial and urban areas as the means to force a general collapse of the German economy and morale, the extensive information compiled by the British Ministry of Economic Warfare (MEW) and Air Ministry Air Intelligence tended to address the enemy's economic and industrial capabilities from a perspective devoid of technical detail.[102]

In contrast, American daylight precision bombing depended upon a determination of the critical systems within the enemy's industrial and military structure, evaluation of specific targets within these broad categories, and the ability to destroy these precise targets most effectively and efficiently. This required detailed information and analyses not only pinpointing the critical targets within broad industries but also addressing the vulnerabilities of specific targets such that operational planners could focus on the most critical elements of any given target.[103]

After the December 1942 shift of Colonel Hughes and his target branch, the Eighth's Assistant Chief of Staff for Plans, A–5, became a critical link between intelligence and operations with primary responsibility for coordinating target matters and operational planning with the British as well as within the Eighth

---

*A separate air intelligence specialty, flak intelligence, dealt with mapping and studying the layout of AA defenses.

Air Force. His responsibilities included refining target priorities, target analysis and tactical planning (including coordination of tactical planning with operational capabilities and current intelligence), preparing target maps and objective folders, coordinating with American and British economic warfare units, and operational analysis.[104] Because of the industrial-economic nature of strategic air targets, the A–5 Target Section routinely dealt with the British MEW, the U.S. Board of Economic Warfare (BEW), and the Research and Analysis Branch of the American OSS, in addition to more conventional military intelligence groups. The two economic warfare agencies had been created by their respective governments to provide direction to possible economic measures against the Axis powers. Each agency had an extensive staff whose functions included monitoring and analyzing the enemy's actual and potential economic condition. The Research and Analysis Branch, OSS, provided much the same function with somewhat more emphasis on the implications for military operations.

Although the amount and accuracy of target information became increasingly sophisticated as the air war developed, some early missions had the advantage of extensive data. For VIII Bomber Command's highly successful raid on the Billancourt Renault military transport factory on April 7, 1943, the MEW secured from Lloyd's of London, who held the insurance policy on the factory, "detailed plans . . . [including] every factory building, vehicle assembly and engine shop, every forge, foundry, and paintshop."[105]

As early as July 1942, Hughes, at the time still working in Eighth Air Force A–2, began to search for a way to obtain the specific data upon which to base target recommendations and to plan attacks. The OSS Research and Analysis Branch and the Economic Warfare Division of the BEW each agreed to provide two or three individuals to staff a new organization, the EOU.[106] Operating in the American Embassy in London, administered by the BEW, and initially composed of civilians (many of whom were commissioned shortly thereafter), EOU worked directly for the Target Section of HQ Eighth Air Force, first in A–2 and then in A–5.[107]

The EOU filled the gap between the policy of precision bombing and the lack of precise data. To accomplish this task, Hughes directed EOU in September to provide detailed analyses of designated targets. These studies were to include the "importance of [a particular] plant within [an] industry, functions of buildings, vulnerability of processes, probable rate of recovery after successful attack, and the sections of the target which should constitute the proper objective of attack."[108] Out of this guidance evolved the aiming-point reports, one of EOU's principal contributions to the CBO. Beginning with ball bearings, synthetic rubber, tires, and oil, the EOU broadened its scope in the new year to include the aircraft industry against which Eighth Air Force would expend so much effort in the next 18 months. As of May 1944, EOU personnel they had produced 285 aiming-point reports.[109] At war's end, the Eighth Air

Force history credited the EOU with "the minutely detailed research into the operation, design and construction of every individual target which the Eighth Air Force decided to destroy by bombing."[110]

The basis for these reports included the full range of MEW and BEW data as well as Eighth Air Force operations research studies on bomb loading and fuzing. The members of EOU eventually gained complete access as well to Air Ministry operational intelligence, including ground reports and photointerpretation reports. The comment in the unit's own history that one of its members had to use "ineffable tact" in acquiring information from "the somewhat reluctant Air Ministry Intelligence" suggests, however, that such openness did not come immediately.[111] EOU personnel visited representative plants within the United Kingdom, spoke with industrialists of appropriate industries, and attempted to extrapolate lessons on target destruction from the results of earlier *Luftwaffe* attacks.[112] The aiming-point reports provided an essential link between intelligence and operations by offering a framework for organizing information and a way to think about the precision bombardment of specific targets.[113] More specifically, the reports constituted much of the material that went into the development of individual target folders, and they provided the information upon which VIII Bomber Command selected not only precise aiming points for bomb release, but also the types of bombs and fuzes for each target.[114]

Feedback on the effects of an attack was as important as selecting the proper target and the means by which to attack it. This broad issue of damage assessment actually involved three related aspects: the extent of the physical damage to the target, the effect of this destruction on that target's output, and the impact of this reduced production or repair capability on the total German war effort. At the initiative of Colonel Hughes, now Eighth Air Force Assistant Chief of Staff for Plans (A–5), one approach to this problem was the evolution of yet another Anglo-American agency capable of supporting the intelligence and analysis requirements of American bombing operations.[115]

The British Ministry of Home Security had formed the Research and Experiment (R.E.) Department in 1940 to reduce the effects of the *Luftwaffe*'s bombing on British industrial production by studying plant construction and layout. In July 1942 a new section, R.E.8, had begun scientific analysis of the vulnerability of German industrial targets and the impact of RAF Bomber Command's attacks. To meet the growing demands of an expanding war, in the spring of 1943 R.E.8 became an Allied agency, with Americans incorporated into it and EOU providing the link with Eighth Air Force and VIII Bomber Command targeteers. By August 1943, fifteen Americans were assigned to R.E.8.[116] Relying primarily on aerial photography and interpretation, R.E.8 analyzed the number and distribution of bombs on the target; the damage to structures, facilities, and production capabilities; the effectiveness of weapons to determine suitability of specific bombs against particular types of targets; and the probable recovery time and estimated production lost.[117] EOU took this

Building an Air Intelligence Organization

analysis and, correlating it with economic data from such agencies as MEW and BEW, attempted to determine the impact of the lost production or repair capability on the German war effort.

Damage assessment was fundamental to the conduct of precision bombing since it influenced decisions on which targets to strike, at what intervals, and with what forces. The entire process was fraught with difficulty and uncertainty. In the first place, it depended on prior intelligence about the nature and overall condition of the German economy, which was itself incomplete and in some fundamental ways inaccurate. It involved assumptions, derived from macroeconomic analysis, about the relative importance of individual targets within broad target categories. In a more technical sense, postattack analysis, often limited to aerial photographs taken tens of thousands of feet above the target, had to differentiate between the more apparent physical damage done to the structures themselves and the real impact of such damage on the capabilities of the target (i.e., production output and repair capability). Additionally, the amount of time required for the enemy to repair any given facility was at best an educated guess.

In time, ULTRA would contribute significantly to the Allied analytical capability by supplementing photographic evidence, suggesting new perspectives on such evidence, or offering information unobtainable from the air. Although few of the photointerpreters at Medmenham were aware of it because of the tight compartmentalization of ULTRA, data regularly flowed between the code breakers and intelligence officers at BP and the CIU.[118] In early American bombing operations, ULTRA did not contribute greatly to damage assessments because the Germans sent most of the information necessary to evaluate the effect of bombing by land lines and through civilian channels. Reports subject to ULTRA interception were often based on first impressions, when the rubble had not yet been cleared and actual damage not fully determined. Too, individuals sending postattack reports had reasons for either exaggerating or downplaying the extent of the damage.[119]

Damage assessment became increasingly proficient over time. Interpreting physical damage was always easier than extrapolating the impact of the damage on the target's output or the effect of that result on the enemy's overall industrial production, and thus military capability. Two examples from this early period of operations illustrate the difficulties involved. On March 22, 1943, 73 B–17s of the 91st, 303d, and 305th Bomb Groups dropped 536 1,000-pound bombs on the submarine construction yard at Vegesack. Eaker wrote jubilantly to Arnold that RAF postattack evaluation had determined, in Eaker's words, "the Vegesack yard has been put out for a year by one raid of less than 100 heavy bombers."[120] Supporting the RAF assessment was a Royal Naval Intelligence Division (NID) report that noted severe damage to several submarines as well. A follow-on NID evaluation the next month revealed that these earlier estimates had been too optimistic and that repairs to the yard had progressed more rapidly than projected.[121]

A more tragic example of the difficulties in the collection and assessment of air intelligence was the VIII Bomber Command strike against a Focke-Wulf factory at Bremen on April 17, 1943. Motive for the attack was an assessment that this facility was producing 80 FW 190s and 35 FW 135s a month, supposedly 34 percent of Germany's total Focke-Wulf output. The 107 B–17 attackers met the stiffest opposition to date; 159 men and 15 aircraft were lost, twice the total of any previous day. Alleviating the pain of these losses was the initial assessment that the force had destroyed or damaged half of the factory.[122] When the CIU studied poststrike photographs over a period of several weeks, it became obvious the Germans had not taken steps to repair the supposedly valuable plant. This warning flag led to an extensive analysis that provided, according to the EOU history, "incontrovertible evidence" that the primary FW 190 production facility was at Marienburg, far to the east, and that whatever capability had existed at Bremen had been moved several months before the raid.[123]

Eighth Air Force: Early Operations

What made the development of air intelligence organizations and capabilities at once so demanding and so critical was the fact that it was occurring in the midst of combat operations. As a result, the relationship between intelligence, planning, and operations was reciprocal from the start. While intelligence contributed to the planning and successful execution of air operations, the demands of the air war affected the organization of intelligence, defined the types of intelligence required, and shaped the manner in which it was employed.

In his instructions to the commanding general of Eighth Air Force, European theater commander Maj. Gen. Dwight Eisenhower stated, "The mission of the Eighth Air Force, in collaboration with the Royal Air Force, is to initiate immediately the maximum degree of air operations with a view to obtaining and maintaining domination of the air over Western France by 1 April 1943, and [to] be prepared to furnish the maximum support to the forward movement of U.S. Ground Forces by late summer 1943."[124] Spaatz's directive to Ira Eaker was more comprehensive, and presumptuous: "The Eighth Air Force bomber effort will be aimed at the destruction of the enemy's will to fight and to eliminate his means of continuing the struggle."[125]

Recognizing the requirement for a break-in period for the fledgling force, in the summer of 1942 American and British air leaders identified an initial group of twenty-nine targets in occupied territory. These were selected primarily because they were "within short range and consistent with the requirement of remoteness from built up areas and freedom from excessive flak." They included aircraft repair facilities, airfields, marshaling yards, shipyards, and power stations.[126] According to Eaker, targets for specific missions would be chosen by a conference of British and American commanders and would depend on "the target's relation to the conditions of the war and the necessity of destroying them . . . [and] on practicality of attacks as regards defense, loss of bombers, operating radii of bombers and weather."[127] Since Eaker's A-2 and A-5 had only begun the process of collating detailed target information, it is not surprising that Eaker observed in his report that in these early missions "the Bomber Commander picked the day's targets based solely on two considerations: first, the weather both in the United Kingdom and over possible target areas, and secondly, the size of the force available."[128]

American air planners in the United Kingdom were not long in developing more sophisticated criteria and looking at a broader range of targets. In mid-August 1942, Col. Henry Berliner, Spaatz's Chief of Plans, recommended that the command's general objective should be the German transportation system in Europe, since the very extent of this system would ensure available targets regardless of weather. More precise objectives should be fighter assembly plants, the Ruhr power plants, and submarine installations.[129] Both the plans and intelligence staffs had already begun studies on German air bases and production facilities in western Europe, and shortly EOU would turn to ball bearings, oil, and rubber. To the dismay of all American airmen, effective implementation of *any* offensive air plan was suddenly delayed by the decisions to invade North Africa, i.e., Operation TORCH, and to attack German U-boat bases with any means possible, including the use of strategic air forces.

The condition of American military forces in the late summer of 1942 meant that TORCH would dramatically affect Eighth Air Force's organization and operation. In addition to the reallocation of units already in the United Kingdom, U.S.-based units earmarked for the Eighth were absorbed into a newly created Twelfth Air Force. All elements of Eighth Air Force and subordinate commands provided maximum support to Twelfth. Although this would prove most burdensome on VIII Fighter and Support Commands, it meant the loss of the only two experienced bomb groups.[130] In addition to planes, equipment, and time, the Eighth sacrificed people. Eighth Air Force intelligence contributed its chief, Colonel McDonald, as well as officers and airmen skilled in operations intelligence, war-room procedures, counterintelligence, and photointerpretation. In the words of the command's historian, these losses left "gaps that could not easily be filled for some time to come." The VIII Bomber Command's A-2 gave up key individuals and also organized an intelligence school for 65 new officers assigned to Twelfth.[131] In all, Twelfth took 27,000 men and 1,072 aircraft, with the result that by December 1 the Eighth had only 27,000 men and 248 heavy bombers and had flown only 23 missions in 3 1/2 months.[132]

Piercing the Fog

Even before the Northwest African invasion, but closely associated with it, the Eighth attacked German submarine bases. The battle for the Atlantic had been a seesaw struggle from the beginning of the war, a struggle that throughout much of 1942 had gone against the Allies. The decision to launch TORCH only increased the dire necessity to gain the upper hand. On October 13, 1942, having just been appointed commander of the Allied invasion force, General Eisenhower put into written form instructions he had discussed previously with General Spaatz. Eisenhower's directive admitted what Spaatz must have expressed forcefully in previous discussions: "The German Air Force must be constantly pounded [to gain air superiority]." Nevertheless, no other objective "should rank above the effort to defeat the German submarine . . . [which] I consider . . . to be one of the two basic requirements to the winning of the war." Accordingly, Spaatz was to initiate "effective action against the submarine ports in the Bay of Biscay."[133] Spaatz, in turn, directed VIII Bomber Command to concentrate its efforts against the German submarine operating bases at Brest, Saint Nazaire, Lorient, Bordeaux, and La Pallice.[134]

Eaker had already outlined what he called Plans for Anti-Submarine Bombing and forwarded them to Spaatz in mid-October. "Without a basic force of 10 heavy bomber groups," he wrote, "it would not be possible to deny these ports to the enemy."[135] His staff had made an extensive analysis of communications systems, shed construction, power units, living quarters and other auxiliary functions which indicated that it would be possible to disrupt critical activities at these bases to deny the enemy their effective use. According to this study, since the heavily reinforced concrete pens could not be destroyed, attacks should concentrate on vital work and support activities located outside the shelters as well as the locks that controlled movement to and from the protected pens.[136] The bomber commander admitted these operations had to be considered an "experiment," but, he stated, they were ones "we are anxious to undertake."[137]

In undertaking this campaign, the Eighth's planners relied heavily on their Allies for intelligence. Specific target information came primarily from RAF and Royal Navy photographs and photointerpretation reports as well as reports from on the scene observers, including pictures smuggled out by the French underground.[138] Operational intelligence personnel met with representatives of the Interservice Topographical Section at Oxford for details on geographical features and with Admiralty officials on building construction within the U-boat bases, including the super-reinforced concrete shelters.[139] American planners also referred to several British studies. The first was a MEW report of July 21, 1942. Based on RAF experiences, this study focused primarily on submarine construction yards and factories producing submarine component parts, neither of which it considered particularly attractive targets. The report was similarly discouraging with regard to U-boat operating bases in western Europe, estimating that vital activities were or could be protected and that redundant systems would make permanent damage difficult. "When these factors are considered in combination," it concluded, "the prospects of causing major disruptions to submarine operations by aerial bombardment of bases would not seem to be especially good, though some harassing action is no doubt possible and effective within limits."[140]

Less than two weeks later, on the basis of a similar study of RAF operations against submarine yards in 1941 and port-area attacks in 1942, Bomber Operations, Air Ministry, concluded that even if successful, attacks on construction facilities would take a minimum of nine months to affect the war at sea because of the number of submarines already undergoing sea trials. Expressing more hope than studied assessment, the Bomber Operations report concluded, "It appears that by far the most profitable method of countering submarines at the present is by harrying them at sea or attacking their operating bases."[141]

By the end of November, after VIII Bomber Command had flown ten missions against the Biscay targets, intelligence assessments remained mixed. From the beginning, the Royal Navy had provided the thrust behind the campaign. Thus, it was not surprising that an Admiralty Intelligence Board report of November 20 referred to the "disorganization" that had resulted from the eight attacks to that date, or that it concluded, "It seems probable that this fine series of actions, if sustained, will have a considerable influence on the enemy's U-boat effort."[142] Several days later another naval intelligence report reviewing the recent attacks on Lorient and Saint Nazaire, on November 22 and 23, respectively, concluded that they had been "important successes" and predicted that "these ports will be completely dislocated in time provided that the attacks can be kept up."[143]

Airmen, both British and American, were less positive. In January, Lt. Col. Harris B. Hull, still VIII Bomber Command A–2 and himself a veteran of missions over the submarine pens, was in Washington telling the Air Staff and the Joint Staff, "These g—— d—— submarine pens are killing us."[144] The obvious emphasis being placed on these five bases, in fact, had allowed the Germans to concentrate dense and increasingly effective defenses. By the end of 1942, VIII Bomber Command losses averaged about 8 percent per raid.[145]

Based on photointerpretation reports and other sources (including ULTRA), British air intelligence offered a much more guarded assessment than the Royal Navy of the impact of the ten raids conducted between November 7 and 23. Five attacks on Saint Nazaire had resulted in delays and shifts in repair work. The facilities appeared to be at full capacity by December 9, and there had been "no noticeable reduction" in the number of operating U-boats. Pointing out the difficulties of permanently closing ports, as evidenced by German failures against Malta and the RAF's own problems against Bengazi, the report stated such operations could have a significant impact only if the attacks were far heavier and "sustained over a long period" and if the number of U-boats sunk at sea increased. Until this last condition was met, the effort to strike either construction yards or bases "will be quite disproportionate to the results."[146]

In response to a request from Arnold for an assessment of all aspects of antisubmarine operations by air, in January 1943 Eighth Air Force's A–5 produced the most extensive analysis to date. The report recommended against attacks on component parts factories (because of locations and redundancies) and construction yards (because of the lag in operational impact). Although complete destruction was not possible, planners concluded that the five operating bases "appear to be by far the most profitable targets." By seriously crippling "vulnerable points . . . continuous and frequent attacks on these bases" could keep them "dislocated and greatly increase the turn-around time of the U-boats," which would decrease the number of boats operating at any given time.[147]

The report then analyzed the potential value of attacking submarines transiting the Bay of Biscay and the demonstrated value of defensive and offensive air patrols in support of convoys. It would be impossible, the planners concluded, to destroy the U-boat threat in the next twelve months regardless of the method of air operations. Therefore, the problem was one of keeping losses to an acceptable level. "The problem . . . becomes one of control." For this, primary emphasis should be on "convoy air protection, supplemented by air attacks on submarines in transit and regular air attacks on the operating bases." Sorties of 50 bombers per week against each operating base, a total weekly

Col. Harris B. Hull

Building an Air Intelligence Organization

effort of 250 sorties, would be "ample to secure a very material decrease in the operating efficiency of these installations within a reasonable time."[148]

Whether this assessment reflected the views of senior commanders is an interesting question. According to several individuals working with him, Spaatz was "absolutely livid" over the diversion of resources to this mission.[149] In a long letter on the subject to Edward Mason of the OSS, Chandler Morse, head of the EOU in London, observed, "The 8th Air Force is extremely unhappy over its directive to attack submarines . . . " since, despite heavy losses and diversion from its primary mission against targets in Germany, the campaign did not appear to be having any effect. Referring specifically to the January 16 report to Arnold, Morse offered his opinion that this memo "tends to make attacks on bases appear to be more successful than the officers at WIDE WING [HQ Eighth Air Force] really believe they are."[150] At the same time, however, Eaker was writing to Arnold that he believed the campaign "has had a material effect" on the reduction in shipping losses.[151]

By the middle of January, then, assessments of the value of heavy-bomber attacks on the Biscay operating bases varied widely. The only near consensus was that construction yards were not worthwhile targets, at least in the short run (less than a year). Nevertheless, in the Casablanca Directive of January 21, 1943, the Anglo-American CCS made submarine construction yards the first priority for the Allied bomber offensive. Although not specifically listed, the chiefs clearly considered the operating bases in France within the category of targets that merited concentrated efforts because of "great importance either from the political or military" point of view.[152] The RAF's ACAS, Operations urged Eighth Air Force to focus future attacks on Biscay bases when weather prevented attacks on submarine construction yards in northern Germany.[153] In all, submarine facilities were the target for 63 percent of the total tonnage that VIII Bomber Command dropped in the first quarter of 1943 and 52 percent of the total expended during the second quarter.[154]

In the six months after the Casablanca conference in January 1943, the Allies gained the upper hand in the Atlantic. A variety of measures contributed to what proved the decisive swing in a pendulum that had moved back and forth for several years. The breaking of the German Navy's Enigma code, the introduction of improved tactics and technical equipment (including extensive defensive and offensive air patrols), and the sheer expansion of resources led to a dramatic reduction in shipping losses by the late spring of 1943. Evidence on the impact of air strikes against U-boat bases in France remained inconclusive, but at best they slowed down the turnaround times of operating boats and, to that extent, had some effect on the trend of events. German records indicate the attacks on the construction yards by either VIII or RAF Bomber Commands only negligibly affected the production of U-boats.[155]

The Allied air campaign against German U-boats illustrates several points about air intelligence. In the first, basic policy decisions, especially with regard to construction yards, were not taken primarily on intelligence assessments. The seriousness of the crisis, perhaps the most serious of the war for the western Allies, provided the justification for these diversions. Assessments made before and after the attacks demonstrated the uncertain nature of intelligence and the problems of evaluating what one sees, let alone of projecting what might happen. Clearly, there was no consensus on the impact, actual or potential, of these attacks. In no small way, this was a problem that affected strategic air operations throughout the war: inherent difficulties involved not only assessing physical damage but also interpreting the impact this damage had on the capability of the target. Finally, the submarine campaign, especially during its early months, proved once again that intelligence, even when correct, could not fully compensate for the lack of adequate operational capability. All of the studies suggested that the level of air attacks needed was simply impossible with the resources available to VIII Bomber Command.

Countering the German Air Force

While U-boats remained the top air priority for the Combined Chiefs until the spring of 1943, they never had that status for American airmen, either in Washington or in England. For Americans, the objective of strategic air power was to destroy German industrial and military capability through daylight, high-altitude, precision attacks on the German homeland. Since the chief obstacle to accomplishing this objective was the GAF, it stood at the top of every AAF target priority list.* According to the Director of Intelligence, USSTAF, "it was always the first duty of Air Intelligence to know accurately the strength, disposition and capabilities of the G.A.F."[156] Reflecting this importance, Eighth Air Force intelligence (later USSTAF) published a weekly special report focused solely on Axis air forces. As they set out to prove their doctrine of strategic air power, American airmen seriously misjudged the capabilities and potential strength of their opponents.

In an August 1942 report to General Spaatz summarizing the first four B–17 missions—all shallow penetrations into France—Eaker confidently asserted, "I am now thoroughly convinced . . . successful bombing operations can be conducted beyond the range of fighter protection."[157] Four months later, Eaker, now Commanding General, Eighth Air Force, forwarded to Arnold a study on the GAF compiled by his intelligence section. This report, he declared, "shows . . . quite clearly, that this all-conquering, all-powerful monster, the G.A.F., has passed its peak and is now on the way downhill." Responding to Arnold's concern that the Germans might mass 1,200 aircraft in North Africa

---

*Although *Luftwaffe* was the official name for the German Air Force during the war, Allied documents generally referred to it by the acronym "GAF" or "G.A.F."

and simply overwhelm Allied air forces there, Eaker added, "there is no probability of that. . . . The simple truth of the matter is that we now have the German Air Force licked."[158] Beyond the naturally positive attitude characteristic of most commanders, Eaker and his subordinates based such assertions upon a series of intelligence estimates, not all of them of impeccable origin.

The EOU history is probably correct that "in the course of the war, no aspect of intelligence received wider, more continuous, and more devoted attention than the German Air Force."[159] But the winter of 1942–1943 was only a midway point in the evolution of air intelligence. In these early months of operations, the Americans depended on a British air intelligence structure that was still refining its capabilities. Before the outbreak of war in 1939, Hitler had convinced the democracies that the *Luftwaffe* was much larger in number and capability than was actually the case. Early in 1942, when British air intelligence determined that the 1940–1941 estimates had badly overstated German aircraft production, British intelligence officers established new methods of analysis. Then the pendulum actually swung the other way, and from the spring of 1942 until early 1943, GAF fighter production was underestimated.[160]

Contributing to this tendency to underestimate was the flawed assumption that the German economy had been operating at full capacity from the outset of the war. Not until 1943 did the MEW shift from its long-held position that the German armaments industry was already in decline.[161] It would also be mid-1943 before the Allies discovered the reorganization of the German aircraft industry that Albert Speer and Erhard Milch had undertaken in 1942. Compounding the difficulties of assessing the potential strength of the *Luftwaffe* was the division of responsibilities within the British intelligence community. The MEW was responsible for estimates on the capacity of the German aircraft industry while the Air Ministry Air Intelligence evaluated the actual output and the operational state of the GAF (including OB, disposition, and wastage).[162]

ULTRA could prove a comprehensive source of accurate intelligence on the GAF, but it was of limited value through 1942. Because of the location of enemy fighter units and the level of air activity, most message traffic went by land lines rather than airwaves as it did in other theaters.[163] British intelligence followed the movement of *Luftwaffe* units from other theaters into western Europe. Once they were in position, the amount of strategic information dropped considerably. Only in the summer of 1943, when the collection and evaluation of all signals intelligence permitted radiotelegraph (R/T) intercepts to be correlated with ULTRA messages, were intelligence officers able to produce consistently reliable results.[164]

Until then, the low estimates of GAF strength produced in the fall of 1942 and in early 1943 seemingly were supported by several sources. As early as the spring of 1942, ULTRA had revealed a growing manpower shortage in the GAF. In the fall of 1942, ULTRA and other sources accurately assessed a decline in German single-engine fighters on the western front as Berlin shifted resources to the Mediterranean and Soviet Union. Having risen from just under 300 fighters in early 1942 to more than 500 by fall, the *Luftwaffe* ended the year with 435 fighter aircraft in the west.[165]

Another reason for the optimism that characterized early Eighth Air Force operations was the exaggerated claims of enemy aircraft shot down during bomber missions. Air-to-air combat between multiengine bombers and swarms of fighters was a new phenomenon. The British had only limited experience with it before they turned to night operations. The Americans had little to refer to when they established procedures to review, record, and report the results of these air battles. It was impossible to reconstruct completely events that occurred in the swirling melee of aerial combat with numerous gunners firing at fast-moving, dangerous fighters. By any standards, the figures from the early missions should have raised eyebrows. Even Carl Spaatz, less inclined to false optimism than many, wrote to his former A–5, Colonel Berliner, that American air forces in Europe had destroyed 1,200 German aircraft by March 1943.[166]

In December, Hap Arnold suggested that Eaker take a closer look at the numbers and methods for recording claims, reminding the latter there was "too much at stake" to be inaccurate.[167] The increase in intelligence officers qualified to debrief returning aircrews, the greater experience of the crews themselves, and the implementation of stricter parameters for determining verified fighter kills reduced the discrepancies between claims and actual losses, but the latter remained well below the former. Eaker, fully aware of the confusion of combat and also the importance of morale among the men he had to send day after day into those air battles, never seemed as concerned with this issue as others did.[168] In a letter to General Stratemeyer, then Chief of Air Staff, on the latest criteria for kills, he could relate the tongue-in-cheek story of the gunner who refused to claim a German fighter which exploded in front of his gunsights because "I didn't see the s.o.b. hit the ground."[169] With better ULTRA information, the importance of aircrew claims would become less significant in an intelligence sense. The importance of morale would not.

The early miscalculations of the GAF and aircraft industry, and their significance, would not become obvious until the summer and fall of 1943. From the beginning, these errors influenced the way in which the AAF sought to achieve its objectives in Europe. In December 1942, Arnold wrote to Spaatz that evidence of a decline in the GAF indicated "the necessity of forcing Germany if it is possible into an air war of extermination."[170] Senior intelligence officers in the theater contributed to this focus on "extermination." In a special report on German and Italian air OBs, Colonel McDonald, still Eighth Air Force A–2, noted it was becoming increasingly evident that the GAF was conserving fighters while it built up its strength. "The above confirms," he concluded, "that our policy during the winter months should more and more be directed to force the enemy into combat in order to continue our policy of attrition of the G.A.F."[171]

Building an Air Intelligence Organization

In these statements lies the resolution of the apparent discrepancy between assertions that the GAF was "on the way downhill" and constant emphasis on German air power as the first target for strategic air operations. In the fall of 1942, American airmen sought to ensure that the GAF remained in decline. If allowed to recuperate from the blows Americans thought they were inflicting, the *Luftwaffe* might become a formidable opponent. By the spring of 1943 Allied intelligence had begun to detect the rise in actual fighter strength in western Europe and to glimpse the increases in single-engine fighter production. In January they received agent reports of a meeting of fighter group commanders that clearly indicated an expansion of the German fighter force. These reports also provided the first indication of the development of the Me 262, Me 163, He 280, and the 30mm cannon.[172] In March, ULTRA revealed fighter units moving to the west from Russia; the next month came information of similar moves from the Mediterranean.[173]

Precise figures were not necessary to realize that Eighth Air Force's daylight bombing offensive had captured Germany's attention. Casualty figures from each mission provided a clear enough indication. The result was not only continued emphasis on the GAF but a realization that extermination through aerial combat would not suffice. From this realization would come a renewed emphasis on attacking single-engine fighter production. Even with this new awareness, intelligence estimates continued to lag behind German production and disposition. While Allied estimates for the first half of 1943 stood at 595 units per month, German factories were producing an average of 753. This disparity increased throughout the year. Thus, when intelligence projected a German monthly production of single-engine fighters in the second half of 1943 at 645, the enemy actually produced 851, over 200 more than the estimate.[174]

How an earlier understanding of the real production capabilities of the German aircraft industry and a more realistic appraisal of enemy losses in the daylight bombing campaign would have influenced that campaign is a moot point. American air leaders were committed to a daylight, precision bombing campaign, and it is unlikely they would have flinched even had they had a more accurate picture. Such insight would almost certainly have prompted an even stronger focus on the aircraft industry and a livelier appreciation of the need to revisit supposedly destroyed factories more frequently.[175] It might have hastened the development of a long-range escort fighter. A more difficult question is whether political and military leaders other than airmen would have supported the strategic air offensive had they known what it would entail. Given the continued opposition to strategic air operations within the U.S. Army and Navy, it is conceivable that more accurate air intelligence would have resulted in less extensive air operations.

Intelligence Implications for the Strategic Air Campaign in Europe

According to AWPD–1, American air power in the European Theater would "wage a sustained air offensive against German military power, supplemented by air offensives against other regions under enemy control which contribute toward that power."[176] Whether that objective still obtained in the summer of 1942 was open to debate, for harsh reality had replaced theoretical assumptions. The United States was not only at war, but the early months of that war had gone quite differently than had been anticipated, with the Axis powers seemingly dominant in every theater. In the midst of these military, political, and economic pressures, the AAF had to rearticulate the role of air power and identify the resources necessary for this role.

In August 1942, President Roosevelt requested the AAF, through General George C. Marshall, Army Chief of Staff, to advise him of the total number and types of combat aircraft required to gain "complete air ascendancy over the enemy." These calculations would be part of a larger reassessment of "the proper relationship of air power to the Navy and our ground forces."[177] Accordingly, Marshall and Arnold directed Brig. Gen. Haywood S. Hansell, a principal in the drafting of AWPD–1, to return from England "within 48 hours" to determine the "objectives[,] the destruction of which will guarantee air ascendancy over [the] enemy."[178] Hansell, accompanied by Major Hull (VIII Bomber Command A–2), Lt. Col. Richard Hughes (Eighth Air Force Assistant A–2), and RAF Group Captain A. C. Sharp (RAF liaison with HQ Eighth Air Force), landed in the United States in late August, and in eleven days they hammered out what became AWPD–42.[179]

AWPD–42 was, like its predecessor, primarily a requirements document intended to determine the aircraft, manpower, and matériel needed to defeat the Axis. Its planners identified a total of 177 targets in Europe that, if attacked with a fully mature force in 66,045 bomber sorties over a six-month period, would produce destruction of the GAF, depletion of the German submarine force, and disruption of the German war economy. Where AWPD–1 had suggested that strategic air operations might themselves bring about Germany's collapse, AWPD–42 accepted the air offensive as a prelude to an ultimate ground assault that could come only after the enemy had been sufficiently weakened through air bombardment. Accordingly, American strategic air forces were to concentrate on the "systematic destruction of selected vital elements of the German military and industrial machine through precision bombing in daylight," while the RAF continued its "mass air attacks of industrial *areas* at night. . . ."[180]

In addition to conceding an eventual amphibious assault on Fortress Europe, AWPD–42 differed somewhat from the earlier plan in its selection of vital elements of the German war effort. According to AWPD–1, the priority assigned targets in Europe was the GAF, the electric power system, transportation systems (rail, road, water), refineries and synthetic oil plants, and, more generally, the morale of the German people. AWPD–42 identified as "overriding intermediate objectives" aircraft assembly plants and engine factories, followed by submarine construction yards, transportation, electric power, oil, aluminum, and synthetic rubber, collectively grouped as primary targets. A brief comparison of the two lists confirms that, with the exception of the submarine yards, the changes were not significant. The flip-flopping of electric power and transportation merely reversed their previous order, and oil retained its position relative to both. In AWPD–1, aluminum had appeared as a subset of targets selected to "neutralize" the *Luftwaffe*. In the new plan aluminum was now one of "three of the major commodities required by Germany in the prosecution of her war effort." The addition of synthetic rubber reflected current thinking in the British MEW that this was a bottleneck industry. With the RAF now concentrating on German morale, that target priority disappeared from AWPD–42.[181]

The most significant difference between the two plans—the inclusion in AWPD–42 of submarine construction yards—reflected broad strategic considerations rather than intelligence analyses. The major air intelligence studies available at the time had stressed both the difficulty of permanently damaging submarine yards and the nine- to twelve-month period that would elapse before such attacks would impact significantly on the battle in the Atlantic.[182] According to Hansell, inclusion of the U-boat yards was "testimony to the terrible toll of Allied shipping by German submarines in 1942. It also recognized the concern, interest, and power of the naval leaders whose authority would influence the adoption of the plan by the Joint Chiefs."[183] In view of the opposition of senior air leaders to the diversion of heavy bombers to the antisubmarine campaign, it is fair to suggest the yards' inclusion as priority targets stemmed from an awareness that any plan that did not include them was doomed from the start.

The operational assumptions that underlay AWPD–42 reflected the still incomplete intelligence available to air planners as well as their still limited base of experience. The prevailing interpretation of the German economy as already strained to the breaking point and incapable of further expansion—and the inability to foresee the steps a nation engaged in a total war might take to continue that struggle—is at least implicit throughout. In addressing transportation, for example, the planners concluded this "vital link" was "at present taxed to its maximum capacity."[184] Within six months, several more complete analyses of the German rail system would indicate that some 30 percent of the traffic it carried was "not essential" to the war effort.[185] Both the operational assumptions and their strategic conclusions were predicated, moreover, on a schedule of force development and operations that did not occur. Despite the efforts of Hansell and others, AWPD–42 failed to resolve the issue of what strategic air power could and should do in the fight against the Axis powers. Within the new organizations supporting the JCS, the other services questioned both the data and the assumptions upon which airmen based strategic bombing plans, and AWPD–42 never became a joint document.[186]

To counter skepticism expressed in the several joint committees and to prevent it from reaching higher, General Fairchild suggested to General Arnold the creation of a group that, through detailed, quantitative analysis of the most current and comprehensive intelligence available, would provide convincing rationale for the selection of strategic air targets.[187] On December 9, 1942, Arnold directed Col. Byron E. Gates, Director of Management Control, HQ AAF, to convene a board of select individuals for the purpose of "analyzing the rate of progressive deterioration" that sustained offensive air operations might impose upon the German war effort. Specifically, the group was to provide him with an estimate "as to the date when this deterioration will have progressed to a point to permit a successful invasion of Western Europe."[188] Thus was born the Advisory Committee on Bombardment, later renamed the COA.

To many, including Hansell (now back in England), Arnold's decision to make management control rather than A–2 or A–5 responsible for this task came "to the surprise and dismay of all concerned, including Fairchild."[189] Apparently, however, Fairchild not only conceived the committee, but he influenced its position within the Air Staff. According to Col. Guido Perera, Gates's executive officer, Fairchild had first raised the subject in Gates's office informally on December 3, 1942.[190] Logical reasons existed for such an arrangement. The military had recently become aware of the new technique of operations research, and the assignment of several analysts to the Office of Management Control provided personnel with some of the skills the study would require. The inclusion of civilians was in line with the prevailing idea that military officers had neither the training nor the time to devote to such economic analysis.[191] Also, some indication exists that Fairchild had not been impressed with the quality of the intelligence papers submitted to the JIC.[192] He and Arnold may have believed the establishment of a group outside the normal intelligence and plans organizations, especially one including prominent civilians, would carry greater weight with the other services and with political leaders such as the Secretary of War and the President.

Regardless of the motives, Gates and Perera, who would play key roles, set to their task with a will. Even before receiving Arnold's official directive, they had contacted Elihu Root, Jr., a respected and well-placed New York lawyer, to ask his participation. Learning that Colonel Moss of the HQ AAF A–2 staff had already been discussing targeting with Dr. Edward Mead Earle, a military historian at Princeton University, they invited Earle to sit on the committee.[193] In addition to Earle and Root, the civilian members were Fowler Hamilton, chief of the BEW; Edward S. Mason, head of the OSS Research and Analysis section; and Thomas W. Lamont, an influential member of New York's banking community. Joining Gates and Perera as military representatives were Colonel Sorenson, AC/AS, Intelligence; Colonel Moss, chief of the Targets Information section of HQ AAF A–2; Lt. Col. Thomas G. Lanphier of the Air Unit in G–2's MID; and Maj. W. Barton Leach, a lawyer serving as an operations analyst under Gates.[194]

The committee cast a broad net in its search for information. Within two weeks, its members had divided potential enemy target systems into three priorities according to their importance to the German war effort, their vulnerability, and the timeliness of impact, and it formed subcommittees to work on detailed studies of the German aircraft, oil, transportation, electric power, coke, and rubber industries, as well as on an overall interpretation of the western Axis economy. Eventually, committee members would address nineteen German industries. In addition, a force requirements subcommittee was to evaluate the resources necessary to achieve the destruction of whichever targets the committee recommended.

In areas in which HQ AAF A–2 had already done considerable work, most notably in electric power, oil, transportation, and rubber, the committee drew heavily upon these sources. Other agencies and organizations that provided material included the BEW, the Army's G–2, the OSS, the Departments of Commerce and State, the American Institute of Mining and Metallurgical Engineers, and the Administrator of Export Control. Reports from the MEW and the Air Ministry, already being sent to the British Embassy in Washington, were made available to the subcommittees. In addition to already completed studies and collected materials, the subcommittees called upon industrialists, economists, and financiers from America and abroad with expertise in key industries. In several instances, these men had actually operated factories in the targeted industries in Europe and Africa.[195] For example, information on the ball-bearing factories at Schweinfurt came from individuals who had worked for SKF, the Swedish firm that had owned these plants prior to their takeover by the German government.[196]

To acquire additional data and gain an operational perspective, Perera, Leach, Hamilton, and Root flew to England in late January 1943. They were greeted with frosty suspicion and concerns that their task involved potential security breaches, duplication of effort, and would impose an undue burden on the British, with whom Eighth Air Force had established close ties. American planners and intelligence officers in the United Kingdom also feared Washington was trying to assume a function—the collection and assessment of intelligence—which was better performed in the United Kingdom. It appeared that this group, especially through the force requirements subcommittee, was attempting to make operational judgments that were the prerogative of operators and planners.[197] To resolve some of the apprehensions, committee representatives agreed that their final report would not address specific force requirements or "operational factors which were particularly in the province of the Eighth Air Force. . . ."[198]

The visitors received full access to Eighth Air Force data and could talk directly and frankly with British officials. The history of the COA implies that these meetings eventually achieved agreement on both the principal targets and the priority assigned to them. All agreed "for security reasons" that the list as finally presented to General Arnold would not be in priority order. This statement was simply a way of agreeing to disagree, since Eighth Air Force and the COA could not reach any consensus on target priorities. It was common knowledge at the time that the list reflected the committee's order of priority.[199]

The committee submitted its report to the commanding general on March 8, 1943. In the jointly signed memorandum that accompanied it, committee members admitted that the limited combat experience of Eighth Air Force and the uncertainty of future resource allocations precluded an answer to Arnold's question as to the date by which air bombardment would permit a successful invasion. They stressed the importance of attacking with "relentless determination" a few "really essential industries or Services" rather than trying to cover everything, and they reviewed the criteria upon which the committee members had based their target recommendations: indispensability of a system to the enemy's war effort; current production, capacity to increase production, and stocks on hand; requirements for the specific product for various degrees of military activity; number, distribution, and vulnerability of vital installations; recuperative possibilities of the industry; and time lag between destruction of installations and desired impact on the enemy's military efforts. The memorandum stressed the need for a closely coordinated British and American target selection process, and it emphasized the latitude required "with respect to operational factors such as weather, diversion of attention, and concealment of bombing design." Accordingly, the selection of specific targets should "be left to the responsible authorities in England, subject only to such directives as may be called for by broad strategic considerations."[200]

The report itself consisted of a general discussion of the identified nineteen systems, an explanation of the process of evaluation and selection, and summaries of the subcommittee reports. The emphasis on careful selection of a few systems and the comments that accompanied each target system indicate that the following was the committee's priority, ranked from highest to lowest: single-engine fighter aircraft, ball bearings, petroleum products, grinding wheels and abrasives, nonferrous metals, synthetic rubber and rubber tires, submarine construction plants and bases, military transport vehicles, transportation, coking plants, iron and steel, machine tools, electric power, electrical equipment, optical precision instruments, chemicals, food, nitrogen, and AA and antitank artillery.

A comparison of the COA report and AWPD–42 completed only six months earlier reveals significant differences. Most notably, the committee put ball bearings in second priority, while it downgraded submarine yards and bases to seventh position, and transportation and electric power to ninth and thirteenth

Building an Air Intelligence Organization

places respectively. Of greatest interest was the removal of transportation and electric power from the COA's top group. Both targets had been prominently identified in AWPD–1 and AWPD–42, and postwar analysis showed them to have been potential bottleneck systems. In his response to Arnold's request for an assessment of the report, Spaatz reiterated his long-standing conviction that the German transportation system should be the single, most important target after the GAF.[201] After the war, General Hansell revealed he had had serious reservations about the COA report in these areas, calling the failure to press for attacks on electric power "a cardinal mistake."[202] Despite the committee's promise not to dabble in matters more appropriately the concern of operators, the COA's recommendations regarding electric power and transportation were predicated on assumed operational capabilities rather than on the intrinsic value of either system.

With regard to electric power, the committee agreed with AWPD–42's assessment of Germany's dependency on electric power. Its members observed, however, "in almost no instance is any single industry dependent upon one generating plant but rather upon a network which pools the greater part of the electrical energy within an area." From this they concluded that even within the two most important industrial areas (Rhine-Ruhr and central Germany) too many targets precluded bombing's having a continuous impact. Similarly, while admitting transportation was "a vital industry, serious disruption of which would cause ultimate economic and military collapse," the report concluded "at no point did the transportation system appear to offer a field of objectives within the scope of any projected operating air force."[203] Nor was the committee alone in these assessments. In February 1943, the British MEW concluded both systems were too widely dispersed to be effective targets.[204] In a special report dated January 5, 1943, the American EOU noted, "Basic industries like steel, power, and transport are not desirable targets because the available air strength does not permit penetration through their very extensive protective zones."[205]

One explanation for the differences between the recommendations of the COA and AWPD–42 lies simply in the time each group had to complete its task. In eleven days the AWPD–42 team could not undertake the detailed studies upon which the COA's report drew, few of which had even been completed by August 1942. While Hansell and his colleagues had encompassed the global struggle, the COA focused specifically on the strategic air war against Germany. There were differences in approach as well. Committee analysts believed they were to determine target systems that would allow an invasion of western Europe in the shortest time. In at least two specific areas, this framework definitely affected their conclusions. The committee relegated transportation to a low priority on the basis that air bombardment would lack decisive impact in 1943. According to the transportation subcommittee report, if invasion were delayed into 1944, "the general attack [on transportation] might offer real opportunities to achieve a state of imminent collapse within the Axis economy...."[206] The COA also accepted submarine yards as a suitable target over the long haul, but it placed the yards in seventh position because it believed an operational impact on the yards would require at least a year's worth of substantial attacks. In these areas, then, the COA report reflected the demands of operations affecting intelligence assessments, rather than the other way around.

Perhaps most important in assessing differences between AWPD–42 and the COA report was the inherent uncertainty of the whole intelligence process, especially at the strategic level. Charles Webster and Noble Frankland, authors of the official British history of the strategic air war against Germany, underscored precisely this point in their own discussion of the committee's recommendations and its critics: "Those criticisms show how much of the economic planning always depended on assumptions which could not be verified in the circumstances of the time."[207]

Although the committee had been unable to provide Arnold the date by which a strategic air campaign would make possible an invasion of Europe, it nonetheless played an important role in the development of that campaign. While the subcommittees had struggled to identify the proper objectives for air operations against Germany, Allied military and political leaders meeting at Casablanca in January had addressed the broader issue of the place of that campaign within the Grand Alliance's overall strategy. As a result of the persuasive arguments of Ira Eaker, the conferees agreed that Eighth Air Force should continue its daylight bombing program in conjunction with RAF night operations. VIII Bomber Command would operate independently of, but in close coordination with, RAF Bomber Command. The CCS would themselves determine the overall priority of targets, with the RAF Chief of Staff acting as their executive agent.

The combined policy paper that these decisions produced, the Casablanca Directive, defined the objective of strategic air operations in Europe as "the progressive destruction and dislocation of the German military, industrial, and economic system, and the undermining of the morale of the German people to a point where their capacity for armed resistance is fatally weakened." The directive called for a comprehensive plan to accomplish these objectives. In the interim, it established the following target priorities, ranked as before: German submarine construction yards, German aircraft industry, transportation, oil, and other elements of the German war industry.[208]

For air power, the decision to continue the American experiment with daylight precision bombing was the most significant aspect of Casablanca. In planning the execution of such operations, however, the Casablanca Directive provided only general guidance. Translation of this broad direction into operational objectives and plans would, especially on the American side, come through Eaker's plan for the CBO prepared in the spring of 1943 (see Chapter

Building an Air Intelligence Organization

4). The Report of the Committee of Operations Analysts featured mightily in the development of this plan.

TORCH and Northwest Africa

The hopes of American airmen for the rapid development of a strategic air offensive against Nazi Germany had been set back even before VIII Bomber Command dropped its first bomb on occupied Europe. AWPD–1 and AWPD–42 had assumed that up to two and a half years would elapse before Allied land forces would be ready to move against the *Wehrmacht*. In contrast, air planners argued they could begin building a force immediately and have it at full strength in eighteen to twenty-one months. Whatever the economic and military strengths of these assumptions, however, they failed to include relevant political considerations. For it was political rather than military concerns that led President Roosevelt and Prime Minister Churchill to override their military advisors and order an amphibious assault into North Africa in the fall of 1942.

North Africa provided a testing ground from which would come invaluable lessons for the larger battles on and over the European continent. The TORCH decision, by irrevocably committing the United States to the defeat of Germany first, also controlled the drain of air resources to the Pacific. In this sense, it offered airmen greater freedom to send American air assets across the Atlantic: they thought the buildup was to conduct a strategic air offensive against Germany. By taking resources and emphasis from Eighth Air Force, TORCH delayed the execution of this offensive. Air power would prove essential to success in North Africa, but in a much lesser role than the one propounded for it by instructors in the Air Corps Tactical School. Air intelligence would take on new forms and be used in different ways. It would be no less central to the resulting victory.

The value of intelligence in the early phases of TORCH was mixed. Even before TORCH had been ordered, both the Air Staff and the Army MID had considered possible German moves into Spain.[209] In September 1942, Twelfth Air Force's A–2 estimated the Germans could put 250 combat aircraft into Spain for operations against Gibraltar or convoys moving through the straits. If the Spanish consented, which A–2 considered a good possibility, the GAF could begin operations from Spanish bases as early as five days after the landings.[210] The British Joint Planning Staff argued on August 5, 1942, that Germany could not move forces into Spain until she had stabilized the situation on the eastern front. There would be no threat of German air attacks from either Spain or the Balearic Islands for at least a month after the invasion forces landed.[211] On October 6, the British JIC reaffirmed the assessments that Franco would not permit the Germans free access to Spain and the Germans were not prepared to force entry.[212] In the weeks before the invasion, information from both ULTRA and Y intercepts allowed Allied intelligence to track the shift of short-range fighters and antishipping air units from the eastern Mediterranean, Germany, and Norway into Sicily and Sardinia. Such information reinforced Allied confidence that Berlin, while aware that Allied troops were preparing to move, assumed they were headed farther east, to Malta or possibly into Tripolitania.[213]

The immediate threat was not the GAF, but the Vichy French forces who still controlled North Africa. Despite several sensitive and sometimes dangerous meetings with French leaders in Africa to convince them not to resist the landings, Allied commanders had to assume military opposition. Twelfth Air Force included the French in Africa under the heading of enemy strength in the TORCH operations plan. The intelligence annex to Field Order No. 1 identified some 560 French aircraft in north and west Africa, with about 90 in the target area around Oran. While the anticipated level of effort was thought by some to be in the range of 60 to 90 sorties per day from D-day to D+4 and to decline rapidly thereafter, Twelfth Air Force intelligence officers considered these figures conservative and believed the French capable of doubling that number. Because, as the annex noted, "no indications [are] that token resistance only will be encountered," the intelligence specialists stressed that all planning should be based on the "assumption that our assault will be bitterly contested."[214] (In the event, the Royal Navy's Fleet Air Arm destroyed a large part of the French Air Force in the initial attacks, and French air activity had virtually ended by D+2.)

Success in correctly assessing the lack of German opposition during the landings on November 7 was offset by the failure to predict the enemy's reaction. Assuming the Germans would not reduce their strength in other theaters, the British JIC had concluded a month before the invasion that no substantial buildup of Axis air forces would occur in North Africa. In October, British Air Ministry Intelligence predicted the enemy would not put more than 515 fighter aircraft against Allied forces. As of December 12th, by drawing resources from the eastern front, the *Luftwaffe* had more than 850 aircraft operating in the region. Many were based in Tunisia itself, which gave them decided advantages because of the limited number of airfields in eastern Algeria for Allied fighters and fighter-bombers.[215]

Once operations began, the Allies had "prompt, full and completely reliable intelligence of the rate of the Axis buildup...."[216] Within two days of the initial landings, French sources in North Africa as well as ULTRA intercepts revealed the German decision to move ground troops, close air support, and fighter units into Tunisia. By the middle of the month, the Allies knew the Germans were moving the technologically superior FW 190 into the theater. Complementing ULTRA in the acquisition of this information were photoreconnaissance flights over Sicily and Sardinia, Y intercepts, and agent reports.[217] The early weeks of TORCH illustrate that intelligence by itself is rarely sufficient to determine the outcome of battle. Despite the accurate picture ULTRA provided on the GAF, Allied air forces were unable to take full advantage of this tool. The small

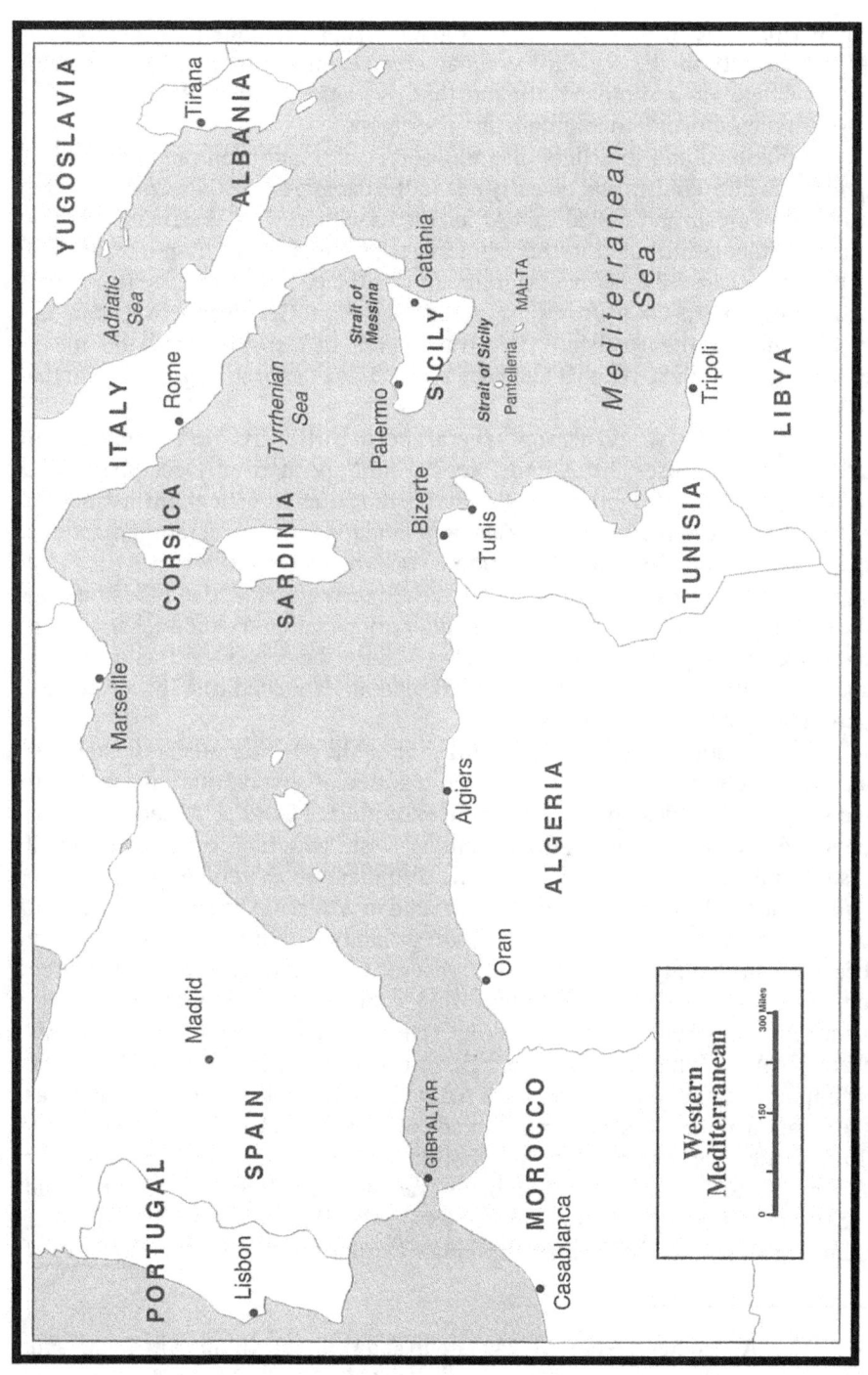

number of airfields and the lack of logistical support limited the number of Allied aircraft in the forward combat area. Compounding this numerical disadvantage was a command structure that, by fragmenting available air assets, allowed the *Luftwaffe* to maintain air superiority.

Operational and logistical planning for TORCH had been predicated on a quick rush into Tunisia and an early end to the campaign. By November 28 the drive into Tunisia had stalled, and Allied forces withdrew to Algeria to regroup. Many factors contributed to the failure to take Tunisia. From an intelligence perspective, certainly the most significant was the failure to foresee the extent and rapidity of the GAF's response. According to Lt. Gen. Kenneth Anderson, commander of the British First Army which had spearheaded the move eastward, it was the GAF that had been the decisive factor in bogging down the advance.[218]

Although they would attempt several abortive offensives in December, for all practical purposes the Allied forces would spend from December 1942 through the end of January 1943 establishing the logistical infrastructure necessary for sustained operations and implementing a series of reorganizations that would eventually provide the framework for success in North Africa and subsequently in western Europe. From these exertions came two milestones in the history of air power: the development of organizational structures to permit the effective employment of air assets within a theater as well as the more specific control of air-ground operations, and an expanded role for air power, particularly strategic air forces.

The evolution of Allied air organization in the Mediterranean theater was a convoluted process that extended over a period of several months, and itself the subject of many studies. During the execution of TORCH, Allied air forces operated as two separate organizations with geographically determined responsibilities: the British Eastern Air Command in eastern Algeria and the American Twelfth Air Force in Morocco and in western Algiers. With the shift of Twelfth Air Force eastward to support ground operations, this arrangement became increasingly unwieldy. Through a series of gradual steps in the winter of 1942–1943, Air Marshal Arthur Tedder emerged as the theater air commander in charge of Mediterranean Air Command (MAC). Subordinate to MAC were NAAF, Malta Air Force, and Eastern Air Command (Cairo). From the standpoint of air operations in North Africa in 1942–1943, the pivotal step was the creation of the NAAF under command of Maj. Gen. Carl Spaatz in February 1943. Under this arrangement, the subordinate Northwest African Strategic Air Force (NASAF), Northwest African Tactical Air Force (NATAF), and Northwest African Coastal Air Force (NACAF) focused on functional rather than on geographically oriented missions.* Responsibility for the air defense of

---

*NATAF, composed of RAF 242 Group and U.S. XII Air Support Command, was committed to the direct support of Allied land forces. NASAF, commanded by

Building an Air Intelligence Organization

North Africa, antisubmarine operations, and protection of friendly shipping rested with NACAF, which contained RAF and USAAF fighter units. At the same time, centralized direction from NAAF could adjust and redirect each force's efforts as necessary. NAAF also took direct control of the new Allied air reconnaissance organization, the Northwest African Photographic Reconnaissance Wing (NAPRW).[219]

The establishment of NAAF resulted in a marked change in the handling and use of air intelligence in North Africa. Before its creation, the focal point of all intelligence, including air, had been the G–2 of Allied Forces Headquarters (AFHQ). Until late December, both targets and forces to be employed against them had been determined at a daily meeting at AFHQ.[220] At the insistence of Spaatz and his chief American intelligence officer, McDonald, these functions now shifted to HQ NAAF. Spaatz himself recorded in his diary the stand they took to ensure that NAAF became *the* operating air headquarters in Northwest Africa. Referring to a meeting on February 18, 1943, to discuss the responsibilities of MAC and NAAF, Spaatz recorded, "[the] position was taken that Northwest African Air Forces had to have all the intelligence functions that were essential for the control of operations. . . ."[221] McDonald established a full intelligence section incorporating combat intelligence, target intelligence, POW interrogations, counterintelligence, Y-Service, and ULTRA.[222] To this organization went the responsibilities for monitoring the condition and activities of enemy air forces, providing intelligence inputs to target selection, preparing and disseminating intelligence summaries and reports, handling capture intelligence (POW reports), and coordinating photoreconnaissance requests and results.[223] NAAF undertook to produce its own target materials. Before the invasion, HQ AAF A–2 had compiled a "considerable volume of target information" judged "of the highest practical usefulness."[224] The airmen now found that objective folders and target charts from Washington were "of little value for they are too broad and general" or arrived too late because emphasis had been placed on appearance at the expense of information and timeliness.[225]

The Allies intended the Intelligence Division of NAAF to be the centerpiece of air intelligence in the theater. It maintained liaison with G–2, AFHQ, for signals intelligence on enemy air signals traffic and the Air Interrogation Center in Algiers for POW-generated intelligence. The division also coordi-

---

Maj. Gen. James Doolittle, despite its designation as a "strategic air force," in actuality conducted interdiction and counterair operations through attacks on enemy shipping and port facilities and airfields in Tunisia, Sicily, Sardinia, and the Italian mainland. While the RAF contributed two Wellington squadrons, the core of NASAF was XII Bomber Command. In the course of these reorganizations, Twelfth Air Force was relegated to an appendage of NAAF; most of its people were absorbed into the latter's staff.

nated photoreconnaissance requests and operations with the NAPRW. While dissemination of intelligence to subordinate commands was an essential function of NAAF A–2, inadequate quantities of materials, poor communications, and perhaps an overriding orientation toward providing information up the chain resulted in significant problems. Reports from operational groups and squadrons in February and March contained frequent complaints that the units were receiving neither specific target information nor general intelligence on enemy forces. On at least one occasion, the 97th Bomb Group had embarked on a mission with no intelligence other than target coordinates.[226] Of particular importance to fighter units was the lack of materials for aircraft recognition training, a weakness on which more than one observer commented as late as May.[227]

Reinforcing the perception that A–2's attention was focused on its internal responsibilities within NAAF headquarters were the observations of Lt. Col. P. M. Barr, chief of the HQ AAF A–2 Operational Intelligence Division. Barr spent from mid-February to early April 1943 on an extensive inspection of American and Allied air intelligence units from AFHQ to AAF squadrons in the field. His report was a model of clarity, comprehensiveness, and lessons to be learned. According to Barr, the potential usefulness of the NAAF Intelligence Division "was reduced by distance from the front, preoccupation with administrative detail, lack of personal contact with the forward groups, [and] poor communications. . . ."[228] Although his recommendations that the number of operational intelligence personnel be significantly reduced and that they be moved to forward positions were not acted upon at the time (perhaps because the campaign ended shortly thereafter), subsequent observers noted qualitative improvements in the dissemination of air intelligence.* Referring to the last weeks of the campaign, several U.S. Navy intelligence officers reported "a well integrated round circle system is apparent [lower echelons to headquarters and back]. . . no lower echelon can function without it."[229]

Two vehicles that NAAF employed to improve intelligence dissemination were the *Daily Intelligence Summary* and the *Weekly Intelligence Report*. The first of these presented very condensed summaries of enemy air and ground situations and activities, but their primary focus was on updating objective folder data based on visual observations and photointerpretation reports. The weekly report addressed the enemy situation in greater detail, including OB, airdrome status, and losses, as well as reviewing Allied air operations. Particularly useful was the technical and tactical intelligence in these reports.[230] Providing a detailed description of the new FW 190, the report of March 15, 1943, described it as "a major technical advance over earlier radial-engined

---

*Barr's suggestions corresponded very closely with the arrangement Spaatz and McDonald would establish for Advanced Headquarters, United States Strategic Air Forces in Europe, when they moved to France in the fall of 1944.

Building an Air Intelligence Organization

fighters." Two weeks later, the report gave a description of the He 177, including photos and data on wing configuration and loading, armament, fuel capacity, and speed. The Me 323 transport, which would become a primary target in the later stages of the campaign, was introduced in a weekly report on February 23 as "really a glider with engines." Equally valuable was the information on trends in enemy tactics. As early as December 5, 1942, the *Weekly Intelligence Summary* for Twelfth Air Force warned that enemy fighters in France were reported to be engaging B–17s in frontal attacks. Later NAAF reports included comments from *Luftwaffe* POWs on tactics debates within German fighter units.[231]

In contrast to the inefficiencies found at A–2, NAAF, Colonel Barr judged intelligence at NASAF to be "very thoroughly organized, [and] in close touch with subordinate groups. . . ." While administrative and reporting duties were not neglected, they were not allowed to interfere with "the essential and primary duty" of providing Maj. Gen. James H. Doolittle, his staff, and his group commanders "up-to-date evaluated information on the disposition, defenses, tactics, and targets of the enemy."[232] (Doolittle's appreciation of intelligence would be further reflected in 1944 when he would insist on having an ULTRA representative assigned to Eighth Air Force.)

The period from January 1943 until the final surrender of Axis forces in North Africa reflected the versatility and flexibility of air power. Within the broad objectives assigned by higher headquarters, Spaatz and his subordinate commanders switched their focus to meet the changing theater situation by striking airfields and ports in Tunisia, ships at sea, and ports and airfields in Sicily, Sardinia, and Italy. Weather, force size, developments in the ground war, and logistics all influenced the expanding air activity, but essential to its success was timely, accurate, and comprehensive intelligence. To obtain this intelligence, air commanders called upon a wide range of capabilities that included photoreconnaissance, agent reports, POW interrogations, aircrew reports, radio intercepts, and ULTRA.

Combat experience quickly revealed that the command's basic need in planning and operations was regular aerial photography of proposed targets. Urged on by Spaatz and Air Vice Marshal Arthur Coningham, commander of NATAF, General Eisenhower pleaded with the British Chiefs in January 1943 for additional photoreconnaissance capability, asserting that high-performance reconnaissance was "absolutely essential" in the effort to reduce enemy lines of communication into Tunisia.[233] At an air commanders' conference two months later, Spaatz stressed that regular reconnaissance over the Sicilian straits and the Tyrrhenian Sea was key to an effective antishipping campaign, whereby the Allies would deny supplies and reinforcements to Axis forces in North Africa. Noting that photoreconnaissance missions were already being flown over the Italian port cities of Genoa, Leghorn, Taranto, Bari, and Naples, Doolittle said he was prepared to launch heavy bombers within six hours when photographs identified appropriate targets.[234] At a similar meeting on February 19, Coningham linked photoreconnaissance to the allocation of scarce resources; he argued for preattack reconnaissance to avoid launching missions against airfields that no longer held enemy aircraft.[235]

The initial period of growing pains caused by inexperienced operators, inadequate equipment, and poor staff arrangements soon passed. Intercepted GAF radio transmissions sent in the clear (i.e., uncoded) or via low-grade code or cryptography soon became the norm.[236] Because the Allies had not properly planned a defensive radar-warning net in North Africa, such interceptions provided the only tactical warning of incoming *Luftwaffe* raids for some time.[237] Y-Service correlation of R/T intercepts with other sources such as radar and ULTRA not only warned of attack but also gave valuable information on enemy tactics, disposition of air patrols, and even morale. Axis radio transmissions studied over extended periods increased knowledge of the enemy. Because the importance of radio interception had not been adequately appreciated in American air intelligence planning, British Y-Service detachments served American headquarters such as XII Air Support Command.[238]

POW interrogations yielded a wealth of information. Interrogation of POWs and investigation of their downed aircraft provided maps and charts depicting projected Axis attacks, locations of active airfields, maintenance and repair capabilities, status of the *Luftwaffe*'s training programs, technical capabilities of its equipment, tactical developments, and the condition of Axis morale. In one case, Allied intelligence acquired an instruction manual for the He 177, complete with photographs.[239] Captured documents also revealed that the German high command and the GAF had *increased* the training of fighter pilots.[240]

In contrast to western Europe, ULTRA played a crucial role in the air war in North Africa from the very beginning because it was the best developed of all sources and methods from the time of the Allies' initial landings. It was largely ULTRA that indicated the enemy had misread the invasion force's destination. This source became no less important once the opposing forces were engaged. In terms of air warfare, ULTRA offered a treasure house of information. "We had," admitted Group Captain R. H. Humphreys, the senior ULTRA officer at NAAF, "advance timing of every intention and move of the German Air Force in Africa and Italy, and as many moves and intentions of Italian forces as fell into joint Italo-German programmes."[241] ULTRA'S insights matched to Y-Service reports allowed Allied commanders to eavesdrop on damage reports from enemy airdromes. This led to a full understanding of the effectiveness of their attacks and to suggestions of when and where to repeat them.[242]

The picture ULTRA provided on Axis shipping was at least as valuable as its dissection of the GAF. So effective had BP become by this third winter of the war that, together with SIS reports and photoreconnaissance, Eisenhower, Tedder, and their staffs had a virtually complete record of the shipping between

Building an Air Intelligence Organization

Tunis, Bizerta, Italy, and Sicily, often down to the cargoes of individual vessels.[243] ULTRA's reports on the daily supply situation of German ground and air forces gave commanders like Doolittle an almost unparalleled luxury in selecting air interdiction targets.

Considering the apparently all-pervasive nature of ULTRA, one must resist the temptation to ascribe Allied victory in North Africa to this source alone. ULTRA was a unique means of looking inside the enemy's command structure and his logistical apparatus. But this capability, invaluable as it was, did not itself guarantee the outcome. ULTRA was most useful when it could be combined with one of the many other sources of intelligence to corroborate, confirm, explain, or establish a link between seemingly disparate pieces of a puzzle. Group Captain Humphreys stressed in his postwar evaluation that the basis of Allied intelligence success had been "the comprehensive fusion of Intelligence from all sources, clarified by the powerful light cast upon the whole situation by 'U.'"[244]

As the lack of Allied progress from November through February demonstrated, even the best intelligence could not replace inadequate planning and force employment. The very uniqueness of this source limited its immediate tactical value, especially in the antishipping campaign. To prevent the enemy from realizing that his high-level messages were being read, commanders approved no mission unless it could be explained by a solidly plausible second source of which the enemy should have been reasonably aware. No ship could be attacked unless the enemy would be able to understand the attack on some basis other than the possible compromise of encrypted messages. One of the values of reconnaissance was that it provided this second alternative source. Even so, commanders with access to ULTRA information could not send too many reconnaissance flights directly to specific locations identified by ULTRA. Most ULTRA targets were covered with general missions not limited to these specific locations. Naval surface forces and fighter sweeps operated within the same parameters.[245]

Despite these elaborate precautionary deceptions, the increasing effectiveness of the interdiction campaign eventually raised serious questions in the minds of some enemy commanders. In March 1943, Field Marshal Albrecht Kesselring charged recent convoys had been "betrayed to the enemy." As evidence, he pointed out that Allied heavy bombers had recently appeared north of Bizerta just as a convoy was transiting that area, and an Allied surface force turned up where no enemy activity had been observed "for weeks."[246] Fortunately for the Allies, the Germans were so confident of the security of their Enigma machine that they concluded after investigation that Italian forces had inadvertently leaked information. Rommel especially seems to have been predisposed to accuse the Italians of duplicity. His and similar attitudes very possibly hampered any attempt at hardheaded countermeasures.[247] Shortly before his death, in his notes of his campaigns, Rommel speculated on the source of British knowledge of German plans to attack in Egypt on or about August 25, 1942. Neither Rommel nor anyone else followed the question forcefully.

As with any source of intelligence, ULTRA was only as good as those who used it. Possession of ULTRA material did not necessarily result in its proper interpretation. For example, knowledge of the opposing air and ground OB convinced Allied commanders that the enemy would remain on the defensive as the new year opened. Having thus attributed to the Germans a course of action which stemmed from their own interpretation of the right thing to do, ULTRA possessors were ill prepared for the series of offensive thrusts that began in late January and culminated in the near disaster at Kasserine Pass.[248] In this instance, concurrent changes in the Axis command structure had muddied the intelligence picture. It reflected once more the danger of neglecting the possibility that the enemy's analysis of his capability and of the overall situation might lead him to courses of action wholly different from those anticipated. Consequently, developments in January–February 1943 illustrate the important point that throughout the war ULTRA almost always provided better information on the German enemy's quantitative status rather than providing insight into German enemy commanders' intentions.

In the early weeks of TORCH, the primary contribution of the Allied air forces was close air support for advancing ground forces and airfield attacks to reduce the enemy's buildup. Doolittle's American Twelfth Air Force had played only a small part in the TORCH invasion. Subsequently concentrated in western Algeria and Morocco in anticipation of possible Axis operations from Spain, the Twelfth had not been heavily involved in the initial eastward thrust. The rapid German buildup and the shift of American ground forces to the southern flank of the Allied line pulled American air units east.

The need to slow the insertion of Axis units and supplies into Tunisia led to attacks on enemy ports in Africa. Through the winter of 1942 and spring of 1943 these initial efforts at interdiction evolved into one of air power's major roles in North Africa. With NATAF concentrating on defensive and offensive support for ground operations, the heavy and medium bombers and their escorts of the NASAF pursued their responsibility for interdiction of Axis sea, land, and air lines of communication and supply to and from Tunisia.[249] Heavy and medium bombers as well as A–20s, DB–7s, and P–38s hit Tunisian ports in December, but the increasing density of enemy defenses drove the attackers to higher altitudes and eventually limited these strikes to the B–17s and B–24s. Although the heavies were not used exclusively in this role, they tended to focus on port facilities and vessels in port, whereas the medium bombers and their escorts sought out ships at sea.

Despite the advantages ULTRA provided, the antishipping campaign started slowly. Throughout the winter, bad weather made it difficult to launch the force, let alone to see and hit a target. Ships at sea proved difficult targets even when located. The initial Allied attacks compelled Kesselring to use convoys heavily protected by air cover and Siebel ferries which had been adapted to carry batteries of AA artillery. Just as Allied aircrews began to master air-to-sea operations, the Axis benefited from two developments that temporarily swung the advantage to their side: German occupation of Vichy France provided 450,000 additional tons of shipping, including desperately needed oil tankers, and Rommel's withdrawal from Tripolitania allowed the Axis to close the vulnerable run to Tripoli, which freed bottoms for the shorter, safer Sicily-to-Tunisia operation.[250]

The B–25s of NASAF initiated the aerial portion of the antishipping campaign on January 11, 1943, followed by the B–26s several days later. The first sinking did not occur until January 20. After several successful attacks, the medium bombers went from January 29 to February 9 without sinking an enemy merchant vessel. Another dry spell lasted from February 10th to 21st.[251] Improvements in the weather and an increasing skill at correlating intelligence and operational capability produced marked improvements. In March, the Axis stepped up the number of sailings, but the Allies destroyed, in port or at sea, 50 percent of these ships, this in contrast to the less than 20 percent rate of the previous month. American air forces were not solely responsible for these results; the extensive naval activity included two-thirds of the Royal Navy's submarines.[252]

Incorporating supply specialists into the targeting process allowed Doolittle to focus more specifically on critical cargoes, thus enhancing overall results. Here ULTRA was at its best. The sinking of the tanker *Thorsheimer* in late February, based on ULTRA guidance, accounted for 70 percent of the known Axis fuel shipment to Tunisia that month. The next month, again thanks to ULTRA, the Axis delivered only about one-third of the fuel requirements to the energy-starved German and Italian ground and air forces.[253]

While the medium bombers took to sea, B–17s and B–24s concentrated on the ports, attacking ships and destroying unloading equipment and storage facilities. Through January and February, the focus of these attacks was Tunis and Bizerta. By mid-March, having begun to drive the Axis to shallower vessels at smaller ports and eventually to over-the-beach operations, NASAF reached into Sicily and Sardinia. In the meantime, B–24s of the Ninth Air Force operating from Tripoli bombed targets in Italy and Sicily, including ferry slips and equipment, submarine bases, and port facilities.[254] Apparently tipped off by an RAF reconnaissance report, Ninth launched three attacks against Catania. Demonstrating the relative and at times quixotic nature of precision bombing, the attackers severely damaged port facilities, but they failed to sink the tanker that was their principal target.[255]

In addition to their interdiction role against enemy shipping, Allied air forces continued to operate against enemy air capabilities with both the NASAF and the NATAF. Using ULTRA as well as visual means and photoreconnaissance, they concentrated on offensive strikes against Axis airfields as the most effective means to achieve air supremacy. When RAF Middle East passed on intelligence that the *Luftwaffe* was concentrating aircraft at a single field at Castel Benito, XII Bomber Command struck with thirteen B–17s and a heavy P–38 escort and claimed 14 enemy aircraft destroyed, 3 probably destroyed, and 1 damaged. A similar attack on El Aouina four days later resulted in 12 aircraft destroyed, 19 damaged, and an ammunition dump exploded.[256]

During Eighth Army's attack on the German-held Mareth Line in southern Tunisia, NATAF focused its entire effort on Axis airfields to free the Western Desert Air Force (the British component of NATAF), allowing it to concentrate on ground support missions.[257] When visual reconnaissance showed the enemy in full daytime retreat, the Allied tactical air forces quickly shifted focus. On April 7 fighters destroyed more than 200 motor vehicles; a similar effort followed the next day, before bad weather provided the retreating forces with natural cover. By the middle of March, the enemy offered little air opposition. Axis fighters that remained in Tunisia were increasingly dedicated to sporadic attacks on Allied ground forces.[258]

While NATAF concentrated on Tunisian airfields, the NASAF'S heavy bombers were at work against enemy airfields outside Tunisia. Based largely on information from ULTRA, supplemented by photoreconnaissance and agent reports, Doolittle's men raided airfields around Palermo and elsewhere in Sicily. By April, NASAF shifted its attention primarily to bases in Sicily, Sardinia, and Italy.[259] In part, these efforts were preparations for Operation HUSKY, the upcoming amphibious assault on Sicily. They had another purpose as well. With Allied air and surface forces strangling the movement of supplies by sea, the Axis turned increasingly to air transport. German airlift became a new priority for air operations. On April 4th, for example, a large-scale attack by B–17s against Capodichino airdrome destroyed or damaged 25 of the 50 transport aircraft caught on the ground.[260]

The most spectacular single strike against the air shuttle effort occurred in early April. In mid-March, in preparation for a massive operation designed to destroy transports and their escorts in the air and on the ground, NASAF intelligence began monitoring Axis air transport movements across the Straits of Sicily to Tunis. ULTRA provided information on cargo, routes, timing, departure and arrival airfields, and defensive measures. Y intercepts contributed details on tactical control and procedures. These were supplemented by weather and photoreconnaissance missions, reports from bomber and fighter crews, and POW interrogations. Routine strikes continued, but the Allied commanders made special efforts not to tip off the enemy to the impending blow.

NASAF launched Operation FLAX on April 5th. Throughout the day, 287 sorties by B–17s, B–26s, and P–38s attacked enemy transports and their escorts, dropped fragmentation bombs on airfields in Sicily and Tunisia, and even damaged a merchant convoy. At a cost of 6 aircraft, NASAF claimed 201

Building an Air Intelligence Organization

enemy aircraft, 161 of them caught on the ground.[261] Although German records identify about half that number, even this lower figure would represent a major blow to an air force already reeling. Nor was this the only coordinated strike of its kind. NASAF executed smaller versions of FLAX the next week. Meanwhile, the Western Desert Air Force had established a radar net over the Cape Bon Peninsula and relied on it to vector fighters against Axis air transports, which suffered heavy losses several days' running. When the tactical air forces downed all 21 Me 323s in a single convoy on April 22d, the Germans ceased daylight air transport operations.[262]

Air power had been a decisive factor in the Allied victory in North Africa, and intelligence, in its several forms, had been critical to that success. At command levels, ULTRA offered insights into the enemy's perspective of the invasion and then enabled Allied leaders to monitor enemy responses. Throughout the campaign it provided information of enemy capabilities and vulnerabilities attainable in no other way, and it was instrumental in guiding the interdiction and counterair campaigns of the NASAF and the NATAF.

While ULTRA was indispensable to command decisions, in tactical execution, other forms of intelligence came into their own and, as the campaign progressed, were used more effectively. Among these, photoreconnaissance was the most obvious; its development illustrates the interrelatedness of ULTRA with other sources. Intercepted messages might reveal movement times and general locations of targets, but mission planners and operators needed precise configurations of target facilities and exact locations (e.g., of ships in harbor) if they were to achieve maximum results with each mission. Similarly, the tactical and technical information on enemy tactics and capabilities provided by crash investigation and POW interrogation were essential to effective air-to-air combat.

One of the most overlooked but important evolutionary steps in air intelligence in North Africa involved the mechanics of the collection, evaluation, and dissemination processes. The shift in targeting from AFHQ to NAAF and its commands, like improvements in the dissemination of intelligence to combat groups and squadrons, reflected growing awareness of the importance of intelligence in air operations at all levels. How this new understanding would translate into operations over the Continent remained to be seen.

CHAPTER 4

The European Theater of Operations, 1943–1945

BY THE SPRING OF 1943, the war in Europe had changed considerably since the Eighth Bomber Command cadre had landed in England. The two-pronged Allied offensive from the Western Desert and the Atlantic Ocean had cleared the Axis from North Africa and prepared the way for the invasion of Sicily. The German *Sixth Army* had surrendered at Stalingrad, and the Red Army had begun what would be its inexorable push westward. At sea, the battle for the Atlantic had turned in favor of the Allies.

That the winter of 1942–1943 had marked the turning was not so obvious at the time as it has become in hindsight. Control of the Atlantic, for instance, had already changed hands several times, and there was no guarantee it would not do so again. Despite the Red Army's victory at Stalingrad, its offensive capability and the intentions of the Soviet dictator, Joseph Stalin, remained unknown. Nowhere did the Grand Alliance have as much as a toehold on the European continent. Not until August, with Italy showing signs of dropping out of the war, would the Americans agree to postpone the cross-channel invasion in favor of continued Mediterranean operations. The decision to invade the Italian mainland after Sicily ensured that Allied forces would remain engaged in the Mediterranean beyond the summer of 1943. Moreover, the western Allies, particularly the United States, could not focus their full attention and resources on Europe, for they were engaged in an equally desperate and undecided struggle throughout the Pacific and Asia.

American airmen would enter the second half of the war with extensive experience in both strategic and tactical operations. Deficiencies in tactical command and control arrangements had been corrected in North Africa, and the new system for air-ground cooperation would prove its worth first in the Mediterranean and later in northwest Europe. In the Mediterranean area, the success of the intensive counterair campaign led to German withdrawal of fighter units from southern and then central Italy in the fall of 1943. From this time forward, Allied tactical air forces concentrated primarily on interdiction and close air support. Even the American Fifteenth Air Force, established in

Piercing the Fog

November 1943 to provide another arm of the strategic air campaign against the Third Reich, flew 53 percent of its missions against German lines of communication.[1] The combined air commands established in North Africa would continue throughout the war, only changing their names from Northwest African to Mediterranean when they moved to Italy. They would continue to provide policy and overall guidance, while each nation's tactical air forces generally provided direct support to their own ground armies.

In the strategic air war against Germany, the spring of 1943 saw the initiation of the CBO. Based in the first instance on the report of the COA as amended by the Eaker Plan, in practice the American daylight strategic bombing campaign would continue to be influenced by operational considerations such as force size, weather, and the unanticipated strengthening of the German air defenses. The most important organizational development in the strategic air war was the creation in December 1943 of the USSTAF. Under the command of Lt. Gen. Carl A. Spaatz, HQ USSTAF was to provide coordination and centralized control to both Eighth and Fifteenth Air Forces. Despite this reorganization, Anglo-American political and military leaders clearly viewed the strategic bombing campaign as an adjunct to land force operations against Germany. This relationship was underscored in the spring of 1944 when the CCS placed strategic as well as tactical air forces under the operational control of the Supreme Allied Commander for Operation OVERLORD—the amphibious assault on the continent.

Technologically, the most important event in this period was the arrival of the long-range P–51 escort fighter. The impact was magnified by the simultaneous arrival of enough heavy bombers to inflict serious damage on German targets day after day instead of only several days a month. The first result of this combination was the reduction of the *Luftwaffe* from being capable of preventing effective attacks on selected targets to being a serious nuisance. In the same period the oil industry was finally recognized by Allied decision makers as the most critical element of the enemy's industrial and military potential.

The full impact of this recognition and these new operational capabilities would be delayed by two diversions imposed from above. The first was General Eisenhower's decision directing the strategic bombers to focus on German transportation networks in France and the Low Countries in support of OVERLORD. The second was the emphasis placed on destruction of the German V-weapons. While some strategic missions continued to be flown against targets in Germany, it was not until the autumn of 1944 that the full weight of American daylight bombing would fall upon the German oil industry. Even then, a large percentage of strategic missions were directed against targets selected for their near-term impact on the ground situation. The introduction of German jet aircraft, although raising serious concern when American airmen realized the war would not end in 1944, came too late to have any practical effect.

The Allied landing on the coast of France had opened a new phase in the air war in northwest Europe. Despite concerns regarding the capability of the *Luftwaffe,* preinvasion identification of airfields and monitoring of enemy air movements nullified this threat. By summer, the GAF presence facing the western Allies was greatly diminished; much of the GAF was committed to the air defense of the Reich or to operations on the eastern front. Allied tactical air forces could concentrate on interdiction and close air support virtually unopposed in the air.

For air intelligence, what was perhaps most significant about the European theater was that there were several distinct air wars being waged there. Initially, these consisted of a tactical one in the Mediterranean and a strategic one from the United Kingdom. With the implementation of Operation OVERLORD, and especially after the breakout in July 1944, there developed yet a third air war. This was also an air-to-ground war, but one that called for support of fast-moving armored units in contrast to the grinding push up the Italian peninsula. The importance of these distinctions is that the intelligence requirements and, therefore, the intelligence organizations differed significantly. The range of demands made on air intelligence directly paralleled the types and complexity of operations the several air forces were called upon to execute. The sources upon which intelligence drew varied as well. The last two years of the war witnessed a maturation of intelligence analysis and application in a process initiated before the summer of 1943, which matched the evolution of the command structures. The most noticeable change in American air intelligence in this period was the incorporation of Americans into the ULTRA system. Coincidental with this was the growing role of ULTRA in overall air intelligence. With or without ULTRA, successful air intelligence depended upon the fusion of the full array of potential sources.

Mediterranean Theater: 1943–1945

For a year after the victory in North Africa, air operations in the Mediterranean theater and the demands made on air intelligence remained significantly different from those in the United Kingdom. During most of the first two years of USAAF operations, American airmen in England focused almost solely on strategic air operations without having to concern themselves with tactical support for land forces. In contrast, from the beginning of Operation TORCH, support for ground operations remained the principal function of Allied air forces in the Mediterranean.

When the Allied high command decided to invade Sicily (Operation HUSKY, begun July 9, 1943), Allied air forces, especially the NASAF, were heavily involved in the neutralization of Axis air power and in interdiction. NASAF was already directing its full attention across the Mediterranean when the Axis forces in Tunisia surrendered in May 1943. Since operations in support of HUSKY involved targets long since made familiar in repeated attacks, the role of intelligence was to focus on those targets most directly related to the coming invasion.[2]

On June 4, 1943, the air intelligence section of Force 141 (the planning organization for HUSKY) prepared a paper for NAAF's A-2 entitled "Bombing of Communications—(In Support of Army Operations)." The paper focused on the vulnerable points in Sicily's road and railway systems, whose destruction would delay enemy movements during the assault phase. It contained a detailed discussion of individual targets with maps and annotated photographs.[3] Using this information, updated primarily by photoreconnaissance and Y intercepts, NASAF and Ninth Air Force flew between June 18 and 30 almost 1,000 sorties against supply areas, terminal ports, and marshaling yards in Sicily and along the west coast of Italy, as well as in Sardinia and Corsica.[4]

Allied commanders and their planners believed command of the air was a prerequisite to a successful assault on Sicily. Air intelligence had not only to determine the strength and capability of the opposing force, but also to suggest how best to defeat it. Estimates of Axis air strength fluctuated in the weeks preceding the invasion. The original plan for HUSKY, prepared in March 1943, assumed a total *Luftwaffe* force of 1,200 aircraft in the theater by the end of April, of which some 840 would be in the Sicily-Sardinia-Pantelleria region. By May, estimates stood at 695 in the central Mediterranean area. A week before the landing, the air intelligence staff of the British JIC, using ULTRA-provided figures, arrived at an estimate of 990 German aircraft when, in fact, there were 960. Based primarily on low-grade SIGINT, the British accurately assessed an Italian strength of approximately 700 aircraft of all types.[5] To assist in the reduction of this threat, NAAF intelligence in May identified "the principal targets (i.e., airfields, assembly points, and factories) which, if destroyed, would contribute to the neutralization of the enemy air force operating in Italy, Sardinia, and Sicily."[6] The targets NASAF bombers and fighter-bombers struck over the next three months coincided with those laid out in the intelligence study, modified daily throughout the course of Operation HUSKY as new information became available.

To prepare for HUSKY, the Allies established a small combat intelligence staff to handle only the most critical intelligence aspects at a combined MAC-NAAF command post at La Marsa. The monitoring of the Axis air forces during HUSKY provides an excellent example of how an intelligence picture can be built up through a coordination of its constituent parts. According to Group Captain Humphreys, the chief intelligence officer of MAC, who headed the command post intelligence unit, "'U' kept us very fully informed of . . . [the] frequent re-dispersal of G.A.F. units." At the same time, he stressed, "the very closest ... coordination of 'U,' 'Y,' and Photo Recce sources was necessary. . . ."[7]

British and American flyers photographed daily, sometimes twice a day, airfields on Sicily and Italy, with the results of their efforts used to confirm information acquired by ULTRA or Y. For example, while ULTRA picked up the order for GAF units to withdraw from Sicily and move up the lower part of Italy under pressure of Allied air strikes, it was the Y-Service that tracked virtually every aircraft movement. This information guided photoreconnaissance missions that, by confirming the arrival of enemy units at rear bases, provided the information necessary to direct attacks on these installations.[8] Y-Service intercepts discovered at least one airfield.

Of particular importance for operational planning was the analysis intelligence provided on the enemy's air defense systems. Information on the German radar network and flak defenses came from aircraft called ferrets designed to carry equipment analyze radar capabilities. The AAF's first ferret aircraft in the Mediterranean were B–17s modified to be electronic intelligence collection aircraft, as based on extensive work being done at the Naval Research Laboratory in Washington, D.C., and at the AAF's Aircraft Radio Laboratory at Wright Field, Ohio. By the fall of 1943, three such aircraft were on station in the region. Each carried directional antennas and a series of receiver sets that allowed it to monitor the frequencies used by a variety of German early warning and gun control radars. With this equipment, the aircrews could plot the location of radars associated with enemy air defenses. The intelligence staff also used the results of Y-Service monitoring of radio transmissions, of pilot debriefings, and of photointerpretation.[9] By June 1943, according to the chief Y officer, the Allies were "fully conversant with all the activities of the enemy's early warning system, its extent and efficiency, and the strength and location of any opposition likely to be encountered. . . ."[10] This knowledge allowed intelligence to recommend to operations the best routes to and from targets to avoid enemy defenses. It was also used to knock out elements of that defensive system, including AA batteries and fighters as well as radar. It also allowed for effective jamming on the proper frequencies, while concurrent Y intercepts indicated the success of such jamming.[11]

Even allowing for the fact that the Germans by this point in the war considered the Mediterranean a secondary war front, the wide-ranging Allied knowledge of Axis air operations and air defenses was remarkable. This understanding allowed a range of military options that the Allies could use to their distinct advantage. The influence of intelligence on planning could clearly be seen as HUSKY drew near. Between June 15 and July 7, 1943, Allied air forces conducted fourteen different raids against portions of the German air defense network. As a result of these attacks, Colonel McDonald concluded in his after-action report, "The enemy's radar defenses in Sicily were crippled to the extent that the south and southwest sections of the island [from which direction the assault forces came] were virtually unprotected."[12]

SIGINT continued to play an important role during the invasion. Beginning on July 10, Y-Service broadcast reports every half hour on enemy aircraft movements to new fields, the arrival of reinforcements, enemy sightings of Allied ships, forecasts of likely targets, airfield serviceability, and unit status reports. By monitoring enemy fighter frequencies, Y-Service not only provided alerts to attacking aircraft but often included the number of attackers, direction of attack, and altitude.[13]

As in most campaigns, the contribution of air intelligence in the invasion of Sicily cannot be measured precisely, particularly since the degree of theater air superiority the Allies now held would, at the least, have insured against defeat. Group Captain Humphreys was essentially correct when he suggested after the war that the "extremely close co-operation between Operations and Intelligence" certainly contributed to the withdrawal of the *Luftwaffe* "at an early date, in the hope of living to fight the battle of Italy."[14]

The Allied decision to continue operations in the Mediterranean after HUSKY—to engage in a battle for Italy—represented a significant shift in strategy. Although the British had contemplated for some time the strategic value of continued activity in this theater, the JCS had opposed such proposals as serving only to delay what they considered the decisive European operation: a cross-channel invasion into the heart of Fortress Europe. During the spring of 1943, however, the Chief of Naval Operations had accepted further Mediterranean operations.[15] In the summer, new intelligence regarding the German aircraft industry persuaded a reluctant General Arnold to shift his position as well.

Arnold had opposed any, let alone more, operations in the Mediterranean because he feared they would draw resources from the United Kingdom and his CBO.[16] Not surprisingly, his RAF counterpart, Air Marshal Charles Portal, had been only halfhearted in his support of this issue for the same reasons. Increasing evidence, first provided through ULTRA, of German decisions to increase production of single-engine fighters (which actually began in March 1943) led both airmen to reevaluate their positions. Most of these aircraft factories lay in southern Germany, out of reach of bombers based in the United Kingdom but well within range of airfields in northern Italy.

In late July 1943, Portal directed his liaison officer in Washington to point out to Arnold ULTRA evidence that suggested factories at Regensburg and Wiener-Neustadt "are now producing about 55% of all German single-engine fighters and further expansion is to be expected. . . ."[17] By early August the RAF representative in Washington could report: "Arnold . . . aware of the German fighter expansion . . . and of the locality of targets in Eastern Europe out of range of bombers based in England. His views are peculiarly like yours. . . . By using a bomber force from northern Italy, we will more easily be able to attack

The European Theater of Operations

the vital fighter aircraft factories."[18] By this time, the overthrow of Mussolini, on July 24, 1943, had made such an operation almost inevitable. Within days of Mussolini's fall, the Combined Chiefs approved General Eisenhower's plan for the invasion of Italy, Operation AVALANCHE, set for September 8–9.[19]

AVALANCHE marked no major break in an already established pattern for the employment of air forces and the intelligence necessary to support them. As with the step from North Africa to Sicily, the move to the mainland represented a continuation of what Allied air forces were already doing: maintaining command of the air and interdicting German efforts to resupply and reinforce ground combat units in central and southern Italy. One significant difference distinguished AVALANCHE from its predecessors: the counterair battle Allied air forces had been waging against the Axis for nearly a year was overwhelmingly successful. During the week prior to AVALANCHE, NASAF flew fifty missions; on only sixteen did it find GAF opposition.[20]

Instead of the intense counterairfield operations characteristic of the pre-HUSKY period, in late August and early September the Allies relied on SIGINT (both Y and ULTRA) and photoreconnaissance for guidance on hitting key airfields. Following reports of a GAF buildup around Salerno on September 14, B–17s, B–24s, and A–20s flew 700 sorties against fields identified by SIGINT and confirmed by photoreconnaissance. Five days later, Y-Service intercepts revealed an overcrowding of GAF bombers on fields around Foggia because of bad weather. Ninety-one P–38s backed by RAF Wellington bombers attacked the next morning, destroying 45 and seriously damaging another 17 enemy bombers.[21]

While providing positive intelligence by monitoring the buildup of enemy air forces at certain bases, SIGINT and photoreconnaissance combined to indicate areas that did not need to be attacked. Guided by SIGINT cues, photoreconnaissance missions over airfields in Sardinia in late August confirmed the evacuation of GAF units. Such knowledge allowed air planners to reallocate resources against more useful targets. In addition to the role of SIGINT in locating and monitoring enemy air units, ULTRA continued to indicate the effectiveness of the ongoing interdiction program as it created localized shortages that hampered GAF operations.[22]

The result of this aggressive and highly effective cooperation between operations and intelligence was the demise of the GAF in Italy. After Salerno, the German *Tenth Army* would demonstrate a tenacity on the defensive that made a mockery of early Allied expectations for Italy, but they would do so with virtually no air support. With the German high command's decision in October to transfer fighter forces to the eastern front (a decision picked up by ULTRA), the character of the air war in Italy changed dramatically.[23] So great was Allied command of the air over Italy that an American special security officer visiting Fifteenth Air Force in January 1944 could comment cavalierly that the *Luftwaffe* was so weak "[our] raids are naturally planned with little regard for the possible opposition."[24]

With the decline of the *Luftwaffe* and the slow advance of the Allied armies in Italy up the peninsula, "the story of air operations," as the official USAAF history observed, "tends to assume the aspect of a repetitious and monotonous routine."[25] In addition to providing close air support coordinated with ground force headquarters, Allied Tactical Air Force fighters and fighter-bombers concentrated on gun positions, road and rail bridges, vehicles, and bivouac areas along and close to the battle line, while fighter-bombers and medium bombers reached out to strike lines of communication and transportation networks.

For their part, the strategic air force's support for land operations would largely involve attacks against railways in central and northern Italy. Occasionally in the fall of 1943 and more so the following year, American heavy bombers participated in the CBO against Germany, primarily through attacks on aircraft factories and oil refineries. Although the Balkan Air Force would be largely a British organization, by the middle of 1944 American bombers flew numerous missions into the Balkans and southeastern Europe in support of the Soviet Army. To carry out this last type of operation more effectively, the Americans set up a base at Poltava, Russia, to and from which they conducted what was known as Operation FRANTIC. Despite the hopes of those who initiated it, FRANTIC remained a limited shuttle-bombing effort whose primary significance was to demonstrate how difficult it was to deal with the Soviets, even as allies.

In January 1944, now that Carl Spaatz was back in England to oversee both Eighth Air Force and Fifteenth Air Force as commander of USSTAF, Arnold sent Lt. Gen. Ira C. Eaker to command the MAAF, which had been established the previous month. As the theater air arm under the Supreme Allied Commander, Mediterranean Theater of Operations, MAAF, absorbed the old Northwest African Strategic, Tactical, and Coastal Air Forces, whose names were changed by the substitution of "Mediterranean" for "Northwest African." The commanders of Mediterranean Allied Tactical Air Force (MATAF) and Mediterranean Allied Strategic Air Force (MASAF) were Americans who doubled as the commanders of the dominant American organization within their respective air force. Maj. Gen. John K. (Jack) Cannon commanded MATAF and Twelfth Air Force, while Maj. Gen. Nathan Twining served as the commanding general of Fifteenth Air Force and of MASAF. Mediterranean Allied Coastal Air Force (MACAF) remained under the command of RAF Air Vice Marshal Hugh P. Lloyd.[26]

The most significant organizational changes occurred within the American air forces. Twelfth Air Force gave up its heavy bombers and became a tactical air force under MATAF. The recipient of these bomber units as well as others subsequently sent to the theater was Fifteenth Air Force. Fifteenth Air Force was to strike those targets beyond the reach of U.K.-based forces or those

Lt. Gen. John K. Cannon   Col. Karl L. Polifka

shielded by the poor flying weather that prevailed over much of northern and central Europe each winter.

Within MAAF, all operational units retained their national identity and received administrative and logistics support through national channels, with operational tasks coming from the respective Allied Air Force headquarters. The combined elements of HQ MAAF were limited to the operations and intelligence section and the signals section, whose relatively small staffs provided the operational ties between MAAF and the subordinate Allied air forces. The latter also consisted of small Anglo-American staffs superimposed upon national combat and support units.[27]

The intelligence section of MAAF may have been a combined organization, but it had a distinctly British flavor. The chief intelligence officer was British, as was the chief signals officer, while the deputy chief intelligence officer was the American Harris Hull, whom Eaker had brought with him from Eighth Air Force. As of the autumn of 1944, most intelligence officers were British, with the exception of the target subsection. Permanently assigned personnel were supplemented by individuals temporarily assigned to Italy from the Air Ministry Air Intelligence (Enemy Aircraft Production section), the MEW, and the American EOU for strategic targeting.[28] Primarily a policy and directive organization, HQ MAAF intelligence also retained control of elements that spanned the spectrum of air operations including photoreconnaissance and photointerpretation, technical intelligence, and interrogation of air POWs. The British influence within MAAF intelligence was reflected in the arrangements for handling ULTRA. Until the summer of 1944, Hull was the only American officer in A–2 cleared for ULTRA. In May 1944, the target subsection at HQ MAAF (Adv.) had no American officers indoctrinated to receive and handle ULTRA.[29]

In general, the MAAF intelligence office was primarily concerned with information accumulation and dissemination in the form of digests, appreciations, and special reports, rather than with analyzing intelligence for operational decision making, which was primarily done at the next lower level.[30]

Given the emphasis on targeting, particularly in relation to the interdiction campaign, it is not surprising that photoreconnaissance and photointerpretation assumed a high priority at all levels of Mediterranean air commands. An ULTRA observer in the summer of 1944 evaluated photoreconnaissance as "probably the most valuable source" of intelligence in this theater because it could advise on what targets to hit and assess the effectiveness of subsequent strikes. ULTRA not only could provide assistance on where to take aerial photographs, but often it could "enable one to exercise superior wisdom" in reading photos.[31]

The MAPRW, composed of Allied photoreconnaissance units and commanded by American Col. Karl Polifka, performed reconnaissance missions for all operational commands at the beginning of 1944. Before he departed the theater in January 1944, George McDonald, NAAF's A–2, had also established the Mediterranean Photo Interpretation Centre. Under HQ MAAF intelligence, the center contained land and air representatives who met regularly to establish policy and determine priorities for photoreconnaissance. As an indication of the expanded demands imposed by both air and land forces on photoreconnaissance and photointerpretation, the Mediterranean Photo Interpretation Centre eventually serviced as many as 120 distinct organizations.[32]

The SIGINT section at HQ MAAF had been formed originally as part of the MAC in March 1943 to control and direct all air organizations engaged in intercepting, processing, and distributing intelligence gathered from enemy low-grade SIGINT, radar, and navigational aids. American SIGINT units in the Mediterranean by spring 1944 included the 849th Company, Signal Intelligence Service, U.S. Army, and the 16th Reconnaissance Squadron, USAAF, whose mission was to fly the ferret aircraft to locate and intercept enemy radar and navigation aids for Allied exploitation. Operational flying units received SIGINT directly from a nearby signals unit or from the central MAAF signal intelligence section, which directly transmitted low-grade intelligence to a specific unit and issued periodic general and special reports.[33]

The air headquarters most intimately involved in the overall planning of interdiction operations was the MATAF. Because the tactical commands—XII TAC and Desert Air Force—worked directly with their respective land components (U.S. Fifth Army and British Eighth Army), MATAF's primary operational responsibility on a day-to-day basis was control of the medium bomber force which, by the summer of 1944, was almost entirely American. Because of this arrangement, the relationship between the intelligence sections in MATAF and Twelfth Air Force was highly complementary,[34] with MATAF intelligence responsible for providing current (combat) intelligence and target selection data. Although the organization was manned primarily by Americans, the deputy to the chief intelligence officer was the only American cleared to handle ULTRA in the summer of 1944.

Reflecting the importance of photoreconnaissance in the targeting process and the need for responsiveness in the execution and interpretation of tactical reconnaissance missions, the 3d Photo Reconnaissance Group (U.S. AAF) and the XII Air Force Photo Center came under the direct control of the chief intelligence officer of the MATAF in the spring of 1944.[35] By October 1944, Fifteenth Air Force and the MASAF had direct control over the U.S. AAF 15th Photo Group, reflecting a decentralization of photoreconnaissance and interpretation that mirrored the American rather than the British approach to the two functions.[36]

By summer 1944, the 3d Photo Reconnaissance Group had developed mosaics of all Italy east of 3.5 degrees longitude, and of practically every important railway and road. Coverage included annotated photos of principal lines of communication (including marshaling yards and bridges), ports, airfields, troop emplacements, gun positions, and ammunition dumps.[37] This extensive coverage would provide the basic intelligence upon which to plan and execute specific missions, augmented by SIGINT and human intelligence (HUMINT) reports. This complete target coverage would become increasingly important because MATAF would assume responsibility for all interdiction operations within Italy by the fall of 1944.

While MATAF carried out current intelligence and target selection and evaluation, Twelfth Air Force A–2 provided support in personnel and intelligence materials.*[38] The Twelfth Air Force A–2 served also as the deputy chief intelligence officer, MATAF, and spent much of his time at headquarters there.[39]

Through 1944, Twelfth Air Force headquarters had an operational intelligence section that focused on analysis and long-term studies and published intelligence summaries and special reports. A detailed study by this office of the Italian railway system and the alternative road network was incorporated into the planning for Operation STRANGLE two months later. In

---

*Indicative of how closely MATAF and Twelfth Air Force Intelligence were linked, the Twelfth Air Force history contains a section on "HQ, M.A.T.A.F., Intelligence Function" and consistently refers to MATAF Intelligence as "Advanced Headquarters" or "Advanced Operating Headquarters."

Piercing the Fog

November 1944, Twelfth Air Force intelligence officers interviewed Italian railway officials to obtain information on the location of transformer stations and the use of electric locomotives on the critical Brenner Pass line into Germany. This intelligence was incorporated into MATAF planning for Operation BOLERO, the American plan to build up forces in Great Britain for an early invasion of the Continent.[40]

An additional source for tactical air forces was the air section at HQ, Allied Armies in Italy (AAI). Using ULTRA, which was exceptionally comprehensive in monitoring German Army units, this section compiled lists of the enemy's land OB as well as assessed his supply and communications situations. The air section maintained photointerpretation reports; materials on airdromes and radar installations; flak reports; and card indexes on roads, railroads, bridges, and ports. OSS reports to the air section headquarters as well as to the tactical and strategic air forces headquarters proved especially valuable for air operations into the Balkans. Based on this intelligence, the HQ AAI air section recommended priorities of target systems and specific targets such as ammunition dumps, supply depots, and rail sections.[41]

In contrast to the organization of the tactical air forces, in which the Allied air headquarters played the dominant intelligence role, the American Fifteenth Air Force headquarters was the focal point for heavy bomber operations. This arrangement reflected the overwhelming preponderance of American bomber forces in the theater. Because of the commitment to the CBO, knowledge of the GAF OB and its capabilities was of greater significance for Fifteenth Air Force than it was for the tactical forces. Most intelligence work related to targeting: analyzing photographs, collating agent reports, studying the economic value of possible objectives, and evaluating bomb damage.[42] As a result of the Fifteenth's broad responsibilities, targets for the bombers ranged from bridges to marshaling yards, from oil refineries to aircraft factories, and from airfields to ammunition dumps. Compounding the normal difficulties of intelligence were conditions that made the Mediterranean theater unique. These included the number of different countries in the area of responsibility, the mix of Allied units involved in air operations, and the variety and number of sources of intelligence, which made correlation and analysis particularly challenging. Considering that Fifteenth Air Force intelligence received reports and information from some sixty-five agencies and staffs just within the theater, ULTRA'S greatest use was in the winnowing of information from other sources.[43]

The U.S. ULTRA representative at HQ Fifteenth Air Force evaluated his source's primary contribution as one of "negative influence." Most of the information received through ULTRA channels, he observed, was available in other sources (e.g., aerial photography, agent reports, or Y intercepts). The difference was that ULTRA lacked much of the incorrect information which the others contained. What ULTRA provided to the local liaison officer was the ability to advise his superiors "what *not* to rely on" from these other sources.[44]

The European Theater of Operations

Despite ULTRA's key role, in the spring of 1944 no one in the target section of Fifteenth Air Force headquarters was cleared to handle it. The special security officer, whose primary purpose was to monitor the enemy's air OB and handle ULTRA for the commanding general, frequently assisted headquarters personnel with his special wisdom, obtained as a result of his special access to sensitive material.[45] Later that summer, an indoctrinated officer joined the target section with responsibility to coordinate and blend ULTRA into other intelligence.

General strategic targeting guidance for Fifteenth Air Force was provided in directives from the Commanding General, USSTAF. Except for joint Eighth Air Force–Fifteenth Air Force operations, each air force commander had considerable leeway in selecting specific targets within the overall parameters. The heart of the intelligence assessment–planning–operations process at Fifteenth Air Force was the daily planning meeting (also called the targeting meeting) attended at 11 o'clock each morning by some thirty officers. Earlier in the day, the A–2 had met with members of his section to assess developments over the past twenty-four hours, review damage resulting from previous strikes, and select recommended targets in coordination with weather and operations. The A–3 generally chaired the 11 o'clock meeting in the capacity of a deputy for operations. After the weather officer outlined the areas available for operations, intelligence presented the recommended list of targets and the rationale for their selection. The ULTRA officer projected the probable GAF reaction under the guise of an enemy OB expert, and the flak officer addressed known concentrations of AA batteries. After detailed questions and answers, the A–3 made his decision and dictated an operations order. According to the Fifteenth Air Force's history, "In general, whenever there were reasonable prospects of success, the recommendations of A–2 were accepted."[46]

With the German decision to contend the length of the peninsula rather than to retreat northward and the Allied decision to focus on western Europe in 1944, the war in Italy became a slugging contest marked by skillful German defenses and slow Allied advances. Even before the first Allied infantryman came ashore at Salerno, airmen had recognized that the primary role of air power in this theater—after the GAF's defeat—would be interdiction. Bombing the lines of communication in Italy had been ongoing since the previous spring in support first of the North Africa campaign and then of Operation HUSKY. In June 1943, NAAF intelligence officers concluded, "Railroad targets as a category assume an importance second only to targets affecting the neutralization of the enemy air potential." The officers reasoned that if the Axis rail net was destroyed, "a collapse would be inevitable."[47] Between June 1943 and the end of the year, numerous diversions sidetracked the development of a systematic interdiction campaign. In a special intelligence report published the day before Christmas, Colonel McDonald provided what would be the thrust of air operations in Italy for the rest of the war. McDonald concluded that interdiction efforts to date had been relatively ineffective because they had lacked focus and thus a concentration of effort. Limited results underscored the need for "complete, simultaneous and continuous interdiction of rail traffic supplying the enemy forces in central Italy." Not content simply to suggest the need for a directed interdiction effort, McDonald identified six specific targets south of the La Spezia–Rimini line and recommended a schedule for attack based on his intelligence analysis.[48]

McDonald called the area south of the La Spezia–Rimini line the key to reducing the enemy's ground capability. The region had relatively few rail lines, and these contained vulnerable targets and potential bottlenecks. It was located at just the right distance from the combat zone to force the enemy to use military trucks, thereby reducing his logistic flow and forcing an increased consumption of valuable fuel. The region's relatively short distance from American air bases would allow the use of medium as well as heavy bombers for interdiction. Thus, McDonald concluded, this region should be the overriding objective of Allied interdiction efforts even if it meant neglecting other communication systems farther north in the Po Valley and across the Alps.

The creation of MAAF and the reassignment of Spaatz and McDonald to England in January 1944 did not alter the direction McDonald's paper had laid out. Operation STRANGLE, initiated in mid-March 1944, followed his recommendations closely. Subsequent interdiction campaigns, while gradually shifting ever northward, adhered to the same principles. Precisely how to conduct this interdiction campaign would prove contentious. It was also one in which intelligence—in the form of recommendations of methods and of postattack analysis leading to modifications of operational techniques—would play an important role.

The question of how best to attack the enemy's transportation network in Italy centered on whether it was more effective to concentrate on saturation bombing of marshaling yards or to focus more precise attacks on bottlenecks such as bridges and viaducts. The central figure in this debate was British professor Solly Zuckerman, a special advisor to Air Marshal Tedder who had acquired a reputation as a bombing genius because of somewhat fortuitous circumstances surrounding the Italian surrender of the island of Pantelleria in June 1943. In December 1943, Zuckerman prepared a paper advocating marshaling yards as the best targets within the Italian railway system. The basis for this position was his analysis of air operations in Sicily.[49] Shortly after he submitted this report, Zuckerman returned with Tedder to England, where the air marshal became Deputy Supreme Allied Commander for Operation OVERLORD. Zuckerman's ideas lingered.

In February 1944, Brig. Gen. Lauris Norstad, Eaker's director of operations at MAAF, forwarded to the deputy air commander-in-chief intelligence reports indicating that the Germans were getting some 85 percent of their supplies by rail. Citing the Zuckerman paper, Norstad pointed out that MAAF operations research studies concurred that bridges were not economical targets and supported Zuckerman's thesis that rail centers (i.e., marshaling yards) were

The aerial interdiction campaign known as Operation STRANGLE was waged the length of the Italian boot ahead of the slogging ground war. This railroad bridge *(above)* on the outskirts of Bologna became inoperative after being bombed. Four spans are down, with two more sagging. Lest the enemy air force be forgotten, a stick of bombs cratered the runway at Pisa. Completely destroyed was this railroad viaduct at Arezzo, where only a few stubs of supports remain.

Lt. Gen. Earle E. Partridge

more appropriate.[50] General Norstad was not listening to his intelligence analysts. Against the Zuckerman thesis were ranged not only Norstad's own target section at HQ MAAF but also the intelligence sections of Twelfth Air Force/MATAF and of AFHQ. One month before Norstad sent his letter, a Twelfth Air Force A–2 study of operations since the Sicily campaign (which it considered a special situation) had concluded, "Marshalling yards must now be conceded to be poor targets for the ends sought in the Italian Theater of Operations."[51] In early February a detailed OSS report on air operations between October and December 1943 reinforced the value of attacks on bridges: "The efficiency of bridge attacks in creating total blockage is . . . six to seven times greater than that of yard attacks."[52]

Nor were Allied assessments the only source for such conclusions. In mid-November, a captured member of the German General Staff in Italy stated during interrogation, "Bombing of communications in northern ITALY has had little effect on the supply situation." According to the report on this interrogation, except for two specific key yards "source does NOT believe that rail traffic in ITALY could be paralyzed by the bombing of selected marshalling yards" since trains were formed up in Germany and sent directly to *Tenth Army* units, without the need to be reformed or marshaled in Italy. Even after heavy attacks at rail centers, one or two military lines were generally reopened quite rapidly.

In place of marshaling yards, the captured officer listed six targets (four bridges, one rail junction, and one main station) for attack.*[53]

The interdiction principles McDonald had suggested in December 1943 were employed in a very limited geographical area in January and February 1944 in support of the Allied landing at Anzio. They were incorporated into a broader interdiction program with the initiation of Operation STRANGLE in March 1944. The extent of the employment of all elements of MAAF against German lines of communication were reflected in assessments of this network by the intelligence sections of each of the major Allied air headquarters as well as by the major operational units. Even before these plans, senior airmen had suggested what intelligence had to provide to plan and execute an effective interdiction campaign. As early as October 1943, Brig. Gen. Earle Partridge, Chief of Staff, XII Bomber Command, "urgently recommended" the accumulation of intelligence on the German supply situation in Italy as it related to rail facilities. He suggested such questions as Where did military traffic originate? What were the principal routes by which enemy supplies and reinforcements flowed into central Italy? and Where were the major railheads and depots?[54]

In response, HQ Twelfth Air Force A–2 prepared a "Suggested Plan for Making Impossible the Military Utilization of Italian Railways by the Enemy" dated January 15, 1944.[55] More limited analyses of lines of communication vulnerabilities flowed from HQ MAAF in weekly rail traffic assessments and from the 42d Wing (U.S. AAF) intelligence section.[56] In the preoperation planning for STRANGLE, the principal sources of information were photoreconnaissance, studies of the Italian railway system, and analyses of previous missions conducted against identified portions of the rail and road nets. These included Inter-Service Topographical Department reports on segments of the Italian railway, Photoreconnaissance Centre interpretation reports, conferences with officials of the Italian State Railway, economic analyses by EOU, and operational mission summaries.[57]

Despite the array of opposition, the initial STRANGLE directive adhered to the priority of marshaling yards over bridges. As the campaign progressed, the weight of assessed evidence, as reflected in periodic analyses compiled by intelligence and operations staffs, fell more and more on the side of the bridge theory.[58] By April 1, Eaker had concluded that bridges and viaducts had been found to be more useful targets than marshaling yards because they were more difficult to repair and presented more effective obstacles to movement when damaged.[59] Air assault by itself could not achieve complete interdiction.

By the last stages of STRANGLE, an OSS study concluded, "Even very effective attack on enemy supply lines will not produce results until the issue

---

*It seems likely Colonel McDonald had seen the results of this interrogation in December, since the prisoner's recommendations for an interdiction campaign in central Italy were mirrored in McDonald's special report of December 24, 1943.

is forced by assault." While air interdiction could not totally cut off lines of communication, the disruption caused by forcing the enemy to use improvised methods for moving his supplies appeared to put him in the position of being unable to respond adequately to increased pressures on the ground. The OSS report concluded: "Until the capacity of the enemy to supply and reinforce his troops in Italy has been tested . . . it can only be said that a vulnerability of unknown intensity has been established. . . ."[60]

Although Operation DIADEM—a major Allied land offensive launched May 11, 1944—succeeded in reaching Rome on June 2, the Germans were able to establish yet another defensive position across the peninsula. The process of air interdiction and slow, methodical land operations continued in Italy until the last weeks of the war. The pattern of air intelligence evidenced in STRANGLE remained largely unchanged. Intelligence determined the key nodes in the transportation networks within and leading into Italy, estimated the impact of their destruction or damage, and evaluated the effectiveness of operations conducted against them.

Photoreconnaissance remained the backbone of target folders and the primary basis for the initial selection of targets and for reattacks. Agent reports continued to suggest the frequency of rail and road movement and thus guided the selection of the most significant bottlenecks. ULTRA provided some guidance for specific attacks, primarily through indications of shortages or difficulties in getting supplies through. Given the nature of the numerous small targets that were the objectives of Twelfth Air Force/MATAF, many of these attacks were never reported through ULTRA channels. According to one ULTRA-indoctrinated observer, the real role of ULTRA lay at the policy rather than the operating level: ULTRA's most important contribution was in providing Allied commanders with the sense of how well air interdiction was accomplishing the task of cutting the enemy's supply lines.[61]

The organization and roles of air intelligence in the Mediterranean theater reflected both the structure of air commands in that theater and the evolving emphasis of air operations. The Allies made greater use of combined air commands in North Africa and Italy than they did when operating from the United Kingdom or in western Europe after June 1944. Air intelligence reflected this. The initial reliance on British experience continued to be evident in the composition of intelligence sections within Allied air headquarters; however, the growing preponderance of American forces made itself felt in several ways, such as in the prominence of Fifteenth Air Force over MASAF and in the number of American intelligence officers assigned to targeting sections in Allied air commands. At the tactical level, Twelfth Air Force not only remained responsible for the planning and conduct of operations by its subordinate units, but its intelligence staff was increasingly integrated with that of MATAF.

Air intelligence during operations in Sicily and Italy reflected experience in the acquisition and dissemination of intelligence gained during the campaign for North Africa. Operations from July 1943 onward demonstrated an integration of intelligence and a breadth of dissemination far superior to activities during TORCH and in the early months of 1943. In contrast to observations on the mishandling of air intelligence in North Africa, by the spring of 1944 observers reported smoothly functioning intelligence sections ranging from single individuals to elaborate organizations akin to small air ministries.

With the demise of the GAF in Italy, air intelligence focused almost entirely on interdiction and close air support. The major exception was the strategic role of the Fifteenth Air Force, much of whose intelligence came from BP and USSTAF, although A-2 did develop independent sources and conducted analyses based on their own requirements and perceptions. Intelligence for ground support missions continued to come from multiple sources. Twelfth Air Force's direct support for Fifth Army relied heavily on ground force information and photoreconnaissance in addition to ULTRA, which was extremely complete regarding the condition and location of the German Army in Italy. Interdiction missions were based on an ever-growing store of photographic intelligence (both for mission planning and poststrike analysis), Army and Air Force SIGINT, and ground observations (agent reports). ULTRA provided an appreciation of the overall effectiveness of the interdiction campaign and thus the impetus to continue the attacks.

Perhaps the most striking aspect of air intelligence and air operations in Italy was their limited impact. Despite the increasing sophistication and sheer size of intelligence organizations and their smooth functioning, air power was not in itself sufficient to secure victory in what was essentially a land war. Air intelligence may have been an integral part of the intelligence planning–operations process, but the overriding fact was that contemporary air power by itself could not win the dogged, dug-in type of war the enemy fought in Italy after the fall of 1943.

Strategic Air Operations in Europe: Spring 1943 to Spring 1944

The Casablanca Directive for Anglo-American strategic air operations in Europe had called for a complete reconsideration of the employment of Allied strategic air power. The report the COA submitted to Arnold on March 8, 1943, served as the catalyst for this reconsideration and the subsequent broad basis for the CBO. General Arnold instructed General Eaker, then commanding the Eighth Air Force, to evaluate the report and, modifying it as necessary, to develop a plan for implementing a strategic air campaign to so weaken Germany that an invasion of Europe would become possible. Eaker appointed a board of Eighth Air Force and RAF officers chaired by Brig. Gen. Haywood S. Hansell, Jr., now Commander, 1st Bombardment Wing, to execute this task.[62] In addition to Hansell, the board included Brig. Gen. Frederick L. Anderson (Commander, 4th Bombardment Wing), Air Commodore Sidney Bufton (Air Ministry Director of Bomber Operations), Col. Charles Cabell (Arnold's special assistant who had carried the report to England), Col. Richard Hughes (Eighth Air Force Chief of Plans and Targeting), two other Americans, and a British wing commander.[63]

The result of this group's deliberations, officially designated "The Combined Bomber Offensive from the United Kingdom" but commonly referred to as the Eaker Plan, was an amalgam of previous recommendations and plans modified by the perspective gained from operational exposure. Well aware of the strength of the *Luftwaffe* as an obstacle to *any* strategic bombing campaign, the planners inserted German fighter strength as an intermediate objective to be attacked previous to or simultaneously with operations against the primary objectives: i.e., German submarine yards and operating bases, the remainder of the German aircraft industry, ball-bearing plants, and oil fields (contingent upon the ability to attack the refineries at Ploesti, Romania). As secondary objectives, chosen because their locations outside Germany made them suitable for weather alternates and as break-in missions for new bomber crews, the board selected tire and rubber production facilities.[64] On the basis of these priorities, the experience gained since the fall of 1942, and the assumption (subsequently proved erroneous) that American and British bomber forces would conduct a complementary and coordinated offensive, Eaker's board identified seventy-six specific targets and laid out a program for force development and employment from April 1943 to the invasion of western Europe, which it projected for May 1944.

The influence of the COA report on the Eaker board's recommendations, and thus on Eighth Air Force operations, reflected not so much the force of its logic as it reflected two other factors: the predisposition of board members to certain COA recommendations and, more subtly but equally important, perceptions of the COA's role. The recommendation to make ball bearings a priority target, for example, was readily accepted because both British and American intelligence analysts and planners in England had themselves identified this industry as a critical component system.[65] On two other COA recommendations, transportation and electric power systems, opinion appears to have differed. For at least one individual, Haywood Hansell, it was the committee's function rather than its arguments that was persuasive; for Hansell, the low priority the COA accorded these systems had "come as a shock." He acceded to this prioritization because he was "reluctant . . . to challenge the intelligence structure which bore such wide and vital support." Open disagreement, he feared, would undermine the confidence General Arnold was attempting to create in the "scientific" objectivity of the strategic bombing process.⁶⁶ He was willing to accept recommendations with which he did not fully agree in order to support the soundness of the selection method.

The inclusion of oil as a hedged priority target contingent on Ploesti raids reflected the current assessment of the importance of oil (which was correct) and the estimated critical levels of German reserves (which were still not nearly so severe as the Allies thought). The Ploesti consideration was a reminder the Allies were as yet incapable of seriously affecting the enemy's oil industry from bases in the United Kingdom. The recognition of Ploesti's crucial position within the German oil industry would prompt not only the spectacular raid by American B–24s from North Africa in August 1943, but also what eventually would almost amount to a campaign in itself against this complex, beginning in late 1943.

One aspect of strategic air operations receiving unanimous agreement was the need to destroy the GAF as quickly as possible. This operational goal and others that followed greatly influenced the shape and the substance of air intelligence. In their letter transmitting the Eaker Plan to the CCS, the JCS noted, "If the growth of the German fighter strength is not arrested quickly, it may become literally impossible to carry out the destruction planned and thus to create the conditions necessary for ultimate decisive action by our combined forces on the Continent."⁶⁷ According to the American chiefs, intelligence indicated that while German bomber strength over the past nine months had declined from 1,760 to 1,450, fighters had increased from 1,690 to 1,710, in spite of heavy losses in Russia and North Africa. Production over the past four months had risen from 720 to 810 fighters per month, and the GAF had increased its fighter strength by 44 percent since December 1941. At Casablanca, Arnold's background book had contained an intelligence assessment that "no increase in I.E. [the effective unit] strength [of the GAF] is to be expected."⁶⁸ Now, just four months later, the JCS noted that the enemy was producing on average 108 fighters beyond his monthly losses. If this trend continued, the Allies might face a total fighter force numbering 3,000 by spring 1944.

In addition to numerical growth, Allied intelligence had detected a significant redisposition of the enemy fighter force. The number of fighters opposing Allied bombers flying from England had doubled (from 420 to 830) in the past 18 months. The impact, the Americans pointed out, was being felt not just in the number of casualties taken by the daylight bomber force, but "especially in terms of reduced tactical effectiveness." The bombs simply were not hitting the target often enough. While these figures were not entirely accurate, they represented the parameters within which Allied leaders made their decisions. Their overall significance was obvious enough for the Combined Chiefs to declare, "German fighter strength must be considered as an *Intermediate* objective second to none in priority."⁶⁹

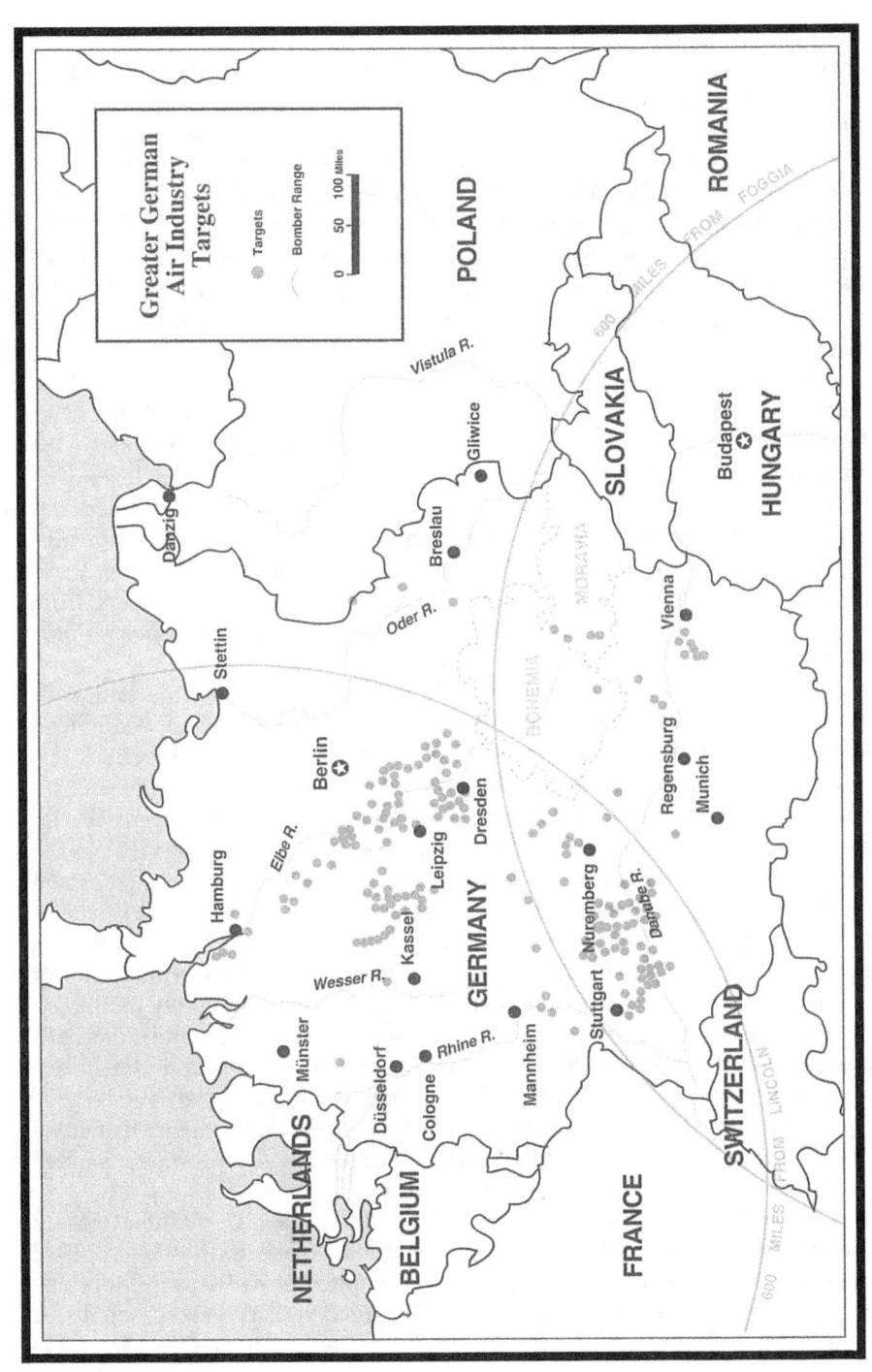

Piercing the Fog

The Combined Chiefs approved the CBO, designated "Operation POINTBLANK," on May 18, 1943, and appointed the Chief of Air Staff, RAF, as their executive agent to direct both British and American bomber forces. Although POINTBLANK was not directed solely against the GAF and related industries, these would be *the* primary objective for Eighth Air Force over the next year. Intelligence analyses of the enemy had illuminated the primary objectives, yet weather, operational limitations, and diversions from this objective restricted what the AAF could accomplish. Between July and October 1943, Eighth Air Force mounted only seven effective strikes against the German aircraft industry and a handful more against closely related industries such as ball bearings.

To coordinate the effort against the *Luftwaffe,* the Allies established the Jockey Committee in June 1943. Initially chaired by the RAF Director of Intelligence and later by the senior American intelligence officer assigned to the Air Ministry, Col. Kingman Douglass, this committee included officers from RAF Director of Bomber Operations and Director of Intelligence; Americans assigned to the Air Ministry; and representatives of the operational commands, beginning with VIII Bomber Command and RAF Bomber Command and expanding eventually to include intelligence and operations officers from Eighth Air Force, USSTAF, Supreme Headquarters Allied Expeditionary Force (SHAEF), Fifteenth Air Force, and Ninth Air Force.[70]

The purpose of the Jockey Committee was to monitor via intelligence analyses the German aircraft industry and GAF operations and to recommend appropriate targets within the framework of the POINTBLANK directive. The group blended operational and intelligence perspectives and concerns by combining representatives of the operational commands with specialists who analyzed the enemy's aircraft industry. Between June 1943 and April 1945 the committee met every Tuesday morning to review the past week's attacks and the latest intelligence from all sources regarding new targets, GAF supply problems, training, and tactical developments and trends.[71] Based on this review, the committee distributed target schedules on the German aircraft industry (broken out by component, engine, and airframe assembly facilities), towns associated with this industry (for RAF Bomber Command), the ball-bearing industry, repair facilities, and enemy airfields in the occupied territories and in Germany. The original objective had been to limit each list to 30 targets. By September 1944, each contained up to 100 targets as the enemy expanded his force and dispersed his installations and the Allied bomber forces expanded and achieved the capability to strike deeper into Germany.[72]

As with all intelligence organizations, the Jockey Committee was to provide information upon which commanders could make the most appropriate operational decisions. The schedules the committee provided were only one important factor. In December 1944, Maj. Gen. Frederick Anderson, Deputy for Operations, USSTAF, reminded his Eighth Air Force commander, Maj. Gen.

James Doolittle, "These 'JOCKEYS' are not a directive. They are issued weekly by the Air Ministry for information only . . ." to give commanders an idea of "Air Ministry opinion on the relative importance of G.A.F. targets."[73] Through the summer of 1943 the gap between what intelligence indicated should be done and the operational limitations that restricted what was possible remained broad. Three months before the POINTBLANK directive, Colonel Hughes had advised Eaker, "Our primary target should be the German Fighter Force in the air, and on the ground, and the industry which supports it."[74] To effectively attack enemy fighters required an offensive capability that did not exist; Eighth Air Force could reach only 43 percent of the fighter assembly plants and 25 percent of the fighter-engine production plants.[75]

While British and American economic analysts correctly recommended fighter engines as the key target in the aircraft industry, intelligence information regarding the location of engine factories was vaguer than that which indicated aircraft assembly plants. Analysts believed that the German authorities had concentrated engine factories around Berlin and Vienna, thus putting them out of range of Great Britain–based forces. Intelligence officers estimated some 60 percent of single-engine fighter airframe production was concentrated in eight plants located within striking distance of East Anglia.[76] The critical need to gain air superiority also dictated an emphasis on airframe assembly rather than on engines because analysts believed effective strikes against this subsystem would hurt the GAF's combat effectiveness within a month, as opposed to a two- to three-month lag in the case of engines.[77]

Lacking fighter escort, long-range capability, and experienced crews in the summer of 1943, Eaker sent his force primarily against targets in occupied Europe rather than over Germany. The Eighth Air Force's heavy bombers flew only nine effective missions into Germany in June and July, four of which had as primary targets submarine yards and shipyards and port areas. Despite these rather meager statistics, Eaker could take heart in the fact that his air force hit targets in Germany on five of the last seven days of July, including major assaults on aircraft assembly concentrations.[78]

One of the disturbing trends intelligence monitored in the summer of 1943 was the change in location of German aircraft production, especially fighters. In mid-August, McDonald received a report from the OSS research and analysis branch warning him that over the past two years aircraft production "has shifted markedly eastward." Only 12 percent of single-engine fighter production was now occurring within 500 miles of London. The enemy was now building 80 percent of his air force within 400 miles of northern Italy. The Allies could expect this trend to continue, since the potential benefits of the manufacturing layout to the Axis outweighed the temporary disruptions.[79]

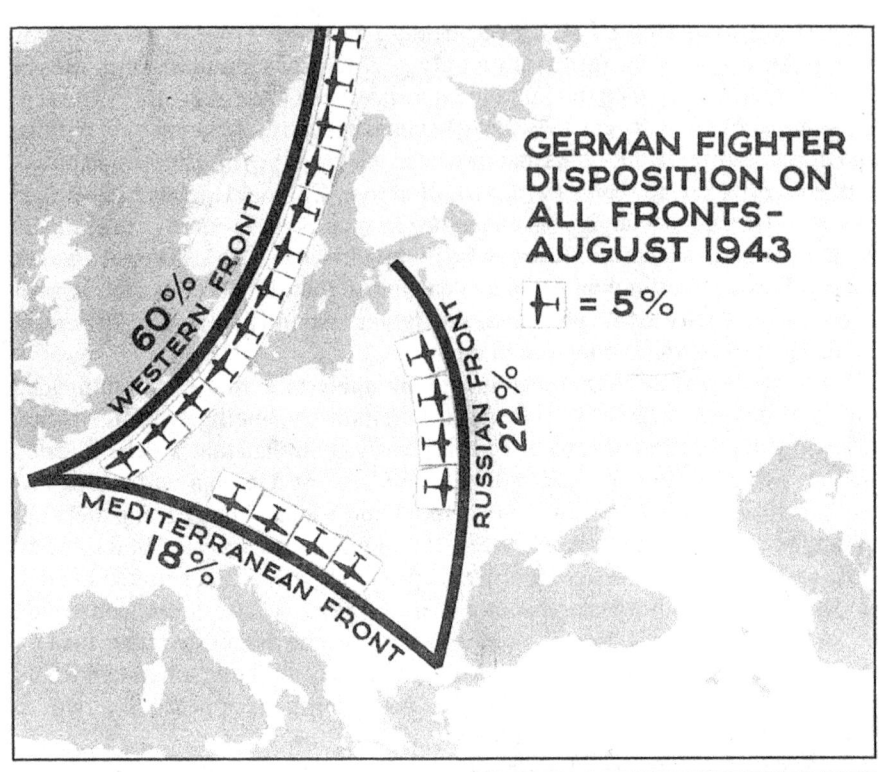

The Combined Bomber Offensive began in spring 1943. By August this Eighth Air Force briefing chart shows the *Luftwaffe* pulling back fighter units from the hard-pressed Russian and Italian fronts to defend the Fatherland. From an airman's standpoint, the first target set was the enemy's air power. Airfields were bombed—Avord, France *(center left)*, a fighter-bomber base *(lower left)*, and the airfield at Otopeni, Italy. So effective were these raids that this photo in May 1945 *(above)* shows a collection of wrecked German aircraft stretching almost to the horizon. The other prong of the attack on the *Luftwaffe* centered on aircraft production. Below, the aircraft engine factory at Strasbourg was flattened. The Fieseler plant near Kassel produced parts for FW 190s until it was destroyed. The huge Fallersleben Works *(bottom left)* made wings for Ju 88s until it was damaged. And there were scores of bomb hits on the Focke Wulf assembly plant at Hanover.

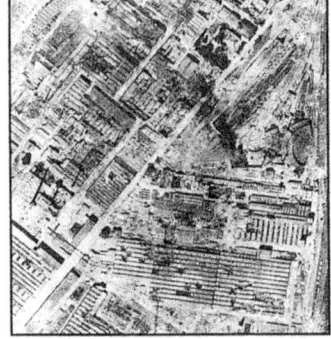

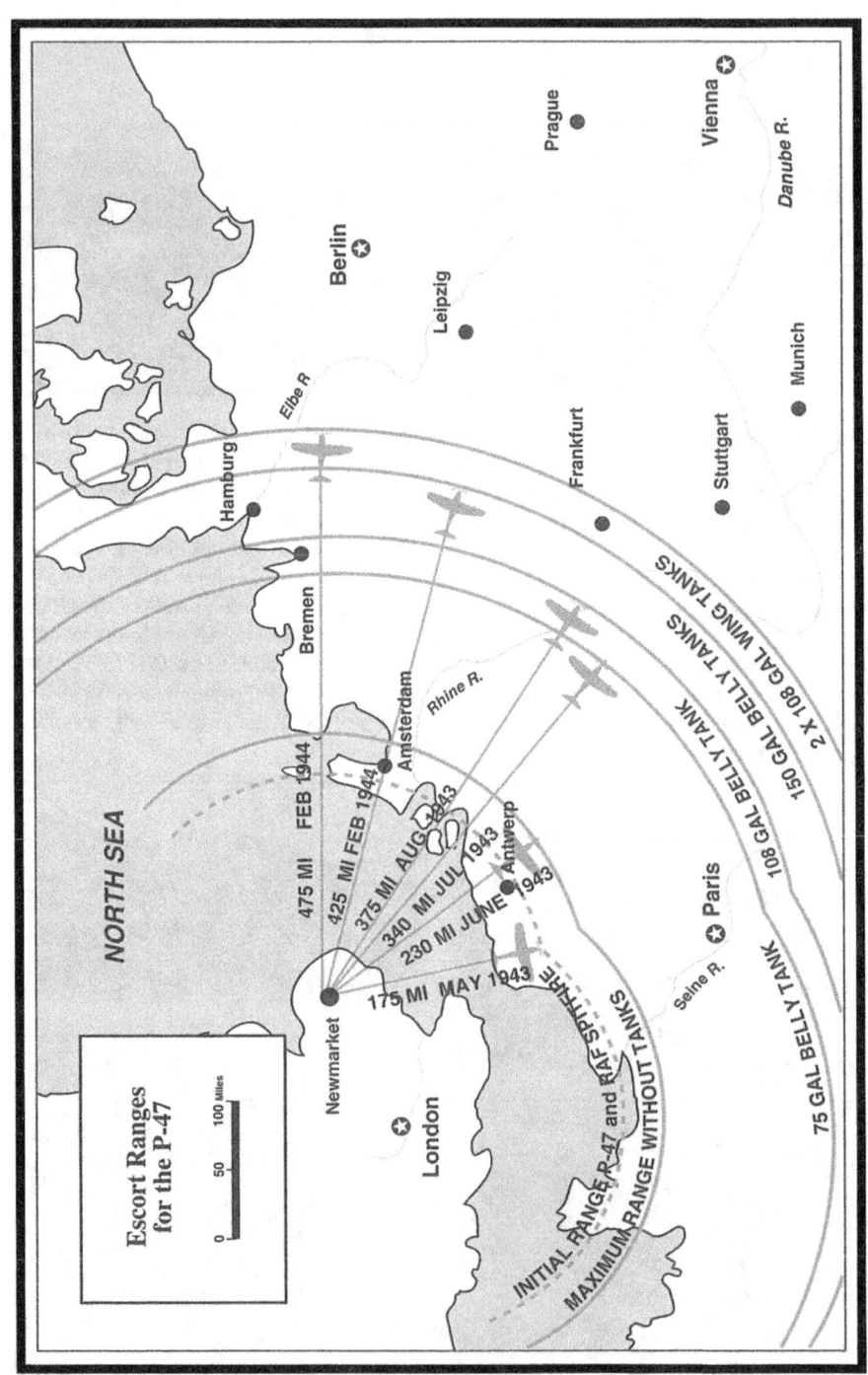

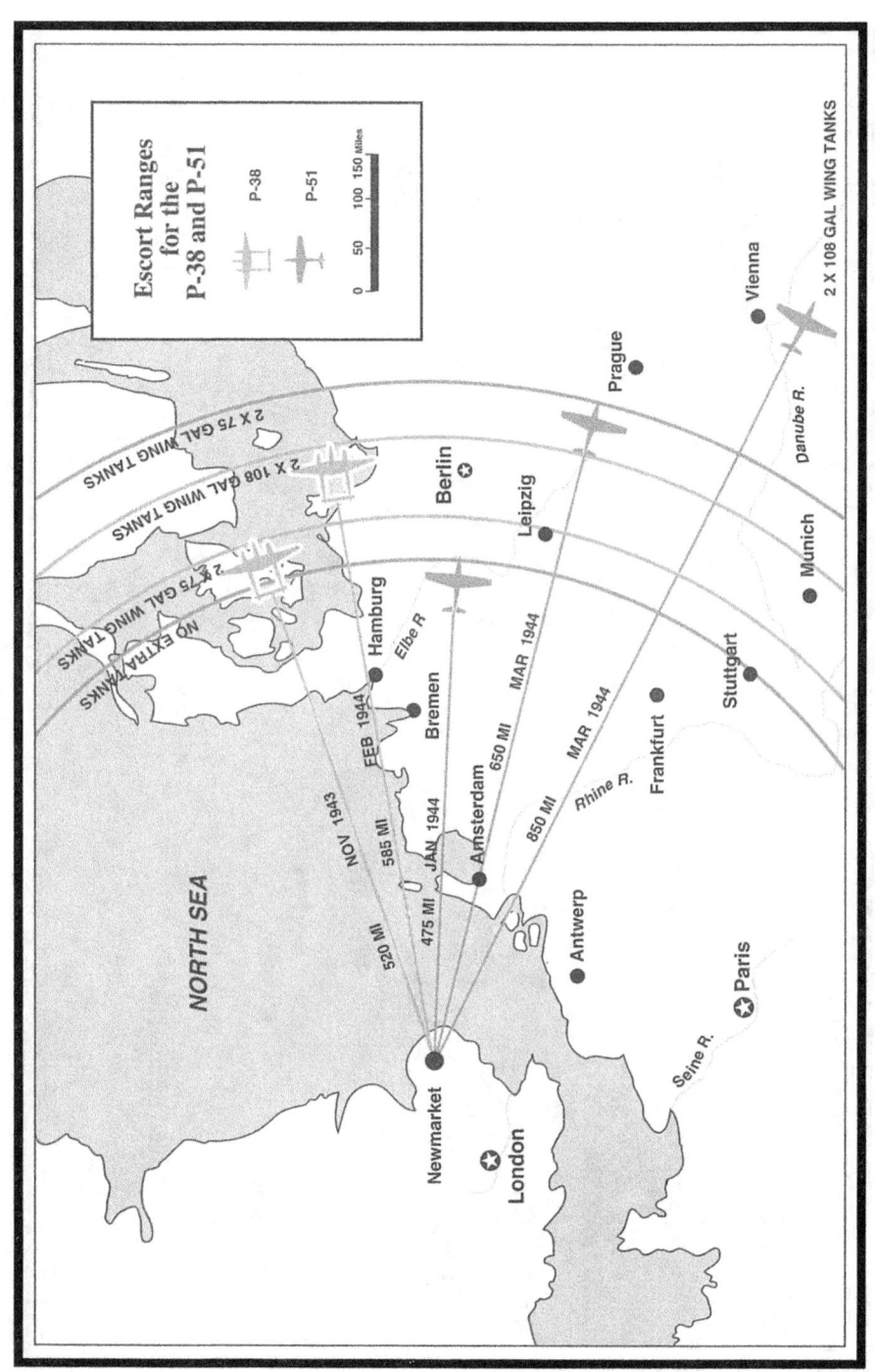

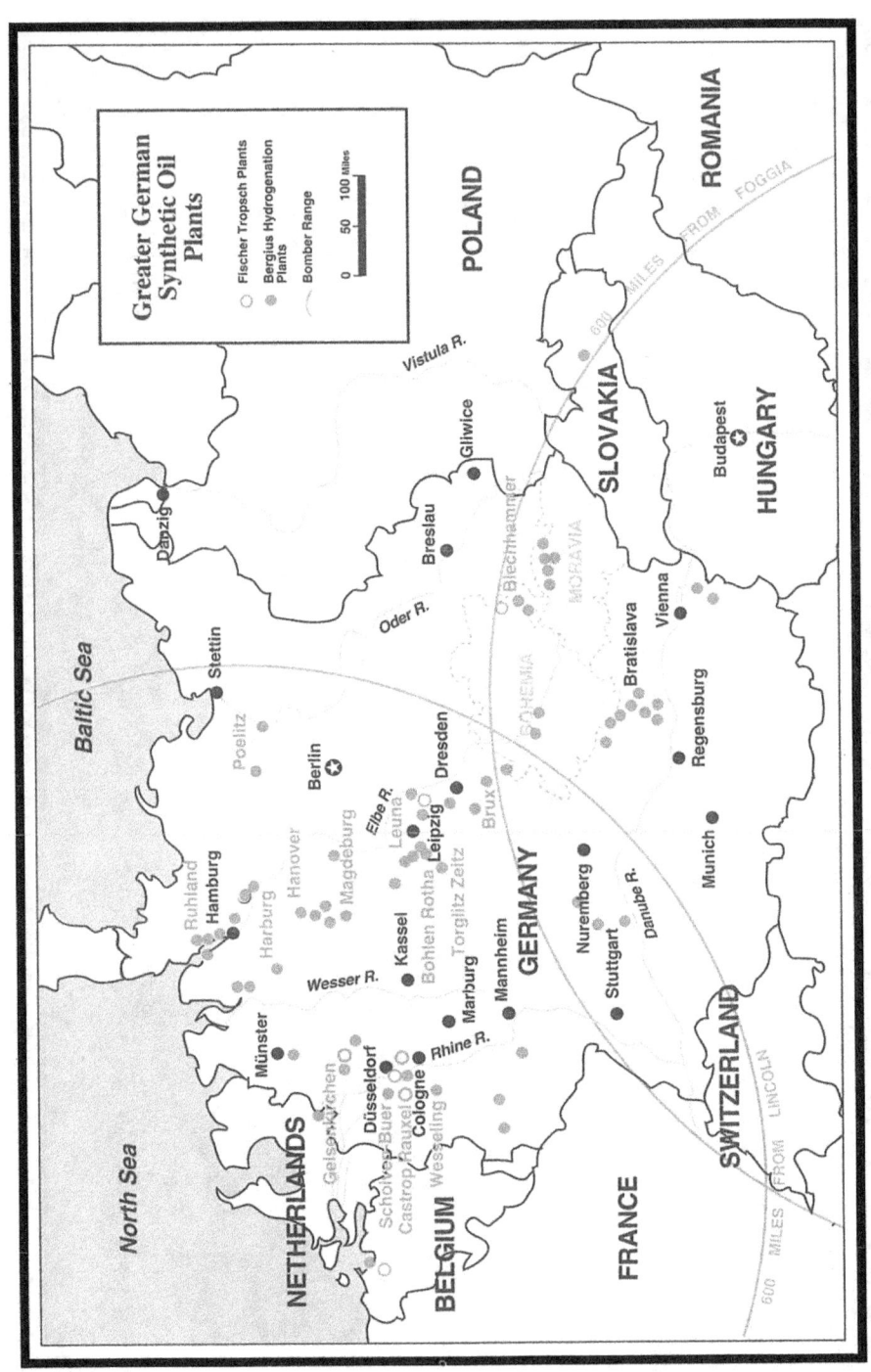

The European Theater of Operations

Coincidentally, on the day this report was released, American bombers struck major targets identified in it. On July 14, 1943, Eaker had written to Spaatz and Brereton (Ninth Air Force commander in North Africa) proposing a joint attack by both Eighth and Ninth Air Forces against German aircraft factories in southern Germany. Referring to an Air Ministry intelligence report passed to him by Portal, Eaker noted Messerschmitt factories in this area were producing 48 percent of the monthly German single-engine fighters (160 Bf 109s per month at Wiener Neustadt and 170 at Regensburg). Eaker believed that a successful double strike would have "a decisive effect on German single engine fighter production" and would result in a "drastic strategic redistribution" of *Luftwaffe* defenses at the expense of capabilities on either the Mediterranean or eastern fronts. Finally, the Eighth Air Force commander noted, RAF A.I.3 studies of the target factories, their defenses, and vulnerabilities reported both locations "virtually undefended."[80] Eaker's suggested joint attack found favor, but as events transpired, the two forces did not conduct their attacks on the same day. Ninth Air Force struck Wiener Neustadt on 13 August. Four days later nearly 125 B–17s from England hit the Messerschmitt factory at Regensburg and flew on to land in North Africa, while some 200 more attacked the ball-bearing factories at Schweinfurt. The decision to combine these targets stemmed from operational considerations, but the reasons for including ball-bearing factories at all was based on considerable intelligence analysis of German aircraft production.

The COA report of March 1943 had placed ball bearings immediately below fighter production as a strategic air target system. Planners and intelligence analysts in the United Kingdom had come to the same conclusion. Assessing possible targets within the total German aircraft production system, Eaker's chief of plans, Colonel Hughes, had advised the commanding general in early March, "A curtailment of bearing production would seriously interrupt the output of aircraft."[81] According to an EOU analysis, "The European ball-bearing industry probably represents the optimum target for an attack against [German] war production as a whole."[82] Intelligence also estimated that 73 percent of the enemy's ball bearings came from six easily identified and relatively vulnerable areas, with 42 percent of the total produced at the Schweinfurt factories.[83] Because of the nature of the machine tools required for this process, the EOU analysts argued, recuperation and repair of factories would take a long time. The impact of these delays would be enhanced because of the supposedly limited stocks in reserve.[84]

Despite serious losses in the August raids that called into question the intelligence pronouncement of virtually defenseless targets, two months later Eaker sent the heavy bombers back to Schweinfurt on what would be the costliest battle for the American strategic bombing forces during the war.* This

---

*On August 17, Eaker dispatched 367 B–17s and lost 60, or 16 percent, of the

Piercing the Fog

October 14th attack has been considered by many the nadir of the American strategic bombing campaign against Germany. Looking back in May 1945, the staff of the Eighth Air Force directorate of intelligence concluded, "On 14 October 1943, the Eighth temporarily lost air superiority in the major target areas of Germany."[85] Four years later the official Air Force history of the war concurred in almost the same words.[86] Senior leaders at the time certainly did not see it that way. In a cable to Arnold the day after the battle, Eaker admitted losses had been heavy, but he said, "there is no discouragement here. We are convinced that when the totals are drawn yesterday's losses will be far outweighed by the value of the enemy material destroyed." As to the day being a defeat in the air, Eaker argued that the mission "does not represent disaster. It does indicate that the air battle has reached its climax. . . . We must continue the battle with unrelenting fury."[87] Eaker was not alone in his assessment. Arnold cabled back his belief the GAF had been backed into a corner. George Marshall, a man not given to easy praise, wired Eaker, "I like the tone of your message. *No* great battle is won without heavy fighting and inevitable losses."[88]

Eaker and the other senior leaders based their optimism on a variety of intelligence indicators. The first-strike analysis of photographs taken during the attack led the Eighth Air Force staff to conclude that 75 percent of the target had been destroyed.[89] Eaker wrote another letter to Arnold declaring that unless the photographs "are very deceiving, we shall find the three ballbearing factories at Schweinfurt are out of business for a long, long time."[90] The initial CIU analysis, also based on strike photos, noted that the brunt of the attack "fell solidly on the target area," with at least 100 hits in the main complex. Smoke and fires, however, prevented analysts from making overall damage assessments.[91] Following a reconnaissance flight over the target area five days after the attack, a second CIU report identified "very heavy and concentrated damage" within all three factories and assorted other buildings, as well as heavy damage to adjacent marshaling yards.[92] More conservative than the American analysts, who believed overall German ball-bearing production had been cut by 40 percent, a JIC report concluded the attacks on Schweinfurt would probably result in a 15 to 20 percent decline in supplies over the next six months.[93]

The Allied failure to reattack quickly enough (in this case, the result of a long stretch of bad weather, overly optimistic assessments of damage, and operational limitations) allowed the Germans to recover. The Allies had misinterpreted the reserves available to the Germans and their ability to draw upon alternative sources in Sweden and Switzerland. Despite the massive external damage, only some 10 percent of the critical machine tools within were severely damaged. The survival of the enemy's equipment and the respite

---

force. On October 14, Eighth Air Force lost another 60 bombers with 128 others damaged from an initial force of 320. Some 640 crewmen were killed, seriously wounded, or missing.

The European Theater of Operations

before the Allies' next attack allowed the Germans to disperse their ball-bearing industry to the extent they would not suffer severe shortages until the last, collapsing weeks of the war.[94]

While American air leaders may have believed, as Eaker wrote to Arnold in October, "We now have our teeth in the Hun Air Force's neck," at least those stationed in England were well aware the enemy still had plenty of bite of his own.[95] In seven days in October, Eighth Air Force lost 160 bombers. While the GAF suffered as well, it clearly had greater strength and resiliency than past estimates had credited to it. The very day of the Schweinfurt battle Arnold had written to Eaker suggesting the GAF was on the verge of collapse. Despite his optimistic assertions of the 15th, Eaker responded to this misperception by declaring there were "no definite indications" of an imminent collapse of the GAF, although there was evidence of "severe strain and some signs of eventual collapse."[96] A month later McDonald felt compelled to write to Maj. Gen. Clayton Bissell, the AAF's A–2, to correct what McDonald sensed to be Washington's misguided belief the *Luftwaffe* was about to "crack up." The GAF's situation, he wrote, "is undoubtedly serious, but cannot at the moment be said to be disastrous."[97] McDonald's comments may well have been inspired by a report issued by Bissell's office on October 18 declaring boldly that "aerial supremacy on a continental scale had been won."[98]

What made the assessment of German air strength difficult was the incomplete nature of intelligence as well as the conflicting interpretations made of it. The most useful source for strategic air intelligence in this period, photoreconnaissance and photointerpretation, rarely yielded complete information. Despite the best efforts of the interpreters, there remained a tendency to overestimate the actual impact of damage on a target's productive capability, even when evaluations of structural damage were correct. Efforts to determine production levels through alternative means such as analysis of serial numbers, by estimating production by plant size, and agent reports became increasingly difficult with the dispersal of production facilities from the prewar locations.[99] In this area, ULTRA could play only a limited role, since German aircraft and associated production information was rarely passed through the military channels from which BP garnered most of its intercepts.[100]

Complaints by two individuals intimately involved in the intelligence targeting process underscored the difficulties the dispersal of the German fighter-aircraft industry presented to the bomber commanders. In an after-action report on Operation ARGUMENT prepared early in 1944, both Colonel Hughes, chief targeteer for Eighth Air Force and then for USSTAF, and the Air Ministry Director of Intelligence (Research) commented on "the decline in the quality of intelligence on German fighter production since the middle part of 1943." Hughes admitted that information on the Focke-Wulf plants in eastern Germany and Poland prior to Big Week had been "most tentative."[101]

Compounding the problem was the fact that British Air Ministry Intelligence, upon which Eighth Air Force and then USSTAF largely depended, still could not always agree among its own divisions on how to interpret data that came to them. While ULTRA provided reliable figures on unit strengths, the Allies had no equally reliable method for comparing these figures with actual or planned production. It was important to know the strength of the enemy, but it was equally necessary to reduce that strength by a combination of attrition and destruction of production facilities. The American position on this issue was succinctly summarized by McDonald in a letter to HQ AAF in July 1944: "Our only concern is to find out how much of the German Air Force is left to fight and where we can bomb the production that sustains it." Then, echoing similar comments by Hughes, he expressed the opinion of USSTAF that "there is actually more production than they [Air Ministry] have yet been able to find."[102]

What ULTRA did provide was extremely accurate data on unit strength, on the German decision to reduce their bomber forces in favor of fighters, and on the enemy's efforts to strengthen their home air defenses at the expense of *Luftwaffe* operations in the Mediterranean region and in the USSR. By November 1943, Allied intelligence counted some 1,700 single-engine fighters confronting them in western Europe, including the German homeland. Considering the August 1943 monthly production rate of 800, the *Luftwaffe* could replace itself every two months. By returning to the July production rate of 1,050, it could lose fighters at October's rate and still increase its force.[103] This calculation reinforced the necessity to continue to attack production rather than to simply seek attrition through aerial combat. The most forceful evidence that the GAF would rebuild, given the opportunity, came not from SIGINT but from HUMINT. In September 1943, the former Italian representative with the German Ministry of Aircraft Production informed the Allies in great detail of German efforts to increase fighter production. Through the implementation of assembly lines, their goal was to go from the 500 fighters produced in January 1943 to 2,000 a month by late 1944 and to 3,000 monthly by April 1945.[104] In light of the costs the GAF had imposed on the heavy bombers with a production rate of 800–1,000 per month in 1943, such figures must have been truly frightening.

In the last week of 1943, McDonald's intelligence staff in the newly formed MAAF summarized Allied interpretations of the *Luftwaffe*'s current status and what Allied heavy bombers might face in the coming year. According to this analysis, the air offensive against the German fighter industry had reached a critical phase. The attacks in July, August, and October had, McDonald's staff believed, "seriously upset" German aircraft production. The difference between the planned monthly output for November of 1,000 and the estimated actual production of 650, or a total of some 1,500 fighters not produced over a four-month period, demonstrated this. Equally significant, these attacks had "thoroughly disrupted" the enemy's intended program of expansion. Although the enemy was "staggering from the blows received to date," it would recover if the Allies failed to pursue the offensive relentlessly. Precise estimates were difficult to project since "less is known in detail about current FW 190 production due to . . . plant movements and the lack of photo coverage." Without continued pressure, the report concluded, the enemy would probably be producing 900 fighters per month by February 1944. The cushion of excess capacity and new machinery that had given the enemy "remarkable powers of recuperation" had been badly damaged; future recovery would be inevitably slower. "It appears well within the capabilities of Allied air power to deliver a fatal blow to the German fighter force through additional attacks on the aircraft industry."[105]

McDonald soon had the opportunity to argue this case closer to the real centers of power than he had in Tunisia. In January 1944 he accompanied General Spaatz to the United Kingdom where he became Director of Intelligence, USSTAF. This resulted from American airmen's efforts to get a single air commander responsible for all American strategic air forces in the European and Mediterranean theaters. The arrangement gave Spaatz operational direction over the Eighth and Fifteenth Air Forces and administrative control over the Eighth and Ninth. The Ninth had just moved to England to become a tactical force in support of the approaching Operation OVERLORD.

In the USSTAF, the director of intelligence came under the deputy commanding general for operations, as did the directors of plans, operations, and weather services. Targeting (still headed by Colonel Hughes) was now part of the directorate of intelligence rather than of plans. Key personnel adjustments that attended this reorganization include General Anderson's appointment as Deputy Commanding General for Operations. Maj. Gen. James Doolittle became Commanding General, Eighth Air Force, replacing Eaker, the new Commanding General, MAAF. USSTAF was established effective January 1, 1944.*[106]

That Spaatz intended to continue the effort against the German fighter force and its production sources was clear from his initial directives. On January 11, 1944, he advised the commanders of Eighth and Fifteenth Air Forces that the priorities of his strategic air forces would be, in rank order, the destruction of fighter airframe and component factories, German fighters "in the air and on the ground," and the ball-bearing industry.[107] In the United Kingdom, planning for operations against the GAF and its supporting industries had never stopped. By mid-November, an Anglo-American committee coordinating mission planning had identified seven priority targets for attack at the earliest moment. All but one involved aircraft production.[108] By November 23, VIII Bomber Command in A–2 had prepared a list of nine priority targets (each with an alternate) within the framework of a major counterair campaign, now code named Operation

---

*After a brief period as USSAFE, the official abbreviation became USSTAF.

ARGUMENT. The list consisted of twelve different target complexes for heavy bombers flying from England. Of these, ten were component or airframe assembly plants, one was a ball-bearing complex, and the last, a major rubber production complex.[109] Before leaving the Mediterranean, McDonald had identified ten priority targets based on intelligence and distance from air bases in Italy. Nine of the ten were aircraft or ball-bearing facilities; the tenth was the massive oil refining complex at Ploesti.[110]

Execution of an operation of the magnitude that airmen now contemplated required a reasonable period of good weather both over the targets and at the operating bases. Persistently bad weather prevailed over Europe from mid-October 1943 until mid-February 1944. While this delayed ARGUMENT, it provided time for the arrival of new bomber groups and the introduction of the long-range P–51s, capable of escorting the B–17s and B–24s deep into Germany and back.

When the weather broke in the third week of February, American bomber forces possessed what they had previously lacked: weapons in sufficient number to strike targets that needed to be attacked. On February 20, they began to exercise their capability. On five of the next six days, Eighth Air Force heavy bombers, in formations of up to 600 aircraft with hundreds of escort fighters, hit all 12 of the major target complexes identified the previous fall, as well as 2 of the 10 McDonald had highlighted. Operating under the same directives from Spaatz, Fifteenth Air Force struck the Messerschmitt complexes at Regensburg and Wiener Neustadt and the aircraft component and ball-bearing plants at Steyr, all on McDonald's list. In addition, RAF bombers conducted major night attacks against five cities close to several of these complexes.*[111] From the standpoint of intelligence, the February period that came to be called Big Week represented a crucial point. American strategic air forces could now hit the targets identified as critical to victory in the air war and thus to Allied victory in Europe. In another, although not wholly correct sense, it marked a new beginning, for the assessed impact of these attacks on the GAF and German aircraft production would condition to a large extent what Eighth and Fifteenth Air Forces did in the future.

The first USSTAF intelligence assessment of Operation ARGUMENT was completed on February 26, 1944. "The fighting value of these units [*Luftwaffe* fighter units in western Europe and Germany] has been substantially reduced . . ." with serviceability down to 50 percent.[112] This emphasis on fighting value rather than simple numerical strength, although difficult to define, would become an increasingly important measure in how the American air command-

---

*Senior commanders had been prepared to take losses of as many as 200 bombers in a single mission, but losses for the week totaled 226 bombers and 28 fighters, with approximately 2,600 crew members killed, seriously wounded, or missing in action.

ers evaluated the *Luftwaffe*. It necessitated a subjective weighing of a variety of factors, such as combat experience, training levels, serviceability, and morale. This increasingly sophisticated approach explained in part why senior airmen such as Spaatz and Anderson would watch GAF fighter strength increase in the summer and fall of 1944 without diverting their primary attention from the oil campaign.

In a teletype conference between HQ USSTAF and HQ AAF on February 27, General Anderson, repeating almost verbatim a paper prepared by the directorate of intelligence, suggested Big Week had cost the Germans 60 percent of their single-engine and 80 percent of their twin-engine fighter production. The German high command had only two choices: either defend high-value targets and watch combat losses rise even higher, or withhold forces to reduce wastage and suffer the destruction of industrial capacity and hence military capability. Allied objectives could best be attained by continuing to assault the enemy's vital production centers to draw defensive fighters into the air.[113]

Within a week a more detailed USSTAF intelligence analysis not only confirmed this assessment, but it provided further impetus for a new approach to strategic air operations. The air intelligence summary for March 5, 1944, concluded that Big Week had cost the enemy 50 percent of his replacements. An EOU study completed at the same time concluded that Big Week had reduced the production of single-engine fighters from 950 to 250 per month and that of twin-engine fighters from 225 to 50 a month; ball-bearing production was at 45 percent of the pre–Big Week level.[114] The GAF had lost some 300 fighters in combat, estimated to represent a tenth of the *Luftwaffe*'s fighter strength. The recognition that the GAF was suffering heavy attrition in the air produced in March a fundamental shift in operational planning. Instead of seeking routes to avoid German defenses, operational planners deliberately set out to directly engage them. On the basis of these intelligence assessments, Spaatz and his chief staff officers also turned to other targets, most notably oil.

Ironically, while the decision to shift from the German aircraft industry to oil proved correct, it was based on intelligence assessments that were too optimistic. The Big Week assaults had destroyed 75 percent of the buildings in the target areas. As in the previous October, however, significant portions of the critical machinery proved salvageable. Big Week accelerated the dispersal of industrial facilities begun some six months earlier. As a result of salvage operations, previous dispersal, and failure to reattack the damaged factories, the massive assault in February actually delayed German production less than the lighter and more sporadic raids of August and October had.[115] The decision to draw the GAF into combat in the spring of 1944 proved strikingly successful. *Luftflotte Reich,* responsible for the air defense of the Fatherland, lost 225 aircraft in February, 236 in March, and 343 in April, to which must be added an additional 338 German fighters lost in France and Belgium between February and May.[116]

Although ULTRA provided little evidence of the impact of Big Week on aircraft production, the reallocation of fighter units indicated Germany's concern. On February 26, the Germans withdrew JG–27 from the Balkans for homeland air defense.[117] A week later, *Luftflotte 2* on the eastern front was advised it would be losing two of its *gruppen* to *Luftflotte Reich* as well.[118] Throughout the spring, ULTRA provided indications that *Luftwaffe* units were losing 15–30 percent of their engaging forces.[119] On March 19, a message from the Air Officer for Fighters referred to "the strained manpower situation in units operating in defence of the Reich" and called for experienced volunteers from other units, especially those with skill in ground attack and with bombers.[120] The next month, *Fliegerkorps I,* hard-pressed by the Red Air Force on the eastern front, was ordered to send fourteen pilots, "including 2 to 4 aces," to *Luftflotte Reich,* in return for newly qualified replacements.[121]

The dispersal of aircraft factories, now in full effect, went largely, though not totally, unannounced by ULTRA. A message from the Japanese naval attaché in Germany not only confirmed the attrition being suffered by the fighter force, but it referred to the "transfer of plant carried out in expectation of intensification of enemy air raids. . . ."[122] In terms of SIGINT, Berlin remained a most productive center for American MAGIC throughout the war. The Japanese Ambassador to Germany from February 1941 to May 1945 was Lt. Gen. Hiroshi Oshima. Oshima regularly sent messages to Tokyo detailing his discussions with high-ranking Germans and his observations made in the field. He sent his reports encrypted by the PURPLE machine, and just as regularly, the Americans in Washington read his remarks.[123] The Allies also became aware, through reports of GAF unit strengths, that production of fighter aircraft was again on the rise. This fact continued to be weighed against the tentative opposition the bomber raids now faced. Taken together, the evidence provided justification for Spaatz to relegate strategic air operations against the German aircraft industry to a level necessary to keep the GAF at its current state.

Allied airmen had never intended the defeat of the *Luftwaffe* to be an end in itself, only a necessary step to opening the German economic and industrial bases to the full weight of strategic air power. Even before the implementation of Operation ARGUMENT, USSTAF leaders had initiated steps to determine "subsequent operations [necessary] to complete the breakdown of German power and will to resist." On February 12, 1944, General Anderson, Deputy Commander for Operations, directed a special planning committee of senior officers from operations (Brig. Gen. Charles Cabell), plans (Col. C. G. Williams), and intelligence (Colonel Hughes) to define new objectives for the CBO, including the role of strategic air forces in the invasion of northwest Europe.[124]

In preparing their report, the committee members relied heavily on a detailed study by the EOU. Prepared primarily by Capt. Harold J. Barnett, this report pointed out that operational constraints had previously limited effective attacks on target systems. With the increasing size, escort capability, and extended range of the American bomber force and the concomitant decline of the GAF, target systems that contained as many as fifty or sixty individual targets now had become feasible. For this reason, oil, which had always been considered an important target but one too dispersed and beyond range to have been assigned a top priority, now assumed new importance. After reviewing in detail the ten primary target systems, Barnett concluded oil had moved conclusively to the forefront. "No other target system," he asserted, "holds such great promise for hastening German defeat."[125] A successful oil campaign would have a decisive impact on the enemy's industrial and military capabilities. It would reduce industrial production across the board, decrease strategic mobility of the German Army (and thus support OVERLORD), hamper air operations, and in general reduce the *Wehrmacht*'s tactical air-ground combat capability. The destruction of twenty-three synthetic plants and thirty-two refineries, an objective now within the Eighth's and Fifteenth's capabilities, would result in "virtually zero" production within six months.[126]

Accepting the basic premises, conclusions, and even much of the language of Barnett's study, the committee placed the petroleum industry (with special emphasis on gasoline) as first priority, arguing that the projected objective of a 50-percent reduction within six months would provide the "maximum opportunity" for strategic bomber forces to affect the German ground forces. Continued policing of the enemy's fighter and ball-bearing industries would provide Allied air superiority and deny the GAF an effective air-ground capability. According to the planners, the strategic forces would shift to attacks against the German transportation networks in occupied Europe in the three weeks immediately preceding D-day as they continued to keep the *Luftwaffe* on the defensive in the skies over Germany.[127]

Intelligence sources outside USSTAF agreed with the committee's conclusions. At the request of the Air Ministry, the MEW evaluated the USSTAF plan. While differing in some statistical data and suggesting a slightly different timing, MEW replied, "Our final conclusion differs little from that of [USSTAF] . . . . We fully endorse their expectations of the strategic results which would follow [from concentrating on the oil industry]. . . ."[128] As evidence of the state of German petroleum, in a report on the MEW position, EOU included the text of a German order signed by the quartermaster general of the high command of the German Army. Stressing the need to avoid a crisis in motor fuel, the message concluded, "The Order of the Hour for motor fuel . . . is: *Economize now whenever possible.*" According to EOU, both the urgency of the message and its origin "make it one of the most striking evidences of the German oil position which we have thus far received."[129] Shortly thereafter,

The oil fields in Romania and adjacent refineries made up the richest single oil complex in Nazi-held Europe. Only heavy bombers based in Italy could attack the complex. The Concordia Vega refinery at Ploesti is shown above after being bombed by B–24s from the Fifteenth Air Force. The other major source of German oil was the series of synthetic oil plants built deep in Germany. On this page are the synthetic oil plants at Magdeburg *(above left)* and Misburg on the canal near Hanover. On the opposite page are the two synthetic oil refineries in the area of Gelsenkirchen *(top)*. Only the bullet-shaped bomb shelter *(center left)* is unmarked at Scholven Buer *(left)*, and the oil tank farm at Bottrop is flattened. At bottom is a photo taken on the ground at Merseburg–Leuna refinery after the area was taken, showing its maze of broken pipes.

Spaatz used this same example to make the identical point to General Eisenhower when he sent Eisenhower the plan for the completion of the CBO.

Unanimity did not mark this shift in priorities among either operators or intelligence analysts. In a draft paper for the Chief of Air Staff, RAF, the director of bomber operations argued that it was better to continue to focus on the GAF with the aim of "achieving an *overwhelming* degree of air superiority." Plants not yet attacked, repair depots, fighter airfields, and GAF facilities and personnel in occupied territories should remain priority targets. Still, the paper conceded, "Oil is the best additional target system" since destroying it would "gravely impair the mobility of the German Armed Forces on all fronts."[130] The COA had argued as recently as mid-January against revising the priority of oil because production was so much in excess in Axis-dominated Europe that its destruction would not affect the enemy's general combat capability for more than six months, and attacking the oil industry would not markedly reduce his aviation gasoline supplies for ten to eleven months.[131]

The question of when an oil campaign would affect German combat capability was crucial. With the Combined Chiefs' decision to place all Allied air forces, strategic as well as tactical, under the Supreme Allied Commander in March 1944, the overriding issue was how best to use strategic air power in support of Operation OVERLORD. USSTAF commanders and staff officers were well aware that OVERLORD had taken center stage, with General Eisenhower now controlling the employment of their force. Both the plan for the completion of the CBO and Spaatz's letter sending it to Eisenhower stressed the impact of an oil campaign (as well as other targets included in the plan) on the Germans' overall military capability. Spaatz emphasized that the purpose of the proposed plan was to provide "maximum support for OVERLORD...."[132] The plan itself, after offering what it considered a "conservative assessment" of the requirements for policing the enemy's fighter aircraft capability, stressed, "Oil offers the most promising system of attack . . . to bring the German armies to the point where their defeat in the field will be assured...."[133]

Unfortunately for American airmen, the oil plan was not the only proposal for the employment of strategic air forces before the Supreme Allied Commander in February and March of 1944. Air Marshal Leigh-Mallory, commander of the AEAF, had already forwarded a plan to concentrate all Allied air forces against the Axis transportation network in western Europe for the three months preceding D-day. (USSTAF was not opposed to attacks on lines of communication; it thought three weeks of concentrated assault would suffice.) The urgency with which USSTAF prepared their oil plan undoubtedly stemmed in part from their strong opposition to the AEAF proposal. The debate over Leigh-Mallory's transportation plan had been ongoing since January, weeks before the oil plan was completed.

What might have been the decisive issue of this debate—the question of whether to concentrate on marshaling yards (as the AEAF proposed, now supported by Professor Zuckerman) or to concentrate on bridges and other bottleneck targets (as advocated most strongly by EOU)—was not an issue at the highest levels. The preponderance of current intelligence by this time favored the latter, which would have released the heavy bombers, since they were not suited for such precision attacks. Spaatz chose not to contest the issue;[134] rather he elected to stress that attacks on oil represented the most effective application of strategic air forces to support OVERLORD in the belief that three weeks would be sufficient to retard a German buildup in Normandy.*

Once the issue became broadly one of transportation versus oil, it was almost inevitable that Eisenhower would opt against the USSTAF proposal. In the first place, Tedder, his own deputy, as well as Leigh-Mallory (both senior RAF officers) strongly favored the transportation strategy. These individuals emphasized the gamble involved in the USSTAF approach: if three weeks were *not* sufficient to block the German lines of communication, there would be no time to recover, and the mighty endeavor would be lost. In contrast, by marshaling *all* their air forces for three months, the Allies might at the very least be assured they had not wasted any resources.

Another contentious issue was timing. None of the senior proponents of the oil campaign talked in terms of fewer than six months for it to have an effect. In his own presentation to Eisenhower, Spaatz essentially admitted the real impact would not be on the immediate tactical capability of the German defenders in the invasion area; it would be the campaign's effect on German mobility—strategic and tactical—in the critical period *after* D-day. Perhaps more than any other event, this debate reflected the fundamental differences in perspective between strategic airmen and tactical (ground and air) commanders. When the former focused on the period after D-day, they were missing the point. Eisenhower, as the supreme commander, focused on what was acknowledged would be the decisive event of the war in Europe, a successful foothold on the continent, not on the sequence of events thereafter.

Eisenhower made his decision on March 25: strategic and tactical air forces would attack the German transportation network in western Europe. Spaatz accepted his superior's decision. Yet, within weeks of the successful Allied invasion, oil would again become the primary target of American strategic air forces. Operation OVERLORD was not the only diversion to American efforts to prosecute the CBO. By the spring of 1944, threats from the German V–1 flying bomb and V–2 rocket had imposed serious demands on American and British air resources as well.

---

*In his book *Pre-Invasion Bombing Strategy* (Austin, Tex., 1981), Professor Walter Rostow, who was intimately involved in this debate, presents a cogent, though not unbiased, argument against the whole Zuckerman thesis. He favors the plan his own EOU organization prepared for the employment of tactical forces against bridges.

The bombing offensive against the German rail system was ordered by General Eisenhower. Its main purpose was to deny supplies to the German army. At Celle *(above left)* and Fulda *(above right)* and Ulm *(below)*, railroad marshaling yards were hit. The railroad bridges at Celle were dropped by Ninth Air Force medium bombers. The marshaling yards at Muhldorf *(right)* in southern Germany were punished by the Fifteenth Air Force. Cologne *(below right)* and Berlin marshaling yards were hit by the Eighth Air Force and the RAF.

Piercing the Fog

Rumors of German efforts to develop revolutionary long-range air weapons had surfaced occasionally since the beginning of the war. By late 1942, they had begun to filter into British intelligence channels in numbers too great to be ignored. Despite the creation of a high-level committee and the mobilization of extensive intelligence resources, by the summer of 1943 the British possessed only limited knowledge about the characteristics, capabilities, or production of these weapons. They knew that Peenemunde, an installation on the Baltic Sea, was the center of German research activity for these V-weapons. They had reason to believe (though without consensus until November 1943) that at least two different systems were in development. The identification of unusual installations under construction in northern France gave probable, but indefinite, evidence for the program at Peenemunde.[135]

The intelligence the British had acquired to this point came overwhelmingly from ground reports (agents in Germany, France, Switzerland, and Poland) and photoreconnaissance and photointerpretation. The popular misconception that Allied intelligence, through ULTRA, had a direct tap into every facet of the Axis war effort falls apart when it comes to the V–1 and V–2 developments. Not only did the Allies never acquire a complete picture of these weapons (if one includes production aspects), but SIGINT played a distinctly secondary role. HUMINT from ground observers offered many of the initial tips that alerted intelligence officers and scientists to focus in a certain direction, but photoreconnaissance and photointerpretation provided the incontrovertible visual evidence. In the course of the V-weapon campaign, British and American photoreconnaissance completely blanketed a 7,500-square-mile portion of France four times, photographed more than 100 selected locations weekly, overflew Peenemunde 50 times, and took 1,250,000 photographs.[136]

Still uncertain as to precisely what was occurring either at Peenemunde or in France, the British decided in mid-August 1943 to attack both locations. RAF Bomber Command launched a major assault on Peenemunde the night of August 17/18, inflicting severe damage and heavy casualties. At the request of the British, Eighth Air Force attacked a large construction site near Watten, France, on August 27. When poststrike coverage showed little damage, the heavy bombers returned on September 7.[137] While the Allies would continue to monitor Watten and similar sites (which were to have been launch facilities for the V–2 rocket), their attacks convinced the enemy to abandon these sites in favor of ones less obvious. This represented a major change in launching plans, and the Germans experienced serious technical difficulties, so that the V–2 program fell increasingly behind schedule.

How much the Americans knew about the development of the German rocket and flying bomb programs through the summer of 1943 is moot. In its extensive discussion of the V-weapons, the official British history suggested that not until October 1943 did the Americans receive information on these developments "apart from what had appeared in general intelligence reports and

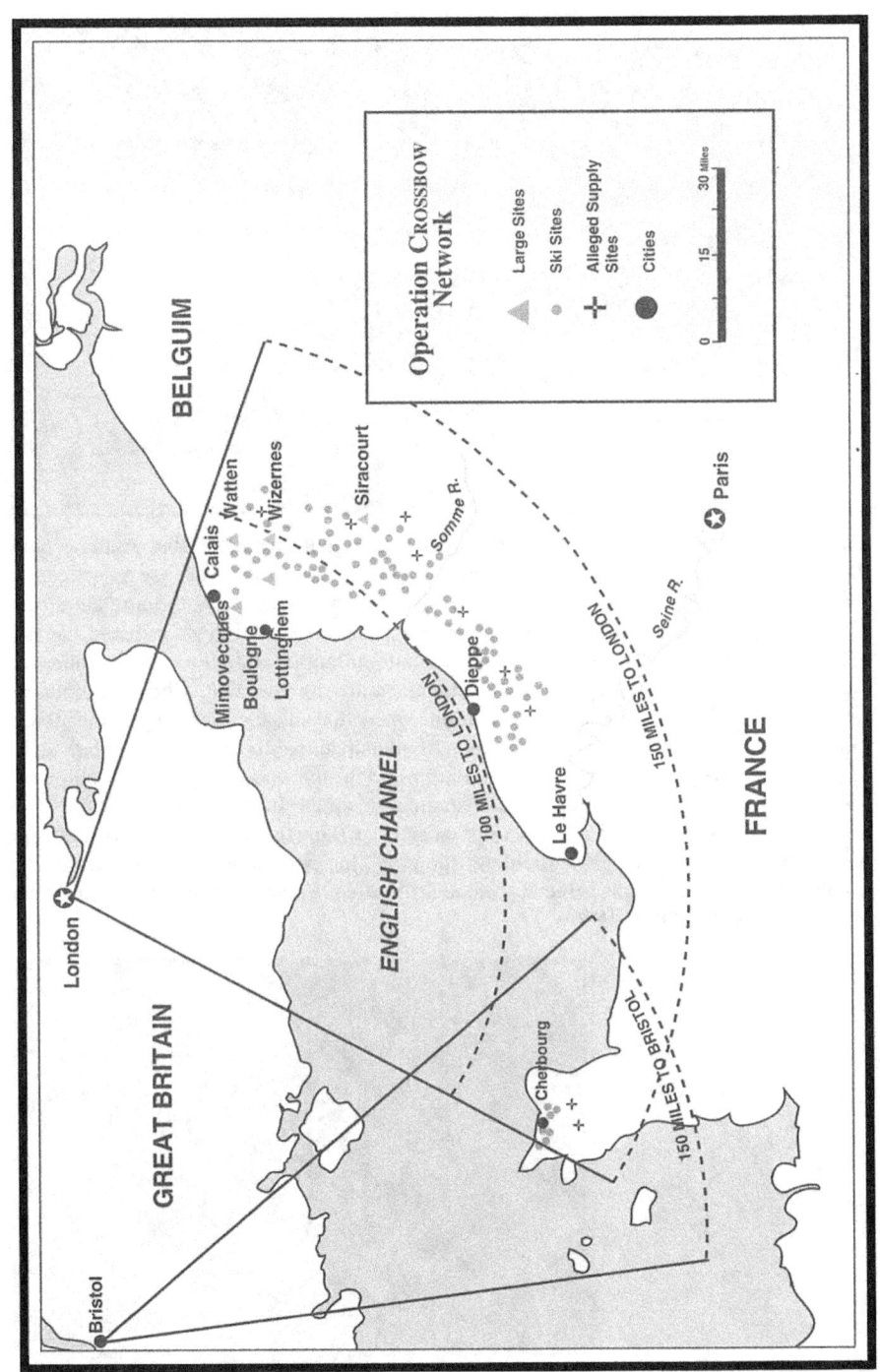

The German secret weapon program was of deep concern to Allied military and civilian leaders. Particularly worried were the British, since they were the targets. One of the most extensive photointelligence efforts of the war sought information about the research, production, and sites for these weapons. Above, American officers can be seen inspecting the assembly line for V–1s in an underground factory at Nordhausen. Below is one of the hundreds of "ski" launch ramps for the V–1. The light-colored building at the bottom was the control room where the missile was armed and given guidance instructions. About three-quarters of an inch above the building is a dark strip which is a heavily camouflaged ski launch ramp. On the opposite page is a photo of the German research and testing site at Peenemunde on the Baltic coast, where the V–1 and V–2 were born. The V–2 missile is seen at *A,* launch towers are at *B,* and the assembly building is *C.* In the middle of the page, the same site is shown after being bombed. At the lower right is the V–1 depot at Watten, France, still under construction when overrun in August 1944.

prisoner of war interrogations. . . ."[138] Lt. Gen. Ira Eaker, in his report covering Eighth Air Force activities from February 1942 through December 1943, noted only that the Eighth had been asked to draw up and execute plans for the August and September operations.[139] On August 11, 1943, Col. Richard Hughes, then the Eighth Air Force chief of plans, but an officer with extensive intelligence experience with Eaker, attended a meeting in the office of the RAF's ACAS, Operations, at which an attack was specifically discussed. According to the minutes of that meeting, Hughes reported that "by arrangement" no directive had been or would be issued to the commanding general, but that "General Anderson" (presumably Brig. Gen. Orvil A. Anderson, then chairman of the Anglo-American committee to coordinate air operations) was "conversant with the whole position in regard to BODYLINE," the code name for the British attempt to define the existence of and the threat posed by the V–2.[140]

In October 1943 Prime Minister Churchill informed President Roosevelt by message of the intelligence gathered on the V-weapons, and the British Chiefs of Staff agreed to pass intelligence to senior American leaders in Washington and England. Several days later the MEW was authorized to discuss the subject with the EOU and other appropriate American agencies. An Anglo-American committee, now operating under the code name CROSSBOW, was organized in November.[141]

New surprises awaited the Allies. Through October and early November, CIU interpreters, advised that the size of the V-weapons required rail transport, pored over photographs of northern France, looking for activity around railroad tracks. The first week in November, a French construction supervisor passed along the location of eight unusual sites on which he was working. Photoreconnaissance flown on the basis of this tip revealed all eight sites, each including several long buildings with an upward curving end, from which they collectively produced the name ski sites. None was near a rail line. With the characteristic buildings to alert them and the knowledge that they needed to expand their search away from railheads, the interpreters went back to previous photographs. Within 48 hours they identified 26 additional ski sites. By mid-December, more than 75 sites had been discovered.[142]

Although these sites might be related to the pilotless aircraft or flying bomb, this was not confirmed until the end of November 1943 when CIU made a dual discovery, the first link between buildings at Peenemunde and those at the ski sites. Alerted to look for "a very small aircraft, smaller than a fighter," keen-eyed British interpreter Constance Babington-Smith went back to photographs of Peenemunde taken the previous June and picked out a small, winged projectile leaning against a wall. Several days later another was seen on a launch ramp.[143]

Having determined the flying bomb represented the more immediate threat, the Allies decided in early December to strike 26 ski sites judged to be at least half complete.* The opening move of operations, which would continue until the end of August 1944, came the day before Christmas when 724 USAAF heavy bombers and 600 fighter-bombers and escorts attacked 24 sites in northwest France.[144] American medium bombers and fighter-bombers of Ninth and Eighth Air Forces and British tactical air forces conducted continual operations against these facilities, while Eighth Air Force heavy bombers went against them when weather prevented POINTBLANK missions. Guidance for these operations came from target lists sent out by the RAF ACAS, Operations.[145] By the end of May, the Allies considered 82 of 96 identified sites "neutralized." Of these, Ninth Air Force had taken out 39; Eighth Air Force, 35; and the British tactical air forces, the remaining 33.[146]

What the Allies did not know was that the initial attacks in December had convinced the Germans to abandon the ski sites as active locations and to undertake repairs only for deception. As had been the case after the earlier destruction of the V–2 rocket site at Watten, the enemy shifted to modified, prefabricated installations, much more difficult to detect and destroy. Not until late April 1944 did photointerpreters at CIU stumble upon the first of these modified sites. Although agent reports had mentioned them as early as February, the mistaken belief that the V–1s could be launched only from the relatively complex ski sites had led scientists and photointerpreters to overlook alternate sites. Once again, the trap of assuming the enemy will do what the observer wants, not what the enemy himself wants, had hindered the correct interpretion. Now provided with some idea of what the needle looked like, photointerpreters went back to the haystack. By D-day they had positively identified 61 modified sites. By this time, agent reports mentioned more than 100 such installations.[147] The Germans opened their flying bomb offensive from the modified sites on the night of June 13, 1944, one week after D-day.

Attempts to blunt the German offensive by attacking the modified sites met with only limited success and resulted in increasing frustration as it became obvious that the enemy could prepare launch facilities faster than the Allies could identify and destroy them. This frustration was accentuated by the timing of events. Every sortie flown against the V–1 sites was a sortie not available to support Allied forces struggling for a foothold on the continent. American airmen had particularly opposed employment of strategic air forces against V–1 and V–2 sites. To the extent that heavy bombers had to be used against the V-weapons, storage and construction locations were more appropriate targets.[148] Unfortunately, intelligence regarding the locations of such installations was extremely limited. On the basis primarily of agent reports and POW informa-

---

*To assist in determining how to attack these sites most effectively, the USAAF constructed in twelve days and at a cost of $1 million a complete replica of one facility at Eglin Army Airfield, Florida, on the basis of photographs and structural estimates.

tion, along with some ULTRA guidance, Eighth Air Force bombers attacked suspected supply depots at Nucourt and Saint Leu-d'Esserent in France in late June, with RAF Bomber Command following up several nights later. Such was the paucity of intelligence that several other missions, flown mostly by Bomber Command, turned out to have gone against inactive locations.[149]

On the basis of EOU/MEW analysis derived from American OSS and British Special Intelligence Service agents, Polish intelligence, British sources in Switzerland, and estimates of reduced output of goods formerly produced in suspected plants, Eighth Air Force and RAF Bomber Command also flew several missions into Germany itself. Most combined British and American tactical air forces missions continued to be against the modified launch sites as they were discovered.[150]

Throughout this period, the British had controlled the intelligence-gathering and analysis processes and the operational decisions on targeting. When the Air Ministry sought to modify the CROSSBOW arrangements in mid-July, the Americans took the opportunity to initiate a fundamental reorganization. The British suggested that CROSSBOW come under their Assistant Director of Intelligence (Science), Dr. R. V. Jones, with an American scientist as his deputy.[151] The Americans insisted on a combined British-American committee composed of uniformed operational and intelligence representatives from the Air Ministry and HQ USSTAF.

In a personal memorandum to Maj. Gen. Frederick Anderson, McDonald poured out his exasperation over the handling of the V-weapon situation. Referring to the "impractical applications of security" which had always pervaded BODYLINE and CROSSBOW, McDonald enumerated examples of a persistent failure by the British to keep their American counterparts involved or even informed. These included "inadequate dissemination of intelligence," "misapplication of forces," the "lag over damage assessment . . . [which] resulted in unnecessary duplication of attack and wasteful bombing effort," and "too little voice by this headquarters in matters of CROSSBOW policy."[152] After a series of memoranda and, undoubtedly, personal discussions among McDonald, Anderson, and Spaatz and between HQ USSTAF and the RAF (as well as Tedder in his role as Deputy Supreme Allied Commander), McDonald summarized the American position in a letter to his Air Ministry counterpart, the ACAS (I): "Frankly, I do not believe that anything less than a joint and balanced Anglo-American CROSSBOW Committee, formed exclusively from representatives of the Air Staff and USSTAF . . . will answer the requirement."[153]

The new CROSSBOW committee, organized along the lines the Americans had suggested, held its first meeting on July 21, 1944. Out of this session came a reordering of priorities. The weight of evidence was now clearly against efforts to knock out the modified sites. A USSTAF intelligence paper dated July 16, 1944, admitted they were as yet unable to fully evaluate the impact of air strikes against handling and storage areas, but it suggested that "strategic attacks on the basic industries producing components" appeared more effective than attacks on the launch sites.[154] Later that month, a combined operations planning committee suggested that even extensive attacks of these sites were neither efficient nor effective and could not prevent the enemy from launching at least thirty missiles a day from as yet unidentified locations. This committee reiterated that supply depots in France and Belgium and factories in Germany were better targets.[155]

During the last week in July the joint CROSSBOW committee concluded, "The attack by large formations [against launch sites] was wasteful and unlikely to bring about any marked reduction in the enemy's scale of attack."[156] Seeking to limit operations against launch sites to harassing attacks primarily by tactical forces, the committee recommended as first priority a series of supply depots, followed by two special fuel dumps linked to the V-1 supply system, and then five assumed factories in Germany and eastern France.[157] As it turned out, the question of control over CROSSBOW operations and intelligence became largely a dead issue within six weeks after the new committee was formed. The ground advance into northern France and the Low Countries in August and September forced the Germans to withdraw their remaining V-1s. Eighth Air Force flew its last CROSSBOW mission on August 30, 1944.[158]

Although Allied attention had focused primarily on the flying bomb in the spring and summer of 1944, the V-2 rocket remained ominously in the shadows. The V-2 had been discovered first, but accurate information remained scarce. Alerted by Polish underground sources of German flight testing at Blizna, the Allies flew the first reconnaissance mission over that target in April 1944.[159] Reports from the Poles, some ULTRA decrypts of an infrequently broken German Army code, and POW interrogations finally gave the Allies by June 1944 a fairly accurate picture of the characteristics, performance, and development of the V-2.[160] When the first V-2 rocket hit England on September 8, 1944, however, the Germans had developed, as the director of the V-2 program later admitted, the capability to fire the weapon from "a bit of planking on a forest track, or the overgrown track itself."[161] An attempt to ferret out launching positions and attack them from the air, especially with bombers, was obviously futile.

Although Eighth and Ninth Air Force bombers were directed against several V-2-related targets, including production centers and liquid oxygen plants in Germany and France, their impact was negligible.[162] Despite the enormous effort that had gone into comprehending the V-2, intelligence had provided only a limited guidance to its operations, and air attacks had only limited impact on the enemy's program. That the V-2 had so little effect on the war turned out to be the result of German technical problems, the inherent limitations of the weapon itself, and the advance of the Allied ground armies.

Emphasis on the V-weapons in the winter of 1943–1944 stemmed from two concerns. The first was the social and political issue of the effect of large-scale, even if inaccurate, air attacks on London. The second involved the potential impact of these weapons on the massive land, naval, and air forces being assembled for the assault on Fortress Europe which was scheduled for late spring. The precise roles of air power in this mighty endeavor were the subject of extensive and sometimes acrimonious debate. That air power would be crucial to Allied success, no one doubted.

OVERLORD and Tactical Air Operations in Western Europe: 1944–1945

Air support for the invasion of France began long before the first Allied soldiers came ashore at Normandy on June 6, 1944. In the broadest sense, the objective of the CBO was the progressive destruction of Germany's capability and will to wage war so as to, in the words of the plan guiding the CBO, "permit initiation of final combined operations on the continent."[163] Debilitating the GAF via Operation POINTBLANK served this purpose by allowing the strategic air forces to attack other elements of the enemy's war industries and economy and by providing command of the air for Allied land and tactical air operations. More directly, in the months preceding D-day, Allied strategic and tactical air forces engaged primarily in operations that prepared northwest France for the invasion.

Planning for tactical air operations imposed new requirements on air intelligence organizations in the United Kingdom. Until the spring of 1944, RAF and USAAF intelligence agencies were overwhelmingly concerned either with the *Luftwaffe* as a defensive force or with the identification and evaluation of strategic air targets. Now, support for OVERLORD required information not only on the GAF in its offensive and ground support roles but also on the German ground forces and their logistical system. While continuing to fulfill strategic functions, air intelligence now assumed three additional responsibilities: assessing the response of the GAF to the invasion; identifying and monitoring targets for tactical air operations; and providing information, primarily through photoreconnaissance, for Allied ground forces.

What made the air activity before OVERLORD/NEPTUNE different from previous amphibious operations was the magnitude of the effort.*[164] American

---

*OVERLORD was the code name for all the activities involved in the invasion of western Europe; NEPTUNE referred more narrowly to the crossing of the English Channel and the landings at Normandy. Allied commands in England tended to use the term "NEPTUNE" more frequently than the now-common "OVERLORD."

After the ground breakout from the Normandy invasion beaches, the Allies had tactical air superiority. This photo of wrecked German equipment at the Falaise Gap shows the punch of tactical air power in support of ground forces. Below, the German fighter field at Frankfurt was peppered by the Ninth Air Force. Meanwhile, the aerial interdiction campaign continued to play havoc with German attempts to reinforce and supply their troops. This railroad bridge at Blois, France, is one of hundreds of highway and railroad bridges destroyed.

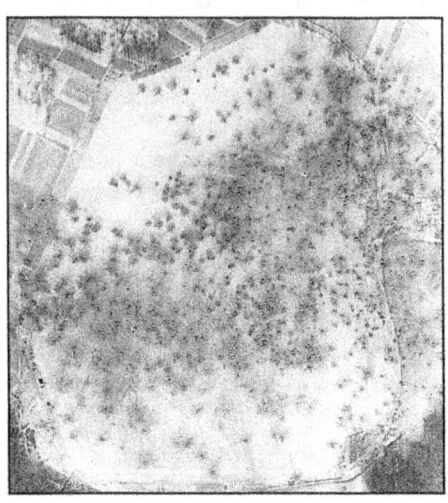

Eighth and Ninth Air Forces were heavily involved in these operations, the latter almost exclusively so. While their B–17s and B–24s continued to attack German aircraft factories through much of April, in May their attention turned to marshaling yards and airfields in France, Belgium, and the western part of Germany. Beginning on May 21, VIII Fighter Command's P–47s and P–51s joined the Ninth Air Force in extensive attacks on rail bridges. As part of Operation FORTITUDE, the deception plan to convince the defenders that the real attack would come in the Pas de Calais region, twice as many bombs were dropped on targets north of the Seine as were dropped to the south. Obviously, this increased the burden on intelligence as much as it did on operations.[165]

Despite participation by the heavy bombers and their escorts, Ninth Air Force made the principal American air contribution to OVERLORD before and after D-day. As directed by Eisenhower, the Ninth's primary objective was the German transportation network in France and Belgium. In the two months before D-day, medium bombers, fighter-bombers, and strafing fighters also struck more than sixty airfields and sought to neutralize German coastal batteries. Reconnaissance elements flew more than 400 sorties against gun emplacements, beach defenses, transportation points, airfields, and other targets.[166] Once the forces were ashore at Normandy, Ninth Air Force became deeply involved in the collection and analysis of intelligence, including the establishment of a SIGINT capability and mobile photoreconnaissance and analysis facilities to meet the demands for immediate responses to fluid combat situations. During preinvasion operations, however, both the Eighth and Ninth relied on previously established intelligence organizations.[167]

Photographic reconnaissance remained the primary source for monitoring static targets such as bridges, marshaling yards, and airfields. Hundreds of reconnaissance missions had pinpointed virtually every useful target within the German transportation system. As these targets became the focus of air attack, aerial reconnaissance and agent reports were the main sources of information on specific attacks and constituted the means to determine when reattacks were necessary. ULTRA provided some details on individual targets, but it was more valuable for its insight on the German assessment of conditions.[168]

The location of almost all airfields in northwest Europe had been identified by a combined Anglo-American section within Air Ministry Intelligence, and a watch was maintained on them by the airfield section of the CIU as well as by the French underground. By the spring of 1944, these organizations provided not only locations but capacities, facilities, and even designations of appropriate aiming points. At the same time, SIGINT followed the movement of enemy flying units. In the first week of May, ULTRA revealed the installations to which units from Germany and other regions would move in the event of an invasion. Two weeks later, it provided intelligence on the distribution of fuel, ammunition, and bombs.[169] Results of the ongoing campaign against German airfields were revealed by all these sources.

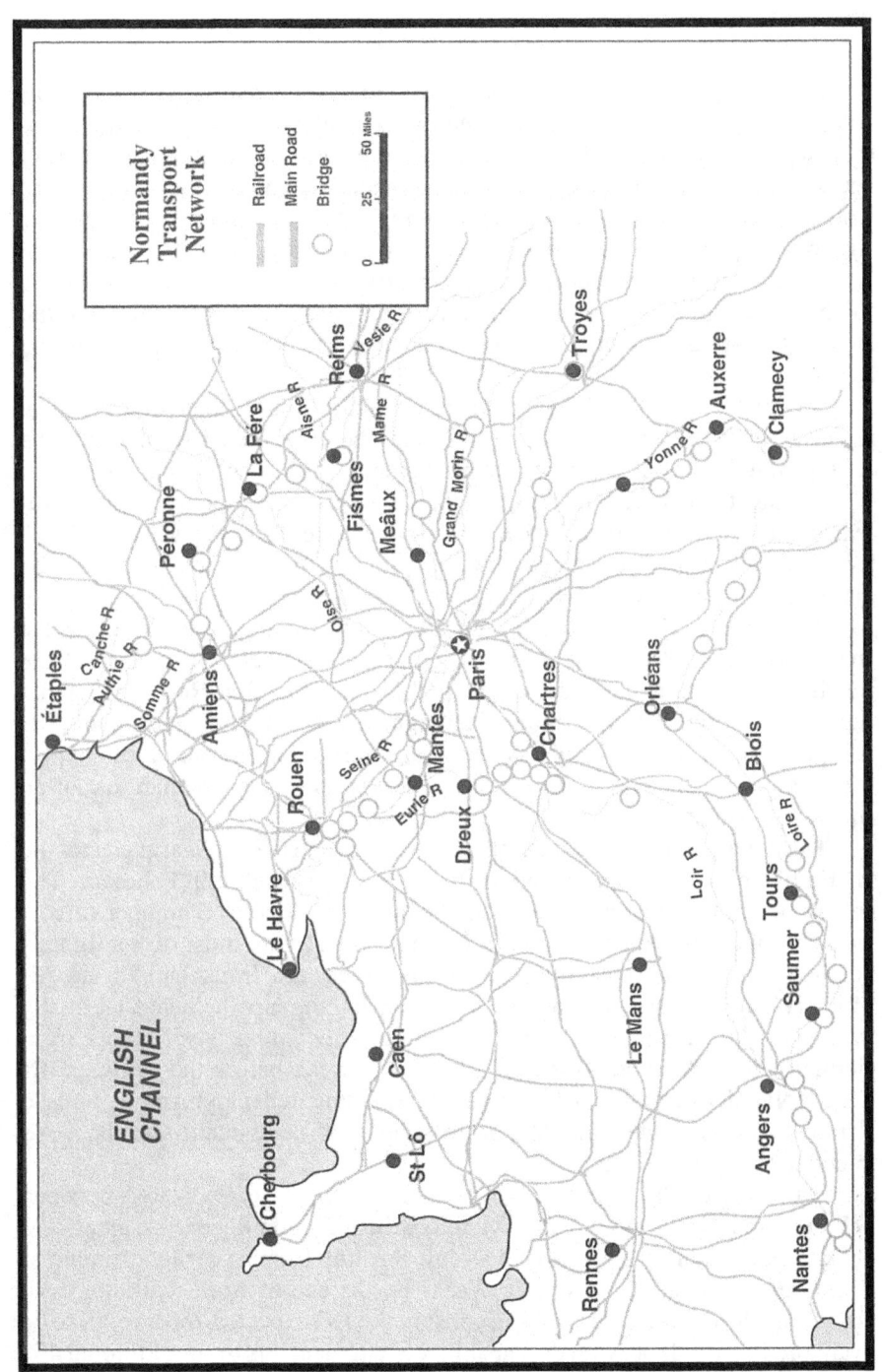

Evaluations of the *Luftwaffe* prior to June reflected different perceptions within Allied intelligence agencies regarding the intentions of the German high command. Given the mobility of air forces, the question of intent had a direct bearing on overall capability. If Hitler intended to contest the invasion, he would be more likely to move fighter units into the combat zone and thus significantly increase the level of operations. Should he decide to contain the Allies within a small beachhead rather than trying to prevent their achieving a foothold, this might call for a smaller air reaction. A larger percentage of the already hard-pressed fighter force could then be retained for air defense of the Reich.

An Air Ministry (A.I.3[b]) appreciation in mid-March noted that "no final forecast [of GAF strength] can at this stage be attempted." It appeared the enemy would not commit more than 50–60 percent of its single-engine fighter force against the initial landing so that it might "attempt to preserve [a] reasonably effective fighter force for the air defence of Germany at a later date." Even a major effort in conjunction with a ground counterattack "could not be maintained in the face of Allied air superiority and heavy casualties."[170] One month later, the AEAF's plan for the Normandy landing concluded that the enemy would withhold most of his day and night fighters for defense of the Reich and protection of his bases and lines of communication. Recognizing that fighting value rather than numerical strength was the critical determinant, the AEAF looked at the *Luftwaffe*'s "stamina, reserves and recent close-support exposure" and concluded, "This value is certain to be far less than that of an equivalent Allied force."[171]

The Ninth Air Force's plan for NEPTUNE issued in late April argued that the GAF fighter force had not recovered from the blows dealt it in February. The enemy would face the invasion with a "dangerously depleted bomber force," with an unimpressive ground attack capability, and with most of his fighter-bomber units already heavily engaged on the eastern front. Unlike the Air Ministry and AEAF assessments, American intelligence believed Germany "will strip her defenses to a bare minimum," including day fighters from Germany, to prevent an Allied lodgment.[172] A week before the landings, IX TAC pointed to recent GAF messages regarding redeployment to unused airfields and defensive construction in support of assessment that the GAF intended to contest the issue.[173]

Estimates of the *Luftwaffe*'s first-line strength also fluctuated between February and May 1944. In early March, British air intelligence assumed 850 operational aircraft in the region at D-day, the drop from an earlier estimate of 1,450 due to the successes of Big Week. By the end of April, with the GAF conserving its numbers by avoiding combat, the JIC expected 750 aircraft to be available by early June, with the capability to augment this by an additional 450

The European Theater of Operations

within four days. Finally, piecing together information from photoreconnaissance, ULTRA, low-grade SIGINT, and agents, Allied intelligence the day before the attack provided a final estimate of 1,015 aircraft immediately available. The listed strength of *Luftflotte 3* in France and the Low Countries at the end of May was 891, with an increase to 1,300 by D+10.[174] According to a USSTAF study on ULTRA during the war, the greatest contribution of this source in the months before D-day was the picture it gradually built up regarding the GAF's logistical difficulties, training problems, and command arrangements.[175] It was this insight that allowed Allied intelligence to assess the weaknesses of the *Luftwaffe* that lay behind the numbers. More recently, an excellent study of ULTRA and the campaign in western Europe by a former intelligence officer in BP's Hut 3 during this period also concluded, "The most striking evidence in German Air Force [messages] during the later spring was on shortages of all kinds."[176]

Most senior American airmen approached D-day not at all confident that the GAF would play the negligible role it did. In late April, Arnold admitted to Spaatz that "my feeling [is] that a great air battle will take place during the first three or four days of OVERLORD."[177] At a weekly air commanders-in-chief meeting less than two weeks before NEPTUNE, and the same week intelligence suggested the *Luftwaffe* would not be fully committed, Spaatz thought the enemy "might well be prepared to uncover occupied Europe altogether and bring all his fighters . . . to the Western Front."[178] The *Luftwaffe*'s actual performance against NEPTUNE was weaker than even the most optimistic Allied predictions. This was a consequence of Big Week and the subsequent air combat during attacks against German industry. The extensive operations against German air bases in France and the Low Countries by Allied air forces in April and May also contributed to the disorganization that afflicted the *Luftwaffe*.

Another contribution was the assistance intelligence provided tactical air operations against the GAF fighter and bomber forces beginning on June 6. The successful monitoring of the location, status, and intentions of the opposing air force paid handsome dividends. Knowing where GAF units earmarked for the combat zone were to go, and sometimes even when they would arrive, Allied air forces could discombobulate their opponents before they could mount an effective engagement. On June 8, *Fliegerkorps II* informed Berlin that it had received nine new fighter units, and it reported their strengths and locations. The next day, the same headquarters reported "serious losses in personnel and equipment due to attacks on airfields."[179] The ability to blend ULTRA with Y intercepts enabled the Allies to determine, often precisely, the arrival times of GAF units, and thus to determine when to attack them just as they were landing at their receiving bases.[180] Throughout the month of June, Allied air headquarters were able to read, according to an ULTRA-indoctrinated intelligence officer, "innumerable commands for movement and operations. . . ."[181] These did not provide a total picture of the enemy because some messages were not received

Piercing the Fog

or decrypted, and because, in the confusion of combat, enemy units sometimes failed to send reports, or they sent incomplete or inaccurate data. Within 36 hours of the invasion, Allied intelligence had identified some 300 of the 400–450 aircraft the Germans would move into the Normandy region by June 10.[182]

Domination of the GAF that had been established in the opening days of NEPTUNE continued through the summer, although the ability to monitor frequently, often instantaneously, active airfields and their condition was not always possible. When it was, it allowed commanders and intelligence officers an unprecedented look at the enemy's intentions and his ability to execute them, his losses, and the status of his aircraft and equipment.[183] These effects were felt in several ways. First, if a decrypted message was seen in time and evaluated correctly, it could provide guidance for mission planning. Messages such as the one sent to subordinate units by *Jagdkorps II* on August 26 directing operations for the next day contained not only the type of missions and the areas of operation, but the location and altitude of rendezvous points as well.[184] Similarly, the approval from an unidentified headquarters of Melsbroek and Chievres airfields in Belgium as collection points for FW 190s and Bf 109s provided the appropriate Allied target officers with invaluable information.[185] Often such messages were received too late to provide immediate operational direction.

For this reason, ULTRA's more valuable contribution continued to be confirmation of and insight into the effects of operations against the GAF. On July 9, BP decrypted a message from Goering decreeing that "because of the intolerable loss in unit commanders" these officers would fly only "when the significance of the operation and number of aircraft employed make it necessary."[186] In early August, just as the Allied armies began their breakout from Normandy, *Jagdkorps II* (responsible for close support to the German Army) advised Berlin it was pulling back four of its best *gruppen* for rest and refit.[187] Considering the desperate situation confronting the German Army, such a move must have been seen by Allied air commanders as a clear indication of the *Luftwaffe*'s battered condition. Two weeks later, this same headquarters advised its superiors that it could not participate effectively in the battle at Falaise because units were repeatedly attacked as they tried to take off. Two groups had lost twenty-two planes in this way in one day.[188]

Tactical SIGINT proved especially valuable in operations against the already weakened GAF. With the establishment of Detachment 3, 3d Radio Squadron (Mobile), on the continent only three days after the initial landings, USAAF tactical air forces began independent signals interception, although they continued to maintain links with British units. The focal point for this undertaking, much of which was time-sensitive, was the SIGINT officer located at IX TAC fighter control, who was in direct contact with airborne aircraft and HQ IX TAC.[189]

The European Theater of Operations

Intelligence gained through radio intercepts could often contribute to immediate air action. According to the IX TAC history, intercepted SIGINT passed to aircraft already in the air resulted in the claimed destruction of 180 enemy planes between June 1944 and March 1945. This figure does not include the results of missions planned specifically to take advantage of a second benefit of SIGINT: the analyses of enemy operational patterns. Such analyses enabled intelligence officers to predict enemy actions. On October 6, 1944, for example, the IX TAC SIGINT officer advised fighter control that enemy aircraft operating around Aachen would most probably return to base by flying directly from Aachen to Bonn. Scrambled fighters, directed to intercept the enemy en route when the latter were low on fuel and out of ammunition, shot down twenty.[190]

By mid-August the condition of the opposing air force was obvious. At the highest theater air level, General McDonald wrote, "It does not appear to be an overconfident statement that the German Air Force is at present time powerless to influence our Allied ground armies' operations."[191] At the cutting edge of air operations, the special security officer assigned to First Tactical Air Force operating with the Sixth Army Group observed, "Allied air operations almost completely disregarded the GAF."[192]

During the first days of NEPTUNE, in addition to neutralizing enemy air power, Allied air forces provided direct support to troops on the beach and focused on isolating the battle areas through interdiction. In the fluid situation that prevailed, intelligence arrived from several sources. The photoreconnaissance that had covered all of northern France in the preceding months now guided fighter-bombers and medium bombers against bridges that had not been destroyed for deception purposes, including the important spans across the Loire River. Visual reconnaissance proved the most important source for the transient intelligence needed to discover and attack troops on the move. At the same time, ULTRA decrypts and intercepts of German Army low-grade radio signals both eased the task of tracking enemy formations. Most accommodating in this regard was a German army inspector general's report only two weeks before D-day that provided the location of every major German armor unit in France and the Low Countries.[193]

On June 16, Captain Kindleberger, a member of the EOU and at the time working as an ULTRA handler with 21st Army Group, prepared an interim assessment of German reserve movement by rail, listing the location of virtually all enemy units then moving toward Normandy. The information contained in this document came from photointelligence, tactical air reconnaissance, air liaison officers assigned to U.S. Army units, and visual reports by Eighth Air Force fighters on escort duty with bombers, as well as from SIGINT.[194]

The successful landing of Allied ground troops in Normandy on June 6, 1944, opened a new dimension to the air war in western Europe and thus placed new demands on air intelligence. The nature of air intelligence in support of

Piercing the Fog

ground operations differed considerably from that required for strategic air operations. The intimate relationship between air and ground action, and the transient nature of tactical targets, necessitated an intelligence organization structured for the rapid collection, evaluation, and distribution of information. In contrast to the strategic air forces, for whom the *Luftwaffe* remained a serious—if weakened—adversary, tactical airmen and the armies they supported went about their tasks largely unconcerned with attack from the air.[195]

The principle of colocated air and ground equivalent headquarters contributed significantly to the effective application of air intelligence to the land war. Except for brief periods of rapid movement, General Hoyt Vandenberg's Ninth Air Force remained with General Omar Bradley's 12th Army Group, while IX TAC and later XIX and XXIX TAC were colocated with First, Third, and Ninth Armies, respectively. For the invasion of southern France in August (Operation DRAGOON), XII TAC was shifted from Italy to support the American Seventh Army and later the Allied Sixth Army Group as part of First Tactical Air Force (Prov.). Because of the relationship between the tactical air commands and the armies they supported, much of the day-to-day decision making, including targeting, took place between the headquarters of those organizations. Ninth Air Force was responsible for providing overall policy and direction and for reallocating subordinate units to meet special operational requirements. Unless directed specifically by SHAEF, the Ninth Air Force commander or his representative (usually the director of operations) made air operations decisions at the morning meeting held with 12th Army Group. These decisions routinely were based on the intelligence report and Bradley's plan of attack.[196]

Ninth Air Force made simultaneous daily mission decisions, since it controlled the IX Bomber Command's eleven medium-bomber groups. Until September, much of the intelligence guidance for the employment of the medium bombers came from a special security officer assigned to the target section of AEAF's advanced headquarters. From this position Maj. Lucius Buck coordinated with 12th Army Group Targets, Ninth Air Force A–2 and A–3, SHAEF G–2 Targets, and the Air Ministry to blend ULTRA, tactical photointerpretation reports, ground reports, and POW interrogations into tactical target lists. With the disbandment of HQ AEAF and the incorporation of its intelligence section into the new Air Staff, SHAEF, Buck was assigned to Ninth Air Force, but he operated from the Air Ministry where he performed the same functions. By September the focus of his efforts, and those of the IX Bomber Command, was petroleum, oil, and lubricants (POL) depots; ammunition dumps; and military transport parks. At the beginning of December, USSTAF and SHAEF as well as Ninth Air Force and the tactical air commands received Buck's target lists.[197]

From the time IX TAC landed at Normandy on D+2, the first tactical air command to do so, intelligence was fully integrated into air-ground operations.

The European Theater of Operations

A–2 and A–3 occupied the same tent, which also included First Army's G–2 (Air) and G–3 (Air).[198] The IX TAC's A–2 office consisted of sections handling operational intelligence, air OB, targets, reconnaissance, signals, flak, counterintelligence, and administration.[199] Operational intelligence dealt with reports of enemy ground formations. Much of this information came from visual reconnaissance transmitted by radio from aircraft in flight, and it then passed immediately to G–2 (Air) and G–3 (Air) and thence through the Army's communications net as well as to appropriate IX TAC units. Operational intelligence officers briefed the commander and his staff each evening on the day's operations to provide the basis for the next day's mission planning.[200]

Tactical reconnaissance, already important in the preinvasion period, assumed even greater significance once land operations began. Through the summer of 1944, most current reconnaissance for the employment of air forces derived from visual tactical air reports. This emphasis resulted from two conditions. Static targets (gun positions, airfields, bridges, and key rail segments) had been thoroughly covered in the months prior to D-day, and existing tactical target dossiers included photographs. Periodic checks assessed the current status of these targets and their condition after being attacked. Most targets during NEPTUNE and the subsequent breakout and race across France were enemy troops and vehicles on the move. Visual reconnaissance passed through interlinked Allied army-air forces communications nets enabled the most timely reaction to these fleeting targets.

This is not to say photoreconnaissance could be or was ignored, particularly in the weeks before the breakout. In his report of German rail movements approaching Normandy, Kindleberger had stressed the value of poststrike photoreconnaissance to confirm pilot visual reports. By verifying claims of damage, he advised, reconnaissance could enable operations to cancel preplanned missions against already destroyed lines and permit a more concentrated effort against those the enemy was still using or was about to repair.[201] The Army had an ever-expanding requirement for photoreconnaissance to assist in the planning of land operations. So great was this demand that within a month of D-day, IX TAC and First Army had jointly designated a full-time Army reconnaissance officer assigned to A–3 to coordinate reconnaissance requests among the IX TAC A–2 and A–3, 67th Tactical Reconnaissance Group (TRG), and First Army.[202] In addition, the Army maintained a ground liaison officer with the 67th TRG to assist in detailed mission planning. Because the various tactical air command headquarters relied on their Army counterparts for intelligence on the German Army, air intelligence officers kept only limited files on this subject.[203]

When stiffening resistance slowed the Allied advances along the German border in early fall, photoreconnaissance increased in importance. Joint air-land operations required complete coverage to permit detailed planning. Fighter-bombers and medium bombers needed photographs of assigned targets to

Piercing the Fog

execute their missions effectively. Because they were now beyond the regions covered extensively before June, the IX TAC reconnaissance section's primary task became the preparation of photomosaics, maps, and annotated target photos for the target section. In addition, this section evaluated bomb damage, analyzed, in cooperation with A–3, the effects of special bombing techniques, and prepared, in conjunction with the target section, target dossiers and mission folders.[204]

Unless 12th Army Group or Ninth Air Force directed a specific operation or the reallocation of forces from one tactical air command to another, the army and tactical air commanders and their key staff officers made the daily target decisions.[205] Major Buck's list served as the basic compilation for selecting targets. As with other such lists, the source of any specific bit of information was often difficult to ascertain. In his postwar report, Buck admitted that while ULTRA provided "the basic and most reliable material," he blended this with other sources before he forwarded his recommendations to Ninth Air Force and the tactical air commands.[206] SHAEF G–2 also published periodic revisions to a master interdiction handbook, which identified bridges and viaducts by location, indicated their structural characteristics, previous damage, and flak defenses, and included other appropriate assessments.[207] Not surprisingly, because the overwhelming portion of targets involved the German Army, most of the ULTRA intelligence came through army channels and was presented by the army SSO assigned to the appropriate headquarters.

While photoreconnaissance and other sources focused on static locations, ULTRA provided glimpses of more fleeting targets. In one of its most spectacular offerings, ULTRA revealed the location of the German headquarters responsible for controlling all panzer divisions sent against the Allies in the opening days of NEPTUNE. Based on this intelligence, an especially effective air strike caused such damage and casualties as to remove that critical command center for two weeks.[208] Similarly, a decrypt pinpointing a concentration of military vehicles camouflaged in a wooded area in eastern France two months later was passed to the XIX TAC A–2. After the original source was protected by an air reconnaissance mission, the subsequent air attack destroyed an estimated 400 vehicles.[209]

Among the most significant insights ULTRA offered were the locations of fuel and ammunition dumps. These installations, often difficult to detect from the air, provided the lifeblood of the German forces. Even here, mission planners still needed photographs to pinpoint precise locations since decrypts generally identified only an area. For example, a series of messages in late August 1944 referred to a fuel depot at Givet, France, without providing an exact location in the village or surrounding area.[210] ULTRA could be more precise on occasion. On August 26, BP signaled the decrypt of a request for a locomotive and tank cars to move oil from Pont sec de Passy, near Lezinnes,

The European Theater of Operations

France, to Dijon.²¹¹ Since the commands received this signal three days after the original German transmission, it may or may not have provided a useful target.

Because of the German need to communicate hurriedly in what was at times a chaotic retreat and the nature of German radio traffic being passed, those who read ULTRA saw much disarray. This led to mistaken impressions that the German military was about to collapse. The Allies could not tap into the landline communications within Germany by which the high command was beginning, by early September, to reorganize and rebuild its forces. Ironically, while trying to reconstitute themselves, the German Army and GAF provided intelligence contributing to their continued destruction. As the Germans identified their locations and unit strengths, they enabled Allied planners to focus their air strikes and then to assess the resulting courses of action.

Although the battle for Germany would last almost eight more months, with only two exceptions, air intelligence had found its niche. These two instances were the Ardennes counteroffensive in mid-December and the *Luftwaffe*'s dawn attack against Allied air bases on January 1, 1945.

The German offensive in December represented not just an air intelligence failure but a failure of Allied intelligence overall. Taken together, the ULTRA decrypts available on German air and land movements provided enough clues to suggest the possibility of a German offensive. In late October, in fact, British air intelligence, keying on the precision of the German language in several messages and on more general evidence of an air buildup, concluded the enemy was preparing a spoiling attack rather than, as almost universally believed, simply strengthening his defensive positions or organizing for an attempted counteroffensive after the Allies crossed the Roer River.²¹² Six weeks later, in the face of continued *Luftwaffe* emphasis on Reich air defense, air intelligence concluded on December 6, "The original plan for [a] 'lightening [*sic*] blow' and sudden attack in the west may with some certainty be said to have lapsed. . . ."²¹³

The problem was not a lack of evidence that something was afoot. Of this there was plenty, not only in ULTRA but in the hundreds of visual and photoreconnaissance reports of extensive ground forces activities and rail movements within Germany.²¹⁴ The problem was an alternative explanation toward which Allied intelligence was too easily lulled. Convinced the enemy was too weak for offensive action, both air and ground intelligence officers chose to believe he was merely strengthening his defenses in the hope of holding off the western Allies through the winter.²¹⁵

That the GAF intended to engage in extensive ground support in this region was evident from late October, and increasingly so by the end of November. An extensive reorganization established a command structure geared for such operations. In the last week of October ULTRA advised the Allies that the GAF was stocking airfields north of Aachen with fuel and ammunition.²¹⁶ In contradistinction to earlier dispositions of fighter units to enhance home air defense, by mid-November it became clear that fighters, perhaps as many as 850, were being shifted or prepared for movement to the west.[217] Units were directed to ensure the capability to equip fighters for ground attack on short notice. One such directive even referred to a "special project" as the reason for these steps.[218]

What made these messages difficult to assess properly, or made them too easy to misinterpret, was the fact that virtually all the steps being taken or ordered were consistent with the employment of the *Luftwaffe* in support of defensive ground operations. Given any rational evaluation of the probabilities of success and the consequences of failure of a spoiling attack, a major German offensive made no sense. The failure was not one of not recognizing signs of the impending thrust; rather, the culprit was the wish that the enemy would do as the analysts and commanders thought he should, not as the enemy himself wanted. Field Marshal Bernard Montgomery was right when he stated (ironically, on the day the attack began) that the German Army "has not the transport or the petrol that would be necessary for [extensive] mobile operations. . . ."[219] He was wrong in assuming Hitler would operate under such an assessment.

In the initial days of the German offensive, the biggest problem air intelligence faced was determining the relative positions of the opposing troops. Terrible weather (which prevented aerial reconnaissance), the rapidity of enemy movement, and the loss of contact with forward troops in the confusion of the first days made close support of American forces difficult. Once the weather broke, just before Christmas, the task of air intelligence, and air operations, became easier. Tactical photographic and visual reconnaissance of marshaling yards in Germany provided targets for heavy and medium bombers. For close support and interdiction in the immediate battle area, the most valuable source was visual reconnaissance since, as General Lee recalled, "It was [just] a question of what you could see on the ground."[220]

The last major German air attack—a dawn strike of some 700 aircraft against Allied bases in Holland and Belgium—came the morning of January 1, 1945. According to a history of the war, the attack, which destroyed about 150 aircraft and damaged more than 100 others, caught Allied intelligence off guard.[221] The British history of the war stated simply, "The GAF achieved surprise in a major attack on Allied airfields on 1 January. . . ."[222] Whether this strike could have been, or indeed was, foreseen remains unanswered. Several ULTRA messages referred to GAF units practicing for low-level strikes against airfields in December.[223] One of the ULTRA special security officers assigned to Ninth Air Force wrote in his after-action report that he had used ULTRA decrypts to convince the commanding general of an impending strike, and American fighters were in the air that morning. The director of operations for Ninth Air Force recalled he had gotten no indication of such an operation, and that it caught everyone off guard.[224] At any rate, the German New Year's assault had a very limited effect on the now massive Allied air superiority, while quick reactions by Allied pilots cost the *Luftwaffe* some 300 planes.

Strategic Air Operations: Summer 1944 to Spring 1945

By September 1944, the Allied ground offensive had progressed far beyond expectations. The prevailing opinion in the Allied camp was that the war with Germany would be over by the end of the year. In the middle of the month, the CCS removed the strategic air forces from Eisenhower's control and placed them under the Chiefs of Staff, RAF and AAF. The Deputy Chief of Air Staff and the Commanding General, USSTAF, were to serve as their executive agents. In practical terms, this shift had little impact either on operations or on the collection, evaluation, and dissemination of strategic air intelligence. Within weeks of securing a foothold in France, Eisenhower had given Spaatz a virtual free hand to employ his strategic air weapon.[225] By August the primary objective of that employment clearly was the destruction of the enemy's petroleum industry and its reserve capacity.

Although he had implemented Eisenhower's instructions to employ Eighth Air Force against the German transportation network in western Europe in support of OVERLORD, the USSTAF commander and his staff continued to focus on the German oil industry. In opposing the AEAF transportation program in the early months of 1944, USSTAF leaders had argued that only by threatening a system vitally important to Germany would the GAF be drawn into continued air combat. Failure to so challenge the *Luftwaffe* would negate the impact of Big Week by providing the enemy an opportunity to rebuild. Such rebuilding appeared to be underway by the spring of 1944. In a memorandum to the deputy commanding general for operations on April 9, McDonald noted the losses of the enemy fighter force in the first three months of 1944 had been 11 percent higher than in the previous year because of the expanded American daylight bombing campaign. The German high command realized this and had begun to withhold fighters for homeland defense, even when this meant that strikes against peripheral targets went unmolested. "Only maximum scale operations deep in Germany," warned the director of intelligence, "assure us the excess of wastage over production which is indispensable to the reduction of the German Air Force."[226]

Spaatz was absolutely convinced of the need to keep the GAF in a weakened state lest his bombers face a revitalized foe after OVERLORD. He threatened to resign unless he received authorization to conduct sufficient strikes to draw the enemy into battle and further weaken his industrial base.[227] Eisenhower consented; on May 12, 28, and 29, Eighth Air Force struck oil complexes in Germany. In the same period, Fifteenth Air Force hit the refineries at Ploesti. The German reaction to these raids, revealed through photoreconnaissance and ULTRA, provided incontestable evidence of the validity of concentrating on the petroleum industry. The decrypt of a GAF operations staff message the day after the May 12 attack on the refinery at Leuna revealed the transfer of flak batteries from aircraft production facilities at Oschersleben, Wiener Neustadt, and Leipzig-Erla to various synthetic oil plants. That the enemy was willing to reduce protection of his aircraft factories provided the clearest possible indication of the importance he attached to oil.[228]

By June 10, 1944, USSTAF had prepared its plan for the employment of the strategic air forces, which Spaatz personally carried to Eisenhower and Tedder on the 13th. The drafters of this plan, among them operations and intelligence officers, argued that events of the past sixty days had demonstrated tactical air forces could effectively support operations in France. Spaatz's people stated, "the German Air Force is no longer able to prevent the destruction by our air forces of any system of targets which we may now select." The key now was to determine on which system to concentrate. After reviewing the list of possible target systems, the planners concluded that attacks on the petroleum industry, with emphasis on gasoline, would most dramatically affect the enemy's combat capability across the board.[229]

Within weeks of the May attacks on oil targets, intelligence organizations outside USSTAF supported Spaatz in redirecting American strategic air efforts. As part of an analysis of the Allied interdiction program and recommendations for future operations, Eisenhower's own SHAEF G–2 identified oil as the strategic target that would most decisively affect the enemy's combat capability. While not totally ignoring the interdiction campaign, this report, based on an earlier EOU study, recommended that American heavy bombers also be directed against refineries, synthetic oil plants, and fuel dumps throughout western Europe.[230] In Washington, the COA was more emphatic. Directed by the AC/AS, Plans, to reassess their original March 1943 report in the light of the changed situation in Europe, the committee opined in June 1944, "Oil is clearly the most important strategic target after the policing of aircraft."[231]

Although Eisenhower issued no formal directive, he and Spaatz obviously had reached an agreement by the middle of June. Eighth Air Force conducted four major attacks in both June and July against the German oil industry. In August, it increased this number to nine assaults on refineries and other facilities in addition to extensive fighter-bomber attacks by Ninth Air Force against fuel depots in Germany, France, and Belgium.*[232] To provide targeting recommendations and to monitor the effectiveness of this expanding oil

---

*Between May 1, 1944, and March 31, 1945, Eighth and Fifteenth Air Forces and RAF Bomber Command conducted 555 separate attacks on 133 oil industry targets, plus numerous raids on reserve oil depots and POL dumps. Nevertheless, Eighth Air Force's 222 oil-related attacks constituted only 13 percent of its total tonnage dropped in this period.

The European Theater of Operations

campaign, the Allies created a Joint Oil Targets Committee in July. In early August, General McDonald forwarded to the USSTAF deputy for operations the first comprehensive assessment of this group. Assuming a base level of 100 percent production in April 1944, the oil targets committee estimated this had been cut to 80 percent in May, to 58 percent in June (revised to 50 percent the next month), and to 49.5 percent in July (with an anticipated downward revision as more complete data became available). The committee also suggested that failure to continue operations at the same level would enable the enemy's production to rise as high as 68.5 percent by the end of August.[233]

Given the difficulties of assessing physical damage, let alone the impact of any given strike on production, the precision with which analysts rendered their estimates was questionable. Just two months earlier, in a message prepared by his director of intelligence, Spaatz had admitted to General Arnold his continuing difficulties in evaluating the damage being done to production capacities, in assessing the impact on the enemy's combat capabilities, and in estimating repair times. Moreover, he pointed out, such analysis was never instantaneous because weather often delayed poststrike reconnaissance missions. Referring specifically to the oil attacks in May, he observed the targets struck on May 12 had not been photographed until twelve days later.[234] Postwar analysis would reveal that the Allies' estimates of German oil production, consumption, and reserves were all too high, although the various errors tended to cancel out one another.[235] While the statistics were not always correct, the general trend was clear enough. More to the point, Allied intelligence was now beginning to obtain authoritative evidence of the operational impact of the oil campaign.

While indications of the effectiveness of these operations came through a variety of channels, Enigma was by far the dominant source. As early as June 5, 1944, the GAF operations staff advised subordinate units that because of "encroachment into the production of a/c fuel by enemy action . . . it has been necessary to break into the strategic reserves."[236] While this reserve was larger and the actual consumption of oil less than the Allies had estimated, such a step was seen as indicative of the potential the oil campaign offered. A month later, *Reichsmarshall* Herman Goering, decreed, "Drastic economy [in fuel use] is absolutely essential."[237] That same month, because of fuel shortages and directly contradicting previously standard procedures, the Germans ordered aircraft not to fly away from bases where attacks were expected.[238] Nor were combat units engaged against Allied forces in France exempt. In mid-July *Luftflotte 3* announced its intention to remove fuel stored at inactive bases, a measure that would severely restrict operational flexibility.[239] A month later, that same headquarters announced, "Damage to fuel production demands a further considerably greater reduction of all flying activities . . . [only] fighter operations in the course of air defense remain unrestricted."[240]

By autumn, it was becoming increasingly obvious that a shortage of fuel rather than a lack of either pilots or airplanes was the primary factor in restricting the *Luftwaffe*'s operations. On September 2, *Jagdkorps II*, which supported German armies in the west, reported 285 serviceable aircraft, but it added that two groups could not fly that day "owing to lack of fuel." That these units were now operating on airfields in Germany suggested that fuel shortages were systemwide and not merely the result of transportation dislocations in forward areas.[241] Supporting functions suffered even more drastically. The director of one of the GAF's technical armament branches announced in October, "All aircraft dry and no testing or ferrying possible."[242] According to a USSTAF-directed study on ULTRA and American air operations, from September onward "the files . . . become an almost continuous chronicle of oil shortage everywhere."[243] Still, it must have been particularly satisfying for those who put forward the oil plan to read a message of November 18 announcing orders, probably from Goering: "Operations are to be ruthlessly cut down, i.e., operations must only take place when the weather situation and other prerequisites guarantee promise of success."[244] In the face of such evidence, there could be little doubt in the air commanders' minds of oil's continued priority.

Well before ULTRA began to provide information on the effects of oil shortages on the *Luftwaffe,* Spaatz had shifted the focus of American strategic bombing from the German aircraft industry and the GAF itself. In response to those who had cautioned against too hasty a de-emphasis on the GAF, the commanding general declared in April 1944, "The requisite intensity of Counter-Air Force actions . . . must now be judged by the principal Air Commanders only."[245] Relying largely on ULTRA decrypts, Spaatz advised his Air Force commanders on September 1 that, except for jet production installations, the German aircraft industry was not a priority target because the lack of fuel and qualified pilots, not airframes, was what was hindering German air operations.[246] ULTRA and other sources certainly supported this confidence, but the condition of the GAF was evident from its relative inactivity as well. Spaatz and his senior officers did not need special intelligence to tell them a force that refused to seriously contest attacks on its homeland was a force in trouble. In a letter to Arnold a month after OVERLORD, Spaatz commented on "the latent weakness of the German Air Force," observing, "It even appears that the effectiveness of POINTBLANK was greater than we had anticipated."[247]

Intelligence assessments from a variety of agencies through the fall of 1944 continued to confirm this assessment. In October, the EOU noted an increase in the production of single-engine fighters from between 500 and 600 a month earlier in the year to 1,400 a month. The economic analysts argued that neither production nor first-line strength was critical. Because petroleum shortages affected both operations and training, without which the expanding fleet would be impotent, the heavy bombers should continue to concentrate on oil. Fighter and fighter-bomber attacks on training bases continued to contribute to the

The European Theater of Operations

already serious delays in the *Luftwaffe*'s training program.[248] Also in October, a detailed study by the Air Ministry's A.I.3(b) section suggested even a projected increase from 2,000 to 2,600 single-engine fighters would not represent a serious problem for Allied operations overall. Recognizing that the introduction of jet aircraft would increase "the enemy's ability on occasion to inflict loss," A.I.3(b) concluded that jets would probably be used for ground attack and therefore they constituted "no appreciable threat to daylight raids" through the end of December.[249]

The USSTAF director of operations incorporated the evaluations of both EOU and A.I.3(b) into a report to the deputy commander for operations in early November. He argued that the threat to deep penetration attacks would certainly be no more and probably be less serious than it had been in the previous year. That the enemy fighter force was not operating to capacity dictated unrelenting efforts against oil.[250] Contributing further to the reluctance to attack the aircraft industry was the recognition that its dispersal was the most successful defensive measure the enemy had undertaken.[251]

Although USSTAF succeeded after the summer of 1944 in maintaining the German oil industry and all its components as the number one priority, the last phase of the strategic air war in Europe was marked by an expanding and often shifting array of target categories. The selection of these targets and their varying priorities, determined largely by developments in the land war, increased the demands on all aspects of intelligence. These demands included recommending priorities among and within target systems, preparing vastly increased amounts of materials to support individual operations, and the ever-expanding requirements to analyze bomb damage and monitor the condition of previously hit areas.

When ordnance depots became a priority for the strategic air bombers, for example, the Allied CIU at Medmenham developed more than a hundred new objective folders (in hundreds of copies each). Between early December 1944 and February 1945, emphasis on the German transportation system resulted in almost 200 new targets, from bridges to marshaling yards to stations.[252] In January 1945 the Eighth Air Force A–2 advised USSTAF it would need four times the already prodigious photoreconnaissance support it had received over the past few months.[253]

To identify the most significant targets and recommend priorities for them, the Allies created the Combined Strategic Targets Committee (CSTC) in October 1944. The CSTC incorporated as "working committees" the Joint Oil Targets and Jockey Committees, as well as several new groups that emerged and sometimes rather quickly disbanded to meet the changing situation in the winter of 1944–1945: POL depots, army equipment, armored fighting vehicles (AFVs), and communications (e.g., transportation). Composed of intelligence and operations representatives of those commands involved in conducting strategic air operations (including SHAEF), the CSTC was charged to provide

Piercing the Fog

"advice as to priorities between the different systems of strategic objectives, and the priorities of targets within these systems."[254] On behalf of the RAF Deputy Chief of Air Staff and the Commanding General, USSTAF, the committee published a weekly priority list similar to the original Jockey schedules. Between September and November, ordnance, military transportation, and AFV production followed oil on the strategic target priority list. These three were taken off the list on November 1 with the decision to concentrate on the German transportation system. In February, when intelligence indicated a rise in production of AFVs, they were reinstated, and a specific working committee was created to monitor armored vehicles.

Intelligence on these systems came from now well-established sources. USSTAF relied on the EOU's general intelligence unit to analyze German military equipment production.[255] Photoreconnaissance and photointerpretation agencies increased their work still further. In contrast to earlier periods, ULTRA provided extensive quantitative and qualitative information on attacks against individual targets, which contributed to accurate assessments. Much of this information derived from decrypted police messages and codes now used by military-industrial agencies created to coordinate production with military requirements.[256] Cross-checking ULTRA information with photointerpretation resulted in more accurate assessments and more effective subsequent targeting decisions.[257] The insight ULTRA now provided on the overall state of German production and resources had strategic implications as well. Messages such as the one from *Oberkommando der Wehrmacht* (the German high command) on January 10, 1945, advising that because of critical shortages of ammunition it would be possible only to supply active sectors while economizing elsewhere, surely contributed to the CSTC recommendation that month to reinstate ammunition to priority status.[258]

In response to the broadening target base, in January 1945 the USSTAF director of intelligence expanded the daily briefing to the commanding general to include considerable target intelligence, and he instituted special weekly briefings to inform key staff officers of the status of target systems and important individual targets. Although USSTAF was not responsible for selection of ground-support targets, the operational intelligence section established a special tactical targets subsection to keep Spaatz and his senior officers informed of the ground situation and of important ground targets. This group worked closely with the target committees in London and at SHAEF.

USSTAF intelligence also expanded the distribution of information to subordinate commands, both strategic and tactical, to assist them in targeting. American officers assigned to the Air Ministry were already sending a daily OB to the tactical air forces and commands; it provided enemy units' strength, locations, and type of aircraft as well as a daily airfield activity report. In the winter of 1944–1945, the USSTAF Air Ministry section sent daily signals on the status of important ammunition dumps, ordnance, and POL depots; military

The European Theater of Operations

training and barracks areas; panzer reequipment depots; headquarters; and traffic concentrations and routes.[259]

In November 1944, the question of transportation as a valid strategic target surfaced again. Largely at the insistence of Tedder, the entire German transportation network assumed second priority for American strategic air operations. Spaatz issued a new directive to his air forces commanders to this effect, but USSTAF intelligence vehemently opposed SHAEF's insistence on transportation, which continued into the new year.[260] The issue was not whether the transportation system was critical, but whether strategic air forces could achieve measurable results by attacking it. An overwhelming portion of those agencies that provided data to USSTAF intelligence agreed that the transportation system simply was too big and had too much excess capacity and reserves to be attacked effectively.[261] The minutes of a meeting of civilian and military railroad experts in late October concluded, "No railroad expert present offered any system of rail transportation targets which he considered, if attacked, would produce the effect desired by the Deputy Supreme Commander, i.e., the isolation of the armies from their sources of supply." In January 1945 the communications working committee of CSTC determined even heavy attacks on a limited portion of Germany would not be profitable.[262]

Earlier that month, McDonald had forwarded a memorandum to General Anderson offering "an Intelligence appraisal of the immediate Strategic Air aims of the U.S. Air Forces." According to McDonald, the direction that the SHAEF staff was providing American strategic air power "is not showing the results which might be expected of the expenditure of such a huge force," rather, it was detracting from the more important oil program. Asserting "the Air Forces are faced currently with deciding the length of this war," McDonald "strongly" recommended "overriding priority" be given immediately to successful attacks on active gasoline producers and jet engine manufacturing centers.[263]

The urgency that McDonald placed on jet aircraft production reflected the most serious concern of American airmen in the winter of 1944–1945. The imponderable factor in the assessments of the GAF in the fall of 1944 was the impact that large numbers of jet fighters might have on the enemy's potency. The Allies had long been aware of German efforts to develop revolutionary new aircraft. British intelligence reports from agents in Germany as early as the summer of 1940 referred to work on gas-turbine engines. By late 1942 the British knew from POW interrogations and agent reports forwarded by the air attaché in Berne, Switzerland, that both Messerschmitt and Heinkel were trying to develop jet- or rocket-powered aircraft. Photointerpreters at Medmenham had discovered an aircraft matching the description of a prototype at a Heinkel factory.[264] In June 1943, advised to be on the lookout for "something queer," a photointerpreter had spotted four small tailless aircraft at Peenemunde which turned out to be Me 163s. The first Me 262 was discovered by photointerpreters early in 1944.[265]

Through the rest of 1943 and into 1944, Allied intelligence continued to receive reports of a variety of jet aircraft, several of which they expected to appear in limited service during 1944. These included the He 280 (which never reached production), the Arado Ar 234 (which came into service primarily in a reconnaissance version in the summer of 1944), the Me 163 (a short-range, rocket-powered interceptor that proved of limited value), and the Me 262 (potentially the most serious threat). The bulk of the information on these aircraft came from HUMINT sources (often confirmed by photoreconnaissance) and captured documents (including notes of a lecture by General Adolph Galland given in Caen, France, in 1943). By early 1944 the Allies had firm information on the Me 262's engines, airframe, armament, and flight characteristics as well as extensive data on the Me 163.[266] Because none of these machines was yet operational, ULTRA provided few insights. But by the middle of July, with both the Me 163 and Me 262 operational (although not yet in service with combat squadrons), Air Ministry Intelligence warned, "The development of jet-propulsion in Germany is assuming important proportions."[267] Y intercepts in early October 1944 gave advanced warning that the Me 262 was going into combat units in both its fighter-bomber and its interceptor roles. American daylight bomber formations experienced their first assault by Me 262s on November 1.[268]

While Hitler had intended to employ the Me 262 (and the Ar 234) as ground-attack weapons, American airmen focused on its potential as a fighter-interceptor. In July, Spaatz wrote to Arnold advising that the employment of large numbers of jets in this role would give the initiative in the strategic air war back to the *Luftwaffe*.[269] By September, the USSTAF commander deemed the potential danger sufficiently acute to advise his superior of the measures he intended to take, should the situation "reach the point where losses become intolerable."[270] For the moment, the primary threat was to Allied reconnaissance. Of ten MAAF reconnaissance missions flown in the Munich area the week preceding Spaatz's letter, Me 262s had succeeded in shooting down three of the six they attacked.

One way to reduce the looming threat was to attack the sources of these new weapons. In his directive to the commanders of Eighth and Fifteenth Air Forces on September 1, Spaatz had given jet production installations a priority second only to oil.[271] By the end of the month, it was obvious that dispersal and the movement to underground production centers (for which jets were given top priority) limited the effectiveness of such attacks, and these installations were dropped from their original priority.[272] Under the prevailing assumption that the war would be over by the end of the year, in the first week of November Spaatz's director of operations agreed with an assessment by A.I.3(b) that there appeared to be "no appreciable threat to daylight raids by 1st January 1945."[273]

The European Theater of Operations

Even the knowledge gained in early December that Hitler had approved conversion of ground-attack Me 262s to the fighter mode initially caused little concern, since this was assumed to be a slow process.[274]

The stunning psychological shock of the Ardennes offensive and the surprise aerial attack on Allied airfields the morning of January 1, 1945, caused a dramatic reassessment of the air situation by Allied intelligence. With the end of the war no longer just over the horizon, developments that had seemed unlikely now took on a different cast. The conversion of Me 262 ground-attack aircraft to interceptors armed with four cannon was in itself cause for concern.[275] Even more disconcerting were reports from workers and officials at the jet production facilities at Strasbourg and a long decrypt from the Japanese naval attaché on the intended scope of Me 262 production.[276] The impact of this new perspective was felt almost immediately. Before the end of December, the first sixteen targets on the weekly Jockey list related to jet production, while the daily airfield attack list emphasized facilities used for jet operations or training.[277] On December 29, McDonald forwarded to the deputy commander for operations an Air Ministry estimate that the GAF possessed 100–125 Me 262s and the potential for 325–400 by April, with possible production of 250 per month from April through June.[278]

In a memorandum to the commanding general, USSTAF, as the new year opened, McDonald warned that jet fighters now constituted "a serious threat" since "a staggering proportion" of German effort was being funneled into this project. McDonald believed that if the war continued until summer, jet interceptors could "completely upset the present balance of aerial power." To preclude this, the Allies had to initiate immediate countermeasures, even at the expense of other target systems. These steps, a worried McDonald urged, should include continued emphasis on oil (especially jet aviation fuel), attacks on jet production facilities wherever they were suspected, and (in contrast to his own opposition to attacks on airfields generally) operations against German airfields used for jet testing, training, and operations. The Eighth and Fifteenth Air Forces, the intelligence chief concluded, must "be given unequivocal directive to place German jet targets on a priority second only to oil."[279]

Responding to the threat, one week later General Spaatz made jet fighters "primary objectives for attack." Writing to Arnold, he noted that while his January 16 directive addressed several target systems, the primary change was "the restoration of the G.A.F. and primarily that of its jet aircraft production, training and operational establishments...." As justification for his decision, with which the Air Staff apparently did not agree, Spaatz repeated the figures McDonald had provided on the potential growth of the German jet fighter force by summer.[280] Despite the flurry of concern, actual operations against jet facilities did not increase significantly; two-thirds of the heavy bomber attacks in January continued in direct support of land operations (principally against rail targets and ammunition depots). The following month, as part of a massive bombardment of targets throughout Germany, Allied air forces effectively reduced jet fighter production to negligible proportions.[281]

The impact of these mortal blows appeared in a recommendation by McDonald to General Anderson in mid-March 1945. Reviewing the GAF's response to daylight bombing since the first of the year, the intelligence director noted that of 55 heavy bomber missions, only 13 had met any reaction; 33 bombers were confirmed as lost to enemy fighters, either conventional or jet. The latest reports suggested that the Germans, who had moved more than half their conventional fighters to the eastern front in January, could devote no more than 125 Me 262s to defensive operations before the end of April. Even those would be unable to concentrate because of fuel shortages and installation damages.[282] In marked contrast to his previous emphasis on the requirement for strong escort support, which he had argued only a few months before was the only reason American bombers could continue deep raids, McDonald now recommended Eighth Air Force fighters could be better employed for "more direct cooperation with the ground forces."[283]

Shortly thereafter, the Jockey Committee in its final meeting concluded the GAF was no longer a worthwhile target.[284] On April 16, 1945, Spaatz directed that in the absence of appropriate strategic targets, American strategic air forces would operate in support of the advancing Allied armies. Three weeks later Germany surrendered.

CHAPTER 5

The Pacific and Far East, 1942–1945

BEFORE THE WAR, the American and Allied understanding of Japanese air warfare capabilities was woefully incomplete, seemingly hampered by a tendency to overlook Japanese accomplishments and ignore available facts. A Zero (Zeke) fighter shot down in China in May 1941 yielded valuable data on its range, speed, armament, and oxygen system. This information came originally from Claire L. Chennault, serving in China as Chiang Kai-shek's air advisor, and had gone, in turn, to the Army, U.S. Navy, and British government, reaching British air headquarters in Singapore before the war. Yet when war broke out, the Zero's performance surprised the RAF's fighter pilots in Malaya. Taxed heavily in Europe and Africa, the RAF had no squadron intelligence officers in Malaya, and the small headquarters staff in Singapore could not cope with all the demands forced upon it by the growing possibility of war in the Far East. Nobody briefed the pilots, who were first to suffer.

At about the same time, the American air intelligence operation in the Philippines had its own troubles. The dichotomy between the Army's and Navy's intelligence operations in Manila that may have hampered the defense of the islands in the face of the Japanese attack also contributed to the destruction at Clark Field. Yet despite the confusion, and in the face of the advancing Japanese, radio intercept services of the Army and Navy continued to operate in the Philippines until late March 1942. The Army unit on Corregidor sent Y intercepts to the Army ground forces on Bataan and to the remnants of AAF units there and on Mindanao.[1]

Throughout the Pacific and Asian war, intelligence information was paramount in guiding the various commanders' decisions on air operations. The destruction of a Japanese convoy off New Guinea in the March 1943 battle of the Bismarck Sea had its origin in the U.S. Navy's interception of Japanese messages, as did the successful ambush of Admiral Yamamoto Isoroku, commander-in-chief of the Japanese Combined Fleet. The air defense of Guadalcanal, largely a Navy-Marine effort but with AAF participation, depended in part on intercepts of Japanese radio messages and on information sent from Australian coast watchers hiding on Japanese-controlled islands. In

Piercing the Fog

the central and southwest Pacific, the U.S. Navy and Army, with Allied forces' participation, created SIGINT organizations charged with watching Japanese activity across a huge expanse of ocean and land areas.

The United States, the British Commonwealth, and the NEI all entered the war against Japan within hours in December 1941. Japanese air forces attacked Hawaii on December 7 and the Philippines and Malaya a few hours later (on December 8, Singapore time). On the 8th, Japan's Army landed in Malaya; a few days later her soldiers came ashore in the Philippines. Simultaneously, the Japanese began moving along the Chinese coast toward Hong Kong. By Christmas, the Allies' situation had deteriorated markedly, with General MacArthur's forces abandoning Manila. Shortly thereafter, Hong Kong and Wake Island fell, and Japanese troops pushed south through Malaya toward Singapore. To stem Japanese advances and pull together the Allies, General Marshall recommended creation of a single unified command for the SPA and the SWPA. Shortly thereafter, the American-British-Dutch-Australian (ABDA) Command came into existence; its commander was the British general Archibald P. Wavell. Wavell's staff officers from all services in the four nations hurried to set up a coherent command structure, but these patchwork solutions were far too late. Retreat in the Philippines led to eventual surrender, as it did in Malaya. Even before the fall of Singapore, the Japanese had set out to seize the oil-rich NEI. The Japanese Army took the oil refinery at Palembang, Sumatra, by air assault on February 16, 1942. On March 2, the Allies evacuated Java, bringing to an end the ABDA Command.[2]

Japanese military and naval forces now threatened to cut the lines of communication between North America and Australia–New Zealand by an advance through the Solomon Islands to Fiji. Japan also threatened Australia directly, organizing an invasion force to take Port Moresby, New Guinea. Many in Australia feared that if Port Moresby was lost, the Australian Northern Territory town of Darwin would be next. The Allies discerned the Japanese intent through a series of messages decrypted at Pearl Harbor and Washington, and they blocked the Port Moresby invasion force's advance at the battle of the Coral Sea in May 1942.[3]

The rapid Japanese expansion surprised even Japan's senior admirals and generals; their outward push slowed as the military took stock of the situation and of the effects of both the battle of the Coral Sea—May 7 and 8, 1942—and then the battle of Midway—June 4 and 5, 1942. The war in the Pacific and in the CBI area now assumed its long-term shape: successful prosecution by either side depended on the adroit use of land-based and naval air power. The destruction at Pearl Harbor, followed on December 10, 1941, by the Japanese sinking of the Royal Navy's battleships *Prince of Wales* and *Repulse* off the Malayan coast, graphically demonstrated the key role of aircraft to the remaining doubters.

The Pacific and Far East

In the Pacific and the Far East, the AAF fought a conflict very unlike the one in Europe and the Mediterranean. The war against Japan was many wars in four or more different theaters (depending upon how one defines the term "theater"), with differing commanders, administrative and logistic systems, and varying enemy capabilities. Reflecting the mixture of sea, terrain, weather, friendly and enemy units, and the distances over which airmen of all services waged war, the air intelligence structures that supported the fighting came to be as diverse as the theaters. To carry the fighting to the Japanese, the AAF created a number of commands throughout the Pacific-Asian region. First priority went to the defense of the sea lines of communication to New Zealand and Australia. To cover part of this responsibility, the Allies created the SWPA, commanded by General MacArthur, on April 18, 1942. MacArthur's responsibilities included operations in Australia and the East Indies. To the east and north of MacArthur's command stretched the SPA and the POA, commanded by Admiral Chester W. Nimitz. Unlike the SWPA and CBI theaters, where the AAF operated as integrated air commands, Nimitz and the Navy often subordinated the AAF's numbered air forces to naval commanders who usually broke them into group or squadron components more amenable to the Navy's style of fighting with various task forces.[4]

The South and Southwest Pacific

Throughout most of the 1930s, American military and naval planning for the Pacific assumed that Japan's geographic location and regional strength of numbers would allow her initially to overrun American outposts in the Philippines and islands of the central Pacific. By the summer of 1941, however, thinking in Washington had shifted to the idea of successfully defending at least the Philippines. At the heart of this revised strategy was air power, particularly the assumed capabilities of the B–17s just beginning to roll off production line. By the end of 1941 the United States lacked not only sufficient numbers of B–17s but also the command and intelligence structure to properly employ what was available.

The air power projected for the Philippines was an issue of considerable debate throughout 1941. American airmen believed that, in the event of war with Japan, they should operate within the context of the overall strategic defensive dictated by the Europe-first policy. Discussions in Washington had considered Japanese naval and air bases on and around Formosa and the mandated islands as possible targets. Col. Harold L. George, already sent to the Philippines to assist in air planning, decided the one hope for the islands' defense lay in hitting the Japanese before they could land. The Americans possessed virtually no information to execute either of these ideas. In May 1941, for example, the sum total of air intelligence about Formosa was an empty

Piercing the Fog

file marked Objective Folder No. 1. Existing air intelligence in Manila consisted of a few oblique and vertical photographs of the sod airfields in the Philippines and some file coverage of districts of supposedly military importance. The Office of the Chief of Air Corps had already begun trying to prepare industrial target reports covering the Japanese home islands in the fall of 1941.[5]

In contrast to photographic or economic intelligence, SIGINT had been active in the Philippines, albeit with only limited success. When Japanese military operations began in the Shanghai area in 1932, the U.S. Army Signal Corps began operating a radio-intercept station at Fort Santiago, Manila. In the mid-1930s a detachment of the 2d Signal Service Company handled radio interceptions at Fort McKinley, near Manila. The beginning of a successful era of radio intelligence dated from the arrival of Maj. Joe R. Sherr as chief of the detachment in July 1940. Sherr's station forwarded raw radio intercepts to Washington; it also discovered and plotted the locations of Japanese radio nets that were significant to the defense of the Philippines.[6]

The U.S. Navy also operated a signal intelligence unit, code named CAST, on Corregidor. Under Lt. Comdr. Rudolph J. Fabian, this organization concentrated on breaking Japanese diplomatic radio traffic, since it possessed a PURPLE machine. By an agreement of May 1941, Sherr's Army detachment did the interceptions while CAST concentrated on decoding or decrypting. With the establishment of HQ USAF Far East, Lt. Harold W. Brown customarily carried intercepted messages to MacArthur's Chief of Staff, Brig. Gen. Richard K. Sutherland, who scanned them and, if he saw anything that would interest General MacArthur, directed that they be taken to him. Time proved the limiting factor in this system. A message intercepted on one day went to Corregidor on a second; a translation came back from the Navy on a third day, if it was decodable. Sundays and holidays often delayed deliveries another day, since the Navy usually took these days off.[7]

Even before Scherr's detachment noted a sharp increase in Japanese diplomatic traffic in early December, American commanders in the Philippines had become aware of increased Japanese military and naval activity. On the evening of November 27, G–2 in Manila reported a formation of Japanese planes flying at high altitude over Central Luzon, presumably detected by one of the two radar sets operating at Iba (northwest of Clark Field) and at Manila. Serious defense readiness began on November 28, including sea patrols by B–17s over waters off Northern Luzon. Unidentified high-flying aircraft were over Clark Field before dawn on the mornings of December 2 and 3, and early in the morning hours of December 3 the Iba station plotted radar tracks off the Luzon coast. It was not definite that the aerial intruders were Japanese, but American offshore aerial patrols revealed large numbers of Japanese transports and cargo ships in harbors and at sea, confirming the general assumption that something impended.[8]

The Pacific and Far East

On the evening of December 7, Manila time, the Army signal detachment intercepted a Tokyo instruction message identifiable as relevant to an earlier message of particular concern to American intelligence in Washington. Sherr sent the instruction message to Washington and also to the Navy SIGINT unit on Corregidor for translation. When Lieutenant Brown got the translated message on the morning of December 8 at Manila, he read a notification that Japan was going to war. By the time Brown reached Sutherland's office, the Philippines were already under attack. Sutherland sarcastically told Brown to take his explanation to MacArthur, who was even then on the telephone hearing a report of the bombing of Clark Field. Brown explained that even though he had not gotten timely translations from Corregidor, Washington had the untranslated messages well before the Japanese attack at Pearl Harbor. "I made my explanation to the General," Brown reminisced, "He said: 'Thank you, Son,' and I left. He never moved a muscle or changed his expression during my explanation."[9]

In the Philippines it was December 8, shortly after 0300 (0830 on December 7 in Hawaii), when a commercial radio station picked up a report of the Japanese attack at Pearl Harbor. On Formosa, inclement flying weather had delayed Japanese plans for execution of before-dawn strikes against the Philippines. The American Far East Air Force (FEAF) could attack against Formosa, and FEAF's chief of staff took objective target folders to MacArthur's headquarters at Fort Santiago in Manila. Maj. Gen. Lewis H. Brereton, FEAF Commander, arrived about five in the morning and, according to his recollection, asked Sutherland to get MacArthur's authority to carry out offensive action as soon as possible. What then happened has long remained controversial and subject to conflicting recollections. Sutherland remembered that Brereton had not wanted to attack without first having photographs, which the initial objective folders lacked. The American bomber commander, Col. Eugene L. Eubank, would later recall that the folders were "definitely poor."[10]

It was Brereton's recollection that the gist of advice he received from Sutherland was this: "We can't attack till we're fired upon." General MacArthur stated much later he had not been told of any desire on Brereton's part to launch an immediate air strike, but he would have disapproved it in any event. "My orders," MacArthur stated, "were explicit not to initiate hostilities against the Japanese. . . . Instructions from Washington were very definite to wait until the Japanese made the first 'overt' move." At midday on December 8, while the Americans deliberated, a Japanese attack destroyed half of their air force on the ground at Clark Field in one disastrous strike.[11]

At about noon on December 8, the Iba radar picked up two flights of Japanese aircraft bearing down on it from across the China Sea. Despite the early warning, American fighter reaction was quite tardy. A flight of Japanese medium bombers flew directly over the radar station, reducing it to scrap with clusters of daisy-cutter bombs. With radar thus blinded, the 2d Signal Service

Piercing the Fog

Company detachment became the sole early-warning capability as American forces withdrew into Bataan and Corregidor. Lieutenant Brown could not translate what he heard, but by monitoring Japanese voice nets and learning to identify call signs, he could often calculate when and where a raid was pending. He also became expert in predicting the appearance of Japanese air reconnaissance planes over Corregidor, enabling AA gunners to shoot down at least six of them. Capture of Japanese air-ground code books on Bataan allowed the small radio intelligence office on Corregidor to monitor the signal nets of the enemy in the Philippines and provide early warnings which sometimes caused enemy losses. In April 1942 Brown and his detachment left the Philippines for Australia.[12]

The stunning Japanese victories in the opening weeks of the war led to a major reorganization of American forces in the Pacific in the spring of 1942. On April 18, MacArthur assumed command of the SWPA with headquarters in Melbourne (later, in Brisbane), Australia. The first problem in Australia was to provide coordination with the Australian armed forces, most of whom had been fighting in the Mediterranean since 1940; the remnants of a few Dutch units which had escaped the NEI; and the bedraggled American AAF flying units that had avoided destruction in the Philippines and Java. Lt. Gen. George H. Brett assumed command of Allied Air Forces SWPA (AAFSWPA) on April 20, with command over all American AAF units in Australia and operational control over all Royal Australian Air Force (RAAF) and NEI Army Air Force combat units.[13]

In the early months of combat, the Americans could contribute very little to air intelligence. It was natural that an Australian, Air Commodore Joseph E. Hewitt, RAAF, became Director of Intelligence for AAFSWPA, with Lt. Col. Reginald F. Vance of the American AAF as his assistant director. Within the American air units, intelligence officers were flyers who spent time on combat intelligence duties between missions or while grounded. The RAAF had a nucleus of air combat intelligence officers who had served with the RAF in England and the Middle East. American air combat intelligence officers who had trained in the United States began to arrive in July 1942, and more came during the late summer and fall.[14]

Early in 1942, Allied offensive air activity consisted of scattered raids, not to destroy the enemy but to deceive him as to Allied strength. Defensive actions sought to turn back the enemy before he could do too much damage. The scattered offensive raids were against better-known strong points, but the effects were largely uncorroborated by photography. Intelligence consisted of pilot observations pinpointed on makeshift maps. Port Moresby, on the southeastern New Guinea coast, became the main base of air operations. A staff of intelligence officers there performed all briefings and interrogations of crews flying from or through the forward field. Reports flowed back to the AAFSWPA Directorate of Intelligence, which began in May 1942 to publish them in a semiweekly serial, *The Allied Air Forces SWPA Intelligence Summary*, that included general-situation reviews plus reports of Allied and enemy air activities.[15]

While Allied airmen sought to keep the Japanese at bay in the spring of 1942, MacArthur and his staff set about putting GHQ SWPA in order. The G–2, Brig. Gen. Charles A. Willoughby, had accompanied MacArthur from Corregidor. Willoughby had been commissioned in 1915 and had seen service on the Mexican border and in World War I. He had attracted MacArthur's attention as a lecturer in military history at the C&GSS during the years when MacArthur had emphasized the value of historical analysis. Rising in rank to major general, Willoughby remained MacArthur's intelligence officer through World War II and the Korean conflict. In his own words, he was dedicated to "strenuous efforts to maintain and defend basic staff principles, particularly the absolute centralization of intelligence and the operational control of all GHQ intelligence agencies." Willoughby organized the Allied intelligence resources within G–2 into the Allied Geographical Section, which prepared maps, guidebooks, and terrain profiles; the Allied Translator and Interpreter Section, which worked mainly on captured documents; the Allied Intelligence Bureau, which handled general intelligence, coast watchers, and clandestine guerrilla activities; and the CB, which handled SIGINT.[16]

MacArthur was convinced of the value of SIGINT. On April 1, ten days after reaching Melbourne, he radioed Washington: "Investigation discloses that a central allied signal intelligence section is required for the interception and cryptoanalyzing [*sic*] of Japanese intelligence. The time delay and transmission uncertainties incident to sending intercepted material to Washington and elsewhere dictate that this work be handled locally. Allied forces here are organizing such a bureau." Even before the establishment of GHQ SWPA, MacArthur had both Dutch and Australian SIGINT analysts plus two American special intelligence organizations in action. Survivors of Sherr's 2d Signal Service Company detachment accompanied MacArthur's party in the escape from the Philippines. Commander Fabian brought seventy-five men of CAST to Australia by submarine and established them in Melbourne with their PURPLE machine. The Navy unit, now called BELCONNEN, was primarily responsible to the FRUPac in Pearl Harbor and to Washington, but it also translated for SWPA, as it had done in Manila.[17]

In August 1942, General Kenney became General MacArthur's air commander in the Southwest Pacific. MacArthur had not, so Kenney believed, fully understood and appreciated the potential of air power. To make matters worse, MacArthur and his previous air commander, General Brett, were estranged, hardly ever speaking. The Allied ground and air units in Australia and New Guinea were tired from the fighting and retreats of early 1942. Kenney believed that he could reverse the dispirited state of the airmen; he was a confident, experienced flyer who sought subordinates that he called "operators."

Piercing the Fog

General George C. Kenney   General Nathan F. Twining

By that term he meant a flyer who understood airplanes, who would take risks, break the rules when an advantage was to be gained by doing so, and would not ignore the opportunity if some modest thievery would benefit the man's squadron or group. Kenney greatly appreciated someone who could use air power in bold, unexpected, and successful, ways. Within days of assuming command of the AAFSWPA, Kenney promised MacArthur he would bomb Rabaul's airfields with his ramshackle collection of B–17s on the day of the Allied landing at Lunga Point, Guadalcanal (to keep Japanese aviators away from the 1st Marine Division and its supporting ships as the men moved ashore). Kenney carried out his promise, much to MacArthur's joy and surprise. That attack on Rabaul marked the first, and rather insignificant, use by Kenney of intercepted Japanese message traffic. After the raid, Kenney read with satisfaction the reply of the Japanese commander at Rabaul to a request for help from the Japanese on Guadalcanal and neighboring Tulagi: the American attack caused too much disruption at the airfields; there could be no air strikes on the landing force for some days.[18]

George Kenney soon became the dominant AAF commander in the region (his public stature approached only by that of Maj. Gen. Claire L. Chennault), and he remained so throughout the war. General Hansell, one of Arnold's closest advisors in planning the war's operations and immensely influential in organizing the B–29 force, said of Kenney: "He did things with air forces that left airmen gasping. MacArthur owed much of his brilliant success in the Southwest Pacific to General Kenney's imaginative performance." Kenney, although he became very close to MacArthur, was not a member of the inner

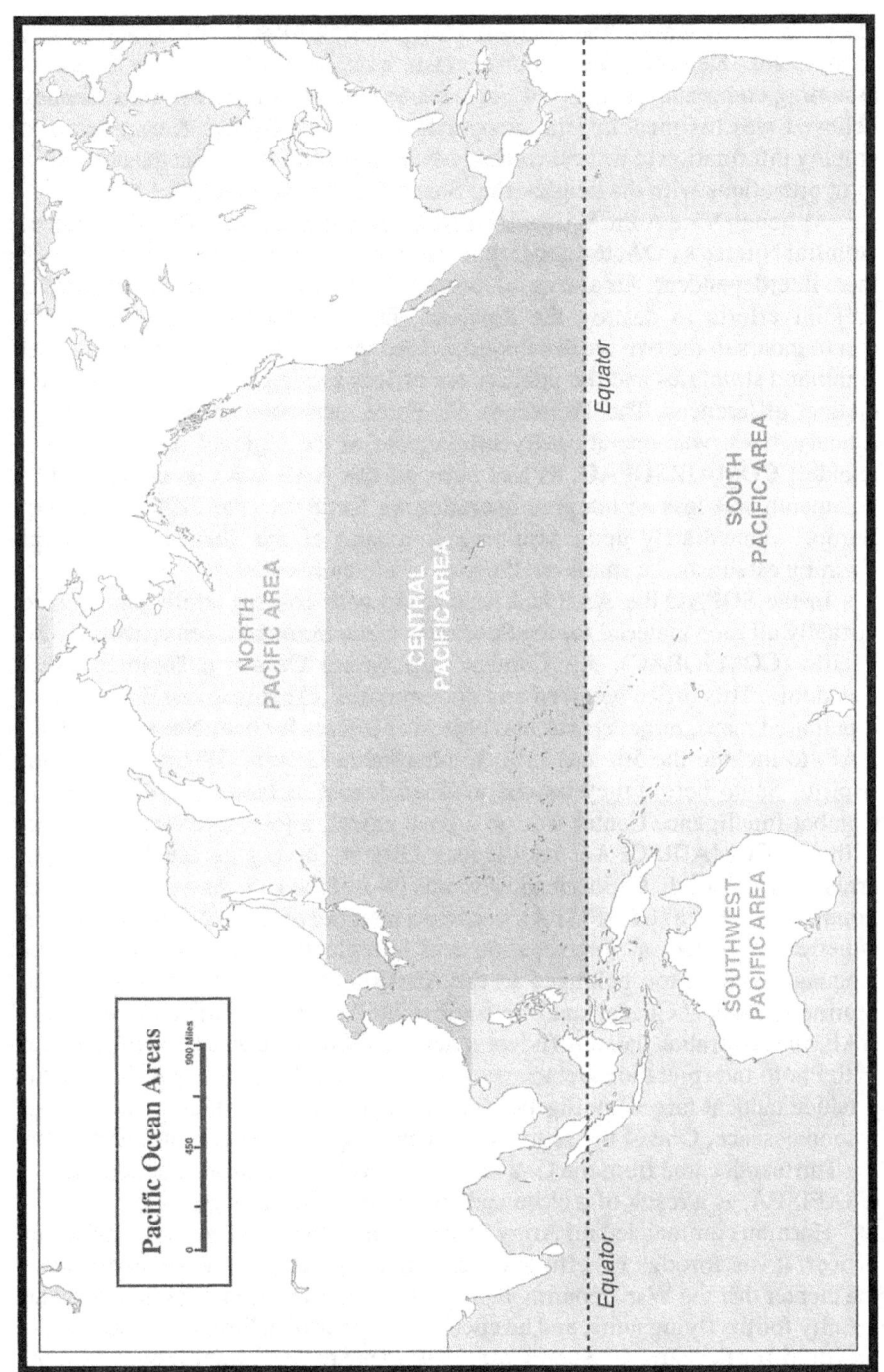

circle that surrounded the general and played endlessly on MacArthur's weaknesses. Kenney's well-known clash with Sutherland within hours of assuming command of AAF not only caused Sutherland to stop what Kenney believed was his meddling in air operations, but it also left Kenney free to employ information to its best combat advantage, both within his theater and in joint operations with the neighboring South Pacific (SOPAC).[19]

Although Vice Adm. William F. Halsey commanded the SOPAC as part of Admiral Nimitz's POA, the geographic proximity of the SPA and SWPA made them interdependent. Air and naval forces from the two commands participated in joint efforts to destroy the Japanese. Despite the fact that the AAF's commanders in the two areas enjoyed a close relationship, the operational and command structures and the intelligence offices serving in each demonstrated distinct differences. The Thirteenth Air Force, activated in the Solomons in January 1943, was operationally subordinate to the regional naval air commander, COMAIRSOPAC, as had been all the AAF units in the area. The Thirteenth was less an integral, operating air force than the Fifth or those in Europe. Immediately upon assuming command of the Thirteenth, General Twining established a small intelligence office on his staff.[20]

In the SOPAC the AAF had little to do with combat intelligence, since virtually all such material for the Solomons came from the Commander, South Pacific (COMSOPAC), Air Combat Intelligence Center at Noumea, New Caledonia. This office received and disseminated all combat intelligence, and it prepared maps, target charts, and objective folders for both Navy air and the AAF, to include the 5th and 11th Bombardment Groups (H) operating from Espiritu Santo before they moved to Guadalcanal in January 1943. The Air Combat Intelligence Center was, to a great extent, a joint intelligence center, with the COMAIRSOPAC Intelligence Officer serving as the J–2. In this arrangement, Col. L. C. Sherman, who was G–2 of the U.S. Army Forces in the South Pacific Area (USAFISPA), became a member of the J–2 committee. The Americans created an interrogation and interpretation section as a theater language pool; it too belonged to the Air Combat Intelligence Center. The Marine air wing at Guadalcanal ran combat intelligence operations, with Army, AAF, and Australian liaison officers attached, to which the AAF contributed the 12th Photo Interpretation Detachment. The Thirteenth Air Force A–2 staff did produce tactical target intelligence, based largely on its own and Navy aerial reconnaissance. One of the primary sources of operational air intelligence for the Thirteenth came from the G–2 of Lt. Gen. Millard Harmon's headquarters, USAFISPA, as a result of a close and continuing relationship.[21]

Harmon commanded all Army forces in the region and was himself an air officer. It was through his efforts to centralize control of AAF air resources in the theater that the War Department had created the Thirteenth. Harmon felt an affinity for the flying units, and he encouraged Sherman, his G–2, to do all that he could for the airmen. Sherman greatly expanded the intelligence support throughout the area, spending considerable time at Thirteenth headquarters whenever he was needed. Sherman's staff prepared air OB and other operational air intelligence for both Harmon and Twining. Because Admiral Halsey's intelligence officer would not provide Harmon's staff with a regular flow of ULTRA, early in 1943 and over the objections of Halsey's intelligence officer, Sherman arranged with General Willoughby to receive locally derived and Washington SIGINT information from Brisbane. Sherman sent as much of this material as possible to Twining and the Thirteenth Air Force A–2.[22]

In 1942 and 1943, the SPA and SWPA commands maintained operational and intelligence liaison to obtain mutual support. Especially in the early operations on Guadalcanal, the services of SWPA's Australian coast watchers, who used battery-powered or crude pedal-driven radio transmitters to send their observations down the Solomons chain, were of great utility. Although the watchers were under SWPA's Allied Intelligence Bureau, the Australians stationed an officer with COMSOPAC as coast-watcher coordinator. Despite the command liaison, reports continued to describe problems in intelligence and operational liaison between forward echelons in each theater. In Brisbane, Col. Benjamin Cain, who eventually became Fifth Air Force A–2, asserted that SWPA gave the U.S. Navy all the intelligence it obtained but said the Navy frequently held up distribution when it did not think SWPA needed to know. Cain was not willing to lay any blame on old Army-Navy rivalries. "The trouble actually was," he reminisced, "the fact that it took so long to realize how much each one of the services needed the other." Such benevolent views as Cain's were not universal. Given his proclivity for centralized control, it was not surprising that Willoughby had stronger feelings. "The Navy" he complained in 1945, "has shrouded the whole enterprise [SIGINT] in mystery, excluding other services and rigidly centralizing the whole enterprise. . . . the Melbourne station is under direct orders of Washington, is not bound by local responsibilities, forwards what they select, and when it suits them. The possibility of erroneous or incomplete selection is as evident now as it was in 1941."[23]

After the June 1944 reorganization that brought Thirteenth Air Force into General Kenney's new FEAF, Thirteenth's intelligence office drew upon the resources of the AAF Directorate of Intelligence. The Thirteenth's A–2 throughout World War II lacked functions peculiar to other A–2 organizations. The Thirteenth's staff was well suited to using technical data to aid the flying groups in drawing up tactical air operations plans and to aid them in avoiding Japanese defenses while attacking.

The American Fifth Air Force also had an intelligence section, but unlike his appreciation for the work of Hewitt and the Australians, Kenney often groused about the Fifth A–2's lack of ability. As late as May 5, 1943, he noted that he needed a Fifth Air Force intelligence officer to give him "more intelligence and imagination than I have now." He appointed Cain, a trusted

Piercing the Fog

Lt. Gen. Millard F. Harmon

Lieutenant Ennis C. Whitehead

acquaintance and Hewitt's American deputy, to the job. Cain now filled both jobs simultaneously. The Fifth Air Force A–2 office was in most respects a part of the Fifth's staff, but in practical terms it functioned more as a go-between, channeling information rather than creating new analytical studies, target folders, and directives. Located in Brisbane near GHQ SWPA's G–2, Hewitt's office, and the intelligence office of the RAAF, the Fifth's A–2 gathered information from the two higher echelons and passed it to the Fifth Air Force Advanced Echelon (ADVON) at Port Moresby. In New Guinea, Brig. Gen. Ennis C. Whitehead's ADVON had another A–2 section that worked with operational airmen in the Fifth Bomber and Fifth Fighter Commands (later with the 1st, 2d, and 3d Air Task Forces when Kenney reorganized his operation). Unlike the main Fifth Air Force's A–2 operation, much original analytical work came from the ADVON's A–2. A radio intelligence unit listened to Japanese air operations radio transmissions, A–2 staff members processed reconnaissance and strike photography and made target charts, and other ADVON personnel kept an enemy air OB up to date using much locally derived data. Over time, the ADVON's staff came to handle all immediate operational and tactical air intelligence, while Hewitt's staff concentrated more on long-range planning, analyses, and administration. The Allies handled special intelligence from decrypted radio intercepts and radio traffic analysis more freely than in any other war theater. For example, Fifth Air Force ADVON's daily summary of principal activities often carried an appendix summarizing all types of CB and AAF radio intercept data on Japanese air movements. Often the summaries contained airfield-by-airfield tallies of Japanese Army and Navy Air Force strengths. Whitehead and his men found the information invaluable in planning their daily flying activities.[24]

The G–2 office at GHQ SWPA was far more comprehensive, collecting information within the theater and from outside sources. After the June 15, 1944, amalgamation of Thirteenth Air Force into the new FEAF, the Fifth and Thirteenth A–2s operated in the same associated and subordinated fashion.[25]

In the SWPA, the main responsibility for escape and evasion lay with the GHQ's G–2, MIS–X, a covert Australian-American group in Brisbane that trained selected AAF personnel in escape methods. The organization also aided in POW escapes and assisted in the recovery of airmen downed in neutral or friendly but hard-to-reach territory. At every opportunity, MIS–X agents also collected and reported intelligence data. Escape and evasion training given by MIS–X or the Fifth Air Force staff included distributing escape and evasion kits and establishing how evaders could reach one of the prepositioned, presupplied locations. Working with coast watchers, MIS–X activities returned several hundred flyers left afoot in the jungles of New Guinea.[26] The chart on the next page depicts the organization of the office of the G–2 SWPA.

In the Philippines, MIS–X joined with local guerrilla units to recover stranded flyers and rescue inmates of some of the more isolated Japanese prison camps. As the Allies moved into the Philippine Islands, General Kenney's men began to operate adjacent to and at times in coordination with the Fourteenth Air Force in China. With those operations came the prospect of aircraft being lost over China and coastal Chinese waters. A MIS–X annex to an AAF intelligence summary noted the cooperation between the commands and the fact that the strong anti-Japanese attitude among the Chinese made evading capture in China a very good possibility. Airmen had been rescued from such seemingly unlikely places as downtown Hong Kong. Many such rescues were effected through agents or teams of the U.S. Naval Group China, the Fourteenth Air Force, or a British unit formed from Hong Kong escapees and operating in south China. Although some bandit chiefs in China caused trouble for Americans who were forced down, communist and nationalist guerrillas were prepared to aid Americans afoot in the country. Most of the operators of small sailing boats in the waters off China's coast were friendly. The rather spotty control by the Japanese of Chinese lands meant that Allied escape and evasion efforts throughout most of the area near the SWPA and China Theater junction stood a good chance of success.[27]

One of Kenney's most important early sources of information was the coast-watcher section of the Allied Intelligence Bureau. Although well known for their work in the Solomons and islands as far north as New Britain, coast watchers also patrolled New Guinea and reported regularly on Japanese air movements. An invaluable resource early in the war, the coast watchers supplemented radar, often providing information for areas where radar sets did not exist or long before radar could pick up a Japanese raid. Radar's improve-

Organization: G–2, Southwest Pacific Area
(Melbourne - Brisbane)
May–September 1942

Chief of Staff

Assistant Chief of Staff G–2

Theater Intelligence
- Executive Section
- Administrative Section
- Operations Section
  - Intelligence Summaries
  - Ground Section
  - Navy Section
  - Air Section
- Battle Order Section
- Plans and Estimate Section
- Drafting Section
- Publication Section
- Liaison with Allied Intelligence Sections
  - Director of Naval Intelligence (Navy)
  - Director of Naval Intelligence (Land Headquarters)
  - Director of Naval Intelligence (Air)
  - G–2, Sixth Army

War Department Intelligence
- Allied Translator and Interpreter Section
- Allied Geographical Section
- Allied Intelligence Bureau
  - Philippine Regional Section
  - Netherlands East Indies Regional Section
  - Northeast Regional Section (Dutch New Guinea)
  - Special Operations (British)
  - Secret Intelligence (British)
- Liaison, Miscellaneous Agencies
  - Political Warfare Committee
  - Office of War Information
  - Far Eastern Liaison Office
  - Combined Operational Intelligence Center (Australia)
  - Press Relations
  - G–2, U.S. AAF, Far East
    - Counterintelligence
    - Censorship

ments over visual and aural detection had become evident during the Battle of Britain in 1940, but the radar sets of World War II had limited range, were bulky and heavy, and experienced interference from ground reflection and atmospheric phenomena. Coast watchers observed Japanese airfields from nearby positions or from semipermanent posts along commonly used Japanese air routes. These men often reported flights of Japanese aircraft in ample time for radar sets to make contact and allow the takeoff of defending fighters. This HUMINT source remained important until supplanted by a growing skill at Y-Service interception early in 1944. The increasing ability to use radio intelligence became particularly important in the campaign against Rabaul and Kavieng, for coast watchers could not provide the constant flow of information from those Japanese-held regions.[28] The chart on the next page shows the organization of the Fifth Air Force's A–2 office.

Despite Kenney's early dissatisfaction with his American air intelligence staff, the Fifth Air Force A–2 served as an important intelligence agency, providing primarily visual and photoreconnaissance, plus weather reporting and forecasting. The Fifth's intelligence capabilities grew so that by 1944 the organization was highly proficient at intercepting low-level radio traffic. Fifth Air Force intelligence specialists had created an excellent air OB file, as well as analyses of patterns of operation and airfields used by their enemy. A card file developed over two years' time recorded by aircraft serial number some 4,000 Japanese planes in the New Guinea–NEI–New Britain region. When a Japanese pilot took off, intercept specialists listened to his radio call, recorded his aircraft's number, checked the aircraft's type and history of normal use (for example, it might be a transport that ordinarily flew between Rabaul and New Guinea), and predicted with good accuracy its probable destination and time of arrival. If the Japanese aircraft were combat types, the intelligence files revealed what targets they had previously hit, and when. This information then went to the operations staff, who could, in turn, prepare Allied fighters to meet an attack. Reports from coast watchers of Japanese air movements frequently served to confirm the intelligence specialists' predictions and increase the chances for a successful interception.[29] The air commanders in the region became avid users of air intelligence and used the disparate sources of information to plan the continuing air campaigns.

In Whitehead, Fifth Air Force ADVON commander in New Guinea, and Paul B. Wurtsmith, initial commander of V Fighter Command, Kenney found two excellent men in whom he trusted and to whom he delegated a great deal of authority. Kenney had the ability to pick good subordinates, then exercise the good sense to let them do the best job they could while he supported them fully. Supremely confident, Kenney was also very opinionated; those who got on his wrong side could have great difficulty getting back into favor.

Throughout the war, Kenney kept a daily diary supplemented when he was away by comments from his aide or secretary, and which in 1945 he expanded

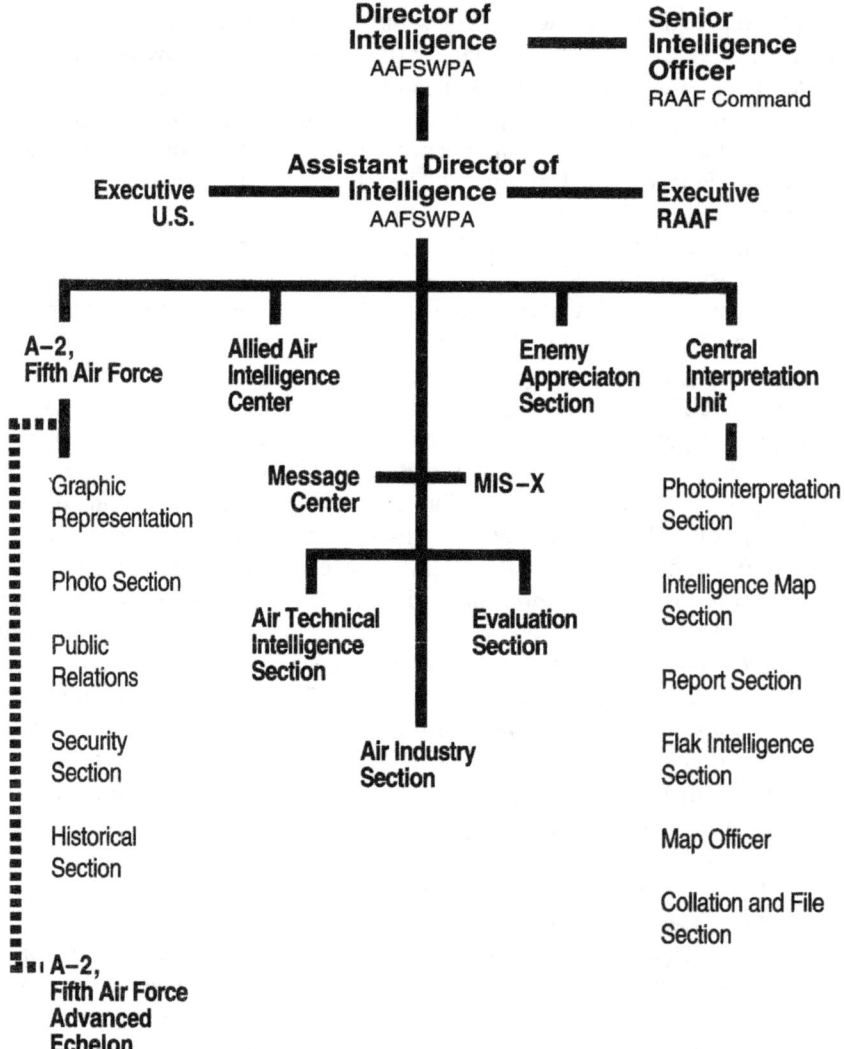

to include information from Japanese or USSBS records of air attacks made by his men. This collection held copies of correspondence and messages, plus assorted items such as orders and memoranda. Kenney sometimes noted the source of his information about the enemy: that from Japanese messages he referred to as "hot information" or "the latest dope." Sometimes he used the word "ultra," referring to what the local Allied code breakers had delivered or to decrypted information from the Navy at Pearl Harbor or from MIS in Washington. In this regard Kenney was unique among AAF commanders, although he reflected the generally lax security procedures in the command. Intelligence leads from several sources prompted Kenney and Whitehead to make some important decisions. Kenney's November 1942 proposal to fly troops to Dobodura and then supply them by air as they attacked Buna was based on his knowledge that no Japanese were within fifteen miles of the proposed landing ground. Heavy aerial fighting in the Solomon Islands meant that Japanese air forces would be limited in their ability to support their army in the Buna-Dobodura area. Fifth Air Force attacks on Rabaul, 450 miles from Port Moresby, further hampered Japanese air opposition.[30]

The Papuan campaign followed the successful ground defenses of the Port Moresby–Milne Bay area in September 1942. The feasibility of carrying out a concerted effort to take Buna and Gona was questioned by some at GHQ in Australia because of logistics difficulties and the lack of roads in the area. Kenney's limited troop carriers could move only about half the needed supplies, with the remainder going by sea to landing areas south of Buna. Despite the problems and weeks of vicious, bloody fighting, the Allied campaign culminated in late January 1943 with the capture of Buna and Gona by American 32d Division and Australian 7th Division infantrymen.[31]

In 1942, Japanese attention centered primarily on the Solomon Islands; they had few combat aircraft on New Guinea. Some days they had no more than sixteen on the island; rarely were there more than twice that number. Aerial reconnaissance by Fifth Air Force B–17s or B–24s tracked the airfields along the Japanese-held coast and at New Britain's bases as well. When in 1943 the number of Japanese aircraft listed in the Fifth's *Daily Summary of Principal Activities* increased to the point that the enemy presented a danger, the well-stocked Japanese airfields became the target of Whitehead's bombers—if not at Kenney's direct insistence, then as a result of his well-understood policy of destroying opposing air forces before they could strike Allied airfields. The intelligence information supporting such operations normally came from theater sources such as aerial observation and photography supplemented by radio traffic analysis. As the war progressed and as American skills in decrypting Japanese message traffic increased, important information appeared from outside the Southwest Pacific theater. One such series of reports came originally from the U.S. Navy and was to have a significant impact on Fifth Air Force for the remainder of the war.[32]

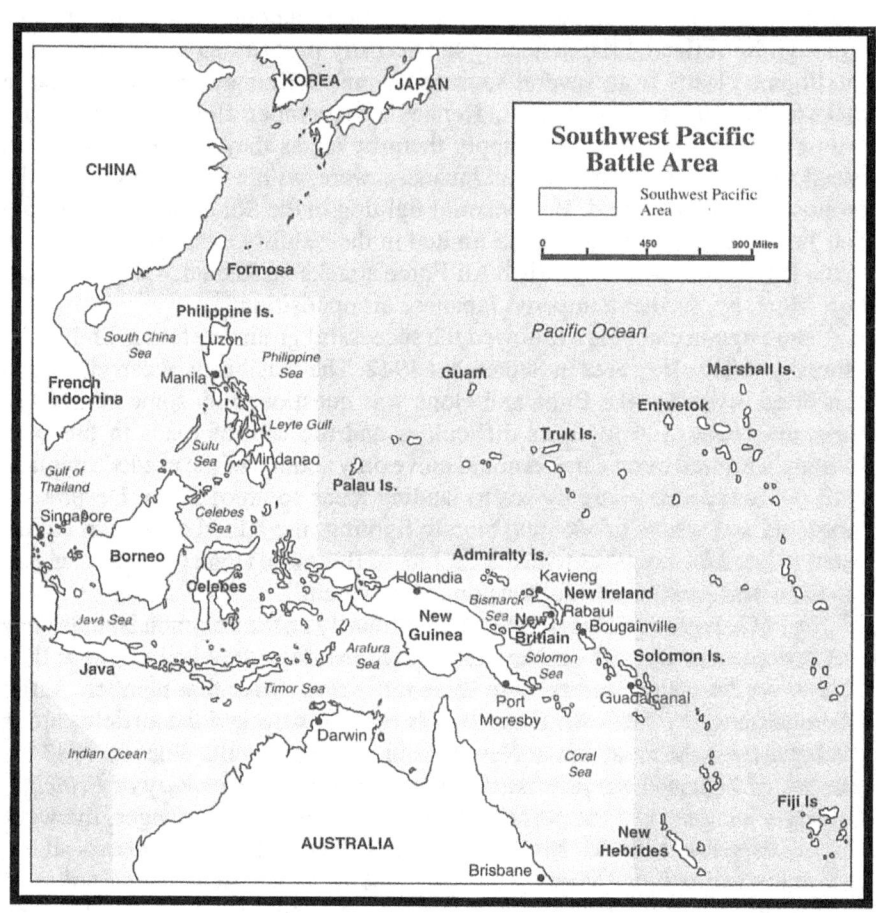

The Pacific and Far East

On January 3, 1943, Kenney saw a message that inspired him to try to cut the Japanese supply lines between Rabaul and New Guinea. The Japanese commander intended to run a convoy to Lae from Rabaul, and Kenney suspected that it was the beginning of an attempt to push the Allies out of New Guinea. Kenney believed that such a heavy blow could force the Allies out of the Pacific war. Directing a reduced bombing effort to allow time to restore his B–17 force, Kenney increased reconnaissance flights while sending all of the operational bombers he could muster to attack Rabaul harbor with, so he thought, the destruction of one ship and damage to six others on January 5. The next day, P–38s with 1,000-pound bombs attacked a convoy of five transports and five destroyers. No ship was hit. This disappointment was soon overcome.[33]

In late February 1943, Fifth Air Force reconnaissance of Rabaul harbor showed increasing numbers of ships; on the 22d, airmen photographed seventy-nine craft of assorted sizes. General Kenney badly wanted to attack them using his newly modified B–25C–1 commerce raiders. His aircraft specialist, Maj. Paul I. Gunn, affectionately called Pappy because he was likely in his mid-forties, had installed eight forward-firing, .50-caliber machine guns in the noses of the aircraft. Kenney itched to try out his new weapon; using both the machine guns and low-altitude skip-bombing tactics, he intended to hit Rabaul as soon as bad weather abated. In MacArthur's office on the 25th, however, Kenney read a Japanese message, intercepted and forwarded by the U.S. Navy, that completely altered his plans. The Japanese intended to move some 6,900 soldiers to Lae to bolster the existing garrison of 3,500, using the prospect of stormy weather to cover the convoy. The possibility of so many fresh troops facing the tired and depleted American and Australian divisions caused General MacArthur serious concern.[34]

Following an afternoon session in Brisbane with MacArthur on the 25th, Kenney sent a courier to Port Moresby with a letter for Whitehead, telling him about the intended convoy and its possible sailing date (between March 5 and 12). Kenney went on to tell his subordinate to postpone the Rabaul raid, prepare for the customary preconvoy Japanese air attack by as many as 100 planes, step up reconnaissance of and attacks on all Japanese airfields on New Guinea and New Britain usable by Japanese fighters, and scale back flying as much as possible to allow preparation of as many B–17s, B–25s, and P–38s as possible at the advanced Dobodura airfield. Flying the B–25s and P–38s to Dobodura was a precaution Kenney took to ensure that unpredictable heavy weather over the Owen Stanley Mountains did not interfere with the strike at the convoy. Because of weather fronts that could cover ships, Kenney thought the Japanese might move before the 5th. Having missed most of the January convoy to Lae and knowing of the new Japanese intentions, Kenney did not want this chance to slip away.[35]

Piercing the Fog

One of the burning ships from the Japanese convoy that Generals Kenney and Whitehead caught off Finschhaven, which they bombed. All eight transports carrying a division of reinforcements sunk, as did four of the eight destroyer escorts. The Battle of the Bismarck Sea was the first major air victory in the Southwest Pacific.

On February 26, Kenney flew to Port Moresby. There he and Whitehead traced the routes of all previous Japanese convoys from Rabaul to New Guinea. Comparing the tracks of earlier convoys, the range of Allied aircraft, and the expected weather, the two men decided to hit the ships as they passed Finschhaven, New Guinea, probably at 10:30 AM one day during the first week of March. P–40 and A–20 aircraft that could not reach the convoy would beat down Japanese air operations at Lae to protect the attack. Kenney directed that crews and squadron commanders practice tactics and run a full dress rehearsal on February 28.[36]

Kenney was pleased as he watched crews practice on the afternoon of the 27th. That same day a reconnaissance aircraft found a break in the clouds through which the observers counted seven vessels thirty miles southeast of St. Mathias Island. Kenney speculated that the ships could be the ones for which he and his men waited, but the weather was still too bad for anything more than continued surveillance.[37]

On the 28th, Kenney's men briefed him on Japanese air strength: 115 on New Britain, 51 on New Ireland, 177 in the Solomon Islands, 206 in the NEI, and 35 in New Guinea. The low figure for New Guinea was normal; on January 31 only 16 enemy aircraft had been reported on the huge island. That was one of the things that worried Kenney. He viewed Japan's air forces as immensely flexible, able to shift quickly from base to base, to come through his sketchy air warning system and hit him with great effect, given the the chance and an able commander. Japanese airmen commonly attacked Allied positions on New

Guinea from Rabaul, and Kenney's worry about Japanese air power potential made him closely watch air intelligence reports that he could use to best advantage. Telling Whitehead to continue with preparations, Kenney returned to Brisbane to prepare for a trip to Washington where he and Sutherland were to meet with the JCS and the representatives of other Pacific commands to discuss Pacific strategy. While preparing for the trip, Kenney told MacArthur of the state of preparations for the attack; he also worried about the weather, which had blocked any reconnaissance sightings that day.[38]

On March 1, the convoy passed out of the heavy weather. Late in the afternoon, a B-24's crew once again saw it. The next day, a series of high- and low-level attacks by the Americans and Australians, followed by Navy PT boats, destroyed the Japanese ships. Kenney and Whitehead had hit the convoy exactly where they had planned, off Finschhaven. They sent their men in under the expected Japanese air cover and achieved complete surprise. All eight of the cargo ships burned and sank in the two days of fighting. By the time Navy PT boats mopped up, four of the original eight destroyer escorts had escaped. Subsequent Japanese messages indicated that they may have rescued as many as 4,500 soldiers, most landing in New Guinea. Those who survived reached Lae without food or equipment, where they faced eventual starvation.[39]

Kenney and MacArthur claimed a much higher toll of Japanese ships based on the conflicting report of the aircrews. The original Fifth Air Force estimate was that as many as fourteen merchantmen had been destroyed with troop losses exceeding 12,000. Continued scrutiny of enemy radio messages and translations of documents captured later in the year at Lae reduced the total in both categories, but the full information remained secret for some time. In March 1943 MacArthur and Kenney were exultant. MacArthur, flush with the adroit use of intelligence analysis, made the very most of the victory in his communique. Japan's military leaders were shocked, for they expected at worst that half of the convoy would get through. Although the Japanese lost most of an infantry division, the battle itself was far more significant for its long-term effects on American air operations in the region. Kenney left for the Washington meeting at dawn on March 4. When he arrived there he was no longer a minor air commander in an isolated and neglected theater; he was the most important AAF hero since the Doolittle raid on Japan the year before. On landing, Generals Marshall and Arnold met and congratulated him. Later that month his picture appeared on the cover of *Life* magazine.[40] The outcome of Kenney's reading of the Japanese messages was to go well beyond congratulations, greatly affecting the size and prestige of the AAF in the SPA and SWPA.

Called to the White House on March 17, Kenney told President Roosevelt about the Southwest Pacific Theater. Answering Roosevelt's questions, Kenney said he needed more airplanes, crews, and supplies if he were to continue the war at the present pace. A few days before, Kenney had made such a pitch to Arnold. "No," said the commanding general and his staff; virtually the entire aircraft production was needed for Europe, for Allies, and for flight training in the States. None could be found for MacArthur's area. The day after Kenney visited Roosevelt, the president invited Arnold to the White House. After that visit, things changed; aircraft became available. Roosevelt, so taken with Kenney's success, made the pitch for reinforcements more effectively than could the airman. He did so in such a way that he evidently convinced Arnold that Kenney had not gone over his head. Neither Kenney's notes nor correspondence from the AAF's chief showed bitterness or anger by Arnold at being urged to change aircraft allocations. Arnold seems to have been sympathetic to Kenney's position and to have believed it important to remain on Roosevelt's good side, where he had not always been in the past. Arnold needed air commanders like Kenney who could use air power; thus far in the war Army air power had had few conspicous successes. Arnold knew that Kenney's success at divining the Japanese plans that led to the Bismarck Sea battle changed Kenney's position radically, and as a consequence, the fortunes of the American air forces grew not only in the SWPA, but in the adjoining SPA as well.[41]

On March 22, Arnold met Kenney and told him he would get the 380th Bomb Group (B–24s) previously scheduled for England. In addition, two medium-bomber groups, two fighter groups, and the 375th Troop Carrier Group would come to him. At that time, nobody wanted the new P–47s. Kenney, starved for planes and anxious to increase his force, gladly took them as the first of his new fighter groups. Twining's Thirteenth Air Force in the SOPAC got additional units, too, "to keep peace in the family," Kenney said.* By the end of 1943, Kenney expected to have new authorizations for about 500 planes. Supplies and crews would follow, as would greater opportunities for himself, and for General Twining in the neighboring SOPAC, to carry the war to the Japanese.[42]

In the months following the Bismarck Sea battle, the Allies maintained their surveillance of Japanese shipping. Half a dozen B–24s and B–17s made daily flights, checking ports along the New Guinea coast and the coast of New Britain as well. Reconnaissance, radio traffic analysis, and interception led to antishipping attacks on April 6, 12, and 15 and again in May. The strain on the aircraft was great; in-commission strength declined steadily, which compelled Whitehead to restrict flying to attacks on targets that intelligence sources had confirmed. The pressure on the Japanese told; in mid-May they altered their logistics strategy. Intercepted radio traffic indicated that the Japanese were changing their policy of sending supplies and reinforcements by ship to a policy of using small barges with fighter cover. In response, the Allies changed too,

---

*Aircraft bound for Australia first reached South Pacific bases where they were often redirected to the Thirteenth Air Force, with consequent friction and complaints. Kenney's and Arnold's agreement that included Twining's force was an adept political move as well as an operationally important one.

The Pacific and Far East

altering their tactics to barge hunting. Finding and sinking small boats can be uneconomical, especially when fighters are needed to protect the B–25s. The Allies therefore followed a campaign of attacking both Japanese airfields and barges. This forced the Japanese to again change their pattern for supplying their army in New Guinea. Supplies to Lae arrived more frequently by submarine and were unloaded at night when Allied air patrols were ineffective. Convoys sailed from Palau and landed farther west, at Wewak, the location of a major collection of Japanese airfields. Sensing an increasing Allied threat, the Japanese began reinforcing their main Army garrisons, primarily in the Wewak area.[43] The Allied pressure on Japan's New Guinea positions, and Japanese unwillingness to be forced into retreat, set the stage for major air, land, and sea fighting in New Guinea and adjacent islands through the latter part of 1943 and the first six months of 1944.

In the SOPAC theater during 1942, Navy domination of the interservice command structure meant that AAF squadrons supported amphibious operations, such as the fighting on Guadalcanal and later on New Georgia, as pieces of a Navy task force. Later, the same task force organization continued to pit AAF airmen against the Japanese in the Solomons, but under Navy control, not as an integral Thirteenth Air Force.[44] So different from the AAF's doctrine on air employment were the Navy's ideas that Twining, as Thirteenth Air Force commander, could not work like his counterpart Kenney. Twining felt frustrated for some time, although he and Harmon worked diligently as good team players. Relations between the AAF and the Navy remained good with the AAF officers having a strong voice in decision making.[45]

During the summer of 1942, few AAF units were in the SOPAC. Those present were stationed and organized in various fashions depending entirely on the needs of the moment. A squadron of AAF P–39s and P–400s* moved to Guadalcanal on August 22, once the Marines had secured and restored the airfield. These aircraft lacked the performance needed to contest the skies with the Japanese Zeros, so they assumed instead a largely ground-support role in the fighting for the island.[46]

Beginning late in 1942, occasional intelligence information reached Guadalcanal from the Navy in Pearl Harbor; much of it referred to Japanese naval movements or air traffic into Rabaul as opposed to air operations information having direct combat application. Air OB intelligence when matched to aerial reconnaissance of the Japanese airfield complex on New Britain allowed for continuing bomber attacks on Rabaul's airdromes. Bombers from both the SPA and SWPA attacked as part of an intertheater effort to beat down the threatening Japanese air forces.[47] On November 22, 1942, after

---

*An export version of the early model P–39, originally intended for Great Britain.

269

considerable delay caused by the loss of equipment in an air crash, the Navy opened an intercept and direction-finding station on Guadalcanal.[48] Both the intercept station and coast watchers supplemented radar to warn of approaching enemy formations.

Air defense of the southern Solomons was crucial to preventing the Japanese from retaking Guadalcanal, and it depended to a great extent on the adept use of radar to identify approaching threats, supplemented by operational intelligence from coast watchers hiding all along the Solomons chain. These men observed and counted Japanese bomber and fighter flights going south, then radioed operations officers on Guadalcanal. Interceptors, primarily Navy and Marine, rose to make a single pass at the bombers before diving to safety. After an attack, as the Japanese pilots flew home, the coast watchers again counted formations and aircraft, radioing Guadalcanal with information that helped confirm or deny the pilots' and AA gunners' reports of enemy aircraft shot down.[49]

Recording of the patterns of Japanese flights by the intelligence officers on Guadalcanal had significant operational implications. Because of the distance from Rabaul, Japanese strikes usually arrived over the island's Henderson Field between 11 AM and 1 PM. This knowledge, coupled to coast-watcher reports and radar confirmation, gave the air commanders time to alert the pilots and crews for the coming fights.[50]

Pilots' observations and reconnaissance data were always important in governing the ways in which Air Commander Solomons (COMAIRSOLS) officers directed the use of U.S. Army air power in the Solomons. On December 5, 1942, two AAF P–39 pilots sighted the partially camouflaged construction at a new Japanese airfield at Munda, New Georgia, confirming coast-watcher reports of activity there. That confirmation brought heavy and continuing bombardment and strafing of the field. Soon after the Japanese began to use Munda, they found their position untenable. By the end of the year, Munda only serviced aircraft; none could be stationed there and survive the air attacks.[51]

One of the most adept and controversial interservice uses of intelligence resulted in the ambush and death of the Japanese Combined Fleet's Commander-in-Chief, Admiral Yamamoto. On April 14, 1943, American radio intercept operators picked up a Japanese message that, when decoded, revealed Yamamoto's plans for a visit to his forces in the northern Solomons; also included was his travel itinerary. In Honolulu, Admiral Nimitz weighed the risks and possibilities of air interception with his intelligence chief, Cmdr. Edwin T. Layton. Seeing a golden opportunity to dispose of his enemy counterpart, to kill the man who planned the attack on Pearl Harbor, and deal the Japanese Navy's morale a heavy blow, Nimitz ordered commanders in the Solomons to ambush Yamamoto if they thought they could make the long flight. The only fighter aircraft capable of such an extended overwater run were the AAF's P–38s at Guadalcanal. Immediately, planning began. At dawn on April

The Pacific and Far East

18, the pilots took off, flying northward at extremely low altitude and carrying external fuel tanks on their planes to give them the needed range.[52]

By 9:34 AM, sixteen P–38 Lightning fighters intercepted two Japanese Mitsubishi Betty bombers and six Zero fighters over Bougainville Island. In the ensuing swirl of aerial fighting, the Americans destroyed both bombers. Killed in the first bomber as it crashed into Bougainville's jungles was Admiral Yamamoto. The successful ambush of Yamamoto later became one of the most highly publicized incidents of the Pacific war. This action also endangered America's ability to read Japan's encrypted message traffic. Virtually everyone involved in the killing of Yamamoto, including the P–38's ground crews, came to know the source of the information. The British were aghast that American policy permitted such a risk. As it was, officials at BP withheld full disclosure of their operation for several months. Had the story reached Japan from any source, and had the Japanese realized its significance, they could have altered their radio transmission practices and foreclosed an extremely valuable Allied insight into their planning. Fortunately, the Japanese failed to understand the true nature of the attack. Ambushes such as the one that killed Yamamoto were unusual events, not central to the war effort. Over time, a more methodical use of technical information came to expand on the reports obtained from ULTRA.

Electronic intelligence gathering efforts began in the Pacific war only after the capture of some Japanese equipment in August 1942 at Guadalcanal. A badly damaged Mark 1 Model 1 radar set found at Henderson Field was quickly packed and sent to the Naval Research Laboratory at Anacostia, in Washington, D.C. Soon, the Navy sent a team with airborne radar intercept equipment to the SOPAC. This team made the first ferret flight in search of Japanese installations in the region, flying an AAF B–17 from Espiritu Santo to Guadalcanal, Bougainville, and returning on October 31, 1942. Other flights in November carried Allied crews but found no enemy radar signals. Since the teams collected no evidence of Japanese radar, operational interest in the Pacific temporarily waned. Development of more effective electronic search aircraft continued in the United States, and they subsequently deployed to North Africa.

At about the same time that the airborne searches were underway in the Solomons, a Navy submarine carrying similar radio-receiving equipment picked up radar signals while on patrol off Japan. The earlier absence of radar reception by the airborne teams resulted in much uncertainty over whether the Japanese in the area lacked extensive radar equipment or if the early detection sets simply would not pick up the signals. The ferret aircraft, generally B–24s or Catalina flying boats, carried radar frequency analyzers plus equipment to determine the relative bearing of the radar set and to measure its pulse width and pulse repetition frequency. Not until late 1943 did the subject receive much attention in SPA and SWPA. Then, seeing the potential importance of mapping enemy radar as a way to avoid AA gun defenses, G–2 SWPA formed its Section 22 to control and coordinate all Allied airborne radar and radio intelligence gathering

271

in the theater. In addition to local use by AAF intelligence and operations officers, Section 22 sent information it collected to Washington, to the Radio Research Laboratory in Massachusetts, and to neighboring theaters, particularly to the CBI. In January 1944, two ferret B–24s arrived in New Guinea for service with Section 22. By early 1944, the Allies had located radar installations on New Britain (especially near Rabaul), New Ireland, Bougainville, and the north coast of New Guinea. The map, however, showed few stations, most with the same type of early warning equipment.

Not until the capture of Kwajalein Island in February 1944 did the Allies realize the full range of Japanese radar production and employment. Even then, their comprehension of Japan's technical advances came only with the discovery of a large pile of documents and a few pieces of equipment. In the SWPA, aircrews and commanders showed little concern for the potential danger of radar to them or to their aircraft. Their view was colored by the relatively few numbers and types of enemy sets scattered across a very extensive geographic area.[53] Wide use of radar locations and incorporation of this fact in flight planning awaited the advent of very-heavy bomber operations in China and India.

The Thirteenth Air Force's participation in the war in the Solomons continued under COMSOPAC's auspices until mid-1944. Until then, the Thirteenth flew with Navy and Marine Corps squadrons of the SOPAC and with AAF from the Southwest Pacific to strike progressively harder blows at Rabaul. Rabaul, the major Japanese air and naval installation, occupied a harbor and airdrome facilities at the eastern end of New Britain. Also on the island, Japanese forces had constructed airfields at Gasmata, Arawe, Cape Gloucester, and elsewhere. Destruction of these installations became Halsey's goal as his SOPAC forces moved north through the Solomon Islands. Virtually daily, SPA and SWPA crews reconnoitered the bases, recording shipping at sea and in harbors as well as any activity at the shore sites. Allied radio intercept specialists noted communications of planes and ships to and from Rabaul, Truk, and other areas. Each day, the *Special Intelligence Bulletin* (*SIB*) at MacArthur's headquarters reported the activity and commented on important changes.[54]

On July 25, 1943, Nathan Twining became COMAIRSOLS under an arrangement that gave each service a chance to have one of its own in charge for a few months at a time. Twining's assignment cemented the close relations that had developed between the Thirteenth Air Force and the SOPAC command. By the following September, Twining had observed that daytime attacks on Japanese shipping in the Solomons had prompted the enemy to shift the bulk of his transport operations to nighttime. To counter this and make the ocean areas as dangerous as possible for the enemy, Brig. Gen. Ray L. Owens, commander of the Thirteenth while Twining filled the COMAIRSOLS job, added more

Two of the coordinated air attacks on Rabaul in late 1943 by aircraft from the Southwest Pacific Theater and the South Pacific Theater. Above, the ship in the foreground in a Nachi-class heavy cruiser. It is pictured just getting underway. A few minutes later, as it was steaming toward the mouth of the harbor, a 1,000-pound bomb hit it amidship and turned the ship on its side. Below, the whole shoreline of Simpson Bay on which the Rabaul airfields were located seems to be ablaze after it was bombed and strafed. The all-important airfields are under the smoke at the left side of the photo.

Piercing the Fog

radar-equipped B–24 low-altitude bombers to the task of searching out and destroying this shipping.[55]

Late in 1943, a series of coordinated air strikes made by South and Southwest Pacific bombers and fighters hit Rabaul in an effort to close or greatly reduce this most threatening Japanese position. Daily Allied radio and teletype exchanges, meetings of the theaters' senior staff members, and communications between Halsey and MacArthur ensured that target information and attack plans were coordinated, with little conflict between the air groups sent on the raids. Especially toward year's end, defense of Rabaul became a battle of attrition for the Japanese naval air force. Allied intelligence judged quantitatively and type of aircraft at Rabaul's airdromes and the flow of reinforcements by air and sea. Kenney, Twining, Whitehead, and Rear Adm. Aubrey Fitch, Halsey's air commander, contemplated the abilities of the new Japanese pilots relative to those of the pilots who had been in the region earlier in an effort to determine the true state of Japanese combat capability. The leaders concluded that across the board the new Japanese flyers could not match those of early 1942, the result of heavy losses incurred by a small group of elite pilots. In October, Admiral Halsey mounted an amphibious assault on Bougainville Island, landing at Empress Augusta Bay on November 1. A smaller landing in the Treasury Islands on October 27, 1943, had preceded the Bougainville operation. MacArthur had agreed with Halsey that SWPA air forces would reduce the threat of Japanese air reaction from Rabaul, Kavieng, Buka Island, and other associated airfields, while Halsey's airmen, including those from the Thirteenth, protected the landing sites and troops going ashore. Progressively harder attacks on the Japanese positions began on October 15. On November 2, fighters and bombers from both SPA and SWPA staged the heaviest strike to date on Rabaul's airfields and harbor.[56]

In preparing their plans for Bougainville and Rabaul, the Allies had access to considerable information on newly developed Japanese aircraft and the organization and operating locations of Japan's air forces. The recent Allied capture of Lae, Salamaua, and Finschhafen had driven the Japanese Army Air Force in New Guinea to the west. Successful AAF efforts to render useless the Japanese airfield at Cape Gloucester on New Britain's western tip (lying between Rabaul and the Allies' New Guinea airfields) had largely succeeded. Kenney, on November 2, summed up Japan's projected air strength in a letter to Whitehead at Port Moresby. Kenney surmised, based on air OB estimates (derived largely from ULTRA) and Y intercepts, that as of November 3, Japan would have 200 to 215 operational fighters and 60 to 70 bombers, most stationed at Rabaul but a substantial number also located at Kavieng on nearby New Ireland. Kenney added, "There is constant evidence picked up by Y Intelligence and by DF [direction finding] that heavy reinforcements are on the way or projected for an early date to move into the area from the Empire." To keep the Japanese on the defensive, Admiral Fitch used Thirteenth Air Force

The Pacific and Far East

plus Navy and Marine squadrons to bomb Rabaul as well as to attack radar warning sites on its approaches as often as possible. AAF joined in the attack from New Guinea, catching many newly arrived Japanese ships in the harbor on November 5. The timing was not coincidental; Allied intelligence analysts had forecast the Japanese naval force's arrival from radio intercepts.

Thirteenth Air Force received its intelligence material from several sources, depending on the particular mission to be undertaken. For example, Halsey ordered the November 11, 1943, raid on Rabaul by the Thirteenth's heavy bombers and naval carrier aircraft to support the force operating at Empress Augusta Bay. He decided on the time and composition of the attacking force based on his understanding from ULTRA of the Japanese presence. Responding to Halsey, the Thirteenth's planners picked their target aiming points from recent photography of Rabaul and surrounding airfields. This was important, for, as heavy bombers were to go in first to reduce opposition, their strikes had to be as accurate as possible. Carrier aircraft were to follow and work over shipping and other targets. So detailed was the intelligence and so effective the planning for these air strikes that by the end of the month, Rabaul ceased to be a major threat, although the Thirteenth and other SOPAC air units made periodic reconnaissance attacks. The Japanese now tried to counter Allied gains by shifting the focus of their operations to western New Guinea, Truk, and the mandated Pacific islands.[57]

As it became apparent that Rabaul's garrison was increasingly isolated and less able to present a major threat, the Thirteenth's aircraft turned to the Caroline Islands. On March 29, B–24s made the first daylight bomb run over Truk Atoll, littering the airfield on Eten Island with aircraft destroyed on the ground. On June 15, 1944, control of the Thirteenth Air Force passed to Kenney and the new FEAF, but the force continued to support Navy operations in the Carolines, Saipan, and Yap Islands. The new AAF organization gave the Thirteenth's A–2 a greater influence in combat operations planning.[58]

As the Thirteenth cooperated in multiservice operations in the Solomons, the AAF continued to fight successfully in New Guinea. By May 1943, intelligence collection and assessment became so well developed that Whitehead regularly received a flow of reports of Japanese air activity almost as quickly as the Japanese moved. On May 14, at dusk, the general knew that a few hours earlier Japanese aircraft had landed at Lae. That night he sent a squadron from Dobodura to attempt to destroy the newly arrived enemy. Bad weather precluded any success, however. The next morning, Whitehead tried again, this time with a flight of A–20s. Once more bad weather interfered. On the 15th, the intelligence staff passed Whitehead another report (probably based on coastwatcher observations and the interception of Japanese air traffic control radio transmissions) of nine bombers refueling at Lae, followed by their departure to the southeast at 4:21 PM. Such a flow of intelligence data made the jobs of air

Piercing the Fog

commanders in the SWPA easier, and it certainly gave them an invaluable edge in the air war. As Whitehead sought a chance to bomb his enemy during those days, he, at the same time, saw to it that Japanese attacks on Allied positions often met airborne Allied fighters guided by Y intercepts, as happened at Oro Bay on May 14th. Many times these interceptions took a heavy toll of enemy bombers.[59]

Throughout 1943 and into May 1944 the pattern continued. Coast watchers in the Solomon Islands and on New Guinea reported air movements; radio interception and radar confirmed them and supplied additional information. Allied airmen rose to the attack or struck at Japanese airfields to preempt other attacks. Coast watchers, men who risked their lives hiding in the jungles, sent a steady flow of increasingly valuable information. Years later, Francis Gideon, who had served as Kenney's deputy A–3, commended the coast watchers as a superb source of warning of Japanese air movements or impending attacks. Often these men hid on hills or mountains above Japanese airfields and reported their observations by radio. The Japanese knew of their presence and sought to catch them at every opportunity. When search teams or natives loyal to the Japanese captured a coast watcher, he was invariably killed.[60] The high-risk coast-watching jobs, however, were not to last forever. By the spring of 1944, radio intercept had supplanted coast watchers as the primary source of information. Electronic eavesdropping had many advantages, not the least of which was its ability to reach far behind the lines to collect information from places denied to coast watchers or where too few lookouts could be effective for long periods. This became readily apparent as the Japanese pulled back from some of their forward positions.

In 1943, as the Allied land forces moved west along New Guinea's coast toward Salamaua and Lae, the focus of Japanese air activity shifted to Wewak. There, a complex of four airdromes—Wewak, But, Dagua, and Boram—supported the bulk of Japanese air operations in New Guinea. Radio intercepts had plotted Japanese flying patterns, OB studies had listed probable numbers and types of aircraft at the fields, and visual and photoreconnaissance had confirmed the count: 225 aircraft populated the airdromes on April 15, 1943. For the next several months, the Japanese and Allied air forces fought each other in a struggle for air superiority. The outcome was by no means preordained, for Kenney did not waver in his fear that an adept Japanese air commander could strike his bases a mortal blow. Kenney had his engineers rush construction of a new airfield at Marilinan, close enough to Wewak that he could use it to support the major operation needed to destroy the extensive Japanese aviation there.[61] The Allies planned the attacks on Wewak's airfields with a full understanding of Japanese flying habits drawn from careful study of air traffic control radio conversations and extensive study of Japanese aerial practices.

In the predawn hours of August 17, 1943, forty-eight Allied heavy bombers hit the Wewak airfields. In midmorning, with fighters flying from Marilinan for

The Pacific and Far East

protection, the Allies returned with B–25s and P–38s. On the 18th an even larger raid hit the airfields in what General Whitehead described as the culmination of months of watching. The Wewak attacks were preemptive strikes to reduce the growing Japanese threat to Marilinan and to the Allied ground offensive aimed at the capture of Lae. When, after several days of pounding, the Japanese commander at Wewak called Rabaul for help, Whitehead's people listened in. That night, Whitehead assured Kenney that whatever the Japanese attempted, he and his men would be ready.[62]

In the ground war and at sea, the situation was similar. Radio traffic analysis led the Allies to watch out for Japanese barge traffic supplying and reinforcing Lae from Rabaul. Barge-hunting aircrews promptly shot up whatever seaborne traffic they encountered. When he read a Japanese message mentioning a land evacuation of Lae, Kenney quickly wrote a note to Whitehead, telling him to watch the area and attack at every opportunity. The notes that General Kenney made in his daily jottings and frequent letters to Whitehead leave clear the impression that these two men knew a great deal of what the Japanese intended. Armed with that knowledge, they pursued their enemy relentlessly across central and western New Guinea.[63]

By mid-February 1944, MacArthur was ready to drive west to retake the remainder of New Guinea. At the same time, Halsey's SOPAC forces occupied Green Island and then Emirau, in quick succession. In the process of judging the needs of the war's coming months, Kenney concluded that the Japanese-held Admiralty Islands, principally Manus and Los Negros, could be an Allied air base that would control Kavieng and Rabaul, ending serious Japanese attempts to use those locations in any important fashion. From Lorengau and Momote airfields in the Admiralties heavy bombers could reach Truk, Woleai, and other Japanese strongholds. Kenney also believed that taking Los Negros would obviate the need for a difficult amphibious attack on Kavieng. From Manus, Allied aircraft could reach Tadji and Hollandia, so Kenney concluded there would be no need to take the Hansa Bay area of New Guinea either. With so much success at exploiting intelligence on the Japanese, Kenney's confidence set him up for a rude shock.

Contemplating the Admiralty idea, Kenney turned to two widely used intelligence sources. Extensive aerial surveillance of Los Negros on February 23 and 24 reported little Japanese activity. In low flights over the island for long periods, aircrews saw no signs of Japanese activity. Based on aerial reports, Whitehead estimated Japanese strength at about 300. The *SIB*s had mentioned the Admiralties only sparingly for weeks, so Kenney doubted there was a substantial enemy force there. On the 24th, he approached MacArthur with the idea of sending a small force by destroyer to Los Negros, landing the troops with close air support and, if they found little Japanese opposition, taking the island quickly. Kenney added that if the Japanese there appeared in strength, the reconnaissance in force could be recalled with little lost. Willoughby, however, disagreed with Whitehead's low estimate of Japanese forces, offering instead his opinion of some 4,050 troops on Los Negros. After an hour and a half's discussion by MacArthur, Kenney, Vice Adm. Thomas D. Kinkaid (MacArthur's naval commander), and Chamberlin, MacArthur accepted Kenney's proposal, and set the action for February 29. With little time available, planning and force preparation began immediately.[64]

To obtain additional information, a scouting party from Lt. Gen. Walter Krueger's Sixth Army went ashore on Los Negros on February 27. Picked up the next morning by a Catalina flying boat, the men returned to report that, in Kenney's phrase, "the place is lousy with Japs." Kenney discounted the possible danger, quieting the fears of Whitehead and Whitehead's chief of staff, Col. Merian C. Cooper, by pointing out that any soldiers on the island would naturally have been where the patrol encountered them just to avoid the bombing attacks around Momote airdrome. Kenney also believed that the area the scouts checked was far too small to reflect the true enemy situation. Moreover, aerial reconnaissance of Wewak and Tadji airfields revealed no aircraft staging forward from Hollandia that could hazard the landing force. Kenney continued his belief in the value of taking Los Negros and then Manus, writing in his notes that he was certain that his scheme would succeed. Plans had advanced so far, with troops of the 1st Cavalry and Seabees embarked, that MacArthur, aboard the cruiser *Phoenix* to observe the operation, was reluctant to change at that late date based on the patrol's report.[65]

In fact, Col. Ezaki Yoshio, the Japanese commander on Los Negros, had hidden his 4,000 or so men in the jungle, forbidding both AA fire or movement during daylight and prohibiting any repairs to trails, roads, or structures damaged by bombardment. The island appeared largely deserted by the Japanese, with much of the apparent evidence favoring Kenney's suggested course of action. The Allied force of about 1,000 men landed shortly after 8 AM on the 29th, quickly quieted the initial opposition with help from naval gunfire, and took Momote airdrome and the surrounding area. At that point, MacArthur decided to move ahead with the Admiralties' seizure, sending for the backup reinforcements. Because of bad weather with low clouds, Whitehead's B–25s and fighters could give only limited support. That night, the Japanese began a series of heavy but uncoordinated attacks, with enemy soldiers recapturing part of the airfield. The following day, clearing weather allowed bombing and strafing in support of the 1st Cavalry Division's men on the ground. Forced onto the defensive by the more numerous enemy, the Allies dug in at positions around a reduced perimeter, where grim and desperate fighting blunted the force of the Japanese reaction. Reinforcements arrived on March 2, but the stubborn enemy resistance continued as the Japanese fought to the last. Air operations from Momote began with light aircraft using the field as early as the 6th. By March 8, most of the struggle for Los Negros was over. The focus of fighting then shifted to neighboring Manus Island. The main struggle for Manus lasted from the 15th to the 18th of March, with continued but diminishing fighting across the island until May 18. Total Japanese losses probably exceeded 4,300, with only 75 taken prisoner.[66]

The fight for the Admiralties had been heavier than expected, with poor weather initially delaying the air support promised by Fifth Air Force. Casualties in the taking of Los Negros reached 61 Americans of the 1st Cavalry Division and Navy Seabees dead, and 244 wounded. Overall losses in the Admiralties operation reached 326 dead 1,189 wounded, with 4 missing. The Japanese defense, doomed in any event because the Allies had cut off hope of support or reinforcements, failed at Los Negros when Colonel Ezaki could not coordinate his units and mass his force. Because of his reputation and confidence, Kenney's suggestion of the 24th prevailed in the planning council and again at the time of final decision on the 28th, but the cost was higher and the struggle longer than either Kenney or MacArthur had anticipated. The decision to proceed with the Los Negros landing seems to have been a case of discounting many of the unknowns with insufficient attention paid to an analytical scrutiny of OB tables. The OB calculations, made over time from a variety of sources—including ULTRA, captured document examination, radio direction finding, and traffic analysis—were less clearly visible, although they were strongly supported by the patrol's report. Kenney's February 28th conclusion and MacArthur's concurrence seem to have stemmed from a desire not to divert themselves from a course of action already in motion, rather than from a hard weighing of data followed by force planning and preparation.[67]

Although the force assembled for the Los Negros landing could have been stronger, thus giving the Allies a greater advantage, from Kenney's perspective, and from the course of the war as seen at the time, the taking of the islands was well worth the risk and effort. The use of the Admiralties allowed SOPAC planners, with the support of the JCS in Washington, to prepare a landing at Hollandia for mid-April and an assault on Mindanao in the Philippines by mid-November. Seizure of Kavieng was canceled, averting a costly fight there, and the Admiralty Islands' Seeadler Harbor became a major Allied naval support base. Planning for Hollandia, already well underway by March 6, dispensed with the intended landings at Wewak and Hansa Bay. As soon as the Admiralty airfields were ready, Kenney based the Thirteenth Air Task Force there. (The Thirteenth Air Task Force was a temporary designation for the Thirteenth Air Force units Kenney employed before he acquired the whole air force in the major reorganization of mid-1944.) From the Admiralties, the Thirteenth flew missions against Japanese-held bases to the north. Kenney's original proposal obtained MacArthur's agreement because of Kenney's prestige in MacArthur's eyes, yet Kenney's decision, made without full recognition of Japanese strength and with initially too few forces, became painful in light of the heavier than expected losses and the time required for its completion.

Piercing the Fog

The Allied landing at Hollandia followed soon after the capture of Manus, occurring on April 22, 1944. For this operation, Kenney's AAF staff planned much differently. Hollandia, as a result of recent Japanese retreats westward, had become the major forward Japanese Army Air Force base facing MacArthur's men. Although the object of repeated aerial attacks early in 1944, the enemy's base remained a substantial threat. Allied intelligence assessed its ground defense strength at about 8,654 general troops and 7,650 airmen, of which the analysts described 2,250 as air duty personnel. As of April 7, Allied commanders believed that Japan's *Eighteenth Army* headquarters was moving to Hollandia from Wewak. The Japanese base operation structure at Wewak appeared rather resilient, retaining the ability to quickly repair some forms of damage to the dirt-surfaced landing areas. A B–24 strike the morning of March 31 had left two of three runways unusable, but all returned to service by that afternoon. To buttress their air capability, the Japanese could draw from airfields at Sarmi and Wakde, the four airdromes near Wewak, the airdrome at Tadji, and the one in the Vogelkop area. SIGINT also indicated that the Japanese were surveying other airfield sites in western New Guinea as well.[68]

Kenney and Whitehead focused their concern not so much on Hollandia itself, which they believed they could control via air attack, but rather on the base and air support structure to the rear that the Japanese seemed to be strengthening. Kenney worried about Japanese efforts to improve their combat aircraft and the rate at which they could assemble reinforcements from the NEI, the Philippines, and the home islands, and direct them against the Allies. Knowledge of the rather weak strength of the ground garrison at Hollandia and the tactical dispositions that would necessarily disperse that strength when fighting began promised victory for the Army. Signals intercepts indicated, but did not confirm, a possible shortage of aviation gasoline on the Davao-Galela-Ambon-Hollandia route. Such a shortage, the product of Allied air and naval antishipping efforts, also promised to delay air reinforcement in western New Guinea. Unfortunately, the reported shortage could not be confirmed. Experience had shown, however, that the enemy could marshal considerable air power when necessary.

On March 8, Whitehead advised Kenney that the Japanese were keeping about 100 fighters at Hollandia and he reminded his commander that the previous October replacements had come to Rabaul at about 200 per week. At that rate, Whitehead's 150 P–38s had been worn down during the space of about three weeks. For the projected Hollandia campaign, Whitehead calculated that just 50 new fighters a week would be very dangerous because he had only 32 long-range P–38s and 177 operational B–24s available. To find the most recent information on Japanese air capability, Kenney asked his A–2, Colonel Cain, to make a special air OB study. The study took some preparation, and, in the meantime, Admiral Nimitz, meeting with MacArthur in Brisbane on March 27, expressed grave fears of a possible Japanese air force reaction to the Hollandia

The Pacific and Far East

landing. Nimitz's carriers would be supporting the Hollandia effort, and he did not want to send them into an area dominated by Japanese land-bases air power. Nimitz also pointed out that his fast carriers, upon which the Sixth Army would depend for air cover, would have to leave on D+2 for refueling, and could not be back until D+8.[69]

Responding to Nimitz's fears, Kenney promised air superiority at Hollandia by April 5th. This promise drew some skepticism, as AAF bases were too far away to permit effective fighter cover. In making the promise, Kenney also noted that to maintain that superiority in the face of possible retaliation, he needed to have ready for operational use airdromes seized at Hollandia, Aitape, or Tadji by D+2. Kenney had not spoken rashly, for by the day of the meeting he and Whitehead had already begun the process of reducing Japanese air power. First, Kenney had directed his air depot expert, Col. Victor Bertrandais, to make extra wing tanks for at least 75 of the older P–38s. This work was nearing completion on the 27th. He had also instructed Whitehead to let the fighters fly no farther than Tadji and to let them remain over Tadji for no more than fifteen minutes for any reason, even if it meant quitting combat. By this he hoped to deceive the Japanese into thinking his aircraft lacked sufficient range to threaten Hollandia, and thereby allow the enemy to feel safe enough to keep large numbers of their airplanes there. The airmen moved the P–38s to Nadzab, as close to Hollandia as they could be based. The Australians moved P–40s to Momote in the Admiralties to block attacks from Rabaul and Kavieng. From March 11 to 25 the Allies once again repeatedly bombed the four Wewak bases that lay between Nadzab and Hollandia. During that period, 2,666 sorties destroyed an estimated 88 enemy aircraft and, more importantly, ended the usefulness of Wewak to the Japanese. Lt. Gen. Teramoto Kunachi, commanding the *Fourth Air Army* at Wewak, seeing the futility of trying to keep Wewak open, abandoned the area and moved his headquarters to Hollandia on March 25th. Allied losses over Wewak totaled only 4 bombers and 2 fighters for the 15 days.

On March 30, when GHQ AAF learned from ULTRA of Japanese expectations of an attack along the New Guinea coast between Madang and Wewak, the Allies decided to foster this notion with some deception. Without letting up on the air suppression campaign, the Australians and Americans began making superfluous attacks in the region, encouraging the Japanese to believe what they were already predisposed to accept. The deception also involved dropping parachute dummies and simulating night photography with illumination or flash bombs. The Navy increased PT boat activity and left rubber boats ashore in selected spots to create the impression that scouting parties had landed. Sporadic and seemingly ill-conceived single-plane night attacks on Hollandia (with intentionally inaccurate bombing) brought some derisive remarks from Radio Tokyo, to Kenney's delight. Daylight aerial photography of Hollandia airfields indicated the Japanese were going for the bait, increasing their aircraft

Piercing the Fog

at the fields there and parking them in the unprotected open, even closely together. For good measure, on the 18th and 19th of March, Allied airmen destroyed most of a convoy bound from Hollandia to Wewak.[70]

On the morning of March 30th the air offensive against Hollandia, preparatory to Allied seizure of the area, began. The first waves of heavy bombers took out the newly emplaced and rather threatening AA gun positions surrounding the Hollandia airfields. Photoanalysis had just recently revealed the presence of the guns, and Kenney promptly made them first priority. Next to be hit were the fuel storage areas and parked aircraft. Poststrike aerial photography showed 118 aircraft destroyed or badly damaged on the first day. By the end of the second day of heavy attacks, the score had risen to 219. At the same time, Kenney received ULTRA information that the Japanese had already begun moving replacements toward Hollandia. Previously arranged carrier-based air attacks by Nimitz's fleet on Palau, Yap, Ulithi, and Woleai, plus Thirteenth Air Task Force B–24 bombardment of Woleai, restrained some of the flow of aircraft by forcing the Japanese to hold many air units in either the NEI or the Philippines, ready to ward off a possible major thrust in the Central Pacific. Allied Air Forces Y-Service monitoring Japanese transmissions from the Hollandia area learned that on March 30 the base had just 18 minutes' warning of the approaching raid, allowing commanders to send 40 interceptors into the air. The defending aircraft appeared disorganized. On the second day, warning increased to 70 minutes. Despite the added time, only 30 fighters rose to

Maj. Gen. Victor Bertrandais

The Pacific and Far East

intercept, and AA fire was generally inaccurate. Against an attack on April 4, the Japanese commander sent up 30 fighters, but he mustered only slight AA fire. The April 4th strike was so conclusive that Hollandia no longer presented a threat. Continued raids preceding the April 22 landing by Sixth Army kept the airfields from any but the lightest and most occasional use.[71]

On April 18, Cain brought Kenney the report on regional enemy air strength. The data confirmed Kenney's previous opinion of the potential danger and Whitehead's fears, leaving Kenney feeling uneasy. Cain advised him that given adequate organization and using the western New Guinea bases, the Japanese could put 50 fighters and 50 bombers over Tanamerah and Hollandia on the morning of D+3, when the carriers had gone but possibly before the engineers had readied the Japanese fields for Allied use. Three enemy cruisers at Manokwari indicated to Kenney the possibility that they might be preparing for the Allied advance. The location of Japanese supply dumps and AA fire from the Tanamerah Bay areas also left him apprehensive of the reception the Army would receive on coming ashore. After reviewing the material, Kenney spoke to Sutherland to recommend bringing the escort carriers from Aitape on D+2 to cover the area when the fast carriers left in the evening. Kenney judged that if Lt. Gen. Robert Eichelberger's men failed to clear the beaches and reach the Hollandia airfields by D+3 and if the Tadji or Tami airdromes could not be taken and put to use by D+2, the Japanese air forces had a chance to inflict a substantial disaster on the Allies. Worse yet, Kenney would have few alternatives since most of his bases lay too far to the rear for an effective reaction.[72] For the moment, however, he and Whitehead had done all they could. The only thing left was to await events, and watch the landing.

The actual taking of Aitape, Hollandia, and the three airfields inland from Hollandia near Lake Sentani proved anticlimactic. General Teramoto had already moved, this time to Menado in the Celebes, where he hoped to rally a counterattack. He could not. Japanese ground resistance at Hollandia collapsed, with logistics the most serious problem for the Allies. The beaches were difficult to use, and roads to the inland airfields were no more than long, narrow morasses that did not allow even jeep travel. Although the airfields fell on April 26, most supplies had to be hand carried or airlifted for some days while Army engineers constructed an acceptable road. The former Japanese airfield at Aitape, meanwhile, had been repaired by RAAF engineers and was ready for use by fighters on April 24. Restoration of the Hollandia fields took longer, their first use coming on May 3. Overall, the Hollandia airdromes disappointed the airmen; none could serve adequately as a major airfield because of the swampy terrain and poor roads. Even the two harbors, at Tanamerah and Hollandia proper, were only marginally useful. The Allied commanders soon forgot these disappointments as they continued moving west. By mid-August, MacArthur controlled virtually all of New Guinea, with the Philippines the next major target for the combined Southwest Pacific and Thirteenth Air Forces.[73]

Piercing the Fog

Once secure in New Guinea and then the Halmahera Islands, Allied commanders drew up formal plans for the assault on the Philippines, Formosa, and China. As part of this process, the planners reviewed the continuing ULTRA disclosures and other information, learning a number of key factors in Japan's regional defense planning. By mid-September 1944, continuing Allied guerrilla raids on Japanese garrisons in the Philippines allowed greater opportunity for intelligence gathering that might supplement the more detached analyses from Brisbane. Assessments drawn from ULTRA led the Allies to believe that Japan was carrying out a strategic withdrawal of air units to Formosa, Luzon, and the home islands, with a consequent reduction in air defenses south of Luzon, especially the Visayan Islands in the central Philippines. The Japanese air reaction to carrier air strikes on Yap, Palau, and elsewhere, as reflected in intercepted messages, seemed one of semiparalysis. Japanese commanders seemed unable to mount any significant air operations. Despite the fact that Japanese naval intelligence had located an Allied carrier task force within 300 miles of Leyte, they made no response. The opposite seemed to be true, with a strengthening of the Formosa–home islands defense line.

The absence of substantial message traffic to Balikpapan in eastern Borneo indicated a reduction of air defenses around the major oil production and refinery complex there. Direct evidence from ULTRA illustrated some regional oil, aviation gasoline, and naval fuel stockpiles. For example, the Japanese Army Air Force aviation gasoline storage capacity in the Philippines stood at 6.6 million gallons in the Manila area (enough to fuel 166 medium bombers for 30 days), 5.8 million gallons at Hondagua in southeastern Luzon, 3.2 million gallons at Iloilo, and 2.4 million gallons at Cebu. The Japanese Navy's air arm also had storage at Manila, Cebu, and Davao. The Allies surmised correctly that this storage pattern reflected the relative importance of these areas in Japanese air operations planning. Balikpapan itself held stocks of an extremely large amount of aviation gasoline—9.9 million gallons—plus 67,894 tons of fuel oil. The amounts stored in Borneo, however, were not there for operational use. This matériel represented a shipping backlog, a result of the constantly constricting hold that the Allied air and submarine forces had on Japanese logistics lines.[74]

Japan's difficulties in moving fuel to various places along her outer Empire defense perimeter, and her growing and very serious problems in troop transport and general shipping, prove the efficacy of Allied aerial and submarine attacks on her merchant fleet as it moved through the Pacific. From this information and long experience in the area, Kenney saw a chance to make Japan's problems even more severe. He believed that the RAAF's April 1944 mining raids on Balikpapan's harbor had badly disrupted transfer of fuel supplies, and he pleaded unsuccessfully for two groups of B–29s to be based temporarily in Australia for an attack on Borneo's oil production. To facilitate acceptance in Washington of his B–29 suggestion, Kenney had even gone so far as to build

The Pacific and Far East

a suitable base in northern Australia and to offer it as an operating site until better locations could be had. Kenney wanted to get hold of the superbombers and put them to use in his theater, and he saw oil as the best target to promote the idea. In Washington, Arnold had refused the request, fearing that once a theater commander controlled the new bombers he would not release them. That would be the end of the strategic bombing command just then beginning operations, and perhaps the end of an independent postwar air force as well.[75]

Failing to get B–29s, Kenney decided to use his own B–24s flying from newly captured Sansapor Island, off the northern shore of the westernmost part of New Guinea. The first two of these raids on Balikpapan—on September 30 and October 3, 1944—badly damaged refining plants and storage capacity, but they encountered heavier than expected aerial opposition. The Japanese were not as impotent in the area as Kenney had thought. Reliance on the absence of radio intercepts as an indicator of lack of opposition had misled Kenney into a belief that the project would be easier than it was. Intercepted messages on October 5 revealed that the Japanese Naval Air Force's *381 Group* had gone so far as to establish an airborne fighter patrol on the approaches to the refinery, with links to outlying radar stations. On October 8, ULTRA revealed the presence of the *341 Group* near Balikpapan as well. Not wishing to risk bombers and crews unnecessarily, Fifth and Thirteenth Air Force B–24 group commanders altered flight formations to tighten the assembly of aircraft and give greater mutual protection for the October 10th and 14th attacks.* Long-range P–38s and P–47s hastily moved to forward airdromes and flew as escorts. Despite intense aerial combat, the bombers inflicted additional severe damage on Balikpapan's refinery and storage areas. Overall, the raids cost twenty-two B–24s and nine accompanying fighters, a stiff price for the SWPA but light in terms of some loss rates in Europe. The attacks proved their worth, crippling production at the Borneo facility and setting the stage for the assault on the Philippines.[76]

Shortly after Nimitz's forces captured Guam and Saipan and had moved on to bombarding Iwo Jima and the Bonin Islands, MacArthur was ready to land in the Philippines. Promoted by intelligence indicating Japanese weakness on Leyte and by the interplay between the major Allied commands in the Pacific, the landing came a month earlier than first planned—on October 20, 1944. In mid-September, Admiral Halsey's men, in rescuing a pilot shot down over Leyte, heard from natives that no Japanese were on the island. On the basis of this and other information, Halsey suggested to Nimitz that they forego landings on Yap and Ulithi and move instead to Leyte. Nimitz deferred to MacArthur,

---

*In support of the raid, air-sea rescue including submarines and Catalina flying boats kept station well inside Japanese-held territory to recover downed airmen. Those craft rescued most of the crewmen shot down on the two final attacks.

as Leyte was within the SWPA, and in a complicated discussion between the Joint Staff, Nimitz's staff, and MacArthur's people, Leyte became the place of first landing during the American return to the Philippines. MacArthur had long intended to retake the archipelago, but two of his subordinates made the decision while he was at sea and the crew of the ship was observing radio silence. Kenney and Sutherland, prompted by the possibility that Nimitz would seek approval if the SWPA commander seemed reluctant, took it upon themselves to decide on the Leyte operation and to so inform the JCS on September 16. MacArthur quickly agreed on his return the next day.[77]

Kenney decided the Leyte question in the belief that he would have the upper hand in any air campaign. He seems to have done so based on the ULTRA indications of Japan's strategic withdrawal to the northern Philippines–Formosa–home islands, Japan's decidedly defensive air dispositions and types of aircraft in the Philippines that would limit offensive reactions, and her rate of aircraft loss and diminishing pilot and aircraft replacement capability. The FEAF commander had concluded that Japanese air power in the Philippines "was shot," although he could not rule out a successful Japanese reaction to the projected landings. Of most concern to Kenney was the need to quickly seize and expand airfields on Leyte to provide land-based air cover to the men ashore. Until bases were in use, the Navy's aircraft—limited in number, range, and firepower and flying from carriers vulnerable to air, surface, and submarine attack—would have to bear the load of protection, for Fifth and Thirteenth Air Forces had too few airfields within operational range of Leyte. Preparatory air attacks by Halsey's carriers against Japanese bases on Luzon had resulted in reportedly large losses of enemy aircraft. Although the Allies knew the Japanese defensive dispositions and their air, land, and sea OB, they were uncertain of the way the Japanese would use those forces when they responded to the direction of Allied moves. Moreover, Allied intelligence estimated that by October 20 the Japanese had 27,000 soldiers on Leyte and adjacent Samar. This number of Japanese, far more than Halsey's information, was not in itself a major danger to the projected landings. The risk to the Allies was from naval and air counterstrikes.[78]

Allied landing forces initially had little trouble on Leyte, seizing Tacloban on October 20th and Dulag on the 21st. Immediately, work began on airfields at both sites. Confusion ashore, with equipment and supplies piled on the beaches, delayed construction of the vital bases. On the 23d, Seventh Fleet intelligence officers discerned a major Japanese fleet seemingly headed toward Leyte, partly from Brunei, with the remainder coming through the Surigao Strait. The ensuing battle for Leyte Gulf forced American naval aircraft from four small escort carriers into a desperate fight. The success of the Navy flyers, and Japanese misperceptions of the American fleet's locations, resulted in an Allied victory that fended off a potentially highly destructive Japanese foray into the center of the vulnerable landing force. Finally, on October 26, thirty-

The Pacific and Far East

four P–38s of the Fifth Air Force arrived at Tacloban. Shortly thereafter, heavy seasonal rains set in, bringing airfield expansion and construction almost to a halt for several weeks.[79]

With the conclusion of the major naval engagements, the air war, marked by fierce Japanese assaults on the uncompleted landing grounds, assumed a tempo not fully anticipated by the Allies. Japanese attacks and horrible airfield conditions quickly left but eight P–38s. Reacting to the danger, Fifth and Thirteenth Air Force bombers and fighters flying from Morotai turned against Japanese airfields in the Visayan Islands near Leyte. In addition, on November 5 and 6, Admiral Halsey's replenished heavy carrier force struck Luzon bases to wear down the Japanese reaction and reduce pressure on the Allied airmen and infantry on Leyte.[80] The Japanese bent every effort to reinforce their Leyte garrison under cover of the bad weather and in the face of still weak Allied air forces on the islands. Kenney and his commanders, realizing the difficulty in which Lt. Gen. Walter Krueger's Sixth Army found itself, used every available combat airplane that they could move to Leyte. ULTRA reported the sailings, and repeated air strikes sank much of the shipping. At this point, Allied ULTRA intervened again, detailing a new Japanese weapon, the organized suicide squadrons (*kamikaze*) of the Japanese Naval Air Force. A single pilot flying one of these planes could badly damage or disable even the heaviest ship. The Japanese suicide aircraft, however, were just part of what ULTRA indicated was a much more impressive air power effort.

To contend with the danger that the Allied operation presented, the Japanese hastily organized what they called the *T Attack Force*. That group was a collection of largely naval air squadrons supplemented by Army air units and commanded in Philippine operations by a Japanese naval air officer, whom the Allies thought to be Rear Adm. Tsunoda Koshiro. The offensive nature of the *T Attack Force* became apparent from ULTRA intercepts about October 23. Subsequently, the Allies estimated the air task force to consist of about 604 fighters and 624 bombers; it was the aerial counterpart of the Japanese Navy surface task force that had tried to disrupt the amphibious landing fleet in the battle of the Philippine Sea. By late October, the Japanese had impressed Allied air intelligence officers and commanders alike with the deftness and tenacity of their employment of offensive air power; the SWPA *SIB* for October 31/November 1 carried the cautionary note, "The gravity of the threat requires the most stringent counter-measures."[81] Despite Japan's diminishing strength, the Japanese had rallied a sizable air task group within 48 hours of the main Allied landing.

The *T Attack Force* struck hard at the precarious Allied lodgment, and the Japanese believed their air onslaught and continued combat over Allied airfields on Leyte had damaged the invasion; this belief spurred them to added efforts. So effective were the Japanese and so difficult the weather and airfield conditions that on October 28 Kenney characterized the situation as critical. He

Piercing the Fog

and Halsey directed every available AAF and Navy fighter toward the intense air battle. ULTRA had made clear by November that the Japanese were taking aircraft from every source remaining to them for Philippine defense. Moreover, the Allies could track three separate fleet striking forces with one heavy and three light carriers plus three hybrid or transport carriers the Japanese had converted from battleships and cruisers. Only repeated air attacks on these fleets kept them at a distance.[82]

One consistent characteristic noted by Allied intercept analysts was the Japanese proclivity to strongly overstate Allied losses, understate their own, and to act on these mistaken beliefs. This tendency and the continued ability of Kenney to read enemy reactions allowed him a clear picture of the battle's progress. It also allowed Halsey, Kenney, and their subordinates to hit hard at the Japanese and continue to drain aircraft and pilots from Japan's defense resources. By November 11, the improving landing fields led the FEAF commander to assume a more favorable outlook. Once the Allies could base a substantial air capability on Leyte, they brought the main Japanese threat under control.[83]

The bloody struggle for Leyte became an Allied victory largely because ULTRA's insights allowed the better armed, largely American, land-sea-air force to be massed against the depleted Japanese capability to react. The *T Attack Force,* heavily damaged in the air war and with diminishing fervor for battle, began to withhold units on Formosa and Japan. On November 11, the Americans intercepted and decrypted a MAGIC diplomatic message from Japanese Foreign Minister Shigemitsu Namoru to his ambassador in Moscow, Sato Naotake. In that message, Shigemitsu acknowledged most pessimistically Japan's declining power in the face of growing Allied strength. In fact, Japanese air capability in the Visayas had peaked in early November, about the time that Kenney noted the improved airfield situation on Leyte. Although Kenney did not see the MAGIC decrypt for some days, it must have given him considerable satisfaction that his perception of the tactical situation matched the beliefs of the Japanese Foreign Minister.[84]

The *T Attack Force,* that instrument of Japanese air power that had seemed such a threat, apparently retreated from the Philippines after its commitment and subsequent heavy losses in the battle for Leyte. A paucity of references to it in Japanese message traffic coincided with a lessening of enemy aircraft seen aloft by Allied pilots. By December 15, Japanese radio traffic to the unit had almost ceased, to be replaced by messages directed to the *H–3 Attack Force,* and to the *K Attack Force.* The *H–3 Attack Force* had not been committed to battle, but the Allies took it to be another air task force of undetermined size and composition, probably made up of navy and army squadrons with *kamikaze* units. From operational assessments and intelligence analysis of downed enemy aircraft, Allied airmen noted the arrival of new types of Japanese fighters. These aircraft were too few and their pilots too inexperienced to affect the trend of the war.

The Pacific and Far East

Allied leaders assessed Japan as losing the struggle for air superiority over the Philippines as a whole. In this period, ULTRA picked up information that three Japanese Army divisions were moving to or had arrived in Luzon from Manchuria or the home islands. Not only were the Japanese reinforcing Luzon, until well into November they had continued to send troops to Leyte by sea routes very vulnerable to Allied air and naval attack. It was against this diminished but most determined Japanese opposition that MacArthur's headquarters made final plans for the capture of Mindoro, to be quickly followed by that of Luzon.[85]

The Mindoro landing preceded the Luzon invasion partly to secure landing fields closer to the main Japanese bases near Manila and Clark Field. Mindoro showed that the Japanese were far from ready to give up. Renewed Japanese air retaliation, in Kenney's words, "fooled everyone," as the Japanese "came to Mindoro" to disrupt Allied shipping. Once again, Allied commanders misread their enemy who, they assumed, would do what the Allies thought best, not what the Japanese believed they must do. The Japanese counterblows failed in the main because of desperate Allied aerial opposition and superb Army engineer construction efforts at building airfields. The first Allied fighter group landed on Mindoro on December 20, 1944; others followed as quickly as landing fields could be prepared. Japanese air attacks continued to threaten the island position, but bad weather gave some cover, and airfield expansion finally created enough landing areas to fend off the Japanese and provide an adequate base for the Luzon seizure. By year's end, Marine 12th Air Group Corsairs flying from Samar Island joined AAF aircraft on Leyte and Mindoro. On December 17 and 18, General Yamashita Tomoyuki's *Fourteenth Area Army* headquarters in Manila transmitted a long message in several parts, conceding Allied success in Leyte. Yamashita cited as the final blow the taking of Ormoc by the American 77th Division. In the same transmission, Yamashita noted the impending success of the Mindoro operation. The way to Luzon via an amphibious landing at Lingayen was now open.[86]

As Allied forces assembled for the convoy to Lingayen, the intelligence staff estimated Japanese air strength on Formosa and in the Ryukyu Islands at about 400 aircraft. Another 500 were probably in China, mostly around Hangkow and Canton. References in Japanese message traffic to several addresses such as the *K Attack Force* and the *T-1 Attack Force* indicated continued movement of planes and men as well as plans to use air task forces, but the sizes and compositions of the forces remained in doubt. Except for some of the planes needed to cope with Chennault's Fourteenth Air Force, the collection of Japanese striking strength represented a substantial threat to the convoy and the landing operation. The Japanese had anticipated an Allied landing at Lingayen. They had themselves used the bay when they took the Philippines in 1941. Unfortunately for the Japanese commanders, however, they had to consider the possibility of other, at least limited, landings where geography permitted, as there could be no assurance that any location was the main point of attack. Japanese warning messages in mid-November had, in fact, pointed out a number of possibilities, which the Allies at least briefly considered using. Lingayen, however, was the place best suited for the landing. The main Allied force consisting of two corps reached Lingayen on January 7. Ground resistance was light; air retaliation was not—it began several days before the beach assault as the main body of Allied vessels moved west of Luzon and minesweepers cleared the channels and approaches to Lingayen Bay. Japanese suicide pilots tried to destroy as much of the invading amphibious fleet as possible, while Yamashita completed his defensive preparations. Overall, *kamikaze* pilots, joined this time by fast, 20-foot-long suicide boats, sank seven Allied ships, including an escort carrier. Three battleships, four more escort carriers, two American heavy cruisers, and an Australian cruiser suffered damage, as did several other vessels. Despite the losses, Allied shipping was not deterred, and Allied troops and support units quickly came ashore.[87]

The desperate suicide attacks prior to and during the landings at Lingayen were the last organized Japanese air opposition on Luzon. Although Japanese airmen based on Formosa remained a threat, the air war for the Philippines soon ended. Allied capture of airdromes, first at Mangaladan and Lingayen, then at Clark Field on January 28, coincided with the Fifth Air Force's first B–24 day attack on Formosa, on January 21. Gathering his thoughts as he looked back over the fighting, Kenney noted that when the Army reached Clark, a quick count found some 500 wrecked Japanese aircraft. Later a more formal survey of Clark, Nichols, and Nielson Fields reported 1,505 nonflyable or destroyed airplanes. The combined AAF-Navy counterair campaign not only destroyed hundreds of aircraft, it had left many more partly flyable but missing vital parts, and no opportunity for ground crews to repair them.[88]

Consolidation of American power in the Philippines was the final wartime campaign for the FEAF, save for a continuing series of strikes on an ever smaller array of Japanese shipping and on Japanese positions along the coast of China. FEAF attacks on Japanese land targets continued until Japan surrendered in the summer of 1945; attacks on both land and sea targets were coordinated with the Navy and the Fourteenth Air Force. Kenney, now a full general, participated in the preparations for the final assault on Japan proper, once Okinawa had been secured by Nimitz's POA forces. Preparations for taking Japan included a reorganization of United States forces, with all AAF in the Pacific except the Twentieth slated for transfer to FEAF. Acrimonious infighting between the Army and Navy, much of it centering on the two strong-willed leaders, Nimitz and MacArthur, delayed the reorganization. Despite the arguments, FEAF's bombers moved to Okinawa to carry out limited attacks on Kyushu before the Japanese surrender.

The Pacific and Far East

Throughout the almost four years of conflict in the SPA and SWPA, the AAF demonstrated a growing skill in collecting air intelligence information from a wide variety of sources, analyzing the data, and using it in the relentless pursuit of Japan. In retrospect, much more remains in terms of knowledge of day-to-day planning and decision-making factors for the Fifth and Thirteenth Air Forces than can be seen for any other AAF segment of the Pacific and Far East theaters. In good measure, this resulted from the combined effects of George Kenney's note taking and correspondence with Ennis Whitehead, his longtime, trusted subordinate. Throughout the fighting, the interplay between air operations and intelligence was helped by the flow of ULTRA information appearing in the special intelligence bulletins from GHQ, which highlighted the trends that seemed either most promising or most dangerous. Application of intelligence to air planning and to coordinated, joint-force Allied undertakings became highly sophisticated, able to rapidly consume information on Japanese forces and quickly apply it. Nonetheless, as shown by Japan's unexpectedly strong defense of the Philippines, intelligence could not provide the final answers to war planning and execution; that could come only from an understanding of combat and of the enemy, and an awareness of and willingness to take risks.

Risk taking is the essence of warfare, and risk taking was standard practice in the Southwest Pacific, often promoted by Kenney's personality. Generally, Kenney decided his course of action after considerable thought, based on substantial current operational intelligence data. Beginning in 1943, for example, Kenney and Whitehead often had a good knowledge of Japanese air strengths and locations. As a result, when they drew up plans, the chances for success usually favored the Allied airmen. Success was not always foreordained, however. Neither Kenney nor Whitehead predicted the difficult situation in the Admiralties that almost backfired on them or the unexpected Japanese aerial defense at Balikpapan that surprised them. Another surprise was the Japanese reaction to the Leyte and Mindoro landings as exemplified by the *T Attack Force*'s rapid formation and deployment to battle. One of the few times that George Kenney seems to have had after-the-fact misgivings, as reflected in his private notes, was over the perhaps too hasty assault on the Admiralties, although the prize was clearly worth the action. The heavy defense of Balikpapan caused Kenney concern, and he personally went to talk to and reassure the bomber aircrews before the final two attacks. In the case of Balikpapan, the refinery was a worthwhile target, but in going after it he had judged the absence of radio traffic to be the indicator of weak defenses—it was not.

The Japanese reaction to the invasion of the Philippines came, as Kenney said, as a surprise to everyone. Indications from intelligence could not provide information from an absent source; in this case, the Japanese *T Attack Force* formed at the last minute. A hastily cobbled-together fighting unit, the *T Attack Force* reacted quickly from a base on Formosa to give the Japanese a strong capability for a concentrated thrust. By that time in the war, however, Allied strength was such that Japan's defeat was virtually certain. The Allies, understanding that they were in a hard fight nevertheless, were bolstered by the fact that the potential consequences arising from a miscalculation were far less than would have been the case in 1943.

Assessing the Watchers: The Allied View of Japanese Air Intelligence

Allied intelligence specialists were not alone in scrutinizing their enemy, although the Japanese did it much differently and with less emphasis. One of the tasks for Allied air intelligence was to watch this enemy effort and remain alert to both its imperfections and the implications of its successes. Air commanders could then assess the threat that Japanese intelligence presented to their own operations. Fortunately for the Allies, the Japanese, especially the Imperial Japanese Army, had traditionally discounted the value of intelligence analyses, its officers preferring the show of bravado associated with offensive warfare. The tendency of Japanese Army leaders was to dismiss intelligence as having negligible importance. The thinking of these men was colored by admiration of German military tactics, their own arrogance, and a general disdain for military forces of all Western nations except Germany.[89]

An example of the state of Japan's air intelligence at the beginning of the Pacific War was her lack of knowledge of Great Britain's military posture in the prized colony of Malaya. On November 22, 1941, sixteen days before the beginning of hostilities, Lt. Col. Tsuji Masanobu, chief of Lt. Gen. Yamashita Tomoyuki's Operations Planning Staff, personally overflew British installations in Northern Malaya. Tsuji had to make the trip because he lacked adequate maps to plan the campaign. The size and development of the bases he saw on his flight caused him to recommend substantial changes to the *Twenty-fifth Army*'s plans. As a result, the Japanese reinforced their Army Air Force units intended for the attack. They then quickly captured Kota Bharu and Alor Star once hostilities began in order to deprive the RAF of major operating sites. One can only commend Tsuji's initiative and accomplishments, but the very fact that Yamashita's senior planner had to make the flight himself spoke poorly of the Japanese Army's grasp of the importance of air and ground intelligence organization. After the initial Japanese victories, its army had learned little. In early 1942, *Southern Army* headquarters, then in Singapore, saw little reason to keep the capability it had, merging the intelligence section into and making it a minor part of the operations staff.[90]

The AAF in the Pacific and Far East did not, however, face an entirely inadequate enemy intelligence structure. The Japanese used sources and methods similar to those used by the Allied organizations, including coast

The Pacific and Far East

watchers, photoreconnaissance, agent reports, and radio intelligence units, using radio methods throughout the war zone. Japanese deception involved quite good attempts at using English speakers on tactical radio nets to confuse or mislead Allied pilots and ground forces. In addition, skilled Japanese interrogators extracted valuable data from POWs, many of whom, because of the widespread aerial fighting, were airmen. Although some Japanese units, like the *Southern Army,* could dismiss intelligence studies, others pursued it. Even *Southern Army* realized its error and recreated an intelligence section early in 1944. By then, however, it was too late for such a move to influence the war's direction.[91]

For radio intercept work, each major Japanese army headquarters had assigned to it their version of a Y-Service unit that dealt with coded or encrypted British, American, or Chinese message traffic. The larger and more important the headquarters, the larger and better equipped the intercept section was. These field units proliferated, but they were by no means as successful as were the comparable Allied organizations. Allied ULTRA could occasionally trace Japan's sources and use of radio intercept data. An early March 1944 decryption of Japanese radio messages confirmed that their surveillance and study of Allied air operations involved direction finding and traffic analysis done as CB did in Brisbane and as the radio intercept squadron did at Fifth Air Force ADVON's operational headquarters in New Guinea. Allied interpreters who studied the messages concluded, however, that no evidence suggested the Japanese were successful in breaking important, high-level codes or ciphers.[92] This meant that the Japanese, despite some monumental American blunders in keeping secrets, remained unaware of the true nature and extent of Allied ULTRA operations. Many of Japan's most valuable intelligence accomplishments came from their efforts to counter Allied air power. Japanese cryptographers often broke low-level air operations codes. For example, they were able to predict B–29 actions in China by reading messages directing the turning on of aircraft homing beacons.

In the SWPA, reports of Japanese intelligence activities unearthed by ULTRA appeared in Willoughby's daily *SIB*s. As much as possible, the Allies tracked the location of Japanese radio intercept units, noting that the removal of one from Rabaul to Truk early in 1944 possibly indicated the decline in the Rabaul unit's relative importance in Japanese plans and the perception that Nimitz's carrier and amphibious forces posed the greater threat to the Pacific islands. On the other hand, the move could have resulted simply from Japan's wish to avoid risking the valuable unit to the heavy and continuing air attacks by Admiral Halsey's carrier aircraft and by Kenney's bombers and fighters. Despite the apparent move of the radio intelligence unit, some capability remained at Rabaul, for it was there that the Japanese gained some of their best radio intercept data on B–29 operations from the Marianas. Throughout the war, knowledge of Japanese radio intelligence activities remained fragmentary, with

Piercing the Fog

Allied understanding of enemy Y-Services dependent on not only interception of Japanese messages, but also the ability to decrypt the system in use.[93]

The Japanese at times gained valuable and specific air information from captured flyers, as could be seen in the February 1944 report to Tokyo on Allied air strength in North Australia. That Japanese report, based upon interrogation of a first lieutenant copilot of a B–24, identified the AAF's 380th Group commanded by a Colonel Miller (the 380th Bombardment Group commanded by Col. William A. Miller) with assigned 528, 529, 530, and 531 squadrons (actually, the 328, 329, 330, and 331 squadrons) at RAAF Long and RAAF Fenton, near Darwin. The Japanese also understood that fifty planes were in the group. To that, Allied analysts commented in the *SIB* synopsis, "The enemy's information is high grade." The knowledge that the Japanese had of the 380th's home station triggered from Allied analysts warnings of a possible Japanese parachute assault on the airfields. Both Long and Fenton were in range of Japanese transport aircraft, and available fragmentary evidence indicated the presence of the *1st* and *2d Raider Groups*, both parachute units, in New Guinea. (The *1st Raider Group,* also known as the *1st Parachute Brigade,* had captured Palembang airfield on Sumatra in February 1942.) The Japanese made no parachute attack on the Australian airfields, but Darwin was the subject of aerial bombardment on a number of occasions at about the same time.[94] POW interrogations yielded other data as well.

At about the same time that they captured the lieutenant copilot of the B–24, the Japanese got hold of another American, a colonel, commander of a heavy bomber group in the Thirteenth Air Force. This unfortunate man faced questioning first at Rabaul, then possibly in New Guinea, before Tokyo directed his transfer there. In the process of interrogation, the Japanese gained information on aircraft loss rates, personnel, flying accidents, air-sea rescue procedures, and the development and possible use in the Pacific of B–29s. Willoughby's *SIB* for February 24, 1944, cited the information Japan had gained from the American officer regarding AAF strength in the SOPAC theater as of about December 30, 1943:

Aircraft Types	Japanese Information	Actual Strength
P–38, P–39, P–40, and Spitfire	200	190
B–25	60	74
B–24	96	146
B–24, radar equipped*	8	8
Total	364	418

*Bombers equipped for low-level sea search and attack of Japanese merchant shipping.

The Pacific and Far East

The information gained by the Japanese was very good and probably represented operational strengths, with the differences between their estimates and the actual strengths possibly being airplanes in depot maintenance or reserve. Little wonder in light of this information that Kenney had been concerned a year previously when the Japanese shot down Brig. Gen. Kenneth Walker's B–17 after a raid on Rabaul on January 5, 1943. Walker probably had limited if any knowledge of the growing but as yet not fully developed radio-intercept intelligence activity in the Pacific. Despite that, his capture might have had serious consequences as even then the secrecy surrounding the subject was rather loosely handled. Fortunately for the Allies (and unfortunately for the general), Walker was never found, apparently having died in the crash.[95]

Although the Japanese had disregarded the creation of strategic intelligence organizations to the detriment of their long-term plans and operations, they remained capable of tactical accomplishments that gave them insights into Allied air operations. Kenney's knowledge of his enemy's understanding of Allied capabilities certainly played a part, although probably minor, in his own plan formulation.

Moreover, the Japanese were not so arrogant as to completely disregard the dangers of Allied intelligence successes. After the March 10, 1944, sinking of a small Japanese freighter, the Japanese sought out one of the ship's officers and queried him about the code books the ship carried. They then reminded all concerned of the dangers to shipping and troops in transit should code information fall into the wrong hands. Later in March, after the destruction of a convoy to Wewak and the coincident loss of its cryptographic materials, the Japanese changed their sea transport cryptographic system, reducing temporarily the Allied use of this source. They still did not realize the true ability of the Allies to read their enciphered messages.[96]

Intelligence specialists at CB and Fifth Air Force headquarters lacked a complete understanding of Japanese information, but they continued to learn of enemy capabilities and tactics as they read his radio signals. The Allies determined, for example, that the Japanese had ascertained from the lieutenant who had flown the B–24 that Allied airmen changed radio frequencies and call signs on each mission. Routine Japanese Y-Service work indicated that the Fifth and Thirteenth Air Forces coordinated operations, and that Japanese forces should be on the alert against large-scale operations in New Guinea and the Solomons after mid-March 1944. The Japanese discerned the direction of Allied intentions correctly, although they were unable to anticipate precisely what would happen or to deflect the Allied campaign. On March 20, Admiral Halsey's SOPAC units landed on Emirau Island near the major Japanese base at Kavieng. In a March 25–27 conference in Brisbane, MacArthur, Nimitz, Halsey, Kenney, and other senior officers discussed major upcoming operations. On April 22, MacArthur landed his Sixth Army at Hollandia and nearby locations. The Hollandia effort had been preceded by a major Allied Air Forces

Piercing the Fog

attack on the airfields in the vicinity, and it required substantial support from Halsey and Nimitz in the way of shipping and naval protection, much of which was directed by radio. Partly to cover MacArthur, Nimitz's Central Pacific carrier task forces, supported by the Seventh and Thirteenth Air Forces, struck Japanese-held islands including Truk, Guam, Woleai, and Yap. Late in March, the Japanese reported by radio that they had learned (probably again from their colonel captive) about American fighter and bomber tactics and of the functions of the radar analysis aircraft known as ferrets.[97]

The full extent of Japan's military intelligence capability and accomplishments remains obscured in the wreckage of her defeat and the large-scale destruction of records at the time of her surrender in 1945. Yet, the Japanese were not without an understanding of the AAF's operations in the Pacific, and one should not assume they were uncertain of Allied capability. Although less sophisticated than the Allied SIGINT system, Japan's radio intercept teams accurately predicted and followed American attacks directed against their homeland. Hampered by the general lack of regard, even disdain, for intelligence as a field of military endeavor, some adroit Japanese analysts nevertheless reached surprising conclusions as to their enemy's intentions. At least one such conclusion probably could not have been more correct had the Japanese had an ULTRA of their own equal to the SWPA's CB. As the Allies drew up their plans for the projected November 1945 landing on Kyushu, Maj. Hori Eizo, who served on the Imperial Army's General Staff and was an accepted expert on MacArthur's planning tendencies, predicted the landing beaches with uncanny, even unsettling, accuracy, based upon his thorough studies of past Allied campaigns. Working in smaller groups and with fewer resources than their Allied counterparts, Japanese air intelligence officers kept a close watch on AAF combat operations, all the while the Allies' ULTRA system was allowing Kenney's senior staff to watch over the shoulders of the Japanese analysts at work.[98]

CHAPTER 6

Taking the Offensive: From China-Burma-India to the B–29 Campaign

As WAS THE CASE IN THE SWPA, intelligence gathering and interpretation played a large role in turning the tide against the Japanese in the POA and in the Far East. In the CBI Theater and in the Central Pacific Area, intelligence was crucial to successful Allied air operations. Although intelligence contributed to target planning in the B–29 strategic air campaign against Japan, intelligence was lacking in regard to the location of specific industry in the home islands. With the switch to low-level, night incendiary attacks, detailed intelligence gathering became much less crucial.

In the CBI Theater, the AAF's operations came to be divided initially between the Tenth Air Force's China Air Task Force (CATF) and the India Air Task Force (IATF). In time, the CATF became the Fourteenth Air Force under Maj. Gen. Claire L. Chennault. The IATF and its parent Tenth became part of the region's very complex Anglo-American command structure. These two air forces operated at the end of the longest logistics line of the war. Together the Tenth and the Fourteenth comprised the bulk of the American commitment to the theater, yet they remained small when compared to the AAF combat commands in Europe. As the two air forces and men struggled to improvise flying operations, their intelligence gathering and application struggled also, adapting innovative and unique practices. In fact, unusual methods of gathering and using intelligence were to become hallmarks of the AAF in the CBI region.

In China, the application of tactical air power could be effective in that vast land only if valid target information was available. Some of that information, and damage assessment as well, came from special teams sent to infiltrate Japanese-held territory and report by radio on enemy activity. More sophisticated intelligence gathering later came to be used in China and Burma as AAF ferret aircraft scouted and mapped Japanese radar stations, giving the aircraft crews the opportunity to escape or minimize the damage incurred after interception or from AA fire. By August 1945, the AAF's commanders had extensive knowledge of their enemy. That flow of information had been increasing for several years.

For the Americans, CBI was a wartime theater at the bottom of the priority list. Faced in early 1942 with a crumbling battle structure in North Africa and Japanese advances in the Pacific, the Allies could spare little for India and China. The matériel and manpower that did arrive came to a region so far distant from Europe and the United States that whatever arrived had traveled the longest supply line of any in the war. Logistics problems were matched by a command structure so complex and so beset with military and political difficulties and personal conflicts that commanding it could only be a protean task. American air involvement in the CBI began with one U.S. Army air force, the Tenth. In 1942, the Tenth Air Force's commander organized two branches: the CATF under Brig. Gen. Claire Chennault and the IATF under Brig. Gen. Clayton Bissell. Chennault was an abrasive character, very much disliked by many in the old Army Air Corps. Bissell too had numerous detractors, Kenney among them. When, in August of 1942, Bissell became commanding general of the Tenth, problems arose between him and Chennault. The American theater commander, Lt. Gen. Joseph W. Stilwell, no amateur when it came to making caustic remarks and holding sharp opinions, maintained a prickly (at times bitter) relationship with Chennault. Stilwell also despised and distrusted China's leader, Generalissimo Chiang Kai-shek and was suspicious of the relationship between Chiang and Chennault. Chennault reciprocated the bitterness in his feelings toward Stilwell. Stilwell was also impatient with the British military authorities in India, while Chiang suspected the British had designs on China; Chiang rarely cooperated with British officials.[1]

Stilwell affords an example of the extreme complexity that afflicted the CBI Theater's command structure and the various ways intelligence could be interpreted under differing circumstances. He was, for instance, both the commanding general of all American forces in the CBI Theater and the chief of staff to Generalissimo Chiang in China. As Commander, Northern Combat Area Command (which consisted of Chinese divisions), Stilwell was subordinate to the British commander of all Allied land forces in Burma, over whom he (Stilwell) was simultaneously superior in his role as Deputy Supreme Allied Commander, South East Asia.

This command jumble extended to air forces as well. Created in February 1942, the American Tenth Air Force, headquartered in India, was responsible for all American air units in the theater until March 1943, when the Americans created Fourteenth Air Force in China at Chiang's insistence. The attempt in August 1942 to resolve what were essentially personality difficulties among senior American commanders by subdividing air into the India-Burma (Tenth Air Force) and China (Fourteenth Air Force) sectors under the overall direction of Maj. Gen. George E. Stratemeyer had been only partially successful.

Piercing the Fog

Chennault, commanding the Fourteenth Air Force, retained direct access to both Chiang Kai-shek and President Roosevelt. By the end of 1943, a new Eastern Air Command (EAC), the air component of Allied Command, South East Asia, would be superimposed on this already complex structure.

The convoluted command and vituperative relationships among the numbered air force commanders during this period appear to have had relatively little impact on the relationship between intelligence and air operations. It is possible to address air intelligence, planning, and operations through 1943 by adopting the AAF's own India-Burma/China approach. Certainly, overlaps occurred. Both Tenth and Fourteenth Air Forces defended the air transport route over the Himalayas. Different interpretations of Japanese activities and subsequent differences over where to employ limited resources marked the real break between Chennault and Bissell. The realities of geography and the nature of the tasks assigned make the India-Burma/China separation useful.

Early air intelligence operations in India and China were handicapped by both the hasty organization of the American air forces and their lack of trained personnel. Chennault's first A–2 in the CATF was Col. Merian C. Cooper. Cooper, highly respected by many in the AAF, was a man of great energy and varied talents who had served in France with the Air Service during World War I and who fought in Poland during that country's war with the Soviet Union. Later Cooper went to Hollywood, where he produced and directed motion pictures (among his best remembered were *The Four Feathers* and *King Kong*). Cooper was a prodigious worker who served simultaneously as Chennault's A–2, his chief of staff, and A–3. Cooper's abilities were greatly admired by George Kenney who later arranged with Washington for Cooper's assignment to SWPA. As intelligence officer, Cooper for some time had only two assistants, 2d Lt. Martin Hubler and 2d Lt. John Birch. The latter was a resident missionary who had helped some of the Doolittle raiders to safety and then had been commissioned in the AAF. In China, the AAF lacked photointelligence; had few target folders, which were poor; and depended almost entirely on Chinese forces for target and threat data. Matters began in India in a similar fashion, with few trained intelligence specialists and little growth in the number of people available for such work. By early 1943, HQ IATF had only three intelligence officers assigned, matching the general poverty of the field in China. Subordinate bomber and fighter groups had a few intelligence officers on their staffs and in squadrons, and most were untrained in the specialty. In India the Americans relied initially on British and Indian intelligence resources.[2]

In 1942, the threadbare air intelligence arrangement did not adversely affect the small American air operations in the CBI Theater, as the Japanese Army ground forces and shipping targets were rather plentiful and the CATF's mission was not an offensive one. But the limited number of trained people kept a strain on the A–2 staffs, especially in China. At the time, the Tenth Air Force's primary task was defensive: protect the India-China air ferry route and

Taking the Offensive

defend the air bases in Assam. The force was quite small in comparison to that in Europe or North Africa, with but a handful of bomber and fighter groups (105 fighters, 12 medium bombers, and 4 reconnaissance planes authorized for China in September 1942). The inadequate staff size became a bone of contention between Chennault and Bissell. Chennault's isolated position made it difficult for him to find alternative intelligence sources, and he was vulnerable to Japanese offensives. He was also acutely sensitive to any perceived attempt to keep his organization in a secondary role. Chennault pressed his need for additional intelligence officers into 1943. Bissell, for his part, endorsed Chennault's requests to Washington, but approval came slowly. Not until the end of 1942 did AAF headquarters authorize a basic A–2 staff for the CATF, and then it remained small.[3]

The commanders' individual personalities played an important role in intelligence application and air operations in the CBI. Bissell, for instance, did not want to have a technical intelligence office in Tenth Air Force, and for reasons that remain unclear, he was not warm to the idea of strong technical intelligence liaison with the RAF. The results impeded the flow of knowledge gained from captured Japanese equipment or crashed aircraft. Bissell operated his air force in a predominantly British theater, and he returned to Washington in August 1943. Thus the foibles of his personality had little lasting influence on the command. Chennault, in his determination to run his show his way and to maintain as much pressure on the Japanese as he could, seemed to misjudge Japan's capability and intent to react to the successful depredations of his minuscule air force in 1943. Late in that year he found his eastern bases threatened by a Japanese army offensive that reduced his ability to continue the air campaign.[4]

Intelligence operations also reflected the theater's command arrangements. Chennault's CATF and Fourteenth Air Force developed a far-flung information-gathering service in China that drew upon Chinese military and civilian sources, its own reconnaissance capability, and the unusual but highly effective Air Ground Forces Resources and Technical Staff (AGFRTS) organization.* In India and Burma, duplication between the various Allied air forces became common, a concern for General Stratemeyer who succeeded Bissell at Tenth Air Force and thought the arrangement could be much more efficient. In June 1944, Stratemeyer remarked in a letter to the local OSS commander that ". . . there have been several [air] intelligence agencies working in the same area under independent direction, covering the same general subject." At times, five different offices sought help from Stratemeyer's headquarters for the same intelligence job. The wasteful and inefficient situation that Stratemeyer wanted

---

*The AGFRTS was a joint Fourteenth Air Force–OSS operation. AGFRTS sent agents far afield to acquire intelligence for the Allies, including target data for the Fourteenth Air Force.

Piercing the Fog

Maj. Gen. Clayton L. Bissell

to streamline resulted from the numerous Allied air forces; each was seeking to complete its mission without much coordination.[5] The chart on the facing page illustrates the extent of the complicated air intelligence fuctions that grew over time in the CBI.

Signal intelligence played a growing part in the CBI fighting, especially from 1943 on. As in other theaters, SIGINT came in several forms and found varying uses. MAGIC diplomatic decrypts told the Allies of Japanese intentions to expand Burma's railroad system, of the changes in Japanese command, and of the scheduled movements of divisions to reinforce the front. Knowing the enemy's plans was one thing; finding appropriate targets in the jungle and elsewhere suitable for air attack was a vastly different issue. Regarding target location, SIGINT was less valuable, so the airmen turned first to HUMINT in the form of agents able to provide precise data on target locations and types, and then to follow up with damage assessments. Low-level radio intercepts and reading of commercial wireless telegraph traffic also indicated how effective air raids were, not only in and around Rangoon and Bangkok but in the major Japanese-occupied cities of China as well.[6]

Despite the use of SIGINT, operational and tactical air intelligence collection in the CBI area depended largely upon photoreconnaissance, flight reports from air crews, and POW interrogations. Agents or contacts in Japanese-occupied areas occasionally provided supplemental data, but this source was not substantial until later in the war. SIGINT assumed greater importance when the first ULTRA representative, Maj. J.F.B. Runnalls, arrived in New Delhi from Washington on December 19, 1943. In Delhi, Runnalls joined a British theater intelligence organization already engaged in deciphering enemy transmissions, and he was heavily influenced by England's experience in Europe and North

Comparative Air Intelligence Functions in China-Burma-India *
1944

	Order of Battle	Target Data	Technical Intelligence	Airfields and Ports	Current Intelligence	Damage Assessment	Photointelligence	Radar Countermeasures and Flak Intelligence
Air Command Southeast Asia	■	■	■	■	■	■	■	
Eastern Air Command †		■			■	■		■
HQ USAAF, India-Burma Sector †	■	■						
Strategic Air Force (Tenth AF)		■			■		■	■
Tactical Air Force					■			
Troop Carrier Command					■			
XX Bomber Command		■						■
Fourteenth Air Force	■	■	■	■	■	■	■	■
Air Transport Command, USAAF				■				
Chinese Air Force	■				■			
Ground Intelligence Sections ††	■	■						

* The comparisons on this chart were drawn by the Joint Intelligence Collection Agency (JICA), CBI, in early 1944. JICA's operation served to streamline somewhat the flow of data between the welter of air intelligence offices. Prior to JICA's presence there was, for example, no exchange of nonoperational intelligence between India and China. Thus, the several A–2 staffs lacked a full understanding of the enemy's capabilities in the adjoining theaters. This figure illustrates the numbers and types of offices that applied intelligence data to operational needs. To fully understand the complexity of intelligence operations in the CBI, one must also consider the various information-gathering organizations such as the Office of Strategic Services and the Special Operations Executive as well as the joint cryptanalysis center in Delhi with its subordinate listening posts near Burma and China.

† Used the same A–2 staff at Eastern Air Command.

†† GHQ India, South East Asia Command, G–2 Rear and G–2 Forward Echelons, U.S. Forces, Chinese G–2

Piercing the Fog

Africa. Interception and decoding of Japanese low-level radio messages played a part in determining the AAF's planning and tactics in the CBI from as early as May 1942. At that time, the Americans learned of Japanese plans to move air units north from Malaya and the NEI. They launched attacks on airfields in Japanese territory. On October 25, 1942, Chennault's B–25s raided Hong Kong in one of the heaviest strikes that the CATF had yet made. The *MAGIC Diplomatic Summary* in Washington had reported ample Japanese shipping in the harbor, and such information could have been sent to Chennault via the United States' military mission in China. An equally likely source was the Chinese military. The precise origin of information was almost irrelevant, because Japanese targets in Hong Kong, Canton, and Hanoi, French Indochina, were plentiful. Hanoi had been the target for B–25s and P–40s on September 25, when CATF intelligence estimates warned of substantial Japanese fighter defenses. On that attack, Chennault's operations planners sent along extra fighters for protection. The precaution proved wise when ten Japanese interceptors had to be driven off; the Americans suffered no losses that day.[7]

While carrying the aerial campaign against Japanese shipping and airfields in southeastern China and French Indochina, Chennault also pursued the primary mission assigned him: defense of the aerial route from Assam, India, to Kunming, China. Acting under instructions from Tenth Air Force, Chennault's air reconnaissance crews photographed and observed Japanese airfields in northern Burma. That information, supplemented by the RAF in India, allowed Chennault and Colonel Cooper to assess Japanese regional air capabilities late in 1942. Based on these studies, Chennault and Bissell both believed the Japanese threat to be increasingly dangerous, with Japan able to operate as many as 350 aircraft in the area. Bissell reported his understanding of the growing threat to Stilwell, who was engaged in trying to obtain British approval and support for the training of 45,000 Chinese troops in India. Stilwell hoped to use these Chinese divisions for an offensive in conjunction with British Indian forces beginning in February 1943. Bissell warned Stilwell on October 8, 1942, that the AAF's air reconnaissance fleet was too small in size and too limited in range to be able to prevent a surprise should the Japanese decide to move forcefully into the area. Despite the problems, the airmen kept watch on Japanese troop increases west of the Salween River in November.[8]

To plan, execute, and evaluate these and other early missions in the CBI, American air commanders relied on a variety of intelligence sources. Among them, the most important during the first year of the war were British. The official relationship between American and British airmen in the India-Burma Campaign differed from the one that existed in North Africa and the United Kingdom. No Allied air command such as NAAF existed until the creation of EAC in December 1943. Nor were personnel integrated in the manner of the British Air Ministry and HQ Eighth Air Force. From the opening stages of the Japanese attack into Burma, Allied airmen operating from India engaged in extensive coordination and cooperation. At Barrackpore, representatives of the operating commands—RAF Bengal Command and Tenth Air Force's IATF—met daily to coordinate their efforts and plan air operations.

The two commands routinely exchanged intelligence. India and Burma had long been part of the Empire, and the British had maintained an extensive presence throughout Asia for decades. It was logical that they would be responsible for maps; exceptions to this agreement were Manchuria, northern China, and Siberia, the responsibilities of the U.S. War Department.[9] Before the American forces achieved their own photoreconnaissance capability, they relied heavily on the British product. Later, Allied units shared photoreconnaissance and photointerpretation responsibilities and resources. In early 1942, the British photointerpretation school at Karachi provided training for AAF personnel before the first Harrisburg-trained intelligence officers arrived.[10] IATF headquarters informed subordinate units that, until the AAF Intelligence Service could prepare and distribute air objective and target folders, the RAF would perform this task. The folders would be supplemented by a weekly *Target Information Summary* compiled jointly from American and British sources.[11] By the summer of 1942, Tenth Air Force reported some success in preparing objective folders by having an AAF officer visit RAF headquarters each morning, with the RAF reciprocating in the afternoon.[12]

The lack of planning and operational materials such as target folders and charts became obvious with the effort to mount offensive operations in the fall of 1942. In November, the 436th Bomb Squadron highlighted the poverty of information by requesting all the photographs of Burma that Tenth Air Force could spare, since "this item is sadly lacking in this department."[13] In December 1942, the IATF intelligence officer wrote to HQ Tenth Air Force that he and subordinate units urgently needed target folders for Burma, French Indochina, and Thailand.[14] Six months showed no improvement; the intelligence officer of the 7th Bomb Group (H) complained that his unit had recently been sent against three oil fields and three towns for which "in no case were adequate photographs or target maps available."[15]

Part of this problem reflected the difficult logistics in the region. At a Washington conference for Pacific Air Forces intelligence officers, an HQ AAF A–2 representative noted that material they had forwarded in December 1942 had not been available for an attack on Japanese-controlled mines in Thailand in April 1943. The Tenth Air Force representative responded that the information was still not available when he had left India for the conference in September.[16] At the same conference, CBI intelligence officers argued that in general their units had material on targets in Japan that were out of reach, but they experienced a severe shortage of materials on targets their forces could strike. This paucity of Washington-generated target intelligence and the subsequent requirement to develop in-theater resources placed even heavier demands on photoreconnaissance and photointerpretation.

Piercing the Fog

To facilitate identification of and successful attacks on Japanese airdromes, Tenth Air Force daily intelligence extracts and weekly intelligence summaries kept units advised of the pattern of enemy airfield construction and methods of camouflage and dispersal. A February 1943 annex to the weekly summary described in detail the enemy's standard pattern for laying out major airdromes and satellite fields and advised on which areas the attackers should focus.[17] In March 1943 the summary noted that the Japanese had begun to shift their aircraft parking from revetments to wide dispersal and to conceal them using villages and natural features as cover.[18]

Intelligence on technical capabilities and tactics of the Japanese air forces enabled friendly forces to devise effective methods to combat them. The best source for such information was Chennault's American Volunteer Group (AVG). Although few AVG pilots remained in the theater after that organization ceased operation, summaries and evaluations of their experiences circulated widely. In August 1942, the Director of Intelligence Service, HQ AAF, distributed an extensive report, "Information on Tactics of A.V.G.," which contained interviews with pilots, extracts of combat debriefs, and a report on AVG experiences and activities previously compiled by Tenth Air Force.[19]

Technical data also provided tactical information useful for combating Japanese flyers. Analysis of the location of pieces of destroyed aircraft suggested structural weaknesses in Japanese bombers, most notably the absence of self-sealing fuel tanks and inadequate wing-fuselage joinings. This information led to suggestions that fighter pilots and gunners should aim for the inner wing tanks since, even if they missed the fuel, they might hit the joints and cause the plane to come apart in midair.[20] The results of flight tests on a captured Japanese Mitsubishi A6M Zero fighter conducted in the United States late in 1942 revealed that the aircraft's excellent roll capability at low speeds decreased significantly as speed increased.[21]

The aerial mining of the Rangoon River afforded an example of the use of alternative sources of intelligence. This operation, using the Royal Navy's mines and enthusiastic British support, significantly retarded river traffic and the movement of Japanese supplies. The Allies based the raid on little more than the thoughtful use of readily available information. In January, while considering mining the river, planners first analyzed Burma's available lines of communication. Alternate port facilities were few, and there was but a single railroad north from Rangoon that forwarded supplies sent by ship. The ocean approaches to Rangoon were open, with ships difficult to intercept by bomber patrols; thus the Gulf of Thailand was not amenable to an aerial blockade. The planners quickly realized that the relatively shallow Rangoon River was a natural funnel; closing it held great promise of cutting supply traffic to Japanese forces in the north. Within days, B–24s flying up the river under a full moon at low tide dropped forty mines, set to delay arming for from two to twelve days, into the river channel. The results were hard to judge in terms of ships

Taking the Offensive

destroyed, but photoreconnaissance noted a sharp diminution of river traffic. The Allied authorities judged the effort so successful that similar flights renewed the mines periodically.[22]

Elsewhere in Burma and Thailand, visual aerial reconnaissance and aerial photography provided the bulk of information needed for mission planning through 1943. Analysis of the Burmese transportation system (with which the British were thoroughly familiar as the country's colonial masters) revealed that a handful of roads and railways carried most of the Japanese supplies from Rangoon to the Burma front. Few alternatives existed to the limited network, and the AAF made specific points of interest, such as bridges and railroad tunnels, the object of frequent surveillance. From analysis and comparison of operations and intelligence reports, the Allies noted that cutting the railroad's single main line north from Rangoon virtually stopped traffic for the time that it took repairs to be made. Recognizing the opportunity to hamper Japanese logistics efforts, the Allies decided on a campaign to destroy key railway repair facilities, locomotives, and rolling stock. The effort capitalized initially on both the isolation of the Burmese railway system from the systems of neighboring countries and the few alternatives available to the Japanese. In March 1944, Col. John R. Sutherland, the Tenth Air Force's A–3, proposed an ambitious bombing of bridges and long stretches of single-line track with well-spaced bombs delivered from low level. Sutherland intended to use all of his P–51s, P–38s, B–25s, and B–24s to cut the railway in at least 329 places along 411 miles of track. Sutherland estimated that such an effort would require the Japanese to move 312 tons of rails to make repairs. Simultaneously, attacks on railway repair facilities and rolling stock would otherwise diminish the ability of the railroad to function. Sutherland's plan depended upon accurate and frequent photoreconnaissance that the AAF supplied in abundance.[23]

The Tenth Air Force commander did not carry out Sutherland's plan as originally conceived—a single concerted effort with sustained follow-ups to prevent the Japanese from reopening the vital supply link. The railroad, however, became and remained through 1944 and 1945 a prime attack target for the very reasons that first attracted Sutherland: its vulnerability due to its single-track layout and a lack of alternate routes. The continued pursuit of the railroad campaign did not mean that Allied operations in India and Burma were overly harmonious. The differing goals of the British and the Americans in the region created frequent problems that detracted from a united application of intelligence in the air war.

For some time, the Allied war effort in India and Burma had suffered from friction between the British, interested in defending India and recovering lost territory, and the Americans, who had interests in China, the Philippines, and elsewhere and who saw the local fighting as part of a greater Pacific war. Almost as troublesome were overlapping military functions, intelligence among them. To reduce the overlap and generally improve air efforts against the

Piercing the Fog

Japanese in India and Burma, the Allies created EAC as part of and subordinate to Air Command South East Asia. Stratemeyer assumed command of EAC on December 15, 1943, bringing the operational portions of RAF Bengal Command and Tenth Air Force into one organization. This new alignment created a more effective air campaign against the Japanese, but it also demanded increased efficiency from the supporting intelligence offices, several of which Stratemeyer combined as the Intelligence Section, HQ EAC, under the Office of the Assistant Chief of Staff, Operations, Plans, Training and Intelligence. The intelligence chief was Wing Comdr. A. T. Richardson, RAF; his deputy, Lt. Col. Wilkes D. Kelly of the AAF.[24]

Within a short time after creation of EAC, a number of plans were well underway to increase the effectiveness of the intelligence functions serving the Allied air forces. A Combined Photographic Interpretation Centre (CPIC) South East Asia came into being on May 1, 1944. That center collected the talents of photoanalysts from the AAF, the RAF, the Royal Navy's Eastern Fleet, and the British Army. Detachments from the center served the bomber forces at EAC's strategic and tactical air forces headquarters. Smaller photointerpretation detachments at times worked with individual groups and squadrons as the need arose. The XX Bomber Command, because of its special mission and its control by General Arnold in Washington, retained its own photointerpretation capability. In many ways, the CPIC was the Southeast Asia equivalent of the CIU at Medmenham, England, and was inspired in its origin by the accomplishments of the CIU in the United Kingdom.[25] The chart on the facing page shows how the CPIC related to the Air Command South East Asia.

Even before EAC's existence, local efforts by the RAF's and AAF's technical intelligence officers had sought to enlarge the scope and accomplishments of their field of endeavor. At a technical intelligence conference held in New Delhi in August of 1943, several lower-ranking British and American officers agreed upon a number of initiatives to speed and improve each others' knowledge of Japanese aircraft and air operations equipment. The meeting produced much closer liaison between the two services and a routing of RAF technical analysis reports to Tenth Air Force. After Bissell's departure for Washington, the technical side of intelligence continued to grow. The example of the CPIC led to a similar organization designed to improve the handling of technical intelligence. Proposed by Air Command South East Asia in the spring of 1944, the Allies set up the Technical Air Intelligence Centre with headquarters in New Delhi. The center was patterned on the parent organization at the Air Ministry in London, but the command hoped it would duplicate the success of similar Allied organizations in the Southwest Pacific and Central Pacific commands. The technical intelligence organization had an RAF chief with a deputy from the AAF and another deputy from the U.S. Navy. The field headquarters located at Calcutta, with a varying number of field units covering

Relationship of Combined Photographic Interpretation Centre and Its Units to Eastern Air Command

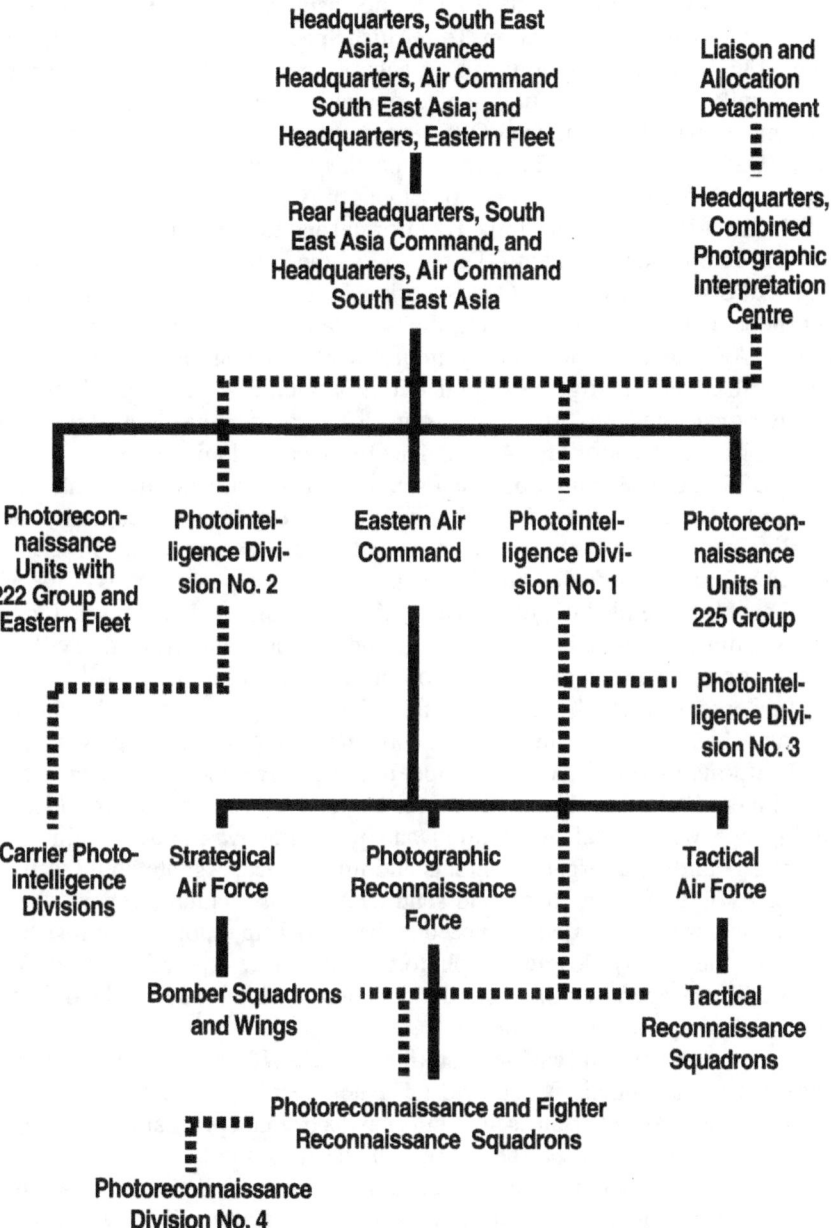

the territory east of the Bramaputra River and other locations that might, from time to time, prove useful.[26]

As the Allies became more proficient in organizing intelligence gathering and analysis in the theater, they made increasingly greater use of agents in Burma as a source of information. The British Special Operations Executive ran Force 136, incorporating within it aspects of agent infiltration, a long-range patrol unit, and political intelligence operations throughout the region. In September 1942, the American OSS sent about twenty agents to eastern India as its Detachment 101. That was to be the beginning of an increasingly important OSS operation that became a locus of AAF air intelligence collection both in India-Burma and in China. By informal and formal agreements between the OSS commander William J. Donovan and the British, as well as due to the course of events, most of the OSS's work occurred in northern Burma, China, and Indochina. From mid-1944 on, the two clandestine organizations became prime AAF sources, although they did not work as a combined unit. OSS and the British covert intelligence organizations in Southeast Asia and China often collided over questions that arose from differences between American and British postwar intentions for Asia and the European colonial empires. By mid-1944, OSS had in Burma more than 400 Americans supervising some 6,000 Kachin tribesmen. Reports from this widespread organization came by radio detailing targets with such refinement (so many feet or yards in a given direction from a specific landmark) that pilots carrying photographs of the area could spot the intended target with ease. Agent reports had exceptional value: they pinpointed the location of equipment and supplies camouflaged in villages, jungles, or fields, hidden from aerial observation and photography.[27]

In September 1944, Lt. Col. Emile Z. Berman, the Tenth Air Force's assistant chief of staff for intelligence estimated that "at least 80 percent of all [our] information on Japanese Camps, dumps, movements, etc., came from Detachment 101." The only other sources Berman had for tactical ground target intelligence were aerial observation and photography; neither could be as accurate regarding a target's contents and importance. Agents could at times reenter an area after an attack and send back precise damage reports.[28] That level of assessment equaled or exceeded the follow-up reports from resistance teams in the highly developed photoreconnaissance operation in Europe. HUMINT from agents on the ground in Japanese territory was not the only area where Allied operations excelled.

Like the escape and evasion operations in the SWPA, the Allies cooperated closely in similar functions in the CBI Theater, despite their other differences. In Burma, the AAF set up an escape and evasion training program soon after the Tenth Air Force arrived on the scene. Almost from the beginning, the sheer numbers of British and American agents in Burma and the large areas of northern Burma inhabited by friendly Kachin and Karen tribes helped in the rescue and recovery of downed pilots. Detachment 101 provided regular

Taking the Offensive

information on towns and regions that were pro-Allies or pro-Japanese, the locations of OSS agent teams and covert OSS airstrips, and other places where rescue would be likely or possible. Once an aircrew was known to be down, their commander sent their general location to detachment headquarters, which in turn alerted its agents in the vicinity to begin a search. Occasionally, trained OSS people parachuted into the jungle to guide lost airmen to safety. By mid-September 1944, Detachment 101 teams had aided more than 180 Tenth Air Force airmen in returning.[29]

To better coordinate rescues in Burma and Thailand, in April 1944 the Allies combined their escape and evasion functions in the India and Southeast Asia commands into what they called the E Group. E Group had roots in the area going back to men who had escaped from Hong Kong in 1942. The unit subsumed the MIS–X and M.I.9 work of the Southeast Asia, India, East, and South Africa commands and the Eastern Fleet, but it worked primarily in the Southeast Asia regions, where the fighting gave it the most opportunity to show its combined skills. The new organization was similar to one used in Europe; it kept close liaison with Detachment 101, Force 136, and air-sea rescue, and it was responsible for all escape and evasion training of ground, sea, and air forces. In addition, E Group organized and implemented all arrangements for contacting or effecting the release of POWs or evaders in enemy territory.[30]

E Group's commander was a British officer; his deputy was an American. The small staff totaled but thirteen officers, about equally drawn from the armies and air forces in the area, with a number of enlisted radio operators and administrative workers. As the size of E Group indicated, the organization did not itself operate large numbers of rescue teams or stations. Primarily, E Group, in addition to its extensive training efforts, took reports of lost aircraft and arranged with the most appropriate Allied force to complete the rescue or recovery of the men downed.[31]

As the Allied airmen fashioned their ground target selection process, they also paid a great deal of attention to the enemy's air defenses. From crew reports, photography, and agent reports, officers plotted the locations of gun sites. Suspected radar locations were collected into a similar listing. Radar station plots became more accurate as the XX Bomber Command began flying ferret missions in the summer of 1944. By October 1944, the AFF had elaborate networks that intercepted Japanese air traffic control radio messages, analyzed their source and content, and reported to British and American commanders the activities of the Japanese Army Air Force. By tracking Japanese air operations and aircraft strength at various places, General Stratemeyer at EAC headquarters and his subordinate air commanders could readily anticipate Japanese reactions to Allied operations.[32]

Y-Service radio intercept collection for the air forces in India-Burma was primarily an RAF responsibility, done by wireless telegraph units at Comilla, Chittagong, and Imphal. The AAF's 5th Radio Squadron (Mobile) was a

311

latecomer, initially lacking the experience and resources of the RAF in India, but by late in the war it had built a sizable SIGINT analysis center in Delhi. Each of the British units worked independently, covering all of central Burma, an obvious and wasteful duplication of effort. In October 1944, the Director of Signals Intelligence, Air Command South East Asia, created the Tactical Air Intelligence Centre (TAIC), a cover name for a radio intercept central operation along much the same lines as the theater's central photographic and technical intelligence units. The TAIC had a CB at Comilla (probably inspired by the Far East CB that intercepted high-grade ULTRA traffic) for cryptanalysis, evaluation, and collation. The units at Imphal and Chittagong, relieved from other responsibilities, performed aircraft search and frequency monitoring. Comilla also became the center for direction finding. Daily and weekly reports of Japanese Army Air Force operations went from the CB to Air Command South East Asia, to EAC, to the Strategic Air Force, and to the 3d Tactical Air Force. The overall effect of this organizational change, even though late in the war, was to concentrate work by specialty area, increase the effectiveness of the Allied air forces' radio intercept intelligence capability, and raise the general understanding of the Japanese air OB and Japanese Army Air Force operations and capabilities in Burma.[33]

The constant Allied air attacks in Burma, supported by a well-honed intelligence-gathering and analysis structure, placed mounting pressure on the Japanese defense line and reduced enemy air operations. By May 1945, Stratemeyer could write to Arnold that so far into the year there had been ". . . no escorted daylight [Japanese] bomber missions" against Allied targets and that ". . . attacks on our forward fields and positions have steadily decreased both in strength and effect." Because Stratemeyer could not watch every Japanese airfield nor read the minds of enemy air commanders, he remained cautious as to the overall abilities of the Japanese to strike at his own bases and other Allied positions.[34]

China and the Fourteenth Air Force

North and east of the Himalayas, the Allies fought a different war in China. Mostly an air operation, the U.S. Navy also had a substantial presence in the form of guerrilla teams and a far-flung intelligence organization. The Fourteenth Air Force kept an intelligence operation that usually complemented the Navy's. In China, as opposed to India-Burma, air intelligence was not fragmented; all of it, Chinese and American alike, flowed to General Chennault, as his was the major air command in the country. From the very beginning of AAF operations in China, Chennault faced two problems that always dictated his use of intelligence: his air force was and remained very small, and logistics were such

Taking the Offensive

a problem that he often could not have ordered his men to fly no matter how lucrative a target the intelligence people found.[35]

The enormous Japanese presence on the Chinese mainland offered a plethora of tactical and strategic strike opportunities. The Japanese military had operated in China for years; they had airfields in abundance, and as they laid out new ones, word of their locations filtered back to Kunming through various channels. Harbors and shipping facilities were always available to strike, as were Japanese troop dispositions, supply columns, and barracks. In the last half of 1942 and in early 1943, Chennault's problem lay in sorting out the best targets. The old AVG, which formed the small cadre that became the Fourteenth, had been an air defense force, using P–40s largely to shoot down Japanese aircraft. In the fall of 1942, the newly formed AAF contingent began to receive B–25 medium bombers and increase the use of P–40s as dive bombers. Both of its new activites required better and faster intelligence analysis, but enhancing support services in this far corner of the world took time. Chennault's staff grew slowly, and his A–2 office suffered from severe shortages of qualified specialists.[36]

Late in 1942, Chennault's A–2, Colonel Cooper, left China for home and medical treatment. At about the same time, Cooper's assistant, Lieutenant Hubler, departed also. Only Lieutenant Birch was left to fill target and combat intelligence tasks. One other officer, 1st Lt. Gerald E. Reed, worked in security and counterintelligence, at that time a normal part of an A–2 office in the AAF. These two officers constituted the entire CATF intelligence staff until a new contingent arrived from the United States to form a team that would operate Fourteenth Air Force's intelligence section for most of the remainder of the war. At year's end, Lt. Col. Jesse C. Williams became Assistant Chief of Staff, A–2, and Capt. Wilfred J. Smith assisted Williams and worked on operational intelligence and objective folders. (Smith later commanded the AGFRTS, the unit that gathered information in the field, directed close air support and air attacks deep into Japanese-held territory, rescued downed airmen, and carried out demolitions and radio direction finding.) Capt. Richard Taylor prepared situation maps and wrote intelligence summaries and extracts. Capt. Morgan B. O'Connor began the AAF photointerpretation work in China, relying on pictures taken by four F–4 aircraft that had arrived in November 1942.* In 1943, 1st Lt. Carl G. Nelson arrived from Washington as a qualified technical intelligence officer to track down enemy war equipment. Four enlisted men—Corporals Nelson, Okerberg, and Varey, and Private Arnegard—typed, drafted reports, and created charts and graphs. In January 1943, Chennault sought formal authorizations for his existing intelligence staff plus two more intelligence officers for each fighter group and bomber group; two for each combat flying squadron to perform briefing, interrogation, and liaison; and two

---

*The F–4 was a P–38 stripped of guns and modified for photography.

313

for the photo squadron. For the photointerpreters, Chennault noted an especial need, as "photo interpretation is particularly valuable in this area as it is the only unbiased source of available information."[37]

When Chennault's organization joined the AAF in July 1942, there came with it a widespread, unsophisticated but very effective intelligence function, the air-raid warning net. Devised by Chennault when he served as Chiang's air advisor between 1937 and 1941, it was patterned on the British observer corps system used during and after World War I. The Chinese air warning net comprised hundreds of people across thousands of miles of territory facing Japanese-occupied China who, when they heard aircraft overhead, called in by radio or telephone with their reports. By plotting the locations of the calls, the Americans tracked the enemy's approach. If the aircraft had been sighted and counted, so much the better. The warning notice was the important fact, however, for it gave immediately useful tactical intelligence and allowed the pilots to scramble their aircraft to meet the incoming attack in time to break up the formation and reduce bombing accuracy. Bissell considered the warning system so important that on September 25, 1942, he wrote Chennault from India telling him to keep it operating "without interruption or decrease in efficiency." With Tenth Air Force approval, the warning net became a special fighter control squadron and a formal, integral part of the CATF.[38] Despite having formal status, the air warning service aided only air defense; it could do little to influence the Fourteenth's offensive mission.

Early in 1943, Chennault's chief of intelligence, Colonel Williams, noted that much work had yet to be done to make the Fourteenth's intelligence analysis information truly supportive of air operations. Aerial photography continued as the primary source, but Williams wanted trained U.S. Army intelligence officers assigned to Chinese forces along the Burma and Indochina borders to sort out good reports before requesting air support. He wanted to strengthen his technical intelligence ability to correctly assess recovered Japanese aircraft and equipment. At the same time, Williams asked once again for authorization and assignment of group and squadron air intelligence officers so that they could prepare adequate target objective material and properly prepare aircrews for combat missions.[39]

Some of the problems that Chennault and his commanders faced in China were simply not amenable to solution. Air technical intelligence always suffered because many of the areas where Japanese airplanes crashed were distant, isolated, and hard for the few recovery teams to reach. The local natives prized the aircraft metal and would carry it away almost as soon as it was cool enough to touch. Even by the end of 1943, with at least the formal support of the Chinese government, air technical intelligence teams still had difficulty recovering parts of downed airplanes.[40]

Japanese military authorities had been aware from as early as the April 1942 Doolittle raid that Allied airfields in China were a threat not only to their

Taking the Offensive

field armies, but to Japan itself. Shortly after Doolittle's attack alarmed the Japanese homeland, the Japanese Army decided to clean out bases in Chekiang and Szechwan that could be used by the Americans and to capture railway equipment that they needed elsewhere in China. The operation, mounted mostly in Chekiang Province, reached the railroad objectives and took airfields at Yushan, Chuhsien, and Lishui by the end of August. The Japanese withdrew to conserve strength in the face of fighting in the Solomons and New Guinea. Renewed Japanese advances began again in February 1943, this time to capture Yangtse River shipping that they could use to alleviate shortages of water transport elsewhere. During both campaigns, Chennault's men fought with interdiction and counterair missions whenever the air transport pilots hauled in enough gasoline and spare parts to support flying. At the end of May 1943, the Japanese once again withdrew to more defensible positions. In both the 1942 and 1943 efforts, the Japanese did not intend to hold all the territory they took. China was far too vast for the Japanese Army Air Force to offer a stiff defense everywhere. Chennault's men, then, had the advantage of being able to pick the place of attack.[41] Selecting the points of attack depended, in turn, on the employment of a widespread intelligence network and first-rate analysis and interpretation. In Chennault's eyes, better use of air intelligence would come with a separate Army Air Force in China.

In the spring of 1943, Chennault heard that his operation was to be a separate command. He would become a major general, no longer under Bissell's control. In July 1943, when Washington split the CBI Theater into the distinct sectors of India-Burma and China, much of the reason for doing so resided in satisfying Chiang's insistence on independence for Chennault. When Bissell returned to Washington, Stratemeyer became the India-Burma air commander, with advisory authority over Chennault's operations, but he had no real power to directly influence the Fourteenth Air Force.[42] Chennault now began to make increasing use of the growing interservice intelligence capability in China, a capability that ultimately benefited both the AAF and the Navy.

Chennault had long sought to strike enemy shipping and had in fact done so since 1942, but his small air force had been hampered by constant supply problems. The Fourteenth was so hard pressed for fuel, tires, spare engines, and parts that its squadrons could not fly patrols seeking randomly located ships in the open waters off China. Search techniques for finding random targets in a given region of the ocean had been developed by the Allies in Atlantic operations and were ideal for use in China. To make the best use of available aircraft, the Fourteenth's B–24 and B–25 patrol bombers needed to be directed to an area where the probability of success was reasonably high. The tactics were well understood, but success required sophisticated, methodical implementation, something Chennault had been unable to afford on a large scale. The

Piercing the Fog

The seas off the southern and central coast of China were the logistics pathway of the Japanese Empire, connecting the home islands with the indispensable raw materials that an industrial power must have—oil, rubber, minerals, and food. This richness of targets attracted Allied aircraft from several theaters. At *left,* the Fifth Air Force attacks a Japanese ship off the China coast; *below,* B–25s from the Fourteenth Air Force bomb a Japanese frigate.

Fourteenth's A–2 office and Commodore Milton E. Miles's U.S. Naval Group China, gave Chennault much of the answer to his problem.*[43]

---

*Adm. Ernest J. King had sent Miles to China in 1942 to organize a guerrilla warfare operation to obtain information on the China coast and support any eventual landing in China by the Navy. Miles organized the Sino-American Cooperative

Taking the Offensive

The cooperation between Miles's naval group and Chennault's airmen began early in 1943 with the detailing by Miles of two naval officers to the Fourteenth Air Force staff to perform photointerpretation work. In return, the Fourteenth seeded harbors and waters along the coast of Japanese-occupied China and northern Indochina with Navy mines flown in over the Hump from India. In October 1943, a Navy-AAF mining raid (Miles's mine experts were aboard the bombers) closed Haiphong harbor by sinking a fleeing ship in the entrance channel. The harbor remained at least partially closed for the remainder of the war. By May 1944, Miles had ninety-eight men working in what he called his "14th Naval unit" doing jobs that included photointelligence (in conjunction with the Army's 18th Photointerpretation Unit); planning the delivery of and charting minefields; providing radio intelligence, air combat intelligence, and air technical intelligence; and rescuing downed or imprisoned flyers. The last-mentioned operation was done with the Chinese under the auspices of the Sino-American Cooperative Organization (SACO) teams. Some of the information that Miles's people developed from this working arrangement, they passed to Navy agencies to support submarine attacks on Japanese shipping and the battles incident to the Allied campaign in the Philippines.[44]

Chennault's planning staff in Kunming derived their information about merchant shipping from the use of aerial reconnaissance, from Commodore Miles's SACO coast watchers, and from the intercept and direction-finding teams of Fleet Radio Unit, China, at Kunming. Proximity to Chennault's headquarters (and the close relationship that grew between the Fourteenth's A–2 and the Navy) created an ideal situation. Coast-watcher reports sent by radio or telephone correlated with other data and yielded the cues needed to search out ships either in convoy or sailing alone. The waters that received most attention were the most heavily used Japanese merchant seaways; thus the chances of success in sinking enemy shipping were greatly enhanced. Between October 1943 and May 1944 the Fourteenth claimed the sinking of 83,100 tons of shipping. With the arrival in China of a squadron of B–24s equipped with sea-search radar similar to the type used by the Thirteenth Air Force in the SOPAC, the Fourteenth combined naval intelligence information with radar-directed, low-altitude attacks that sent tonnage claims to 248,665 between May 24 and October 31, 1944.* The campaign from the bases in eastern China against Japanese merchant shipping far exceeded similar low-altitude bombing operations of the Fifth and Thirteenth Air Forces in the SWPA and SPA.[45] Much of the credit for success was due to the artful ULTRA intelligence analysis that sent the bombers, unknown to their crews, to the most lucrative areas.

Organization (SACO) and a far-flung intelligence-gathering operation.

*Claims for sinkings had to be supported by a confirmed sighting of sinking or at night by an explosion and fire. With the use of radar, confirmation could be a target's disappearance from the radar scope, subsequent to an attack and bomb hit.

Piercing the Fog

On February 22, 1944, the SWPA SIB carried the comment, "Due to air attacks by [our] China-based planes [Japanese] shipping along the China coast has been routed; beginning February 18, 100 miles off-shore."[46] The intercept confirmed the success of Chennault's and Miles's antishipping campaign, employing both aerial attacks on ships at sea and in harbors, and the aerial mining of harbors and select sea lanes. But what the Japanese thought to be a corrective action sent their ships into deeper water where American submarines waited. ULTRA via Honolulu had directed the submarines to the position of enemy shipping. Much of Honolulu's information had come from China. The growing threat to shipping and airfields represented by the Fourteenth could hardly be ignored by the Japanese military authorities in China. The results, in fact, were already being seen on the Chinese mainland.

By September 1943, Japanese leaders knew that they had to deal with the American airfields supporting the Fourteenth Air Force, whose depredations continued to harm their army. The Japanese wished also to pressure China into withdrawing her forces from northern Burma. This time Japan intended to "deal a crushing blow to the enemy"[47] in a strong, well-coordinated campaign. The Japanese generals assessed the Fourteenth's strength at about 500 combat aircraft, quite a bit above the Fourteenth's summertime operational totals. Among the targets were airfields at Kweilin and Liuchosien. The operation, titled "*Ichi-go*," was to be prepared in strict secrecy. Despite the security, the Japanese concluded that their enemy understood what was transpiring even before *Ichi-go* was under way, although they were mystified as to how the information had leaked out. However much of the Japanese plan Chennault knew, the garrulous, offensive-minded general seems to have overestimated the ability of the small Fourteenth Air Force to carry the load that China could not, and he seems to have underestimated the Japanese Army's reaction to his success and its capacity for a sustained drive aimed at his eastern China airfields. The Japanese were also wary of the possible use of Chinese airfields by long-range bombers; this was added incentive to chase out the Americans. Chennault's 68th Composite Wing's bases came under increasing danger from the Japanese early in 1944.[48] Even if Chennault miscalculated Japanese intent, it is difficult to see how he could have acted differently. To have withheld the Fourteenth from the fighting was not in Chennault's nature, nor would it have been acceptable in the eyes of Arnold or Roosevelt.

As the Japanese moved toward Chennault's bases, he made increasing use of one of his most important intelligence assets, the 5329th AGFRTS. AGFRTS, staffed largely by people from Fourteenth Air Force and operating as a joint AAF-OSS venture, spread agents and radio direction-finding teams across much of Japanese-occupied China, including major ports and key cities. The Fourteenth carried AGFRTS on its books as an AAF unit, but from its inception in April 1944, AGFRTS was strongly influenced by the OSS. The organization quickly became an important part of Fourteenth Air Force's

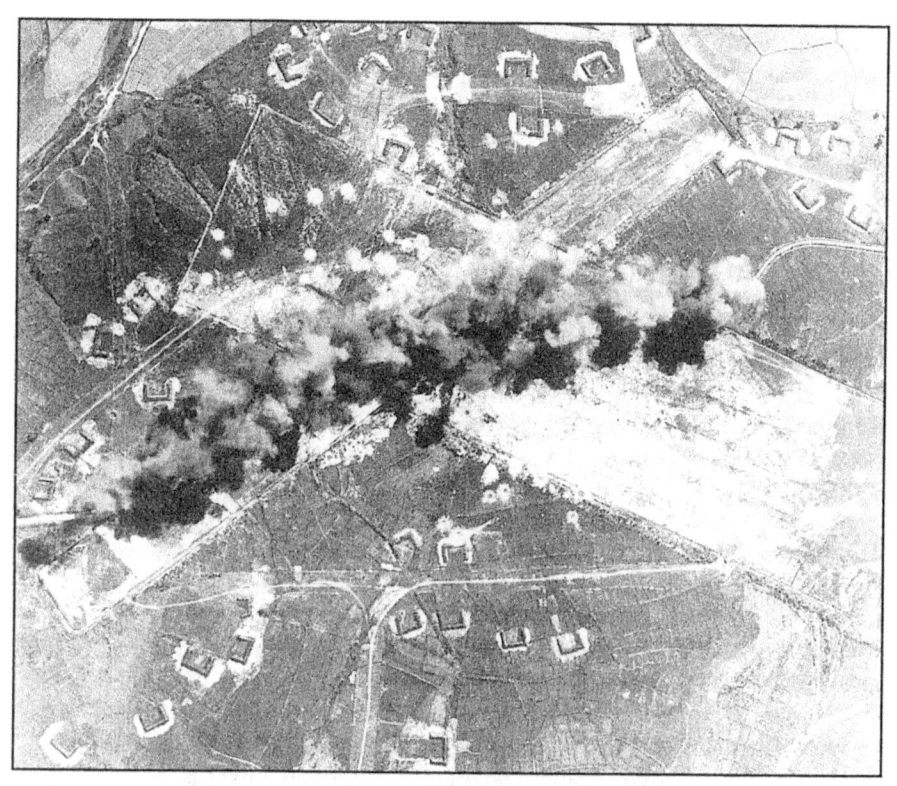

Fourteenth Air Force B–25s bomb the runways of Laiwing Airport in China.

Brig. Gen. Clinton D. Vincent

Piercing the Fog

intelligence structure, something of a rival to the Navy's unit in China that also supported Chennault. AGFRTS, in addition to its OSS-peculiar duties aimed at disrupting Japanese control, provided the airmen with weather reports and information on lucrative targets such as ships and major Japanese troop movements. Liaison teams serving with Chinese field army headquarters reviewed, validated, and forwarded requests for air support and supplied information upon which interdiction and close support missions could be planned.[49]

Of special importance during the Japanese offensive of 1944 were the AGFRTS and Naval Group China agent reports that gave the location of Japanese front lines and information on infiltration tactics and supply columns. Using these reports, Brig. Gen. Clinton D. Vincent, commander of the 68th Composite Wing, launched frequent attacks on the enemy columns nearing his bases. Other reports allowed Vincent's men to strike Japanese supply depots and transshipment points. As if they were not busy enough, AGFRTS field teams also assisted in the rescue and return of downed Allied airmen.[50]

In the spring of 1944, to support forward air operations, the Fourteenth Air Force's intelligence officer moved a section of his operation to Lianshan to coordinate more rapidly with the field intelligence teams and to expedite photointerpretation. As the Japanese pressed their offensive in the Tungting Lake region, they forced evacuation of several Fourteenth Air Force bases. Working with the 68th Composite Wing and the Fourteenth Air Force's Air Service Command, AGFRTS agents began systematic destruction of roads and bridges as they reported Japanese positions and movements. Lacking coherent information from the rapidly deteriorating Chinese Army, Vincent had to depend on the field people and observations by his aircrews for warning and information upon which to plan evacuation of Lingling and Hengyang airfields. The Japanese advance had disrupted the ground situation, making it difficult for AGFRTS teams to provide a constant flow of information. At the advanced Fourteenth Air Force intelligence center, field team reports, photography, Chinese military information, and other data were reviewed, sorted, and melded into usable assessments of enemy movements and probable intentions. The result was a speedy processing of information during the Japanese offensive that allowed a series of interdiction strikes from early December 1944 through March 1945. A bombardment of Hangkow's docks and warehouses by Maj. Gen. Curtis E. LeMay's China-based B–29s supplemented the Fourteenth's attempts to deflect the Japanese drive.[51]

By mid-November 1944, most of the major American air bases in eastern China had fallen to the Japanese. Even before then, however, the Americans began to make changes in the theater's command and intelligence structure. In October 1944, Chiang Kai-shek rid himself of a long festering sore when he succeeded in getting President Roosevelt to recall Stilwell, replacing him with Lt. Gen. Albert C. Wedemeyer. This was when the CBI Theater became the

Taking the Offensive

Maj. Gen. Claire Chennault meets his new theater commander, Lt. Gen. Albert C. Wedemeyer.

India-Burma Theater and the China Theater. Wedemeyer took charge of the latter, simultaneously becoming Chiang's chief of staff. With the change in theater alignment came a change in the OSS's (and AGFRTS's) position. Previously, Stilwell, grudgingly, to be sure, but to keep peace with Chiang and because of his duties in India, allowed Chiang and Chennault to go about their business more or less undisturbed. It was logical then that AGFRTS should be in effect part of the Fourteenth Air Force, as that was the only military organization that it served directly. Wedemeyer prepared for a move of the Tenth Air Force to China later in 1945, and he decided to take greater control of military operations in that country. Wedemeyer had his staff supervise AGFRTS's functions and those of the Naval Group China in January 1945. In February, the new theater commander established an air intelligence section in his S–2 office in Chungking, staffing it partly with experienced people from Chennault's air force, but generally excluding Miles's Navy group.[52]

Both Chennault and Miles objected loudly. Miles believed his operations were restricted so as to force him and his men out of China. The final six months of the war in China engendered bitterness in Miles, as his organization slowly lost the position it had created over several years. The close relationship between AGFRTS and the Fourteenth deteriorated into quibbling and finger pointing. In a letter of February 4, 1945, Chennault reiterated to Wedemeyer his need for AGFRTS and his fears that it would no longer furnish the information and services his airmen had for so long put to good use. Chennault closed by asking, rather petulantly, for the return to his command of those people from the Fourteenth who originally staffed AGFRTS the year before and who now wanted to leave the OSS.[53]

Despite the troubles that arose with the new command arrangement in China, the relationship beteen the Naval Group China, AGFRTS, and the Fourteenth Air Force continued to yield information upon which commanders could make decisions. Chennault also had alternate sources on which to rely as the war entered its final months. To apply greater pressure on the Japanese, and to make militarily valueless the areas they occupied, the Fourteenth Air Force engaged in a campaign to destroy railroads. The impetus for the effort came originally from the JTG in Washington. In one of its first projects related to the Fourteenth, the JTG assessed both the economic and military impact of a railroad interdiction campaign in China. Concluding that the Japanese used large areas of China proper (excluding Manchuria) as a source of raw materials, the group decided that any effort to attack scattered quarries, mines, and agricultural collection points would not be economically worthwhile. On the other hand, certain rail lines provided the bulk of military transportation for Japan's army in China, especially south of the Yangtze River. The JTG recommended dividing the Chinese rail system into different zones and then concentrating air attacks within selected zones on railway lines, bridges, and other facilities upon which the Japanese depended. Such tactics would make repairs very difficult. When one zone's rail lines were out, the effort would target another. The first railways recommended for saturation attacks were those from Peking to Hangkow, from Tientsin to Pukow, and from Tatung to Puchow. The group's members reasoned that if these lines, which had heavy military use, were destroyed, lateral and ancillary lines would have only local importance. Only certain segments of the three lines need be attacked to make the plan effective.[54]

The JTG recommended that efforts by fighters to strafe locomotives and water towers would be an added benefit because such attacks were easy to make, were economical, and would force a heavy load on repair facilities. To achieve military success and to meet the Fourteenth Air Force's mission of directly supporting the Chinese armies, Chennault's staff had to choose the specific segments carefully and closely coordinate the resultant attacks with the ground forces. The JTG's studies also allowed Chennault to better manage the always critical fuel supply by avoiding superfluous or uneconomical raids.[55]

The resulting fighter sweeps early in 1945 destroyed some 145 locomotives plus a good number of bridges, railway lines, and rolling stock. Attacks on nearby roads and canals prevented their use as alternate routes. When intelligence reports indicated that the Japanese were taking damaged locomotives to shops in north China, B–24s hit those shops and adjacent railyards in

Taking the Offensive

March 1945. When the operations planners judged that B–24 strikes consumed too much fuel, Chennault ceased using the large aircraft and moved them to India to haul supplies over the mountains. Fighters took over the railway attack task, but they, too, soon had to reduce their efforts to conserve gasoline. The rail targets remained known to Chennault and available, but he lacked the means to destroy them as rapidly as he wished. This was the same situation that had obtained so often in China since the AAF's arrival in July 1942. Always ready to fight the Japanese, the American airmen had too few aircraft, too little gasoline, or too much of a need for parts and aircraft tires. The Fourteenth's bombardment and attack planning had been a function partly of knowing the enemy's whereabouts, but more importantly it was a question of how much of a force could be mustered on any given day to hit the most worthwhile targets.[56]

Despite the supply problems, the Fourteenth had hit rail targets successfully, and senior military leaders in Washington drew on ULTRA to oversee the extent of those successes. General Marshall's understanding of the railway interdiction plan became the basis for some of the discussions at Potsdam in July 1945. At the Allied Tripartite Meeting on July 24, Marshall told the Soviets of the AAF's destruction of railroads in Japanese-controlled China as he encouraged the Soviet leadership to draw up plans to enter the war in Asia. He noted that the bombing and sabotage had by that time substantially reduced Japan's ability to move troops from China proper to counter Soviet moves in Manchuria. The Americans told also of the 500,000 Japanese troops that they believed were on Kyushu, but they pointed out that naval and AAF mining of Japanese waters had cut Japan's ability to move her army from the home islands. Arnold then added remarks that outlined rather specifically Japan's current air operations, her air logistics situation, and her ability to continue air warfare; like Marshall, Arnold based his account on ULTRA intercepts plus photographic reconnaissance of Japan's airfields.[57]

Although Chennault had formal access to ULTRA information from at least March 1944, a special security officer did not arrive at Fourteenth Air Force headquarters in Kunming, China, until October of that year. Before then, such ULTRA information as Chennault saw came to him via the special security representative in New Delhi, India, or from Stilwell's office in Chungking which was served, in turn, by the radio facilities of the U.S. Naval Group China. Because of the distance and time required to carry the material, Fourteenth Air Force probably received little ULTRA data on a regular basis before March 1944. The amount of other intelligence information derived from Japanese message traffic available to the Fourteenth Air Force is unclear. Occasional data reached Chennault, as in the December 1942 message from Washington. Miles, discreet in discussing SIGINT, also hinted in his memoirs that his communication people decrypted information valuable to the AAF in China and elsewhere in the Pacific.

With an SSO in Kunming, this changed. Regular Japanese air OB estimates arrived from the War Department in 1945, as they did in other AAF commands in the Pacific. Low-level radio interception and traffic analysis by Navy, Army, and OSS personnel was much more common and of more immediate use. Even with B–24 heavy bombers assigned, General Chennault ran an air force that was far more tactical than strategic, so his need for intelligence centered on material for ready use. When the B–29s of the XX Bomber Command flew from Chengtu, they could use more sensitive information. Yet even this demand in China was far less than that of the air forces in other Pacific theaters.[58]

Several factors affected the ways that air intelligence analyses influenced Chennault's war in China. The Fourteenth's A–2 did basically the same work as the planners and staff officers elsewhere, but with substantially less ULTRA content until well into 1944. Agent teams watching and reporting on Japanese-held areas paralleled similar efforts in Europe and the Southwest Pacific, but porous control by the Japanese of areas they occupied in China made the work of such teams broader in scope and of more importance to the Fourteenth than to other major AAF units, even to the Tenth Air Force in Burma's jungles and mountains.

The Central Pacific

Intelligence studies and support for air operations in the Navy-controlled POA came largely from the MIS in Washington and from the Intelligence Center, Pacific Ocean Area (ICPOA), in Honolulu. ICPOA, and its associated FRUPac, was part of Admiral Nimitz's headquarters and grew from the prewar Combat Information Center originally used to track the movements of enemy and Allied ships into an all-encompassing intelligence-gathering and analysis organization. On September 7, 1943, in recognition of its multiservice composition and analysis role, ICPOA became the Joint Intelligence Center, Pacific Ocean Areas (JICPOA). In many ways, JICPOA was Nimitz's version of MacArthur's G–2 SWPA in Australia; it served primarily the main Navy theaters—the SOPAC Area and the POA—but it provided considerable information (especially on enemy OB) throughout the Pacific. JICPOA and G–2 SWPA maintained a good working relationship with much mutual interchange that affected the course of the war. The great distances and long travel times in the Pacific enforced a separation on the two organizations that limited the joint effort's effectiveness.[59]

Radio intelligence quickly became a prime source of information, most of which went to support the Navy's surface and submarine fleets. Air intelligence, too, came from JICPOA, but it was applied differently than was the CB's product in Brisbane. The Navy task force organizations in the POA included naval, Marine, and AAF air units, but these organizations were subordinate to their task force commanders. The Seventh Air Force functioned as an integral operational air unit even less than had the Thirteenth under SOPAC. The Seventh's groups and squadrons flew for the various task forces, while the headquarters gave administrative and logistic support. Although the Seventh Air Force's position (or plight, depending upon one's point of view) caused other AAF leaders like General Kenney much grief throughout the war years, the organization served Admiral Nimitz well and suited the Navy's operational style. The Seventh's commander, Maj. Gen. Willis Hale, rarely used intelligence in forming plans and assigning tasks until late in the war. These functions fell instead to the various air commanders of the task forces.[60]

The air intelligence produced by JICPOA and used by the Seventh's groups included regular interception of Japanese weather reports from an excellent system of observation, air OB information, and air operations analyses, plus a variety of charts, maps, books, and similar materials. The Seventh Air Force's intelligence officer had little to do with original analysis; early in the war he served largely as a briefer and an information conduit. Not until the campaign for the Gilberts late in 1943 and the Marshalls early in 1944 did the Seventh's intelligence section achieve any real importance; even then it was still subordinate to the Navy's air operations and did little to influence war planning. Although size comparisons can mislead, the number of people authorized for the Seventh Air Force's A–2 section varied between 1943 and 1945 from one-fourth to less than one-half that of the Fifth Air Force ADVON A–2 in New Guinea. In April 1943, of the 10 officers assigned to the Seventh Air Force's A–2 section in Honolulu, 1 worked with combat intelligence, 2 handled the command's public relations matters, 6 were photointerpreters, and 1 did counterintelligence. The director and his administrative and executive help rounded out the officer authorizations, while 24 enlisted men completed the staff. A July 1943 request to increase the A–2 section's strength to 27 officers and 57 enlisted found favor locally, but not at AAF headquarters in Washington, which saw little reason to assign scarce talents to offices that did secondary work. The demands of the Gilbert and Marshall Islands campaigns taxed the limited intelligence staff, which leaned increasingly on the resources of JICPOA, especially for radio-intercept data, air OB formulations, and technical intelligence. In recognition of the large amount of photointerpreter work being done by the Seventh both in Hawaii and at its advance echelon on Tarawa, the AAF added a photographic intelligence detachment on February 7, 1944. The detachment had authorizations for 43 officers and 49 enlisted. All personnel had to come from General Hale's own organizational resources; the supply of trained people was slim.

The situation on Hale's staff reflected in part the very haphazard growth of the A–2 section through the first two years of fighting. The state of the intelligence office's manpower strength also reflected the reluctance of the AAF's headquarters to assign people to jobs that could or should be accomplished by Admiral Nimitz's joint center. Washington's reluctance to add to

Piercing the Fog

General Hale's strength was probably increased by the realization that any such additions could be drained away by the theater commander, if he so desired. There remained a compelling bureaucratic reason to send qualified intelligence officers and men to other locations where they could have a more direct and continuing effect on Air Force operations.[61]

Despite the troubles, the Seventh contributed substantial operational air intelligence to the Gilbert Islands campaign as photoreconnaissance aircraft overflew Japanese-occupied islands, recording enemy positions and activities. Aerial reconnaissance by the Seventh's B–24 crews provided information crucial to Admiral Nimitz's planning for the Marshall Islands campaign. When photographs showed that the Japanese had failed to adequately fortify Kwajalein and Eniwetok, those islands instead of the more heavily protected Wotje and Maloelap became the targets of amphibious landings. Nimitz's bold stroke into the center of the Marshalls group succeeded after extensive bombardment by Seventh Air Force B–24s.[62]

For the taking of the Gilbert Islands, code named Operation GALVANIC, the Seventh's bomber force became Task Group 57.2, commanded by Hale, and the fighters became part of Task Group 57.4, the Ellice Defense and Utility Group, under Marine Brig. Gen. L. G. Merritt. Hale's bombers neutralized Japanese airfields on Tarawa and Makin Islands and made photoreconnaissance missions in support of Task Force (TF) 57's commander, Vice Adm. John H. Hoover. Other targets selected to prevent significant Japanese interference with GALVANIC were Kwajalein, Maloelap, Mille, and Jaluit. Tactical intelligence to support these missions came from the Seventh's A–2, who compiled maps, aerial photographs, and weather information and passed on information from the headquarters of Admirals Nimitz and Hoover.[63]

Continuing AAF expressions of concern for the integrity of Seventh Air Force led in 1944 to an alteration of the command arrangement in the Central Pacific. On May 1, Nimitz created TF 59 which comprised all shore-based aircraft in the forward area except for the Army and Navy transport commands. Hale assumed the command of TF 59, simultaneously becoming also COMAIRFORWARD; he relinquished command of the Seventh, which then fell to Brig. Gen. Robert W. Douglas, Jr. These changes gave the AAF partial operational control of its assets, although TF 59 remained a subordinate part of Admiral Hoover's TF 57. Although the Navy in the Pacific still controlled Hale's force, the change allowed Hale a greater degree of operational direction of his men. The small-island targets, widely scattered across thousands of miles of ocean, and Nimitz's overall strategy frustrated Hale's ambitions and limited the AAF's practical application of intelligence data developed both in Honolulu and by the Seventh's own reconnaissance efforts.[64]

On August 1, 1944, to prepare for the arrival of B–29s in the Pacific, the War Department created Army Air Forces Pacific Ocean Area (AAFPOA). The

Taking the Offensive

Maj. Gen. Willis H. Hale

Maj. Gen. Robert W. Douglass, Jr.

new organization absorbed the support and services units of Seventh Air Force, leaving the Seventh only the VII Bomber and VII Fighter Commands. General Harmon became AAFPOA's commander and Deputy Commander of Twentieth Air Force. Harmon's charge from Washington was to coordinate support for both the Seventh and the XXI Bomber Command. In reality, AAFPOA was an agency to satisfy Nimitz's insistence on control of theater air operations through the task forces while streamlining the logistic and administrative support of the B–29 organization. Harmon's position was to be roughly analogous to, though much less influential than, the positions of Generals Spaatz, Eaker, and Kenney in other theaters, where they responded to theater commanders for all air operations.[65]

The AAFPOA arrangement, however, was not entirely a paper command. AAFPOA's staff included a Directorate of Intelligence as part of the office of the Deputy Chief of Staff for Plans and Operations. Though similar to intelligence operations set up by the AAF elsewhere in the Pacific and CBI, it lacked several specific services. Technical intelligence officers on AAFPOA's roster served at JICPOA, where a joint Army-Navy team pursued information from crashed or captured Japanese aircraft and equipment. Flak analysis was also a joint undertaking at JICPOA because of the vital interest in the subject by Army, Navy, and Marine aviators. The Special Intelligence Branch at AAFPOA collated AA defense information, commonly called flakintel, and delivered it to XXI Bomber Command and Seventh Air Force units that operated near Japanese-held territory. Along with the flakintel information, the

Piercing the Fog

Special Intelligence Branch designed and had built flak computers that could be used to determine AA artillery patterns at several altitudes from 15,000 feet to 30,000 feet. These computers aided mission planners in determining the safest route to a target area. The Special Intelligence Branch also kept close contact with the Directorate of Communications, whose job included radar countermeasures (RCM) analyses. From the data supplied by the communicators, AAFPOA A–2 prepared radar coverage maps to supplement the flakintel information sent to field units. To reduce danger to the B–29s on bombing runs over Japan, the XXI Bomber Command and AAFPOA's VII Fighter Command cooperated to reduce Japanese radar coverage.

Beginning in mid-May, the Bomber Command extended RCM flights to cover much of Japan. First, RCM B–29s picked up radar signals and found their points of origin by triangulation. Nisei radio operators on board listened to the associated Japanese radio transmissions to and from the stations. Once the bomber crews plotted the information, the B–29 command passed the data to AAFPOA's VII Fighter Command. Based on information from the RCM aircraft, P–51s of the 15th Fighter Group struck radar stations on Chichi Jima with strafing, rocket, and dive-bombing attacks on June 27, 28, and 29, 1945. The weather was too poor to observe results, but the operations highlighted the prompt exploitation by one air command of intelligence collected by another.[66]

AAF-Navy cooperation carried out by the Seventh could also be seen in the aerial minelaying around the Bonin Islands during November and December of 1944. At other times, Seventh Air Force B–24s and P–47s attacked shipping and Japanese airfields on Iwo Jima, Haha Jima, and the Pagan Islands. Many armed reconnaissance missions near the Bonins sought targets in those waters. At other times, Seventh Air Force B–24s and P–38s escorted Navy or AAF reconnaissance aircraft overflying Japanese-held islands. On May 25, 1945, VII Fighter Command and its subordinate units came under control of Twentieth Air Force as the latter carried out strategic bombing of Japan. From that day, the long-range P–47s flew more and more frequently against Japanese home island targets. In mid-July, the remainder of the Seventh became part of General Kenney's FEAF on Okinawa. Only at the very end of the war did the Seventh become an integral air force, able to use intelligence information to plan its own operations. By then there was no war left to fight.[67]

In April 1945, JICPOA's Air Estimates Group moved from Hawaii to Guam to support the advanced theater headquarters there. That move broadened the flow of intelligence to the AAF as the XXI Bomber Command received better and more frequent estimates of Japanese air strength and dispositions in the home islands. This improved intelligence and resulted in better mission planning for the remainder of the war. The close proximity to FEAF's operations in the Philippines also increased cooperation between JICPOA and G–2 SWPA in preparation for the final assault on Japan.[68]

B–29 Operations Against Japan

During the autumn of 1942, General Arnold traveled through the Pacific, visiting his air forces, commanders, and men in the SWPA, SOPAC, and Central Pacific. He sought the air power views not only of the flyers but also of MacArthur, Nimitz, and Halsey. As a result of the trip, as he noted after the war, Arnold concluded that lack of a unified command meant that the AAF's new very long-range, very heavy B–29 bombers due to become operational in 1944 could be easily misused by a theater commander searching for a quick solution to local problems. To ensure their most effective employment, Arnold believed he would have to retain control of the B–29s once they were deployed. The alternative would be fragmentation of the force and dispersion of B–29s among several commands; worse still, the B–29s would be controlled by commanders who were not airmen. That Pacific trip may have planted the seed for control of the XX Bomber Command and later the Twentieth Air Force in Arnold's mind, but immediate and constant nourishment for the idea came from operational frustrations in Europe. Despite elaborate theories for heavy bomber employment, the AAF had not, by the end of 1943, clearly demonstrated the undisputed value of strategic air power. The American air generals in North Africa and Europe faced pressure to break up numbered air forces and use airplanes to satisfy the desires of ground commanders clamoring for tactical support. Some Army generals believed that B–17 and B–24 bombers should support frontline troops; others denied that strategic air power was a significant factor in the war. As Arnold and his key supporters steadfastly held to a belief in the importance of an independent strategic bombardment force, intelligence analysis became a key element in the complicated relationships of interservice competition, air power advocacy, and operational preparations.[69]

Faced with the possibility that the war might end without the AAF proving its strategic worth, and losing thereby the chance for continued autonomy, not to mention independence, Arnold and several supporters, including Brig. Gens. Haywood S. Hansell, Jr., and Laurence S. Kuter, began a doctrinal offensive in Washington to convince the joint chiefs and senior policy makers of the value of precision bombardment. At the Cairo conference in December 1943, Hansell continued to push for an independent strategic bombardment force, and he successfully persuaded the combined staff planners that instead of the final victory against Japan depending upon invasion of the home islands, "the defeat of Japan may be accomplished by air and sea blockade and intensive air bombardment from progressively advanced bases."[70]

Arnold persuaded the JCS to retain control of the new, very heavy bomber force and to make him, Arnold, its commander and their executive agent in directing its operation. This not only kept the B–29s out of the hands of admirals and generals who would be tempted to use the new aircraft in tactical

Piercing the Fog

Maj. Gen. Laurence S. Kuter

roles, it also created a pressing need for intelligence that would guide Washington in developing target lists and effective operational plans.[71]

Even before command arrangements for the Twentieth Air Force had been resolved, Arnold told the COA to recommend appropriate targets. The committee's work followed an even earlier target study done by the Air Forces Intelligence Service. Arnold's desire was to have the committee verify independently the Air Staff's analysis, which had selected fifty-seven main targets and had a target-industry priority list of aircraft, nonferrous metals, naval bases and shipyards, iron and steel, petroleum, chemicals, automobile engines, and rubber. The COA began work in May 1943 to assess each different industry, seeking to determine the following in each case:

- The indispensability of its product to Japan's war economy.

- The industry's position as to current production, production capacity, and stocks on hand.

- Japan's requirements for various degrees of military activity.

- The possibility of successful substitution or decrease in use of products without affecting front line strength.

- The number, locations, and vulnerabilities of vital installations within each industry.

- That industry's recuperative power.

- The time lag between destruction of installations and the desired effect on frontline strength.[72]

The study, by its nature, required substantial understanding of the industrial, transportation, and military relationships in Japanese society. This knowledge remained skimpy and ill-defined.

In September 1943, the COA began working with Hansell, who had by then become the Chief of Staff of the XX Bomber Command, the unit that was to deploy to India and China and be the first to use the B–29 in the war. The committee sought information as to the new airplane's capabilities which gave, in turn, a chance for the XX Bomber Command to correlate its intelligence actions with those of the COA.[73] In making its assessments, the committee faced difficult problems. Information on Japan was fragmented, limited, and of undetermined worth. In some cases it quickly became clear that analyses would have to be drawn inferentially, by comparing Japan's supposed industrial operation with that of America and of other countries. The members labored throughout the summer and fall of 1943 to assemble material and form their recommendations.[74]

The Cairo conference of Allied leaders in November and December 1943 became the first stage on which the COA's recommendations about Japan would play. To achieve an immediate role for the B–29s, Generals Arnold, Hansell, and Kuter presented their employment proposal based upon a preliminary assessment from the COA of the Japanese iron and steel industry and its vulnerability to attacks on coke ovens in Manchuria. These ovens at Anshan and Penshian (near Mukden) produced 56 percent of Japan's coke. Since coke does not last in open storage, the committee believed that destruction or disablement of the ovens (they could be damaged by shock from near misses and take up to two years to repair) would have a substantial effect on sheet steel fabrication, and thereby reduce shipbuilding. The Allied leaders at Cairo approved use of B–29s for attacks on Japanese industry; with that approval came a plan to base the aircraft in India, stage them through bases at Chengtu, China, and hit the ovens along with other targets. The plan, called MATTERHORN, was to be carried out by the XX Bomber Command under Brig. Gen. Kenneth B. Wolfe.*[75]

---

*Preparation of an earlier version of the MATTERHORN plan miscarried because of logistics problems. In that plan, 280 B–29s would fly from Chinese bases near Chengtu, supported by 2,000 B–24s converted to cargo duties. Such an amount of

Piercing the Fog

MATTERHORN had immediate importance to Arnold, Hansell, and Kuter for reasons other than the pure wish to carry the war directly to Japan. In Australia, and on visits to Washington, Kenney agitated for assignment of B–29s to him, to be based in Darwin. With Kenney's continued interest and prestige, and MacArthur's support, the JCS might see their way to giving Kenney his wish. In China, Chennault wanted the B–29s so he could strike farther and hit more targets than were possible with B–24s. With Chiang's support and Roosevelt's sympathy, Chennault might get some of the new aircraft too. Hansell abhorred the idea of giving B–29s to local commanders; he knew that the B–29s were difficult to handle and had many developmental problems, and he feared, like Arnold, that once so lost, the strategic bombers might never be recovered for integral air operations. Moreover, JCS planners and even Air Staff members had considerable sympathy for such a use as Kenney proposed. Thus, the pressure on Arnold and his supporters to make a success of long-range bombing continued to increase.[76]

On February 6, 1944, as the organization and training of the XX Bomber Command continued, COA members rendered an early opinion on the use of very heavy bombers to the Air Staff. They prepared a memo listing their best opinion of the primary target systems within range of possible bases at Chengtu, Davao, and Saipan:

- Merchant shipping and harbor concentrations.

- Coke production in Manchuria, amounting to 56 percent of the total Japanese production.

- Urban industrial areas.

- Aircraft production, because all of the most important targets in the industry group could be hit from Saipan. (Virtually none, however, could be reached from Chengtu.)

- Antifriction bearings, also because the major targets in this category could be reached from Saipan.

- Electronics, because the industry was not well established in Japan, had little redundancy, and because of evident problems in production and distribution of parts such as radio and radar tubes.[77]

---

flying from India to China was too impractical, and Arnold judged it not worth the cost.

Taking the Offensive

The list produced in early 1944 resulted from considerable debate between members of the COA and representatives of the Air Staff intelligence office and the Navy. The Air Staff's intelligence people had advocated more emphasis on electronic systems and oil production. The February recommendations were something of a compromise, noting that attacks on oil were primarily a function of reducing shipping capability. Oil transport was ideally suited for submarine and air interdiction which, in turn, could be well cued by ULTRA sources, of which the COA was unaware. Electronics remained fairly high on the list, but the committee did not view electricity as a primary target because of Japan's decentralized power grids. In addition, the main hydroelectric plants were too well constructed and would probably withstand bombardment.[78] On April 6, the JCS issued a directive that cited the COA's target list as the one best suited for the B-29s. The JCS paper noted that the most promising early uses for the bombers were the Manchurian coke ovens and petroleum refineries in the NEI, primarily those at Palembang. Throughout 1944, the COA continued to study target systems in the light of newly developed intelligence information.[79]

The XX Bomber Command prepared for its deployment to China. One of the key members of the COA, Col. Guido Perera, became a permanent representative of the COA to the staff of the newly activated Twentieth Air Force, thus integrating more closely intelligence, COA evaluation, and operational employment of the B-29s. Hansell, the Twentieth's chief of staff, relied a great deal on the committee's advice.[80]

The first B-29 in a combat theater landed in India in April 1944; the first B-29 combat mission was a shakedown raid on Bangkok, Thailand, on June 5. Tactical operations of the XX Bomber Command from bases in China also began in June. Chengtu was the only base from which the B-29s could reach key Japanese facilities, and only a few were within range from there. Following the recommendations of the COA, on June 15, 1944, the coke ovens at the Imperial Iron and Steel Works at Yawata, Japan, became the first mission's primary target; secondary were the nearby coke and raw materials loading facilities at Laoyao harbor. Following the COA's recommendations and the lead of General Kenney (but with a target Kenney believed to be incorrect),* the oil refinery at Palembang was the next target, along with the Moesi River, which the B-29 crews mined to restrict river traffic to Palembang. The B-29s made but a single raid on Palembang, staging through Ceylon. The attack inflicted

---

*Kenney had argued for Balikpapan because his intelligence information showed it to be a far more important producer of oil products for the Japanese. Balikpapan, however, was beyond the range of B-29s flying from Ceylon. To hit Balikpapan, the aircraft would have had to use the base at Darwin, which Arnold and his people remained reluctant to do. Part of the reason for the target decision seems to have been the continuing fear that MacArthur, at Kenney's urging, might have tried to keep the planes in his theater and under his control.

little damage on the refinery, but all of the mines fell into the river channel. The XX Bomber Command directed subsequent missions at iron and steel plants at Anshan, Manchuria. Operations from China were few, as logistics problems and the difficulty of using the new, not fully developed B–29 greatly restricted flying. Frequent poor weather over the targets further hindered the overtaxed operations. Weather information had always been an important element in intelligence planning. Now it assumed an even greater role, yet there was no way to accurately forecast weather en route to or over a target so far away.

The problems were not unanticipated, and the XX Bomber Command's intelligence officers sought to alleviate some over which they had a measure of control. Chinese and Allied observation stations gathered and reported current weather data in an attempt to understand the Japanese cloud cover and winds they would encounter.[81] Much of the spring of 1944 saw the target section of the Assistant Chief of Staff, Intelligence of the XX Bomber Command preparing and assembling route and target materials, both radar and visual. By May 18, the individual bomb groups knew of steel and aluminum targets in Manchuria; they even had stereoscopic photographs. Four days later, the flyers had a preliminary estimate of the state of Japan's petroleum production. The operational intelligence section of the A–2 office prepared information on Japanese fighter tactics and combined that data with the enemy air OB in the areas of China and Japan over which the B–29s would fly. The staff reviewed or prepared air and ground rescue plans and issued training materials and equipment to aid crew members in escape and evasion should their aircraft be shot or forced down. The information was to stand many of the crews in good stead in the coming months.

In August 1944, a XX Bomber Command staff reorganization abolished the position of Assistant Chief of Staff, A–2, substituting a tri-deputy organization. Part of the reason this change was possible was the heavy involvement of the Air Staff A–2 in Washington, who did much of the target analysis work for the Twentieth Air Force. Intelligence in the XX Bomber Command became a section reduced in size under the Deputy Chief of Staff, Operations. Col. James D. Garcia became its chief. Some of the duties previously managed by A–2, such as search and rescue, moved to other staff agencies. To accommodate the smaller intelligence office, the commander discontinued various reports. During busy periods, outside personnel not fully employed elsewhere (and not necessarily qualified in intelligence work) were pressed into service.[82] In spite of the growing influence of Washington, a number of things simply could not be done outside of India and China.

The AAF and the Navy had since 1942 slowly expanded and improved their electronic warfare capabilities. Often the two services had worked together, reaping joint benefits. One result was that the B–29s came from the factory ready to incorporate a wide variety of radar and RCM equipment. On June 29, 1944, B–29s equipped with radar-detection and warning sets began

Taking the Offensive

recording the locations and characteristics of Japanese radar stations. The ferret aircraft continued to fly with each bombing mission; they also flew alone to map Japanese electronic defenses in eastern China and Manchuria, and later in the home islands. Data from these early recording missions and similar flights in Burma had considerably broadened Allied understanding of Japanese radar. The American bomber crews quickly began using their detection equipment to avoid AA defenses by taking evasive action when their ships came under observation and fire.[83]

Maps of AA gun positions prepared by the A–2 supplemented the radar information. The maps issued to flight crews indicated the locations, types of guns, their estimated number, and any detected patterns of movement between locations. Within a short time, the Americans had drawn fairly comprehensive maps of enemy defenses. This information allowed for flight planning that took advantage of open areas to reduce the likelihood of detection and the risk of aircraft damage by Japanese gunfire. At the same time, a flight of B–29 photoreconnaissance aircraft greatly improved target information by mapping large areas of China, Manchuria, and Korea. To support MacArthur's drive through the Philippines and Nimitz's seizure of Okinawa, the photo B–29s also covered both Okinawa and Luzon.[84]

By the summer of 1944, Japan's strategic position no longer seemed as favorable as it had been a year earlier. In order to capitalize on any apparent weakness, General Arnold directed committee analysts to review their report and either validate their original recommendations or create a new target priority list. In that review, completed on October 10, 1944, the committee recommended B–29 attacks on the Japanese aircraft industry and urban industrial areas and, where feasible, their mining of sea lanes. In a disquieting note, the COA observed that "lack of information remains a major obstacle to careful target selection." To correct the problem, it recommended increased efforts at reconnaissance and other information gathering, such as POW interrogations and technical analyses of captured documents and equipment.[85] The problem of inadequate knowledge of Japanese target areas was shortly to assume greater importance.

The COA's recommendations, and the information gathering and mapping done by the XX Bomber Command's intelligence staff, became the basis of B–29 operations from Chengtu. As a result of his unhappiness over the performance of the bombers, Arnold fired General Wolfe (who returned to the States) and replaced him with General LeMay on August 29, 1944. LeMay was a known perfectionist. He insisted on mission accomplishment, but his demands conflicted with the very imperfect understanding of enemy targets.[86]

In the Pacific, east of China, B–29s of Hansell's XXI Bomber Command began landing on Saipan in mid-October 1944, as soon after that island's capture as their airfields were ready. When Hansell's crews arrived, they, like LeMay's, found target information poor. Photoreconnaissance of Japan had

335

Piercing the Fog

Maj. Gen. Kenneth B. Wolfe

Brig. Gen. Curtis E. LeMay

been nil except for the limited work done by XX Bomber Command flying from China. Radar maps were not ready, either, so early radar bombing had to depend on educated guesses by the bombardiers as much as on anything else. The XXI Bomber Command stood ready to bomb Japan, but Hansell lacked much of the target data and weather information to do a credible job.[87]

Not until November 1, 1944, did Hansell have a photoreconnaissance version of the B–29 (called the F–13) to survey Japan. On that day, the first plane of that type in the Pacific arrived from the United States, and the crew made an immediate run over Japan. Luckily, the weather was clear. The men took some 7,000 pictures of the Tokyo and Nagoya areas. There followed in the next few days 16 more photography runs, some of which found virtually complete cloud cover, obscuring the land below. Cloud cover was to become an increasingly greater problem for the B–29s, forcing commanders into decisions made from a narrowing list of options. Although Japanese air defenses made a concerted effort to attack the reconnaissance aircraft, either their fighter controllers and pilots could not gauge correctly the F–13's speed and altitude, or their fighters could not reach the high-flying airplane. By November 24, the date of the XXI's first mission to bomb Japan, enough information existed to plot the main targets. The first target for Hansell's bombers was the Musashino plant of the Nakajima Aircraft Company, located near Tokyo. Based on studies of maker's plates from crashed Japanese aircraft, air intelligence specialists believed that the plant produced an estimated 30–40 percent of all Japanese aircraft engines. Besides its being a major weapons production facility, the Americans believed that if they struck a plant close to Tokyo, the will of the

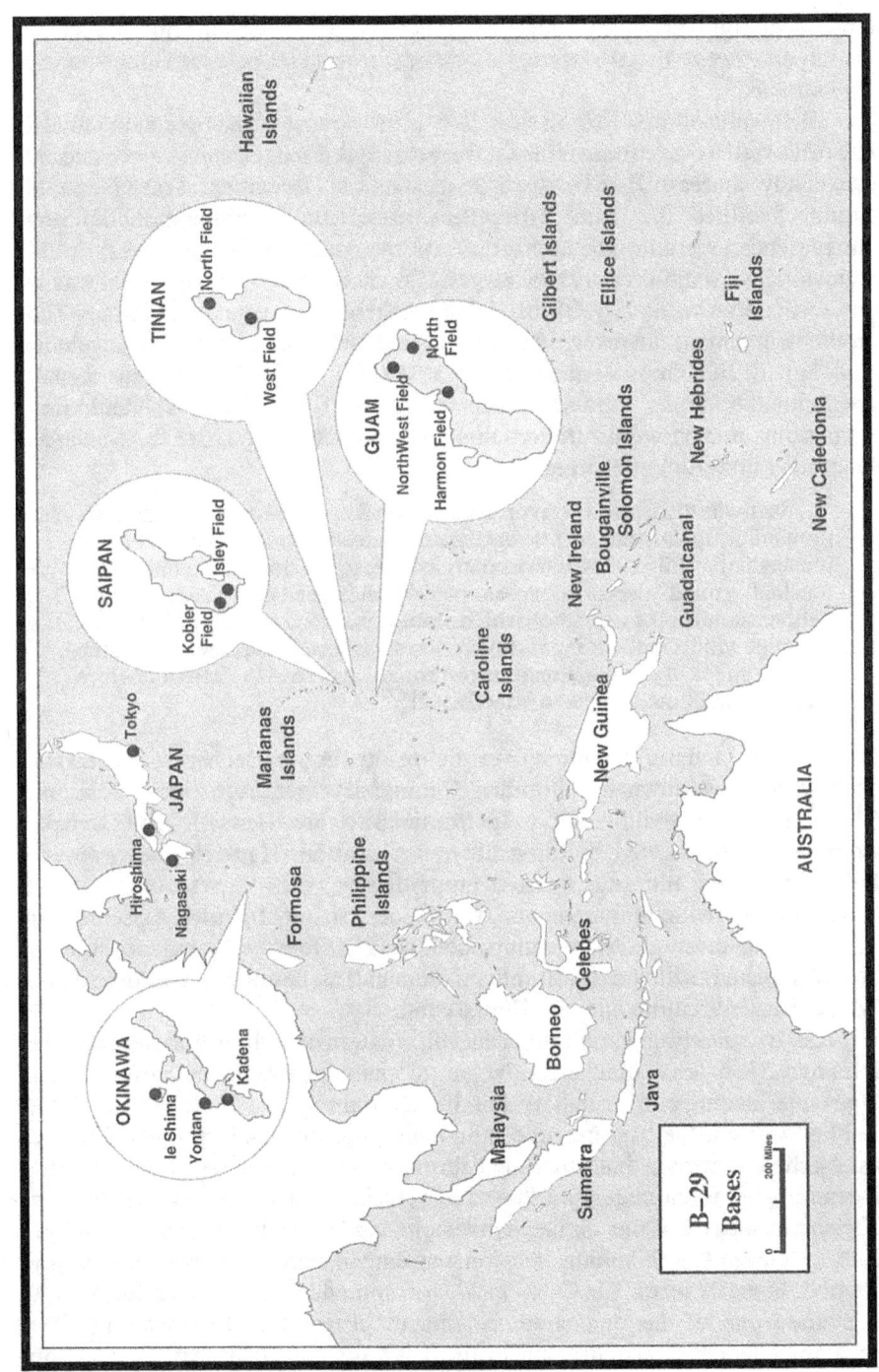

Japanese to fight might be weakened. At the very least, the attack on Musashino would serve notice that the strategic bomber force had the power to hit whatever it wanted to.[88]

The results of that first mission, like those of most of the precision attacks that followed in the ensuing months, were disappointing. Despite an occasional reasonably successful strike, such as the one on December 18 at Nagoya's aircraft facilities, the main difficulties arose from a combination of crew inexperience, operating the aircraft at extreme range limits, and, worst of all, atmospheric conditions over the targets. Cloud cover was no new problem for the AAF; air crews had lived with it for more than two years over Europe. The problem in Japan, however, was compounded by the extreme wind velocities—up to 200 knots—encountered at 25,000 to 30,000 feet, the normal preplanned bombing altitudes. Attempting to fly in tight, self-defending formations in such winds proved almost impossible; worse, if the formation succeeded in finding the target,

> . . . drift was difficult to correct and bomb runs had to be charted directly upwind or downwind. Attacking Japan's best-defended cities directly in the teeth of a 200-knot wind was unthinkable; going downwind the B–29s reached ground speeds in excess of 500 miles per hour, in which case neither bombsights nor bombardiers could function properly. Moreover, the high winds made it impossible for crews to make a second pass if the run-in failed; if a navigational error brought a plane in downwind from target it might not be able to attack at all.[89]

Early in January, impatient over the results thus far achieved and having decided to close down XX Bomber Command's operations from India and China, Arnold moved the unit to the Marianas to join Hansell's XXI Bomber Command and directed a full-scale reorganization. Hansell was relieved; LeMay replaced him and reported immediately, with the remainder of his command following in increments over the next several months. As senior air officer in the theater, LeMay commanded the XXI Bomber Command, soon to be redesignated, with the XX Bomber Command, as Twentieth Air Force. Like Wolfe, Hansell returned the the United States.

LeMay quickly departed from Hansell's pattern of high-altitude attacks. He introduced low-level attacks and began to conduct experiments with various types and loadings of incendiary bombs. On the night of March 9/10, 1945, LeMay sent out the first massive, low-level, night incendiary raid. The raid established a pattern that continued through July, interrupted by a lengthy incendiary bomb shortage, by a short diversion in April of bombing airfields on Kyushu in support of the Okinawa invasion, and by the minelaying campaign. LeMay's incendiary bombing decision was long in coming, having been amply studied for many years. The COA's 1943 recommendations on Japanese targets contained one of the first endorsements of urban-area fire bombing. The recommendation appeared again in the 1944 review of the earlier work on

Taking the Offensive

Japan. The committee assumed, for the first part of its report, that Japan was to be defeated by combined aerial bombardment and naval blockade, to include mining of the seaways. In its report to Arnold, the COA reiterated the refrain that ran through its deliberations the previous year, telling the commanding general that a "lack of intelligence remains a major obstacle to careful target selection." Nevertheless, the committee also recommended a strategic bombing campaign to encompass antishipping attacks and attacks on the aircraft industry, as well as attacks on urban areas, followed by a review to determine what changes might then be needed. For the second portion of the report, which dealt with an invasion of Japan, the COA recommended "an attack on the aircraft industry and on urban industrial areas and an intensification of the attack on shipping by all available methods [including B–29s]."[90] During the same time, AAF intelligence officers prepared several studies along similar lines, but with more specifics.

Lacking full knowledge of Japan, the A–2 staff based their calculations supporting urban area attack recommendations on the damage inflicted by the RAF Bomber Command on German cities during 1943. The data that air intelligence used came from appraisals of aerial photographs of German cities and industrial areas, the tonnage of bombs dropped, and reports originating from unspecified *ground intelligence* sources (much of it apparently ULTRA) on the continent. Using this information, and comparing the relationships between urban area destruction and apparent effects on industrial production for the hardest hit cities, the A–2's vulnerability specialists tried to determine the probable impact of urban attacks. Their work was inconclusive. They believed, however, that to affect production, bombardment had to destroy at least 30 percent of the housing that supported it. Extrapolating from the effects of the September 1, 1923, earthquake and fire that destroyed much of Tokyo and Yokohama, A–2 analysts prepared some rough guidelines for attacking Japanese urban areas. The COA then modified these guidelines in their November 1944 revised report on Japan. The committee concluded that attacks would be effective if "On each urban industrial area they were pressed to the point of over fifty percent damage within about a month, and attacks on the most important urban industrial areas were completed within two or three months."[91]

The idea of firebombing Japanese cities was more than just an analytical proposal by some of the A–2 staff forwarded by the COA; it caught on within the AAF at a much more practical level. Late in 1943 the Chemical Warfare Service began a series of incendiary bomb tests at Dugway Proving Ground, Utah. The tests involved, so the AAF's senior chemical officer told the chief of the air staff, a prototype village, ". . . the construction of which was as nearly Japanese as could be reproduced in this country."[92] By dropping large quantities of various types of incendiary bombs on the village, the Chemical Warfare Service concluded that the six-pound, oil-filled bomb probably would be most effective on Japanese urban areas. Separately, in January 1944, Arnold visited

Piercing the Fog

Eglin Army Air Field, Florida; while there, he initiated another effort to test incendiary weapons for use on Japan. These latter evaluations continued into the summer of 1944, using as targets several small, wooden villages constructed for the purpose. At Eglin, the testing showed promise as a means of predicting the damage that combustible buildings would sustain when hit by certain mixtures of high-explosive and incendiary bombs. Again, as in Utah the previous year, the six-pound bomb was most effective at starting a conflagration that existing firefighting equipment could not control. As demonstrated at Dugway and Eglin, the potential for incendiary attacks matched the prospects in the COA's examination of the topic, but the final decision on the matter came about for reasons far more complex than just weather and winds, or the nature of Japanese targets.[93]

Although the primary B–29 offensive had gotten underway from the Marianas in November 1944, the results had not met expectations. The number of sorties was less than desired, while target damage seemed to be less than necessary to reduce Japan's continued resistance. High winds, poor weather, the need for more crew training, and disappointing accuracy from radar bombing—all contributed to the poor showing. In Washington, Arnold experienced increasing pressure to make the B–29s live up to his claims. Between September 1942, when the new aircraft first flew, and the start of operations in China in 1944, the B–29 had shown continued development problems. The Wright R–3350 engine was prone to catch fire, and many types of equipment subassemblies could not be delivered to meet assembly-line demands. Tools and necessary ground equipment for the huge airplane were in short supply, and the AAF lacked the experience needed to absorb the aircraft, with its attendant development difficulties, and to create operational bomber groups. The B–29s failed to meet Arnold's expectations when flying from Chinese bases, and he replaced the first commander there with LeMay, who showed decided promise as a tough organizer and leader. Yet congressional critics and doubtful senior military officers were prepared to compare the high and growing costs of the B–29 program to its continued troubles. Arnold, as the airplane's main proponent, was their chief target.[94] All of these factors plus the generally accepted intelligence analysis that postulated Japanese manufacturing dependence on innumerable small workshops in urban areas surrounding the factories combined over time to move the American strategic air campaign away from precision daylight bombing.

There appears to have been no operations order issued by Twentieth Air Force headquarters in Washington to start the urban bombing campaign directed at destroying many of Japan's major cities. There are, however, substantial records that trace the process of the decision and illustrate the role of intelligence in that process. LeMay had become familiar with the potential represented by incendiary bombs while in Europe, and in December 1944 his B–29s in China teamed up with Chennault's Fourteenth Air Force to destroy with incendiaries large portions of the Japanese dock and storage areas along the Yangtze River in Hankow. In that raid, the B–29s arrived over the target in four distinct groups, each carrying a different type of incendiary bomb, as if to test which was best. Confusion in scheduling and as a result of heavy smoke raised by the first bombs dropped caused several sections of aircraft to miss their targets, considerably diminishing the effectiveness of the raid. Nevertheless, riverfront buildings and some other Chinese-occupied parts of the city suffered extensive damage. Interviewed twenty years after the war, LeMay took only partial credit for the decision to use incendiaries on Japanese cities in 1945, saying it was a "combination of several people's ideas."[95]

Brig. Gen. Lauris Norstad, serving in Washington as Twentieth Air Force's chief of staff, seems to have been one of those to whom LeMay referred, a key player in the evolution of the firebombing decision. Norstad's position made him the intermediary, not only between the ever-impatient Arnold and his proxies in the Pacific—first Hansell and then LeMay—but also between the A–2, the JTG, and the operational commanders. Relying on the A–2's and COA's analyses and the plans for the Twentieth that envisioned urban-area attacks as a last resort, Norstad had agitated for incendiary bombing since November. The apparent success at Hankow fortified his position. Pushed by Norstad toward a fire raid on Nagoya, Hansell objected that the tactic was inappropriate and not compatible with the mission of "destruction of primary targets by sustained air attacks using precision bombing methods both visual and radar." Hansell's case was not strong; he still lacked the intelligence needed to locate enough primary targets to bring the Japanese to conclude the war. Norstad relented temporarily, but he continued to discuss the matter with

Brig. Gen. Lauris Norstad

Piercing the Fog

Arnold, telling him on January 2, 1945, of an incendiary test set for the near future.[96] That test, made by Hansell the next day, proved inconclusive; clouds and smoke obscured the scene from photoreconnaissance and from the intelligence officers on Guam for some days.

Summoned from China to Guam early in January, Curtis LeMay found he was to replace Hansell. Arnold, pressed by the JCS to get results with the B–29s and increasingly frustrated with what he viewed as a lagging effort, had decided on a new commander. Because Arnold did not wish to fire Hansell himself, Norstad carried the message to both men in the Marianas. Within a few days, Arnold suffered a serious heart attack and was temporarily removed from participation in the course of the decision. For his part, LeMay knew full well that he was expected to find success, and to do so soon. Although incendiary attacks occurred only after much discussion in Washington, the final decision resulted from a chain of circumstances. LeMay, seeing little chance of success for precision bombing because of the winds aloft and heavy cloud cover over Japan, decided to use night, low-level delivery of incendiary bombs, beginning with a March 9/10, 1945, raid on Tokyo. That decision, though LeMay's in form, had a much different substance. In April 1945, LeMay wrote Arnold that ". . . during my first six weeks [at XXI Bomber Command in the Marianas] we had one operational shot at a target." LeMay added that he found the poor weather, which nullified any chance for precision, high-altitude bombing by almost constantly obscuring the targets, to be his ". . . worst operational enemy."[97] LeMay well understood the stress under which Arnold operated as commander of the Washington-controlled Twentieth Air Force, a radical departure from the rule that the theater commander would control all military assets in the area. Both men desired intensely that the strategic air force succeed in its mission of forcing Japan's capitulation before the scheduled November 1945 invasion of Kyushu, Japan's southernmost main island.

Reading the COA and A–2 analytical studies of the layout and composition of major Japanese cities, LeMay believed that incendiary attacks would succeed. The test bombing of January, although inconclusive, had yielded some encouraging results along the lines predicted, supporting the work in Washington and at the proving grounds in Florida and Utah. Local intelligence analysis of Japanese flak defenses indicated to LeMay that they were much lighter and less accurate than those he and his men had faced over Germany. By opting for a night attack, LeMay further reduced the risk; intelligence studies and the air OB summary, produced from ULTRA by MIS, indicated that Japan had a negligible radar-directed night-fighter capability. General LeMay believed that he could afford a low-level approach that stood a good chance of success, yet one that did not depend upon the poorly developed art of long-distance meteorology. LeMay's decision seized upon the clearest course of action, one long spelled out in studies of targets and Japanese defenses that both the Air Staff and his staff on Guam had made. The first major fire raid on Tokyo

Taking the Offensive

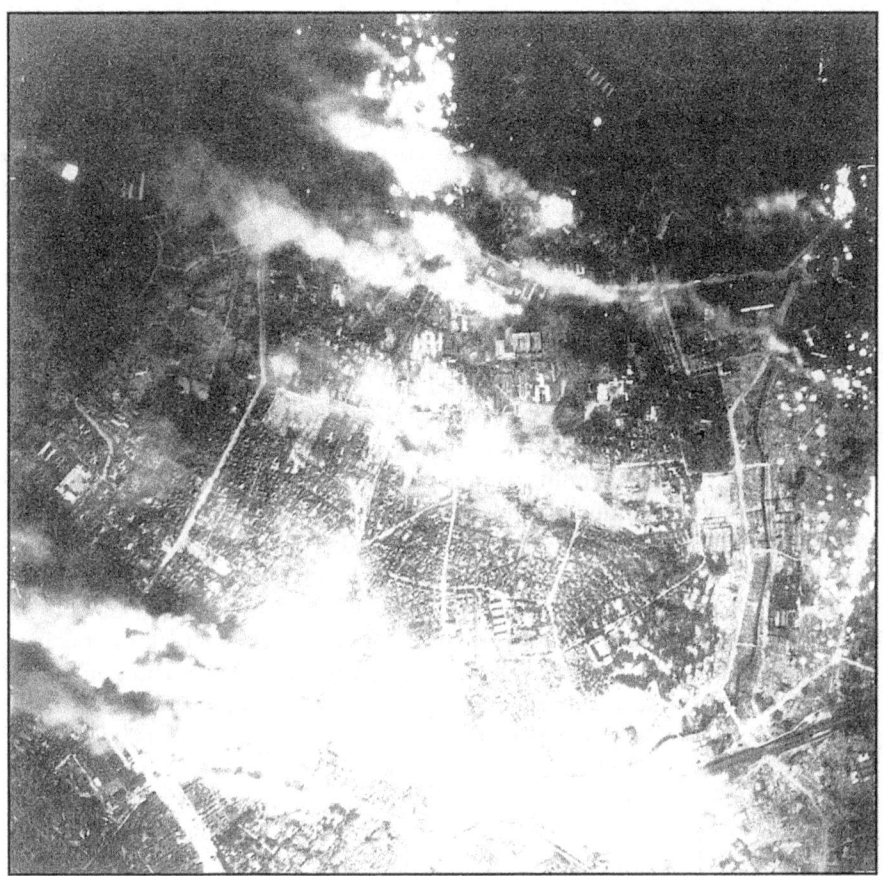

Photo of one of the fire-bomb raids on Tokyo by Twentieth Air Force B-29s.

consumed one-fourth of the city's buildings; in terms of casualties, it was the single most destructive attack upon any Japanese city during the war. Much of the specific target planning for that raid and others following it had been done in Washington, where the Air Staff selected the impact areas as a compromise between industrial importance and susceptibility to fire. But the Air Staff's deliberations had long suffered from an incomplete understanding of Japan. As the planners' confidence in the tactic grew, they placed greater stress on hitting the industrial areas in the major Japanese cities.[98]

Urban-area attacks were necessary to end the war sooner than would have occurred otherwise, and despite the continuing discussion of the propriety of firebombs as weapons used this way, those who decided the issue in 1945 did so after extended consideration. LeMay himself was careful to reason through the many tactical aspects of the problem. Although he has stated publicly that he alone made the final decision on the use of incendiary weapons on Japanese cities, he had reached that point as the final player in a year's long process of group dynamics.[99]

Precedent in the AAF existed for LeMay's action, as did substantial pressure for it from the highest levels in the service. When he carried the news of LeMay's appointment to command the XXI Bomber Command on Guam, Lauris Norstad told him to solve the training problems, deal with the high winds and bad weather, and get the job done, or, as LeMay recalled, "If you don't get results, you'll be fired. If you don't get results, also, there'll never be any Strategic Air Forces of the Pacific. . . . If you don't get results it will mean eventually a mass amphibious invasion of Japan, to cost probably half a million more American lives."[100]

Norstad's remarks could not be taken lightly. The weapons had been shipped to the Pacific and were available, and there seems to have been a clear acceptance by General Arnold that the tactic was to be used. The Eighth Air Force had dropped a limited number of incendiary weapons on German targets, notably the heavy attack on transportation and administration centers of Berlin on February 3, 1945.[101] In the Far East, the Hangkow raid and the test incendiary bombing of Nagoya, made over Haywood Hansell's objections, indicated a willingness to depart from the doctrinal policy of attacking specific military or war-support targets with precision bombing. Precision bombing had not been very accurate, and the constant pressure of proving that the B–29 was worth its cost led first to Norstad's and then to LeMay's decision to use firebombing. The immediate reasons for the attacks on Japan's urban areas derived not just from bureaucratic and political pressures, but also from the demands of warfare and the wish to use the fastest, most effective method to end the war. In this regard, the perceived lack of intelligence about Japanese targets that existed for years at the A–2 office in the Pentagon and later on Guam played strongly in the minds of all the participants. The lack of clarity about the targets, and about Japan's true capacity to resist to the end by inflicting heavy losses on an invader, was a powerful consideration.

XXI Bomber Command's difficulties with the weather over Japan were complicated by the fact that even in late 1944, no liaison existed between the Joint Intelligence Center in Honolulu and the Twentieth Air Force, even though JICPOA had for years been reading the Japanese weather observation radio traffic. In fact, for much of Hansell's time with the XXI Bomber Command, no SSO was available to support him. When finally an SSO did arrive at Hansell's headquarters, he had to fill in for the A–2 and assistant A–2, both of whom were delayed by an air crash on Eniwetok. This meant that the SSO, Maj. Charles T. Kingston, could do little else until early January.[102] When JICPOA's Air Estimates Group moved from Hawaii to Guam in April 1945, special intelligence became much more readily available to the airmen. By then ULTRA's capabilities had, in many ways, become superfluous.[103]

Taking the Offensive

The crew of the B–29 Enola Gay. Col. Paul W. Tibbetts *(center, wearing khakis)* was commander of the 509th Composite Bomb Group and pilot on the first mission to drop an atomic bomb.

One of the most productive AAF uses of intelligence late in the war benefited the antishipping campaign. This joint AAF-Navy effort drew upon the previous Seventh Air Force experience in the Bonins and saw an extensive seeding of naval mines by B–29s. The newly laid minefields radically affected Japanese shipping by either sinking a number of vessels that had the misfortune to encounter them or isolating ships in harbors with unswept approaches. Japanese records reported that the aerial mining campaign sank or badly damaged 670 ships, including 65 combat ships, after March 1, 1945. Mines accounted for 63 percent of all Japanese merchant shipping losses during the final half-year of the war. Aerial delivery of naval mines depended heavily on adequate intelligence. The 313th Bombardment Wing carried the mines to Japan's ports and the Inland Sea, based on an assessment of the most vulnerable sea lanes and harbors and an analysis of Japanese mine-clearing efforts. An extensive target study indicated that delivery was best made at night from altitudes of 5,000–8,000 feet. Follow-up reconnaissance surveys indicated where the Japanese had swept channels. Regular remining promptly closed these routes. The result was an almost complete cessation of Japanese shipping after March 1945.[104]

On July 19, 1945, General Carl A. Spaatz arrived on Guam to command the newly organized U.S. Army Strategic Air Forces (USASTAF), composed of the Twentieth and the Eighth Air Forces plus much of AAFPOA's staff and support functions. The Eighth had recently transferred without aircraft from Europe and was to be equipped with B–29s on Okinawa. The creation of the Strategic Air Forces did not, however, bring all of the intelligence planning under its headquarters' A–2, Brig. Gen. Norris B. Harbold. Harbold served as one of five assistant chiefs of staff: A–1 was personnel and administration; A–2, intelligence; A–3, operations; A–4, transportation, supply, maintenance, and logistics; and A–5 encompassed strategic planning and policy, organizational requirements, unit moves, and plans liaison. Under General Spaatz's direction, the headquarters staff was to be streamlined, with its effort confined to planning and supervising the Eighth and Twentieth. Also in the headquarters were seven special sections, including a Joint Target Committee. Clearly, Spaatz wanted to recreate his successful European experiences in the Pacific. The A–2's function in this arrangement was to direct the collection, evaluation, and dissemination of information about the enemy's capabilities. The A–2 office had divisions dealing with operations reporting, air liaison, special intelligence, central evaluation and interpretation, photoreconnaissance, target matters, processing, interpretation and reproduction of photographic and related materials, and intelligence liaison. Twenty officers performed all of this work; in the headquarters, only the A–5, with eleven officers, was smaller. Spaatz expected that much of the staff work, including intelligence, would be done by the two numbered air forces.[105]

The task facing the Strategic Air Forces' planners was clear: effect the final defeat of Japan. Although nobody foresaw Japan's immediate collapse, the warfighting means available to the USASTAF included a wholly new type of weapon—nuclear explosives. The 509th Composite Group, selected and trained to drop the atomic weapons, had its headquarters in a compound on North Field, Tinian, where it awaited word to fly its missions. Spaatz, on leaving Washington, brought instructions that the atomic bombing was to begin after August 3; he also received the target list based upon planning done in Washington. There was little more for him to do except carry out the instructions, although he did have the authority to select the day and time to accord with weather and tactical considerations. LeMay, who had recently become Chief of Staff, Twentieth Air Force, saw to the final mission planning, meeting with the 509th's commander, Col. Paul W. Tibbets, and the bombardier, Maj. Thomas Ferebee, to select the aiming point for Hiroshima. The Aioi Bridge, near *Second Army* headquarters, was the best and most recognizable spot; it had been amply depicted in aerial reconnaissance photographs. Weather over Japan, the old bugaboo for the B–29s from as far back as the China operations, remained the key factor. When

Taking the Offensive

The mushroom-shaped cloud from the second and last atomic bomb dropped on Japan—target Nagasaki.

on August 5 the forecast for Hiroshima seemed favorable, Spaatz decided to go the next day. En route to Hiroshima, the three B–29s avoided heavy flak concentrations. On board, the RCM specialist checked to see that the frequencies where the bomb's radar proximity fuze operated were clear; they were, and there was no danger of a premature detonation. Finding the clouds broken enough to allow visual release, Major Ferebee dropped the weapon at 8:15 AM Hiroshima time.[106]

CHAPTER 7

Planning the Defeat of Japan: The A–2 in Washington, 1943–1945

BASED UPON THE EXPERIENCES of the first two years of fighting, the AAF had matured considerably by the spring of 1943. Similarly, the Air Staff's intelligence capabilities and performance matured. Close relationships had grown between the offices of A–2 and RAF intelligence, as well as with the U.S. Navy and theater air commanders. Still lingering were the competing interests of the War Department's G–2 and its air section; that competition continued to trouble air intelligence throughout the remaining war years as the nascent AAF's leaders sought to assert their independence.

By early 1943, the COA, based upon intelligence information available for Germany, completed one of the most far-reaching analytical efforts of the war, with recommendations for the air campaign in Europe (see Chapter 4). General Arnold received the committee's report in March 1943 and sent it immediately to Ira Eaker, his air commander in London. There Eaker, his staff, and RAF representatives extensively reviewed the COA's work. Eaker then flew to Washington and, on May 18, presented his views of the report to the JCS and the CCS. Both groups of senior officers, already familiar with the scope and purposes of the COA's work, approved it as written that day.[1] The approved report and Eaker's plan accompanying it became the basis for the Allied CBO that continued virtually to the end of the fighting in Europe. The completion of the committee's report was one of the last major efforts of the Air Staff A–2 to participate in the field of operational intelligence for Europe and the Mediterranean. For the remainder of the war, the A–2's office worked to influence the planning and operations against the Japanese in the Pacific war.

In Europe, the air intelligence functions of the Eighth, Ninth, Twelfth, and Fifteenth Air Forces increasingly gained confidence throughout the final years of the conflict. The American air intelligence staffs of the numbered air forces worked under the tutelage of the more experienced and extensive RAF intelligence structure and personnel, with the Allied air operations guided by centralized analysis of the German and Italian enemies. From its inception, operational air intelligence for the CBO was done largely in London, with some completed in Italy for use by the Fifteenth Air Force. ULTRA material drawn from Japanese sources flowed from Washington to Europe on completion of the Anglo-American intelligence-sharing agreement in mid-1943. The eastward flow, however, was far less than the amount of similar material on Germany derived by the British Government Code and Cypher School's ULTRA operation at BP.

The success of the air intelligence arrangement in the European-Mediterranean region led the Anglo-American Allies to divide intelligence worldwide along more formal lines. In February 1944, the RAF, U.S. Navy, U.S. Army's G–2, and AAF concluded an agreement giving the Americans primary responsibility for air intelligence collection and analysis in support of the war with Japan. Despite the intelligence rivalries, the Americans had come to realize that dividing intelligence activities among the agencies best able to meet the particular requirements of that field would be the most effective way to pursue the gathering of information about Japanese capabilities and intentions. Deciding how to apportion those responsibilities was not a simple task.

Tactical air warfare in the Pacific and Far East was the province of the Navy, of Marine Corps aviation, of the AAF's numbered air forces' commanders, and of the various Allied air forces. That region, far from Washington, had no central air intelligence function, although the different AAF commands produced some first-rate analytical products and exchanged information with one another and with Nimitz's Navy headquarters in Honolulu. Radio intercept operations of the Army and Navy in Washington and Honolulu sponsored the very important collection and preparation of periodic air OB lists, which supported the various tactical air campaigns. Much more work had to be done to support the planned strategic bomber offensive of the Twentieth Air Force. AAF headquarters in Washington also served as the staff of the Twentieth, and the A–2 quickly assumed a significant part of the role of intelligence support for the B–29 very long-range bomber program. The problems facing the target planners were considerable, for they had little data about Japan on which to base a coherent analysis or to create target charts. This had already been recognized in the spring of 1943 when a major reorganization of the A–2 office aimed at improving intelligence production. That reorganization, however, was but one of many that accompanied the changes incident upon the relentless Allied prosecution of the war against Japan.[2]

The period 1943–1945 in Washington saw five men serve as AC/AS, Intelligence, a turnover rate that produced problems. Brig. Gen. Edgar P. Sorenson held the job from June 22, 1942, until October 22, 1943; he served also as a member of the COA. He seems to have left in some disfavor, as Arnold was not happy with the overall state of air intelligence and possibly also with Sorenson's opposition to the COA's recommendations about Japan and to the COA's very existence. The next incumbent, Maj. Gen. Clayton Bissell, served for only a few months before handing the job to Brig. Gen. Thomas D. White

Planning the Defeat of Japan

General Thomas D. White

Maj. Gen. James P. Hodges

(later to become Air Force Chief of Staff). White held the post for nine months, from January 5 to September 4, 1944, during which he tried unsuccessfully to get G–2 to relinquish the function of air intelligence to his office. Before returning to the Pacific, White sent a memo to General McDonald in London, at the bottom of which he wrote a postscript, "I have never had an unhappier job tho' few people know it; A–2 will forever suck hind tit in the AAF."[3] That thought would have held cold comfort for White's successor, Maj. Gen. James P. Hodges, who got the job September 2, 1944, after his B–24s in France, pressed into a tactical role to help the Allied breakout in Normandy, released their bombs in confusion away from the bomb line, killing Lt. Gen. Leslie J. McNair and a number of others. Hodges's tenure lasted less than a year, and when he left on June 1, 1945, Maj. Gen. Elwood R. Quesada returned from Europe and command of the IX TAC to take the job.

The wartime incumbents of the A–2 office were not chosen at random, nor were they without experience for the taxing job. Bissell, for all of his fusty personality and the dislike he engendered in people like Kenney and Chennault (see Chapters 5 and 6), was in Arnold's eyes, "an excellent staff officer who carefully worked out every operation before he undertook it, or said he could not do it."[4] White, during the interwar years, had served as air attaché to France and the Soviet Union. His experience and judgment were so well regarded that in August 1939 the chief of the Air Corps' Plans Division requested he be appointed to a board of officers to study "the scope and form of the military intelligence required for the initial operations of Air Corps units; as to the means of obtaining and processing the information required, and as to the Air Corps intelligence procedure." Despite the embarrassment attendant on General Hodges's transfer from Europe to the A–2 job, he, too, had been requested as a member of the August 1939 intelligence study board. Hodges as well as White understood the relationship among intelligence collection, analysis, and dissemination for air operations.[5]

Arnold, the commanding general who presided over the AAF throughout the war, quickly came to appreciate the importance of comprehensive, well-founded air intelligence. At first he lacked the time to pursue the subject extensively and was not privy to all the intelligence that pertained to the AAF. Writing after the war, he noted that before the conflict began, ". . . one of the most wasteful weaknesses in our whole setup was our lack of a proper Air Intelligence Organization. . . . I know now there were American journalists and ordinary travelers in Germany who knew more about the *Luftwaffe*'s preparations than I, the Assistant Chief of the United States Army Air Corps." Arnold's postwar assessment of the information gained from the Spanish Civil War was that the U.S. Army's flyers knew less than half of what they should have about German air operations. He regretted that the Army had no effective way to rectify that situation, since the attaché system usually provided only the most cursory and inadequate reports.[6]

Before the war, Arnold was busy trying to coax money from Congress and obtain support within the Army for greater aircraft production and crew training. He did not then have access to the products of what came to be called the MAGIC *Diplomatic Summaries* and to the other decryption efforts that were, as yet, extremely limited. As Arnold admitted in his postwar autobiography, he did not fully understand the thrust of the Japanese air and naval expansion within her mandated Pacific territories. He quickly acquired a greater appreciation of intelligence; it was he who arranged for the aerial photography of Japanese islands by B–17s en route to the Philippines in November 1941. In 1942, when he dispatched Cooper to be Chennault's chief of staff (Cooper simultaneously served as the A–2 in China), Arnold took advantage of Colonel Cooper's prewar experience in Russia. Cooper, the peripatetic adventurer, flyer, and motion-picture director, was to learn all he could of the Soviet-Japanese situation in Siberia, including the locations of Soviet airfields the United States might be able to use. He was to report his information directly and secretly to Arnold.[7]

Throughout the war, Arnold continued his personal intelligence-gathering efforts, either through agents like Colonel Cooper or personally in his conversations with other commanders or world leaders. The commanding general remained displeased with the official arrangement of his A–2's relationship to the War Department's G–2. The G–2, so he believed, had not allowed the AAF's intelligence office freedom of operation to perform air intelligence work as it saw fit because the G–2 feared such duplication would

Planning the Defeat of Japan

diminish its own authority and position. Before the war, Arnold noted, G–2 had not allowed the AAF to assemble its own target folders on locations in possible enemy countries. Later, when the AAF desperately needed such information, the service had to seek out knowledgeable civilians who had worked on the financing or construction of facilities in Germany and Italy. When Arnold or his people had particular trouble getting data on Japan or Japanese-occupied areas, he often turned to Brig. Gen. William Donovan, whose OSS he respected, but even that source was not overly fruitful. In summary, Arnold came to believe that the intelligence departments of the old Army and the old Navy were not prepared for the new kind of warfare, nor were they ready to adapt to the needs of a large, modern air force in a global conflict. At the same time, the inability of the War Department's G–2 to comprehend the needs of aerial warfare left the AAF's intelligence office in the difficult position of trying to make up for lost opportunities while meeting resistance within the Army itself to its growing responsibilities.[8]

General Arnold's access to ULTRA information (and access by the people on the AAF's staff in Washington) came slowly. At the time of Pearl Harbor, he did not see the decrypted Japanese messages, although he had occasionally heard bits and pieces of information in conversations with General Marshall or Admiral Stark. After the Japanese attack, the AAF Commanding General regularly read the *MAGIC Diplomatic Summaries,* yet in September 1943, when C Section of Special Branch began to draw from ULTRA, appending a military and naval supplement to the *MAGIC Summary* for select readers, Arnold was not among them. In February 1944, a separate Japanese (later called the Far East) summary appeared along with a European summary, replacing the military and naval supplements. Although at some point Arnold and his staff began reading the ULTRA-based supplements, the date is unclear, as no records of the specific grant of access exist. Originally, only the Chief of Staff, the Army's Assistant Chief of Staff, Operations Plans, and the G–2 received the MAGIC supplements and the summaries.[9] George Marshall did not during the war grant Arnold formal access to ULTRA, but clearly Arnold learned of the effort, probably from several sources. It is very difficult to believe, for instance, that George Kenney in March 1943 would have talked to his commanding general, whom he had known well for many years, described the battle of the Bismarck Sea, and not mentioned the origin of MacArthur's information that had led to the victory. Arnold surely would have realized the implications of what he heard. Again, when in July 1943, Air Chief Marshal Portal, chief of the RAF's Air Staff, sent his emissary to Arnold's office to discuss the nature and location of expanded German fighter production, most probably the intelligence source for that information was stated, if mutedly.[10]

Arnold's lack of complete access to the sensitive intelligence material was not the serious impediment it might have been. ULTRA-derived operational intelligence went from Great Britain to Washington, but only slowly at first. In

Piercing the Fog

the fall of 1943, cryptographic intelligence played a far less important role in Washington than it did in Europe. For the AAF staff, concerned more with logistics, training, and deployment matters, this hardly constituted a serious flaw in their day-to-day work or in the AAF's headquarters operations.

From his Washington office, Arnold kept a close eye on his men in the field. The air commanders in war theaters, and Allied airmen as well, could expect to hear from him if he believed their judgment wanting. In the autumn of 1943, he became exasperated at what he saw as the inadequate use of combat intelligence during the Regensburg raid. Before the attack on Regensburg, Arnold had been pushing Ira Eaker to step up the level of bombing directed at GAF production sources as a way of reducing Germany's air power prior to an invasion of Europe. At the same time, Arnold had sought to have Portal use his RAF fighter force offensively, to help protect the bombers as far as their range would allow. On October 14, 1943, he wrote Portal to express some of his unhappiness with the progress of the CBO. After chiding Portal for not following up on his previous pleas for greater fighter involvement, Arnold remonstrated:

> In the case of the Regensburg raid [of August 17, in which the Eighth Air Force lost thirty-six B–17s], for example, it was known in England that fighters had moved south from Denmark and north from Brest to German and northern French bases to meet the Regensburg bombers and to stop them on their withdrawal. At the time, we apparently had the great majority of the German fighter force on known airdromes refueling at known periods of time. Nothing was done about it. Why should not all of our medium bombers and vast numbers of your Spits (equipped with belly tanks and bombs) have smashed the Germans while they were pinned to their refueling airdromes?[11]

The difficulty of organizing such a precise fighter and medium-bomber attack on a truly fleeting target, and the possibility that doing so might have tipped off the *Luftwaffe* to the compromise of its encrypted radio transmissions, seems not to have influenced Arnold's opinion. The biting tone of the letter was pure Hap Arnold, reflecting the pressure under which he operated and his ever-present drive for accomplishment. The letter also showed his wish that intelligence data be used promptly and advantageously, an attitude which he retained throughout the war. It is possible, and perhaps likely, that this incident between Arnold and Portal brought Arnold's full, formal initiation into the ULTRA world. Based on Arnold's remarks to Portal, it is doubtful that he was fully aware of the extent, function, and rules regarding the sensitivity of ULTRA in mid-October. Yet he could not have been excluded indefinitely, and Portal, or perhaps Spaatz seeking to avert future conflict, may have suggested Arnold's entry into ULTRA knowledge. At some point after October 1943 (possibly in December 1943 or January 1944), the AAF's commanding general and his A–2 regularly saw and understood the origin of the special signals intelligence attachments to the *MAGIC Summaries*.[12]

Planning the Defeat of Japan

Knowledge of ULTRA was not a panacea by any means. The A–2 knew, but could not tell his staff, who continued to labor at projects that brought them into contact and conflict with those in the G–2 office who had broader knowledge of many aspects of air intelligence. At the same time, and mitigating some of the problems, improvements in the systematic handling and preparation of intelligence information sped the delivery of analytical products to the AAF's field commanders.

Organization and Interservice Relationships

The Air Staff reorganization of March 29, 1943, greatly broadened the A–2 office's scope of affairs, giving the air staff's intelligence operation new stature and opening avenues for expanded work. The combat liaison branch of the Operational Intelligence Division became a separate division teamed with training coordination. The former Administrative Division disappeared and a new Historical Division came into being. The latter division represented AAF headquarters' method of meeting President Roosevelt's and General Arnold's directions to record the operations and activities of the war, something that had not been done in the conflict in Europe until after the 1917–1918 American involvement there. Where the reform of the War Department in March 1942 had created equal AAF, Army Ground Forces, and Army Service Forces, these changes one year later resolved some of the nagging problems that various air staff offices believed impeded their ability to function effectively.[13]

The AAF Intelligence Service (AFIS), the operating agency working under the A–2 since 1942, lost its separate identity. From March 1942, the AFIS and the A–2 had some overlapping functions; in the spring of 1943, Arnold combined those AFIS activities most directly related to staff intelligence with the A–2. Some other tasks went elsewhere. For example, the supervision of policies related to the safeguarding of military information and the processing of security clearances for training shifted to the Air Provost Marshal's office. With few other changes, the March 1943 reorganization shaped the A–2 office's form and function for the remainder of the war years. Unlike the 1943 reorganization, lesser changes of 1944 and 1945 within the A–2 office related to the need to change focus periodically to provide data to the operating commands, primarily the Twentieth Air Force, engaged in the strategic campaign in the Pacific war.[14] The A–2 was the Twentieth Air Force's A–2 as well, and much of the Air Staff's intelligence work was related to the B–29 operation. The chart on the facing page shows the A–2 office's functions after the 1943 reorganization.

Through 1943, many senior officers working in military and naval intelligence in Washington saw the duplication of work by several agencies. The overlap was especially evident in the relations between the WDGS's

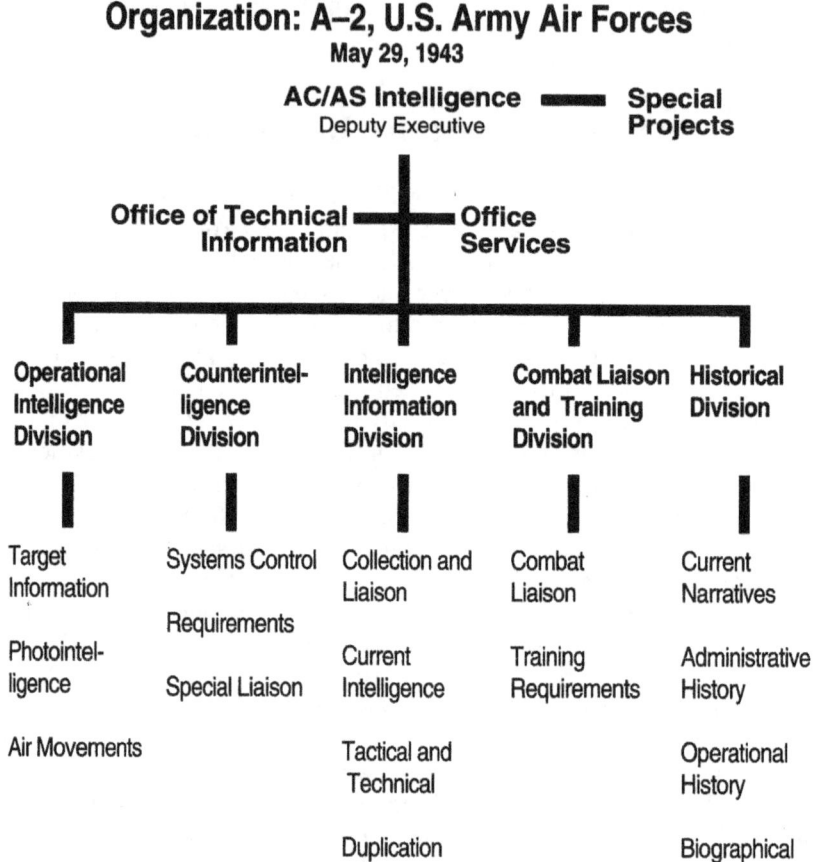

Planning the Defeat of Japan

Assistant Chief of Staff, G–2, whose MIS had a substantial air analysis unit, and the office of the AC/AS, Intelligence. In some areas, the two intelligence offices complemented one another's work; in other areas, they clashed. The MIS air unit used the closely controlled ULTRA intercepts to create estimates of enemy and neutral air OB, which it provided to the Air Staff in the form of finished studies and reports. For the AAF, the question revolved around more than the bureaucratic intricacies of a few agencies in and near Washington. Many airmen saw G–2's position as contributing to their subservience. The March 1943 Air Staff reorganization centralized the AAF's intelligence in one office. As a consequence, the A–2 could improve his product and tend to problems outside his office, such as the restrictions that the War Department's G–2 imposed on his domain.[15]

In the autumn of 1943, after he returned from India, Clayton Bissell became the AAF's chief intelligence officer. Bissell held the job for only a few months. During his tenure from October until early January 1944 he proposed to Maj. Gen. George V. Strong, the War Department G–2, that the responsibilities for joint intelligence matters related to Japanese air intelligence be more clearly defined for each of the services. Strong moved slowly on the proposal because he and Bissell could not agree on how to handle sensitive radio intercept data and compile Japanese Army air OB. The air OB came from radio intercept, and its compilation had to be controlled similarly. The Army was most reluctant to imperil the security of this prized source by allowing an excessive amount of direct knowledge and access. In January, Bissell replaced Strong as G–2, with Brig. Gen. Thomas D. White named as A–2. Now the G–2 and A–2 were both airmen, and both saw the chance to improve interagency relationships. Bissell dropped the radio intercept and air OB questions from the joint intelligence proposal, and together he and White gained support of the JCS's JIC for a coordinating group, the Ad Hoc Committee, to oversee air intelligence. That group would soon include RAF representation.[16]

On February 24, 1944, Air Vice Marshal F. F. Inglis, the RAF's ACAS (I), and Rear Adm. R. E. Schuirman, the U.S. Navy's Director of Intelligence, with Bissell and White, signed the air intelligence working agreement. By its terms, an Allied, primarily RAF, center in London controlled air intelligence about Germany. A similar setup in Washington was to handle information on the Japanese, but it was almost entirely American in staffing and control. The agreement recognized the existing situation based on the two Anglo-American ULTRA intercept centers, but it did not itself address the sensitive cryptanalysis questions. Both the Americans and the RAF would keep all interested parties of both countries, especially theater commanders, fully apprised of crucial air intelligence matters. The new agreement also formalized the preeminent place of the Americans in the Pacific war's intelligence arrangements. The Anglo-American agreement did not greatly affect the positions of the air intelligence offices in MacArthur's command, in Nimitz's Central Pacific, or in the CBI. In the first two cases, MacArthur and Nimitz were very senior officers with strong personalities; their command structures were too well insulated and tightly controlled by their staffs. In the last instance, CBI was too far removed from Washington; both the Americans and British were too busy elsewhere, and Lord Louis Montbatten's South East Asia Command had a firm hold on affairs in his region.[17]

The agreement was the basis for regularizing over time the methods of handling and securing ULTRA and conforming it to the manner that the British had developed at BP. Where handling systems in the SWPA had previously been rather lax in comparison with those found in Europe and the Mediterranean, the agreement formed the basis for new, more stringent and more technically secure procedures that used approved War Department transmission equipment and circuits. New sensitivity about handling ULTRA was followed by the arrival from MIS in Washington of Army SSOs to serve in many more places in the Pacific and Far East than they had served previously. At last, SSOs could now be found with MacArthur's GHQ, at Kenney's FEAF headquarters, and at the headquarters of both the Fifth and Thirteenth Air Forces. In mid-November 1944, the SSO assigned to GHQ SWPA, Capt. Phil Graham, wrote to Colonel Clarke in Washington that Kenney was very happy with the additional service, especially the direct access to OB compilations and the special studies such as those on jet propulsion and aviation fuel additives like butanol that had now become available. At first hesitant about the intrusion into his territory, Graham noted that FEAF's A-2, Colonel Cain, became a willing, even happy, user of the MIS services. Understanding the nature of Japanese alcohol and butanol production led to a Fifth Air Force campaign to destroy such manufacturing sites on Formosa. By mid-July 1945, 75 percent of alcohol production capacity on Formosa had been eliminated, and Fifth Air Force units were paying special attention to shipping the product to Japan. RAF SLUs also arrived in Australia to give Australian forces their own ULTRA transmission systems, to allow Australia direct access to ULTRA data from London, and to lessen Australia's dependence on what had become the American-dominated intelligence operation at GHQ SWPA. Although some might have looked upon the RAF SLUs in Australia as a violation of the agreement, more than anything else, the service they provided was largely one of secure transmission, an extension of the British Commonwealth's facilities from India. The RAF SLUs did, however, accompany Australian forces to Morotai and New Guinea late in 1944.[18]

The agreement did not automatically clarify questions of authority in Washington, nor did all of these changes occur in rapid order. After the signing of the document, several weeks passed during which the intelligence staffs haggled over responsibility, until the members of the JCS JIC finally settled the issue in July 1944. The Americans divided air intelligence assessment tasks among the various service offices they believed best able to deal with specific areas. AAF intelligence acquired primary responsibility for the following: enemy airfield information and reporting; air facilities and air route data through Alaska and Siberia to China and through Asia or Africa to Japan; aviation target material; and target damage assessment of strategic targets (except shipping). The Army G–2 became responsible for aerial photointerpretation for the SWPA and Asiatic theaters, for POW interrogation, for processing captured Japanese documents, and for aircraft nameplate analysis (i.e., determining production rate and location of manufacture). The Director of Naval Intelligence dealt with air facilities and route data across the Pacific to Japan and China; for building terrain and relief models (used for crew target recognition training); for the status and target damage assessment of Japanese shipping (a natural outgrowth of naval ULTRA); for aerial photointerpretation covering North, Central, and South Pacific theaters; and for technical intelligence (i.e., the study of captured Japanese equipment and weapons).[19]

Many of the senior AAF staff officers in Washington thought the agreement satisfactory if only because it protected the most important AAF concerns, most notably, strategic intelligence to support the B–29 program. Some objected, with one of the strongest opinions coming from General McDonald, Spaatz's intelligence chief in London. In June 1944, McDonald had learned of the agreement before all of the organizational details had been settled when he saw an Air Ministry directive on the subject. The British officer who composed the paper in London, Group Capt. A. J. Miley, was under the impression that the agreement gave the U.S. Navy "primary responsibility on behalf of both British and U.S. Services for intelligence on the Japanese Air Forces." McDonald, seeing the official British document, became livid. He wrote White a highly critical letter (apparently with Spaatz's approval and support), noting that he and others found "it difficult to see the propriety of the Navy's position in this over-all air intelligence [arrangement]." McDonald believed that the AAF had by far the best U.S. air intelligence organization, and he held that giving the show to the Navy was "an anachronism almost too discordant to suffer." McDonald's real concern, and possibly also that of Spaatz and others in USSTAF, came at the end of the letter when he said, "It seems to me that when a Service gives away dominion over its intelligence . . . it has in fact given up its independence." Independence for the AAF was the burr under McDonald's saddle blanket, and infringement pained him. The airmen's unhappiness with domination by the Army had come to the surface as McDonald saw the AAF once more on the outside. General White settled the immediate problem with a call to the director of intelligence at the British Joint Staff Mission across town, and he cabled McDonald the same night to point out the error and calm the people in Europe. That did not resolve the irritation at the more deep-seated issues.[20] The problem of G–2—A–2 relations remained at the surface of the A–2 staff's work throughout the war.

Piercing the Fog

White was quite aggressive in trying to set up his A–2 operation as a separate and independent function, but it was an almost constant struggle. On February 7, 1944, White wrote to the Chief of the Air Staff to comment on both General Arnold's and his own lack of confidence in and dissatisfaction with the AAF's air intelligence. Arnold's specific feelings of unease centered on preparation for the B–29 air campaign against Japan, upon which he had staked his reputation and the Air Forces' future. Arnold had earlier made these feelings known when he had assigned the COA to review the A–2's work. Some in the A–2 office, including possibly Sorenson himself, resented the intrusion of the outside analysts. The commanding general's feelings probably contributed to Sorenson's reassignment in October 1943, but Arnold continued to find fault with his intelligence office. The extent to which Arnold's unhappiness, if any, contributed to Bissell's short stay as A–2 is hard to judge. He was replaced by White in January 1944.[21] It was White who set about trying to effect a major refocusing of the A–2 office toward the war against Japan and postwar operations.

White went further than just seconding Arnold's apprehensions, expressing his belief that the A–2 had too many extraneous functions and an excessive and needless interest in Europe, where McDonald's people were doing good work with the RAF, and that it was poorly prepared to assure good quality air intelligence analyses. Hardly had the ink dried on the first letter when White again wrote to the Chief of Air Staff to discuss his views of the relationship between G–2 and A–2. In the latter correspondence, White pointed out that Arnold needed a completely integrated and uninhibited intelligence staff, and until he got such, he could not be a full partner on the JCS. Whereas the Army and Navy chiefs had independent intelligence, White contended that the AAF was largely dependent upon G–2 and was organized on a pre-1941 basis. By the latter remark, he seemed to mean that the A–2 lacked permanent status within the Army and that it was not equal to G–2 and ONI. In closing, White advocated the transfer of all air intelligence responsibility from G–2 to A–2. The proposal faced an enormous bureaucratic resistance from well-entrenched opponents. White's proposal failed, for to have allowed the transfer would also have raised the question of an independent Air Force. That idea was premature in the midst of a war for which the military had just become organized and fully effective.[22]

White's focus, and Arnold's too, remained on the war with Japan. They believed that long-range air power could be decisive in the Pacific and that demonstrating it could set the stage for postwar Air Force independence. To pursue that issue and to plan appropriately, the two men needed adequate strategic targeting information, and their subordinate commanders and A–2s in the field needed good tactical intelligence. In an air war, where both sides had fast-moving, destructive operations, radio intelligence became increasingly important.

Army Air Forces' Y-Service

Shortly after the war began, the Army had created and assigned to the AAF five signal intelligence companies. The AAF found these companies satisfactory so long as they worked within the United States, where they served as stationary operating agencies of numbered air forces. Their primary function was to intercept encrypted, coded, and voice transmissions; they also performed radio direction finding. It soon became apparent that these companies could be valuable overseas in gathering air intelligence; they began moving to combat areas in 1943, where AAF headquarters attached them to numbered air force headquarters. Once in the combat areas, the commanders realized that the table of organization dictated companies that were clumsy and ill-suited to the mobile type of air warfare of the early 1940s. By the summer of 1943, the AC/AS, Intelligence staff believed that a number of changes should be implemented. To start with, Maj. Virgil O. Johnson returned to Washington from New Guinea where he had served as a radio intercept expert in General Whitehead's Fifth Air Force advanced headquarters. Johnson's new task was to help formulate plans for an entirely new AAF radio intercept organization. Both G–2 and the Signal Security Agency gave initial, informal approval to the undertaking; the Army's intelligence staff knew that they needed to make some changes to better support the field air units, and overseas commanders were anxious to have better radio intercept operations. Johnson, on his arrival in Washington, delivered a letter from Whitehead, pleading for much improved support. Whitehead was not alone, for late in 1943 Brig. Gen. Howard Davidson sent Hap Arnold a letter from Tenth Air Force in India seeking better intercept assets. Although Davidson had a radio intercept squadron, it could not do what he needed because it lacked Japanese language specialists who could translate and make useful the information overheard by the operators. Davidson closed his letter by telling Arnold, "The Japanese are great talkers over the radio [while in flight], but unfortunately we have no way of knowing what they are saying."[23]

The resulting Air Staff actions altered the original companies into what were known as radio squadrons, mobile—units that could move rapidly with the area air headquarters and do more of the things that air generals needed. The new squadrons were larger, acting as would an air force signal intelligence service or signal security agency unit, providing not only intercept and direction finding but also translation, analysis, and evaluation for the air commander. Each squadron served an air headquarters that was unique as to region, mission, and composition; thus each squadron differed in what it did and how well it did it. Typical, if one could use that word for one of these units, was the 1st Radio Squadron (Mobile), which in August 1943 superseded the 138th Signal Radio Intercept Company in New Guinea. The squadron was fortunate in that it inherited much that SWPA's CB had helped set up for the AAFSWPA

Piercing the Fog

Maj. Gen. Howard C. Davidson

operation. At the air headquarters the squadron had seventy-nine men. Intercept operators fed messages captured in the clear or in low-grade code or cipher to the analysis section, which in turn translated or decoded for the intelligence evaluation section. From there, the evaluators sent information to Fifth Air Force headquarters, to the AA command, or to the air defense fighter controllers. Messages of higher grade cipher were transferred to Brisbane for decryption and analysis. Other sections of the squadron repaired equipment, encrypted and transmitted messages, or performed various support functions. Detachments from the squadron served Thirteenth Air Force or various advanced air headquarters in New Guinea or the Philippine Islands.[24]

In addition to the decryption work in the Philippines, the 1st Radio Squadron's direction-finding teams ran an around-the-clock listening service that covered the Japanese Army and Navy air forces' operations. Overhearing enemy transmissions, translators noted the content. Direction-finding teams simultaneously reported locations of probable enemy airfields or the bearing of approaching aircraft beyond radar range so that operations planners could schedule air strikes or direct fighters to intercept. Similarly, in Europe after D-day, the 3d Radio Squadron worked as an adjunct of the Ninth Air Force, feeding reports of radio intercepts to the A–2. Detachments of the squadron did the same for the IX and XIX TACs' A–2s and for the intelligence officers of subordinate air units. This arrangement of squadrons deployed worldwide formed, in effect, a signals intelligence service that remained at the disposal of the air force commanders. All radio squadrons could and did pass encrypted information at the air commanders' behest, and they scrutinized the various air forces' radio practices to detect possible faulty American tendencies that could provide information to the enemy. Such overseas units, scattered across Europe, the Mediterranean, CBI, and the Pacific, formed the basis of an AAF tactical Y-Service. Other squadrons, like the 6th, assigned to Fourth Air Force at Hamilton Field, and stationed in the hills above Daly City, California, immediately south of San Francisco, worked on a more strategic level. This squadron intercepted Japanese and other countries' transmissions and forwarded them to Arlington Hall Station in Virginia for decryption and analysis.[25]

On a more extensive plane, the A–2 increasingly drew radio intelligence from MIS in Washington after the spring of 1943, when the Allies began to have more success with Japanese Army cryptology. Most of the decrypted message information, except for that read by the A–2 himself (who became an ULTRA recipient), was in finished form, i.e., it came to the Air Staff as reports or assessments of German or Japanese capabilities and intentions. Within the A–2 office by war's end was a small department, the Special Sources Section, Collection Branch, that received and handled MAGIC diplomatic decrypts but not the more general, operationally related ULTRA. Access to the MAGIC material was tightly controlled. Although the Collection Branch's chief and the executive officer knew of the material's existence, neither had authorization to see it. The most important for the A–2 staff was, of course, ULTRA related to the Japanese air war, as that part of the conflict was A–2's main task. Despite the increased use of the ULTRA source, the AAF's intelligence analysts remained frustrated throughout the final two years of the conflict, both because of the method by which MIS conveyed Japanese ULTRA to them, and because of the secrecy and restrictions imposed on its use.

MAGIC decrypts, rewritten for use by the A–2, tended to cover specific topics extracted from regular diplomatic radio traffic, whereas the rest of the ULTRA resembled that being taken by the British from German messages. Because ULTRA was too fragmentary in its decrypted form, G–2 could not prepare analyses or reports from a particular message or even groups of messages. The best intelligence from Japanese Army ULTRA was very often derived from the long process of decrypting, collating, analyzing, and refining, very much like that which the MIS's Anglo-American counterpart carried on at BP. Final information, e.g., the OB summaries, thus reached A–2 without notation of source, and without explanation of the reasons for restrictions on its use and dissemination. Fueling their grumbling was not knowing the reasons for the reports' formats and the constraints on freedom to use the data as the A–2 staff saw fit. The worst part, of course, was that the normal air intelligence officers could not be let in on the secret, even by the A–2 himself, who knew the source.[26] The A–2 analysts, not knowing the origin, could not trust the product.

Still, secrecy and source protection alone did not explain entirely the dissatisfaction, for Hodges and Quesada, themselves ULTRA readers, made

Piercing the Fog

similar observations. Much of the problem centered on the uncertain availability of the material related to work that was vital to the A–2 but over which the AAF had no control. An excellent example of this type of report was the air OB compilations, prepared by a small group of officers in Special Branch. In April 1944 this function became even more centralized and further from the AAF's control and understanding when preparation of the weekly Japanese air estimate shifted from G–2's air unit to Special Branch. Beginning in November, Special Branch published and circulated to the Air Staff a combined Japanese Army-Navy air strength list. The list had appended to it a detailed section on estimates not only of Japanese air capabilities but also of intentions, based upon the current situation. Other reports to the Air Staff from MIS contained information on Japanese plans and operations, major changes in air dispositions, new types of aircraft, weapons, defenses, tactics, supply, and aircraft production and replacement. Much of the data on Japanese shipping that made possible the air and submarine antishipping campaign came from the MAGIC Diplomatic Summary and other military ULTRA assessments. Reference to the combined Japanese Army-Navy air forces report was the only way in which planners in Washington, Honolulu, and elsewhere could grasp fully the true state of Japanese air power. The irony was that from early 1943 on, as air intelligence improved, the Japanese became less and less able to carry on air warfare. The heavy losses of their best pilots in the long and bitter Solomon Islands campaign greatly reduced the overall experience of the flyers. The declining level of Japanese capabilities was not clearly perceived everywhere. The issue at hand was winning the war, and the A–2's people chafed under their perception that they were restrained from meeting the challenge and their frustration of knowing that another air intelligence staff, whose size and sources they did not fully comprehend, was doing the work that they should have been doing.[27]

Far East Target Analysis

At the time that the AAF organized the Eighth Air Force and Arnold sent Spaatz to England, the AAF also delineated responsibility for studying potential targets. Information for industrial objectives in Europe was to be handled by the Eighth and the RAF. The Far East, and especially the Japanese home islands, was the province of the A–2, although some European analyses would be done by the Air Staff. Theater A–2s in the Pacific and CBI exercised their own local authority on problems peculiar to their areas or operations. In March 1943, the Air Staff received from the AIS its first target study of Japan, Korea, and Manchuria, recommending fifty-seven key targets from a priority list including aircraft production, nonferrous metals, naval bases and shipyards, iron and steel, petroleum, chemicals, automotive assembly, and rubber processing. The basic information supporting the intelligence services study came from the BEW and

MID. At the urging of General Fairchild and over Sorenson's objections, who thought his men's study sufficient, the COA also began to analyze the target vulnerabilities of Japanese industry. Throughout the study, the COA and A–2 worked together, exchanging information and opinions. Colonel Moss, an A–2 officer highly regarded by people like Haywood Hansell, also worked with the COA and was a regular link between the two organizations.[28] The COA applied the same methodology it had used in scrutinizing Germany the previous year. For the Japan study, senior committee members believed it necessary to have naval representation on the analytical teams, so they approached the office of Admiral Ernest J. King's staff chief. The Navy agreed to the idea, but it was slow to appoint members. Not until mid-July 1943 did three naval officers join the main committee. As an illustration of the range of experience on the committee, one of the men, Capt. H. W. Wick, was career Navy; another, Comdr. Francis Bitter, had come to war service from MIT and was an air technical analyst in the office of the Deputy Chief of Naval Operations, Air. The third, Lt. Comdr. Albert E. Hindmarsh, was normally a professor of history at Harvard. Hindmarsh was then serving in the ONI.[29]

The committee's analytic approach for the German and Japanese studies has already been described. One difference between the Japanese and German studies was their consideration of the possibility of attacks on urban areas. In fact, the area attack idea had been under quite serious discussion by COA members since May 1943. The idea also had support within the A–2 office, which prepared a report for the COA on the expected effects of incendiary attacks on Japanese industry. Mr. Horatio Bond, of the Office of Civilian Defense, and Mr. R. N. Ewell, of the National Defense Research Committee, worked with the A–2 staff preparing the substance of the report. The A–2 report reasoned that "Japanese war industry was more highly concentrated in a few key cities than was the case in Germany, that these cities were far more inflammable than those in Germany, and that 1690 tons of incendiaries, effectively placed, would be sufficient to destroy 20 of the most important cities of Japan, having a total population of 16,600,000." The report went on to state that these urban areas contained 74 percent of the priority sites that appeared in the A–2's March 1943 report on Japanese targets. The full committee, not having independently analyzed the whole question of incendiary city attacks, simply adopted the A–2 report. But the COA found it difficult to express in precise terms the effect of urban area attacks, holding that such targets should be considered important, "though not one taking priority over precision target systems." There appeared throughout the record of the committee's examinations a recurrent theme: a paucity of precise information about Japan.[30]

The COA's report and recommendations placing the destruction of coking facilities high on the air operations target list became a topic of discussion at the Joint Staff plans office in Washington while the Cairo conference was underway in November 1943. Haywood Hansell, in Cairo, had requested confirmation of a Joint Staff planners' cable to him and others at the conference, expressing doubt as to the COA's conclusions on the effects of attacking coke ovens.* After conferring with Colonel Moss of A–2 and COA and with General Bissell, Moss's new superior at A–2, the Joint Staff plans office replied to Hansell that destruction of three coke plants representing 61 percent of Japan's capacity would immediately reduce steel production by 25 percent. This would result in an estimated 53 percent reduction in Japanese steel production for the twelve months after destruction. Certain members of the COA believed that the cable to Cairo was inaccurate and that it understated both the number of plants that should be hit and the effects of such attacks. Nevertheless, the confirming cable from the Joint Staff plans office, based upon A–2's approval, helped Hansell establish the MATTERHORN plan for B–29 operations in China and India.[31]

Shortly thereafter, the Air Staff intelligence office and the COA renewed their rivalry. On December 4, 1943, the Joint War Plans Committee of the JCS sought from the JCS's JIC an analysis of the optimum timing and deployment of B–29s against the Japanese targets listed in the COA's report. The JIC, in turn, referred the question to A–2 and to Commander Bitter at the office of the Deputy Chief of Naval Operations, Air. The A–2's representative, at a meeting on December 18, argued against the conclusion reached by the COA on coking plants as targets, preferring instead to place primary emphasis on selected electric power facilities. The discussions continued until April, when the joint plans office prepared a formal position paper for the JCS stating that the best early use of the B–29s was attacking coke ovens in Manchuria and oil refineries in the NEI, primarily at Palembang. Essentially the joint planners overlooked the A–2's wishes and endorsed the COA recommendations on shipping, the petroleum industry in the NEI, iron and steel in the form of coke ovens, urban industrial areas, aircraft plants, antifriction bearings, and electronics.[32] The problem remained of finding and identifying precise target sites.

The COA's conclusion late in 1943 that the Allies possessed insufficient information about Japan to go beyond general target objective studies and make careful target selections assumed greater significance in light of the AAF's operational experience in Europe. The precision bombardment of Germany had not succeeded to the extent that the air war planners had hoped, in large measure due to difficulties of weather and because German defenses impeded the use of optical bombsights. The Norden sights were not always effective from the

---

*Col. Perera, one of the few full-time members of the COA, intimated in memoirs drafted long after the war that the first cable to Cairo came at the instigation of some in A–2 who opposed the COA's activity. Perera, a Boston attorney in civilian life, continued in his memoirs to explore very guardedly the tense relations between the A–2 office and the COA. Perera believed that Sorenson's opposition to the COA led to his replacement, perhaps at the instigation or urging of Brig. Gen. Laurence S. Kuter, the AC/AS, Plans. Perera, "Washington and War Years," *passim.*

altitudes at which the B–17s and B–24s flew as they evaded German fighters and AA fire. Newly developed radar bomb sights had not improved bombing accuracy. Radar was an immature technology, radar displays were inexact, and systems were too new to be well understood by the crews who used them. The equipment did not always perform as expected and could not compensate for the many problems the bombardiers faced. In the months' long effort to reduce the German synthetic oil refinery complex at Merseburg-Leuna, for example, the use of radar did not overcome problems presented by clouds, undercast, or German smoke screens that covered much of the area around the complex. Since the B–29s were to be equipped with optical and radar aiming devices similar to those used in Europe, the AAF's intelligence analysts and planners had to understand what factors would affect operations over Japan. Japan's weather (knowledge of which was a critical piece of air intelligence) was every bit as unreliable as the weather in northern Europe. Because the aircraft coming off the production lines represented an enormous investment both in terms of dollars and personal credibility, Arnold could not afford to have them stand idle.[33]

As the B–29 formations gained training experience and the time for the air campaign against Japan drew closer, A–2 officers realized they lacked proper target folders of the Far East. Such folders as existed had to be revised to incorporate new material and to respond to requests from field units, especially the Fourteenth Air Force which lacked extensive analysis and production capability. In the spring of 1944, the A–2's Far East Analysis Branch of the Analysis Division headed by Lt. Col. DeForest Van Slyck began work on a comprehensive revision effort, but time was short and growing shorter. Hansell needed objective folders of specific targets, and he desired that the A–2 office prepare a series of large-scale base maps of objective areas from which target charts could be produced in the field. The gathering and analysis of data required the services of offices outside of A–2, such as the OSS, the U.S. Foreign Economic Administration, G–2's MID, Naval Intelligence, and the Air Ministry, among others. Added to the press of time was a dearth of people to do the work and a dependence upon other government agencies (principally MID and the Coast and Geodetic Survey) for printing the necessary material.[34]

The MID's New York office, although little known, played a key part in gathering target intelligence data. A number of U.S. institutions had had extensive dealings with the many Americans who had lived in Europe or worked with German companies. At Colonel Moss's suggestion, the New York office set out to find the companies, banks, executives, or engineers who knew their counterparts in Germany. Banks that had loaned money to companies in Axis or occupied countries, for example, had extensive maps, diagrams, or information about the facilities for which the money had been intended. At MID's request, this information came out of the files for minute scrutiny and use in objective folder preparation. People who knew the regions in question

Piercing the Fog

gave the benefit of their experience to the military. For Europe, the information was extensive, but not so for Japan where few Americans had lived or worked. While German emigrees held important positions in the United States, most who had immigrated from Japan were working-class people. As a general rule, the Japanese-Americans were not trusted, and whatever information they may have had was not so well exploited.[35]

The A–2 staff had built good working relationships with the other services in Washington, and despite the nagging annoyance of the Air Forces' senior officers on the question of service independence, the objective folder and target production effort moved ahead toward the November 1944 goal. The growing interagency effort that represented the Japanese intelligence project led the JCS's Ad Hoc Committee, originally created to settle the problems associated with dividing the Japanese intelligence effort among the services, to propose more closely integrated work on aviation target material and target damage assessment. By mid-May 1944, the Ad Hoc Committee had recommended that these two functions be done within the A–2 office rather than by a new committee or agency, with the consequent bureaucratic tangles and delays. A–2 was the logical location since the AAF's long-range and very long-range bombers would consume the target documentation. In mid-May 1944, Van Slyck and an associate, Maj. Philip G. Bower, met with representatives of the Director of Naval Intelligence to lay the groundwork for cooperation. The Navy intended to prepare target charts of Japan for use by its carrier aircraft, using AAF information. The Navy's plan included employing the target numbering system of A–2, and the naval officers at the meeting suggested the need for a common map-grid numbering system. The common grid would not only simplify joint intelligence preparation and map and chart production, it would allow specific instructions to be sent in short form to all users by cable or radio, thus increasing the services' ability to coordinate attack plans.[36]

The work of the Ad Hoc Committee on Joint Service Intelligence led the JCS to study the worth of a more formal organization for air intelligence of Japan. In September 1944, several recommendations aimed at expediting and streamlining target information led to the creation of the Joint Target Analysis Group (shortened to "Joint Target Group" the following month). The JTG had the mission of integrating and coordinating preattack and postattack intelligence analyses of air targets in the war against Japan. It was also part of the A–2's office, thus keeping central analysis within an existing organization. An AAF brigadier general, John A. Samford, in a new position of Deputy AC/AS for Intelligence for Targets, headed the JTG; all of the group's personnel came from existing offices of the services and agencies whose work it performed. For example, the A–2's Analysis Division handed over to the JTG a substantial portion of its Far East and Tactical and Technical Branches, including the air target material and air target damage assessment work previously addressed by the Ad Hoc Committee. The Navy added a number of similar functions. The

JTG did all of its work in the name of Arnold as Commanding General, AAF. A special panel of consultants stood ready to offer advice. This consultative group comprised several people from the COA, including Colonel McCormack of G–2 whose unique sources of ULTRA information would be most important. In charge of the panel was Dr. Edward Bowles, Arnold's science advisor, who had contributed greatly to the design and use of airborne radar bombing aids and other electronic warfare advances.[37]

The services saw the JTG as an organization created for a specific task—assessing information for the aerial attack on Japan. The group had no table of organization; its member agencies, primarily from the AAF and Navy, contributed personnel at the request of the AC/AS, Intelligence. The group was an analytical body charged with making recommendations on Japanese targets and giving advice to field commanders; it could not direct any actions, but Samford could keep contact with any service or office he felt appropriate. The group's organization and functional authority left it a creature of AAF headquarters and a true staff extension of the AC/AS, Intelligence, with General Arnold and his intelligence chief as, in effect, executive agents overseeing the JTG's operation. For Arnold and the AAF, the importance of the JTG's creation and position was a clear recognition of air power's importance and of the AAF's and the B–29's key roles in air warfare plans of the United States.

The JCS directive gave the JTG a broad selection of responsibilities and functions including preparation and distribution of a list of all air targets important to Japan's general economic and military strength; production and distribution of strategic target information; listing the priority of target systems and specific targets in each system; recommending the most suitable munitions, fuzing, and loads for targets; and indicating the forces to be used against each target. The JTG was charged with preparation of damage assessment reports and reports on the repair and reconstruction of damaged targets; the creation of special studies; and the liaison with using agencies to ensure adequacy and acceptability of the group's work. Among the JTG's first projects were the organization and distribution of the Air Target Index Japanese War, and the adjunct air target system folders, which covered each target or collection of targets described in the index. Because the JTG lacked extensive information on Japan, the European experience in analyzing bomb damage, especially that which the Germans had inflicted on London, became vital to studies of Japanese targets. The JTG's Physical Vulnerability Section, for example, tried to quantify the areas of effectiveness of bomb blast and bombing patterns on industrial areas, industrial structures, and urban areas to form the basis of a comparative analysis applicable to Japan. Many of the people who worked in the Physical Vulnerability section were veterans of the similar British organization in London called R.E.8. Many had also done extensive bomb damage analysis work for the RAF and Eighth Air Force between 1940 and 1944. It was largely from the studies done in Washington that the group devised its recommendations on the mix of high-explosive and incendiary bombs to be dropped and the fuze sensitivities to be considered for each type target.[38]

There were in the handling of Japanese target intelligence by the JTG and the AAF both similarities and significant differences over the work that had been done in Europe. In 1943, when Ira Eaker received the COA's recommendations for attacking Germany, he, as the Eighth Air Force's commanding general, chaired a board in London that approved the COA's work and then prepared an estimate of the forces needed to accomplish the progressive destruction of the targets. Late in April 1943, Eaker flew to Washington and made his recommendations to the CCS. In May, the CCS approved the Anglo-American CBO. In 1944, when the JTG began work, the operations analysts' previous recommendations relative to Japan carried the weight of the committee's prominence and reputation, even though its work had been done from an admittedly poorer base of intelligence data. Although the COA was by now largely out of business, it retained its influence within the JTG by virtue of its stature in Arnold's eyes, the past quality of its work, and the presence of a number of its members on the JTG's panel of consultants. Arnold in this case stood as Eaker had previously done, except that Arnold commanded both the AAF and the Twentieth Air Force and he was determined to see air power through to success in the war. The fragmented air effort in the Pacific also figured prominently. The U.S. Navy (and through it Nimitz and the Seventh Air Force), Marine Corps air, Kenney's FEAF, and the China Theater's Fourteenth Air Force could all be reasonably expected to play an important part in the attack on the Japanese homeland. Sheer logic, if not Arnold's determination, demanded first-rate air intelligence and an effective unit to produce it. Thus the JTG became the prime agency and the AC/AS for Intelligence, the most important player in the effort.[39] The lack of understanding of Japan was to cause continuing difficulty for target analysis. Nowhere was the air intelligence need greater than in the requirement for adequate target photography.

Of all the varied sources of information used by the AAF headquarters intelligence staff, none came in larger amounts than photography from aerial reconnaissance. In the summer of 1945, one of the A–2 officers described it as "probably the most important source or form of air information that came to the headquarters during this war."[40] The officer, Maj. A. W. White of the Air Information Division, speaking to the senior intelligence officer course at the AAF School of Applied Tactics, went on to say that some of the people in the A–2 office were of the opinion that 90 percent of the intelligence used in planning the war against Japan came primarily from AAF and Navy combat photography, with some from the OSS. Estimates such as White's were highly subjective, influenced greatly by the visible volume of material. The piles of photographs did not translate directly into high-quality analysis; in fact, White himself pointed out that the staff spent a great deal of time in sifting and scrutinizing, yet it could not keep up with the growing collection. Clearly, for

Planning the Defeat of Japan

target analysis and damage assessment of the Japanese homeland, first-rate aerial photography was vital, yet it did not begin in substance until November 1944 when Hansell's F–13 crew made their initial flight.

White noted also that the AAF's pictures, most taken from high altitude, were inferior to those of the Navy, usually made from 6,000 to 8,000 feet. The low-altitude photographs were much more useful, for they showed the areas observed in greater detail. The appreciation of photography displayed at headquarters reflected the experience of air commanders in India-Burma and in Europe. Good aerial photography served the target planners well, for despite its drawbacks it was more quickly adaptable to the analytical process than was the written, sometimes more ephemeral or arcane, collection of data from captured documents, POWs, crashed aircraft, and intercepted messages that might indicate the enemy's capabilities or intentions.[41] The dearth of information on Japan, especially photographic, had serious consequences in operations planning, directly affecting decisions on the tactics and types of bombs to be used on Japanese cities.

German and Japanese Interchanges and Implications for the War on Japan

As the Allies moved across France in 1944, Arnold's thoughts centered more and more on how to deal with Japan and the postwar shape of his Air Force. The thoughts became linked in his mind late in the summer as he formulated several ideas dealing with both topics. In September of that year, President Roosevelt directed Secretary of War Stimson to organize an "impartial and expert study of the effects of the aerial attack on Germany."[42] The study, actually one that Arnold sought, was to be all-encompassing, covering both direct, physical damage and the indirect consequences of the CBO on the German economy. In its final form, this study was the product of civilian-led group and came to be called the USSBS. In charge of the survey was Franklin D'Olier, chief executive of the Prudential Insurance Company. The origins of the USSBS were many and diverse; A–2's Target Information Section, in particular Maj. Ralph A. Colbert, chief of its European Branch in early 1944, played a key role. In Colbert's view, his section required a continuing evaluation of the effects of its recommendations regarding targets to be struck. "Plans should be prepared now," he wrote to General White on March 27, 1944, "for the establishment of a Commission of experts, headed by USAAF Intelligence, prepared upon Germany's defeat to conduct an investigation inside Germany that will disclose the true facts concerning the Strategic Aerial Bombardment of Europe. . . ." As things eventually turned out, AC/AS, Plans subsequently took the lead away from A–2 in establishing the survey, but Major Colbert managed to follow up his initial interest by getting himself assigned to the survey and serving in its Economic Section in Europe.[43]

Piercing the Fog

Another group appointed by Arnold to study air warfare issues was the AAF Evaluation Board. Its task was to scrutinize the military aspects of the air campaign in Europe. Neither the Bombing Survey nor the Evaluation Board were intelligence agencies, but Arnold and his A–2 clearly saw the intelligence and data-gathering value of each. To take advantage of the vast amount of German information, the intelligence staff, with widespread support elsewhere on the Air Staff, organized the extensive Post-Hostilities Intelligence Requirements Survey of the German Air Force, and later of the Japanese air forces. The posthostilities study of the Germans was to be done largely by General Spaatz's people in Europe, but several Air Staff offices decided to send additional teams. To coordinate the collection and assessment of the anticipated information, Generals Hodges in Intelligence and Kuter in Plans pushed hard for the central AAF intelligence survey.[44]

According to the collection plan, the primary purpose behind this data-gathering foray was to obtain "all information pertaining to the Japanese Air Force available in Germany."[45] This effort had two main objectives. First, the AAF staff needed to know what technology or understanding of the Allied military Germany had transferred to Japan. ULTRA had, from time to time, indicated that such transfers had been made, primarily by blockade-running submarines. Now the Air Staff believed it imperative that they confirm what had transpired between the Axis partners. With such an understanding, the Allies could then postulate the existence of new or previously unobserved Japanese defenses. The second direction of these studies was to determine from the German bombing experience how Japan, her economy, and her military might hold up under a concentrated Allied onslaught.

The survey teams that descended upon Germany after her surrender in May 1945 found enormous collections of material, among which were indications of the types of data the Axis nations had exchanged. At the German Air Ministry's offices at Berchtesgaden, Allied inspectors found documents that noted limited transfers of air warfare material to Japan between June 1943 and March 1945. Also reaching Washington was a report covering German proximity fuze experimentation based on radio, optic, and acoustic principles. The American investigators in this case noted Japan's apparent awareness of the work, but they doubted Japan had received either substantive data or design models. Proximity fuzes were of concern to the AAF because if Japan had such a capability, she would be able to increase greatly the effectiveness of her AA artillery, thereby threatening the B–29 offensive, which most people believed would continue into 1946. Other areas of specific intelligence and operational interest were the extent to which missile, infrared, radar, and jet engine and aerodynamics technology had reached Japan. The May 1945 capture of the German submarine *U–234* heightened Arnold's interest in the subject of information transfer when it was found that the craft carried several German and Japanese officials plus large amounts of documentation bound for Japan. The flow of material arriving from Germany was so fast that the AAF's specialists in Europe and at Wright Field found it impossible to absorb and study all that they received.[46]

As the previously mentioned studies were underway, at least two other major study groups turned up in Germany seeking information. One was the von Kármán mission, a pet endeavor of Arnold's led by the chief of his Scientific Advisory Group, Dr. Theodore von Kármán. This group had been charged by Arnold to "think in terms of developments to be anticipated over 20 years and thus provide guidance to AAF as to goals to be achieved." As Arnold noted, von Kármán and his people were to observe, correlate, and draw conclusions from all possible enemy developments, those in being or under consideration. Von Kármán's group had no intelligence analysis charter as such, but by the very nature of their work they would deal in such matters. When the von Kármán team members arrived in Europe in May 1945, they ran into another group, Maj. Gen. Clayton Bissell's ALSOS mission.* Bissell had dispatched the ALSOS mission from G–2 to carry out a number of the War Department's scientific intelligence goals, but the primary purpose was to ferret out as much information as possible about Germany's atomic energy development. In addition, the group was to find all available records on enemy scientific research and development, especially those with a military application. This included aeronautical research, but the AAF was not represented on the mission's staff.[47]

Not only were the two teams surprised to find each other making similar inquiries, but an inevitable clash quickly found its way to Washington when the von Kármán group, assisted by Spaatz's representatives, tried to lay claim to material unearthed by the ALSOS team. As a further complication, the U.S. Navy and the British voiced legitimate claims to the German secrets. Arnold instructed his deputy, Eaker, who had recently moved to the new job in Washington, to settle the problem, but to be careful how he did it. Arnold was explicit in stating that he did not object to joint work, nor did he want the ALSOS and von Kármán teams consolidated. He wanted von Kármán's conclusions and recommendations sent directly to AAF headquarters—von Kármán's work was not to be commingled with either ALSOS or ATI reports. Arnold did not object to facts jointly developed being jointly reported. Under no circumstances, however, was any information "which definitely discloses our intentions and programs for future air research and development" to be disclosed to anyone outside of Arnold's Washington domain.[48] Whatever course of action the AAF was to take in postwar operations and development, Arnold wanted it decided by the air leaders first. Arnold seems to have feared that premature disclosure

---

*ALSOS was a cover name for the mission, not an acronym. The team was to determine the extent and success of Germany's nuclear research and to locate other significant scientific intelligence data. Few people knew of the ALSOS mission's existence.

might endanger such plans, and he sought at the outset to protect what he believed was the AAF's proprietary information.

The interservice and interallied competition for information became so intense so quickly, and the volume of material so great, that the orderly collection and analysis process broke down by the end of May. Hodges at one point told Eaker that the entire intelligence collection scheme that was originally to have been governed by G–2 SHAEF was "in a state of chaos."[49] To resolve the problem, Hodges urged immediate action to bring the entire effort under the control of a joint air policy advisory council with an AAF general in charge and also having Navy and National Advisory Committee for Aeronautics members, as well as a representative of the U.S. aircraft industry. In June, an agreement prepared by the CCS gave the British the first good article of each type to be discovered. Spaatz objected, pointing out that many important one-of-a-kind articles had escaped American control. He feared they would be lost for use in the war against Japan if the process was not quickly reversed.* The flow of documents became so great that the question of who would get what soon disappeared. Neither the British nor the Americans could cope with matters independently. The upshot was an agreement between the USSTAF A–2 and the Air Ministry to set up in London the Air Documents Research Center. The newly acquired material could be screened, indexed, and reproduced so that all of the interested Anglo-American agencies could receive copies. Of primary importance in this effort was the locating and examining of material pertinent to the Japanese war. The agreement averted an unseemly squabble between Allies over the intellectual and intelligence spoils of the European war. Eventually an agreement between the RAF's intelligence chief and General McDonald resulted in a process of copying documents so that each country would receive a full set of German records and research reports.[50]

When it came to the B–29 program, Arnold's interest never flagged. He quickly saw the potential for trouble that the German technology transfers represented. He sent LeMay a letter outlining his fears on July 5: "Recent intelligence from Germany," he wrote, "emphasizes the interest the [Japanese] have had in aircraft developments along the lines of the Me 163 and 262." Arnold went on to instruct his subordinate on how to spot evidence of aircraft of unusual design—look for "lengthening of, lengthened or paved runways." Blast marks were especially important, as that ". . . was how we first noted German jets. Use your photo-reconnaissance people, PW [POW] interrogators,

---

*Some of the items cited by Spaatz as unavailable to his people were one Ju 290 airplane believed to be the only surviving example of this four-engine type; one two-stage turbine supercharger; one flyable Ta 152, the two-stage version of the FW 190; one Ju 388, a late development of the Ju 88; one Ho 9 jet-powered flying wing; one Ju 222 featuring a 24-cylinder, radial liquid-cooled engine; and one 48-cylinder aircraft engine.

all sources of intelligence,"⁵¹ continued the note. On Guam, LeMay read Arnold's directive, but he doubted that the commanding general's fears would be translated into much of a threat. As a man respectful of Arnold's position, ability, and temperament, LeMay tried to calm Arnold's apprehensions by replying, "The [Japanese] now have little time for experimentation and development of new aircraft types. Available production must be utilized to its full capacity upon established models and replacement parts and engines." LeMay went on to note his belief, "All available air strength is currently being used to counter, by large scale attacks against massed amphibious forces, an expected invasion of the homeland."⁵²

LeMay correctly assessed the situation, but with the war's end indefinite, Arnold wanted no resurgence of Japanese defenses and tactical ability, not even temporarily. The AAF's commanding general was tired of the war, suffering from heart problems, impatient to a degree rarely seen in other people, and constantly concerned about his Air Force. As accurate as were the air intelligence assessments of Japan's remaining strength, Arnold knew that the reports sent to him daily could be wrong or could have missed important details. By the end of July, the Japanese government showed signs of surrender. The final blows came early in August, delivered by the very-heavy bomber force over which Arnold had worried and fussed for years.⁵³

An early-July air intelligence analysis of Japan's ability to continue the war stated: "Japan's war-making capability is not comparable in strength to that of Germany [toward the end]. It [Japan] is already so weakened that imposition of a high rate of combat expenditure would cause collapse." Japan did not have high combat losses, as she did not face conflict on her home territory except for the AAF-Navy air offensive. The intelligence analysts applying the lessons brought home by some of the USSBS's teams could not predict with any accuracy either the course of combat Japan would follow or the time when the war would end. Nor should they have tried to make such a prediction; that would have violated one of the basic tenets of intelligence analysis and placed them into a position of advocating a particular point of view. Such advocacy could have easily guided them away from other, possibly more productive, endeavors in impartially gathering and assessing information. Because of the indeterminate nature of the Pacific conflict, Maj. Gen. Elwood R. Quesada, recently appointed AC/AS, Intelligence, played his hand conservatively, holding the position that "Japanese war-making capability may retain significant menace for a long time." Quesada had no choice but to adopt that view; he recognized that Japan's leaders alone would have to decide how to continue the fight against the Allies. The USSBS analysts who had returned from Europe to help formulate the final assault on Japan now assumed much of the role formerly held within the AAF by the COA.⁵⁴

Piercing the Fog

A difference of opinion quickly arose as to how to prosecute the air war. The Bombing Survey people, upon returning from Europe, proposed a target list to include, in priority order, the following:

- The Japanese transportation system, including the sea blockade and attacks on coastal shipping and on railways.

- Attacking central ammunition reserves if intelligence could confirm that such reserves were in central dumps and that they could be destroyed.

- Attacking nitrogen and synthetic oil production and any radar, aircraft, propeller, and heavy AA plants remaining.

- Destruction (in 1946) of Japan's rice crop and eliminating coke production at Anshan.

- Attacking urban industrial concentrations, but only if such an attack had at least a one in three chance of hitting any of the above precision targets or if it was probably the most efficient way of destroying precision targets.

The JTG had also analyzed Japan's remaining targets. They did not agree with the USSBS recommendations. The JTG's target groupings placed overwhelming emphasis on rail transportation and shipping, followed by heavy attack on concentrations of end-product industry and then clean-up attacks on radar, airplane engine, and specialized armament industries. Urban attacks figured prominently in the end-product industry category, as the target group's analysis indicated that these industries were very vulnerable to incendiary attacks. The JTG's inner circle seems to have believed strongly that if fire could destroy large quantities of war matériel, it would produce heavy expenditures similar to those caused by heavy combat. Sustained consumption was important to reduce Japan's fighting capacity. To reduce it to a point as low as possible, the JTG harked back to the analysis of Japanese cities as targets because group members believed that Japan's major production and storage facilities were to be found throughout the cities. Furthermore, urban areas lent themselves to bombing in poor weather, since precision bombing was not necessary for such missions.[55]

By mid-1945, intelligence officers and the Air Staff had accepted the operational reality that the weather over Japan simply would not allow the type of precision bombing for which the B–29 force had practiced at home. The JTG disparaged nitrogen and petroleum production as targets. Ammunition fabrication and distribution would suffer, they reasoned, from disrupted

Planning the Defeat of Japan

transportation. By scrutinizing the air OB and comparing it to the observed rate of flying, the JTG's staff became convinced that the Japanese had moved aviation gasoline to where they needed it and had then hidden it and reduced flying to cut consumption to the absolute minimum. The JTG found no profitable targets there. By similar reasoning, food supplies would be needed by the occupation commander to sustain the population under his dominion, so the AAF and Navy had no reason to try to poison the rice crop at the start of the next growing cycle. Overall, the JTG believed that attacks on their targets would accelerate the strain on Japan's economy, leading to collapse when the inevitable engagement of land forces came.[56]

As the intense target studies were being made of Japan, Robert A. Lovett traveled to Europe to view firsthand the war's effects. Lovett served from 1941 to 1945 as Assistant Secretary of War for Air. His primary job was to oversee procurement, but he did much more for the AAF in informal ways. The relationship between the hard-driving, often unreasonable Arnold and the assistant secretary was close, and Lovett thoroughly understood and was a strong supporter of air power. He was also a moderating influence on Arnold, the enfant terrible who drove the AAF through the war as much as he led it. Thus it was that in June 1945, when Lovett returned from his trip, he brought back a series of questions about the AAF's intelligence future that caused the senior air officers in the Pentagon to take notice. Lovett's concern lay with the emerging separation of the AAF from the British intelligence services, from which it had gained so much during the European war. Now that the Air Forces could concentrate on the war in the Far East, Mr. Lovett wanted to know the quality of American air intelligence as compared to that available for the just-concluded war with Germany. He also wanted to know what new organization the staff had planned for the changing situation and how the AAF intended to find the trained intelligence officers needed for the job. Lovett's questions were also instructive in that they revealed his understanding that the U.S. AAF intended to carry as much of the air war as possible. The British presence in the Pacific would be minimal, their continental contacts of no use, and Britain's ULTRA net unproductive. The AAF did not especially want the RAF's operational squadrons in the Pacific, in part due to a lack of airfields on Okinawa and the other islands for the use of the Americans and their allies. The AAF wanted the freedom to prove itself, its aircraft, and its doctrine. That meant an unencumbered campaign based on target lists prepared with good intelligence analysis. If Lovett was going to support his airmen, he needed to know more about how they were going to meet the new requirements.[57]

Eaker and Quesada wasted little time in putting together an answer, and it was one that acknowledged a number of shortcomings. The generals claimed that the British national defense organization with its equal status of army, navy, and air force was much more effective in gathering air intelligence than was the American system. According to Eaker, the Air Ministry's intelligence gathering and assessment had "a certain cohesion and single-mindedness of purpose that is totally lacking in Washington."[58] The most nettlesome problem that Eaker saw in Washington was the JCS's decision in 1944 to fragment intelligence responsibilities among the services. His statement that the British system was intrinsically more effective than the one in America was difficult to prove, but it was a good way to approach the question. What made the British system so responsive, Eaker believed, was its tremendous signals intercept and photointerpretation capabilities so near the fighting, readily available to the military and naval commanders. Eaker and Quesada pointed out that the Pentagon was 7,000 miles from the Pacific fighting and that the Americans had always had a paucity of information about the Japanese. This lack of data made it very difficult to assess targets or predict Japanese reactions to bombing. It was not possible, they contended, for the system in Japan to ever be as good as the one in Europe had been. This argument, as far as air power went, applied mostly to strategic air. Kenney and Nimitz had excellent operational air intelligence. The air war over Japan was soon to become more tactical than strategic with the projected November 1 invasion of the Japanese home islands. In answering Lovett's questions, Eaker and Quesada hit again on one of the AAF's continuing concerns: subordination of the air to the ground army, in this case, of A–2 to G–2.[59]

The two generals contended that the AAF had been enjoined from gathering primary intelligence information, except for photography. Worse, but carefully worded for security reasons, G–2 controlled ULTRA analyses and decrypts, giving the Air Staff only finished studies, not the information from which the reports had been drawn nor information from which air analysts might reach other conclusions. The memo to Lovett stated, "In some cases, G–2 only gives us 'evaluated' information, i.e. conclusions deduced from unknown facts, and restricts us rigidly in the way we use these conclusions."[60] Air attachés were likewise controlled by the War Department, not the AAF, and their effectiveness suffered as a result. Eaker and Quesada opined that many of these deficiencies could be offset by the experience gained in Europe; they also proposed a realigned intelligence office, able to concentrate on the tasks allowed them by the Joint Chiefs and to have in place an air intelligence operation comparable to the Air Ministry in London and capable of supporting an independent air force, should one be organized after the war. As a follow-on to the reorganization, Eaker's letter told Lovett that sufficient intelligence officers from Europe were in training in Florida and at Langley, Virginia, for the Pacific war and for use as posthostility intelligence experts. The latter claim regarding training was true on its face, but was a misconception on Eaker's part. Many of the officers who came to the intelligence training from Europe had been of the impression they were on their way home; others had no interest in participating in yet another war in a far-off place of indeterminate length and

Planning the Defeat of Japan

Maj. Gen. Richard C. Lindsay

unknown sacrifice. These men were unhappy, and their performance showed it; their value as intelligence officers was open to question.[61]

One need not read between many of the lines of the letter to Assistant Secretary Lovett and the supporting documents that accompanied it to see again the airmen's frustration with Army control and all of its attendant encumbrances. This time there was a difference. Unlike General White's organizational agonies of early 1944, there now seemed a real possibility that the AAF would escape from the Army once the war was over. To that end, the AC/AS, Intelligence office shed its unwanted appendages. History, motion picture services, and the operational activities that could be delegated to subordinate commands all disappeared from the organizational chart. The A–2 office now had two branches: the JTG and the Director of Air Intelligence. Organizationally and functionally, the JTG remained the same with its panel of consultants and its evaluation and production divisions. The Director of Air Intelligence had the counterintelligence, intelligence collection, photographic, analysis, and technical intelligence divisions. The spring of 1945 saw AAF intelligence reach its largest size in terms of people assigned. Once the focus of war shifted entirely to Japan and the structure of the strategic air force in the Pacific became firm, that staff began to diminish rapidly. By July 7, 1945, in fact, Spaatz, on his way to take over the new strategic air operation, was advised by his prospective chief of staff, Brig. Gen. Richard C. Lindsay, that Washington's efforts in support of the Pacific war should be limited, replaced by intelligence analysis in the theater, principally at the numbered air forces on Guam and Okinawa. The centrifugal forces that large operating commands created, with local people better apprised of situations, began to draw the work away from AAF headquarters, just as had occurred in Europe several years earlier. Had the war continued, Spaatz's stature and reputation, plus the magnitude of the work to be performed, would probably have drawn the JTG itself (or at least much of its work) to Guam.[62]

Army Air Forces Intelligence and the Atomic Bomb

The United States embarked upon development of atomic energy for military uses at the urging of Albert Einstein and a number of prominent physicists. At first, the work was spread out among a number of facilities under the overall direction of the Office of Scientific Research and Development (OSRD), headed by Dr. Vannevar Bush. In the fall of 1942, atomic research came under the purview of the U.S. Army's Manhattan Engineer District and came to be called the Manhattan Project. Brig. Gen. (later Maj. Gen.) Leslie R. Groves headed the Manhattan District, but he received ample supervision from Bush, Dr. James B. Conant, Chairman of the National Defense Research Committee (part of the OSRD), General Marshall, and Secretary of War Stimson (from May 1, 1943, Stimson had overall responsibility for the endeavor). Over the course of the following few years, Groves also assumed responsibility for all of the security, counterintelligence, and military intelligence related to the United States's development of nuclear physics. Ultimately, of course, President Roosevelt and his successor in 1945, President Harry S. Truman, bore final responsibility for the nuclear development effort, but both kept a loose rein on the work, allowing Stimson and primarily Groves to bear the main effort of guiding the design and construction of the atomic bomb.[63] Concurrently, the AAF assembled and trained the 509th Composite Group to deliver the atomic weapons.

Early in March 1945, Stimson began to take an increasing interest in the employment of the atomic bomb. Since 1942, the Secretary of War had assumed that when completed and tested, such a weapon would be used. On March 5, Stimson conferred with his assistant, Harvey Bundy, and later with Marshall, advising both that within a short time they would be involved with the final decision of whether or not to use the weapon on targets in Japan. At about the same time in early March, Groves and Marshall discussed the bomb's use, Groves pointing out the need to coordinate with the War Department's Operations Planning Division, which Groves had assumed would draw up final plans. Marshall demurred. Citing security needs, he told Groves to do the job within his own organization and to keep the number of people involved to a minimum. Groves then formed a target committee consisting of his deputy, Brig. Gen. Thomas F. Farrell, Lauris Norstad from Arnold's office, three of Groves's subordinates (Col. William P. Fisher, Dr. J. C. Stearns, and Dr. D. M. Dennison), and Dr. William G. Penny of the British team at Los Alamos. Drs. John von Neumann and R. B. Wilson also came from the Los Alamos team to be part of the committee. Maj. J. H. Denny, one of Groves's assistants, filled out the committee's initial membership. Although other men participated in target planning from time to time, this group handled most of the work. Active planning began at a meeting in Washington on April 27.[64]

At the committee's first gathering, immediate problems arose relative to concerns about the weather and the few visual bombing days over Japan each month in the summer. Committee members were concerned with the fact that meteorologists could give at most only twenty-four hours' notice of a possibly good operational day. A second problem was the continuing campaign of the Twentieth Air Force which, if not restricted, would soon bomb all Japanese locations that might be targets. To begin the target selection process, Norstad sent a memorandum to General Samford at the JTG requesting specific data, phrasing his request so as to conceal both the bomb's existence and the planning process then underway. Norstad's memo gave a plausible reason for the inquiry, telling Samford to have his people assess a number of targets suitable for a 12,000-pound British Tallboy high-explosive blast bomb to be detonated at an altitude of 200 feet. In general terms, Norstad said that he wanted Samford's people to select reasonably large urban areas, at least three miles in diameter, having high strategic value on the Japanese main islands between Nagasaki and Tokyo. Norstad added to his request a list of possible sites, including Tokyo Bay, Kyoto, Hiroshima, Nagasaki, Nagoya, Kokura, Sasebo, Yokohama, Kobe, Yawata, Shimonoseki, Yamaguchi, Kawasaki, Fukuoka, and Orabe. The JTG was to eliminate from consideration cities previously destroyed by bombardment.[65]

Notably absent from Norstad's request was the need for any information on defenses. Japanese aerial defenses were not one of the committee's primary concerns, and those considerations it left almost entirely to LeMay and the operational mission planners in the Pacific. There was, throughout the selection process from the earliest date of the target committee's meetings, the desire to strike a city yet undamaged. The reasons were twofold: to destroy a major military-related area in a single attempt that dealt the Japanese Army a heavy blow and then to give the Manhattan District's engineers and physicists the chance to use the damage to compute the effects of the bomb's detonation with more precision than previously possible. What the committee sought as much as a wartime target was a laboratory setting for an operational bombing raid of unprecedented proportions.[66]

Once the target material had been collected by the JTG, three members of the committee, acting under cover of Norstad's Tallboy request, visited the A-2's offices to review the data and prepare a final list. Kyoto, Hiroshima, Nagasaki, Niigata, and Kokura emerged as the best candidates. Kyoto gained the most prominence because of its size, its industry, its location as a center of transportation, and the fact that many government and industrial leaders had evacuated there from other damaged cities. Kyoto was also attractive because

381

of its topography. Lying in a bowl formed by mountains, the committee believed that the bomb's energy would be better focused there than anywhere else. Hiroshima (est. pop. 350,000) was an "Army" city, the committee believed, as well as was a major port. From the target information, the men concluded that the city contained large quartermaster supply depots, had considerable industry, and was the location of several small shipyards. Nagasaki (est. pop. 210,000) was the major shipping and industrial center of Kyushu. Kokura (est. pop. 178,000) had one of the largest Army arsenals and ordnance works and the largest railway shops on Kyushu, with large munitions storage areas to the south. Niigata (est. pop. 150,000) was an important industrial city, making machine tools, diesel engines, and heavy equipment; it was also a key port for shipping to and from the mainland. The initial selection now completed, Manhattan Project member Stearns searched the target data to determine all that he could about the cities, including the exact locations of strategic industries. He also had to obtain the best possible aerial photographs and from them determine the general nature of construction and the contents of the buildings, the heights of prominent structures, and the total square footage of roofs. On May 30, Groves asked General Marshall to direct Arnold to prohibit bombing of the five cities by the Twentieth Air Force; he also asked that MacArthur and Nimitz receive similar instructions.[67]

In the process of target selection, target committee members sought distinctly military reasons for their choices, but they recognized that substantial collateral damage would be incurred by the bomb's detonation. Since the AAF had concluded in its own and from the COA's analyses that Japanese manufacturing was dispersed among many modest shops in urban areas and in regions surrounding industrial sites, the preliminary atomic bomb planning followed the general thrust of the AAF's intelligence assessments of Japanese targets. Not Stearns nor any other Manhattan Project people were intelligence analysts. They accepted for their own purposes the data as presented, and they lacked the time or background to make any independent studies.

Above all, General Arnold was a commander who was not playing a major active role in the atomic bomb targeting decision, not even through Norstad who, though a member of the target committee, was less active than the specialists in the selection procedure. Marshall had given target selection responsibility to Groves and the Manhattan Project people, not the air warfare specialists. From the time that the 509th Composite Group began training in Utah, Groves and Farrell—through the general planning process that worked out the details of the unique mission and then through the target committee—gained substantial operational control of the 509th. Colonel Tibbets, its commander, often attended regular planning meetings at Los Alamos and met with the committee in Washington.[68]

Arnold, Norstad, and LeMay saw the 509th as their unit, and so it was in official terms. Formal transfer of the 509th to the Manhattan District was not in question, and during training Tibbets knew that he and his men would go to the Pacific and fly as part of the AAF's Twentieth Air Force. The Manhattan Engineer District, by virtue of its organization, was incapable of supporting a very-heavy bomber unit. Yet the highly technical, unusual nature of the atomic bomb project and the need for secrecy in target selection made the operational control question a moot point. The flow of the war, General Marshall's desire for security, and the long-assumed intent to use the weapon decided the issue of the 509th's control, just as it did the direction of the atomic weapon decision making. Tibbets, when selected for command of the 509th, was told by Maj. Gen. Uzal G. Ent, the Second Air Force commander, "The only man you're going to be responsible to for getting the job done is General Groves; you've got to satisfy him." At the time that he retired from the Air Force, Tibbets recalled that within the AAF he worked for Arnold, with an intermediary to solve problems, but he rarely saw Arnold. On Tinian, the 509th was attached to the 313th Bomb Wing for logistical support, but Groves solved the operational questions, acting through LeMay.[69]

In addition to the target committee, a second stream of planners and policy makers in this undertaking centered on Stimson, who, like Norstad, was a junction between the Manhattan Project and the AAF. Stimson dealt largely in matters not related to the AAF. His long service in government as well as his education, his somewhat fragile health (he was nearly 78 at the time and suffered heart trouble), and his legal background inclined him toward a preference to stay out of direct military decision making. Discussions between Stimson and Marshall and then between Stimson and Truman had resulted in creation of the Interim Committee, appointed to outline a program of action on the bomb's use. Groves seems to have viewed the Interim Committee as what may be termed the predecessor of the postwar Atomic Energy Commission, but with the function of advising on news releases and drafting postwar legislation on atomic energy. Stimson's concept of the group was quite different; he wished it to set immediate policy, but not until May 28 did the Secretary of War decide to make the atomic bomb his primary concern. Even then, the press of daily business, his health, and his age restricted his ability to concentrate on the problem. Stimson had difficulties stemming from the secrecy of the Manhattan District's true purpose. So few people knew of the atomic bomb project's existence (or the weapon's soon to be completed assembly and initial test) that policy could not be formed with an appreciation of the weapon by all the people involved. This severely limited Stimson's ability to intervene significantly in the planning and operational preparations then underway.[70]

Sometime between the first and sixth of June 1945, President Truman and Secretary Stimson reaffirmed the intent to use the atomic weapons on Japanese targets, based mostly on the view of Stimson and a number of others that the weapon was necessary to avoid American casualties that would be sustained in the invasion of Japan. Stimson was by this time in the midst of a conflicting duality of thinking. On the one hand, he had lectured Arnold on the problems associated with urban-area attacks, and he did not want the United States to gain, as he said, the "reputation of outdoing Hitler in atrocities."[71] On the other hand, he was concerned that the airmen might so bomb Japan that "there would be no good background on which to use the weapon," thus apparently losing the opportunity of convincing the Japanese that further resistance was futile.* On June 19, Stimson met with Under Secretary of State Joseph C. Grew, with whom he often conferred on this and similar questions. These men concluded that it "would be deplorable if we have to go through with the military program with all its stubborn fighting to a finish."[72] They wanted to find a way to induce Japan to surrender, and that way seemed more and more to be the atomic bomb. Warnings to Japan preceding the invasion could, in Stimson's mind, include atomic attack.[73] The nature of that attack and its target, whether city or relatively unpopulated area, Stimson did not say.

Stimson, Marshall, and Truman faced the uncertainties of the new weapon's use in the war with some doubts. ULTRA seems to have been one of the factors that helped them resolve their dilemma. In April 1945, Willoughby had sent MacArthur his estimate that the Japanese would defend Kyushu, site of the projected November landing in the Japanese home islands, with at least eight and probably ten divisions. This was to prove conservative. Through May, June, and July, decrypted Japanese messages analyzed in Washington revealed a burgeoning defense preparation effort on Kyushu. Air and naval suicide units supplemented an assembly of armored brigades and combat divisions transferred from Manchuria and elsewhere in Japan. Newly formed divisions and garrison troops added to the strength. In all, ULTRA identified thirteen of the fourteen Japanese divisions on the island, supported by considerable air power. ULTRA counted 600,000 Japanese with 6,000 to 7,000 aircraft; in fact, the final Japanese total was more nearly 900,000 armed men. Although Japanese air and land forces were no longer the well-armed, efficient fighting units of 1942, the Japanese had demonstrated repeatedly their ferocity and willingness to fight to the death. Stimson's concern, as he noted in his diary, clearly grew when he examined the numbers (although he did not note ULTRA as his source). General Marshall had substantial doubts about the proposed landings as well, and so told Truman at the July Potsdam Conference. Storming ashore in the face of a bloodbath did not appeal to Washington policy makers, who were concerned not only with the immediate cost in dead and wounded but also with the prospect of an uncertain length to the war, with possible Soviet military involvement that

---

*At that time, MAGIC had not yet picked up the messages between Prime Minister Togo in Tokyo and Ambassador Sato in Moscow. Their communications indicated that the Japanese government was willing to consider peace with some conditions, primarily retention of the emperor. MAGIC Diplomatic Extracts, SRH–040. MAGIC intercepts on this topic did not begin until July 11, 1945.

Planning the Defeat of Japan

seemed less appealing with the passage of time. With these factors in mind, Truman approved the use of the weapon late in July 1945.[74]

The initial decision by the president and Stimson to drop the atomic bombs was not made on the basis of intelligence information either provided by or in the possession of the AAF. It seems to have grown from the running course of events. Material on hand in the JTG provided the basis for assessing the prospective targets and preparing for postattack surveys of the cities bombed. Descriptions of this course of events given by both General Groves and Secretary Stimson were remarkably alike in that regard. Senior government officials, having presided over the expenditures of billions of dollars and the creation in several states of technical and scientific complexes unrivaled anywhere, assumed all along that such a weapon, if created, would be used against an enemy power. Probably the only person who could have stopped the use of the atomic bomb during the last weeks before its delivery was the president, and Truman saw no compelling reason to do so in light of the bitter fighting that many thought would last well into 1946. Quite the contrary; Truman, Stimson, and Marshall were deeply concerned about the human cost of an invasion and the subsequent fighting. Truman remarked during a meeting with the JCS on June 18, 1945, that he "hoped that there was a possibility [by using the bomb] of preventing an Okinawa from one end of Japan to another."[75] Admiral William D. Leahy, for most of the war President Roosevelt's personal representative to and a member of the JCS, was equally cautious, fearing that the Americans would suffer as many as 268,000 casualties in fighting for the Japanese home islands (after refined intelligence of Japan's home defenses became available, the medical planners's estimate for treatable casualties—not including dead—rose to over 394,000, just for the invasion of Kyushu).[76]

The question of whether or not the atomic bomb's use was necessary to end the war without an invasion of Japan has never been settled and in all probability can never be. Influential arguments supported the bomb's use: in Secretary Stimson's words, an invasion would "cast the die for a fight to the finish"; use of the bomb was essential to save the lives of Americans who would have to bear the brunt of the effects of the landing and fight across the enemy homeland in terrain favorable to the Japanese defenders. Strong arguments also opposed use of the weapon: Japan had sent peace feelers to the Soviet Union seeking Stalin's intercession to end the war, and the United States knew of the Japanese government's position through reading of MAGIC decrypts. ULTRA had indicated the military collapse of Japan and the military leaders' understanding of their country's peril. But ULTRA-based analyses could not predict enemy actions in so desperate a situation.[77]

Many of the men deciding the issue struggled with questions of military usefulness and moral, ethical, and political implications of the bomb's use. Many had serious doubts. Stimson wavered repeatedly; he clearly saw the atomic bomb as more than just a new weapon that could cause a bigger blast.

Piercing the Fog

On May 31 he met with J. Robert Oppenheimer, Ernest O. Lawrence, Enrico Fermi, and Arthur H. Compton, the most prominent physicists involved in the project. Then, and at other times, Stimson described the atomic bomb as "a revolutionary change that held great promise and great danger for civilization."[78] In the summer of 1945, the true effects of the new weapon were unrealized, and it had not yet acquired the quasi-mystical qualities some would later ascribe to it. More than anything else, the lack of information on Japan dogged the efforts of the A–2 in studying the country and lent little knowledge to the men who decided the question of using atomic weapons.

Planning for the bombing of Japan faced several serious problems. For years the A–2's analysts and the COA had recognized the significantly poorer level of intelligence available for Japan. Unlike their fairly substantial knowledge regarding Germany, where active British aerial photography and data collection efforts preceded the war's beginning, the Americans understood the relationships of the several segments of Japan's industrial base only incompletely. Compounding the problem of insufficient target information, the AAF's strategic bombardment program, while well conceived theoretically, fell victim to an inability to meet the technical demands of precision bombing. In Europe, bombardiers had difficulty finding German targets and then in hitting them accurately, once found. These difficulties were only slightly alleviated when radar was used. Due to its technical immaturity, radar failed to satisfy the needs of Spaatz and his people in Europe. Intelligence could not compensate for the technical deficiencies, but an extensive interplay between technology and intelligence existed. Once the Pacific bombing effort began in earnest, the frailties of the equipment were magnified. The 200-mile-per-hour winds in the jet stream high above Japan prevented accurate visual aiming from nearly 30,000 feet. Radar provided some help, but it could not overcome problems associated with weather over Japan, where clear days were no more frequent than they were over Germany. When General LeMay remarked to Arnold that weather was his worst operational enemy, he added, "Our attempts to bomb precision targets at night have failed because we do not have the proper tools to do the job. Bombardiers have not been able to synchronize on the target with the flares and [bomb] sight we have."[79] Arnold, faced with justifying the cost of the huge strategic bomber force, required results, and he insisted on them when dealing with his subordinates. Facing pressures to use the new aircraft effectively, the military also had to contend with the prospect of fighting Japanese troops on the ground.

From the engagement at Guadalcanal in August 1942, the Japanese had fought American forces in the Pacific bitterly, bravely, and to the death virtually every time contact occurred. The fanatical resistance encountered on Saipan, Iwo Jima, and Okinawa was simply the culmination of long combat experience. Secretary Stimson recognized the cost of a campaign in Japan's home islands when he wrote in his diary the remarks about an invasion casting the die for a fight to the finish. The outcome of that fight, Stimson believed, he would be a high casualty list for America and a Japan left in "a worse shambles than we left Germany."[80] Added to the apprehensions about casualties was the distaste many Americans (including the senior military commanders) felt for Japan, stemming from the Pearl Harbor attack and the brutal behavior of Japan's troops throughout Asia. The mistreatment of American POWs, about whom a good deal of information had filtered back to Washington from Philippine guerrillas via the SWPA G–2, no doubt contributed to this mind-set.[81]

Discussions in mid-June between the JTG and the USSBS served as a forum for airing differing views of the American strategic bombing effort for Japan. The USSBS members who had come back to the United States spent considerable time reviewing the bomber program. Although the bombing survey representatives were reluctant to force upon the AAF lessons drawn from the as yet incompletely analyzed CBO, these joint discussions were fruitful in providing consideration for new directions. Of particular interest was the inference drawn by Quesada that Japan's war-fighting potential did not match Germany's, and that the Japanese had concentrated their much more limited economic assets in specific areas while they lacked resources to defend them. There grew in the opinion of Quesada and the JTG the importance of transportation as a target along with ammunition reserves and petroleum, relegating urban areas to a somewhat lower priority.

Two factors complicated matters for both sides. One was the basic uncertainty about the state of Japan's will and ability to fight on. The Soviets had an interest in the Far East and in participating in the peace settlement; as such, they were reluctant to end the fighting too quickly until they had some part in it. Another complication was the dearth of knowledge about the independent target study and of the air campaign being prepared by the Manhattan Project. Among the few places where these two issues converged was with Lauris Norstad, the Twentieth Air Force's chief of staff and an officer very close to Arnold. Norstad could discuss the atomic weapon secret with only a few people while Arnold was preoccupied with a very busy schedule, his recent heart attack, and the future of the Air Force. Norstad, who had advocated the fire-bombing raids, apparently now became also a champion of the atomic bomb as a key to the AAF's future through a demonstration of air power.

The upshot of all of these discussions and differing opinions came on July 25, when Spaatz received a new air campaign mission directive based on a formal JCS position. Transportation was the first objective, followed, in order, by aircraft production, ammunition storage areas, and urban industrial areas. It was too late to effect a change in the atomic bomb decision; the first weapon was to be released over Hiroshima on August 6. Whatever the change to the air campaign might have been, how quickly such change might have been accomplished, and the results can never be judged with accuracy. That Japan would have capitulated is certain. What is less sure is when and under what circumstances she would have ceased to struggle.[82]

Within days of Japan's surrender announcement, General LeMay wrote Clayton Bissell thanking him for the work that MIS had done in support of the campaign against Japan by the XXI Bomber Command and the Twentieth Air Force. Specifically, LeMay credited to MIS (not entirely correctly) the original concept of aerial mining, the intelligence analysis that supported the effort, and the rapid transfer of information that made readjustment of the mine-laying pattern possible. LeMay also recalled that Washington passed to him via secure radio circuits information available there that allowed for adjustments in target planning as the air campaign progressed. The general was appropriately grateful that MIS had gone so far as to send one of its best photointerpreters to Guam, where he did as-needed, on-the-spot industrial analyses of any of 180 Japanese urban areas. Another specialist came to do the same for studies of Japanese petroleum production. Of particular interest in LeMay's letter was his comment, "When it became evident that the Target Analysis Section of [Twentieth Air Force's] A–2 would have difficulty keeping abreast of the scale of effort maintained by the command, a civilian analyst who for four years had been working on the Japanese industrial systems came to Guam from MIS to help."[83]

LeMay directed his remarks to G–2, not to the air intelligence staff of the AAF. In doing so, he echoed and reinforced the feeling within some parts of the AAF that its air intelligence office had not done well in the war against Japan. Moreover, many in the Army believed that the A–2's function was a wartime expedient, to be disbanded or greatly reduced when peace came. In fact, intelligence assessments of Japan done in Washington did not match the scope and breadth of those made by the Allies in the war with Germany; this was so for many reasons, not all of them properly laid at A–2's doorstep. Japan had concealed much of herself before the war, and for many years she lay far beyond the prying eyes of photoreconnaissance pilots and photointerpreters. Hap Arnold summed up matters after a fashion when, in December 1944, he told the OSS's General Donovan of the necessity for translating the German bombing experience into a method for evaluating the potential effects of attacks on Japan. Using the German information as a basis for study was a perfectly fine idea; the problem was that strategic judgment of Japan still had a long way to go on the eve of the B–29 campaign. The frustration with the lack of adequate data on Japanese target systems, locations, vulnerabilities, and relationships to Japan's economy had a significant effect on the course of the strategic aerial war in the Pacific.[84]

The Reorganization of 1945

By the end of April 1945, the A–2 office in Washington had begun preparing for peace, even as they laid out targets for the final assault on Japan. Although many believed that the AAF's accomplishments and the position of air power in modern war portended an independent air arm for the United States, when this would happen was uncertain. The A–2's survey of the responsibilities and authority of his office, done to answer Assistant Secretary Lovett's questions, reported that authority for air intelligence in the Army remained firmly under the control of the War Department's G–2, with the A–2 operating either as G–2 directed or with G–2's tacit approval because G–2 could not undertake everything it wanted to. The general legal authority for A–2's existence was Army Regulation 95–5, which established the AAF as a major command and authorized Arnold as Commanding General to create the agencies he needed to perform his mission. Despite Arnold's authority, the G–2's office retained virtually all control of intelligence activity, approving very little independent AAF intelligence work, and then only with the understanding that A–2 first determine if the War Department could provide the services and information requested. Theoretically, this was an efficient, logical position for the Army to adopt, but since the G–2 could not hope to do all the work, it hampered the AAF's development to independence and frustrated the A–2's staff. An example of the quandary in which the air intelligence office found itself was liaison with the Navy and other agencies.

During the war, the A–2 had established extensive contacts with the other services. To continue these contacts, A–2 had requested, at G–2's insistence, approval by G–2 of the arrangements, but it had never received a reply. No authority existed for motion-picture production, something in which Hap Arnold believed strongly and which he promoted effectively before and throughout the war years. Nor were the extensive historical analyses begun under the A–2's direction authorized to the depth and scope that the AAF was pursuing them. Air attaché activity remained so tightly under G–2's control that the air intelligence staff questioned whether the AAF could maintain necessary and productive foreign contacts with the return of peace. Other areas of concern remained a lack of radio and radar analysis capability for the air headquarters (as opposed to the gathering of information in the field to be processed by others) and the AAF's ability to control the overall gathering of air intelligence in general.[85]

The ambiguous position of AAF intelligence at the headquarters in Washington stemmed very much from General Arnold's own ambiguous position as a member of the JCS and from the general attitude surrounding the AAF's more or less autonomous position within the American military and naval structure. Since Arnold sat on the JCS, his A–2 served as a member of the JIC along with the other services' chiefs of intelligence. The A–2's position on the JIC was informal; the Army had not provided any explicit authority for such membership. The JCS itself was not a body with a specific charter ordering it to perform certain functions. Almost everything connected with the JCS was equally informal, seen through much of the conflict as wartime expedients. Sensing the approach of independence from the Army and equal status with the Army and Navy in the postwar military, two intelligence chiefs—Hodges and Quesada—prepared for the change.[86] Hodges had begun the studies that were to guide postwar intelligence organizations on the air staff.

Then, immediately following V–J Day (September 2, 1945), Quesada reformed his office, making the last in a series of wartime shifts designed to meet current needs and changing situations. Reduced in size, the A–2 office now contained an Air Information Division, an Air Intelligence Division, and a small Executive Division. It also marked the end of a four-year evolution under the direction of eight men who filled the office or function of the chief of AAF intelligence. With the new ground rules that came into play at the end of the war, Quesada supervised the air intelligence study of foreign air forces, their offensive capabilities in relation to American strategic vulnerability, and their defensive potentials. The office scrutinized the United States's strategic objectives in foreign countries, including their strategic vulnerabilities. The A–2's office also collected information on foreign airfields, meteorology, terrain, logistics, and air operations.[87]

With the end of World War II, the air intelligence office changed its focus from combat data analysis to that of trying to ensure the prevention of strategic, tactical, or technological surprise, and of amassing air intelligence required by the AAF for future war operations. Many of the people who had served throughout the war soon left the service, but enough remained to staff the office's new components. The Air Information Division's collection branch kept many of its wartime functions and had the special task of watching developments related to very high-level security information and signals intelligence. This section did not prepare its own signals intelligence analyses; G–2 still provided them. The air attaché branch assumed greater responsibility for selecting and briefing its new members, an improvement over the absolute control by the G–2. The new Air Intelligence Division contained branches analyzing enemy offensive air power, defensive capabilities, worldwide air facilities, and enemy strategic vulnerabilities. This new branch was essentially the old JTG, scaled down and lacking the other service members and British representatives; the target vulnerability studies it performed were similar to those of its wartime predecessor. The Executive Division directed the administrative, counterintelligence, and plans and policy activities of the office of the A–2. The attention once focused on Germany and Japan and which had been building slowly for two years to a scrutiny of the USSR now assumed greater importance.[88]

Planning the Defeat of Japan

By early 1945, the Soviet Union's role in the defeat of Germany was abundantly clear to senior officers in Washington. Although a difficult and at times perverse and puzzling ally, the USSR had been recognized by the Americans as crucial to the war effort against the European Axis. Clayton Bissell assessed the Soviets' important role in the summer of 1944 when he told General Marshall, "The defeat of Germany this year is dependent primarily on Russian military action and secondarily upon the effectiveness of Anglo-American military operations."[89]

As far back as February 1943, Arnold had harbored ambivalent feelings about the Soviet Union when he advised General Marshall not to give heavy bombers to the Russians. Arnold's primary reason for the recommendation was that he had too few of the aircraft to outfit his own service, the Navy, and the Marine Corps, let alone another country that might not employ them effectively. Arnold told Marshall in this case that he fully supported the policy of helping Stalin so as to hurt Germany. He added that "There is, moreover, a growing uncertainty as to where Russian successes will lead. I for one am willing to accept the risk to us created by possible Russian misuse of aid or abuse of successes, so long as her successes are necessary for our success." Nevertheless, when in May 1945 Arnold turned down a request for P–59 and P–80 jet aircraft from Maj. Gen. S. A. Piskounov, Chief of the Aviation Department, Soviet Government Purchasing Commission, his refusal was not overtly based on distrust of Soviet intentions. He justified the refusal on lack of Munitions Board approval and on the need for British consent, which he did not have.[90]

At a lower level in the AAF, an assessment of Soviet intentions of early 1945 that circulated among the A–2 staff contained doubts about what the Red Army planned in the immediate future vis-à-vis the *Wehrmacht*. The basic thrust of the paper was that nobody understood what to expect from the Soviets, either in Europe or in Asia. It was this uncertainty more than anything else that shaped the AAF's assessment of her enigmatic ally. A minor A–2 staff reorganization proposed for early 1944, for instance, included an officer position to assess events in the Soviet Union, a position separate from the foreign liaison and air OB functions. Perhaps one reason for this action was the need to keep tabs on the huge Allied nation to which America committed large numbers of aircraft and other air warfare–related matériel under Lend-Lease. This could not have been an overriding factor, however, as the A–2 office had little to do with Lend-Lease. The most pressing reason had to have been the uncertainty with which some on the Air Staff viewed the Soviet Union, the difficulties experienced in dealing with her, and the need to know more about the country. Not until Japan had been defeated did the staff have time to assess the state of relations with the Soviet Union, but very quickly questions arose.[91]

Colonel Grinnell Martin, chief of the new Offensive Air Branch of A–2, prepared a short memorandum discussing the strategic vulnerability of the United States in September 1945. That memo noted that, for the foreseeable future, only Canada, the United Kingdom, and the USSR posed a threat to America. Martin dismissed Canada and Great Britain as benevolent, presenting no serious problem. The USSR was another story. Having interned at least two B–29s that had landed in Siberia before their entry into the war against Japan, the Soviets could use the aircraft as patterns for similar aircraft of their own. Based upon American design and manufacturing experiences with the B–29, Colonel Martin predicted that in no less than five years the Soviets would have between 50 and 100 such airplanes operational.[92]

In mid-November of 1945, the G–2 office sent A–2 an estimate of probable developments that might require the use of U.S. forces in the next five to fifteen years. Prominent in the discussion within that report was the emerging conflict between the USSR and the Western Allies. In defining the factors that constituted a threat to the United States, the G–2 analysts drew disturbing parallels between the Soviet activity, both prewar and postwar, and the trends of prewar German actions, including rigid police states, absolute political control, occupation of or attacks upon foreign neighbors (for the USSR, this included the Baltic States, Finland, and Poland), closed economies, and exporting political doctrine inimical to democratic processes.[93]

The report also noted that the war had placed the USSR in a position where from five to fifteen years might be required for the Soviet Union to develop its war-making capability to the point that it could directly threaten the United States. The assessment concluded that a potentially unfriendly Soviet strategic air force would not emerge until about 1950 to 1955 and that the USSR could take until 1960 to recoup its manpower and industrial losses of World War II. Thus, the immediate threat seemed small except for the nearly certain effort by the USSR to push hard to develop a nuclear weapon. The analysts translated this nuclear research and development into a five- to ten-year growth period. Of overriding concern to military planning, according to the report's conclusion, was the lack of understanding by the American people of Soviet intentions. This lack, and the wish of the people to demobilize, meant that little chance existed for maintaining an American armed force able to cope with the clearest possible danger the USSR presented: an ability to move west and occupy large amounts of Europe. With this view of a mixed state of affairs, the AAF entered the postwar period as an enormously strong organization, but as one rapidly declining in size and capability.[94]

CHAPTER 8

Retrospection

INTELLIGENCE PLAYED A CRUCIAL ROLE as the AAF pursued the air war from 1941 to 1945. It provided an analytical framework through which American airmen estimated their opponents, allocated their resources, and calculated the results and impact of their attacks. Consistently throughout the war, intelligence provided substantial clarification of the ambiguities of a war conducted in a new medium. Whatever the difficulties with American air intelligence, it is worth contrasting the American (and British) experience with what occurred in the Italian, German, and Japanese intelligence agencies. Had Allied intelligence capabilities and those of the Axis been reversed, the results of the war, or even of major campaigns, might not have been reversed, but the road to victory would have been far more costly and difficult.

American air intelligence in World War II faced enormous difficulties, none of which was open to easy solution, and few of which were ever completely solved. Paramount was the very nature of the war. Operational commanders and intelligence organizations almost always had to work on the basis of less than complete information, even when interception and decryption of enemy message traffic provided a direct avenue into the enemy's mind. Given the conditions of war, the best intelligence could provide only fleeting glimpses of the enemy's intentions and capabilities; it was then a matter of how well and how imaginatively intelligence formed its estimates of the Axis forces.

From the beginning, large problems confronted American intelligence in the conduct of the air war. The great military organizations of 1943, 1944, and 1945 that crushed the Axis had evolved from minuscule services that possessed virtually no intelligence capabilities in 1940. Surely one of the greatest American triumphs of World War II involved turning America's immense economic potential into military capabilities. Beyond the mobilization problems of an unprepared nation, air intelligence in Washington at the A–2 office found itself hampered by dependence on the War Department's G–2. The Army's close hold on intelligence sources, especially those having to do with special intelligence, caused difficulties. Those impediments were less significant in the various theaters in which the AAF operated. Particularly in Europe, British capabilities and the RAF's position as an independent service were a boon to American tactical and strategic air intelligence. The British provided a model and the extensive cooperation to make American air intelligence more effective and valuable than it otherwise would have been. At war's end, Ira Eaker observed that the British system operated more effectively because of the equal status of the air, land, and naval forces.[1] The way the British integrated their intelligence and operational systems served as a model for Americans into the postwar period. Their experience and contact with the other European powers was what the Americans lacked. In the operating theaters, commanders and subordinates exhibited a level of cooperation not typical of Washington.

The lack of consistent support for the A–2 may have had its strongest impact in the area of intraservice and interservice rivalry that pervaded Washington throughout the war. In the absence of a single, national agency to coordinate intelligence gathering, analysis, and dissemination, the services resorted to measures that alleviated some problems but dealt effectively with only a few. A case in point was the 1944 division of analysis and production tasks between the Army, Navy, RAF, and AAF to reduce duplication and to place some of the work in the most logical areas: in London for Europe and in Washington for Japan. In most instances, the rivalries and turf fights in Washington continued. The OSS could not develop to its full potential because it was excluded not only from certain geographical areas like SWPA, but from functional and analytical tasks as well. Lack of access to ULTRA probably retarded its research work and, moreover, effectively kept the OSS from full partnership in intelligence tasks. The AAF made enormous strides in use of information about the enemy between mid-1941 and September 1945. Of all the sources available, one in particular proved especially useful and flexible in all of the areas around the world where Army airmen fought.

Tactical reconnaissance served as the basis of AAF's intelligence analysis and operational target planning in combat theaters worldwide during World War II. It provided information on terrain, weather, and hydrography (especially for mining sea lanes and ports); location and employment tactics for communication and electronic equipment (such as radar) and the lines of communication among and within enemy units; and location, disposition, composition, movement, and logistical status of enemy air, land, and sea forces. Aerial photography, as an element of reconnaissance, provided an important and consistent source of information about the enemy. This form of information could be viewed by intelligence specialists within hours of its acquisition and immediately compared to previous days' photographs, making a basis for timely tactical decision making. ULTRA, by contrast, was far better suited to strategic decision making or to an air commander's need for overall planning guidance. This conclusion did not always apply; reconnaissance and ULTRA sources provided immediate insights with direct application in certain circumstances.

Neither source could be exclusionary; each complimented other information and analyses.

Although intelligence was crucial to Allied victory, its contribution to the focus and conduct of operations could not be termed the single most decisive factor in winning the air war. The American and British services in Europe and the American success in the Pacific reflected a capacity to integrate intelligence, skillfully and in a timely fashion, into operations. American airmen proved responsive to the contributions that intelligence could make to their campaigns, something that stood in stark contrast to their opponents' ability to incorporate such information. Intelligence involved more than a simple depiction of the enemy and his capabilities in combat. It demanded a willingness to learn from the experiences of others and a capacity to analyze both combat and other lessons honestly. Allied success depended on more than intelligence officers and organizations in the building of a coherent intelligence picture of the Axis enemies.

Doctrine, Intelligence, and Air Power: The Prewar Preparations

In the period between 1920 and 1939, intelligence, as understood today, hardly existed in the United States. Henry Stimson's remark that "gentlemen do not read other gentlemen's mail" as he shut down work aimed at penetrating Japanese diplomatic ciphers was suggestive of the American approach to intelligence during the prewar period. In his political undertakings, President Roosevelt sent special messengers and intelligence gatherers to Europe to pursue his sometimes ambiguous policies. The most important of these emissaries was the future Maj. Gen. William "Wild Bill" Donovan, head of the OSS, who visited Italy in 1935 in an attempt to discover Mussolini's intentions, and perhaps even to enlist him in an anti-German coalition.[2] But, for the most part, American intelligence relied on the routine efforts of military attachés, often poorly supported at American embassies. These military attachés were largely naval and army officers whose knowledge and training predisposed them toward ground and maritime matters, which meant that air intelligence received scant attention. The information that was garnered depended on the reports of junior officers whose training and background did not prepare them to perform sophisticated analyses. Some frightening reports of German air power (such as Charles A. Lindbergh's) in the late 1930s and early 1940s exercised more influence on the popular press than on the government. The reports attributed exaggerated capabilities to potential opponents, particularly to the *Luftwaffe,* and suggested that the United States had little chance of catching up. While such reports attempted to persuade the American people to stay out of a European conflict, they helped Roosevelt mobilize support for the initial buildup of American air and naval power.

Hap Arnold's May 1939 meeting at West Point with Lindbergh was a prime example of the problem facing the AAF. Arnold, dealing with what he believed was a gross lack of information about enemy air power, thought that Lindbergh passed him a great deal of useful material, which he probably did. After all, starting from a baseline of virtually no information, any information helped. But that Arnold personally had to gather intelligence to make his own assessments of the GAF illustrated the magnitude of the problem.

Assistant military attachés for air confronted an almost impossible task in their intelligence-gathering mission. No one possessed a clear conception of what was needed. What was important was often unclear. Considering the technological revolution occurring in the late 1930s, performance characteristics of enemy aircraft and other design developments were enormously important. Equally important were the production capacities of aircraft industries, not to mention the force structures being cast by potential opponents or allies. Any eventual American employment of its Army Air Corps depended on a thorough understanding of the capacity, capabilities, strengths, and weaknesses of enemy economic systems. Little information was available and less was used by the government or Air Corps in their preparation of production plans for strategic bombers in the last years of peace.

Much of the intelligence gathered by the attachés tended to overlook the tactical employment doctrines (e.g., the Germans in the Spanish Civil War) in favor of technical and quantitative intelligence. That any one officer or even a small group of officers serving as attachés could address all these demanding areas was beyond the realm of the possible. Two factors saved American intelligence and its strategic position from disaster. The first was the time and space available for the United States to address critical failings and weaknesses in its intellectual and physical preparations for war. Other people, most notably the British, paid a terrible price learning lessons that Americans could use. Second, at least in Europe, the United States had the inestimable advantage of having the British build an effective intelligence system from which the American military could draw from and then graft onto their own intelligence capabilities.

The American problem in gathering intelligence on potential opponents in the 1930s also suffered from other weaknesses beyond a lack of resources. The Japanese covered their developing air power most effectively, so that American intelligence remained blind to this technological and operational potential. The Japanese largely excluded American observers from territories they controlled, and complexities of the Japanese language as well as differences between Japanese and American cultures made the task of American intelligence analysts all the more difficult. American belief in the inherent superiority of the white race further exacerbated difficulties in understanding the nature of the danger. The estimate of the assistant naval attaché in Tokyo underlined these deeply ingrained prejudices:

> Originality is certainly not a trait of the Japanese and this quite evidently applies to their aviation equipment. Everything is basically of foreign origin—planes, engines, and instruments. They do build well, however, and the results are creditable, but being copied from foreign developments their equipment must necessarily be at least a couple of years behind that of the leading occidental powers. . . . I believe that there is no doubt that we are markedly superior to the Japanese in the air—in piloting skills, in material, and in ability to employ our aircraft effectively on the offense and defense.[3]

The information on the other Axis powers was almost the opposite: too much information of uncertain origin and value. In the 1930s the Germans, through skilled manipulation of observers, proved to be masters in persuading foreign intelligence services that they possessed extraordinary capabilities and potential. The most famous example involved the visit of the chief of staff of the French Air Force, General Joseph Vuillemin, to Germany in August 1938. The aerial display made such a frightening impression on him that he returned to Paris to advise his government that the French Air Force would last barely two weeks against the *Luftwaffe*.[4] Such assessments led the Foreign Minister, George Bonnet, hardly a strong reed himself, to beg the German ambassador in early September 1938 that Germany not put France in a position where she had to honor her treaty obligations—this, at the same time he was delivering a "warning" that a Nazi attack on Czechoslovakia would result in a French declaration of war.[5] The British were no less confused by German claims.[6] One should not be surprised, therefore, that the minimal American effort to estimate the German potential was similarly in error; but the damage was considerably less, for in the long run it had the beneficial impact of speeding up American rearmament, especially in the air, the one arena where a potential enemy might strike directly at the United States.

While the world situation steadily deteriorated in the late 1930s, American airmen, particularly those at ACTS, had evolved a complex theory of air power. That theory strongly influenced the development and conduct of the later American strategic bombing offensives against first Germany and later Japan in the Second World War. American air doctrine rested on two basic premises. The first was that unescorted, large formations of heavily armed bombers could fight their way deep into enemy territory, without suffering exorbitant losses, and then drop their bombs on selected targets with precision. The second, and a related premise, was that the bombers could attack certain specific target sets, the destruction of which would lead to such widespread dislocations that the enemy's economic system would collapse. It was an attractive theory that promised not only justification for an independent air force, but it would also avoid the catastrophic losses of soldiers that had occurred in World War I.[7] The doctrine had important implications for intelligence.

Only combat could test the assumptions on which the first premise rested. The second assumption demanded excellent intelligence on potential enemy economies, and that intelligence did not exist. As Captain White accurately bemoaned in 1938, the general lack of intelligence precluded an air campaign effective in causing economic dislocation.[8] Unfortunately, devotees of strategic bombing at the ACTS never seemed to have recognized the role of intelligence in determining the weak links in an enemy's economic structure. Such economic analysis as did occur largely rested on studies performed on similar American industries. While such studies were useful, they carried with them the danger that conditions peculiar to America were not necessarily mirrored in Germany or Japan.

In fairness to the Americans who developed the concept of precision strategic bombardment, precious little information existed on which *any* analysis could establish a coherent picture of potential opponents. What seems astonishing today in a time of bountiful information was the general lack of intelligence in the United States as World War II broke out. While the American military had some general understanding of the German military and economic situations, ground and maritime intelligence needs were scantily supported. Virtually *no* resources were available for the gathering of air requirements.

The crucial turn came only with the creation of the Air Corps Intelligence Board. The interest of both President Roosevelt and the new Army Chief of Staff, General Marshall, also helped the creation of an air intelligence capability. But the real problem, as with all the services from 1939 through 1942, lay in building an effective intelligence organization from thin air. Here the American penchant for flexibility and unorthodox solutions held particular value.[9] By bringing civilian expertise, such as engineers, professors, lawyers, and economists, into intelligence organizations that grew exponentially, the capabilities of AAF intelligence generally matched the demands that war placed on them. One has only to consider the success of the American ULTRA organization, with talent that included some of the greatest legal minds in the United States, to understand what the skillful addition of civilians to intelligence was able to accomplish. On the negative side, while civilian talent may have made a long-term favorable contribution, it could not address the immediate problems of intelligence shortcomings in the war's early years. The United States paid dearly for such weaknesses in the first six months of its participation in the conflict.

With the outbreak of war in Europe in September 1939, the pace of America's rearmament quickened, but the weaknesses of the American military presented extraordinary problems. The entire structure, operational as well as support, had to be built from scratch. With doctrinal conceptions for air power largely in place, considerable gaps in understanding continued. Particularly dangerous was the air planners' failure to recognize the enemy's potential to organize an effective air defense to thwart American efforts at implementing strategic bombing doctrine or the enormous flexibility that the enemy's economic system possessed. The intelligence organization and knowledge did not exist to support the implementation of AWPD–1. German economic and industrial systems were broadly misunderstood; perhaps more serious was the fact that American airmen were unaware of the extent of their ignorance. The fog and friction of war made it difficult to acquire that knowledge. American air plans for the destruction of the German economy consequently carried with them serious misconceptions from the beginning as to how Germany worked and what its most serious weaknesses were.

The two years preceding America's entry into the war provided time for further preparations and, perhaps more important, the opportunity for the American military to learn from the experiences and mistakes of others. The British, particularly after Churchill became Prime Minister, willingly shared combat and intelligence experiences; American airmen were able to observe the course of the air war over Europe from a front-row seat. Their willingness to learn the lessons of combat achieved at the expense of others was somewhat open to question.

The Battle of Britain provided a laboratory experiment to test the theories of strategic bombing. The *Luftwaffe,* in many ways the most up-to-date air force in the world in 1940 (with technological devices such as blind bombing aids that the RAF and AAF would not possess until 1943), formed up across the English Channel to strike a decisive blow.[10] The Germans, with geographic advantages that Allied air forces would not enjoy until the end of 1944, failed utterly. Why they failed is obvious today, fifty years later, but it may not have been so obvious then. Above all, the Germans did not devise and follow through on a strategy aimed at gaining air superiority. They did not persevere in the face of adversity, and they lacked either a coherent or a strategic approach. Among other important lessons, it was apparent that a modern bomber force could not accomplish its mission in the face of enemy fighters unless it had the protection of a fighter escort. British society and industry proved adaptable, flexible, and resistant to sustained bombardment from the air. The capacity to inflict effective, long-term damage was going to prove far more difficult than prewar air theorists had thought.

American observers saw little of this. American assessments attributed heavy *Luftwaffe* bomber losses to inadequate bomber defenses and airframe size, the low level at which the Germans flew their missions, and to poor formation-flying discipline.[11] AWPD–1 argued the following summer that "by employing large numbers of aircraft with high speed, good defensive power, and high altitude," American bombers would be able to penetrate deep into the heart of Germany without unbearable losses.[12] The impediment that enemy fighters might represent still did not appear in the AAF's plans. Escort fighters lacked drop tanks, and American airmen continued on a course of fighting the Germans with unescorted bomber formations until the second disaster over Schweinfurt in October 1943. As the American official historians suggested, such an oversight "is difficult to account for."[13]

Even before America entered the war, its attention centered on Europe. Among other reasons, Roosevelt and his advisors determined that Germany represented the greatest strategic threat to the security of the United States. Nazi hegemony over the European continent might be irreversible, while the prospect seemed small that Japan could defeat the United States. Europe and Germany were known entities, familiar and calculable to most Americans; therefore the natural proclivity was to concentrate on the known. If American understanding of German capabilities was poor, the understanding of Japan was far worse. Intelligence estimates reported that the Japanese built battleships, airplanes, tanks, and other weapons, but estimators could not conceive that they could come close to the performance of Western technology. Nor could Americans believe that the Japanese could launch effective military operations or understand that they would have a differing approach in their calculations of war risks or of the relationship of means to ends.

The war in the Pacific should hardly have come as a surprise. The last prewar issue of *Time* magazine had the following to say about the situation:

> Everything was ready. From Rangoon to Honolulu every man was at battle stations. And Franklin Roosevelt was at his. This was the last act of the drama. The US position had the single clarity of a stone wall. One nervous twitch of a Japanese trigger, one jump in any direction, one overt act, might be enough. A vast array of armies, of navies, of air fleets were stretched now in the position of track runners, in the tension of the moment before the starter's gun.[14]

Despite the efforts of historians to discover a smoking gun that would implicate the Roosevelt administration in the Pearl Harbor disaster, the real cause of the catastrophe lay in the assumptions and attitudes of American civilians and military. Ignoring Admiral Togo Heihachiro's surprise attack on the Russian Far East Fleet at Port Arthur in 1904, few could imagine that the Japanese would or could launch another surprise attack in 1941.[15] The result was a tactical and operational defeat in the Philippines and Hawaiian Islands. A peacetime mentality clouded the judgment of American commanders. The Pacific fleet at Pearl Harbor had made minimal preparations to resist air attack. The Army (including the AAF) assumed that the Navy was handling matters, despite the fact that the AAF's mission in Hawaii was to protect the fleet.[16]

The real causes of the Pearl Harbor disaster had more to do with faulty assumptions and a general unwillingness to take enemy capabilities seriously than with a failure to gather intelligence. The destruction of American air power in the Philippines resulted from slightly different factors. Pearl Harbor had occurred eight hours earlier; American aircraft remained parked wing tip to wing tip, reflecting a peacetime belief that one will be able to do anything one wants to an adversary in war, while the opponent in turn will be able to do nothing in reply. One can doubt whether more intelligence could have averted disasters in the face of such facile assumptions.

Intelligence and the Air War in Europe

The Japanese attack on Pearl Harbor and Hitler's ill-considered declaration of war on the United States propelled the United States into a two-front war. The German declaration of war allowed Roosevelt to portray the Nazis and Japanese as representing a close alliance (in fact little connection or strategic cooperation existed between the two powers); the Americans were able to pursue a Europe-first strategy with only minor modifications despite the overwhelming desire of the American public to smash the Japanese. As early disasters in both the Atlantic and Pacific underlined, two years of preparation were not sufficient to ready U.S. forces for combat against well-prepared enemies. The resulting deficiencies led to disastrous defeats. The American military faced the difficult tasks of conducting combat operations, rapidly expanding their forces, and building up the logistics and intelligence structure required to support those forces once deployed and in combat.

For the AAF, creation of an intelligence capability represented an especially difficult task: only the most superficial formal air intelligence organization characterized the interwar American military services. While airmen scrambled to remedy the problem, they failed to understand until 1943 how dependent their theories of air power employment were on economic analyses. Ira Eaker's comment that "almost no information regarding targets in Germany, strength, and disposition of the German air force, etc. was available in the United States" defines the intelligence deficit with which the AAF began the air war.[17]

The United States first had to build an intelligence organization that could effectively support operational commanders. Here the American penchant for adaptability and flexibility showed to full advantage. By drawing from a wide variety of civilian backgrounds, the U.S. military created capabilities in a surprisingly short time. The presence of individuals such as Telford Taylor (later a chief prosecutor at Nuremberg, eminent historian of the Third Reich, and leading Wall Street lawyer as well as professor of law at Columbia) and Lewis F. Powell, Jr. (later an Associate Justice of the Supreme Court) suggests the capacity and willingness of the rapidly expanding U.S. intelligence organizations to attract and assign positions of responsibility to first-class talent. But the inchoate American intelligence organizations were ill prepared for the challenges of 1942 and even 1943. They had to learn, as did American combat forces, on the job.

Piercing the Fog

Particularly in the area of targeting and economic analysis, the air intelligence organization had little choice but to depend on outside talent. Here the willingness of the great American universities and their faculties proved crucial. The intellectual competence of the academically trained economists, political scientists, and historians provided a level of skill and expertise that airmen and their counterparts in the other services simply did not possess. The AAF in particular proved willing to reward talent and expertise with appropriate rank and status and to utilize such talent in positions of trust and responsibility.

The initial classes of those selected and schooled as air intelligence officers turned out to be surprisingly good. They were products of a school system that had virtually no experience in the field.[18] The capabilities of the first classes in the intelligence school at Harrisburg had little to do with their schooling; all the students were volunteers from a wide variety of professions and disciplines. Nearly all those trained had been successful in civilian life and were highly motivated volunteers, so it is hard to see how any schooling could have failed. This excellence, unfortunately, soon declined as the number of volunteers was exhausted and as the intelligence school rapidly expanded its student body to accommodate the insatiable demands of combat commands for more intelligence officers. With a rapidly expanding student body, Harrisburg found itself forced to draw its faculty from among its graduates, the best of whom bitterly resented any assignment to remain at the school. One also suspects that as the demand for intelligence officers leveled off, bureaucratic concerns began to determine those who would receive assignment to the basic course. Whatever the weaknesses of the schooling system, in a surprisingly short time the American military, and the AAF in particular, fielded efficient intelligence organizations. At their best, American intelligence officers assigned to the European and Mediterranean theaters stepped in and worked hand in hand with their British intelligence organization counterparts. The American success, similar in many ways to the success of the British, stands in stark contrast to the generally ineffective intelligence undertakings of the Axis.

American air intelligence benefited enormously from its close cooperation with the British. In every aspect of intelligence—from signals, to cryptanalysis, to photoreconnaissance, to the resistance networks, and to economic analysis—Americans found enormously useful the open-handed aid that the British extended. Such British aid was not entirely unselfish; the British desperately needed the support of American industrial production and the eventual participation of American air and ground forces in battling into Fortress Europe. Even before the United States entered the war, the British proved to be remarkably forthcoming with many of the products of their intelligence system (although they remained circumspect with regard to ULTRA). With America's active participation assured by Japan and Germany, the British provided a more systematic form of help to the struggling American forces. As early as spring 1941, the British and Americans cooperated extensively through the MEW on questions dealing with oil and the economic position of the Axis powers. Cooperation on sharing other crucial raw materials was slower to develop; through 1943 the Americans relied heavily on British assessments of the German economic situation.[19]

From the beginning, cooperation between Eighth Air Force's growing intelligence organization and the RAF's already well-organized and skillful intelligence effort was close and fruitful, remaining so to the end of the war. Throughout the war the British Y-Service, responsible for intercepting and determining the location of German radio transmissions, provided its intelligence directly to the U.S. Eighth Air Force as well as to the RAF, much of it (i.e., the intercepted high-grade encrypted messages) going directly to BP, the central analysis agency. Close cooperation between the U.S. War Department and British military intelligence provided a forum through which the British could funnel their experience and capabilities into the growing U.S. intelligence network.[20] The American Air Staff in Washington found the system less than satisfactory since there was a pervasive feeling that the G–2 was filtering out key pieces of the puzzle, not through malice but because of its ignorance of air matters. Key pieces were being filtered out for that reason and to protect ULTRA sources worldwide.

In Europe, direct contacts with British intelligence were enormously important for the development of American air intelligence. Even before the United States entered the war, the RAF had trained eleven AAF officers in the techniques of photographic interpretation. Those officers returned to the United States in October 1941 to help in the creation of an American photoreconnaissance effort.[21] By spring 1942, the British had agreed to establish a combined office with the Eighth Air Force to interpret all photographic intelligence at a common location, the CIU. There, the results of British and American photoreconnaissance over the continent could be gathered, collated, and passed back to the using units.[22] While relations between the British and the Americans were often rocky, the overall impression of American airmen involved was one of unparalleled honesty and openness in the working relationships between the intelligence organizations of these two powers.

By summer 1942, the first American long-range bomber units had arrived in the United Kingdom; almost immediately they launched the first daylight raids onto the continent against targets relatively near their home bases. The British made every effort to persuade American airmen that daylight, unescorted bomber raids against German air defenses would have unwanted results. Certainly the British experience thus far in the war had provided a salient warning. The disastrous raid of Wellington bombers against the Heligoland Bight in December 1939, the heavy losses involved in the 1941 CIRCUS operations by RAF fighters and bombers over the continent, and finally the pummeling of a low-level Lancaster attack on the M.A.N. works in 1942—all lent considerable support to the British position. But American airmen insisted on doing things their way.²³ Still wedded to an untried doctrine, they believed that British bomber formations had never achieved the critical mass required to defend themselves.

American air operations over the continent in summer and fall 1942 rarely moved beyond the framework of a protecting cloak of RAF fighters. Ira Eaker was claiming by late fall that experiences thus far indicated the B–17 could "cope with the German day fighter." On the basis of the first 1,100 sorties, he argued, German fighters were no match for close formations of American bombers; losses on the bombing missions onto the continent had averaged only 1.6 percent. What Eaker failed to mention was that most of those missions had enjoyed heavy fighter support; in raids flown beyond fighter range or when no diversionary efforts were flown, the attacking bombers had suffered a loss rate of 6.4 percent, *and* no missions had yet flown over German territory.²⁴ Yet American intelligence estimates seem to have supported Eaker in his belief that the answer to the problems involved in penetrating deep into the Reich would only require formations consisting of ten bomber groups. In particular, the Americans believed that the *Luftwaffe* had thinned its forces along the outer perimeter of Fortress Europe and that, once past this defensive system, their bomber formations would have a relatively easy time over Germany.

These early Eighth Air Force missions raised two important issues, one dealing with the analysis of intelligence and how doctrinal "belief" clouded judgments; the other, with technological assessments. American air intelligence was hardly an effective or efficient organization at this time; one can wonder how much clout it enjoyed with operational commanders. Not surprisingly, it provided no suggestion that American doctrine might be fundamentally flawed. First, experience thus far in the war suggested that deep penetration bomber raids into Germany *would* have substantial problems unless they were defended by escorting fighters. Intelligence analysts did not argue this point. This state of affairs underlined one of the major difficulties confronting AAF intelligence organizations: their general unwillingness to involve themselves in critiques of the doctrine and performance of their own forces. To do so would probably have involved them in serious disputes with their operational masters. Not doing so may have resulted in needless losses of aircraft and aircrews in both Europe and the Pacific.

The second issue has more to do with technological assessment than with intelligence. Reinforced by the silence of intelligence and operations on questions of basic doctrine, a disastrous effect was the near loss of the daylight strategic bombing campaign. British and American airmen did not believe that a long-range fighter with suitable air-to-air capabilities could be constructed to escort bombers on deep penetration raids into Germany. Churchill had suggested to the Chief of Air Staff in 1941 that long-range escort fighters might be a considerable boon to Bomber Command; Portal, perhaps basing his opinion on the performance of the deficient German Me 110 during the Battle of Britain the previous year, replied that such a fighter could never hold its own against short-range day fighters. A chastened Churchill responded that such a view closed "many doors."[25] American airmen were no more prescient with their intelligence analyses; their reading of loss rates in 1942 suggested that escort fighters were unnecessary. Eighth Air Force attitudes were summed up by a letter that Eaker sent Spaatz in October 1942:

> The second phase, which we are about to enter, is the demonstration that day bombing can be economically executed using general fighter support. . . in getting through the German defensive fighter belt and to help our cripples home through this same belt; the third phase will include deeper penetrations into enemy territory, using long-range fighter accompaniment of the P–38 type in general support only and continuing the use of short-range fighters at critical points on a time schedule; the fourth phase will be a demonstration that bombardment in force—a minimum of 300 bombers—can effectively attack any German target and return without excessive and uneconomical losses. This later phase relies upon mass and the great firepower of the large bombardment formations.[26]

Eaker's letter is remarkable for more than his assumption that great formations of B–17s could defend themselves without protection by escort fighters. It is clear from his letter that, as with the *Luftwaffe*'s intelligence before the Battle of Britain, he assumed enemy defensive forces would array themselves in a narrow and rather well-defined belt, downplaying the German option of a defense in depth.

Luckily for the Americans, their theories were not tested at the end of 1942 and the first half of 1943. Because of Operation TORCH (the landings of Anglo-American forces in Morocco and Algeria) a substantial portion of American air assets was shifted to the Mediterranean, site of one of the crucial air battles of World War II. The impact of the TORCH diversion on American air operations onto the continent was substantial. Between November 1942 and March 1943 Eighth Air Force could launch only two raids of more than 100 bombers, a force by Eaker's own calculation incapable of fighting its way into and back out of the Reich.[27] The shift to the Mediterranean in retrospect was wholly beneficial for American ground and air forces. Leading American airmen and their intelligence officers had to address the problems of air power in joint tactical operations. The doctrine of precision bombing attacks against highly specialized segments of the German economy had little relevance in a theater where those targets were out of range, where the crucial problem from the first involved the winning of air superiority, and where the major mission of Allied air forces after gaining air superiority was to cut the sea lanes of communication supporting Axis forces in North Africa. In Northwest Africa, joint service cooperation was a must, and not surprisingly the leading air and ground commanders emerged to command the landing on the European continent in the next year.

Intelligence was crucial to Allied success in the Mediterranean. Here a close cooperation quickly evolved between British and American intelligence organizations, replicating what was occurring in England. ULTRA was a critical factor,[28] but success came only when it was included among other sources; ULTRA confirmed what Allied commanders already suspected. Other means of intelligence, such as photoreconnaissance, provided a framework for information from ULTRA. ULTRA's continuing success owed much to the extraordinary carelessness of the Germans.[29] Not only did flawed signals discipline on the part of the German military provide the Allies with the cribs that allowed access to the ciphers, but when operations suggested that something was terribly amiss with their signals security, the German intelligence experts consistently assumed that treachery marred the high command or that the Italians were guilty of both incompetence and treachery.[30]

ULTRA, in combination with the other intelligence sources, placed Allied commanders in the position of a man playing poker and knowing with a fair degree of accuracy what cards his opponents held. Had the Germans enjoyed overwhelming superiority (as they had in the Balkans campaign of spring 1941), such intelligence might have done the Allies little good. Given the overwhelming superiority that Anglo-American forces enjoyed in 1943, the excellence of Allied intelligence helped to hasten an inevitable end. Intelligence aided Allied air operations against the *Luftwaffe* by indicating enemy air operations, the disposition of his forces, and his strengths and weaknesses in the theater. In both Tunisia and Sicily, ULTRA and Y sources not only gave the Allies a clear picture of how German forces were deployed, they allowed Allied airmen to maximize their air potential by concentrating attacks on the German air bases. Dispersal fields did the Germans no good, because the Allies knew of their location, often before *Luftwaffe* units could begin operations. Similarly, ULTRA indicated when and where Axis seaborne convoys or air resupply movements would be. By March 1943, Allied air attacks on naval convoys moving from Sicily to Tunisia had become so effective that the Germans and Italians were forced to shut them down entirely; the information as to their exact course and timing made air and naval attacks on such movements doubly effective. The Axis air bridge to Tunisia was no more effective, because Allied air intelligence was consistently on the mark with correspondingly high German and Italian losses. The resulting air attacks severed the lines of communication between Italy and Tunisia and helped bring the campaign in North Africa to a successful conclusion.

The largest contribution of the Mediterranean theater to Allied victory may have been the training and preparation it provided airmen like Spaatz and Doolittle. The war in the Mediterranean did not look like the war posited by prewar doctrine. The interdependence of the services and the importance of cooperation were underlined for all to see. The war for air superiority brought a level of realism about the survivability of the bomber that was not present in England until the autumn of 1943. As early as that spring, Doolittle was pressing Arnold for long-range fighters to support medium and heavy bombers.

He argued that the presence of such fighters would significantly reduce bomber casualties while their use "as intruders would greatly increase the effectiveness of our strategic operations."[31]

While Allied air forces battered the *Luftwaffe* in the Mediterranean, Eighth Air Force finally reached a level of forces that allowed attacks into the Reich. For the first time the theory of self-protecting bomber formations would receive a full test. The problem confronting Eighth Air Force lay in a force structure that was not sufficient to absorb the punishment that the *Luftwaffe* would inflict. Eighth Air Force's strength severely constrained the number of targets it could strike; that number was further reduced by demands in the POINTBLANK directive that mandated high bombing priorities for U-boat construction sites and dockyards; these were not the targets that intelligence studies had indicated held the most profit potential. Thus Eighth Air Force operated with severely restricted target choices.

The limited availability of bombers made the American decision to strike ball-bearing factories, in particular those at Schweinfurt, almost inevitable. Allied intelligence analysts believed no other target system provided so few crucial targets that could by their destruction do such extensive damage to the German economy as a whole. An offensive against the Reich's petroleum industry, in contrast, would have demanded attacks on somewhere between fifty and sixty major targets, while target systems such as electricity or transportation demanded the destruction of an almost infinite number of targets. Destruction of the ball-bearing industry would have a serious impact on aircraft engine production, thus destroying German industry supporting the *Luftwaffe*. The offensive did not develop as air planners had hoped. The damage of the two Schweinfurt raids looked spectacular from the air; reconnaissance flights soon confirmed that the first raid in August 1943 had done substantial damage to the structure of the buildings. The machinery that produced ball bearings was only lightly damaged; photoreconnaissance missions that flew over Schweinfurt in the aftermath of the raid could not reveal this information.

The Germans and their armaments minister, Albert Speer, recognized the attack on Schweinfurt for what it was: an effort to cripple the German economy by taking out one of its critical components. Speer's comments after the war suggested a number of weaknesses in the ability of U.S. air intelligence to assess bomb damage.[32] Damage to the Schweinfurt ball-bearing facilities did indeed look impressive from the air, but the Germans soon recovered production. Other factors mitigated the overall impact of the Schweinfurt attacks. Many of the German armament industries had stocked substantial supplies of ball bearings to meet the vagaries of wartime supply. Swedish and Swiss industrial concerns stepped in and took up much of the German shortfall, and the Germans found a number of ingenious means of getting around their shortages. In other words, human ingenuity under the pressures of war proved adaptable and flexible in finding alternative solutions.[33]

Piercing the Fog

Speer's postwar comments that a more sustained attack on the ball-bearing industry would have led to industrial collapse underlines a fundamental difficulty in the American situation. Even had American air intelligence understood the advantages of more attacks, it is unlikely that much more could have been done. Despite the POINTBLANK directive, Bomber Command was unwilling to cooperate in attacking what its commander viewed as a panacea target, although the British Air Ministry exerted considerable pressure in support of the American attacks on ball bearings.[34] The losses of bombers that Eighth suffered in the August Schweinfurt-Regensburg attack made it impossible for Americans to return to Schweinfurt on a regular basis. When the Americans attacked again in October 1943, German efforts to disperse the industry or to find alternative sources of supply were already underway. The damage inflicted did not compensate for the terrible drubbing that the Eighth's bombers took over Schweinfurt in the second raid, nor did it place the Germans in an impossible situation.

What was occurring in the skies over Germany was an enormous battle of attrition that played an important role in the air victory of 1944. Allied signals intelligence and ULTRA were able to pick up the movement of German day interceptors from the various fronts to defend the skies over the Reich from American attack. But what intelligence could not fully grasp was the level of attrition that Eighth's bombing raids inflicted on the *Luftwaffe*'s fighter forces, in part because so few intelligence officers had exposure to flying, much less air-to-air combat.[35] While American intelligence discounted the wilder reports of bomber crews on the numbers of German fighters shot down, Eighth Air Force was still too optimistic over the summer and fall 1943 on the damage that it was inflicting on its foe.[36] The Germans suffered serious casualties over this period, but not enough to blunt the ferocious defense that they were mounting. The reported level of casualties inflicted on the German fighter force led to serious miscalculations or at least serious overestimates of the level of success. Eaker himself suggested that there was evidence of "severe strain and some signs of eventual collapse." In Washington, Arnold was suggesting that the *Luftwaffe* was on the brink of collapse;[37] others declared, "Aerial supremacy on a continental scale had been won."[38]

American air attacks were severely affecting Germany's strategic situation, both in terms of the serious attrition imposed on the *Luftwaffe* and the effect of bombing on German aircraft production. American aerial attacks became more difficult as the Germans shifted production facilities to the east, making bomber missions longer and more hazardous. Historians have generally tended to underestimate the impact that American bombing had on the production capacity of Germany's aircraft industry, because the Germans counted the repair of seriously damaged aircraft as new production, thus inflating the reports on the number of aircraft produced. If historians face difficulties in this area, the fact that air intelligence personnel during the war experienced the same conundrum should not be surprising. Intelligence could estimate German production on the basis of ULTRA and other sources, but correlation seemed lacking between losses claimed in air-to-air action and the subsequent reports of front-line strength, attrition, and production.[39]

By the end of 1943 the Allies were on the way toward winning the intelligence war. Through a variety of sources, they built a coherent and generally clear picture of the enemy's capabilities and intentions. In the Mediterranean, Allied airmen used that intelligence to win a series of major victories over Axis forces. In the skies over Germany, that advantage did not translate into victory because the targets were too numerous and the bombers too few, and because the *Luftwaffe*'s fighter forces were fighting on their home ground. The attacking bombers still had to deal with the defenders before hitting the targets on which the American precision bombing campaign rested. All the intelligence in the world could not change the fundamental equation of fighter versus bomber.

Indeed, the attack on Schweinfurt in October 1943, the infamous "black Thursday" raid, represented the nadir of the American strategic bombing effort. It came close to ending the daylight campaign, and the damage to the morale of Eighth Air Force was nearly catastrophic. But two improvements in late 1943 changed the balance in the air and gave American airmen the means to execute their plans and make full use of the extraordinary advantages that intelligence would give them in 1944. The first was the steady growth of the bomber force, despite heavy losses, in the period from summer 1943 through summer 1944. While Eaker had at his disposal a daily average of 459 bombers in June 1943, by December the Eighth had more than 1,057 on hand, and by June 1944 the total reached 2,547.[40] The American bomber force could absorb far heavier losses, while attacking progressively larger target sets on a more sustained basis. Finally, a true long-range fighter, the P–51, appeared in the European theater. Long-range fighter escort support now allowed the Americans to attack the *Luftwaffe* anywhere in the skies over the Reich. Although appearance of the P–51 did not lead to any significant decrease in bomber losses until May 1944, it drastically increased the price that the *Luftwaffe* had to pay,[41] eventually resulting in the German fighter force's collapse prior to D-day.

Intelligence was particularly helpful in discerning how Allied changes in tactics affected German defensive capabilities. Doolittle's decision in March 1944 to release escorting fighters from the restrictions of flying close escort missions with the bombers and to allow them to seek out German fighters anywhere and everywhere received considerable support from intelligence. ULTRA messages confirmed that American fighters were causing the Germans difficulties as they attacked airfields and aircraft landing and taking off.[42] ULTRA confirmed that the American air offensive was also causing desperate shortages of pilots, parts, and supplies in the enemy fighter forces.[43]

Piercing the Fog

With the Normandy invasion in June 1944, ULTRA gave away the German movement of fighters to the invasion front and enabled Allied covering forces to destroy many of the German aircraft and much of their supporting infrastructure before the Germans ever got it in place.[44] Similarly, ULTRA indicated on June 9 and 10 the exact location of Geyer von Schweppenburg's *Panzer Group West*'s headquarters.[45] The resulting air attack not only destroyed most of the panzer group's communications equipment, but it also killed seventeen staff officers, including the chief of staff.[46] The strike effectively robbed the Germans of their only organization capable of handling a large number of mobile divisions on the western front.

The greatest contribution of intelligence information in 1944 came on the strategic level. Intelligence kept the focus on the *Luftwaffe* through spring 1944 by pointing out the severe difficulties under which the Germans were operating, while it suggested the extraordinary measures that the enemy was taking to escape those difficulties. By May 1944, Spaatz and Doolittle had persuaded Eisenhower that the German petroleum industry now represented the crucial Achilles' heel of the whole Nazi war effort, military as well as economic. On May 12, Eighth Air Force struck the synthetic oil plants at Zwickau, Merseburg-Leuna, Brux, Lutzkendorf, Bohlen, Zeitz, and Chemnitz. Speer recalled in his memoirs that he immediately warned Hitler of the extraordinary danger:

> The enemy has struck us at one of our weakest points. If they persist at it this time, we will soon no longer have any fuel production worth mentioning. Our one hope is that the other side has an air force general staff as scatterbrained as ours![47]

Speer was being a bit unfair to his own air force and was missing a substantial point: in war it is extraordinarily difficult to estimate the long-range effect of military actions on an enemy's capabilities. This was especially true for the air war up to 1944, where damage was consistently difficult to estimate. The result had been a tendency of airmen to hedge their bets by attacking a number of different target systems in the hope that one would provide the key to success; the *Luftwaffe* high command's conduct of the Battle of Britain was an especially good example of this approach. In terms of the American conduct of the oil offensive in 1944, intelligence, and particularly ULTRA, played a crucial role in keeping the interest of air leaders firmly centered on one target system. At this point, with the vast growth in its force structure, Eighth Air Force, supported by the Fifteenth Air Force in Italy, struck on a continuous basis at the relatively few oil facilities available to Germany.

Within days of the opening of the oil offensive on May 12, BP was forwarding decrypts indicating a substantial movement of flak forces within the Reich to defend the petroleum sites.[48] On May 21, another intercept from an unspecified German source ordered:

> Consumption of mineral oil in every form... be substantially reduced...
> in view of Allied action in Rumania and on German hydrogenation plants;

Retrospection

extensive failures in mineral oil production and a considerable reduction in the June allocation of fuel oil, etc., were to be expected.[49]

By early June, after a second series of strikes had done an even more thorough job of disrupting the German petroleum industry, BP forwarded another ULTRA decrypt from the *Oberkommando der Luftwaffe,* the *Luftwaffe* high command:

> To assume defense of Reich and to prevent gradual collapse of readiness for defense of German air force in east, it has been necessary to break into *OKW (Oberkommando des Wehrmachts*—armed forces high command [oil]) reserves. Extending, therefore, existing regulations ordered that all units to arrange operations so as to manage at least until the beginning of July with present stocks or small allocation which may be possible. Rate of arrival and quantities of July quota still undecided. Only very small quantities available for adjustments, provided Allied situation remains unchanged. In no circumstance can greater allocations be made. Attention again drawn to existing orders for most extreme economy measures and strict supervision of consumption, especially for transport, personal and communications flights.[50]

The special security officer at Eighth Air Force Headquarters underlined after the war ULTRA's contribution to the success of the offensive against oil. His claim that intercepts proving that petroleum shortages resulting from raids were general and not local convinced "all concerned that the air offensive had uncovered a weak spot in the German economy and led to exploitation of this weakness to the fullest extent."[51] For the remainder of the war, ULTRA and photoreconnaissance allowed the Allies to keep close tabs on German repair efforts; follow-on air raids destroyed the German efforts to reconstruct petroleum production facilities. This consistent focus kept the German petroleum industry from recovering from the lethal blow that it had received over the summer.

In the war's last year, intelligence, particularly photoreconnaissance, made major contributions to the waging of the two great transportation plans executed by Allied strategic and tactical air forces.[52] The first isolated the Normandy battlefield and enabled Anglo-American forces to win the logistical race of the buildup. The second was even more successful and led to a general collapse of the German railway system over the winter of 1944–1945; this success prevented the German arms industry from resupplying the weary, badly battered *Wehrmacht* during the winter of 1945. As German defenses rapidly collapsed in spring 1945, fanatical Nazis were unable to wage a last-ditch, desperate struggle on the ruins of the Reich. The execution of the transportation attacks, as well as the intelligence contribution, suggests much about the difficulties in using intelligence effectively and the problems in integrating intelligence into operations.

The first of the transportation campaigns was largely limited to the tactical and operational arena. It sealed off the coastal areas of France from reinforcement and made German logistic difficulties so great as to prevent a rapid

Piercing the Fog

buildup to contest OVERLORD. Contributing to the German failure to reinforce the Normandy battlefront was a successful deception effort that completely misled German intelligence as to the possibility of another landing. Considerable squabbling between the airmen and those advocating landing on the continent centered on the question of how best to isolate the battlefield. Should the brunt of attack be on marshaling yards or on bridges and other choke points? The benefits accrued by either approach are still not entirely clear today. What is clear is that Allied air forces possessed sufficient strength and knowledge to pursue both. By late May, the railroads in the west of France were in a state of complete collapse,[53] leading to the Germans' difficulty in building up to meet the invasion and support the battle of attrition. Throughout the period, ULTRA decrypts indicated to Allied air commanders the extent of damage to the French railways.[54] Photoreconnaissance also revealed the extent to which tactical and strategic air attacks had closed supply routes. The aerial interdiction effort in Normandy succeeded far beyond a similar effort in Italy because of the enormous battle of attrition that occurred with the relentless pressure exercised by the Allied armies seeking a breakout.

In early fall, the success of the Normandy interdiction effort led Eisenhower's deputy, Air Marshal Tedder, to suggest an equivalent campaign to destroy the Reich's transportation system. Tedder ran into substantial opposition from both Air Marshal Arthur T. "Bomber" Harris and Spaatz. Nevertheless, some of the strategic bombing effort bled over into the transportation plan. Bomber Command's main targets were the German population centers, and in the heart of most German cities were located the railway stations and marshaling yards for the *Reichsbahn* (the German railways). Spaatz agreed to support Tedder's plan when bad weather obscured the oil targets and the Eighth could not execute precision bombing attacks.

While considerable information was available on the impact that Allied air attacks had on the French transportation system, air intelligence underutilized ULTRA. In February 1945, a review of ULTRA information, initiated by Air Vice Marshal Norman H. Bottomley, the RAF's Deputy Chief of Air Staff, indicated that the Combined Strategic Targets Committee had systematically suppressed ULTRA data on the *Reichsbahn* and on the German economy, intelligence that underlined the extent of the enemy's difficulties.[55] One relevant message, unused since its decryption in October 1944, indicated that by that date, due to transportation destruction and bottlenecks, "from 30 to 50 percent of all [factories] in West Germany were at a standstill."[56] As one historian of the attack on the German transportation network has suggested:

> Only when the weather improved in January 1945, when it was realized that ULTRA had unlocked important secrets, when Upper Silesia was overrun . . . only then were the paralysis of the *Reichsbahn* and the coal famine perceived and a new consensus formed behind the transportation campaign. Ultimately, after much misunderstanding, segments of the

Retrospection

Allied air intelligence community and all the Allied air commanders agreed to set bombing priorities in line with Tedder's conception.[57]

During late fall and early winter, intelligence organizations minimized their estimates of damage imposed by the offensive against the transportation network; their approach largely reflected a desire to support the views of the commanders of the strategic bombing forces. In effect, they prevented the full fury of Allied air capabilities from destroying the German transportation network before winter began, and thus they may have extended the war by several months. In the end, the German transportation system did collapse in late winter with devastating effects, ending the production of arms; the result was the collapse of Nazi Germany in March and April 1945.[58]

Intelligence and the War in the Pacific

The most crucial difference between air intelligence operations in the European and Pacific theaters lay in the fashion with which American society, specifically its military, judged and estimated their potential opponents, Germany and Japan, both before and during the war. In the former case, many, including the president (who spoke fluent German and read Hitler's speeches in the original),[59] were intimately acquainted with Germany, its history, its society, and its culture. Even in the last years before the outbreak of war, Germany had remained a relatively open society from which Americans could readily acquire much information. Many Americans spoke and read German because of background, education, or family ties. Little of this was true with regard to Japan. Throughout this period the Empire of the Rising Sun remained a society that even westerners who spoke the language found difficult to penetrate. Few westerners tried, and even fewer succeeded, to learn the language. The result was a general ignorance of Japan, its society, and its military institutions; that ignorance, combined with a general sense of racial superiority, led Americans to belittle Japanese capabilities and potential, whether one talked about strategic, operational, tactical, or technological levels of war. That arrogance carried into the post–Pearl Harbor period; the crushing defeat inflicted on the U.S. Navy at Savo Island in August 1942 underlines the persistence of such attitudes well into the war.[60]

Luckily in one area, cryptanalysis, American intelligence had made significant strides before the war, a base on which the country could expand intelligence efforts. Even here, difficulties abounded in language competence and in understanding enemy capabilities and intentions. The Pearl Harbor disaster resulted not from a lack of intelligence, but from a general unwillingness to understand or to recognize its import. Intelligence analysts and operational commanders simply assumed that the Japanese would not (or

Piercing the Fog

perhaps even could not) attack the Hawaiian Islands. Such fundamental misconceptions would have been hard to shake until the bombs began to fall.

Perhaps the greatest single difference between the European theater and the Pacific from the point of view of the American air intelligence effort lay in the very size of the latter. In Europe one can talk of one theater, even though operations were conducted in two distinct areas: the Mediterranean and western Europe. In both, the nature of the enemy and hence the intelligence-gathering efforts remained quite similar throughout the war. From both, the Allies would launch major strategic bombing efforts onto the European continent with similar targets as their objectives. Both areas supported ground and amphibious efforts that struck against enemy land forces able to draw from the resources of the continent. The efforts from the Mediterranean and from England confronted tenacious and effective air defenses on the continent. So one sees a combined intelligence effort which evaluated the same kinds of information. Airmen would transfer from one area to the other with ease; the most famous example is the transfer of Ira Eaker to the Mediterranean and his replacement in Europe by Spaatz and Doolittle from the Mediterranean.

The intelligence situation confronting American airmen in the Pacific was radically different from that which existed in Europe. In the Central and South Pacific, AAF units remained under the control of the Navy; their intelligence organizations consequently were dependent on their sister service. In the SWPA, General Kenney's efforts occurred in an Army theater of operations. In the CBI, the American effort involved considerable interallied difficulties with the British and a clash in strategic goals between American interests that aimed at keeping open the link to China and British interests that aimed at regaining the southeast Asian empire lost so disastrously in the first months of the Pacific War. American airmen in China waged a valiant effort to support a weak and corrupt Chinese nationalist regime as they prepared the base for long-range strategic bombing attacks with B–29s against the Japanese home islands. Within China, a nightmare of conflicting interests, the incapacity of the nationalist government to work with Stilwell, unseemly squabbles between Stilwell and American airmen, and Japanese capabilities combined to make this theater one of the least successful American undertakings of the war. The differing natures and demands of the four Pacific theaters resulted in substantially different organizations as well as substantially different requirements from intelligence. Points of comparison were fewer in the Pacific than they were in Europe.

Of all the American airmen in World War II, George Kenney displayed the greatest adaptability and flexibility in difficult and challenging circumstances. From the tactics of low-level skip bombings against ships to a brilliant operational employment of his resources against the Japanese air base structure, ground forces, and sea lines of communications, Kenney showed himself to be a master of operational art. Crucially important to his success was how he employed intelligence.

Retrospection

From the first, Kenney displayed a keen sense of how intelligence could be used. He was not well served by MacArthur's staff because special intelligence from Honolulu and Washington unfortunately was funneled into the SWPA through General Sutherland. Sutherland in turn passed what he thought was significant to MacArthur directly, often leaving the intelligence organizations, including MacArthur's chief of intelligence, in the dark. Kenney and the air effort were hurt less than might have otherwise occurred. He inherited an air intelligence organization originally created to meet the needs of Field Marshal Wavell's combined command. Kenney was integrated into the extensive British and Australian net which read low-grade Japanese codes and ciphers in the theater, made radio traffic analyses, and gathered intelligence from the effective and efficient coast-watching effort established before the war by the Australians. Kenney's personality, abrasive at times but certainly not imperial, matched Australian sensibilities far better than was true with either MacArthur or most of his staff.

In time, Hewitt, Kenney's intelligence chief, and the SWPA headquarters became responsible for the long-range intelligence planning, while Fifth Air Force's (and eventually Thirteenth Air Force's) intelligence organizations were responsible for the day-to-day operational and tactical intelligence. Throughout the war, Kenney proved himself a commander who consistently and coherently used intelligence to accomplish his mission. Whether it be the reports of coast watchers or the deciphering of high-level messages, he incorporated intelligence to its best advantage to attack Japanese weaknesses, to avoid their strengths, or to deceive the enemy as to his own intentions. The classic example of Kenney's skillful utilization of past and present intelligence undoubtedly came in the Battle of the Bismarck Sea. Past intelligence indicated how the Japanese would probably move a major reinforcing effort, and ULTRA indicated when that move would begin. In combination, Kenney and his subordinates constructed a realistic and effective campaign plan that allowed them to smash the Japanese. This skillful use of intelligence, combined with extraordinary flexibility and adaptability to the actual conditions of war, probably made Kenney's employment of air power the most effective, given the resources employed, of all Allied air power in World War II.

Kenney's first contributions were strikes at Rabaul in 1942 in support of the landings at Guadalcanal; special intelligence almost immediately confirmed for him and MacArthur that the ability of the Japanese to use the airfields at Rabaul had been upset if not reduced. In September 1942, Kenney had flown an infantry regiment into Port Moresby to help defend southern New Guinea, an action that was not exactly in line with the accepted, narrowly defined view of air power held by many within the Army. The interdiction of the Japanese sea lines of communication from Rabaul to New Guinea during the following year showed the talents of Kenney and his very able subordinate, Ennis Whitehead, to their greatest advantage. In that case, the patient collection, collation, and

Piercing the Fog

interpretation of signals and special intelligence indicated that the Japanese were about to make a major move to reinforce Lae. At the same time, a major refitting of American B–25 medium bombers carried out on the scene gave aircrews enhanced capabilities to strike targets at low level. Finally, Kenney and his subordinates (operators as well as intelligence officers) carefully reconstructed the routing that the Japanese had used in previous convoys to Lae. The result of all this care and patience was a devastatingly effective attack on the Japanese convoy, exactly where Kenney and Whitehead had planned to strike (and almost at the exact time). All the supply ships were sunk and a number of Japanese soldiers were rescued, although without arms, ammunition, or supplies they were worse than useless.[61] For the Japanese, the effect of the losses in the battle of the Bismarck Sea were immediate and adverse. Allied success had turned on the extraordinarily competent integration of intelligence with tactical flexibility and adaptation. No better example exists in World War II of the skillful combination of intelligence and operational capabilities in battle.

Despite occasional troubles such as those in the Admiralties and during the first Philippine landings brought on by exuberance and an unwarranted contempt for his enemy's abilities, George Kenney's use of intelligence after the Bismarck Sea operation retained by and large this level of effectiveness because of two factors. First, he picked excellent subordinates and used them well; he gave them the authority and support to get on with the job. In 1943, Kenney's handling of Allied air units broke the back of the Japanese air power operating in New Guinea. By understanding that the heart of the Japanese defensive system lay in their well-stocked bases used to shuttle aircraft back and forth within the theater, he struck at the bases themselves. With the base structure severely debilitated, Japanese air power simply withered, and Kenney's forces gained general air superiority in the skies over New Guinea. The second major factor that allowed General Kenney to continue his successful use of intelligence was the extraordinary extent to which the Allies in SWPA, Pearl Harbor, and Washington had penetrated Japanese signals transmissions. By 1944, intelligence was providing MacArthur and his land, sea, and air forces with a continuing reading of Japan's overall situation and her plans for air operations.

By 1944 the Japanese armed forces were in retreat, but they could still muster a substantial air task force in reaction to Allied landings. The appearance of their task forces came by surprise, since ULTRA had not detected the units well in advance. Despite this unexpected development, Japan's weakness prevented her from sustaining an effective air campaign as a barrier to further Allied advances. Having defeated Japanese air power, the question then became less one of holding air superiority in support of the Philippine campaign than of supporting the Army and Navy in combat with the Japanese ground and naval forces in the Philippine Islands. Again Kenney showed himself to be a master at adapting to the conditions. By the end of the war, he was concentrating his

Retrospection

air power on Okinawa to support Operation OLYMPIC, MacArthur's great invasion of the home islands, scheduled for November 1, 1945. By then Kenney controlled not only Fifth Air Force, but also Thirteenth from the South Pacific and Seventh from the Central Pacific. Such was the high regard with which he was held.

Contrasting the Allied success at intelligence exploitation in the Pacific, the problems in the CBI Theater reflected three distinct difficulties. First, British and American war aims were so divergent as to make military cooperation difficult. The common need to defeat the enemy meant that, at lower levels, useful cooperation occurred. This cooperation was partially due to a growing awareness of the need for more combined air intelligence centers, much like those found in Europe. Second, the organization of the theater left much to be desired (the organization can only be described as being inversely proportional to the size of the forces being led and to their military effectiveness, at least in the early days of the fighting). Finally, one can only note a general lack of geniality and level of trust among senior commanders—Chiang, Stilwell, Wavell, Chennault, and Bissell—that made relationships in the Allied high command in the European theater appear to be problem-free.

Within the CBI Theater, intelligence was critical. In particular, the nature of the terrain in Burma and India made HUMINT particularly important. The clandestine organizations established in this area by the American OSS and the British Special Operations Executive proved crucial in passing useful intelligence to airmen. Allied intelligence officers did an effective job in analyzing the geography of the theater. The mining of the Rangoon estuary on the basis of an analysis of Burmese landforms and railways is an excellent case of how an intelligence organization can spot weaknesses in the enemy's situation merely by thinking through the problem and using information readily at hand. As with other theaters of war, all sources of intelligence proved enormously helpful to air operations; signals intelligence was as useful as it was in other areas. Photoreconnaissance was invaluable in both target selection and damage assessment.

In China an enormous philosophical difference existed between Stilwell and the indigenous political and military leadership (Chiang and his nationalist regime), the latter being supported by one of Stilwell's subordinates, Claire Chennault. Stilwell regarded the creation of a well-trained and disciplined ground force as sine qua non for effective military operations against the Japanese in the theater, but that demanded substantive reform of the Chinese nationalist regime, something that Chiang either would not allow or could not accomplish. In effect, Chennault offered a shortcut for the military and strategic defeat of the Japanese, one that would allow Chiang to husband his strength for the coming struggle against the communists. That shortcut involved the supposed use of air power to redress the deficiencies of Chinese ground forces. Chennault believed that his air units could beat the Japanese first in China with

Piercing the Fog

his Fourteenth Air Force and then in the home islands by B–29 raids launched from Chinese bases. Events proved Stilwell right and Chennault wrong. Chennault overestimated the ability of his air units to carry the load for China and underestimated the Japanese Army's capacity and intent for a sustained drive aimed at his eastern China airfields. When the Japanese recognized the threat of B–29 raids from bases in China, they simply captured the air bases in a great land campaign. The result reflected a considerable intelligence failure at the level where intelligence was the most difficult to perform: strategic and operational assessment. Strategic assessment at the highest levels demanded a real knowledge of one's own allies and one's opponents that involved far more than a simple counting of enemy units; it demanded a knowledge of the language, history, cultures, and politics involved in complex strategic situations.

The last significant air intelligence area in the Pacific was the great strategic bombing campaign launched against the Japanese home islands by the B–29s. Here prewar American ignorance of Japan—some was inevitable, given the secretiveness of Japanese society, and some was self-induced by a belief in racial superiority—came into play. Virtually no aerial photoreconnaissance of the home islands existed until very late in 1944. The initial conceptions for the campaign reflected the flawed prewar precision bombing doctrine. As the COA review of bombing priorities noted in October 1944, "lack of information remains a major obstacle to careful target selection."[62] General LeMay's decision to abandon the initial precision bombing campaign for an approach reminiscent of the British area bombing campaign resulted from the operational realities confronting American airmen. Precision bombing attacks could not be made to work in the face of intense operational problems and the lack of current target and weather information. Aside from operational demands, the AAF leadership was under constant pressure to prove the worth of the B–29 and to justify the creation of an independent service after the war.

The experience and lessons from Allied operations in Europe made their way to Washington and to and throughout the Pacific and Asian war theaters, usually with good results. On the Air Staff, the A–2 and A–3 grew in their abilities and their mutual accomplishments in affecting air planning and operations. In the course of this development, a number of individuals came to prominence in the interplay between intelligence and air operations. The personality of the AAF's commanding general appeared often in the direction and organization of the service. Hap Arnold was a singular character, unmatched by any other individual in the wartime AAF; his interests ranged from design of aircraft and support equipment to tactics and operations of air power. Intelligence in general and the A–2 office in particular received his attention, although his influence may not always have been wholly beneficial. The May 1939 meeting with Lindbergh was but the first of his many independent

On the many different fronts and vastly different circumstances under which the Army Air Forces fought in World War II, a variety of aircraft were pressed into duty for photoreconnaissance, but the mainstay in Europe was the P–38 *(above)*; in the Pacific, the huge distances made the B–29 the favorite, once it became operational. The version of the B–29 shown in the photograph was designated the F–13.

contacts. Another was the instruction to Colonel Cooper to scout the airfield situation in Soviet Siberia and report to Arnold any locations where the AAF might be able to operate against Japan. At the very least, this put Cooper in the position of working on a task unknown to his commander, Claire Chennault. As might be expected, not all of Arnold's freewheeling actions solved problems. Haywood Hansell, a man who worked closely with Arnold in developing war plans and B–29 operations, observed that Arnold "habitually distrusted his own staff. He was always under the impression that there were some brilliant people out there somewhere if he could just get his hands on them." As a result, Arnold often took a suggestion in a draft paper and turned it into policy, disrupting the Air Staff's normal process. These sorts of actions have their place and can keep bureaucratic organizations from self-justifying lethargy. But in Arnold's case, such practices at times negated the value of an air intelligence staff applying hardheaded analysis to a very complex set of problems.[63]

The demands for action and abrupt changes in policy could be detrimental to the effective working of the Air Staff. As an example with far-reaching consequences, Hansell cited the creation of the COA. For all of the potential good that the COA could do, Arnold's perhaps overly quick decision on its organization and purpose may have pushed the group into making operational recommendations for which its members were unqualified, rather than studying intelligence data in a quest for a reasoned analysis of enemy weak points. In Hansell's opinion, even the name of the group was incorrect, implying that it had an operational function.[64]

General White's biting remark of September 1944 that the "A–2 will forever suck hind tit in the AAF"[65] probably arose as much from Arnold's style of leading the service and his unwillingness to take the A–2 office seriously as it did from any other single source, like the G–2's obstructionism or other Air Staff office problems. Hansell was even more critical of the manner in which senior AAF officers treated the relationship between intelligence and command. Hansell believed that most of the AAF's generals spent too much time focusing on operational flying problems and goals and not nearly enough time thinking about targeting and adequately using the intelligence resources at hand. As Hansell pointed out, commanders had to give their intelligence officers instructions on what to look for, the classic essential elements of information (EEIs), to support planning. If a man did not understand the nature of target objectives, Hansell doubted that he could effectively contemplate EEIs and direct the formulation of air warfare plans. Hansell's criticisms along this line also fell on intelligence officers, who, he believed, too often reacted to operational demands and failed to use their analytical expertise and the assets of their offices to examine critically the accomplishments of the force in meeting the enemy. Hansell himself believed such work might have alleviated the heavy losses of bombers attempting to attack strongly defended German targets without fighter escorts.

Hansell's thoughts on these subjects emerged well after the war with all the advantages of hindsight. During the conflict, senior officers could take little time for reflection. Had they been better prepared to do so, such self-critical thinking might have served to prevent Chennault's loss of the eastern China bases in 1944 and other misjudgments elsewhere in the Pacific, as air commanders allowed themselves to assume that the enemy would do as the Americans thought best, rather than do what best suited the enemy's own needs. The operational bent was surely the case for some, Arnold included, but not for all. Hansell singled out Spaatz and Maj. Gen. Frederick Anderson as exceptions. Kenney was operationally oriented, but he and Whitehead were more than capable of understanding the nature and importance of targets, and both gave targets ample thought.[66] Even Chennault can be faulted only partially on this score, as he was forced by logistic circumstances to carefully judge the value of targets before committing precious gasoline to a raid.

Hansell did not stint in criticizing his own go-along attitude, either. He considered his worst wartime mistake to have been failing to oppose the COA's target recommendations that he thought were inappropriate. The most prominent error he saw was the COA's effective removal of Germany's electric power generation capacity from the the CBO target list. At the time, in 1943, Hansell justified his actions as those of a good team player who refused to act to the possible detriment of the AAF, still struggling for serious consideration as a wartime service. He believed that to oppose the COA would challenge the very agency that the AAF had created to study the goals of strategic bombing. The result of strong objections might have been to "have industrial targets and the whole idea of strategic air warfare eliminated altogether" by those on the JCS and elsewhere who did not understand air power. In other words, Hansell was a loyal soldier who supported Arnold and his service, first and foremost. But Hansell may also have considered that his action fostered too many poor ideas, including urban area attacks. His opposition to that tactic seems to have contributed strongly to Arnold's decision to remove him from Guam and the XXI Bomber Command in 1945.[67]

Conclusion

Clearly, intelligence played a crucial role in the Allied victory in World War II and contributed to a shortening of the war. In large part, the success of American air intelligence rested on the significant and timely commitment of resources and sustained effort by senior air commanders, even in the darkest days of 1941 and 1942.

Intelligence did not and could not fully illuminate the enemy's situation.[68] It rendered a significant contribution by suggesting the parameters within which the Germans and Japanese worked, allowing Allied commanders to see with some clarity occurrences in the enemy camps. At the strategic level, it provided the American leadership with a sense of those attacks that were having the most significant effect on the German situation. In 1942 and 1943, the AAF was not in a position to act on such intelligence; the losses at Schweinfurt, for example, prevented repetitions of the attack with sufficient frequency to shut down the German ball-bearing production. Nor could intelligence's knowledge of

Sweden's sale to Germany of ball bearings have led to military interdiction of that source of supply. Consequently, intelligence could not compensate for the gap created by operational or diplomatic weaknesses.

The Schweinfurt raids raised other significant problems for air intelligence analysts, most notably the difficulty of evaluating the economic and strategic effect of attacks on certain target sets. That problem unleashed a host of other questions which depended for their answers on knowledge that even in peacetime would be beyond the ability of intelligence organizations to answer: How dependent is the enemy on any particular industry? What are his alternative sources of supply? How rapidly can he disperse his production? What is the capacity of his industry to repair significant damage? How long will it take him to feel the effects of damage done to particular target sets? Indeed, the enemy himself may have a hard time in calculating his own capacity to adapt to the damage on his military or economic structure. Seeking the answers remained a prime task of intelligence, one not fully resolved, but one met with ingenuity and skill in most instances.

As with strategic intelligence, the growth of operational and tactical air intelligence analysis skills were of considerable help to command planning. It was useful for American airmen to know in 1943 that a substantial portion of the *Luftwaffe*'s fighter force was moving from the eastern and Mediterranean theaters to the defense of the Reich. In a strategic sense, this information suggested that damage to targets selected for daylight bombing was hitting the Germans hard. In an operational sense, such intelligence could not alter the reality that American bombers had to fight their way through an increasingly effective German air defense.

On the tactical level, intelligence had to be timely; by 1944 the cooperation of operations and intelligence had become so refined in the American tactical air forces that the flow of information created frequent, if fleeting, opportunities. Thus, *Luftwaffe* fighter-bomber formations that moved to Normandy following the successful Allied lodgment on June 6 were savaged even before they landed. Similarly, intelligence providing the location of *Panzer Group West* enabled American fighter forces to destroy one of the crucial links in the German command and control system. The significant aspect of intelligence-operations cooperation was the fact that both worked to a high level of understanding for each other's needs and requirements. The close relationship between commanders and their intelligence deputies fostered cooperation that made the whole greater than the sum of its parts. But that level of cooperation was established over a long period and after considerable trial and error. Intelligence was not the servant or handmaiden of operations; it was rather a partner, and that partnership played a major role in winning the war more effectively, quickly, and at less cost.

The American military did an impressive job in creating effective intelligence organizations out of minuscule cadres. First, the British provided

Retrospection

considerable support onto which the American airmen could graft their young intelligence organizations in Europe. Second, with two notable exceptions, weaknesses in intelligence organizations did not lead to any serious failures early in the war. Admittedly, Pearl Harbor and the Philippines were terrible defeats, but distance and the heavy commitment of Axis forces to other theaters had a shielding effect on American military forces. Moreover, America had two full years to prepare for conflict, while its Allies bore the brunt of battle. Had the United States not shortchanged and fragmented its intelligence organizations so badly in the interwar period, it might have significantly mitigated the problems it confronted in building up the intelligence organizations under the pressures of wartime.

NOTES

INTRODUCTION

1. Henry H. Arnold, *Global Mission* (Blue Ridge Summit, Pa., 1989), pp. 188–189.

2. Ray S. Cline, *Secrets, Spies and Scholars, Blueprint of the Essential CIA* (Washington, D.C., 1976), p. 18.

3. Intvw, Col Thomas A. Fabyanic, USAF, Ret, with Maj Gen Haywood S. Hansell, Jr., USAF, Ret, Jan 21, 1987.

4. Hansell intvw, Jan 21, 1987, pp. 4–11; Haywood S. Hansell, Jr., *The Strategic Air War Against Germany and Japan: A Memoir* (Washington, D.C., 1986), pp. 20–44.

5. One of the few exceptions to this rule occurred late in the war and involved the B–29 force. Because Arnold served as the executive agent in charge of this force (the Twentieth Air Force) for the JCS, the Air Staff intelligence office served as the operational A–2.

6. See George W. Goddard, *Overview, A Life-Long Adventure in Aerial Photography* (Garden City, N.Y., 1969) for a review of the development of the AAF's aerial photography capabilities leading to World War II.

7. See Hansell intvw, Jan 21, 1987, p. 26, for the operational problems. Hansell was the first B–29 commander in the Pacific; Curtis E. LeMay commanded the B–29 force in China before he moved to Guam.

8. Von Kármán directed the AAF rocket research project at the California Institute of Technology and would later head for Arnold what became known as the Air Force Scientific Advisory Board.

9. Before 1947, the nation's defense establishment consisted of the Navy Department and the War Department, each with its own secretary. There was no secretary of defense responsible for all of the armed services.

10. For the G–2's position in this matter, see Memo, Col Carter W. Clarke, MIS, to Adm J. R. Redman, Dir Naval Comm, Dec 2, 1943, in *OP–20–G File on Army-Navy Collaboration, 1931–1945*, Special Research History No. 200 (hereafter SRH–200), National Security Agency (NSA), pt 1, pp. 222–225.

11. Memo, E. E. Stone to Dir, Naval Comm, Mar 9, 1943, SRH–200, pt 1, pp. 156–157. The allocation agreement of which Stone spoke was the division of responsibility in 1941 whereby the Army and Navy pursued code and cryptography systems of their opposing Japanese service, with the Army also working on the Japanese diplomatic traffic known as MAGIC. See Chapter 2.

12. The U.S. Navy special operations mission that claimed the life of Admiral Yamamoto Isoroku, commander in chief of the Japanese Combined Fleet, is discussed in Chapter 5. Cf. Anthony Cave Brown, *"C," The Secret Life of Sir Stewart Graham Menzies* (New York, 1987), p. 469, and R. Cargill Hall, *Lightning Over Bougainville: The Yamamoto Mission Reconsidered* (Washington, D.C., 1991), passim.

13. Intvw, John F. Kreis with Forrest C. Pogue, Jan 7, 1991.

Chapter 1

1. Bruce W. Bidwell, *History of the Military Intelligence Division, Department of the Army General Staff: 1775–1941* (Frederick, Md., 1986) (hereafter *History of MID*), pp. 109–118; John Patrick Finnegan, *Military Intelligence: A Pictorial History* (Arlington, Va., 1985), p. 22; Peyton C. March, *The Nation at War* (Garden City, N.Y., 1932), pp. 226–227.

2. Victor H. Cohen, "History of Air Intelligence to 1945" (unfinished Air Force Hist Div MS), USAF Collection 203.6, chap 2, pp. 5–11; Air Matériel Command, "Collation of Air Technical Intelligence Information of the Army Air Arm, 1916–1947," Dec 1948, 203.6, vols 1–10; Concepts Div, Aerospace Studies Institute (ASI), "Air Attaché System," Mar 1964, 239.04621-2, app pp. 40–44. (Hereafter, only the index citation number will be given for material in the possession of the U.S. Air Force when the original document is in the collection at Maxwell AFB, Ala., or a microfilm copy is held by the Air Force History Support Office at Bolling AFB, D.C. When the material cited exists only as an original document located at the Air Force History Support Office, the notation will include the designation "AFHSO" immediately preceding the index number for the specific item.)

3. Concepts Div, ASI, "Air Attaché System," Mar 1964, app pp. 40–44; Russell McFarland, "Foreign Mission," Jul 21, 1919, 203.6, vol 1, doc 36.

4. *Final Report of General John J. Pershing, Commander in Chief American Expeditionary Forces* (Washington, D.C., 1919), p. 16; Maurer Maurer, ed, *The U.S. Air Service in World War I*, vol 1, *The Final Report and a Tactical History* (Washington, D.C., 1978), pp. 214–217.

5. *Final Report of General Pershing*, p. 16; Maurer, *Final Report and Tactical History*, pp. 214–217.

6. Maurer Maurer, *Aviation in the U.S. Army, 1919–1939* (Washington, D.C., 1987), p. xix.

7. Mauer Maurer, comp and ed, *The U.S. Air Service in World War I*, vol 4, *Postwar Review* (Washington, D.C., 1979), pp. 298–303; "Development of the Information Section and Organization of Intelligence Section," 203.6, vol 1, docs 38, 101.

8. Maurer, *Postwar Review*, pp. 298–303; "Development of the Information Section and Organization of Intelligence Section," vol 1, docs 38, 101.

9. Maurer, *Final Report and Tactical History*, pp. 214–217; ltr, Maj James Barnes, Ofc, CA/S (OCAS), AEF, to CA/S (CAS), subj: Recommendation for Information Section, Mar 19, 1918, 203.6, vol 1, doc 30.

10. *Final Report of General Pershing*, p. 15.

11. Thomas G. Ferguson, *British Military Intelligence, 1870–1914* (Frederick, Md., 1984), p. 233, citing Field Marshal Viscount Sir John French, 1914, pp. 43–44.

12. S. F. Wise, *The Official History of the Royal Canadian Air Force*, vol 1, *Canadian Airmen and the First World War* (Toronto, 1981), p. 340. The evaluation of Von Kluck's reliance on supposed Anglo-French intentions appeared in Maj Edwin E. Schwien, *Combat Intelligence, Its Acquisition and Transmission* (Washington, D.C., 1936), pp. 11–13.

13. Erick von Ludendorff, *My War Memories* (London, n.d.), pp. 204–205.

14. Lect, Wing Comdr T. L. Leigh-Mallory, RAF, before the Royal United Service Institution, Aug 21, 1930 (MID, G–2, War Department: Washington, D.C., Sep 24, 1930), 248.501-53.

15. *Final Report of General Pershing*, p. 16.

16. "Organization and Duties of the Office of Air Intelligence, GHQ AEF," pp. 1–17.

17. Ibid.

18. Ibid.

19. Bidwell, *History of MID*, pp. 247–259.

20. Ibid., pp. 300–302.

21. Ltr, Maj Gen Mason M. Patrick, Chief Air Svc AEF, to Dir Mil Aeronautics War Dept (WD), subj: The Future of the Information Section, Air Service A.E.F., Jan 18, 1918, 203.6, vol 2, doc 134; Ofc Dir Air Svc Cir 39, May 13, 1919, 203.6, vol 2, doc 45.

22. Memo, Maj H. M. Hickam for Dir Air Svc, May 22, 1919, 203.6, vol 2, doc 48; Air Svc stencil 4–292, "Function, Information Group," n.d., 203.6, vol 2, doc 49; memo, Col Wm. P. Pearson, Admin ExO Dir Air Svc, for Col [Oscar] Westover, Ofc Dir Air Svc, Apr 7, 1920, 203.6, vol 2, doc 50.

23. Concepts Div, ASI, "Air Attaché System," Mar 1964, pp. 45–46; memo, Hickam for Admin ExO Dir Air Svcs, subj: American Air Attachés Abroad, Mar 17, 1920, 203.6, vol 2, doc 47; Robert F. Futrell, *Ideas, Concepts, Doctrine* (Maxwell AFB, Ala., 1974), p. 21; memo, Asst Chief of Staff (AC/S), WD, for Chief Air Svc, subj: Cooperation with the Services in Obtaining Information from Civilian Channels, Jun 23, 1921, 203.6, vol 2, doc 111.

24. Ltr, Dir MID to Chief Air Svc, Dec 3, 1920, subj: Information Desired by You from Foreign Armies, Dec 3, 1920, 203.6, vol 2, doc 91; ltr, Military Attaché Paris to AC/S G–2, subj: Information Requested by the French Air Service, Apr 25, 1922, 203.6, vol 2, doc 119.

25. Ltr, L. W. McIntosh, Chief Engineering Div, to Chief Air Svc, subj: Air Attachés, Mar 3, 1924; 1st Ind, W. H. Frank, Exec OCAS, to Chief, Engineering Duracon, Mar 10, 1924; 2d Ind, McIntosh to CA/S, Mar 17, 1924, 203.6, vol 2, doc 151.

26. Ltr, Lt V. E. Bertrandais, Off Chief Materiel Div, to Chief Matériel Div, subj: Reports of Aeronautical Activities in France and England, Dec 22, 1928, 203.6, vol 3, doc 77.

27. Cohen, "History of Air Intelligence," chap 4.

28. Ibid.

29. Bidwell, *History of MID*, pp. 327–338.

30. Ibid.

31. Futrell, *Ideas, Concepts, Doctrine*, p. 34.

32. Memo for AC/S, WPD, Air Force Study, Mar 14, 1938, in AAG 321, Misc Staff, Corps or Department.

33. Schwien, *Combat Intelligence*, p. 10.

34. Memos, Lt Col W. R. Weaver, Chief Info Div, for Actg Exec OCAC, Jul 1, 1933, Weaver, for Exec OCAC, Jul 24, 1933, and Lt Col J. W. Chancy, Actg Exec OCAC, for Chief Info Div, Aug 1, 1933, all in 203.6, vol 4, docs 64–68.

35. Memo, Weaver, Chief Info Div, for Actg Exec OCAC, Jul 1, 1933.

36. Memo, Chancy, Actg Exec OCAC, for Chief Info Div, Aug 1, 1933.

37. Bidwell, *History of MID*, pp. 303–304.

38. Cohen, "History of Air Intelligence," chap 6, sec "GHQ Air Force."

39. Ibid.

40. Futrell, *Ideas, Concepts, Doctrine*, p. 40.

41. Ibid., pp. 40–41.

42. Hansell intvw, Jan 21, 1987.

43. Hansell, *Strategic Air War Against Germany and Japan*, pp. 7, 12.

44. Donald Wilson, "Origin of a Theory for Air Strategy," *Aerospace Historian*, Mar 1971, pp. 19–25.

45. Futrell, *Ideas, Concepts, Doctrine*, p. 40.

46. Hansell, *Strategic Air War Against Germany and Japan*, p. 12.

47. ACTS, "Committee Study on the Northeastern Theater, 1935–1936," 248.501–33, 1936.

48. Ibid.

49. ACTS Lect, Capt Robert C. Oliver, Instr Mil Intel, Apr 29, 1939, 248.500 8–13, 1938–1939.

50. ACTS, "Brief Remarks ... by Lieutenant Colonel E. M. Almond, Inf.," Apr 29, 1939, 248.500 8–13, 1938–1939.

51. OCAC, "G–2 Information Prepared by Information Division, 1934–1938," 248.501–57, 1938; Cohen, "History of Air Intelligence," chap 6, sec "GHQ Air Force."

52. Rprt, WDGS G–2, Japan (Aviation—Military), "Annual Aviation Intelli-

gence Report as of July 1, 1935," Aug 8, 1935, MA Tokyo, Rprt 7896, 248.501–65.

53. Rprt, G–2 Japan (Aviation), "Summary of Aeronautical Inspection, May 1–25, 1936," 203.6, vol 4, doc 127; ltr, Maj J. F. Phillips, Nichols Field, Philippine Islands, to Brig Gen A. W. Robbins, Wright Field, Jun 11, 1936, 203.6, vol 4, doc 130.

54. WDGS G–2, "Aviation Statistical Summary [Japan]," Jul 1, 1938, Ref MA Tokyo, No. 235–37, 248.501–65, 1938.

55. Lects, Lt Cdr R. A. Ofstie, "Aviation in the Sino-Japanese War," given at Navy Dept, Jan 1938, 248.501–65, 1937–39; Bemis in William M. Leary, "Assessing the Japanese Threat, Air Intelligence Prior to Pearl Harbor," *Aerospace Historian,* winter 1987, pp. 272–273.

56. Ofstie lects.

57. Rprt, Capt Patrick W. Timberlake, ACTS, "An Analysis of the Air Operations in the Sino-Japanese War," n.d., 248.501–65A.

58. Ltr, C. L. Chennault, Capt USAF Ret, to The Adjutant General (AG), U.S. Army (USA), May 21, 1938, 248.501–65; Leary, "Assessing the Japanese Threat," p. 274.

59. WDGS G–2, "Aviation Statistical Summary [Japan]," Jul 1, 1938.

60. Rprt, Capt Thomas D. White, ACTS, "Japan as an Objective for Air Attack, 1937–1938" (thesis), 248.501–65.

61. Ibid.

62. Claire Lee Chennault, *Way of a Fighter* (New York, 1949), 93–94; Leary, "Assessing the Japanese Threat," p. 274.

63. Hansell intvw, Jan 21, 1987.

64. Diaries, Martin F. Scanlon, 1935–1939, AFHSO, USAF microfilm; Rprt, WDGS G–2 England (Aviation), "Royal Air Force," Apr 1929, MA London, Rprt 25011, 248.501–53.

65. Rprt, WDGS G–2 England (Aviation), "Air Defense," Jan 16, 1939, MA London, Rprt 29764, 248.501–53.

66. Rprt, WDGS G–2 Great Britain (Aviation), "Annual Aviation Intelligence Report as of July 1, 1938," Sep 17, 1938, MA London, Rprt 39638, 248.501–53.

67. Rprt, WDGS G–2 Great Britain (Aviation), "Air Defense System," Mar 29, 1939, MA London, Rprt 40025, 248.501–53.

68. Ibid.

69. Rprt, MID, WDGS G–2 Germany (Aviation), "German Policy Pertaining to Air, General," May 8, 1935, MA Berlin, Rprt 14,065, 248.501–57.

70. Ibid.

71. Ltr, Maj Truman Smith, Military Attaché Berlin, to Chief MID, WDGS, subj: Conditions Existing in the German Air Ministry, Nov 16, 1935, 248.501–57.

72. Telford Taylor, *Munich: The Price of Peace* (New York, 1979), pp. 757–758, 760–762; Truman Smith, "The Facts of Life: A Narrative with Documents," Truman Smith Personal Papers, file, "The Facts of Life: 1893–1946," p. 92.

73. Rprt, WDGS G–2 Germany (Aviation), "Use of Air Force in the 'Anschluss' between Germany and Austria," Mar 19, 1938, MA Berlin, Rprt 15,809, 148.501–57.

74. Rprt, WDGS G–2 France (Aviation), "Spoken Views on National Defense Policy, General Information on European Combat Air Situation," Sep 18, 1938, MA Paris, Rprt 24519–W, 248.211–26.

75. Robert Hessen, ed, *Berlin Alert: The Memoirs and Reports of Truman Smith* (Stanford, Calif., 1984), pp. 118–119.

76. Taylor, *Munich,* pp. 760–761.

77. Matthew Cooper, *The German Air Force, 1933–1945: An Anatomy of Failure* (London, 1981), p. 58.

78. Memo, Lt Col Thomas D. Finley, Chief, Western European Section, WDGS MID, with Capt Townsend Griffiss, subj: The Air Warfare in Spain and Its Effect upon the Air Rearmament, Aug 11, 1938, 248.501–79C.

79. Rprt, Capt Townsend Griffiss, Asst Mil Attaché for Air, Valencia, "Special Report on Spanish Government Air Force," Feb 21, 1937, MA Valencia, Rprt 6471, 248.501–79A.

80. Futrell, *Ideas, Concepts, Doctrine,* p. 45.

81. ACTS, Capt Demas T. Craw, "An Analysis of the Air Operations in the Spanish Civil War, 1937–1938," quoting Maj Gen James E. Fechet, "Has a Modern War Been Fought?" 248.501–790, 1936.

82. Futrell, *Ideas, Concepts, Doctrine,* p. 45.
83. Arnold, *Global Mission,* p. 169.
84. Annual Rprt, WD, *Report of the Secretary of War to the President, 1938* (Washington, D.C., 1938), pp. 29–30.
85. Futrell, *Ideas, Concepts, Doctrine,* p. 46.
86. Maj Gen Sir Kenneth Strong, *Intelligence at the Top: The Recollections of An Intelligence Officer* (Garden City, N.Y., 1969), pp. 23–24.
87. Uri Bialer, *The Shadow of the Bomber: The Fear of Air Attack and British Politics, 1932–1939* (London, 1980), pp. 55–56, 127–160.
88. Arnold, *Global Mission,* p. 169.
89. Williamson Murray, *Strategy for Defeat: The Luftwaffe, 1933–1945* (Baltimore, Md., 1985), pp. 18–23.
90. Futrell, *Ideas, Concepts, Doctrine,* pp. 48–49.
91. Ibid., pp. 49, 51.
92. Lect, Capt Robert C. Oliver, ACTS, "Military Intelligence MI–1–C," Apr 3, 1939, 248.5008–1, 1938–1939.
93. Ibid.; handwritten lect, Oliver, ACTS, Apr 29, 1939, 248.5008–13, 1938–1939. The Army Command and General Staff School was currently emphasizing a preference of intelligence "capabilities" over "intentions," and the matter would be included in the Army Staff Officer's Field Manual dated Aug 19, 1940. See Bidwell, *History of MID,* p. 512.
94. Oliver handwritten lect, Apr 29, 1939; ACTS, "Military Intelligence Required for Initial Operations of Air Units," n.d., 248.501–25, 1938–1939.
95. Cohen, "History of Air Intelligence," chap 7, p. 8.
96. OCAC, Personnel Order 192, Aug 17, 1939.
97. "Report of a Board of Officers Convened by the Chief of the Air Corps to Consider Air Corps Requirements for Military Intelligence," n.d., 142.0201–1, 1939.
98. Memo, Brig Gen George V. Strong, AC/S WPD, for CAC, subj: Air Corps Intelligence, Oct 5, 1939, 142.0201–1, 1939.
99. Bidwell, *History of MID,* p. 386.
100. Cohen, "History of Air Intelligence," chap 7, pp. 16–17.
101. Bidwell, *History of MID,* p. 305.
102. Memo, Maj Gen H. H. Arnold, CAC, for Chief, Info Sec OCAC, subj: Evaluation of Foreign Information for Air Corps Command and Staff Use, Oct 23, 1940, 145.93–40, Sep 1940–Mar 1941.
103. OCAC, "Organization of Intelligence Division," Dec 1940, 142.021; Hansell, *Strategic Air War Against Germany and Japan,* p. 23.
104. Cohen, "History of Air Intelligence," chap 7, pp. 29–32.
105. Ibid.
106. Hansell, *Strategic Air War Against Germany and Japan,* p. 21.
107. Ibid., pp. 20–21; Hansell intvw, Jan 21, 1987.
108. Cohen, "History of Air Intelligence," chap 7, pp. 32–36.
109. Ibid., pp. 44–46.
110. Ibid., pp. 40–42.
111. "List of Air Corps Attachés and Military Missions," ca. Jan 1942, 142.0201–2, Oct 1939–Jan 1942.
112. Futrell, *Ideas, Concepts, Doctrine,* p. 53.
113. Bidwell, *History of MID,* p. 386.
114. Cohen, "History of Air Intelligence," chap 7, pp. 41–42.
115. Ibid., pp. 45–46; memo, Brig Gen M. F. Scanlon, AC/AS, Intelligence (A–2), for C/AS, subj: Responsibility for Air Intelligence, Sep 8, 1941, 145.91–221, Jun 1941.
116. Bidwell, *History of MID,* p. 306; Cohen, "History of Air Intelligence," chap 7, pp. 48–52.
117. Cohen, "History of Air Intelligence," chap 7, pp. 52–53.
118. Ibid.
119. Futrell, *Ideas, Concepts, Doctrine,* p. 59.
120. Brig Gen Carl Spaatz, C/Plans Div, OCAC, and Col R. C. Candee, C/Intel Div, OCAC, "An Air Estimate of the Situation," Mar 22, 1941, 142.0302–10.
121. Bidwell, *History of MID,* pp. 386–387. In the main, these individuals were not held in high regard by Brig Gen Raymond E. Lee, U.S. Army Military Attaché

Notes to Pages 48–61

to the United Kingdom. See *The Raymond E. Lee Papers*, a 5-volume diary (Carlisle Barracks, Carlisle, Pa.), for Jun 3, 1940, to Jan 23, 1941, and for Apr 8 to Nov 29, 1941, pp. 168, 423, and 467–468. Lee's assessments, however, were influenced perhaps by his negative views on the use of air power for strategic bombing; e.g., see p. 459.

122. Hansell, *Strategic Air War Against Germany and Japan*, p. 24.

123. Ibid., pp. 25–41; Futrell, *Ideas, Concepts, Doctrine*, pp. 59–61.

124. Hansell, *Strategic Air War Against Germany and Japan*, pp. 25–41; Futrell, *Ideas, Concepts, Doctrine*, pp. 59–61.

125. Hansell, *Strategic Air War Against Germany and Japan*, pp. 25–41; Futrell, *Ideas, Concepts, Doctrine*, pp. 59–61.

126. Research Paper, Col C. W. Strand, Air War College, "Philosophy, Concepts and Doctrine for Air Intelligence," Jan 1952, USAF Collection, pp. 20–21.

127. Memo, Maj H. S. Hansell, for Gen Arnold through Gen Chaney, subj: An Air Estimate of the Situation for the Employment of the Air Striking Force in Europe (ABC-1), Aug 11, 1941, 145.96–32, 1941–1942.

128. Hansell intvw, Jan 21, 1987.

129. Arnold, *Global Mission*, pp. 266–273.

130. Rprt, Gen William (Billy) Mitchell (for the Secy War), untitled, unpublished, AFHRC, Gen Ennis Whitehead files.

131. Among those suggesting Japanese involvement are Fred Goener in *Search for Amelia Earhart* (New York, 1966) and Paul Briand in *Daughter in the Sky* (New York, 1960). A contrary view is presented by Elliott R. Thorpe in *East Wind Rain* (Boston, 1969).

132. Intvw, Donald M. Goldstein with Cdr Chihaya Masataka, Feb 1987.

133. "Eleven-Nation Allied Military Tribunal" (unpublished, 1946), National Archives and Records Administration (NA).

134. *Hearings before the Joint Committee on the Investigation of the Pearl Harbor Attack* (hereafter *PHA*), pt 27, pp. 58–65.

135. Ibid., pp. 89–91.

136. Bidwell, *History of MID*, pp. 461–462.

137. *PHA*, pt 27, pp. 54–74.

138. Ibid., pp. 89–90.

139. Ibid., pp. 54–74.

140. Gordon W. Prange, *Pearl Harbor: The Verdict of History* (New York, 1986).

141. Arnold, *Global Mission*, pp. 168–169.

Chapter 2

1. Constance Babington-Smith, *Air Spy: The Story of Photo Intelligence in World War II* (New York, 1957), p. 1.

2. Ursula Powys-Lybbe, *The Eye of Intelligence* (London, 1983), pp. 32–45.

3. Diane T. Putney, ULTRA *and the Army Air Forces in World War II* (Washington, D.C., 1987), p. 80; Patrick Beasley, "ULTRA and the Battle of the Atlantic: The British View," symposium presentation, U.S. Naval Academy, Annapolis, Md., Oct 28, 1977, p.1; David Kahn, *Hitler's Spies: German Military Intelligence in World War II* (New York, 1978), pp. 193–195, 218–222.

4. F. H. Hinsley et al., *British Intelligence in the Second World War: Its Influence on Strategy and Operations* (London, 1981), vol 3, pt 2, pp. 778–780, 946.

5. Putney, ULTRA *and the AAF*, p. 76.

6. Hinsley, *British Intelligence in the Second World War*, vol 3, pt 2, p. 946.

7. Ibid.

8. Ibid., pp. 945–960. Appendix 30 contains the most up-to-date (as of 1988) discussion of the relative contributions of the Poles, French, and British in the cracking of Enigma.

9. Putney, ULTRA *and the AAF*, p. 77.

10. Hinsley, *British Intelligence in the*

Second World War, vol 3, pt 1, pp. 477–482.

11. Peter Calvocoressi, *Top Secret ULTRA* (New York, 1980), p. 6.

12. See Ralph Bennett, *ULTRA in the West: The Normandy Campaign, 1944–45* (New York, 1980), pp. 15–17, for a bibliographic discussion of ULTRA signal records.

13. Ronald Clark, *The Man Who Broke PURPLE* (Boston, Toronto, 1977), pp. 154–157.

14. Thomas Parrish, *The ULTRA Americans: The U.S. Role in Breaking the Nazi Code* (New York, 1986), pp. 94–95.

15. Putney, *ULTRA and the AAF,* pp. 78–81.

16. *Operations of the Military Intelligence Service, War Department, London,* Special Research History No. 110 (hereafter SRH–110), National Security Agency (NSA), pp. 39–40.

17. SRH–110, pp. 40–41.

18. Parrish, *ULTRA Americans,* p. 176.

19. SRH–110, pp. 13–14; *Use of (CX/MSS ULTRA) by the United States War Department, 1943–1945,* SRH–005, pp. 6–9.

20. SRH–110, pp. 44, 18.

21. Putney, *ULTRA and the AAF,* p. 86.

22. SRH–110, pp. 2–4, 18, 33.

23. *Synthesis of Experiences in the Use of ULTRA Intelligence by U.S. Army Field Commanders in the European Theater of Operations,* SRH–006, p. 12.

24. *Marshall Letter to Eisenhower on the Use of ULTRA Intelligence, Mar 15, 1944,* SRH–026.

25. Capt Langdon Van Norden, in *Reports by U.S. Army ULTRA Representatives with Army Field Commands in the European Theater of Operations 1945,* pt 2, SRH–023, p. 114.

26. Lewis F. Powell, Jr., in Putney, *ULTRA and the AAF,* pp. 29–31, 60–61.

27. Rprt, Maj Ansel E. M. Talbert, in SRH–023, p. 26.

28. Intvw, Dr. Robert C. Ehrhart with Gen Robert M. Lee, May 21, 1988, p. 2.

29. Intvw, Dr. Robert C. Ehrhart with Lt Gen Francis Gideon, May 18, 1988, p. 22.

30. Rprt, Maj Harry M. Grove, in SRH–023, p. 104.

31. Rprt, Lt Robert S. Whitlow, in SRH–023, p. 38.

32. Talbert, in SRH–023, p. 26.

33. *Problems of the SSO System in World War II,* SRH–107, pp. 22–23; Talbert, in SRH–023, p. 21.

34. Rprt, Capt Van Norden, in SRH–023, p. 113.

35. See, e.g., Capt Loftus E. Becker, in SRH–023, p. 97.

36. Rprt, Lt Col James D. Fellers, in SRH–023, p. 59.

37. Whitlow, in SRH–023, p. 40.

38. Grove, in SRH–023, p. 107.

39. Fellers, in SRH–023, p. 63.

40. Rprt, Maj Lucius A. Buck, in SRH–023, p. 10.

41. SRH–107, p. 34.

42. Whitlow, in SRH–023, p. 41.

43. Grove, in SRH–023, p. 105.

44. Rprt, Lt Col James D. Fellers, in *Trip Reports Concerning Use of ULTRA in the Mediterranean Theatre, 1943–1944,* SRH–031, p. 7.

45. Rprt, Maj Warrack Wallace, in SRH–031, p. 111.

46. Rprt, Lt Col Rood, in SRH–031, p. 50.

47. Fellers, in SRH–023, p. 66.

48. Rprt, Lt Col John W. Grieggs, in SRH–023, p. 110.

49. Talbert, in SRH–023, pp. 20, 23, 27.

50. Putney, *ULTRA and the AAF,* p. 31.

51. Grove, in SRH–023, p. 104.

52. Whitlow, in SRH–023, p. 45.

53. SRH–006, p. 17.

54. Putney, *ULTRA and the AAF,* p. 11.

55. Grove, in SRH–023, p. 104.

56. Fellers, in SRH–023, p. 67.

57. Rood, in SRH–031, p. 49.

58. SRH–006, p. 18.

59. Whitlow, in SRH–023, p. 44.

60. Rprt, Maj Leo J. Nielson, Jr., in SRH–023, p. 116.

61. SRH–006, p. 6.

62. Fellers, in SRH–031, 6; Powell, in Putney, *ULTRA and the AAF,* app 3, "Excerpt: Recommendations Section from Report on Visit to Operational Air Commands in Mediterranean Theater (4 April–10 May 1944)," p. 170.

63. SRH–031, p. 14.

64. Whitlow, in SRH–023, p. 49.
65. Ibid., p. 44.
66. Putney, ULTRA and the AAF, p. 93.
67. Allied Strategic Air Force Target Planning, SRH–017, p. 15.
68. See, e.g., Grieggs and Fellers, in SRH–023, pp. 110–111 and 47, respectively; Parrish, The ULTRA Americans, pp. 138–139; and Putney, ULTRA and the AAF, p. 70.
69. Bennett, ULTRA in the West, p. 15.
70. Whitlow, in SRH–023, p. 47.
71. Grieggs, in SRH–023, pp. 110–111.
72. Whitlow, in SRH–023, p. 53.
73. Hinsley, British Intelligence in the Second World War, vol 2, p. 273; Bennett, ULTRA in the West, p. 58.
74. SRH–017, p. 3.
75. Powell, in Putney, ULTRA and the AAF, p. 50.
76. Talbert, in SRH–023, p. 31; SRH–017, p. 2.
77. SRH–017, pp. 12, 3, 11.
78. Ibid., p. 11.
79. Ibid., p. 6.
80. Powell, in Putney, ULTRA and the AAF, p. 41.
81. SRH–017, pp. 16, 17.
82. Cited in SRH–017, p. 31.
83. William Haines, ULTRA and the History of the United States Strategic Air Force in Europe vs. the German Air Force (Frederick, Md., 1980) (hereafter Haines Report) p. 61. (This is a commercially printed version of a report prepared by Lt Col William Haines, dated Sep 24, 1945.)
84. Wesley Frank Craven and James Lea Cate, The Army Air Forces in World War II, vol 3, ARGUMENT to V–E Day (Chicago, 1948), pp. 26, 34–48.
85. Ronald Lewin, ULTRA Goes to War (New York, 1978), p. 118.
86. Powell, in Putney, ULTRA and the AAF, pp. 27–28.
87. History of the Intelligence Group, Military Intelligence Service, WDSG, Military Branch, pt 1, SRH–131, pp. 21–23.
88. Powell, in Putney, ULTRA and the AAF, p. 20.
89. Bennett, ULTRA in the West, p. 19.
90. Lee intvw, May 21, 1988, p. 12.
91. Rood, in SRH–023, p. 18.
92. Buck, in SRH–023, p. 11.
93. Rood, in SRH–023, p. 18.
94. Lee intvw, May 21, 1988, p. 7.
95. Rood, in SRH–031, p. 50.
96. Bennett, ULTRA in the West, pp. 162–163.
97. Rood, in SRH–031, p. 50.
98. SRH–017, p. 19.
99. Whitlow, in SRH–023, pp. 44, 48.
100. Fellers, in SRH–031, p. 8.
101. Ibid., p. 19.
102. Rood, in SRH–031, p. 50.
103. Rprt, Maj Hitchcock, SRH–023, p. 52.
104. Rood, in SRH–031, p. 51.
105. SRH–006, p. 25; Putney, ULTRA and the AAF, p. 34.
106. Rood, in SRH–031, p. 17.
107. Intvw, Dr. Thomas Fabyanic with Maj Gen Haywood S. Hansell, Jan 21, 1987, pp. 32–33.
108. War Diary, R&A Br, OSS London, Economic Outpost in the Economic Warfare Division (hereafter OSS War Diary), NA, RG 226, entry 91, vol 5, p. 57.
109. Rood, in SRH–031, p. 52.
110. Minutes, HQ USSTAF/Directorate Intel, "Meeting of A–2's of American Air Forces in Europe, Held 0900–1800 Hours, Jan 23, 1945," Library of Congress (LC), Spaatz Collection, box 121.
111. Glenn B. Infield, Unarmed and Unafraid (New York, 1970), pp. 61–63, 66–67.
112. Infield, Unarmed, p. 70.
113. Roy M. Stanley II, World War II Photo Intelligence (New York, 1981), p. 68.
114. Infield, Unarmed, p. 130.
115. Ltr, Col George D. McDonald to Maj Gen Clayton Bissell, AC/AS, Intelligence, Nov 17, 1943, USAF Academy Library Special Collections (USAFA), Gen George D. McDonald Collection, box 2.
116. Babington-Smith, Air Spy, pp. 181–187, 204.
117. Msg, Spaatz to Eaker, Feb 8, 1944, LC, Spaatz Collection, box 215.
118. Fellers, in SRH–031, p. 7.
119. Infield, Unarmed, p. 92.
120. Stanley, Photo Intelligence, p. 68.
121. Infield, Unarmed, p. 119.

122. "Photo Intelligence," in HQ USSTAF, *History of the Directorate of Intelligence, United States Strategic Air Forces in Europe, January 1944–May 1945,* Sep 8, 1945 (hereafter *History of the Directorate of Intelligence, USSTAF*), LC, Spaatz Collection, box 290.
123. *History of the Directorate of Intelligence, USSTAF.*
124. Babington-Smith, *Air Spy,* p. 69.
125. Ibid., p. 199.
126. "Photographic Reconnaissance and Intelligence," in *History of Directorate of Intelligence, USSTAF,* pp. 5, 7.
127. Babington-Smith, *Air Spy,* p. 167; Infield, *Unarmed,* p. 76.
128. Stanley, *Photo Intelligence,* p. 65.
129. Ibid., pp. 65–70; Infield, *Unarmed,* p. 111.
130. Infield, *Unarmed,* p. 114.
131. Daily Activity Summary, 10th AF, Mar 16, 1942, 830.641.
132. Wesley Frank Craven and James Lea Cate, *The Army Air Forces in World War II,* vol 4, *Guadalcanal to Saipan* (Chicago, 1948), pp. 458, 515.
133. Admin Hist, 12th AF, vol 3, annex 1, "Mediterranean Allied Tactical Air Force," 650.01.
134. Marvin Downey, ed, "History of the Fifteenth Air Force," HQ Air Matériel Command, Dec 20, 1945, 670.01-1.
135. *History of the Directorate of Intelligence, USSTAF.*
136. See, e.g., Spaatz's comments in "Minutes of Conference Held in the Office of Gen. Spaatz on 2 March 1944," LC, Spaatz Collection, box 122.
137. See, e.g., draft letter from Brig Gen George McDonald to ADI (P), dated Feb 15, 1944, contained in *History of the Directorate of Intelligence, USSTAF.*
138. *History of the Directorate of Intelligence, USSTAF.*
139. HQ 8th AF, "Intel Rev, 1944," Jan 9, 1945, 520.602, p. 18.
140. *History of the Directorate of Intelligence, USSTAF.*
141. Minutes, HQ USSTAF/Directorate Intel, "Meeting of A–2's of American Air Forces in Europe."
142. Comments, Elliot Roosevelt, in Ibid.

143. Powys-Lybbe, *Eye of Intelligence,* p. 155.
144. USSBS (Europe), vol 4, *Aircraft Division Industry Report,* NA, RG 243, pp. 48–54, 73–75; ibid., vol 175, *Ammoviawerke Merseburg-Leuna Germany,* NA, RG 243, pp. 209–211; ibid., vol 581, *The Effects of Strategic Bombing on the German War Economy,* NA, RG 243, pp. 44–45.
145. Memo, Col Guido Perera to Maj Gen Kuter, subj: Past Effectiveness and Future Prospects of Eighth Air Force Effort Under POINTBLANK as of 1 August 1943, 520.422B.
146. Babington-Smith, *Air Spy,* pp. 204–205.
147. Powys-Lybbe, *Eye of Intelligence,* pp. 195–197; Hinsley, *British Intelligence in the Second World War,* vol 3, pt 1, p. 424.
148. Babington-Smith, *Air Spy,* p. 190.
149. Powys-Lybbe, *Eye of Intelligence,* p. 172.
150. Ibid., pp. 10, 35.
151. Ibid., p. 142.
152. Ibid., p. 140.
153. Putney, ULTRA *and the AAF,* p. 82; Aileen Clayton, *The Enemy Is Listening* (London, 1980), passim.
154. Hinsley, *British Intelligence in the Second World War,* vol 3, pt 2, p. 781; Parrish, ULTRA *Americans,* pp. 94–97; *History of the Special Branch, MIS, War Department, 1942–1944,* SRH–035, pp. 20–21. In *The Enemy Is Listening,* Clayton gives an account of the integration of American SIGINT into field operations.
155. Rprt, "Airborne R/T Interception by M.A.S.A.F.," Mar 21, 1944, 520.6251–1; rprt, "Status of Y Intelligence in Eighth Air Force," May 1, 1945, 520.6251.
156. Narration, Maj Herbert R. Elsas, A–2 Sec, HQ 8th AF, to Maj Leon Benson, A–2, HQ USSTAF, "Outline History of Operational Employment of Y Service," Jun 6, 1945, and memo, Maj Elsas to Dir Intel HQ 8th AF, [no subj], May 5, 1945, both in LC, Spaatz Collection, Boxes 295, 296, 297.
157. Memo, Elsas to Dir Intel, HQ 8th AF, May 5, 1945.

158. Rprt, Lt Jakob Gotthold, HQ AAF, Air Comm Ofc, "Airborne Interception of R/T Traffic Carried Out with the Fifteenth Air Force," Nov 1, 1944, USAFA, McDonald Collection, box 11.

159. Intvw, Dr. Thomas Fabyanic with Brig Gen Harris B. Hull, Feb 20, 1987.

160. A.I.4, "The Contribution of the Y Service to the Target Germany Campaign of the VIII USAAF," n.d., LC, Spaatz Collection, box 295.

161. HQ 8th AF, Ofc Dir Intel, "Status of Y Intelligence in Eighth Air Force," May 1945, LC, Spaatz Collection, box 295.

162. Clayton, *The Enemy Is Listening*, pp. 269–270.

163. Narration, Elsas, "Outline History of Operational Employment of Y Service," Jun 6, 1945.

164. Rprt, Gotthold, HQ AAF, Air Comm Ofc, "Airborne Interception of R/T Traffic Carried Out with the Fifteenth Air Force."

165. Minutes, "Meeting of A-2's of American Air Forces in Europe."

166. Memo, Elsas to Dir Intel, HQ 8th AF, May 5, 1945.

167. Ltr, Col George D. McDonald to Maj Gen Clayton Bissell, AC/AS, Intelligence, HQ AAF, subj: Development of Radio Intelligence for the Pacific Theatre, Dec 27, 1943, USAFA, McDonald Collection, box 2.

168. Admin Hist, 12th AF, vol 3.

169. Ibid.

170. Ibid.

171. G/C R. H. Humphreys, "The Use of 'U' in the Mediterranean and Northwest African Theatres of War, Oct 1945," in *Reports Received by U.S. War Department on the Use of ULTRA in the European Theater in World War II*, SRH-037.

172. Whitlow, in SRH-023, p. 51.

173. Alexander S. Cochran, Jr., "MAGIC, ULTRA, and the Second World War: Literature, Sources, and Outlook," *Military Affairs*, Apr 1982, pp. 88–92; Edward J. Drea, "ULTRA and the American War Against Japan: A Note on Sources," *Intelligence and National Security*, Jan 1988, pp. 195–204.

174. Hinsley, *British Intelligence in the Second World War*, vol 1; Donald Cameron Watt, "British Intelligence and the Coming of the Second World War," in Ernest R. May, *Knowing One's Enemies* (Princeton, 1984).

175. Lewin, *ULTRA Goes to War;* Ronald Lewin, *The American MAGIC: Codes, Ciphers, and the Defeat of Japan* (New York, 1982).

176. Edward Van Der Rhoer, *Deadly MAGIC* (New York, 1978).

177. Gordon W. Prange, *At Dawn We Slept* (New York, 1981); Roberta Wohlstetler, *Pearl Harbor: Warning and Decision* (Stanford, 1962).

178. *The Role of Radio Intelligence in American-Japanese War, August 1941–September 1942*, SRH-012, vol 2, pp. 233–250, 282–283.

179. Clark, *The Man Who Broke PURPLE.*

180. SRH-035, p. 5.

181. Ibid., p. 16.

182. Alexander S. Cochran, Jr., *The MAGIC Diplomatic Summaries* (New York, 1982).

183. Alexander S. Cochran, Jr., "The Influence of 'MAGIC' Intelligence on Allied Strategy in the Mediterranean," in Craig L. Symonds, *New Aspects of Naval History* (Annapolis, Md., 1980).

184. For instance, see MAGIC Diplomatic Summary (hereafter MDS) 371, Apr 1, 1943, MDS 420, May 20, 1943, MDS 514, Aug 22, 1943, and MDS 535, Sep 12, 1943, all in *MAGIC Summaries*, SRH-549.

185. In particular, see MDS 1027, Jan 16, 1945, MDS 1084–6, Mar 15–16, 1945, and MDS 1104, Apr 3, 1945.

186. Cochran, *MAGIC Diplomatic Summaries.*

187. Douglas M. Horner, "Special Intelligence in the South-West Pacific Area during World War II," *Australian Outlook* 32 (Dec 1978), pp. 315–316; Rprt, "Radio Intelligence in the Fifth Air Force," n.d. [1944], 730.625.

188. SRH-035, p. 31.

189. *The Role of Communications Intelligence in Submarine Warfare in the Pacific,* SRH-011.

190. SRH-035, pp. 41–42.

191. Ibid., pp. 10–16, 26.

192. Ibid., pp. 35–36.
193. Ibid., p. 49.
194. *Japanese Order of Battle Bulletins,* SRH–129.
195. *Proceedings of the Pacific Order of Battle Conferences,* SRH–056, SRH–097, and SRH–098.
196. SRH–035, p. 49.
197. SRH–012, vols 1, 2.
198. *Reminiscence of LTC Howard W. Brown, Aug 1, 1945,* SRH–045.
199. *Narrative of the Combat Intelligence Center, Joint Intelligence Center, Pacific Ocean Area,* SRH–020; W. J. Holmes, *Double-Edged Secrets* (Annapolis, Md., 1979), pp. 112–120.
200. SRH–012.
201. Intvw, with Maj Gen Spencer B. Akin, USA, Sep 12, 1960, US Army Military History Institute Archives (USAMHI), Carlisle Army Barracks, Carlisle, Pa.
202. Information on Central Bureau is found in GHQ Far East Command, *A Brief History of the G–2 Section, GHQ, SWPA and Affiliated Units,* Jul 8, 1948, 710.600, vol 3, pp. 66–69, and Horner, "Special Intelligence in the South-West Pacific Area during World War II," pp. 310–313.
203. Alexander S. Cochran, Jr., "MacArthur, ULTRA, et le guerre du Pacificque", *Revue d'histoire de la guerre mondaile et des conflits contemporains,* Jan 1984.
204. *ULTRA Material in the Blamey Papers,* SRH–219. (This source, like several other SRHs, is a collection of papers in which the pages are unnumbered.)
205. Intvw, A. S. Cochran with Capt A. H. McCollum, Dec 31, 1981. Additional evidence of this transfer is found in the Charles A. Willoughby Papers, USAMHI, and in the Office Diary, 1942–1944, NA, RG 200, Papers of General Sutherland.
206. SRH–219.
207. Ibid.
208. *Brief History of the G–2 Section,* vols 4, 5.
209. Ltr, Marshall to MacArthur, subj: The Use of ULTRA Intelligence, May 23, 1944, in SRH–034.
210. *Use and Dissemination of ULTRA in the Southwest Pacific Area, 1943–1945,* SRH–127.

Chapter 3

1. Testimony, Brig Gen Hayes A. Kroner, Sep 13, 1944, in MIS, War Dept, *U.S. Army Investigations into the Handling of Certain Communications Prior to the Attack on Pearl Harbor, 1944–1945,* SRH–115 (NSA declass, 1981), p. 53.
2. Kroner, in SRH–115.
3. Hearings before the Joint Committee on the Investigation of the Pearl Harbor Attack, Congress of the United States (Washington, D.C., 1946), Seventy-ninth Congress, pt 14, pp. 1368, 1406.
4. Gordon W. Prange, with Donald M. Goldstein and Katherine V. Dillon, *Pearl Harbor: The Verdict of History* (New York, 1986), chap 31, p. 552. See also Wohlstetler, *Pearl Harbor,* p. 74.
5. Testimony, Brig Gen Sherman Miles, in SRH–115, p. 6.
6. Kroner, in SRH–115, p. 56.
7. Miles, Sep 14, 1942, in SRH–115, p. 42.
8. Testimony, Col Rufus Bratton, Sep 14, 1944, in SRH–115, p. 94.
9. Bidwell, *History of MID,* p. 477.
10. Ibid., pp. 475, 471.
11. Ibid., pp. 477, 456.
12. PHA, pt 14, pp. 1368, 1406.
13. Rprt, Army Pearl Harbor Board, Oct 20, 1944, p. 240.
14. Cited in Bidwell, *History of MID,* pp. 480–481.
15. Cited in Prange, *Verdict,* p. 514.
16. WD GO 6, Jan 23, 1942, 203.6, vol

5, pt 2, doc 316; Maj Gen Otto L. Nelson, Jr., *National Security and the General Staff* (Washington, D.C., 1946), p. 399.

17. Nelson, *National Security*, p. 589.

18. Memo for AC/S G–2, subj: Survey of Intelligence Activities and Army Air Forces, Nov 9, 1945, 203.6, vol 8, doc 31.

19. Cohen, "History of Air Intelligence," chap 8.

20. Ibid., chap 9.

21. Ibid.

22. Memo, Lt Harry C. Greene, Jr., Chief, Organizational Planning Div, Management Control, Dec 31, 1943, in 107.99.

23. Ibid.

24. Memo, Brig Gen Thomas D. White, AC/AS, Intelligence, for C/AS AAF, subj: I.G.D. Investigation, Feb 27, 1944, 203.6, vol 7, doc 30.

25. Ibid.

26. Rprt, Wing Comdrs Allom and Luard, "Report of Air Intelligence in the U.S. Army and Its Relationship to Air Intelligence at the Air Ministry," Mar 30, 1942, 203.6, vol 5, pt 2, doc 332.

27. Memo, Lt Col W. W. Dick, Air AG, for C/S (Attn: G–2 Div), subj: Staff Contacts between Army Air Forces and Air Ministry, Jun 25, 1942, 203.6, vol 5, pt 2, doc 363.

28. Memo, Maj Gen George E. Stratemeyer, C/AS, for C/S, subj: Direct Communication between Headquarters, Army Air Forces, and Air Units Not Under Its Command, Oct 7, 1942, 203.6, vol 6, doc 35.

29. Ibid.

30. Memo, Col T. J. Betts, Ofc AC/S G–2, and Col W. M. Burgess, Ofc AC/AS, Intelligence, for AC/S G–2 thru AC/AS, Intelligence, subj: Relationships Between G–2 and the Assistant Chief of Air Staff, Intelligence, in Air Matters, Jul 31, 1943, 203.6, vol 6, doc 220.

31. Rprt, "Informational Intelligence Division, AIS," Nov 1942, 142.01.

32. Memo, White for C/AS, Feb 22, 1944.

33. Rprt, "Organization, Functions and Key Personnel of the Operational Intelligence Division, AFDIS," Nov 7, 1942, 242.01.

34. Final Rprt, Lt Gen Ira C. Eaker, Dec 31, 1943, exhib 6, "Intelligence, Development of A–2 Section VIII Bomber Command, Problems and Solutions," 520.101A.

35. Target Info Br, AC/AS, Intelligence, "Index to Reports and Publications" (hereafter "Index to Rprts & Pubs"), Feb 23, 1943, 142.022–10.

36. Operational Intel Div, A–2, AAF, "Progress Report for October 1942" [amended to include 1943], Nov 7, 1943, 142.01.

37. "Index to Rprts & Pubs."

38. Cohen, "History of Air Intelligence," chap 13.

39. Ibid.

40. "Index to Rprts & Pubs."

41. Routing and Record Sheet, Maj Gen M. S. Fairchild, AF Dir Mil Requirements, to AF Dir Intel, subj: Intelligence Concerning Enemy Capabilities, Oct 4, 1942, 203.6, vol 6, doc 31.

42. Cohen, "History of Air Intelligence," chap 11.

43. Ibid.

44. Ltr, Sorenson to CGs, All Air Forces, et al., subj: Technical Air Intelligence, n.d.

45. Ltr, Cdr S. Teller, Bur Aeronautics, USN, to Col W. M. Burgess, subj: Joint AN Technical Aviation Intelligence Organization—Proposal for Jun 8, 1943, 203.6, vol 6, doc 170.

46. Ltrs, Col George C. McDonald, AC/S A–2, NAAF, to Sorenson, May 6, 1943, and Sorenson to McDonald, May 18, 1943, both 203.6, vol 6, doc 170.

47. Ibid.

48. Memo, Maj Gen O. P. Echols, AC/AS, Matériel, Maintenance, and Distribution, for C/AS, subj: Technical Intelligence, Jun 13, 1943, 203.6, vol 6, doc 190.

49. Memo, Burgess, Chief Informational Intel Div AAF, for Col Bentley, Nov 10, 1943, 203.6, vol 6, doc 105.

50. Memo, AFABI for Dep AC/AS, Intelligence, subj: Technical Section, Nov 3, 1943, 203.6, vol 6, doc 105.

51. Memo, Burgess, Chief Informational Intel Div AAF, for Col Bentley, Nov 10, 1943.

52. AAF Management Control, "Re-

view of the AAF Headquarters Air Intelligence Function," Sep 22, 1943, 107.99.

53. Cohen, "History of Air Intelligence," chap 9.
54. Ibid.
55. Ibid.
56. Brett, in ibid.
57. Brown, in Ltr, Sorenson to McDonald, May 18, 1943.
58. Ibid.
59. Ibid.
60. Final Rprt, Col E. F. Koenig, Comdr AAFAIS, to CG, 1st District, AAF Tech Training Commd, Sep 30, 1942, 266.1–1, 1942.
61. Memo, Lt Col Carl H. Norcross, Asst A–2, VIII Bom Comd, for AC/S, subj: Army Air Forces Intelligence School, Harrisburg, Pennsylvania, Jan 22, 1943, 266.1–1, 1942.
62. Koenig Final Rprt, Sep 30, 1942.
63. Ibid.
64. Memo, Lt Col Norcross for AC/S, A–2, Jan 23, 1943, 266.1–1, 1942.
65. Ibid.
66. Rprt, IG, "AAF Air Intelligence School," Mar 18, 1943, 266.1–1, 1942.
67. Cohen, "History of Air Intelligence," chap 9.
68. Hist, AAF Air Intel School, 1942–1945.
69. Ltr, Sorenson to CG 5th AF, subj: Intelligence Material and Information, Apr 18, 1943, and 1st Ind, Lt Col Benjamin B. Cain, Asst Chief, A–2, 5th AF, Apr 27, 1943, 203.6, vol 6, doc 157.
70. Cohen, "History of Air Intelligence," chap 9.
71. Ibid.
72. Koenig Final Rprt, Sep 30, 1942.
73. Hist, AAF Air Intel School, Oct 29, 1943–Sep 2, 1945, vol 2.
74. Cohen, "History of Air Intelligence," chap 9.
75. Eaker Final Rprt, Dec 31, 1943.
76. Rprt, Air Ministry, Air Historical Br, "Anglo-American Collaboration," Aug 1946, LC, Spaatz Papers, box 70.
77. Rprt, Lt Gen Ira C. Eaker, "USAAF in the United Kingdom, Feb 1942–Dec 1943" (hereafter Eaker Report), LC, Eaker Papers, box 20.
78. Intvw, Dr. Robert C. Ehrhart with Brig Gen Harris B. Hull, USAF, Ret, Feb 13, 1988.
79. See note 76 above.
80. Memo, Lt Col Weicker to C/S, HQ 8th AF, Dec 5, 1943, LC, Spaatz Papers.
81. Intvw, Dr. Edward Hopper, 8th AF Historian, with [General Charles P.] Cabell, Jul 9, 1944, LC, Spaatz Papers, box 135.
82. Eaker to Spaatz, Mar 18, 1942, LC, Spaatz Papers, box 322.
83. Hull intvw, Feb 13, 1988.
84. Hist, 8th AF, *Activation and Establishment, Jan 28, 1942, to Aug 17, 1942* (HQ Eighth Air Force, Feb 1945), 520.01, vol 1, p. 254.
85. Ltr, A–2, HQ 8th AF, to A–1, HQ 8th AF, Apr 21, 1943, LC, Spaatz Papers, box 328.
86. Eaker Report, p. E–2-2.
87. Hinsley, *British Intelligence in the Second World War,* vol 2, p. 51.
88. Ibid., p. 49.
89. Ltr, S/L G. E. Daniel, O.C. RAF, Photo-Interpretation Course, to HQ 10th AF (Attn: Lt Col Wright), Jun 14, 1942, 830.365; Hinsley, *British Intelligence in the Second World War,* vol 2, p. 51.
90. Hinsley, *British Intelligence in the Second World War,* vol 2, p. 51.
91. 8th AF Hist, vol 1.
92. Ltr, Eaker to Air Vice Marshal Medhurst, Mar 27, 1943, LC, Eaker Papers, box 19.
93. 8th AF Hist, vol 1, p. 346.
94. Ibid., pp. 225–226.
95. Eaker Report, p. B–2.
96. Minutes, Committee on Coordination of Air Ops, Oct 5, 1942, LC, Spaatz Papers, box 121; Hull intvw, Feb 20, 1987.
97. Rprt, Maj Gen Ira Eaker, "Fundamental Lessons Learned on the First Ten Heavy Bombardment Raids over Enemy Territory," Oct 2, 1942, 523.609A.
98. 8th AF Hist, vol 1, p. 90.
99. Monthly Intel Rprt, A–2 to VIII Bom Comd C/S, Dec 26, 1942, 523.6042.
100. A–2, VIII Bom Comd, "Sources of Information on German Defense Installations," Dec 14, 1942, LC, Spaatz Papers, box 220.
101. Ltr, Arnold to Eaker, Jan 13, 1943,

and draft A-5 response, n.d., both LC, Eaker Papers, box 16.

102. OSS War Diary, vol 4. See also Sir Charles Webster and Noble Frankland, *The Strategic Air Offensive Against Germany, 1939–1945*, vol 1, *Preparation* (London, 1961).

103. OSS War Diary, vol 4, pp. 13–15.

104. 8th AF Hist, vol 1, pp. 228, 345–346.

105. Powys-Lybbe, *Eye of Intelligence*, p. 155.

106. Memo, Lt Col Hughes to Col Robert Bacon, A-2, HQ 8th AF, Jul 1942, LC, Spaatz Papers, box 120.

107. Intvw, Dr. Bruce C. Hopper with Col Hughes, Sep 15, 1943, LC, Spaatz Papers, box 135.

108. Cited in OSS War Diary, vol 4, p. 20.

109. OSS War Diary, vol 4, pp. 20, 26, 29.

110. 8th AF Hist, vol 1, p. 349.

111. OSS War Diary, vol 4, p. 38.

112. Ibid.

113. Ibid., pp. 29–30.

114. Hughes intvw, Sep 15, 1943.

115. Hist, 8th AF, vol 2, *Experimentation and Frustration, 17 August 1942 to 1 May 1943* (HQ 8th AF, Jul 1945), 520.01, pp. 353–356.

116. Memos, Ministry of Home Security, subj: Brief Outline of Research and Experiments Department, n.d., and subj: American Personnel in R.E.8, Aug 5, 1943, both in LC, Spaatz Papers, box 186.

117. Memo, Ministry of Home Security, subj: Brief Outline of Research and Experiments, n.d.

118. Powys-Lybbe, *Eye of Intelligence*, p. 35.

119. Haines Report, p. 36.

120. Ltr, Eaker to Arnold, Apr 5, 1943, LC, Eaker Papers, box 16.

121. Cited in Hinsley, *British Intelligence in the Second World War*, vol 2, p. 756.

122. "Special Report on Bremen," n.d., LC, Spaatz Papers, box 326; Roger A. Freeman, *Mighty Eighth War Diary* (London, 1981), p. 54.

123. Babington-Smith, *Air Spy*, pp. 184–185; OSS War Diary, vol 4, pp. 63–64.

124. 8th AF Hist, vol 2, p. 8.

125. Ibid.

126. Ibid., p. 5.

127. Ltr, Eaker to Maj Gen James Chaney, CG USAFBI, cited in ibid., p. 41.

128. Eaker Report, p. E-2.

129. Memo, to CG, 8th AF, Aug 1942, LC, Spaatz Papers, box 143.

130. 8th AF Hist, vol 2, p. 16.

131. Ibid., p. 20.

132. Hist, 8th AF, vol 3, *Growth, Development and Operations*, p. 1.

133. Memo, [General Eisenhower] for General Spaatz, Oct 13, 1942, LC, Spaatz Papers, box 16.

134. 8th AF Hist, vol 2, pp. 5–6.

135. Ltr, Eaker to Spaatz, Oct 14, 1942, LC, Spaatz Papers, box 16.

136. Ofc Dir Intel, HQ 8th AF, "Target Priorities of 8th Air Force," May 15, 1945, 520.323–A.

137. Ltr, Eaker to Spaatz, Oct 14, 1942.

138. Eaker Report, p. E-2; folder, Anti-Submarine Intelligence Reports, LC, Spaatz Papers, box 10.

139. Rprts, A-2, VIII Bom Comd, Oct 1942–Jan 1943, 523.604.

140. Rprt, MEW, "Bombing Attacks on the German U-Boat Yards," Jul 21, 1942, LC, Spaatz Papers, box 222.

141. Rprt, RAF Bom Ops, "Submarine Building Yards," Aug 1942, contained in annex C, A-5, HQ 8th AF, "An Appreciation of the Air Effort Against Submarines," Jan 16, 1943, LC, Spaatz Papers, box 71.

142. Intel Rprt, Nov 20, 1942, 523.432.

143. N.I.D. report, n.d., LC, Eaker Papers, box 16.

144. Hull intvw, Feb 20, 1987.

145. HQ 8th AF, "An Evaluation of the Air Effort Against Submarines," Jan 16, 1943, LC, Spaatz Papers, box 297, p. 15.

146. Air Intel Rprt, Jan 7, 1943, cited in Intel Svc, HQ AAF, "An Evaluation of the Air Effort Against Submarines (to Jan 1, 1943)," Feb 12, 1943, 142.042–6.

147. See note 145.

148. Ibid.

149. Hull intvw, Feb 20, 1987.

150. Ltr, Morse to Mason, Feb 10, 1943, 118.1511.

Notes to Pages 145–155

151. Ltr, Eaker to Arnold, Jan 11, 1943, LC, Eaker Papers, box 16.
152. Wesley Frank Craven and James Lea Cate, *The Army Air Forces in World War II*, vol 2, *Europe: TORCH to POINTBLANK* (Chicago, 1948), pp. 305–306.
153. 8th AF Hist, vol 2, p. 6.
154. Craven and Cate, *TORCH to POINTBLANK*, p. 313.
155. Hinsley, *British Intelligence in the Second World War*, vol 2, pp. 754–756.
156. Hist, USSTAF Dir Intel, Jan 1944–May 1945, p. 4, LC, Spaatz Papers, box 297.
157. Rprt, "Accuracy of Bombardment—4 Missions," Aug 27, 1942, LC, Eaker Papers, box 5.
158. Ltr, Eaker to Arnold, Jan 11, 1943, LC, Eaker Papers, box 16.
159. OSS War Diary, vol 4, p. 56.
160. Hinsley, *British Intelligence in the Second World War*, vol 2, 142.
161. Webster and Frankland, vol 1, *Preparation*, p. 476.
162. Hinsley, *British Intelligence in the Second World War*, vol 2, pp. 141–149; OSS War Diary, vol 4, p. 57.
163. Haines Report, pp. 235–236.
164. Hinsley, *British Intelligence in the Second World War*, vol 2, pp. 271–272.
165. Ibib., pp. 238, 521, 517.
166. Ltr, Spaatz to Col Berliner, Mar 26, 1943, LC, Spaatz Papers, box 11.
167. Ltr, Arnold to Eaker, Dec 23, 1942, LC, Eaker Papers, box 16.
168. Hull intvw, Feb 13, 1988; ltr, Eaker to 8th AF A–2, Dec 1943, LC, Eaker Papers, box 17.
169. Ltr, Eaker to Stratemeyer, Jan 30, 1943, LC, Eaker Papers, box 17.
170. Ltr, Arnold to Spaatz, Dec 7, 1942, LC, Spaatz Papers, box 10.
171. Special Rprt No. 9, A–2, HQ 8th AF, 520.6314.
172. Haines Report, p. 18.
173. Hinsley, *British Intelligence in the Second World War*, vol 2, p. 521.
174. Craven and Cate, vol 2, *TORCH to POINTBLANK*, p. 708.
175. Ibid., 708–709.
176. AWPD–1, cited in Haywood, S. Hansell, Jr., *The Air Plan That Defeated Hitler* (Atlanta, Ga., 1972), p. 298.

177. Memo, Pres Roosevelt to Gen Marshall, Aug 24, 1942, 145.82–4.
178. Ltr, Marshall to USFOR-LONDON, n.d., LC, Spaatz Papers, box 66.
179. Hansell, *Strategic Air War Against Germany and Japan*, p. 100; Hull intvw, Feb 13, 1988.
180. AWPD–42, 145.82–42.
181. Ibid.
182. See nn. 140, 141.
183. Hansell, *Strategic Air War Against Germany and Japan*, p. 106.
184. AWPD–42.
185. Air Est, Intel Svc, HQ AAF, "Transportation in Axis Europe," Dec 1, 1942, 142.042.
186. Hansell, *Strategic Air War Against Germany and Japan*, p. 145; intvw, Dr. Thomas Fabyanic with Guido Perera, Jun 10, 1987.
187. Hansell, *Strategic Air War Against Germany and Japan*, p. 148; Perera intvw, Jun, 10, 1987; Hist, COA, Nov 16, 1942–Oct 10, 1944, 118.01.
188. Memo, C/S to Col Gates, Dec 9, 1942, in COA Hist.
189. Hansell, *Strategic Air War Against Germany and Japan*, p. 148.
190. Perera intvw, Jun 10, 1987.
191. COA Hist, pp. 3–4.
192. Perera intvw, Jun 10, 1987.
193. COA Hist, p. 6; Perera intvw, Jun 10, 1987.
194. COA Hist, pp. 6–7.
195. Memo, Howard Bruce to Col Sorenson, subj: Foreign Experts, Dec 12, 1942, 118.051–1.
196. Minutes, Committee Mtg, Jan 15, 1943, 118.151–1.
197. Ltr, Eaker to Andrews, CGETOUSA, Mar 27, 1943, LC, Eaker Papers, box 18; Ltr, Eaker to Perera, Feb 3, 1943, LC, Eaker Papers, box 17; Perera intvw, Jun, 10, 1987.
198. COA Hist, pp. 36–37.
199. Ibid., pp. 36–38; Perera intvw, Jun 10, 1987.
200. Memo, to Gen Arnold, subj: Report of Committee of Operations Analysts with Respect to Economic Targets Within the Western Axis, Mar 8, 1943, 118.01.
201. Ltr, Spaatz to Arnold, Apr 21,

1943, LC, Spaatz Papers, box 111.
202. Hansell intvw, Jan 21, 1987.
203. Rprt, COA, "Economic Targets Within the Western Axis."
204. Webster and Frankland, vol 1, *Preparation,* p. 217.
205. Special Rprt No. 3, EOU, Jan 5, 1943, 118.1511.
206. "Feasibility of Air Attack on European Axis Transport," Jan 21, 1943, 118.04-4.
207. Sir Charles Webster and Noble Frankland, *The Strategic Air Offensive Against Germany, 1939-1945,* vol 2, *Endeavour* (London, 1961), p. 220.
208. CCS 166/1/D, cited in Craven and Cate, vol 2, *TORCH to POINTBLANK* p. 305.
209. Rprt, AS/G2, "An Estimate of Possible Axis Moves into North and North-west Africa," Dec 24, 1941, 119.04-2.5; memo, for AC/S, WPD, subj: C.P.S. 2/2—Super Gymnast, G2/I, Feb 14, 1942, 119.04-2.5.
210. FO 1, Oct 15, 1942, annex 2, 650.327-5.
211. Hinsley, *British Intelligence in the Second World War,* vol 2, p. 465.
212. Ibid., pp. 474-475.
213. Humphreys, "Use of 'U,'" SRH-037.
214. FO 1, Oct 15, 1942, annex 2.
215. Hinsley, *British Intelligence in the Second World War,* vol 2, p. 487.
216. Ibid., p. 489.
217. Ibid., p. 487, 491.
218. Craven and Cate, vol 2, *TORCH to POINTBLANK,* p. 88.
219. Ibid., pp. 162-163.
220. Humphreys, "Use of 'U,'" SRH-037, p. 28; Craven and Cate, vol 2, *TORCH to POINTBLANK,* pp. 120-121.
221. Diary entry, Thurs, Feb 18, 1943, LC, Spaatz Diary, box 10.
222. Humphreys, "Use of 'U,'" SRH-037, p. 28.
223. Lt Col P. M. Barr, Ofc AC/AS, Intelligence, HQ AAF, "Survey of Air Intelligence in North West African Theater, February 12-April 13, 1943" (hereafter Barr Report), 142.0471-2.
224. Barr Report, p. 12.
225. Rprt, Maj Earl Smith, VIII Ftr Comd, "Combat Intelligence in North Africa Theatre of War, Jan 30, 1943," LC, Spaatz Papers, box 121; Barr Report, p. 13.
226. "Visit to 97th Bomb Group, Mar 22, 1943," in Barr Report.
227. Rprt, HQ NAAF A-2, "U.S. Navy Combat Intelligence Officers . . . May 1943, Jun 9, 1943," 612.608.
228. Barr Report, p. 6.
229. Rprt, HQ NAAF A-2, "U.S. Navy Combat Intelligence Officers," p. 3.
230. NAAF, *Weekly Intelligence Report* File, 620.607.
231. NAAF, *Weekly Intelligence Report,* Apr 12, 1943.
232. Barr Report, p. 8.
233. Msg, to C/Ss, Jan 6, 1943, LC, Spaatz Papers, box 10.
234. Minutes, Air Comdrs Conf, Mar 17, 1943, LC, Spaatz Papers, box 10.
235. Ibid., Feb 19, 1943.
236. Hinsley, *British Intelligence in the Second World War,* vol 2, pp. 742-743.
237. Humphreys, "Use of 'U,'" SRH-037, p. 25. See also John F. Kreis, *Air Warfare and Air Base Air Defense, 1914-1973* (Washington, D.C., 1988), pp. 160-169 for a discussion of Allied air defense problems.
238. Rprt, Sq Ldr D. J. Wiseman, CIO, NATAF, "Wireless Intelligence," May 13, 1943, 614.430-2; Barr Report.
239. NAAF, *Weekly Intelligence Summary,* Mar 30, 1943, 650.607.
240. Ibid.
241. Humphreys, "Use of 'U,'" SRH-037, p. 27.
242. Haines Report, pp. 21-22; Humphreys, "Use of 'U,'" SRH-037, p. 25.
243. Hinsley, *British Intelligence in the Second World War,* vol 2, pp. 575-576; Humphreys, "Use of 'U,'" SRH-037, pp. 26-27.
244. Humphreys, "Use of 'U,'" SRH-037, p. 26.
245. Ibid., p. 20. For an example of the lengths to which commanders resorted to conceal ULTRA, see Hugh P. Lloyd, *Briefed to Attack: Malta's Part in African Victory* (London, 1949). Lloyd spent almost eighteen months as the air commander on Malta when he directed a continuing antishipping campaign against Axis

Notes to Pages 165–177

supply lines to North Africa. He not only had to provide a plausible excuse to the Germans and Italians for his search success, he had to provide equally good reasons to his own people, some of whom almost guessed that he had some special source. Lloyd's book, of course, was written well before ULTRA was open knowledge, so he imparts to readers the same cover.

246. Haines Report, p. 26.
247. B. H. Liddell Hart, ed, *The Rommel Papers* (New York, 1953), p. 282.
248. Hinsley, *British Intelligence in the Second World War,* vol 2, pp. 576–577.
249. Ltr, Tedder to CG, NAAF, Mar 7, 1943, LC, Spaatz Papers, box 13.
250. NAAF A–2, *Weekly Intelligence Report,* Feb 28, 1943, 612.607.
251. Craven and Cate, vol 2, *TORCH to POINTBLANK,* 147.
252. Hinsley, *British Intelligence in the Second World War,* vol 2, pp. 607–608.
253. Ibid., pp. 573, 607.
254. Craven and Cate, vol 2, *TORCH to POINTBLANK,* p. 182.
255. Ibid., p. 184.
256. Ibid., p. 151.
257. NATAF, "Situation on Air Plan—Tunisia," n.d., pp. 9, 23–24, 614.430–2.
258. Ibid., pp. 10, 22.
259. Craven and Cate, vol 2, *TORCH to POINTBLANK,* pp. 195, 184.
260. Ibid., p. 192.
261. HQ NASAF, "The Battle of FLAX," Apr 14, 1943, LC, Spaatz Papers, box 10.
262. NATAF, "Situation on Air Plan—Tunisia," p. 30.

CHAPTER 4

1. Marvin Downey, ed, *History of Fifteenth Air Force* (HQ Air Matériel Command, Dec 20, 1946), 670.01–1, p. 303.
2. Craven and Cate, vol 2, *TORCH to POINTBLANK,* p. 419.
3. "Bombing of Communications—(In Support of Army Operations), Air Intelligence Section, Force 141," USAFA, McDonald Collection, box 10.
4. Craven and Cate, vol 2, *TORCH to POINTBLANK,* pp. 435–438.
5. Hinsley, *British Intelligence in the Second World War,* vol 3, pt 1, pp. 80–82.
6. HQ NAAF A–2, "Strategic Analysis—Air," May 13, 1943, 612.317–1.
7. Humphreys, "Use of 'U,'" SRH–037, p. 31.
8. Clayton, *The Enemy Is Listening,* p. 256.
9. Ibid., p. 245; Alfred Price, *The History of U.S. Electronic Warfare* (Arlington, Va., 1984), vol 1, pp. 72–76.
10. Price, *History of U.S. Electronic Warfare,* vol 1, pp. 72–76.
11. Ibid.
12. Contributions of Combat Intelligence.
13. Clayton, *The Enemy Is Listening,* p. 247–248.
14. Humphreys, "Use of 'U,'" SRH–037, p. 31.
15. Craven and Cate, vol 2, *TORCH to POINTBLANK,* p. 285.
16. Personal, C/AS for Welsh, Jul 26, 1943, cited in Alexander Cochran, "Spectre of Defeat: Anglo-American War Planning for the Invasion of Italy in 1943" (Dissertation, 1983).
17. Ibid., p. 410.
18. Cochran, in his "Spectre of Defeat," does an excellent job of addressing this whole subject and is the first to include recently released ULTRA decrypts and assess their influence on Portal and Arnold.
19. Craven and Cate, vol 2, *TORCH to POINTBLANK,* p. 518.
20. Clayton, *The Enemy Is Listening,* p. 283.
21. Ibid., p. 275.

22. Hinsley, *British Intelligence in the Second World War,* vol 3, pt 1, p. 175.
23. Rprt, Lt Col Leslie L. Rood, in SRH–031, p. 49.
24. Craven and Cate, vol 2, *TORCH to POINTBLANK,* p. 576.
25. Craven and Cate, vol 3, *ARGUMENT to V–E Day,* pp. 326–328.
26. Ibid., p. 329.
27. Hist, MAAF, Dec 1943–Sep 1, 1944, vol 5, "Combat Intelligence Data," app A, 622.01-5.
28. Fellers and Rood, both in SRH–031, pp. 6, 50.
29. Rood, in SRH–031, p. 52.
30. Ibid., p. 50.
31. MAAF Hist, Dec 1943–Sep 1944, vol 5, annex 3.
32. Ibid., vol 5, app C.
33. Admin Hist, 12th AF, pt 2, vol 1, annex 1, 650.01-1.
34. Ibid., vol 3, annex 1, "Mediterranean Allied Tactical Air Force."
35. Downey, *History of Fifteenth Air Force,* p. 207.
36. 12th AF Admin Hist, vol 3, annex 1, "Mediterranean Allied Tactical Air Force."
37. Ibid., vol 4, "Historical Record, January–June 1944."
38. Ibid., vol 4, "Historical Record, July–September 1944."
39. Ibid., vol 4, "Historical Record, October 1944–December 1944."
40. Rprt, Maj Warrack Wallace, in SRH–031, pp. 111–112.
41. Rood, in SRH–031, p. 50.
42. Downey, *History of the Fifteenth Air Force,* p. 201.
43. Comments, Maj Murphy, cited by Rood, in SRH–031, p. 50.
44. Rood, in SRH–031, p. 50.
45. Downey, *History of the Fifteenth Air Force,* pp. 222–235; Rood, in SRH–031, p. 49.
46. HQ NAAF A–2, "Strategic Analysis of Italy—Rail," Jun 11, 1943, 622.6111.
47. Special Rprt No. 64, "Communications (Italy): Interdiction of Rail Traffic Supplying Enemy Forces in Central Italy," Dec 24, 1943, USAFA, McDonald Collection, box 10.
48. Rprt, "Air Attacks on Rail and Road Communications," Dec 1943, LC, Spaatz Collection, box 24.
49. Rprt, Dir Ops to Dep Air Commander in Chief, "Interruption of Italian Rail Communications," Feb 13, 1944, LC, Spaatz Collection, box 24.
50. Cited in MAAF Hist, Dec 1943–Sep 1944, vol 1, "Narrative," 622.01–1, p. 191.
51. Memo, Lt R. H. Dorr (OSS) to Col W. F. Chapman, A–3 Sec, HQ MAAF (Adv.), subj: Comments on Air Attack on Marshalling Yards, Feb 8, 1944, LC, Spaatz Collection, box 24.
52. Rprt Extracts, AFHQ, CSDIC [Combined Services Detailed Interrogation Centre], Special Sec, Jan 8, 1944, LC, Spaatz Collection, box 24.
53. Ltr, CG, XII Bom Comd, to CG, 12th AF, subj: Intelligence Requirements in Connection with Current Plans for Interdicting Enemy Lines of Communication, Oct 6, 1945, in *Report on Operation STRANGLE, 19 March–11 May 1944* (HQ MATAF), annex G, 626.430–15.
54. *Report on Operation STRANGLE,* annex D.
55. Ibid., annex G.
56. Ibid., addendum B, "Sources of Information"; *War Diary* (R&A/OSS, London), vol 5, p. 66.
57. "Bridge Busting: A Report on the Tactics of Medium Bombardment as Used in Italy for the Disruption of Rail Traffic," Apr 16, 1944, in *Report on Operation STRANGLE,* annex G.
58. Ltr, Eaker to Devers, Apr 1, 1944, LC, Eaker Collection, box 24.
59. *Report on Operation STRANGLE,* annex J, "Railroad Traffic Interdiction—Central Italy—March–April 1944," n.d.
60. Rood, in SRH–031, p. 51.
61. Ltr, Eaker to Brig Gen Hansell et al., Apr 2, 1943, LC, Eaker Collection, box 17.
62. Hansell, *Air Plan,* p. 157.
63. HQ 8th AF, "The Combined Bomber Offensive from the U.K.," Apr 12, 1943, LC, Spaatz Collection, box 67.
64. "Priorities for Air Attack Among

Economic Targets in 1943," n.d., cited in 8th AF Hist, vol 2.

65. Hansell, *Air Plan,* p. 162.
66. CCS 217, "Plan for Combined Bomber Offensive from the United Kingdom," May 14, 1943, 118.04W.
67. Briefing Book for General Arnold, "German Situation," 1943, 119.01-1.
68. CCS 217.
69. Col Kingman Douglass, "Jockey Committee: Its History and Functions," n.d., LC, Spaatz Collection, box 137.
70. Ibid.
71. Ibid.
72. Ltr, Anderson to Doolittle, subj: G.A.F. Targets, Jockey Committee, No. 80, Dec 28, 1944, LC, Spaatz Collection, box 215.
73. Memo, Col Hughes to Maj Gen Eaker, subj: Relative Priority of the German Aircraft Industry as a Target, Mar 23, 1943, 520.4231C.
74. Memo, Col Hughes to CG, 8th AF, subj: Estimate of Force Required for Attack on German Aircraft Industry, Mar 22 1943, 520.4231C.
75. HQ 8th AF, Dir Intel, "Target Priorities of the Eighth Air Force," May 15, 1945, 520.323-I, p. 11.
76. Memo, Hughes to CG, Mar 22, 2943.
77. Freeman, *Mighty Eighth,* pp. 64–84.
78. Rprt, R&A/OSS, "Geographical Shifts in the German Aircraft Industry," Aug 17, 1943, USAFA, McDonald Collection, box 8.
79. Eaker to CGs, NAAF and 9th AF, Jul 14, 1943, 520.4231D.
80. Memo, Hughes to CG, Mar 22, 1943.
81. EOU, "Handbook of Target Information," n.d. [prepared in spring or summer 1943], LC, Spaatz Collection, box 216.
82. EOU, "War Diary," p. 11.
83. HQ 8th AF, Dir Intel, "Target Priorities of the Eighth Air Force," p. 12.
84. Ibid.
85. Craven and Cate, vol 2, *TORCH to POINTBLANK,* p. 705.
86. Msg, Eaker to Arnold, Oct 15, 1843, LC, Eaker Collection, box 16.
87. Ltrs, Arnold to Eaker, and Marshall to Eaker, both Oct 15, 1943, LC, Eaker Collection, box 16.
88. 8th AF, "Narrative of Operations, 115th Operation," Oct 14, 1943, 520.332.
89. Ltr, Eaker to Arnold, Oct 15, 1943.
90. CIU Interpretation Rprt, Oct 16, 1943, 520.332.
91. Ibid., Oct 20, 1943, 520.332.
92. HQ 8th AF, Dir Intel, "Target Priorities of the Eighth Air Force"; "Joint Intelligence Committee Report," cited in C/AS, RAF, and CG, 8th AF, "The Combined Bomber Offensive Progress Report, February 4, 1943–November 1, 1943," annex P, LC, Spaatz Collection, box 67.
93. Craven and Cate, vol 2, *TORCH to POINTBLANK,* p. 704.
94. Msg, Eaker to Arnold, Oct 15, 1943.
95. Msg, Eaker to Arnold, n.d., Eaker Collection, box 16.
96. Ltr, Col McDonald to AC/AS, Intelligence, subj: State of German Air Forces in Mediterranean Theater, Nov 16, 1943, USAFA, McDonald Collection, box 2.
97. "Current Items of Air Intelligence from AC/AS, A-2, Oct 18, 1944," cited in Craven and Cate, vol 2, *TORCH to POINTBLANK,* p. 712.
98. R&A/OSS, "Major Targets in the German S/E Fighter Aircraft Industry," Aug 17, 1943, USAFA, McDonald Collection, box 8.
99. Haines Report, p. 41.
100. Off Dir Ops, HQ USSTAF, "Information Supplementary to the Outline of Method for Implementation of the 'Big Week,'" n.d., LC, Spaatz Collection, box 169.
101. Ltr, McDonald to Brig Gen Thomas D. White, AC/AS, Intelligence, Jul 23, 1944, USAFA, McDonald Collection, box 2.
102. HQ 8th AF, Dir Intel, "Target Priorities of the Eighth Air Force," p. 9.
103. Cited in ibid., p. 10.
104. Special Intel Rprt [No. 65], HQ MAAF A-2, "Air Attack on German Single-Engine Fighter Production," Dec 26, 1943, USAFA, McDonald Collection, box 9.
105. Craven and Cate, vol 2, *TORCH to POINTBLANK,* pp. 748–754.
106. Directive to CGs, 8th and 15th

AFs, Jan 11, 1944, LC, Spaatz Collection, box 143.

107. Combined Ops Planning Committee, "Tactical Plan for the Air Battle of Leipzig . . . ," Nov 29, 1943, LC, Spaatz Collection, box 147.

108. HQ VIII Bom Comd A-2, "ARGUMENT Target Suggestions," Nov 23, 1943, 520.4231B.

109. Special Intel Rprt [No. 63], HQ NAAF A-2, "Strategic Targets," Dec 24, 1943, 617.608.

110. Craven and Cate, vol 3, *ARGUMENT to V-E Day*, pp. 33-44.

111. Memo, Capt J. C. Reed to Col McDonald, Feb 26, 1944, LC, Spaatz Collection, box 143.

112. Teletype Conf Script, Feb 27, 1944, LC, Spaatz Collection, box 67.

113. "Use of Strategic Air Power After 1 March 1944," Feb 28, 1944, in *War Diary*, pp. 70ff.

114. Craven and Cate, vol 3, *ARGUMENT to V-E Day*, p. 45.

115. Hinsley, *British Intelligence in the Second World War*, vol 3, pt 1, p. 317.

116. Haines Report, p. 82.

117. Ibid., p. 83.

118. Ibid., p. 92.

119. Ibid., p. 86.

120. Ibid., p. 92.

121. Ibid., p. 91.

122. Carl Boyd, "Significance of MAGIC and the Japanese Ambassador to Berlin: (1) The Formative Months Before Pearl Harbor," *Intelligence and National Security*, Jan 1987, pp. 150-151.

123. Memo, Maj Gen F. L. Anderson, Feb 12, 1944, LC, Spaatz Collection, box 61.

124. Rprt, Capt Harold J. Barnett, "The Use of Strategic Air Power after 1 March 1944," pp. 70ff.

125. Ibid.

126. HQ USSTAF, "Plan for Completion of the Combined Bomber Offensive," Mar 5, 1944, LC, Spaatz Collection, box 61.

127. "Petroleum Industry," n.d., atched to Ltr, Capt Kindleberger to Col Hughes, subj: M.E.W. Comment on USSTAF Plan for Attack Against Oil Installations, Mar 25, 1944, LC, Spaatz Collection, box 144.

128. Ltr, Kindleberger to Hughes, Mar 25, 1944.

129. Dir Bom Ops, "Notes on the Employment of the Strategic Bomber Forces Prior to 'OVERLORD,'" Mar 19, 1944, LC, Spaatz Collection, box 144.

130. COA, "Requested Comment on JIC 106/2," Jan 12, 1944, and "Report on German Aviation Gasoline Position," Jan 18, 1944, both in LC, Spaatz Collection, box 67.

131. Ltr, Spaatz to Eisenhower, Mar 5, 1944, LC, Spaatz Collection, box 144.

132. HQ USSTAF, "Plan for the Completion of the Combined Bomber Offensive."

133. See, e.g., Memo, Capt Kindleberger to Col Hughes, subj: Summary Account of Meeting of 25 February 1944, Norfolk House, Feb 26, 1944, LC, Spaatz Collection, box 144, and Memos, Lt R. H. Dorr, USNR, OSS, to Col W. F. Chapmen, A-3, MAAF (Adv.), subj: Comments on Air Attack on Marshalling Yards, Feb 8, 1944, and subj: The Value of Marshalling Yards as Targets: Mediterranean Example, Feb 22, 1944, both cited in EOU, "War Diary," pp. 86-90.

134. AD Ops (SO), "The Battle of the Flying Bomb," n.d., pp. 1-2, and D of I (O), "CROSS-BOW: Summary of Information," Jun 12, 1943, both in LC, Spaatz Collection, box 171; Ltr, Hughes to CG, 8th AF, Aug 11, 1943, LC, Spaatz Collection, box 171; Powys-Lybbe, *Eye of Intelligence*, pp. 90-91, 188, 191; Hinsley, *British Intelligence in the Second World War*, vol 3, pt 1, pp. 371, 363-364, 390-393.

135. "Battle of the Flying Bomb."

136. Hinsley, *British Intelligence in the Second World War*, vol 3, pt 1, p. 385.

137. Ibid., p. 399n.

138. "U.S. Army Air Forces Activities in United Kingdom Covering Period from February 20, 1942, to December 31, 1943," LC, Spaatz Collection, box 20.

139. Minutes, mtg to discuss attack of installations in northern France, Aug 11, 1943, 519.4311.1.

140. Hinsley, *British Intelligence in the Second World War*, vol 3, pt 1, p. 399n.

141. "Battle of the Flying Bomb," p. 2;

Powys-Lybbe, *Eye of Intelligence*, p. 196.
142. Babington-Smith, *Air Spy*, pp. 223, 227–228.
143. Msg, Eaker to Eisenhower, Dec 26, 1943, LC, Spaatz Collection, box 171.
144. See sample lists in CROSSBOW File, 520.323B.
145. "Battle of the Flying Bomb," pp. 5–6. See also R. V. Jones, *The Wizard War, British Scientific Intelligence, 1939–1945* (New York, 1978), chaps 38, 39.
146. Hinsley, *British Intelligence in the Second World War*, vol 3, pt 1, pp. 424–426.
147. EOU, "War Diary," p. 50; Spaatz to Eisenhower, Jun 25, 1944, and Jul 10, 1944, both in LC, Spaatz Collection, box 171.
148. Hinsley, *British Intelligence in the Second World War*, vol 3, pt 2, pp. 538–539.
149. Ibid., p. 542.
150. Ltr, RAF ACAS (I) to Dir Intel, HQ USSTAF, Jul 8 1944, LC, Spaatz Collection, box 171.
151. Memo, McDonald to Maj Gen Anderson, Jul 8, 1944, LC, Spaatz Collection, box 171.
152. Ltr, McDonald to Air Vice Marshal F. F. Inglis, Jul 15, 1944, LC, Spaatz Collection, box 171.
153. "CROSSBOW, 9 July through 15 July 1944," Jul 16, 1944, LC, Spaatz Collection, box 171.
154. Committee on Operations Planning Coordination, "Preliminary Report on the Possibility of Reducing the Flying Bomb Activity to an Acceptable Scale and on the Sterilization of the Large Rocket," Jul 28, 1944, LC, Spaatz Collection, box 149.
155. Cited in Ltr, HQ AEAF to Air Comdrs, Jul 25, 1944, LC, Spaatz Collection, box 172.
156. Hinsley, *British Intelligence in the Second World War*, vol 3, pt 2, pp. 542–543.
157. EOU, "War Diary," p. 51.
158. Powys-Lybbe, *Eye of Intelligence*, p. 192.
159. Hinsley, *British Intelligence in the Second World War*, vol 3, pt 1, pp. 436, 443, 450.
160. Cited in Babington-Smith, *Air Spy*, p. 236.
161. EOU, "War Diary," p. 50.
162. CCS 217.
163. Craven and Cate, vol 3, *ARGUMENT to V–E Day*, pp. 71–72.
164. Freeman, *Mighty Eighth*, pp. 212–259; HQ 8th AF, Dir Intel, "Target Priorities of the Eighth Air Force," p. 72.
165. Rprt, "Ninth Air Force Activities, April Thru June 1944," n.d., LC, Spaatz Collection, box 166.
166. Draft Hist, IX TAC, "A–2," Mar 1945, LC, Quesada Collection, box 3.
167. Hinsley, *British Intelligence in the Second World War*, vol 3, pt 2, pp. 113–114.
168. Ibid., p. 104.
169. A.I.3(b), "Employment of the G.A.F. Against 'OVERLORD,'" Mar 15, 1944, USAFA, McDonald Collection, box 8.
170. HQ AEAF, "Overall Plan for Operation NEPTUNE," Apr 15, 1944, LC, Spaatz Collection, box 166.
171. "Ninth Air Force Plan for Operation NEPTUNE," annex I, "Intelligence," Apr 26, 1944, LC, Spaatz Collection, box 151.
172. IX TAC Ops Plan, May 31, 1944, LC, Spaatz Collection, box 65.
173. Hinsley, *British Intelligence in the Second World War*, vol 3, pt 2, pp. 103–104.
174. Haines Report, p. 120–124.
175. Bennett, *ULTRA in the West*, p. 54.
176. Ltr, Arnold to Spaatz, Apr 24, 1944, LC, Spaatz Collection, box 143.
177. Minutes, mtg of Air Commanders in Chief, May 26, 1944, LC, Spaatz Collection, box 143.
178. Haines Report, p. 110.
179. Lt Col Whitlow, "Commands," pt 2, SRH–023, p. 50.
180. Haines Report, p. 108.
181. Bennett, *ULTRA in the West*, p. 67.
182. Ibid., p. 86; Powell, in Putney, *ULTRA and the AAF*, p. 20.
183. Signal XL 8081, LC, Microfilm Sec, ULTRA Files.
184. Signal XL 8444, LC, Microfilm Sec, ULTRA Files.
185. Haines Report, p. 119.

186. Ibid., p. 128.
187. Ibid., p. 130.
188. Draft Hist, IX TAC, "Signals Intelligence," Mar 1945, LC, Quesada Collection.
189. Ibid.
190. Memo, McDonald to Anderson, Aug 17, 1944, LC, Spaatz Collection, box 143.
191. Rood, in SRH–023, p. 16.
192. Bennett, ULTRA in the West, p. 49.
193. Capt Charles Kindleberger, to G–2 (Air), 21 Army Grp/HQ 2d TAF, "An Interim Report on the Rail Movement of German Reserves," Jun 16, 1944, cited in W. W. Rostow, *Pre-Invasion Bombing Strategy: General Eisenhower's Decision of March 25, 1944* (Austin, Tex., 1981), app F, pp. 122–137.
194. Intvw, Dr. Robert C. Ehrhart with Gen Robert M. Lee, May 21, 1988.
195. Lee intvw, May 21, 1988.
196. Buck, in SRH–023, p. 8.
197. Hists, IX Ftr Comd and IX Air Support Comd, monthly from Oct 1943 through Feb 1945, LC, Quesada Collection, box 2.
198. Draft Hist, IX TAC, "A–2," Mar 1945, LC, Quesada Collection.
199. Draft Hist, IX TAC, "Operations Intelligence," Mar 1945, LC, Quesada Collection.
200. Kindleberger, "Interim Report," in Rostow, *Pre-Invasion Bombing Strategy*.
201. IX Ftr Comd Unit Hist, Jul 1944.
202. Rprts, Fellers, Whitlow, and Grove, all in SRH–023.
203. Draft Hist, IX TAC, "A–2, Recce Sec," Mar 1945, LC, Quesada Collection.
204. Lee intvw, May 21, 1988; Griggs, in SRH–023, p. 34.
205. Buck, in SRH–023, p. 8.
206. SHAEF G–2, "Interdiction Handbook," LC, Spaatz Collection, box 215.
207. Bennett, ULTRA in the West, p. 68.
208. Grove, in SRH–023, p. 108.
209. Signal XL 8339, LC, Microfilm Sec, ULTRA Files.
210. Signal XL 8038, LC, Microfilm Sec, ULTRA Files.
211. Air Sunset 248, Oct 28, 1944, cited in Hinsley, *British Intellligence in the Second World War*, vol 3, pt 2, p. 408.
212. Air Sunset 260, Dec 6, 1944, cited in ibid., p. 428.
213. Craven and Cate, vol 3, ARGUMENT to V–E Day, pp. 675–681.
214. Bennett, ULTRA in the West, pp. 199–201; Hinsley, *British Intelligence in the Second World War*, vol 3, pt 2, pp. 406–438.
215. Hinsley, *British Intelligence in the Second World War*, vol 3, pt 2, p. 406.
216. Air Sunsets 253 (Nov 7, 1944), 254 (Nov 9, 1944), and 255 (Nov 12, 1944), cited in ibid., pp. 901–905.
217. Ibid., pp. 410, 424.
218. Ibid., p. 438.
219. Lee intvw, May 21, 1988, p. 11.
220. Craven and Cate, vol 3, ARGUMENT to V–E Day, p. 665.
221. Hinsley, *British Intelligence in the Second World War*, vol 3, pt 2, p. 442.
222. Haines Report, p. 167.
223. Lee intvw, May 21, 1988.
224. Ltr, Spaatz to Arnold, Sep 30, 1944, LC, Spaatz Collection, box 143.
225. Memo, McDonald to Anderson, Apr 9, 1944, USAFA, McDonald Collection, box 3.
226. Rostow, *Pre-Invasion Bombing Strategy*, p. 56n.
227. Haines Report, pp. 98–99.
228. HQ USSTAF, "Plan for the Employment of the Strategic Air Forces," Jun 10, 1944, LC, Spaatz Collection, box 145.
229. G–2 SHAEF, "Use of Air Power Against Enemy Military Transport and Supplies," Jun 7, 1944, in "Plan of 10 June 1944," annex F, LC, Spaatz Collection, box 145.
230. Memo to AC/AS, Plans, subj: Review of Basic Study, Report of the Committee of Operations Analysts, Mar 8, 1943, Jun 21, 1944, LC, Spaatz Collection, box 67.
231. EOU, "War Diary," p. 23.
232. Memo, McDonald to Anderson, Aug 1, 1944, USAFA, McDonald Collection, box 3.
233. Ltr, Spaatz to Arnold, May 24, 1944, LC, Spaatz Collection, box 143.
234. Charles Webster and Noble Frankland, *Strategic Air Offensive Against Germany, 1939–1945*, vol 3, *Victory* (London, 1961), p. 225.

235. Haines Report, p. 104.
236. Ibid., p. 119.
237. Ibid., p. 117.
238. SRH–017, p. 25.
239. Haines Report, p. 128.
240. Ibid., pp. 134–135.
241. Ibid., p. 150.
242. Ibid., p. 134.
243. Ibid., p. 160.
244. HQ USSTAF, "Plan for the Employment of the Strategic Air Forces," Jun 10, 1944.
245. Spaatz to CGs, 8th and 15th AFs, subj: Target Priorities, Sep 1, 1944, 520.323B.
246. Ltr, Spaatz to Arnold, Jul 17, 1944, USAFA, McDonald Collection, box 3.
247. "A Counter Air Force Program for the Period from Now until the German Collapse," Oct 24, 1944, LC, Spaatz Collection, box 143.
248. A.I.3(b) Air Ministry, "The Threat of the German Air Force to Our Planned Strategic Air Operations," Oct 23, 1944, USAFA, McDonald Collection, box 9.
249. Dir Ops, HQ USSTAF, "The Threat of the German Air Force to Strategic Operations," Nov 5, 1944, USAFA, McDonald Collection, box 9.
250. Minutes, "HQ USSTAF Meeting Regarding the German Air Force," Nov 1, 1944, LC, Spaatz Collection, box 143.
251. Powys-Lybbe, *Eye of Intelligence*, pp. 67–68.
252. Minutes, "Meeting of the A–2s of American Air Forces in Europe," Spaatz Collection, box 121.
253. Memo, subj: Terms of Reference, Oct 13, 1944, LC, Spaatz Collection, box 186.
254. EOU, "War Diary," p. 125.
255. Hinsley, *British Intelligence in the Second World War*, vol 3, pt 1, p. 54.
256. Powell, in Putney, ULTRA *and the AAF*, p. 41.
257. Bennett, ULTRA *in the West*, pp. 226–227.
258. HQ USSTAF, *History of the Directorate of Intelligence, United States Strategic Air Forces in Europe, January 1944–May 1945* (Office of the Directorate of History), LC, Spaatz Collection, box 290.

259. Directive No. 2, Spaatz to CGs, 8th and 15th AFs, "Control of Strategic Air Forces in Europe," Nov 1, 1944, LC, Spaatz Collection, box 146.
260. HQ 8th AF, Dir Intel, "Target Priorities of the Eighth Air Force," pp. 31–32.
261. "Current German Railway Situation and the Problem of Air Attack," Jan 10, 1945, cited in ibid., p. 32.
262. Memo, McDonald to Anderson, Jan 5, 194[5] (misdated 1944), 519.323.
263. Rprt, A.I.2(g), "German Air Force Developments," Jul 19, 1944, USAFA, McDonald Collection, box 9.
264. Babington-Smith, *Air Spy*, pp. 210–211.
265. A–2 3d Bom Div, "Enemy Jet Propelled Aircraft," Aug 25, 1944, 520.651–1; Hinsley, *British Intelligence in the Second World War*, vol 3, pt 1, pp. 348–349.
266. A.I.2(g), "German Air Force Developments," Jul 19, 1944.
267. Hinsley, *British Intelligence in the Second World War*, vol 3, pt 2, p. 597.
268. Ltr, Spaatz to Arnold, Jul 22, 1944, LC, Spaatz Collection, box 143.
269. Ltr, Spaatz to Arnold, Sep 3, 1944, LC, Spaatz Collection, box 143.
270. HQ 8th AF, Dir Intel, "Target Priorities of the Eighth Air Force."
271. Minutes, mtg, "Underground Factories in Germany," Sep 20, 1944, LC, Spaatz Collection, box 215.
272. Dir Ops, "The Threat of the German Air Force to Strategic Operations," Nov 5, 1944, and A.I.3(b), "The Threat of the German Air Force to Our Planned Strategic Air Operations," Oct 23, 1944, both in USAFA, McDonald Collection, box 9.
273. Hinsley, *British Intelligence in the Second World War*, vol 3, pt 2, p. 59.
274. Haines Report, p. 165.
275. Ibid., pp. 166, 172; Hinsley, *British Intelligence in the Second World War*, vol 3, pt 2, p. 600.
276. McDonald to SHAEF Air Staff, Dec 20, 1944, USAFA, McDonald Collection, box 3.
277. Memo, McDonald to Anderson, subj: Estimated Buildup and Use of Me

262s and Ar 234s, Dec 29, 1944, USAFA, McDonald Collection, box 3.
278. Memo, McDonald to Spaatz, subj: Allied Air Supremacy and German Jet Planes, Jan 3, 1945, USAFA, McDonald Collection, box 9.
279. Ltr, Spaatz to Arnold, Jan 10, 1945, 519.3181–1.

280. Craven and Cate, vol 3, ARGUMENT to V–E Day, p. 722.
281. "Analysis of G.A.F. Reactions Since 1 January 1945," Mar 20, 1945, USAFA, McDonald Collection, box 2.
282. Ibid.
283. Douglass, "Jockey Committee."
284. Craven and Cate, vol 3, ARGUMENT to V–E Day, p. 754.

CHAPTER 5

1. U.S. Signal Security Agency, *Reminiscences of Lieutenant Colonel Howard W. Brown,* Aug 14, 1945, SRH–045 (hereafter Brown Report) [this report is also in the Air University Library, M–U43294–32, and has been reprinted in Ronald H. Spector, ed, *Listening to the Enemy* (Wilmington, 1988), pp. 43–76], pp. 42–44; Air Ministry, Draft RAF Narrative, *The Campaigns in the Far East,* AFHSO, vol 2, pp. 62–63. See also John B. Lundstrom, *The First Team,* (Annapolis, Md., 1984), p. 480 for comments on the American understanding of the Zero fighter.
2. S. Woodburn Kirby et al., *History of the Second World War, The War Against Japan,* vol 1, *The Loss of Singapore,* (London, 1957), app 3; Wesley Frank Craven and James Lea Cate, *The Army Air Forces in World War II,* vol 1, *Plans and Early Operations* (Chicago, 1948), pp. 243–245, 366, 376, 396.
3. Craven and Cate, vol 1, *Plans and Early Operations,* pp. 410, 480–483; Ronald Lewin, *The American MAGIC: Codes, Ciphers, and the Defeat of Japan* (New York, 1982), pp. 92–93.
4. Craven and Cate, vol 1, *Plans and Early Operations,* pp. 428–438, 451–454; Ibid., vol 4, *Guadalcanal to Saipan,* pp. 70–74, 88–89, 209–211, 290–291.
5. Craven and Cate, vol 4, *Guadalcanal to Saipan,* pp. 405–434; Allison Ind, *Bataan, The Judgement Seat* (New York, 1944), pp. 2–3, 9–10; Walter D. Edmonds, *They Fought With What They Had: The Story of the Army Air Forces in the Southwest Pacific, 1941–1942* (Boston, 1951; Washington, D.C., 1992), pp. 22–23 [a copy of the WD C/S Memo for the Secy General Staff, subj: Air Offensive Against Japan, Nov 21, 1941, is appended to Rear Adm Edwin T. Layton, with Capt Roger Pineau and John Costello, *"And I Was There," Pearl Harbor and Midway—Breaking the Secrets* (New York, 1985), following p. 528].
6. Brown Report.
7. Ibid.
8. Ibid.
9. Ibid., pp. 50–52.
10. Cited in Robert F. Futrell, "Air Hostilities in the Philippines, 8 December 1941," *Air University Review,* Jan–Feb 1965, pp. 33–45.
11. Edmonds, *They Fought With What They Had,* pp. 80–81; Maj Gen Charles A. Willoughby and John Chamberlin, *MacArthur, 1941–1951* (New York, 1954), pp. 25–26; Futrell, "Air Hostilities in the Philippines," pp. 33–45.
12. Brown Report, pp. 58–67.
13. Craven and Cate, vol 1, *Plans and Early Operations,* pp. 403–426.
14. Air Eval Bd, SWPA, "Fifth Air Force Intelligence Evaluation, Combat Intelligence in SWPA (A General Review of Growth from April 1942 to June 1944)," 706.601–1; intvw, Current Intel Sec A–2, AAF, with Lt Col Reginald F. Vance, Senior Staff Off, Allied Forces, Port Moresby, Sep 11, 1942, in 142.052; HQ Allied Air Forces SWPA Directorate Intel, Serial No. 1, May [19,] 1942 (mis-

dated May 18, 1942).

15. HQ Allied Air Forces SWPA Directorate Intel, Serial No. 1, May [19,] 1942.

16. General Willoughby's story and the narrative of GHQ SWPA Intel is told in the multivolume *Brief History of the G–2 Section, GHQ SWPA, and Affiliated Units* (Tokyo: July 8, 1948), 710.600. Something of a summary appeared in GHQ Far East Comd, *Operations of the Military Intelligence Section GHQ SWPA/FEC/SCAP* [Supreme Commander Allied Powers] (Tokyo: Sep 30, 1950). The quotations are from vol 3, Sep 30, 1950, p. 4, and chap 2, n.p. See also Willoughby and Chamberlain, *MacArthur*.

17. Allison Ind, *Allied Intelligence Bureau, Our Secret Weapon in the War Against Japan* (New York, 1958), pp. 1–13; Lewin, *American MAGIC,* (New York, 1982), pp. 181–184; Desmond J. Ball, "Allied Intelligence Cooperation Involving Australia During World War II," *Australian Outlook,* Dec 1978, pp. 299–309; Horner, "Special Intelligence in the South-West Pacific Area," pp. 310–327; D. M. Horner, *High Command: Australia and Allied Strategy, 1939–1945* (Canberra, 1982), chap 10, "Allied Intelligence Co-operation in the SWPA," pp. 224–246.

18. Papers of General George C. Kenney, entries for Aug 1942, AFHSO (hereafter Kenney Papers); George C. Kenney, *General Kenney Reports* (hereafter *Kenney Reports*) (New York, 1949; Washington, D.C., 1987), pp. 31, 61–62.

19. Haywood S. Hansell, Jr., *The Strategic Air War Against Germany and Japan* (Washington, D.C., 1986), p. 148; Lewin, *American MAGIC*, chap 12; *Reports by U.S. Army ULTRA Representatives with Field Commands in the Southwest Pacific, Pacific Ocean and China Burma India Theaters of Operations 1944–1945,* SRH–032, pp. 5–17; *Kenney Reports,* pp. 26–28, 52–53; Kenney Papers, Aug 4, 1942; *Use and Dissemination of ULTRA in the Southwest Pacific Area, 1943–1945,* SRH–127, pp. 6–28. Kenney's regular, direct access to ULTRA material sent from Washington seems to have begun late in 1943 or 1944. The amount and type of such information he received is difficult to determine; by the time of the Philippine campaign, the SSOs in Brisbane were a conduit for intelligence from China-Burma to the SWPA forces (see SRH–127, pp. 145–148) as well as from outside the theater. In any event, Kenney had daily briefings from his intelligence staff and from the SSO assigned to HQ FEAF. Kenney's papers contain no remarks to the effect that he resented Sutherland's control of special security information or that Sutherland kept anything of importance from him. Kenney knew so much of Sutherland's bad side that he must have understood the SSO problem, yet Kenney had been content to work with theater data and with what MacArthur told him of air operations matters in SSO reports. See also the Brown Report for a description of the beginning of American Army intercept operations in the SWPA.

20. Hist, 13th AF Intel Sec 1943–1945, 750.600.

21. Memo, Van Slyck for Brock, ca. Mar 1943; ltr, Col L. C. Sherman, AC/S G–2, U.S. Army Forces in South Pacific Area (USAFISPA), to Col William C. Bentley, Dep AC/AS, Intelligence, AAF, Mar 5, 1944, vol 7, doc 38, 203.6; ltr, Sherman to AC/S G–2, WDGS, subj: Intelligence Net, South Pacific Area, May 29, 1943, in 705.603.1.

22. Diary, L. C. Sherman, AFHSO, pp. 12, 17, 21, 26–27.

23. Lect, "Intelligence Experience during World War II," Col Benjamin Cain, Dec 10, 1946, Air War College, K239.716246-6.

24. Air Eval Bd, SWPA, "Combat Intelligence in SWPA," Jun 1944, 730.601–2. See also, e.g., 5th AF ADVON, "Summaries of Principal Activities," 730.606. The Summaries for Oct 30 and Nov 26, 1943, are illustrative, but there are many others, including *Brief History of the G–2 Section,* vol 3, p. 31.

25. "Air Forces and Units in SWPA," 706.204; *Brief History of the G–2 Section,* pp. 9–10; 13th AF Intel Sec Hist.

26. Brief History of the G–2 Section, pp. 86–87; Eric A. Feldt, *The Coast Watchers* (New York, 1946), pp. 143,

170, 209–210, 270.

27. Brief History of the G–2 Section, pp. 86–87; HQ Allied Air Force SWPA, suppl No. 1 to MIS-X annex, "Evading Capture in Southeast China," 730.614.

28. Brief History of the G–2 Section, "Introduction," pp. 38–40.

29. Kenney Papers, entries for 1943, passim, and included correspondence with General Whitehead; draft rprt, "Radio Intelligence and the Fifth Air Force," n.d. [1944], 730.625.

30. Kenney Papers, entries for Nov 1942.

31. Craven and Cate, vol 4, *Guadalcanal to Saipan*, pp. 108–127. For the ground campaign in Papua, see Samuel Milner, *Victory in Papua* (Washington, D.C., 1957).

32. See 5th AF ADVON, "Summaries of Principal Activities."

33. See *Brief History of the G–2 Section*, "Introduction"; Kenney Papers, Jan 1–5, 1943.

34. *Kenney Reports*, p. 76; Kenney Papers, entries for Feb 22 and 25, 1943; Samuel Eliot Morison, *History of United States Naval Operations in World War II*, vol 6, *Breaking the Bismarcks Barrier, 22 July 1942–1 May 1944* (Boston, 1950), p. 54. The messages themselves may be seen in *Radio Intelligence in World War II, Tactical Operations in the Pacific Ocean Area, February 1943*, SRH–144, pt 2, pp. 445–448, 531–532, 564–576.

35. Ltr, Kenney to Whitehead, Kenney Papers, Feb 25, 1943.

36. Kenney Papers, entry for Feb 26, 1943.

37. Ibid., entry for Feb. 27, 1943.

38. Ibid., entry for Feb. 28, 1943.

39. Ibid., entries for March 1–4, 1943; Morison, *Breaking the Bismarcks Barrier*, pp. 62–64.

40. *Life* Magazine, Mar 22, 1943. The accompanying article reported the battle in substantial, but inaccurate, detail, repeating the claim of much higher losses than had been sustained; Kenney maintained the incorrect information in his postwar book (*Kenney Reports*, p. 205), although he had access to the correct data in Japan. The original claims by the aviators were erroneous but understandable, given the confusion of combat. Why Kenney did not correct the final account in his book is unknown. Conversation, John Kreis with Capt Roger Pineau, USN, Ret, Apr 1, 1991. Pineau wrote the note on pages 63–64 of Morison's *Breaking the Bismarcks Barrier* and discussed the issue with MacArthur in Japan after the war.

41. Kenney Papers, entries for Mar 10–Apr 6, 1943, including ltr, Arnold to Kenney, Mar 30, 1943; *Kenney Reports*, p. 215.

42. Kenney Papers, entry for Mar 22, 1943.

43. Ibid., entries for Apr and May 1943; *Kenney Reports*, pp. 233–240, 247–248. See also *SWPA Special Intelligence Bulletins* (hereafter *SIBs*), pt 1, SRH–203, May, Jun 1943.

44. Memo, Air Comd, Solomon Islands, Maj Victor Dykes, Jun 1944, 749.01.

45. Intvw, USAF Academy faculty with Gen Nathan Twining, Nov 3, 1967, K239.0512–636; Craven and Cate, vol 1, *Plans and Early Operations*, pp. 451–452; Ibid., vol 2, *Torch to Pointblank*, pp. 88–89, 210–211; Ibid., vol 4, *Guadalcanal to Saipan*, pp. 33–34, 332.

46. Craven and Cate, vol 4, *Guadalcanal to Saipan*, pp. 41–42.

47. Intvw, Dr. Robert Ehrhart with Lt Gen Francis C. Gideon, USAF, Ret, May 20, 1988, pp. 1–2.

48. U.S. Navy Direction Finder Station, Guadalcanal, SRH–188.

49. Kreis, *Air Warfare*, pp. 225–230.

50. Ibid., p. 231.

51. Records, First Marine Div, Daily Intel Summaries, entries for Oct, Nov, Dec 1942, box 8, C 4–3, U.S. Marine Corps Historical Archives.

52. Layton, *"And I Was There,"* pp. 474–476.

53. Price, *History of US Electronic Warfare*, pp. 48–51, 133–153.

54. Gideon intvw, May 20, 1988; *SIBs*, daily entries on air and naval movements, SRH–203.

55. Ltr, Brig Gen Ray L. Owens to COMAIRSOLS (Twining), Sep 18, 1943, LC, Twining Papers, box 121; Craven and Cate, vol 4, *Guadalcanal to Saipan*, pp.

228–229.

56. Ltrs, Kenney to Whitehead, Oct 21, 24, 1943, in Kenney Papers; Craven and Cate, vol 4, *Guadalcanal to Saipan,* pp. 246–255; *SIB*s, Oct 1943 (tracing Japanese air and naval activity and reinforcements of aircraft to the region), SRH–203.

57. Ltrs, Kenney to Whitehead, Oct 19, 21, 24, and Nov 2, 1943, in Kenney Papers; *SIB*s, Nov 1943, SRH–203; Craven and Cate, vol 4, *Guadalcanal to Saipan,* pp. 317–328; ltr, Twining to Arnold, Nov 14, 1943, LC, Twining Papers, box 121.

58. Memo, Air Comd, Solomon Islands, Dykes, Jun 1944; Memo, subj: Brief History of the Thirteenth Air Force, 750.006; Memo, 13th AF Intel Sec, 1943–1945, Jul 1945, 750.006; Kenney Papers, entries for June 10–20, 1944.

59. Kenney Papers, entry for May 17, 1943; Gideon intvw; Feldt, *Coast Watchers,* pp. vii–ix, 270.

60. Feldt, *Coast Watchers.*

61. Ltrs, Kenney to Whitehead, Aug 16, 18, 20, 1943, Kenney Papers.

62. Kenney Papers, entries for Aug 16–18; ltr, Whitehead to Kenney, Aug 21, 1943, Kenney Papers.

63. Ltr, Whitehead to Kenney, Aug 21, 1943; Kenney Papers, entries for Aug and Sep 1943.

64. Kenney Papers, entries for Feb 23–24, 1944; ltr, Kenney to Whitehead, Feb 24, 1944, Kenney Papers; see also *SIB*s, Jan, Feb 1944, SRH–203; John Miller, Jr., *CARTWHEEL: The Reduction of Rabaul* (Washington, D.C., 1959), p. 321.

65. Kenney Papers, Feb 28, 1944.

66. Craven and Cate, vol 4, *Guadalcanal to Saipan,* pp. 555–567; Miller, *CARTWHEEL,* pp. 339–349.

67. Kenney Papers, entries for Mar 6–8, including ltr, Kenney to Whitehead, subj: "Outlining the Hollandia Preparations," Mar 6, 1944; Craven and Cate, vol 4, *Guadalcanal to Saipan,* pp. 571–573. Some of Kenney's misgivings are recounted after the fact in a somewhat ambiguous two-page summary of activities for the time of the Admiralties planning. Although the summary's author is anonymous, it was clearly a person very close to Kenney, perhaps his aide. Kenney Papers; see also Miller, *Cartwheel,* pp. 335, 348–349.

68. *SIB*s, Apr 1–6, 1944, SRH–203.

69. Ibid., Apr 8, 9, 1944; ltrs, Kenney to Whitehead, Mar 6, 1944, and Whitehead to Kenney, Mar 9, 1944, both in Kenney Papers; *Kenney Reports,* p. 377.

70. Memo, 5th AF A–2 to Whitehead and Kenney, subj: Reduction of Wewak, Mar 29, 1944, Kenney Papers; Kenney Papers, entry for Mar 26; *Kenney Reports,* pp. 374–377; Craven and Cate, vol 4, *Guadalcanal to Saipan,* p. 589.

71. *Kenney Reports,* p. 374; msg, Cmdr 5th AF ADVON, to Kenney, Mar 31, 1944, Kenney Papers; Kenney Papers, entries for Mar 30, 31, and Apr 1. For Kenney's information on the indications of Japanese aircraft replacement, see his entry for Apr 17.

72. Kenney Papers, entry for Apr 18, 1944.

73. Craven and Cate, vol 4, *Guadalcanal to Saipan,* pp. 598–609.

74. *SIB*s 496, 497, and 502 for September 15/16, 16/17, and 21/22, 1944, respectively, SRH–203.

75. Craven and Cate, vol 4, *Guadalcanal to Saipan,* pp. 601–602; *Kenney Reports,* pp. 378–379, 419, 426.

76. Wesley Frank Craven and James Lea Cate, *The Army Air Forces in World War II,* vol 5, *MATTERHORN to Nagasaki* (Chicago, 1949), pp. 316–322; *Kenney Reports,* pp. 436–442; *SIB*s 517, 519, Oct 6/7, 8/9 1944, SRH–203.

77. Kenney Papers, Sep 16, 17, 1944.

78. Ibid.; *SIB*s 511, 522, 523, 525, and 530, Sep 30/Oct 1, Oct 11/12, 12/13, 13/14, and 19/20, 1944, respectively, SRH–203.

79. Craven and Cate, vol 5, *MATTERHORN to Nagasaki,* pp. 357–372.

80. Ibid.; Kenney Papers, Nov 24–25, 1944; *SIB* 551, Nov 9/10, 1944, SRH–203.

81. *SIB*s 532, 534, 542, and 543, Oct 21/22, 23/24, 31/Nov 1, and Nov 1/2, 1944, SRH–203.

82. *SIB*s 532, 534, 542, and 543, Oct 21/22, 23/24, 31/Nov 1, and Nov 1/2, 1944, SRH–203; Kenney Papers, Oct 28, Nov 10, 11, 1944.

Notes to Pages 288–300

83. Kenney Papers, Oct 28, Nov 10, 11, 1944.
84. *SIB* 569, Nov 27/28, 1944, SRH–203.
85. *SIB* 586, Dec 14/15, 1944, SRH–203.
86. Craven and Cate, vol 5, *MATTERHORN to Nagasaki*, 393–401; Kenney Papers, Dec 20, 26, 1944; *SIB* 594, Dec 22/23, 1944, SRH–203.
87. *SIB* 596, Dec 24/25, 1944, SRH–203; Kenney Papers, Jan 10, 1945; "Philippine Sea Frontier, Air Intelligence Notes," in Kenney Papers, Jan 1945.
88. Kenney Papers, Jan 21, 1945; Craven and Cate, vol 5, *MATTERHORN to Nagasaki*, pp. 413–415.
89. Alvin D. Coox, "Flawed Perception and Its Effect Upon Operational Thinking: The Case of the Japanese Army, 1937–1941," *Intelligence and Military Operations* (London, 1990), pp. 239–254. See also Michael Howard, *Strategic Deception*, vol 5 in F. H. Hinsley et al., *British Intelligence in the Second World War*, (London, 1990), pp. 203–221. Howard, in discussing deception efforts in the South East Asia Command, illustrates Japanese intelligence flaws similar to those of the Germans, resulting in an overestimation of Allied strength. The overestimating came about for similar reasons: an inadequately developed military intelligence organization unable to pursue hard-headed analytical goals. See also *The Japanese Intelligence System*, Sep 4, 1945, SRH–254.
90. Coox, "Flawed Perception"; Masanobu Tsuji, *Singapore, the Japanese Version*, Margaret E. Lake, trans (Sidney, 1960), pp. 44–52.
91. HQ South East Asia Command, "SEA Translation and Interrogation Centre Bulletins," Nos. 76, 79, May 19, 25, 1945, 820.605; *SIB* 317, Mar 19, 1944, SRH–203; SRH–254, pp. 21, 28A, 52.
92. SRH–254, pp. 21, 28A, 52; *Japanese Signal Intelligence Service*, 3d ed, Nov 1, 1944, SRH–266, pp. 5–14; *SIB* 569, Nov 27/28, 1944, SRH–203.
93. *SIBs* 277, 279, 292, 296, all in Feb 1944, and *SIB* 569, Nov 27/28, 1944, SRH–203. See also SRH–266, pp. 41–46, and SRH–254, pp. 34–38.
94. *SIBs* 277, 279, 292, 296, all in Feb 1944, and *SIB* 569, Nov 27/28, 1944, SRH–203. See also SRH–266, pp. 41–46, and SRH–254, pp. 34–38.
95. *SIBs* 277, 279, 292, 296, all in Feb 1944, SRH–203; Kenney Papers, entries for Jan 5, 1943, and succeeding days.
96. *SIBs* 315, 327, Mar 17, 29, 1944, SRH–203.
97. *SIBs* 296, 308, 311, and 317, SRH–203.
98. See Alvin D. Coox, "Japanese Military Intelligence in the Pacific Theater: Its Non-Revolutionary Nature," and Takahashi Hisashi, "A Case Study: Japanese Intelligence Estimates of China and the Chinese, 1931–1945," *The Intelligence Revolution*, Proceedings of the 13th Military History Symposium, U.S. Air Force Academy, October 1988 (Washington, D.C., 1991), pp. 197–222.

CHAPTER 6

1. Intvw, John F. Kreis with Lt Gen Devol Brett, USAF, Ret, Feb 15, 1985; Robert Lee Scott, Jr., *The Day I Owned the Sky* (New York, Toronto, Sidney, Aukland, 1988), pp. 74–75; Jack Samson, *Chennault* (New York, 1987), pp. 89, 91, 138, 180; Kenney Papers, entry for Jan 18, 1943; Joseph W. Stilwell, *The Stilwell Papers,* edited and arranged by Theodore H. White (New York, 1948), pp. 35–38.
2. *Kenney Reports*, pp. 183, 240–241; draft rprt, "The China Air Task Force," n.d. 862.057; intvw, with Capt John M. Birch, Mar 20, 1945, 14th AF Hist Files, 862.01; ltr, Chennault to Bissell, subj: Tables of Organization, Nov 15, 1942,

864.311.

3. Ltrs, Chennault to Bissell, Nov 15, 1942, and Bissell to Chennault, Nov 25, 1942, both in 864.311; Birch intvw, Mar 20, 1945, p. 9.

4. Rprt, "Technical Intelligence Conference, Aug 10–15, 1943," 830.365.

5. Ltr, Stratemeyer to Lt Col Richard P. Hepner, Chief, OSS, SEAC, Jun 29, 1944, 820.605.

6. Lewin, *American MAGIC*, p. 244.

7. Memo, Target Selection, 10th Air Force Style, n.d. [Feb–Mar 1944], 830.323; SRH–032, p. 81. See also the *MAGIC Diplomatic Summaries* of the period that discuss commercial activity in the area and Japanese reactions to Allied attacks; memo, HQ 10th AF, subj: Information Obtained from Lt Col Boater, G–2 for General Stilwell, Jun 13, 1942, 830.605; rprt, Col Robert L. Scott, Jr., to CG USAAF, "Bomber Escorts and Night Fighter Tactics for China Air Task Force," Dec 22, 1942, 862.3102.

8. Stilwell Papers, pp. 160–165; msgs, Chennault to Bissell and Bissell to Stilwell, Oct 3, 8, 12, and Nov 5, 26, 1943, 864.1621.

9. Rprt, "Intelligence Estimate of the Situation, A–2, Tenth Air Force," Aug 27, 1942, 830.609–1.

10. Daily Activity Summary, 10th AF, Mar 16, 1942, 830.641.

11. "Compilation of Objective Folders, IATF," 827.605.

12. Intel Est, Aug 27, 1942, 830.609–1.

13. Ltr, Intel Ofc, 436th Bom Sq (H), to 10th AF, Nov 22, 1942, 827.605.

14. Ltr, A–2 HQ IATF to 10th AF, Dec 22, 1942, 827.605.

15. Comments, S–2 to IATF CG thru Col Necrason, May 24, 1943, 827.605.

16. Rprt, "Conference with Pacific Air Force's A–2s," Oct 1943, 830.605.

17. 10th AF, WIS, annex A, Feb 28 1943, 830.607.

18. 10th AF, WIS, Mar 20, 1943, 830.607.

19. HQ AAF, Aug 27, 1942, 863.549.

20. 10th AF, WIS, Apr 29, 1943, 830.607.

21. Daily Intel Extr, Jan 13, 1943, 830.6062.

22. Rprt, Col Harold B. Wright to CG, 10th AF, "Dropping of Magnetic Mines in Rangoon River," Jan 13, 1943. See also subsequent reports of Feb 25 and Mar 21, 1943, on the same subject; Craven and Cate, vol 4, *Guadalcanal to Saipan*, pp. 473–474.

23. Memo, Tenth Air Force Targets and Target Selection, Mar 1944, 830.323; memos, Vulnerable Points of the Burma Railroad System, Apr 16 and 19, 1943. See also "Photographic Interpretation Reports" in 830.635.

24. HQ Air Comd, SEA, Policy Directive No. 1, Dec 15, 1943, 862.600; Draft Hist, EAC Intel Sec, 862.600.

25. "Charter of Combined Photographic Interpretation Centre, South East Asia," May 1, 1944, 820.600.

26. Rprt, "Technical Intelligence Conference"; Tenth Air Force Targets and Target Selection; ltr, HQ Air Comd SEA, John Baker, to Maj Gen Stratemeyer, Mar 4, 1944, w/atched Allied Tech Intel Org proposal.

27. Rprt, Lt Col Emile Z. Berman, "Special Report on Activities of Detachment 101, OSS in Relation to Air Force Action in North Burma," 830.601.1; ltr, Stratemeyer to Hepner, Jun 29, 1944; Hist, Det 101, Jul 2, 1944, 859.011; Richard Aldrich, "Imperial Rivalry: British and American Intelligence in Asia, 1942–46," *Intelligence and National Security*, Jan 1, 1989, pp. 22–28.

28. Rprt, Berman, "Special Report on Activities of Det 101, OSS."

29. Rprt, "Average Daily Duties of S–2 Section," Mar 15, 1943, 830.6031; rprt, Berman, "Special Report on Activities of Det 101, OSS."

30. HQ SEAC, "Formation of E Group South East Asia and India Commands," Apr 6, 1944, 805.614; record and routing slip, AAF India-Burma Sector, CBI, Apr 13, 1944, 805.614; rprt, "The 13th Report of F/Lt R. G. Huxtable, 'E' Group Officer," Jan 1945, 805.614.

31. See note 30 above; memo, HQ Strategic Air Force, SEAC, subj: Proposed Tactical Air Intelligence Center, Oct 27, 1944, 820.605; memo, 17th AAF Photo Intel Det, Radar Intel, May 18, 1945,

860.613–1; rprt, HQ XX Bom Comd, "Enemy Ground Defense Bulletin No. 1," Jun 1, 1944, 761.646.

32. Memo, HQ Strategic Air Force, SEAC, Oct 27, 1944; memo, 17th AAF Photo Intel Det, Radar Intel, May 18, 1945; rprt, HQ XX Bom Comd, "Enemy Ground Defense Bulletin No. 1," Jun 1, 1944.

33. Ltr, with attachs, Stratemeyer to A/C F.J.W. Mellersh, HQ Strategic Air Force, and to HQ Air Comd SEA, Oct 27, 1944, 820.605.

34. Ltr, Stratemeyer to CG, USAAF (A–2), subj: Deterioration of the Japanese Air Forces in the India Burma Theater, n.d. [Apr 1945], 820.605.

35. Ltr, Chennault to CG, 10th AF, Jan 8, 1943, 864.311; ltr, Chennault to CG American AAF CBI, subj: Intelligence Reports, Dec 2, 1942, 864.600.1; rprt, HQ China Air Task Force, "Intelligence Summary," Dec 26, 1942, 864.600.1; rprt, China Air Task Force, "Review of A–2 Activities," Dec 31, 1942, 864.311.

36. See note 35 above. Chennault's close personal interest and small size of his operation allowed him a greater involvement in intelligence than was possible for many other commanders. He saw many messages reporting Japanese activities. On some he noted his doubts or requested information. Some intelligence reports that came to him were too vague for action or dealt with areas beyond the reach of his airplanes.

37. Bissell quote in Birch intvw, Mar 20, 1945, pp. 7–10; rprt, HQ CATF A–2, "Review of A–2 Activity, Jul 4–Dec 31, 1942," 864.311; ltr, 1st Lt Carl G. Nelson to Col W. M. Burgess, Dec 16, 1943, 862.6032.1; 1st Ind; ltr, Chennault to CG, 10th U.S. Air Force, Jan 8, 1943, 864.311; ltr, Bissel to Chennault, China Air Task Force, Sep 25, 1942, 864.311.

38. Samson, *Chennault,* p. 91; R. M. Smith, *With Chennault in China* (Blue Ridge Summit, Pa., 1984), pp. 93–105; ltr, Bissel to Chennault, Sep 25, 1942.

39. "Review of A–2 Activities," Dec 31, 1942; ltr, Chennault to CG, 10th AF, Jan 8, 1943.

40. Ltr, 1st Lt Carl C Nelson to Col W. M. Burgess, Dec 16, 1943, 862.6032.1.

41. HQ USA Far East, *Army Operations in China, December 1941–December 1943,* 1956, Japanese Monogr 71, pp. 71, 79–86, 122, 138.

42. Craven and Cate, vol 4, *Guadalcanal to Saipan,* pp. 436–441, 450–451.

43. Bernard Osgood Koopman, *Search and Screening: General Principles with Historic Applications* (New York, 1980), pp. 1-1–23; rprt, AAF Eval Bd, India, Burma, and China Theaters, "Effectiveness of Air Attack Against Japanese Merchant Shipping," Dec 15, 1944, 138.7–4.

44. Milton E. Miles, *A Different Kind of War* (Garden City, N.Y., 1967), pp. 307–316; Oscar P. Fitzgerald, "Naval Group China: A Study of Guerrilla Warfare During World War II" (Unpublished Dissertation, USN Library, Washington, D.C.), pp 72–75.

45. Miles, *Different Kind of War,* pp. 307–322; rprt, Seymour J. Janow, 14th AF Ops Anal Off, to Chennault, subj: LAB [Low-altitude Bombing] Operations, Aug 21, 1944, 862.3102; rprt, AAF Eval Bd, "Effectiveness of Air Attack Against Japanese Merchant Shipping."

46. *SIB* 291, Feb 22, 1944, SRH–203; Miles, *Different Kind of War,* pp. 307–316.

47. Japanese Monogr 71, p. 158.

48. HQ USA Far East, *Army Operations in China, January 1944–August 1945,* 1956, Japanese Monogr 72, pp. 13–30; Craven and Cate, vol 4, *Guadalcanal to Saipan,* pp. 521–525.

49. R. Harris Smith, *OSS: The Secret History of America's First Central Intelligence Agency* (Berkeley, Calif., 1972), p. 261; rprt, 5329th AGFRTS (Prov.), "Organizational Report for July, 1944," 1944, 862.6001; ltr, 24th Stat Control Unit, 14th AF, subj: Strength Report by Base, Jan 15, 1945, 862.204.

50. Msgs, AGFRTS Liaison Team to Wedemeyer, Chennault, Vincent, et al., 862.6311.

51. Rprt, 5329th AGFRTS, "Organizational Report, August—September 1944," 862.6001; Birch intvw, Mar 20, 1945, pp. 14–15.

52. Craven and Cate, vol 5, *MATTERHORN to Nagasaki,* pp. 227–232.; msg,

Wedemeyer to Chennault, Feb 4, 1945, 862.6311; Miles, *Different Kind of War,* pp. 456–473.

53. Ltr, Chennault to Wedemeyer, Feb 4, 1945, 862.609–1.

54. Rprt, OSS, "Strategic Air Campaign Against Railroads in Occupied China," 859.607; see also msg, Wedemeyer to Chennault, No. 32488, Feb 6, 1945.

55. Rprt, OSS, "Strategic Air Campaign Against Railroads in Occupied China"; Craven and Cate, vol 5, MATTERHORN *to Nagasaki,* pp. 262–264.

56. HQ US Forces China Theater, "Periodic G–2 Reports for Feb–Mar 1945," 855.607; Craven and Cate, *MATTERHORN to Nagasaki,* pp. 262–263; Hist, 308th Bom Gp; rprts, Comdr 308th Bom Gp to CG 14th AF, "Mission Reports of Mar 1945."

57. US Dept State, "Minutes of the Tripartite Military Meeting, Jul 24, 1945," in *Foreign Relations of the United States, Diplomatic Papers: The Conference of Berlin, 1945* (Washington, D.C., 1960), pp. 349–351.

58. SRH–032, p. 83; *Procedure for Handling ULTRA Dexter Intelligence in the CBI,* SRH–046, p. 3; HQ 14th AF, A–2 Sec, "Japanese Air Order of Battle in China"; Miles, *Different Kind of War,* pp. 316–318.

59. SRH–020, pp. 4, 9, 10, 12; ltr, Brig Gen J. J. Twitty, JICPOA, to Col F. H. Wilson, G–2, SWPA, in Hist, G–2, SWPA, vol 3 (hereafter Twitty ltrs), pp. 81–83.

60. Craven and Cate, vol 5, *MATTERHORN to Nagasaki,* pp. 534–536; Kenney Papers, entries for Apr 13 and May 10, 1945; HQ AAFPOA, *History of the Air War in the Pacific Ocean Areas* (hereafter *History of AAFPOA–USASTAF*), vol 4, chap 10, "Task Force Organization of AAF Units," 702.01.

61. SRH–020, pp. 4–14; Craven and Cate, vol 5, *MATTERHORN to Nagasaki,* pp. 290–302; Hist, A–2 Sec, HQ 7th AF, "Daily Diary, A–2," 740.600.

62. USSBS (Pacific), "The Seventh and Eleventh Air Forces in the War Against Japan," pp. 5, 16–17; Craven and Cate, vol 5, *MATTERHORN to Nagasaki,* pp. 290–310; rprt, Air Off, USAFICPA, "Seventh Air Force Participation in the GALVANIC Operation, 13 November 1943–6 December 1943," pp. 2–4, 740.306–6A.

63. Craven and Cate, vol 4, *Guadalcanal to Saipan,* pp. 290–310; rprt, Air Off, USAFICPA, "Seventh Air Force Participation in the GALVANIC Operation."

64. Craven and Cate, vol 5, *MATTERHORN to Nagasaki,* pp. 675–677.

65. History of AAFPOA–USASTAF, vol 4, chap 3.

66. Ibid., pp. 525, 593–594; ltr, Brig Gen F. L. Ankenbrandt, subj: Summary of Ferret Operations, 15 to 26 June 1945, Jul 15, 1945, 740.310–5.

67. Craven and Cate, vol 5, *MATTERHORN to Nagasaki,* pp. 692–694; Ellis A. Johnson and David A. Katcher, *Mines against Japan* (Silver Spring, Md., 1973), p. 26.

68. SRH–020, pp. 17–18; Twitty ltrs.

69. Craven and Cate, vol 5, *MATTERHORN to Nagasaki,* pp. 30–40; Arnold, *Global Mission,* pp. 347–348; Hansell, *Strategic Air War Against Germany and Japan,* pp. 139–141.

70. See note 69 above.

71. Hansell, *Strategic Air War against Germany and Japan,* pp. 158–160.

72. COA Hist, p. 63.

73. Ibid., pp. 89–91.

74. Ibid., pp. 59–67; memo, Col A. W. Brock for C/AS A–2, subj: Japanese Target Data, Mar 20, 1943.

75. COA Hist, Tab 40, "Japanese Coke Ovens as a Strategic Bombardment Target," and Tab 42, "Effect of the Destruction of Coke Ovens on Japan's War Effort."

76. COA Hist, Tab 42, pp. 76–78; Kenney Papers, entries for Jan 1944 (covering a visit to Washington, D.C.); Hansell, *Strategic Air War against Germany and Japan,* pp. 141–142.

77. COA Hist, Tab 45, "Strategic Economic Targets for VLR Operations from Davao, Chengtu and Saipan."

78. Ibid., pp. 77–78.

79. Ibid.

80. Ibid., pp. 112–113.

81. Ltr, Kenney to Arnold, Oct 23, 1943, in Kenney Papers.

82. Historical Rprts, HQ XX Bom Comd, A-2 Sec, Jun 7 and Sep 10, 1944, 761.600.
83. Radar Countermeasures Rprts, XX Bom Comd, "Missions 1-24," Jan 1945, 761.907.
84. XX Bom Comd, "Enemy Ground Defense Bulletin," Jun 1, 1944, 761.646; XX Bom Comd, "Radar Coverage Map," Jan 25, 1945, 761.654.1; HQ 20th Air Force, "Plan for Army VLR Photography of the Far East," n.d. [1944]; memo, subj: The Weather Factor in Bombing Japan from Bases in the Marianas and Bonin Islands, 760.626.1; HQ 20th AF, "Flak Intelligence in the Pacific," Jul 29, 1945, 760.646.1; Craven and Cate, vol 5, *MATTERHORN to Nagasaki*, pp. 163-165.
85. COA Hist, pp. 113-115.
86. Craven and Cate, vol 5, *MATTERHORN to Nagasaki*, pp. 157-174.
87. Hansell, *Strategic Air War against Germany and Japan*, p. 212.
88. Ibid., p. 179; *History of AAFPOA-USASTAF*, vol 4, pp. 1-3, 23-24.
89. See Craven and Cate, vol 5, *MATTERHORN to Nagasaki*, pp. 546-576, for the initial campaign from the Marianas and the operational difficulties encountered; the quotation is from p. 576. The preceding and following paragraphs are adapted, with the author's permission, from David MacIsaac, *Strategic Bombing in World War II: The Story of the U.S. Strategic Bombing Survey* (New York, 1976), pp. 105-106.
90. Memo, COA for General Arnold, subj: Revised Report of the Committee of Operations Analysts on Economic Targets in the Far East, Oct 10, 1944, in COA Hist, Tab 97.
91. Prelim Rprt, COA, "The Economic Effect of Attacks in Force on German Urban Areas," 118.04.2.
92. Memo, subj: General Arnold's Directions to AC/AS Operations: Commitments and Requirements from the Chief of the Air Staff, Feb 18, 1944, and ltr, Brig Gen E. Montgomery, Air Chem Off, to C/AS, subj: Test of Incendiaries, Feb 24, 1944, LC, Arnold Papers, box 117.
93. Ibid.; ltr, Brig Gen Mervin E. Gross, Ofc AC/AS, OC&R, subj: Test of Incendiaries, May 5, 1944, LC, Arnold Papers, box 117.
94. Marcelle Size Knaak, *Post-World War II Bombers* (Washington, D.C., 1988), pp. 482-487.
95. Intvw, Col Bill Peck with Gen Curtis E. LeMay, Mar 11, 1965, USAFHRC 785, pp. 6-9. This differs from LeMay's account in his autobiographical *Mission with LeMay*, written by him with McKinlay Kantor (Garden City, N.Y., 1965).
96. Hansell, *Strategic Air War against Germany and Japan*, pp. 217-218; Craven and Cate, vol 5, *MATTERHORN to Nagasaki*, pp. 563-565; memo, Norstad to Arnold, subj: Notes for Conference with the Secretary of War, Jan 2, 1945, AFHSO, Norstad Papers, microfilm reel 32811, frame 477.
97. Ltr, LeMay to Arnold, Apr 5, 1945, LC, LeMay Papers, box 11, Arnold folder.
98. Ibid.; Alvin D. Coox, "The Air Assault on Japan," in *Case Studies in Strategic Bombardment*, R. Cargill Hall, ed (Air Force History and Museum Program, Washington, D.C., forthcoming), chap 4.
99. LeMay, *Mission*, pp. 347-352.
100. Ibid., p. 347.
101. Richard G. Davis, "Operation Thunderclap: The U.S. Army Air Forces and the Bombing of Berlin" (Unpublished MS), AFHSO.
102. Rprt, Maj Charles T. Kingston, in SRH-032, pp. 45-46.
103. SRH-020, p. 17.
104. Johnson and Katcher, *Mines against Japan*, pp. 29, 110, 116; Hansell, *Strategic Air Warfare against Germay and Japan*, pp. 198-200.
105. History, vol 4, chap 11, Reorganization and Changes.
106. R. Mets, *Master of Airpower, General Carl A. Spaatz* (Novato, Calif., 1988), pp. 302-303; Craven and Cate, vol 5, pp. 712-713, 716-717; Wyden, *Day One*, p. 239.

Chapter 7

1. Ltr, Arnold to Harry L. Hopkins, asst to Pres Roosevelt, Mar 25, 1943, LC, Arnold Papers, box 39 (this letter clearly spells out the overall importance with which the AAF's CG viewed the accomplishments of the COA); COA Hist, pp. 44–47; rprts, COA, atched to COA Hist.
2. The clear difference in the amount of staff effort directed by A–2 toward the war with Japan is evident from a review of the records of AC/AS, Intelligence, 142.01f. Although Germany continued to participate in intelligence operations at HQ AAF, the great bulk of the A–2's efforts centered on the question of Japan and preparations for the final assault on that island nation.
3. Memo, White to McDonald, Aug 1, 1944, USAFA, McDonald Collection.
4. Arnold, *Global Mission,* 419.
5. Ltr, C/S, Plans Div, to Exec, OCAC, subj: Appointment of Board of Officers and Travel Orders, Aug 16, 1939, 145.91–414.
6. Arnold, *Global Mission,* pp. 168–169, 174.
7. Ibid., p. 209; Corr, Arnold with Merian C. Cooper, LC, Arnold Papers, box 38, CBI folder, and box 39, Russia folder; SRH–035, pp. 1–2.
8. Arnold, *Global Mission,* pp. 533–535.
9. Ibid., p. 209; SRH–005, pp. 12–13; *History of Military Intelligence Service, WDGS, Reports Unit,* SRH–062, p. 42; ltr, John F. Kreis to Henry Schorreck, Oct 20, 1990, NSA Hist Ofc, and conversation, Kreis with Schorreck, Nov 28, 1990.
10. Intvw, John F. Kreis with Forrest C. Pogue, Jan 7, 1991; see also Personal, C/AS for Welsh, Jul 26, 1943, cited in Cochran, "Spectre of Defeat," p. 410.
11. Ltr, Arnold to Portal, Oct 14, 1943, 145.95. See also ltrs, Arnold to Portal, Sep 25, and Portal to Arnold, Oct 14, 145.95.
12. SRH–005, p. 13.
13. Chase C. Mooney and Edward C. Williamson, "Organization of the Army Air Arm, 1935–1945," USAF Hist Div Study 10, Jul 1956, pp. 40–45.
14. Org charts and notes, Ofc AC/S (I), 1942–1945, 142.01.
15. Memo, for the AC/S, G–2, subj: Relationships between G–2 and the Assistant Chief of Air Staff, Intelligence, in Air Matters, Jul 31, 1943, vol 6, doc 220, 203.6
16. Memo, Gen Bissell for Gen White, Jan 20, 1944, w/atched memo, to C/AS, Jan 22, 1944, subj: Coordination of Japanese Air Intelligence, vol 7, doc 9, 203.6. See also ltr, Bissell to Lt Gen Ira C. Eaker, Feb 2, 1944, in LC, Eaker Collection, box 26, folder, "Correspondence with the War Dept."
17. Memo of Agreement, subj: Responsibility for Coordination of Aviation Intelligence, Feb 24, 1944, 142.0212–1.
18. Ltr, Capt Phil Graham, SSO, GHQ SWPA, to Col Carter W. Clarke, Nov 16, 1944, in *Military Intelligence Service, War Department—Special Security Officer and Other Correspondence Relating to Special Intelligence in the Pacific Ocean Area,* SRH–119, pp. 34–41; Horner, *High Command: Australia and Allied Strategy,* pp. 244–246; Craven and Cate, vol 5, MATTERHORN to NAGASAKI, pp. 482–485.
19. Memo, AC/AS No. 44–59, subj: Changes in Functions of AC/AS Intelligence, Resulting from Agreements of Service Members, JIC, Respecting Japanese Air Intelligence, Jul 18, 1944, 142.0212–1; memo, Brig Gen White for C/AS, subj: Ad Hoc Intelligence Committee, Mar 13, 1944, vol 7, doc 40, 203.6.
20. Ltr, McDonald to White, Jun 4, 1944, w/atched docs and corr, vol 7, doc 69, 203.6.
21. COA Hist, pp. 98–100; ltr, White to C/AS, subj: Japanese Air Intelligence, Feb 7, 1944, 142.0212–2. See also memoirs, Guido R. Perera, "Washington and War Years," 1973, 168.7042, pp. 101– 102, 108, 119.
22. Ltr, White to C/AS, subj: Transfer of Air Intelligence Activities from G–2 to A–2, Feb 28, 1944, vol 7, doc 33, 203.6; ltr, White to C/AS, Feb 7, 1944.
23. Memo, for Chief, Hist Div, AC/AS,

Intelligence, Aug 21, 1943, 142.0212–2; Hist, 1st Radio Sq (Mobile), AFHSO; ltr, Davidson to Arnold, Dec 19, 1943, LC, Arnold Papers, box 105.

24. Hist, 1st Radio Sq (Mobile).

25. Hists, 1st, 3d, 5th, 6th, and 8th Radio Sqs (Mobile).

26. SRH–062, p. 13. See also lect, Maj A. W. White to senior intel offs, AAFSAT, n.d. [summer 1945], 248.502A.

27. SRH–062, pp. 14–16. See also SRH–035, pp. 37–54.

28. Hansell intvw, Jan 21, 1987, pp. 6–7.

29. COA Hist, pp. 2–3, 59–61; memo, Col A. W. Brock, Jr., Dir AAFIS, for C/AS, A–2, Mar 20, 1943, subj: Japanese Target Data, 118.01.

30. COA Hist, pp. 63–64, 73–74, 80, 90–91, 93–94.

31. Ibid., pp. 92–93; Hansell, *Strategic Air War against Germany and Japan*, pp. 145–148.

32. COA Hist, pp. 96–98.

33. "Report on Bombing Accuracy on Operations Against Leuna Synthetic Oil Plant during the Period from May through November 1944," LC, Spaatz Papers, box 77; rprt, Lt Gen Ira C. Eaker, "U.S. Air Force Activities in the U.K., February 1942 to December 31, 1943," LC, Eaker Papers, box 20; Donald R. Baucom, "The Radar War," draft chapter in AFHSO.

34. Minutes, "Conference on 1 October 1943 with Pacific Air Forces A–2s," 142.025–6; memo, for AC/AS, Intelligence, subj: Target Information Publications and Additional Data on Far East Objective Folder Revision Schedule Submitted 18 May 1944, n.d. [May–June 1944], 142.021–3; ltr., Brig Gen Hansell, HQ 20th AF, to AC/AS, Intelligence, subj: Far East Target Data Program of AC/AS Intelligence, May 25, 1944, 142.021–3.

35. Memo, [A–2] to A/CS G–2, subj: Usefulness of MID New York Office to A–2 (bearing the handwritten notation, "Dispatched Mar 29" [1944]), 142.021–3. See also Hansell intvw, Jan 21, 1987, pp. 6–7.

36. Memo, [A–2] to ACS G–2; memos, Capt H. D. Alexander, subj: MID-NY and Target Information Section [AC/AS] Working Procedure, May 22, 1944, and Lt Col De F. Van Slyck for Chief, Anal Div [AC/AS], subj: Plans for Implementation of Ad Hoc Committee's Recommendations, May 15, 1944, 142.021–3.

37. Extract, JCS Decision 1020, Sep 4, 1944, vol 7, doc 110, 203.6; Directive, Joint Target Analysis Group, AC/AS, Intelligence, Sep 11, 1944, LC, Arnold Papers, box 115; memo, Ofc Dir JTG, subj: Current Organization and Projects, Dec 28, 1944, JTG memo 3, vol 7, doc 164, 203.6.

38. Rprt, JTG, Precis, n.d. [1945], 142.6601–4; rprt, J. Bronowski, "The Work of the Joint Target Group," Jul 1945, 142.6601–5 (Dr. Bronowski was the Senior Science Officer of the Research and Experiments Office, Home Office, London, assigned to work with the JTG).

39. Intvw, Hugh N. Ahmann with Gen Lauris Norstad, Feb and Oct 1979, pp. 540–550, K239.0512–1116; LeMay intvw, Mar 11, 1965, pp. 6–9; rprt, Lt Gen Ira Eaker, "U.S. Air Force Activities in the United Kingdom, February 1942 to December 31, 1943," LC, Eaker Papers, box 20.

40. White Lect, n.d. [summer 1945].

41. Ibid.

42. Ltr, Roosevelt to Secy War, Sep 9, 1944, copy in 142.04–15.

43. Colbert, in civilian life a Cleveland attorney, came to AC/AS, Intelligence, from the staff of the Air Intelligence School at Harrisburg. For his career with the Survey, see MacIsaac, *Strategic Bombing in World War II*, pp. 27, 28, 38, 43, 48, 49, 58, 59, 179; for the jurisdictional squabble between Plans and Intelligence, see ibid., chap 2, "A Question Is Raised: How Effective Is Bombing?" pp. 21–29.

44. Ltr, Kuter to Spaatz, subj: Post-Hostilities Intelligence Objectives in Germany, Mar 13, 1945; rprt, Air Staff, "Post-Hostilities Intelligence Requirements Plan," n.d. [Sep–Nov 1944] (this document spells out the types of information desired by several staff offices in Washington); see also ltr, Arnold to Spaatz, Sep 2, 1944, w/atch: "The Objectives of the AAF in Post-Hostilities Planning

and Activities in Europe"; memo, AC/AS, Intelligence, for CAS, subj: Post-Hostilities Air Intelligence Objectives, Oct 6, 1944, all in 142.04–15.

45. Rprt, Air Staff, "Post-Hostilities Intelligence Requirements Plan," n.d.

46. Memos, AC/AS, Intelligence, for Dep CG, AAF, subj: Daily Activity Report, Jun 6, 1945, and subj: Daily Activity Report, Jun 15, 1945, 142.0323. See also the Daily Activity Reports, May 12, 14, and 24, 1945, and the memo from Hodges to Arnold, in 142.0323. The Daily Activity Reports may also be found in LC, Arnold Papers.

47. Memo, Bissell for CG, AAF, subj: Duplication of Effort in War Department Scientific Intelligence, May 12, 1945, vol 7, doc 228, 203.6; memo, Arnold to Eaker, May 22, 1945, in ltr, AC/AS, Matériel and Services, to Dir, AAF Air Tech Svcs Comd, subj: Functions Prescribed for Dr. Theodore H. von Kármán's Scientific Advisory Group by the Commanding General AAF, Jun 23, 1945, vol 8, doc 23, 203.6. (The letter quotes in its entirety the memo describing Arnold's desires for the von Kármán's group. The Arnold memo can also be found in LC, Arnold Papers, box 79.) See also Vincent C. Jones, *Manhattan: The Army and the Atomic Bomb* (Washington, D.C., 1985), p. 286.

48. Memo, Arnold to Eaker, Mar 22, 1945.

49. Memo, Hodges to Eaker, subj: AAF Post Hostilities Intelligence Activities [late May 1945], 142.04–15. (The best copy of the document is barely readable; thus no date can be discerned.)

50. Ltr, Spaatz to Arnold, May 12, 1945, in LC, Arnold Papers, box 115; draft hist, "Air Technical Intelligence," pp. 11-58–11-59, 106.19.

51. Ltr, Arnold to LeMay, Jul 15, 1945, LC, Arnold Papers, box 11.

52. Ltr, LeMay to Arnold, Jul 25, 1945, LC, Arnold Papers, box 11.

53. Norstad intvw, Feb and Oct 1979, pp. 540–550. Arnold was possessed of a ferocious temper and an impatience that knew no bounds, as Norstad so clearly points out. During the war, Arnold drove himself so hard that he suffered several heart attacks. At one point his doctors removed him to Florida to recover and get away from business in the Pentagon. See also ltr, Maj Gen E. R. Quesada to C/AS, Jul 12, 1945, subj: Discussions between D'Olier Committee and Joint Target Group. This letter and the attached "Report on USSBS and JTG Conferences" laid out the Air Staff's assessment of Japan's ability to continue the war. Quesada doubted that Japan could hang on for long.

54. Ltr, Quesada to C/AS, Jul 12, 1945; "Report on USSBS and JTG Conferences."

55. Ltr, Quesada to C/AS, Jul 12, 1945; "Report on USSBS and JTG Conferences."

56. Ltr, Quesada to C/AS, Jul 12, 1945; "Report on USSBS and JTG Conferences."

57. See Norstad intvw, Feb and Oct 1979, p. 563, for the Arnold-Lovett relationship. See entries for Jun 1945 in LC, Kenney Papers, where Lovett describes the problems and plans for airfield preparation for the final assault on Japan. See also ltr, Eaker to Quesada, subj: Intelligence Study, Jun 23, 1945, in LC, Arnold Papers, box 97, and in 142.021–1, as well as ltr, Maj Francis B. O'Mahoney and Capt Raymond K. Perkins to AC/AS, Intelligence, subj: Survey of the Office of the Assistant Chief of Air Staff, Intelligence, Apr 21, 1945.

58. Memo, Eaker to Asst Secy War for Air Lovett, subj: Intelligence Study, Jul 6, 1945.

59. Ibid.

60. Ibid.; draft hist, "Air Technical Intelligence," pp. 11-45–11-49.

61. Memo, Eaker to Asst Secy War for Air Lovett, Jul 6, 1945; draft hist, "Air Technical Intelligence," pp. 11-45–11-49.

62. Ltr, Brig Gen Richard C. Lindsay to Spaatz, subj: USASTAF Intelligence, Jul 7, 1945, in LC, Spaatz Papers, box 11; memo, Brig Gen Louis J. Fortier, WDGS, MID, to AC/S, G–2, subj: Survey of Intelligence Activities of Army Air Forces, Nov 9, 1945, 142.01.

63. Leslie R. Groves, *Now It Can Be Told: The Story of the Manhattan Project*

(New York, 1962), pp. xi–xiii; Diaries of Henry L. Stimson, 50 and 51 (microfilm ed, reel 9) (hereafter Stimson Diaries), entries for Mar 5, Apr 24, 25, and May 28, 1945, Manuscripts and Archives, Yale University Library, New Haven, Conn.; Henry L. Stimson and McGeorge Bundy, *On Active Service in Peace and War* (New York, 1948), p. 613.

64. Groves, *Now It Can Be Told*, pp. 266–267; Records of the Manhattan Engineer District (hereafter MED Records), NA, RG 77, Microfilm Roll M1109, folder 5, sec D, "Report of the Target Committee Meeting, Apr 27, 1945"; Stimson and Bundy, *On Active Service*, p. 613.

65. R&R C/S 20th AF (Norstad) to Dir JTG, subj: Target Information, Apr 27, 1945, and "Report of Target Committee," Apr 27, 1945, both in MED Records.

66. R&R C/S 20th AF (Norstad) to Dir JTG, subj: Target Information, Apr 27, 1945, and "Report of Target Committee," Apr 27, 1945, both in MED Records.

67. Memos, Maj Derry and Dr. N. F. Ramsey to Groves, subj: Summary of Target Committee Meetings of 10 and 11 May, May 12, 1945, and Col John N. Stone to Arnold, subj: Groves Project, Jul 24, 1945 (the Stone memo gave Arnold the specific reasons why the cities had been chosen, except for Kyoto, which by then been stricken from all lists by Stimson), both in MED Records.

68. Groves, *Now It Can Be Told*, chap 19, "Choosing the Target"; see also planning meeting records of the Target Committee for the general course of the 509th's position; intvw, Arthur K. Marmor with Brig Gen Paul W. Tibbets, Jr., Sep 1966, K239.0512-602, pp. 17–22.

69. Tibbets intvw, Sep 1966, pp. 17–22.

70. Stimson Diaries, entries for May 1, 2, 28, 1945; Groves, *Now It Can Be Told*, p. 327.

71. Stimson Diaries, entry for Jun 6, 1945.

72. Ibid., entry for Jun 19, 1945.

73. Ibid., entries for Jun 6, 19, 26–30, 1945.

74. Edward J. Drea, *MacArthur's ULTRA: Codebreaking and the War Against Japan, 1942–1945* (Lawrence, Kans., 1992), pp 202–223. Drea's work is particularly useful in understanding MacArthur's policy and command decisions in the SWPA. It goes beyond the SWPA, however, to open new insights into Washington's decision to use atomic weapons, and it should not be overlooked by a reader interested in this subject.

75. Minutes, JCS mtg with Truman, Jun 18, 1945, NA, RG 165.

76. Ronald R. Spector, *Eagle Against the Sun* (New York, 1985), p. 543.

77. Stimson Diaries, entry for Jul 2, 1945; SWPA *SIB*, Jul 15/16, 1945 (the semimonthly review). For a review of the literature (as of late 1990) relating to the use of this weapon, see J. Samuel Walker, "The Decision to Use the Bomb: A Historiographical Update," *Diplomatic History*, winter 1990, pp. 97–114.

78. Stimson Diaries, entry for May 31, 1945.

79. Ltr, LeMay to Arnold, Jul 25, 1945.

80. Stimson Diaries, entries for Jun 26–30, Jul 2; memo, Norstad to Arnold, subj: Notes for Conference with Secretary of War, Jan 2, 1945, AFHSO, Norstad Papers, microfilm reel 32811, frame 477; ltr, Arnold to Lt Gen Barney M. Giles, C/AS, Feb 16, 1945, AFHSO, Norstad Papers, microfilm reel 32811. Arnold, in writing to Giles, spelled out as clearly as ever his position on why the B–29s had to produce results. Having built nearly 2,000, he could not explain satisfactorily why the AAF could not put even 100 over a target. See also ltr, Arnold to Brig Gen William J. Donovan, OSS, Dec 30, 1944, AFHSO, Norstad Papers, microfilm reel 32811, where Arnold noted that the B–29 operations were carried out on the basis of information from the experience over Germany, not on accurate intelligence of Japan.

81. Schaffer, *Wings of Judgment*, chap 8.

82. Diary entry, Aug 11, 1945, LC, Spaatz Papers, box 21; "Interim Report of U.S. Strategic Bombing Survey," Jun 18, 1945, LC, LeMay Papers, box 11. See also MacIsaac's *Strategic Bombing in World War II* (pp. 99–102) for a discussion of the influence of the USSBS on the future

course of the conventional bombing campaign in the Pacific.

83. Ltr, LeMay to Bissell, Aug 21, 1945, LC, LeMay Papers, box 11.

84. Ltr, Arnold to Donovan, Dec 30, 1944, AFHSO, Norstad Papers, microfilm reel 32811.

85. Internal A–2 rprt, "Survey of the Office of Assistant Chief of Air Staff, Intelligence," Apr 21, 1945, 142.021.1, file, "Memoranda and Correspondence"; see also memo, for Dep Chief, Plans and Policy Staff, subj: Analysis Division—Functions, Organization, Personnel and Policy, Apr 24, 1945, vol 7, doc 217, 203.6.

86. Internal A–2 rprt, "Survey of the Office of Assistant Chief of Air Staff, Intelligence," Apr 21, 1945; see also memo, for Dep Chief, Plans and Policy Staff, subj: Analysis Division—Functions, Organization, Personnel and Policy, Apr 24, 1945; Herman S. Wolk, *Planning and Organizing the Postwar Air Force, 1943–1947* (Washington, D.C., 1984), pp. 31–44.

87. Memo, for AC/S, G–2, subj: Survey of Intelligence Activities of Army Air Forces (which contains an extract of AAFR 20–1, *Organization*, pertaining to the office of A–2), Nov 9, 1945, 142.01.

88. Ibid.

89. Memo, Bissell for C/S, Jul 3, 1944, 142.0302–8.

90. Ltr, Arnold to Marshall, subj: Heavy Bombers for Russia, Feb 26, 1943, LC, Arnold Papers, box 39.

91. Memo, subj: Soviet Intentions in Eastern Europe, n.d. [Dec 1944 or Jan 1945], 142.0302–8; memo, for AC/AS, Intelligence, subj: Reorganization, Feb 4, 1944, 142.0202–13.

92. Memo, Col Grinnell Martin for Air Intel Div (Col Adams), subj: Strategic Vulnerability of the United States, Sep 27, 1945, 142.12–13.

93. Memo, G–2, with cvr ltr of Maj Virgil O. Johnson, AC/AS, Intelligence, Nov 16, 1945, 142.12–1.

94. Ibid.

Chapter 8

1. Memo, Eaker to Asst Secy War for Air, subj: Intelligence Study, Jul 6, 1945.

2. Williamson Murray is indebted to Professor Brian Sullivan of the strategy department of the U.S. Naval War College for bringing this episode to his attention and for underlining its significance.

3. Lects, Lt Cmdr R. A. Ofstie, "Aviation in the Sino-Japanese War," given at the Navy Dept, Jan 1938, 248.501–65, 1937–1939.

4. For General Vuillemin's visit to Germany, see *Documents diplomatique francais,* 2d ser, vol 10, doc 401, 18.8.38, doc 429, 21.8.38, and doc 444, 23.8.38.

5. Akten zur desutschen auswärtgen Politik, ser D, vol 2, doc 377, 26.9.38.

6. For the course of British intelligence estimates as to the German air danger (and danger in general), see Wesley Wark, *The Ultimate Enemy: British Intelligence and Nazi Germany, 1933–1939* (Ithaca, N.Y., 1985).

7. For discussions of the development of air doctrine in the AAF, see Thomas H. Greer, *The Development of Air Doctrine in the Army Air Force, 1917–41* (Maxwell AFB, Ala., 1955), and Thomas Fabyanic, "A Critique of United States Air War Planning, 1941–44" (dissertation, St. Louis University, 1973). See also the discussion in Murray, *Luftwaffe,* app 1.

8. ACTS, Capt Thomas D. White, "Japan as an Objective for Air Attack, 1937–1938," 248.501–65.

9. See Williamson Murray, *The Change in the European Balance of Power, 1938–1939: The Path to Ruin* (Princeton, 1985), chap 1, for an indication of how historians even after the fact have misesti-

mated German economic and military potential. One of the traditional views of Americans is the belief that adaptability, flexibility, and independence have much to do with our success in war. That view has been fundamentally undermined by Martin van Creveld's *Fighting Power: German and U.S. Army Performance, 1939–1945* (Westport, Conn., 1982) which indicates that the performance of American ground units in World War II left much to be desired, especially in comparison with the German Army. Nevertheless, a point is worth making here: American flexibility, adaptability, and independence of mind made major contributions in the support areas: logistics, intelligence, and scientific and technological development. In these areas the skills of civilian life best translate into military effectiveness.

10. For the best account of the Battle of Britain, see Francis K. Mason, *Battle Over Britain* (New York, 1968).

11. Haywood S. Hansell, *The Air Plan That Defeated Hitler* (Atlanta, 1972), pp. 53–54.

12. Craven and Cate, vol 1, *Plans and Early Operations*, p. 149.

13. Ibid., p. 604.

14. *Time*, Dec 8, 1941, p. 15. As it does today, *Time* appeared on the newsstands before the date on the cover. This issue was actually being sold as early as December 4.

15. Such attitudes suggest that the present-day American ignorance of and contempt for history represent a consistent theme in our history. After all, had not the Japanese Navy begun the Russo-Japanese war with a surprise attack on Port Arthur, an attack that was greeted with considerable approval by the American and British press?

16. Bidwell, *History of MID*.

17. Eaker Final Rprt, Dec 31, 1943, exhib 6, "Intelligence Development of A–2 Section VIII Bomber Command, Problems and Solutions."

18. Memo, Lt Col Carl H. Norcross, Asst A–2 VIII Bom Comd, for AC/S, subj: Army Air Forces Intelligence School, Harrisburg, Pennsylvania, Jan 22, 1943, 266.1-1, 1942.

19. Hinsley, *British Intelligence in the Second World War*, vol 2, p. 46.

20. Ibid., pp. 49–50.

21. Ibid., p. 51.

22. Ibid.

23. In fairness to American airmen, no matter how wrongheaded their analysis of the operational arena might have been, it is uncontestable that the daylight bomber offensive was the crucial factor in winning air superiority over the European continent and that, without that air superiority, OVERLORD would have faced nearly insurmountable odds in driving the German Army back from the coast of France. See Murray, *Luftwaffe*, chaps 5, 6.

24. Fabyanic, "Critique of United States Air War Planning," pp. 125–127.

25. Webster and Frankland, vol 1, *Preparation*, p. 177.

26. Ltr, Eaker to Spaatz, Oct 1942, quoted in Fabyanic, "Critique of United States Air War Planning," pp. 129–130.

27. Craven and Cate, vol 2, *TORCH to POINTBLANK*, pp. 670–672.

28. For an outstanding recent study on the impact of ULTRA on the Mediterranean campaign, see Ralph Bennett, *ULTRA and the Mediterranean* (London, 1989).

29. For this side of the story, the reader's attention is drawn to Gordon Welchman's extraordinary book, *The Hut Six Story* (New York, 1982).

30. Haines Report, p. 26. See also Erwin Rommel, *The Rommel Papers*, B. H. Liddell Hart, ed (New York, 1953), pp. 266–268, 282.

31. Ltr, Doolittle to CG AAF thru CG NAAF, subj: Escort Fighters, 22.5.43. For an interesting discussion of the development of fighter escort for bomber formations in the Mediterranean and the early conclusion of Doolittle about the importance of fighter escort, see Bernard Boylan, "The Development of the Long-Range Escort Fighter" (unpublished MS, Maxwell AFB, 1955), AFHRA, pp. 74–76.

32. See Albert Speer, *Inside the Third Reich* (New York, 1970), p. 285.

33. For example, beginning in fall 1943 the Germans began to use roller bearings rather than precision ball bearings in their tank turrets; the former made it more difficult but not impossible to rotate tank turrets. By so doing, the Germans realized a considerable savings of precision ball bearings for more crucial uses.

34. Webster and Frankland, vol 2, *Endeavour*, p. 62.

35. This problem is even more clearly illustrated by reference to the British experience. Toward the end of 1943 some British crews on night missions began to report that they were attacked by German night fighters that had positioned themselves underneath the bomber and had then fired upward with a cannon slanted diagonally behind the cockpit. What British crews were seeing was the highly effective *Schräge Musik* system that the Germans had developed. Because British intelligence officers simply discounted these reports as the work of distraught crews, this valuable information was not generally passed along to those flying the missions.

36. For further discussion, see Murray, *Luftwaffe*, chap 5.

37. Msg, Eaker to Arnold, LC, Eaker Collection, box 16.

38. Rprt, AC/AS, Intelligence, A–2, "Current Items of Air Intelligence," Oct 18, 1944, cited in Craven and Cate, vol 2, *TORCH to POINTBLANK*, p. 712.

39. And it is still almost impossible to correlate these figures since many of the German records were lost in the war and because the *Luftwaffe* was clearly falsifying the records to make its production totals look better when they were presented to the *Führer*.

40. Murray, *Luftwaffe*, tables 33, 50.

41. Ibid., table 50.

42. For ULTRA confirmation, see the messages in ULTRA *History of U.S. Strategic Air Force Europe versus the German Air Force*, SRH–013, pp. 153, 156.

43. Ibid., pp. 155, 157.

44. Murray, *Luftwaffe*, pp. 266–267.

45. Bennett, *ULTRA in the West*, p. 68.

46. L. F. Ellis, *Victory in the West* (London, 1968), vol 1, pp. 271–274.

47. Speer, *Inside the Third Reich*, pp. 346–347.

48. PRO DEFE 3/156, KV 4021, 16.5.44, 0558Z.

49. PRO DEFE 3/159, KV 4762, 21.5.44, 2054Z.

50. PRO DEFE 3/166, KV 6673, 6.6.44, 2356Z.

51. PRO 31/20/16; Maj Ansel M. Talbert, U.S. Army Air Corps, "Handling of ULTRA Information at Headquarters Eighth Air Force," in SRH–023.

52. This comment is based on the first-rate study of the impact of the transportation plan on the German transportation system. Alfred C. Mierzejewski, *The Collapse of the German War Economy, 1944–1945: Allied Air Power and the German National Railway* (Chapel Hill, N.C., 1988).

53. Murray, *Luftwaffe*, tables 55–57.

54. Among many other messages, see PRO DEFE 3/47, KV 3015, 6.5.44, 1316Z; DEFE 3/153, KV 3300, 9.5.44, 2301Z, and KV 3292, 9.5.44, 1659Z; DEFE 3/155, KV 3763, 14.5.44, 0412Z; DEFE 3/158, KV 4690, 21.5.44, 0534Z; DEFE 3/161, KV 5446, 27.5.44, 2131Z; DEFE 3/162, KV 5626, 29.5.44, 1107Z; DEFE 3/162, KV 5622, 29.5.44, 0817Z; DEFE 3/163, KV 5825, 31.5.44, 0039Z; and DEFE 3/163, KV 5999, 1.6.44, 1516Z.

55. Mierzejewski, *Collapse of the German War Economy*, p. 167.

56. Ibid., p. 167.

57. Ibid., p. 162.

58. Mierzejewski's argument on this point is compelling. See ibid., chap 8.

59. Williamson Murray is indebted to Dr. William Emerson, Director of the FDR Library in Hyde Park, New York, for this information.

60. At Savo Island in August 1942, in a night attack, a force of Japanese heavy cruisers sank four American and Australian heavy cruisers with virtually no damage to themselves, despite the fact that the Americans possessed the advantage of radar. The Allied force was caught completely by surprise, *eight* months after the beginning of the war.

61. See Chapter 5.

62. COA Hist, pp. 113–115.
63. Hansell intvw, Jan 21, 1987.
64. Ibid.
65. Ltr., White to McDonald, Aug 1, 1944.
66. Hansell intvw, Jan 21, 1987, pp. 14–15.
67. Ibid., p. 15.
68. This comment should be qualified in one important area: the battle of the Atlantic from the summer to December of 1941. During this period, ULTRA intelligence by itself entirely illuminated the disposition and movement of German U-boats in the North Atlantic. This allowed the Admiralty to move the great convoys entirely around the submarine patrol lines and to reduce drastically British losses. No other factors come into play during this period. For a more specific discussion see Beesley, *Very Special Intelligence,* chap 6.

GLOSSARY

A–2	Assistant Chief of Air Staff, Intelligence (United States); *see also* AC/AS, Intelligence
AA	Antiaircraft
AAF	U.S. Army Air Forces; occasionally, Allied Air Forces (Southwest Pacific Theater)
AAFPOA	Army Air Forces, Pacific Ocean Area
AAFSWPA	Allied Air Forces, Southwest Pacific Area
AAI	Allied Armies in Italy
ABC	American-British Conversations
ABDA	American-British-Dutch-Australian
AC/AS, Intelligence	Assistant Chief of Air Staff, Intelligence (United States); *see also* A–2
ACAS (I)	Assistant Chief of Air Staff, Intelligence (British)
ACTS	Air Corps Tactical School
ADVON	Advanced echelon
AEAF	Allied Expeditionary Air Force
AEF	American Expeditionary Force
AFHQ	Allied Forces Headquarters
AFIS	AAF Intelligence Service
AFV	Armored fighting vehicle
AGFRTS	Air Ground Forces Resources and Technical Staff
A.I.	Air Ministry, Intelligence (British)
AIS	Air Intelligence Service
ALSOS	G–2 Intelligence Summary Mission (Europe)
ATI	Air technical intelligence
AVG	American Volunteer Group
AWPD	Air War Plans Division
BDA	Bomb damage assessment
BEW	Board of Economic Warfare (United States)
BIO	Branch intelligence officer
BP	Bletchley Park
CATF	China Air Task Force
CB	Central Bureau

Piercing the Fog

CBI	China-Burma-India
CBO	Combined Bomber Offensive
CCS	Combined Chiefs of Staff
C&GSS	Command and General Staff School
CIU	Central Interpretation Unit (British)
COA	Committee of Operations Analysts
COMAIRFORWARD	Commander, forward air forces
COMAIRSOLS	Air Commander, Solomons
COMSOPAC	Commander, South Pacific
CPIC	Combined Photographic Interpretation Centre (India)
CSTC	Combined Strategic Targets Committee
DF	Direction finding
EAC	Eastern Air Command
EEI	Essential element of information
EOU	Enemy Objectives Unit
FBI	Federal Bureau of Investigation
FEA	Foreign Economic Administration
FEAF	Far East Air Force (American)
FRUPac	Fleet Radio Unit, Pacific
GAF	German Air Force
GHQ	General Headquarters
HUMIT	Human resources intelligence
IATF	India Air Task Force
ICPOA	Intelligence Center, Pacific Ocean Area
ISAS	Information Section, Air Service
JCS	Joint Chiefs of Staff
JIC	Joint Intelligence Committee
JICA	Joint Intelligence Collection Agency
JICPOA	Joint Intelligence Center, Pacific Ocean Area
JTG	Joint Target Group
MAAF	Mediterranean Allied Air Forces
MAC	Mediterranean Air Command
MACAF	Mediterranean Allied Coastal Air Force
MAGIC	Intercepts from Japanese diplomatic messages

Glossary

MAPRW	Mediterranean Allied Photographic Reconnaissance Wing
MASAF	Mediterranean Allied Strategic Air Force
MATAF	Mediterranean Allied Tactical Air Force
MEW	Ministry of Economic Warfare (British)
MID	Military Intelligence Division
NAAF	Northwest African Air Forces
NACAF	Northwest African Coastal Air Force
NAPRW	Northwest African Photographic Reconnaissance Wing
NASAF	Northwest African Strategic Air Force
NATAF	Northwest African Tactical Air Force
NEI	Netherlands East Indies
NID	Naval Intelligence Division (British)
OB	Order of battle
OCAC	Office of the Chief of Air Corps
OCS	Officer Candidate School
ONI	Office of Naval Intelligence
OSRD	Office of Scientific Research and Development
OSS	Office of Strategic Services
POA	Pacific Ocean Area
POL	Petroleum, oil, and lubricants
POW	Prisoner of war
RAAF	Royal Australian Air Force
RAF	Royal Air Force
RCM	Radar/radio countermeasures
R.E.	Research and Experiment (British)
R/T	Radiotelegraph
SACO	Sino-American Cooperative Organization
SCU	Special communications unit
SHAEF	Supreme Headquarters, Allied Expeditionary Force (Europe)
SIB	*Special Intelligence Bulletin*
SIGINT	Signals intelligence
SIS	Signals Intelligence Service (U.S. Army Signal Corps)
SLU	Special liaison unit
SOPAC	South Pacific
SPA	South Pacific Area
SSO	Special security officer

SWPA	Southwest Pacific Area
TA	Traffic analysis
TAC	Tactical Air Command
TAIC	Technical Air Intelligence Centre (Southeast Asia)
TR	Training Regulation
TRG	Tactical Reconnaissance Group
TO	Table of organization
ULTRA	Material derived from intercepted messages transmitted by the Germans on their Enigma machine
USAFISPA	U.S. Army Forces in the South Pacific Area
USASTAF	U.S. Army Strategic Air Forces
USSBS	United States Strategic Bombing Survey
USSTAF	United States Strategic Air Forces, Europe
WDGS	War Department General Staff
WIR	Weekly Intelligence Report
WIS	Weekly Intelligence Summary
WPD	War Plans Division

BIBLIOGRAPHIC NOTE

PRIMARY SOURCE MATERIALS for this volume came largely from the U.S. Air Force's record collection kept at the Air Force Historical Research Agency, Maxwell Air Force Base, Alabama. A microfilm copy of these records is available at the Air Force History Support Office, Bolling AFB, D.C. In particular, the various files of the Office of the Assistant Chief of Air Staff, Intelligence, contain material related to internal planning and assessment as well as the administration of the office as it evolved through several reorganizations during the war. The records of the AC/AS (I) also contain material related to work with other Air Staff agencies; these documents are crucial to assessing the influence of intelligence on the U.S. Army Air Forces' plans and operations. Closely related to the A–2's file records are the files of the Committee of Operations Analysts. Review of the COA's work is necessary, since the committee exercised a significant influence over the Air Staff's responsibilities related to planning the air war both in the Pacific and Europe. Beginning with 1944, the records of the Joint Target Group (a part of the A–2) become of value in tracing planning for the aerial assault of Japan.

Similarly, the records of the Manhattan Engineer District at the National Archives are important to understand how the district employed the 509th Composite Group and used air intelligence in target planning. The district's records are open to the public, although they are incomplete. Some of the material was withdrawn from microfilming and release because of its sensitivity. For purposes of this study, records of the Manhattan Project that are not available do not appear to be an impediment.

The Library of Congress's Manuscript Division holds a number of collections of wartime officers whose understanding of the relationship of intelligence to the AAF's plans and operations was far-reaching. Paramount are the assembled papers of General of the Air Forces H. H. Arnold, the man who led the service throughout the war. These files were organized largely (though not entirely) by use of the Army's index file system. This is not a serious impediment to a researcher unversed in the system, as a card file gives clues to the possible locations of important items. Also in the Manuscript Division are collections of the papers of Generals Carl A. Spaatz, Ira C. Eaker, Thomas D. White, and Curtis E. LeMay. LeMay's papers are particularly useful for understanding the relationship between intelligence and operations in the Pacific. The papers and diaries of Henry Lewis Stimson are in the Yale

Piercing the Fog

University Library, New Haven, Connecticut. A microfilm copy is available in the Library of Congress's Manuscript Division. The Stimson papers for this period are mostly of a personal nature; few bear on the question of AAF operations and intelligence. The Stimson Diaries, however, are quite different. Stimson made daily and often extensive entries, many of which bear on the atomic bomb decision. Prior permission to cite or quote from the Stimson Diaries must be obtained from the Yale University Library, Manuscripts and Archives Division.

The Ira C. Eaker Collection, useful for its coverage of early strategic air operations out of England, is much skimpier for the time after the general moved to the Mediterranean in January 1944. Most likely this reflects Eaker's focus in his new position on diplomacy and policy in contrast to immediate operational concerns. General Carl Spaatz's papers contain a wealth of material on all aspects of the air wars in both the Mediterranean and European theaters.

The reports and records of the United States Strategic Bombing Survey are found in the National Archives, Record Group 243. They are also available in a few major libraries nationwide. This material is an excellent after-the-fact review of the bombing of Germany and Japan. Little in the reports, however, describes or records the day-to-day intelligence operation by the Air Staff.

In addition, the personal and professional papers of two other key airmen proved valuable for understanding air intelligence in the latter half of the war in Europe. The USAF Academy Library Special Collections section holds the papers of Brig. Gen. George C. McDonald, who served as Spaatz's Chief Intelligence Officer, Northwest African Air Forces, then as Director of Intelligence, United States Strategic Air Forces in Europe, from January 1944 until the end of the war. Although much more limited than either the Eaker or Spaatz Papers, and less well organized internally, they contain some material that does not appear in other collections of papers or in the files of HQ USSTAF contained in the USAF Collection. Also in the Academy's Special Collections are the papers of Maj. Gen. Haywood S. Hansell, Jr. Although limited in content, the papers of Lt. Gen. Elwood R. Quesada held in the Library of Congress contain information that proved most helpful in determining the role of signals intelligence and photointelligence in tactical air operations from the spring of 1944 to the spring of 1945.

Primary sources dealing with ULTRA and MAGIC for both the European and Pacific war fall into two categories. The first includes the National Security Agency Special Research Histories (SRHs), most of which are available at the AFHSO at Bolling AFB. These studies are collections of declassified wartime reports. Essential for an understanding of the handling and application of ULTRA at the various air commands in Europe are SRH–031, *Trip Reports Concerning Use of ULTRA in the Mediterranean Theater, 1943–1944*, and SRH–023, *Reports by U.S. Army ULTRA Representatives with Army Field Commands in the European Theater of Operations, 1945*, part 2. The former

Bibliography

contains reports submitted by Bletchley Park–trained special security officers on their get-acquainted tours of Mediterranean Allied commands prior to their assignments with the U.S. forces in western Europe. The latter contains the after-action reports by SSOs who dealt primarily with air intelligence derived from ULTRA after the invasion of Normandy. What is striking about all these reports are the efforts these individuals exerted during the war to understand ULTRA's place within the broader intelligence framework (even though few had had prior intelligence experience) and the candor of their comments. Also useful are SRH–006, *Synthesis of Experiences in the Use of ULTRA Intelligence by U.S. Army Field Commands in the European Theater of Operations* and SRH–107, *Problems of the SSO System in World War II*. These histories provide useful synopses of such experiences, but they rarely identify the sources of their information, much of which came from SSOs assigned to Army rather than Air Forces commands.

The SRHs and related reports produced by the National Security Agency are of mixed value, requiring careful consideration and judicial use. They are incomplete, censored, and not always objective. Of particular concern when reviewing these special histories is the problem of not always being able to determine why an item was deleted, especially when what appears to be similar information may appear elsewhere in the document. A researcher has no way to compare the the subject matter available with that in other volumes yet to be declassified and released for public review. Most of the writers or compilers had specific goals or assignments as they prepared their volumes. Although these special research histories should be used with great caution, they have value in determining the overall importance of message decryption and the control of ULTRA material in the war against Japan. Some are quite explicit and helpful, such as the message files related to the Battle of the Bismarck Sea and the MAGIC Diplomatic Summaries.

The second major category of primary ULTRA-related material encompasses the intercepted messages themselves, extracts of the messages, and signals sent from intercept facilities to the operational field commands. Those from Bletchley Park are now on file at the British Public Record Office in London. As of December 1988, the Library of Congress held 257 microfilm rolls covering the period November 1941 to May 1945. The signals are grouped strictly chronologically without regard for subject, geographic location, or units involved, and no index is available to assist the researcher other than the microfilm roll list arranged by date. Even more than when they were transmitted (since the original recipients maintained a frame of reference in their heads and in their files), these signals are isolated documents which must be placed within a broader context to be assessed and used properly. Some of the SRHs contain either decrypted messages or the extracts and commentary such as the Willoughby bulletins of the SWPA.

Piercing the Fog

Interviews with Lt. Gen. Francis S. Gideon (wartime Director of Operations, Fifth Air Force) and General Robert M. Lee (Director of Operations, Ninth Air Force, fall of 1944 to war's end) were particularly helpful for the insights they provided into the tight controls imposed on the dissemination and use of ULTRA.

The number of secondary works dealing with ULTRA expands yearly. Of these the most important for the present work have been the first three volumes of *British Intelligence in the Second World War: Its Influence on Strategy and Operations* (F. H. Hinsley *et al.*). Reflecting the increasing quality of ULTRA in the last eighteen months of the war, volume 3 (which was published in two parts) tends to be largely a narrative recitation of ULTRA signals. Without reading the earlier two volumes, the casual reader might overlook the importance of other intelligence tools and organizations. *British Intelligence* is likely to remain the standard work on this subject for both the depth and the breadth of its information.

Little unclassified material is available on USAAF signals intelligence above the basic tactical and technical level, although several SRHs do cover day-by-day activities of some Signals Intelligence Service units. A Draft History, IX Tactical Air Command, dated March 1945, contains several short but informative papers on the tactical air forces' use of Y intelligence. These are contained in the Library of Congress's Lt. Gen. Elwood R. Quesada Collection. The Spaatz Collection contains several documents prepared by American and British officers on the significance of Y-Service for strategic air operations in western Europe. The unit histories of the USAAF's Radio Squadrons (Mobile) vary both in completeness and quality. Several give good data on the Air Force's Y-Service units. Topics covered include organization, stations of service, relationships to the air commanders, and the extent of work performed.

The two most useful sources for providing information on the methodology and role of photographic intelligence in Europe were written by former British WAAF officers intimately involved in activities at Medmenham. Constance Babington-Smith's *Air Spy: The Story of Photo Intelligence in World War II* is personal-account history at its best. It combines Babington-Smith's experiences with methodology and techniques. It also provides concrete examples of the use and misuse of this special resource. *The Eye of Intelligence* by Ursula Powys-Lybbe takes a more detached, clinical approach, organizing chapters not chronologically, but by the various aspects of photointelligence, especially photointerpretation. As could be expected, both focused on the British experience, although *Air Spy* contains good information on key Americans.

For the American side of photointelligence, Roy M. Stanley's *World War II Photo Intelligence* does an excellent job of explaining the technical aspects of photoreconnaissance and interpretation. Of particular value are the numerous photographs and diagrams employed to clarify the text. Although cited only occasionally in this work, the general understanding Stanley's book offers is invaluable. Complementing the technical information presented by Stanley is the narrative approach offered in *Unarmed and Unafraid*. A survey history of air combat reconnaissance, its chapters on World War II are especially useful for providing a sense of the problems American aerial reconnaissance faced in the early period of the war.

Material on both photoreconnaissance and photointerpretation is scattered throughout the records of the numerous air commands contained in the files of the Air Force Historical Research Agency. Useful official material is in the folders on Photo Intelligence in the General Carl Spaatz Collection at the Library of Congress and in the HQ USSTAF "History of the Directorate of Intelligence" in the same collection. Both contain documents regarding the debate over the creation of an independent American photointelligence capability.

The most useful secondary source—indeed, one of the very few—for Y intelligence is *The Enemy Is Listening* by former British WAAF Aileen Clayton. Clayton, like Babington-Smith in photointerpretation, was an early entrant into signals intelligence. She had extensive and intensive experience in Britain and the Mediterranean, and her ability to explain the technical aspects of this somewhat arcane and unromantic aspect of intelligence is unsurpassed.

For the strategic air war in Europe, the USAF's collection of Eighth and Fifteenth Air Force records is essential. Particularly useful both in identifying the main issues and in providing guidance to other primary documents is the multivolume "History of the Eighth Air Force" prepared by that headquarters throughout and immediately after the war. Air Force records in the 142 series, Assistant Chief of Staff, Intelligence, and Predecessors, are useful for providing the Air Staff intelligence perspective on specific issues, including operations against the submarine pens, and detailed studies by the Air Intelligence Service on strategic target systems in Germany. Also invaluable for the European air war is the War Diary of the Research and Analysis Branch, OSS London, volume 5, "Economic Outpost with Economic Warfare Division," RG 226, National Archives. Although written in the "weren't-we-great" style characteristic of many organizational histories, this study is must reading for an understanding of the organization and methodology of the Enemy Objectives Unit, crucial in the Eighth Air Force targeting and damage assessment effort. RG 226 also contains the many detailed target studies prepared by EOU.

Air intelligence in North Africa is more difficult to track through the documents than are operations in and from the United Kingdom. In part this reflects the transient nature of all aspects of North African operations when contrasted with the more permanent organization, location, and facilities available in the UK. Additionally, the several changes in command structures and the joint nature of operations and intelligence necessitate a broad sweep through sources. Important files include those of the Twelfth Air Force (AFHRA Gp 650), Northwest African Air Forces (AFHRA Gp 612), Northwest

Piercing the Fog

African Strategic Air Force (AFHRA Gp 615), and Northwest African Tactical Air Force (AFHRA Gp 614). Particularly useful in understanding the role of ULTRA in North Africa was Group Captain Humphreys's "The Use of 'U' in the Mediterranean and Northwest African Theaters of War," in the National Security Agency's SRH–037, *Reports Received by U.S. War Department on the Use of ULTRA in the European Theater, World War II.*" Volume 2 of Hinsley's *British Intelligence in the Second World War* also provided essential material on signals intelligence, including ULTRA, especially with regard to the antishipping campaign which occupied so much of the strategic air forces' efforts.

The intelligence files of the Fifth, Tenth, and Fourteenth Air Forces contain varying amounts of relevant material about the AAF in the Pacific and CBI, due largely to the difficult conditions and the widespread nature of the war in that region. The operations records of the three numbered air forces usefully supplement the intelligence files. Other records, such as those of AAF Headquarters, provided valuable data, especially in the case of B–29 operations, where many of the general mission objectives were reached based upon the predeployment work of the COA and the Air Staff. The contents of the records of the Seventh and Thirteenth Air Forces are distinctly less productive than those of the Fifth, Tenth, and Fourteenth. This reflects the Navy command structure under which these two organizations worked for much of the war. Most operational decisions of the air units subordinate to the Navy were not taken by the air commanders, and no commander of either Air Force reached the prominence of either Kenney or Chennault. The records reflect the reactions to task force directives, not the extent of or reasons for Air Force planning.

The best single source to trace the thoughts and actions of specific commanders of the Far East region is the collection at the AFHSO known as the George C. Kenney Papers. This aggregate of letters and of diary and journal entries covers events from 1941 through the end of the war. It was supplemented by General Kenney in the months after the war as he incorporated some of it into his book, *The General Kenney Reports*. Used with an understanding of its origin and purpose, this book is almost unmatched among the legacies of America's Pacific air generals for judging the influence of information upon plans and operations. The papers of Generals Nathan Twining and Curtis E. LeMay in the Library of Congress's Manuscript Division proved a most helpful resource, as did the oral histories and individual collections at AFHSO. Especially useful for an understanding of ULTRA and the air-ground relationships in the SWPA is Edward J. Drea's *MacArthur's Ultra*.

Libraries in the Washington, D.C., area, the Library of Congress, Army Library, and the Air Force History library provided a great deal of information about the war. Much of it is operational, with few accounts of intelligence work. In part this is so because of the wartime and postwar strictures on revealing sensitive information. Probably this also reflects the less glamorous aspect of

Bibliography

intelligence studies and their underrated importance when compared to the actions of fighters and bombers.

In the chapter notes, citations referring to material in the possession of the U.S. Air Force, either the original documents at Maxwell AFB, Alabama, or the microfilm copies at Bolling AFB, carry the notation, USAF Collection, followed by the index number the first time that such a reference appears in the book. Thereafter, only the AFHRA index citation number appears. In instances when the documentary material exists only in the original at the AFHSO, the notes carry the notation "AFHSO" and the index number for the specific item. Material in the National Archives carries the notation NA followed by record group and box numbers, as appropriate. Documents in the Library of Congress's Manuscript Division are identified as LC, the name of the collection, such as Arnold Papers, and the appropriate box and folder number.

SELECT BIBLIOGRAPHY

Books

Andrew, Christopher. *Her Majesty's Secret Service: The Making of the British Intelligence Community.* New York: Viking Press, 1986.

────── and David Dilks, eds. *The Missing Dimension: Governments and Intelligence Communities in the Twentieth Century.* Urbana, Ill., and Chicago: University of Chicago Press, 1948.

Arnold, Henry H. *Global Mission.* New York: Harper & Bros., 1949.

Babington-Smith, Constance. *Air Spy: The Story of Photo Intelligence in World War II.* New York: Harper & Bros., 1957.

Bennett, Ralph F. *Ultra in the West: The Normandy Campaign, 1944–45.* New York: Charles Scribner's Sons, 1980.

Bialer, Uri. *The Shadow of the Bomber: The Fear of Air Attacks and British Politics, 1932–1939.* London: Royal Historical Society, 1980.

Bidwell, Bruce W. *History of the Military Intelligence Division, Department of the Army General Staff 1775–1941.* Frederick, Md.: University Publications of America, 1986.

Byrd, Martha. *Chennault: Giving Wings to the Tiger.* Tuscaloosa, Ala.: University of Alabama Press, 1987.

Calvocoressi, Peter. *Top Secret Ultra.* New York: Pantheon Books, 1980.

Chennault, Claire Lee. *Way of a Fighter.* Ed. Robert Hotz. New York: G. P. Putman's Sons, 1949.

Clark, Ronald. *The Man Who Broke Purple.* Boston: Little, Brown & Co., 1977.

Clayton, Aileen. *The Enemy is Listening.* London: Hutchinson & Co., 1980.

Cline, Ray S. *Secrets, Spies and Scholars: Blueprint of the Essential CIA.* Washington, D.C.: Acropolis Books, 1976.

Bibliography

―――. *Washington Command Post: The Operations Division.* U.S. Army in World War II: The War Department. Washington, D.C.: Office of the Chief of Military History, 1951.

Cochran, Alexander S., ed. *The MAGIC Diplomatic Summaries.* New York: Garland Publishing, 1982.

Craven, Wesley Frank and James Lea Cate. *The Army Air Forces in World War II.* 7 vols. Chicago: University of Chicago Press, 1948–1958; Washington, DC: Office of Air Force History, 1982.

Drea, Edward J. *MacArthur's ULTRA: Codebreaking and the War Against Japan, 1942–1945.* Lawrence: University Press of Kansas, 1992.

Edmonds, Walter D. *They Fought With What They Had: The Story of the Army Air Forces in the Southwest Pacific, 1941–1942.* Boston: Little, Brown and Co., 1951.

Ellis, L. F. *Victory in the West.* London: Her Majesty's Stationery Offfice, 1968.

Feldt, Eric A. *The Coast Watchers.* New York: Oxford University Press, 1946.

Ferguson, Thomas G. *British Military Intelligence, 1870–1914.* Frederick, Md.: University Publications of America, 1984.

Finnegan, John Patrick. *Military Intelligence: A Picture History.* Arlington, Va.: History Office, U.S. Army Intelligence and Security Command, 1985.

Freeman, Roger, with Alan Crouchman and Vic Maslen. *Mighty Eighth War Diary.* London: Jane's Publishing Co., 1981.

Futrell, Robert Frank. *Ideas, Concepts, Doctrine: A History of Basic Thinking in the United States Air Force, 1907–1964.* Maxwell AFB, Ala.: Air University, 1974.

Goddard, George W. *Overview: A Life-Long Adventure in Aerial Photography.* Garden City, NY: Doubleday & Co., 1969.

Goldstein, Donald M. "Ennis C. Whitehead, Aerial Tactician." *We Shall Return! MacArthur's Commanders and the Defeat of Japan, 1942–1945.* ed. by William M. Leary. Lexington, KY: University Press of Kentucky, 1988.

Greer, Thomas H. *The Development of Doctrine in the Army Air Arm, 1917–1941.* Maxwell AFB, Ala.: Air University, 1955.

Groves, Leslie R. *Now It Can Be Told, The Story of the Manhattan Project.* New York and Evanston: Harper & Row, 1962.

Hansell, Haywood S., Jr. *The Strategic Air War Against Germany and Japan: A Memoir.* Washington, D.C.: Office of Air Force History, 1986.

Hinsley F. H. et al. *British Intelligence in the Second World War: Its Influence on Strategy and Operations.* 4 vols. New York: Cambridge University Press, 1979–1990.

Holmes, W. J. *Double-Edged Secrets.* Annapolis, Md.: Naval Institute Press, 1979.

Horner, D. M. *High Command: Australia and Allied Strategy, 1939–1945.* Canberra: Australian War Memorial, 1982.

Howard, Michael. *Strategic Deception.* Vol. 5 of *British Intelligence in the Second World War.* London: Her Majesty's Stationery Office, 1990.

Ind, Allison. *Allied Intelligence Bureau: Our Secret Weapon in the War Against Japan.* New York: David McKay Co., 1958.

———. *Bataan: The Judgment Seat.* New York: Macmillan, 1944.

Infield, Glenn B. *Unarmed and Unafraid.* New York: Macmillan, 1970.

Johnson, Ellis A. and Katcher, David A. *Mines Against Japan.* Silver Spring, Md.: Naval Ordnance Laboratory, 1973.

Jones, R. V. *The Wizard War: British Scientific Intelligence, 1935–1945.* New York: Coward, McCann & Geohegan, 1978.

Jones, Vincent C. *Manhattan: The Army and the Atomic Bomb.* Washington, D.C.: Office of the Chief of Military History, 1985.

Kahn, David. *Hitler's Spies: German Military Intelligence in World War II.* New York: Collier Books, 1978.

Kenney, George C. *General Kenney Reports.* New York: Duell, Sloan & Pearce, 1949; Washington, D.C.: Office of Air Force History, 1987.

Kirby, S. Woodburn et al. *The War Against Japan.* 5 vols. London: Her Majesty's Stationery Office, 1957–1969.

Knaack, Marcelle Size. *Post–World War II Bombers, 1945–1973.* Encyclopedia of U.S. Air Force Aircraft and Missile Systems. Washington, D.C.: Office of Air Force History, 1988.

Koopman, Bernard Osgood. *Search and Screening: General Principles with Historic Applications.* New York, Oxford, Sidney, Frankfort, Paris: Pergamon Press, 1980.

Bibliography

Kreis, John F. *Air Warfare and Air Base Air Defense, 1914–1973.* Washington, D.C.: Office of Air Force History, 1988.

Layton, Edwin T., with Roger Pineau and John Costello. *"And I Was There": Pearl Harbor and Midway—Breaking the Secrets.* New York: William Morrow & Co., 1985.

LeMay, Curtis E., and Bill Yenne. *Superfortress: The B–29 and American Air Power.* New York: McGraw-Hill, 1988.

——— and McKinlay Kantor. *Mission With LeMay.* Garden City, N.Y.: Doubleday & Co., 1965.

Lewin, Ronald. *The American Magic: Codes, Ciphers and the Defeat of Japan.* New York: Farrar Strauss Giroux, 1982.

———. *ULTRA Goes to War: The First Account of World War II's Greatest Secret Based on Official Documents.* New York: McGraw-Hill, 1978.

Lundstrom, John B. *The First Team.* Annapolis, Md.: Naval Institute Press, 1984.

Maurer, Maurer, ed. *The U.S. Air Service in World War I.* 4 vols. Washington, D.C.: Office of Air Force History, 1978.

May, Ernest R., ed. *Knowing One's Enemies.* Princeton, N.J.: Princeton University Press, 1984.

Mets, David R. *Master of Airpower: General Carl A. Spaatz.* Novato, Calif.: Presidio Books, 1988.

Mierzejewski, Alfred C. *The Collapse of the German War Economy, 1944–1945: Allied Air Power and the German National Railway.* Chapel Hill: University of North Carolina Press, 1988.

Miles, Milton E. *A Different Kind of War.* Garden City, NY: Doubleday & Co., 1967.

Morison, Samuel Eliot. *History of United States Naval Operations in World War II.* 15 vols. Boston: Little, Brown & Co., 1947–1962.

Morton, Louis. *Strategy and Command: The First Two Years.* Washington: Office of the Chief of Military History, 1962.

Murray, Williamson. *Luftwaffe.* Baltimore, Md.: Nautical & Aviation Press, 1985.

———. *The Change in the European Balance of Power, 1938–1939: The Path to Ruin.* Princeton, N.J.: Princeton University Press, 1985.

Nelson, Otto L. *National Security and the General Staff.* Washington, D.C.: Infantry Journal Press, 1946.

Parrish, Thomas. *The Ultra Americans: The U.S. Role in Breaking the Nazi Code.* New York: Stein & Day, 1986.

Potter, E. B. *Nimitz.* Annapolis, Md.: Naval Institute Press, 1976.

Powye-Lybbe, Ursula. *The Eye of Intelligence.* London: William Kimber, 1983.

Prange, Gordon W., with Donald M. Goldstein and Katherine V. Dillon. *Pearl Harbor: The Verdict of History.* New York: McGraw-Hill Book Company, 1986.

———. *At Dawn We Slept.* New York: McGraw-Hill, 1981.

Price, Alfred. *The History of US Electronic Warfare.* Washington, D.C.: The Association of Old Crows, 1984.

Putney, Diane T., ed. *ULTRA and the Army Air Forces in World War II: An Interview with Associate Justice of the U.S. Supreme Court Lewis F. Powell, Jr.* Washington, D.C.: Office of Air Force History, 1987.

Van der Rhoer, Edward. *Deadly Magic.* New York: Charles Scribner's Sons, 1978.

Rostow, W. W. *Pre-Invasion Bombing Strategy: General Eisenhower's Decision of March 25, 1944.* Austin, Tex.: University of Texas Press, 1981.

Samson, Jack. *Chennault.* New York: Doubleday, 1987.

Schaffer, Ronald. *Wings of Judgment: American Bombing in World War II.* New York: Oxford University Press, 1985.

Scott, Robert Lee. *The Day I Owned The Sky.* New York, Toronto, Sidney, Aukland: Bantam Books, 1988.

Sherry, Michael S. *The Rise of American Air Power: The Creation of Armageddon.* New Haven, Conn.: Yale University Press, 1987.

Smith, Robert M. and Smith, Philip D. *With Chennault in China: A Flying Tiger's Diary.* Blue Ridge Summit, Pa.: TAB Books, 1984.

Smith, R. Harris. *OSS: The Secret History of America's First Central Intelligence Agency.* Berkeley, Los Angeles, London: University of California Press, 1972.

Spector, Ronald H., ed. *Listening to the Enemy.* Wilmington, Del.: Scholarly Resources, Inc., 1988.

———. *The Eagle and the Sun*. New York: Macmillan, Free Press, 1984.

Speer, Albert. *Inside the Third Reich*. Trans. Clara and Richard Winston. New York: Macmillan, 1970.

Stanley, Roy M., II. *World War II Photo Intelligence*. New York: Charles Scribner's Sons, 1981.

Stilwell, Joseph W. *The Stilwell Papers*. Ed. and arranged by Theodore H. White. New York: William Sloan Associates, 1948.

Stimson, Henry L., and McGeorge Bundy. *On Active Service in Peace and War*. New York: Harper & Bros., 1948.

Stripp, Alan. *Codebreaker in the Far East*. London: Frank Cass, 1989.

Sun Tzu. *The Art of War*. Trans. Samuel B. Griffith. Oxford, New York: Oxford University Press, 1963.

Thorpe, Elliott R. *East Wind, Rain: The Intimate Account of an Intelligence Officer in the Pacific, 1939–1949*. Boston: Gambit, Inc., 1969.

Tibbets, Paul W., with Clair Stebbins and Harry Franklin. *The Tibbets Story*. New York: Stein & Day, 1978.

Tsugi, Masanobn. *Singapore, The Japanese Version*. Trans. Margaret E. Lake. Sidney: Ure Smith, 1960.

Wark, Wesley. *The Ultimate Enemy: British Intelligence and Nazi Germany, 1933–1939*. Ithaca, N.Y.: Cornell University Press, 1985.

Webster, Charles, and Noble Frankland. *The Strategic Air Offensive Against Germany, 1939–1945*. 4 vols. London: Her Majesty's Stationery Office, 1961.

Wedemeyer, Albert C. *Wedemeyer Reports!* New York: Henry Holt & Co., 1958.

Welchman, Gordon. *The Hut Six Story*. New York: McGraw-Hill, 1982.

Willoughby, Charles A. and John Chamberlin. *MacArthur, 1941–1951*. New York: McGraw Hill, 1954.

Wise, S.F. *The Official History of the Royal Canadian Air Force*. Toronto: University of Toronto Press, 1980.

Wohlstetter, Roberta. *Pearl Harbor: Warning and Decision*. Stanford, Calif.: Stanford University Press, 1962.

Wyden, Peter. *Day One: Before Hiroshima and After.* New York: Simon & Schuster, 1984.

Articles

Aldrich, Richard. "Imperial Rivalry: British and American Intelligence in Asia, 1942–46." *Intelligence and National Security*, January 1, 1988, pp. 5–55.

Andrew, Christopher. "The Growth of the Australian Intelligence Community and the Anglo-American Connection." *Intelligence and National Security*, April 2, 1989, pp. 213–255.

Cochran, Alexander S., Jr. " 'Magic,' 'Ultra,' and the Second World War: Literature, Sources, and Outlook." *Military Affairs*, April, 1982, pp. 88–92.

Drea, Edward J. "Ultra and the American War Against Japan: A Note on Sources." *Intelligence and National Security*, January 3, 1988, pp. 195–204.

Stripp, Alan. "Breaking Japanese Codes." *Intelligence and National Security*, October 2, 1987, pp. 135–150

INDEX

"Air Estimate of the Situation for the Employment of the Air Striking Force in Europe" (ABC–1), 48–50
A–2, U.S. Army Air Forces
 branches of, 379
 need for independence, 377–79
 organization of, 355–60
 preparations for peace, 389–90
 relation to G–2, 389–90, 393
 responsibilities distinguished from those of G–2, 359
ABC–1 Agreement, 111
Administrator of Export Control, 153
Admiralty Intelligence Board, 143
Admiralty Islands, 277, 291, 416
Advisory Committee on Bombardment (later COA), 152–54
 analysis compared with AWPD–42, 154–57
AEAF, 212–13
Aerial mining, 328
 by B–29s, in Pacific, 345
 Rangoon River, 306–7
Aerial photography
 importance in North Africa, 163
 importance of, 394
Aerial reconnaissance
 in Burma and Thailand, 307
 target photography, importance of, 370–71
Air Board
 bombing role in air power, on, 38–39
Air Combat Intelligence Center, 256
Air Command South East Asia, 308
Air Corps
 aerial photography school established, 81
 creation of, 20
 Information Division, OCAC (later Intelligence Division), 20, 22–23, 41–42
Air Corps Act, 12, 17–18, 21
Air Corps Intelligence Board, 40–41, 398
Air Corps Tactical School, Maxwell Field, 12, 24–28, 50, 126, 397
Aircraft, British
 Mosquito, 81
 Spitfire IX, 81
 Spitfire XII, 81
Aircraft, German
 Ar 234, 244
 Bf 109, 125, 201
 FW 190, 124, 158, 162–63, 197, 205
 He 111, 34
 He 177, 163
 He 280, 149, 244
 Ho 9 jet-powered flying wing, 374
 Ju 52, 34
 Ju 87 Stuka, 34
 Ju 88, 197
 Ju 222, 374
 Ju 290, 374
 Ju 388, 374
 Me 110, 404
 Me 163, 149, 244, 374
 Me 262, 149, 244, 245, 374
 Me 323, 163, 169
 Me 109G, 124
 Ta 152, 374
Aircraft, Japanese, 288
 Mitsubishi Betty bombers, 271
 Nakajima Type 97 (Nate), 31
 Type 96 Mitsubishi (Claude), 30
 Type 99 (Val), 122
 Zero, 247, 271, 306
Aircraft, U.S.
 A–20, 166, 275
 B–17, 25, 51, 106, 139, 166, 168, 175, 201, 206, 226, 249–50, 254, 268, 271, 295, 352, 404–5
 B–24, 166, 167, 192, 206, 210, 226, 267–68, 271, 274–75, 280, 285, 294, 306, 307, 315, 317, 322, 324, 328
 B–25, 167, 265, 269, 277–78, 294, 304, 307, 313, 315, 316, 319, 416
 B–25C–1, 265
 B–26, 167, 168
 B–29, 285, 293, 320, 324, 327–28, 419

483

campaign against Japanese home islands, 418
Enola Gay, 345
Japan's proximity-fuze capability and, 372
MATTERHORN plan for, 366
operations against Japan, 329–47
raids from Chinese bases, 418
reconnaissance, 81–82
DB–7, 166
F–4 (P–38E), 81
F–5 (P–38G/H), 81
F–7, 81
F–9, 81
F–13, 336, 419
P–38, 82, 166, 168, 265, 270–71, 277, 280–81, 287, 294, 307, 328, 419
P–39, 82, 269, 294
P–40, 82, 106, 281, 294, 304, 313
P–47, 226, 268, 328
P–51, 82, 95, 172, 206, 226, 307
P–59, 391
P–80, 391
P–400, 269
Aircraft Radio Laboratory, Wright Field, Ohio, 175
Air Documents Research Center, 374
Air Force General Information Bulletin, 120
Air Forces (numbered). *See* individual air forces, by number
Air Ground Forces Resources and Technical Staff (AGFRTS), 301
5329th, 318–22
Air Intelligence Service (AIS), 117
Airlift, German, 168
Air Matériel Command
Technical Data Laboratory, 122
Air observation
in World War I, 15–16
Air Service
Engineering Division, 18–20
Information Group, 18, 20, 23–24
Air Target Index Japanese War, 369
Air War Plans Division (AWPD), 43
AWPD–1, 46–51, 74, 150–52
AJAX (VIII Fighter Command), 95
Akin, Spencer B., 107
Allied Air Forces Southwest Pacific Area (AAFSWPA)
Directorate of Intelligence, 252–53
Allied Air Forces SWPA Intelligence Summary, 253

Allied Intelligence Bureau, 108, 259, 261
Allied Sixth Army Group, 232
Allied Translator and Interpreter Section, 108–9
Allied Tripartite Meeting, 323
ALSOS mission, 373
American Air Service
aerial photography use, 81
American-British Conversations–1 (ABC–1), 46–47
American-British-Dutch-Australian (ABDA) Command, 248
American Expeditionary Force (AEF)
intelligence in, 11–16
American Far East Air Force (FEAF)
Pearl Harbor attack and, 251
victory in Philippines, 290
American Institute of Mining and Metallurgical Engineers, 153
American Seventh Army, 232
American Volunteer Group (AVG), 87, 306
Anacostia Naval Aircraft Factory, 124
Anderson, Frederick L., 69, 71, 194–95, 205, 222, 421
Big Week, on, 207
Eaker Plan and, 191
planning for European invasion, 208
Anderson, Kenneth, 160
Anderson, Orvil A., 69, 71, 220
Anti-Comintern Pact, 29
Antisubmarine operations
AWPD–42, 151, 156
COA, 156
policy and outcomes, 142–46
ARCADIA conference, 111
Ardennes counteroffensive, 235–36, 245
Armies (numbered). *See* individual armies, by name
Army Air Forces (AAF)
birth of intelligence organization in, 112
disbands Air Staff intelligence operations unit, 6
Evaluation Board, 372
Historical Section, 117
Intelligence Service (AFIS), 355
Proving Ground Command, Eglin Field, Florida, 125
Technical Training Command, 127
Army Air Forces Air Intelligence School (later, Intelligence Division of the School of Applied Tactics), 127, 132, 370, 402

Index

Army Reorganization Act of 1920, 17, 21
Army War College
  on aviation, 36
Arnold, Henry H., 1, 50
  access to sensitive information by, 8–9, 28, 42–43, 103, 353
  ambivalence toward Soviet Union, 391
  and Kenney's requests for reinforcements, 267–68
  appreciation for intelligence, 352
  assessment of Japan's likelihood of attack, 53–54
  character and use of intelligence, 418–20
  creates COA, 6, 420
  details officers to British Air Ministry, 118
  direction and operation of B–29, 329–30
  displeasure with A–2/G–2 relationship, 352–53
  dissatisfaction with AAF intelligence, 360
  enlists outside experts to develop intelligence, 6–7
  fears OVERLORD air battle, 229
  fires General Wolfe, 335
  Hitler's power of intimidation, on, 38
  importance of Joint Target Group to, 369–70
  initiation into ULTRA, 354
  interest in information transfer, 372–75, 388
  perceives decline in GAF, 148, 408
  promotes and defends B–29, 340, 342
  refuses Kenney's requests for B–29s, 285
  reports from Spain, on, 37
  requires access to intelligence, 118–19
  sends bombers to Hawaii to block attack, 51–52
  strategic air campaign to weaken Germany, 190, 202–3
  study groups appointed by, 371–73
  suffers heart attack, 342
  supervision of air commanders, 354
Assistant Chief of Air Staff, A–2
  competition with other service intelligence agencies, 7
  limited knowledge of ULTRA by, 8
  responsibilities of, 4–5
Atomic bomb
  AAF intelligence and, 380–88
Attachés
  military, 18, 20, 28, 31–32
  prewar role of, 395–96
Australia
  7th Division, 263
  handling of intelligence by, 108
Australian Special Wireless Group, 108
Avord, France, 197
AWPD–1, "Munitions Requirement of the AAF," 46–51, 74, 150, 399
AWPD–42, 74, 150–52
  analysis compared with COA's, 154–57
  estimates time for European invasion, 157

B Section, 105–6
Babington-Smith, Constance, 92, 220
Balkan Air Force, 178
Ball bearing industry, 201, 203, 407–8, 422
Barnett, Harold J., 209
Barr, P. M., 162–63
Battle of the Bismarck Sea, 8, 247, 265–68, 415
Battle of Britain, 261, 399, 404
Battle of the Coral Sea, 106–7, 248
Battle of the Marne, 15
Battle of Midway, 8, 248
Battle of Mons, 15
BELCONNEN (Navy signal intelligence), 253
Bemis, Harold, 29
Berliner, Henry, 141
Berman, Emile Z., 310
Bertrandais, Victor E., 20, 281, 282
Betts, T. J., 119
Big Week, 206–8, 228, 229
Birch, John, 300, 313
Bissell, Clayton, 19, 350–51, 360
  AAF chief intelligence officer, 357
  ALSOS mission, 373
  assesses Soviet role in war, 391
  commands IATF, 298, 301–2, 304
  intelligence requirements of, 112
Bitter, Francis, 365–66
Blamey, Thomas, 107
Bolling Field, 127
Bombe machine, 61
Bombing Survey, 376
Bombs
  British Tallboy, 381
Bombsights, 366–67
Bond, Horatio, 365

485

Bonin Islands, 328
Bonnet, George, 397
Bottomley, Norman, 412
Bower, Philip G., 368
Bowles, Edward L., 7
Bradley, Omar, 232
Bratton, Rufus, 115
Brereton, Lewis H., 251
Brett, George H., 42, 126
British Air Ministry, 18
  coordination with, 118
  estimates GAF fighting value, pre-OVERLORD, 228
  technical intelligence section, 122
British Eastern Air Command, 160
British Eighth Army, 181
British Government Code and Cypher School, 8
British Joint Planning Staff, 157
British Royal Flying Corps
  reconnaissance by, 15
Brown, Grover C., 49
Brown, Harold W., 81, 250, 252
Brown, Harvey C., 126
Brux, Czechoslovakia, 92
Bryden, William, 43
Buck, Lucius, 78, 232, 234
Bufton, Sidney, 191
Bullitt, William C., 38
Bundy, Harvey, 380
Burgess, W. M., 119, 125
Bush, Vannevar, 380
Butler, William C., 119

Cabell, Charles, 132
  Eaker Plan and, 191
  planning for European invasion, 208
Cain, Benjamin, 257–58
  special OB study by, 280, 283
  use of MIS services by, 358
Cairo conference, 329, 331, 365
California Institute of Technology, 7
Candee, Robert C., 43, 47
Cannon, John K., 178
Canterbury Digest, 96, 98
Caroline Islands, 275
Casablanca Directive, 74, 145, 156, 190
CAST (Navy signal intelligence), 250
Catalina flying boat, 285
Central Bureau (CB), 107–8
Chandler, Charles DeForest, 14
Chaney, James E., 47
Chemical Warfare Service, 339

Chennault, Claire, 30–31, 247, 254, 321, 417–21
  air-raid warning net of, 314
  antishipping campaign of, 317–18
  commands CATF, 298, 301
  commands Fourteenth Air Force, 297
  intelligence requirements of, 112
  photoreconnaissance equipment available to, 87
  raids Hong Kong, 304
  relationship with AFGFRTS, 321–22
  wants B–29, 332
Chiang Kai-shek, 247, 298, 320, 417
Chicago Herald Tribune, 63, 101
Chihaya Masataka, 52
China
  aid to Americans by, 259
  failures of American undertaking in, 414
  formal assault plans of Allies, 284
  Fourteenth Air Force in, 312–24
  need for valid target information on, 297
China Air Task Force, 87
China-Burma-India (CBI) Theater, 82, 297
  comparative air intelligence functions in, 303
  complexity of command structure, 298, 300
  difficulties in intelligence exploitation in, 417
  low American priority of, 298
  photoreconnaissance in, 87
  split into sectors, 315, 320–21
Churchill, Winston, 50
  ARCADIA conference, 111
  informs Roosevelt of V-weapons, 220
  long-range escort fighter recommendation, 404
  orders assault into North Africa, 157
Clark Air Field, 106
Coast Guard
  cryptanalytical projects of, 4
Coast watchers, 276
Colbert, Ralph A., 371
Colley, A. W., 122, 125
Color-coded war plans, 21–22
Colossus machine, 61
Combined Bomber Offensive (CBO), 76, 349
  broad basis for, 190
  initiation of, 172

Index

objectives, 1944, 208, 224
POINTBLANK, 194, 221
targets of, 197
Combined Bomber Offensive from the United Kingdom. *See* Eaker Plan
Combined Chiefs of Staff (CCS), 118, 370
German fighter strength, on, 192, 194
place all air forces under Supreme Allied Commander, 212
Combined Photographic Interpretation Centre (CPIC) South East Asia, 308–9
Combined Strategic Targets Committee (CSTC), 241–42, 412
Command and General Staff School (C&GSS), Fort Leavenworth, Kansas, 22, 126
Commands (numbered)
VII Bomber, 327
VII Fighter, 327–28
VIII Bomber, 95, 130–31, 134, 137–38, 140–43, 205
VIII Fighter Command, 95, 141, 226
VIII Support Command, 141
XXI Bomber, 327–28, 338, 421
IX Fighter, 98
IX Tactical Air (IX TAC), 230–34, 362
XII Air Support, 164
XII Bomber, 161, 169
XIX Tactical Air (TAC), 66, 67, 362
XX Bomber, 308, 311, 331, 333–34, 338
Committee of Operations Analysts (COA), 152–54
analysis compared with AWPD–42, 154–57
catalyst for reconsideration of air power, 190
endorses urban-area fire bombing, 338–39
influence on CBO, 172, 349
influence on Eaker Plan, 191, 349
influence in JTG, 370
target priorities of, 201, 212, 349
target recommendations for Arnold, 330–33, 335, 421
target study of Japanese industry, 365–66
use of air intelligence by, 6–7
Compton, Arthur H., 386
Computers, flak, 328
Conant, James B., 380
Condor Legion, 35

Coningham, Arthur, 163–64
Cooper, Merian C., 278, 300, 313, 352, 419
Craig, Malin, 37
Crash analysis
difficulty of, in China, 314
Crash intelligence, 122, 124
CROSSBOW, 220, 222
and reorganization of Allied intelligence, 222–23
Cryptanalysis
decipherments of Enigma messages, 60–61
success of West in, 58
Czechoslovakia, 38

Daily Intelligence Summary, 162
Damage assessment
destruction of German aircraft factories, 202, 207
European experience applied to Japan, 369
by R.E.8, 138–40
ULTRA and, 75–76
Dargue, H. A., 26
Davidson, Howard C., 361–62
Dayton, Lewis, A., 130
Dennison, D. M., 380
Denny, J. H., 381
Dilly Project, 84
Direction finding (DF), 57–58
Director of Naval Intelligence, 359
Divisions (numbered)
1st Cavalry, 278–79
9th Bombardment, 70
77th, 289
D'Olier, Franklin, 371
Donovan, William J., 310, 350, 388, 395
Doolittle, James H., 69, 72, 161, 163–65, 195
airfield raids, 168
bombing tactics of, 409
lessons of Mediterranean theater learned by, 406–7, 414
need for photoreconnaissance, 163
persuades Eisenhower to bomb petroleum industry, 410
replaces Eaker, Eighth Air Force, 205
Douglass, Kingman, 194
Douglass, Robert W., Jr., 326
Douhet, Giulio, 37
Dugway Proving Ground, Utah, 339

487

E Group, CBI, 311
Eaker, Ira C., 91, 414
    aircraft factory targets, 201
    antisubmarine plans, 142
    asserts success of unescorted B–17 bombing missions, 404–5
    attacks on German aircraft factories, 201–2
    availability of intelligence, on, 120
    bombing program, 156
    British model for intelligence, 394
    commands MAAF, 178, 205
    conclusions on interdiction, 188
    damage assessment by, 139–40
    directed by Arnold to reduce German air power, 354
    establishes intelligence to complement British agencies, 132
    establishes photointerpretation facility at Mount Farm, 84
    Harrisburg graduates evaluation by, 131
    on intelligence deficit at war's start, 401
    intelligence requirements of, 112
    perceives weakness of GAF, 146–47
    recommends independence for AAF intelligence, 377–79
    size of bomber force available to, 409
    strategic air plan against Germany, 190–91
    target choices, 141
    V-weapons and, 220
Eaker Plan, 74, 172, 190–91, 349, 370
Earhart, Amelia, 52–53
Earle, Edward Mead, 152
Eastern Air Command (EAC), 300, 308–9, 312
Echols, O. P., 125
Economic analysis agencies, 93
Eglin Army Airfield, Florida, 221, 340
Ehrhart, Robert C., 66
Eichelberger, Robert, 283
Eighth Air Force, 67, 74, 76, 349
    A–2 responsibilities, 134–35
    A–5, 136–37
    air campaign against Germany by, 111–12
    attacks V-weapon targets, 222
    bombing German rail system, 214, 226
    briefing chart, 197
    Eaker Plan and, 191
    early intelligence operations of, 140–46
    flaws in bombing doctrine ignored by, 404–5
    mission of, 140
    number of bombers available to, 1943–44, 409
    organizing intelligence in, 132–40
    photographic interpretation capability, 85
    photointelligence, development of, 6
    primary objectives against GAF and aircraft industries, 194, 201
    relation to COA, 153–54
    reliance on British intelligence by, 120–21
    restricted target choices of, 407
    supports Twelfth, 141
    and ULTRA, 9
    use of incendiary weapons in Germany, 344
    use of RAF air intelligence by, 5, 403
    WIDE WING, 134
    Y intelligence in, 95, 98
Einstein, Albert, 380
Eisenhower, Dwight D., 37
    focus on transportation networks, 172
    importance of photoreconnaissance, on, 163
    states mission of Eighth Air Force, 140
    strategic air operations to weaken German industrial base, 237
    submarines as targets, on, 142
    targets German transportation network, 212–14
Eizo, Hori, 296
Electronic warfare capabilities, AAF and Navy, 334
Eleven Nation Military Tribunal, 52–53
Eleventh Air Force, Alaska, 119
Embick, Stanley, 37
Employment of the Air Forces of the Army, TR 440–15, 24–25, 37
Engines
    48-cylinder (German), 374
    Wright–3350, 340
Enigma, 60–62, 145. *See also* ULTRA
Ent, Uzal G., 383
Escape and evasion training, 259
    in CBI Theater, 310–11
Eubank, Eugene L., 251
Ewell, R. N., 365
Ezaki Yoshio, 278–79

Fabian, Rudolph J., 250, 253
Fairchild, Muir S., 12, 123
    air target selection, 152, 365

Index

need for technical intelligence, on, 122
Farrell, Thomas, F., 380
Fechet, James, 36
Federal Bureau of Investigation, 102
   cryptanalytical projects of, 4
Fellers, James, 79
Ferebee, Thomas, 346–47
Fermi, Enrico, 386
Ferret aircraft, 175, 335
Fifteenth Air Force, 70, 76, 79–80, 181, 349
   bombing German rail system, 214
   bombing of oil plants, 210
   heavy bomber operations, 182
   in Mediterranean theater, 178–79
   missions against German communication lines, 172
   photoreconnaissance and interpretation capability, 89
   strategic role of, 190
   targeting strategy, Mediterranean theater, 183
Fifth Air Force, 316, 325
   Admiralties, fight for, 279
   Advanced Echelon (ADVON), 258
   air intelligence used by, 5
   campaign to destroy Japanese alcohol and butanol production, 358
   crash intelligence by, 122
   day-to-day operational and tactical intelligence by, 415
   directorate of intelligence, organization chart, 262
   innovative use of land-based air power by, 112
   intelligence, 257–58
   intelligence methods, resources of, 261
   intelligence section of, 257–58
   Japanese intelligence on, 295
   seeks Harrisburg graduates, 130
Fifth Army, 181
   use of annotated photographs to support, 83
   use of intercept information by, 361–62
Firebombing, 338–44
First Army, 233
First Tactical Air Force, 78
First Tactical Air Force (Prov.), 232
Fisher, William P., 380
Fitch, Aubrey, 274
Flak, 84
Flak maps, 136
Flakintel, 327–28

Fleet Radio Unit, China, 317
Formosa
   formal assault plans of Allies, 284
   lack of intelligence concerning, 249–50
Fort Belvoir, Virginia, 126
Fort McKinley (near Manila), 250
Foulois, Benjamin D., 23
Fourteenth Air Force, 259, 297–98, 367
   campaign to destroy railroads, 322–23
   role in China, 112
   supply problems of, 315, 323
   ULTRA access, 323
   war in China, 312–24
Fourth Air Force, 363
France
   Vichy forces' control of North Africa, 158
Franco, Francisco, 35
Frankland, Noble, 156
French Air Force, 15, 158, 397
Friedman, William F., 63–64, 94
Fuller, H. H., 35
Fuque, Stephen D., 36

Galland, Adolph, 244
Garcia, James D., 334
Gates, Byron E., 26
   bombardment advisory committee, 152
Geerlings, Gerald K., 135
Geheimschreiber (Fish), 61, 76
General Electric, 31
General Motors, 31
George, Harold L., 43, 149
German Air Force (GAF), 33–34
   air campaign countering, 146–49
   Allied underestimates of strength of, 146–49, 203–5, 235, 408
   assessments of preparedness of, 35, 38
   in Battle of Britain, 399, 410
   communications security in, 77
   dawn attack against Allied air bases, 235–36
   domination of by Allies, 229–30
   effectiveness in Tunisia, 160
   fighter strength, production, late 1943, 192
   fighting value estimates, pre-OVERLORD, 228
   in Italy, 177–78
   losses, spring 1944, 207–8
   rebuilding of, 33–34
   reduction of, 1943–45, 172–73
   replacement rates, late 1943, 204

restricts fuel use, 239–40
strength estimates, March 1943, 174
strength for OVERLORD, 228–29
ULTRA information on, 158, 160
ULTRA-provided information on, 77, 78
German Air Ministry
 information on Japan held by, 372
German Ministry of Aircraft Production, 204
German rail system, 214, 225
German weapons
 V–1 flying bomb, 83, 84, 93, 213, 216, 218–21, 223
 V–2 rocket, 83, 91, 93, 213, 216, 218–21, 223
Germany
 aircraft industry, 80, 91–93, 176–77, 408–9
 aircraft industry and production, 194–95, 197, 201, 240–41
 atomic energy development in, 373
 careless signals discipline of, 406
 commanders' speculations on sources of Allied information, 165–66
 confidence in and use of Enigma, 60
 information on, in World War I, 15–16
 intelligence by, 59
 introduction of jet aircraft 172–73
 oil industry, 172
 postwar studies of intelligence in, 371–80
 radar network and flak defenses, 175
 transportation system, 141, 172
Ghormley, Robert L., 47
GHQ Air Force, 23–24
GHQ Southwest Pacific Area
 G–2, MIS–X, 259–60
Gideon, Francis C., 66, 276
Gilbert Islands, 326
Goddard, Robert, 81
Goering, Herman, 33, 239–40
Government Code and Cypher School, Bletchley Park (BP), 59, 61, 65, 72–73, 78
Graham, Phil, 66, 358
Great Britain
 air defense systems, pre-WWII, 32–33
 assistance to American intelligence, 394, 399, 402–3
 claims to German secrets, 373
 control over Enigma-generated intelligence, 62–64, 70
 dominance in MAAF intelligence, 179–80
 dominance of SIGINT, 94–95
 fear of aerial bombing, 38
 friction with Americans, in India and Burma, 307–8
 intelligence in CBI, 300, 304–5
 photoreconnaissance experience, 81
 Secret Intelligence Service, 92
Grew, Joseph C., 384
Griffiss, Townsend, 36
Groups (numbered)
 11 (RAF), 98
 3d Photo Reconnaissance, 181
 5th Bombardment, 256
 7th Bomb Group, 305
 7th Photo Reconnaissance, 85, 89
 10th Reconnaissance, 83–84
 11th Bombardment, 256
 12th Army, 68, 232, 234
 15th Photo, 181
 21st Army, 231
 67th Tactical Reconnaissance (TRG), 233
 71st Reconnaissance Group, 84
 91st Bomb, 139
 97th Bomb, 162
 303d Bomb, 139
 305th Bomb, 139
 375th Troop Carrier, 268
 380th Bomb, 268, 294
 509th Composite, 346, 380, 382–83
Groves, Leslie R., 380, 383, 385
Guadalcanal, 247, 269
 Navy intercept station on, 270
Gunn, Paul I. 265

Hale, Willis H., 325–27
Halsey, William F., 256, 272
 assaults Bougainville, 274
 recommends Leyte landing, 285
 strikes Luzon, 287
Hamilton, Fowler, 152–53
Hamilton Field, 363
Hansell, Haywood S., Jr., 3, 25, 31, 41, 49, 150, 155, 254, 329, 331–33, 336, 338, 365–67, 419–21
 access to RAF intelligence by, 47–49
 air estimate, Europe, 42
 Eaker Plan and, 191
 expanded air attache, 43
 photoreconnaissance, on, 80
Harbold, Norris B., 346
Harmon, Millard F., 256–58, 269, 327

Index

Harris, Arthur T., 412
Harrisburg Academy, 127
Harrisburg Intelligence School, 81, 85
Heligoland Bight, 403
Hewitt, Joseph E., 252, 257–58
Hickam, Horace, 18
Hindmarsh, Albert E., 365
Hiroshima, Japan
  nuclear bombing of, 346, 387–88
Hitler, Adolf, 33, 38
Hodges, James P., 40, 351–52, 363–64, 390
Holland, Harvey N., 128
Hollandia, 279–83, 295
Hoover, John H., 326
Hopkins, Harry, 103
HQ Eighth Air Force
  ULTRA clearance, 66
HQ Mediterranean Allied Tactical Air Force
  photoreconnaissance and interpretation capability, 89
HQ Ninth Air Force
  ULTRA clearance, 66
Hubler, Martin, 300, 313
Hughes, Richard, 69, 134, 136–37, 150, 191, 195, 201, 203, 220
Hull, Harris B., 96, 131, 132, 143–44, 179–80
  authors AWPD–42, 150
Human intelligence (HUMINT)
  agents in Burma, 310
  coast-watchers, 261
  German aircraft replacement rates, on, 204
  importance in CBI Theater, 417
  jet aircraft, on, 244
  Mediterranean theater, in, 181
  target locations and types, Pacific, 302
  V-weapon campaign, on, 216
Humphreys, R. H., 164–65, 174, 176

Iba Air Field, 106
Imperial Defense College, 37
Incendiary bombing against Japan, 338–44
Index Guide for Procurement of Military Intelligence, 28, 39
India
  cryptanalysis center in, 303
  ULTRA representative stationed in, 302–3
India Air Task Force, 87

Inglis, F. F., 357
Intelligence Center, Pacific Ocean Area (ICPOA), 324
Interdiction
  campaign against Italian transportation network, 183–84, 186–89
  North Africa, 166–67
  reliance on photographic intelligence, 190
Interim Committee, 383
Interservice Topographical Section (U.K.), 142
Italy
  German withdrawals from, 171–72
  invasion of, 177–78
  limited impact of air intelligence and air operations, 190
  photoreconnaissance over, 163

Japan
  Allied view of air intelligence of, 292–96
  American attitudes toward, 387, 397, 413
  attitudes and assumptions as limiting use of intelligence, 413–14
  B–29 operations against, 329–47
  coke production, 331, 365–66
  difficulties moving fuel, troops, 284
  encryption systems, 100–101
  estimates of U.S. aircraft types vs. actual strength, 294
  invades China, 29
  JN–25 naval code, 104
  most valuable intelligence accomplishments of, 293
  naval base building by, 52–53
  offensive of 1944, 318–20
  prewar intelligence on, 20–21, 29–30
  primary responsibility for intelligence of, 350
  radar production and employment, 272
  rapid expansion, 1942, 247–49
  rearmament, 53
  resistance to surrender, 386–88
  secrecy surrounding development, 396
  suicide squadrons of, 287
  surprise attacks by, 400
  target study of, 364
  use of small barges with fighter cover, 268–69
  weakness of prewar air intelligence on, 51–52

491

weather as factor in attacks on, 338
weather problems encountered, 344, 346–47
Japanese Air Force
　information available in Germany, 372
Japanese Army
　discounts value of intelligence analyses, 292
　underestimates of strength of, 29–31
Japanese Army Air Force
　gasoline storage capacity in Philippines, 284
Japanese Combined Fleet, 247
Japanese Naval Air Force
　defenses of oil refineries, 285
　kamikaze of, 287, 290
　T Attack Force, 287–88, 291
Japanese Navy
　gasoline storage by, 284
Japanese Order of Battle Bulletins, 105–6
Jet aircraft, 241, 243–46
JICPOA Air Estimates Group, 328
Jockey Committee, 194–95, 241, 246
Joffre, J. J., 15
Johnson, Virgil O., 361
Joint Army-Navy Board, 40, 116
Joint Army-Navy Planning Committee, 116
Joint Chiefs of Staff
　Ad Hoc Committee, 368
　ambiguous position of Arnold and AAF, 389
　chooses COA target list for B–29, 333
　creates Joint Target Group (JTG), 9, 322
Joint Target Analysis Group, 368–69
Joint Intelligence Board, 113
Joint Intelligence Center, Pacific Ocean Areas (JICPOA), 324–25
Joint Intelligence Collection Agency (JICA), 124, 303
Joint Intelligence Committee (JIC), 116
Joint Oil Targets Committee, 239, 241
Joint Photo Reconnaissance Committee, 89–90
Joint Strategic Committee, 116
Joint Target Group, 369–70, 376–77, 380, 387
Joint War Plans Committee, 366
Jones, Bryon Q., 36–37
Jones, R. V., 222

Kamikaze, 287, 290

Kármán, Theodore von, 7, 373
Kasserine Pass, 166
Kelly, Wilkes D., 308
Kendall, Douglas, 88
Kenney, George C., 9, 108, 112
　battle for Leyte, 285–88
　becomes air commander, Southwest Pacific, 253–54, 256
　bombs Rabaul airfields, 254, 265, 269, 415
　diary noting information sources, 261, 263
　interprets intelligence for major victory at Bismarck Sea, 265–68
　Mindoro landing, 289, 291
　presses for assignment of B–29, 332
　requests B–29s for oil production attacks, 284–85
　skillful use of intelligence by, 277, 291, 414–16
　takes Hollandia, 279–83
Kesselring, Albrecht, 165, 167
Kimmel, Husband, 114–15
Kindleberger, Charles, 68, 231, 233
King, Ernest J., 316, 365
Kinkaid, Thomas D., 278
Kingston, Charles T., 344
Koenig, Egmont F., 127–28
Koenig, Theodore, 33–34
Korea
　target study of, 364
Kroner, Hayes A., 113
Krueger, Walter, 287
Kuter, Laurence S., 48, 91, 329–30, 366

Lamont, Thomas W., 152
Lanphier, Thomas G., 153
Launch sites, V-weapons, 217–22
Lawrence, Ernest O., 386
Layton, Edwin T., 270
Leach, W. Barton, 153
League of Nations, 52
Leahy, William D., 103, 385
Lee, Raymond E., 32, 47
Lee, Robert M., 78, 236
Leigh-Mallory, Trafford L. 15, 212–13
LeMay, Curtis E., 320, 335, 336
　509th Composite and, 382–83
　abandons precision bombing, 418
　becomes Chief of Staff, Twentieth Air Force, 346
　comments on Japanese weather, 386
　estimates of Japanese weakness, 375

Index

incendiary bombing by, 338–42
reflects opinion of A–2 problems in Pacific war, 388
Lend-Lease, 391
Leyte, battle for, 285–88, 291
Life magazine, 267
Lindbergh, Charles A., 1, 34–35, 395–96, 418
Lindsay, Richard C., 379
Lingayen, 289–90
Lloyd, Hugh P., 178
Los Negros, 277–79
Lovett, Robert A., 50, 377
  concerns for air intelligence without British assistance, 377–79
Lowe, James T., 41
Lowry Field, Colorado, 81
Ludendorff, Erich, 15
Luftwaffe. See German Air Force
Luzon invasion, 289–90

MacArthur, Douglas, 22
  Army position on air warfare and, 24
  attack on Philippines, 285
  command of, 249
  controls New Guinea, 283
  dismissal of SIGINT from Washington, 109
  infighting with Nimitz, 290
  intercept intelligence priorities, 107–8
  Pearl Harbor attack and, 251
  provision of intelligence to, 416
  seizure of Admiralties, 278–79
MAGIC, 51
  Berlin as center for, 208
  failure to interpret regarding Pearl Harbor, 113
  handling by Special Sources Section, Collection Branch, 363
  Japanese declining power information, 288
  Japanese plans, 1943, 302
  significance in Pacific theater, 99–105
MAGIC Diplomatic Summaries, 8, 103–5, 304, 352, 354, 364
Malaya, 292
Malta Air Force, 160
Manchuria
  target study of, 364
Manhattan Project, 6, 380
Manus Island, 278–79
Mapping, 134–35
  of AA gun positions, Japan, 335
  CBI theater, 305, 335
  Far East targets, 367
  flak maps, 136
  landfall identification maps, 135–36
  perspective target maps, 135
March, Peyton C., 13
Mareth Line, 168
Marine Corps, 269
  12th Air Group Corsairs, 289
  combat intelligence at Guadalcanal, 256
Marshall, George C., 9, 150, 202, 323
  and atomic bomb, 380
  policy regarding Japanese ULTRA, 109
  reluctance to invade Japan, 384
  role in development of intelligence, 398
  SSOs, on, 66
  use of air power, and, 38
  withholds ULTRA access from Arnold, 353
Martin, Grinnell, 391
Mason, Edward S., 145, 152
Massachusetts Institute of Technology, 7
Materials
  laminated methyl methacrylate, 124
MATTERHORN, 331–32, 366
Maxwell Field, Alabama, 12
McCormack, Alfred, 64, 66, 94
  establishes B Section, 105
  Special Branch and, 108
McDonald, George C., 82, 93, 148
  A–2/G–2 relations and, 359
  air intelligence in North Africa, 161
  comments on Sicily, 175–76
  criticizes elaborate folders from Washington, 121
  establishes Mediterranean Photo Interpretation Centre, 180
  frustrations with British intelligence, 222
  priority targets identified by, 206, 243, 245
  sharing of intelligence with RAF, 374
  view of Italian interdiction campaign, 183–84, 188
  view on strength of GAF, 203–5, 231
McNair, Leslie J., 351
McNarney, Joseph T., 18, 42, 46–47
Medhurst, C.E.H., 132
Mediterranean Air Command (MAC), 160
Mediterranean Allied Air Command, 70
Mediterranean Allied Air Forces (MAAF), 178–80
Mediterranean Allied Coastal Air Force

493

(MACAF), 178
Mediterranean Allied Photographic Reconnaissance Wing (MAPRW), 87
Mediterranean Allied Strategic Air Force (MASAF), 178
Mediterranean Allied Tactical Air Force (MATAF), 178, 180–81
Mediterranean Theater, 173–90
Merritt, L. G., 326
Milch, Erhard, 147
Miles, Milton E., 316–18, 321, 323
Miles, Sherman, 28, 114–15
  assessment of Japan's likelihood for attack, 53
  delineation of responsibility for intelligence, 42, 44–45
  technical evaluation, on, 42
Miley, A. J., 359
Miller, William A., 294
Milling, Thomas D., 14
Mining
  by Fourteenth Air Force, 317, 323
Ministry of Economic Warfare (MEW), U.K., 136–38, 155, 209, 220
Mitchell, William (Billy), 18–19, 19
Modeling of targets, 86
Montbatten, Louis, 358
Montgomery, Bernard, 236
Morale
  German, 151
  relation to overestimates of damage claims, 148
Morse, Chandler, 145
Moss, Malcolm W., 41–42, 120, 152–53, 366–67
Munich agreement, 38
Mussolini, Benito, 177, 395

Nagasaki, Japan, 347
Nakajima Aircraft Company, 336, 338
National Defense Research Committee, 365, 380
Naval Group China, 321
Naval Intelligence (OP–20–G), 8
Naval Research Laboratory, Washington, D.C., 175, 271
Navy and National Advisory Committee for Aeronautics, 374
Navy Department
  cryptanalysis by, 21
Nelson, Carl G., 313
NEPTUNE, 224, 228–30, 233
Neumann, John von, 380

New Guinea
  importance of Japanese supply lines to, 265, 269, 416
Nimitz, Chester W., 10, 107
  attack on Yamamoto, 270–71
  command of, 249
  creates TF 59, 326
  fears Japanese air force reaction to Hollandia invasion, 280–81
  infighting with MacArthur, 290
  intelligence available to, 325
Ninth Air Force, 67–68, 70, 78–80, 167, 349
  bombing German rail system, 214, 225–26
  chief American air contributor to OVERLORD, 226
  colocated air and ground equivalent headquarters, 232
  plans for NEPTUNE, 228
  relation to 3d Radio Squadron, 362
Noonan, Fred, 52
Norcross, Carl H., 128–29
Norden bombsight, 366–67
Norstad, Lauris, 184, 187, 341–42, 344, 380
  champions atomic bomb, 387
North Africa
  Operation TORCH, 157–69
  Y intelligence and tactical air operations in, 99
Northwest African Air Forces (NAAF), 82
  A–2 functions, 162
  changes handling of air intelligence in North Africa, 161
  dissemination of information, 162–63
Northwest African Coastal Air Force (NACAF), 160–61
Northwest African Photographic Reconnaissance Wing (NAPRW), 87, 161–62
Northwest African Strategic Air Force (NASAF), 160
  antishipping campaign, in, 166–67
  launches Operation FLAX, 168–69
Northwest African Tactical Air Force (NATAF), 160, 166–68
Nuclear weapons, 346
  AAF intelligence and atomic bomb, 380–88
  Soviet push for, 392

O'Connor, Morgan B., 313

Index

O'Connor, William J., 88
Office of the Assistant Chief of Air Staff, Intelligence (AC/AS, Intelligence)
   A–2 creation, responsibilities, 43, 116–25
   Air Intelligence Service, 116
   duplication of work with G–2, 119
   operational intelligence work of, 119–21
   relations with G–2, 45–46
   technical intelligence, 121–25
   training responsibilities, 129
   see also A–2
Office of Naval Intelligence (ONI) prewar, 102
Office of Scientific Research and Development (OSRD), 380
Office of Strategic Services (OSS), 303
   Detachment 101, 310–11
   Enemy Objectives Unit (EOU), 6, 137–38, 201
   EOU report on feasibility of target systems attack, 209
Officer Candidate School (OCS), 127–28
Ofstie, Ralph A., 29–30
Olive, J. F., Jr., 41
Oliver, Robert C., 39, 40
Operation ARGUMENT, 74, 76–77, 203, 205–8
   USSTAF intelligence assessment of, 206–7
Operation AVALANCHE, 177
Operation BODYLINE, 220, 222
Operation BOLERO, 182
Operation DIADEM, 189
Operation DRAGOON, 232
Operation FLAX, 168–69
Operation FRANTIC, 178
Operation GALVANIC, 326
Operation HUSKY, 168, 173
   coordination of intelligence for, 174–75
Operation OLYMPIC, 417
Operation OVERLORD, 78, 89, 172–73, 212–13, 412
   information requirements, ground and logistical systems, 224
Operation POINTBLANK, 194–95, 224, 407–8
Operation STRANGLE, 181, 184–89
Operation TORCH, 81, 86, 98, 141, 157–69
   air support for ground operations, 173
   impact on American air operations, 405
Oppenheimer, J. Robert, 386

Oshima Hiroshi, 208
Otopeni, Italy, 197
Owens, Ray L., 272–73

Pacific Ocean Area (POA), 107
   Fleet Radio Unit, Pacific (FRUPac), 107
Pacific theater
   evolution of photointelligence in, 87
Partridge, Earle E., 187–88
Patrick, Mason M., 18, 19
Patton, George, 69
Pearl Harbor, 3, 4, 8
   air intelligence implications of, 113–15
   causes for disaster, 400–401, 413–14
   failure of intelligence, as, 52–55
   rise in Japanese activity preceding, 250–51
Penny, William G., 380
Perera, Guido, 91, 152–53, 333, 366
Pershing, John J. 13, 15
Petroleum
   German, 209–12, 237–40, 410–11
   Japanese, 284–85, 334
Philippine Islands, 3, 4, 53, 247–48
   consolidation of American power in, 290
   formal assault plans of Allies, 284
   projected use of air power against, 1930s, 249
   recovery of downed and captured men in, 259
Phillips, James F., 29
Phoenix, 278
Photointelligence, 80–94
   British photointerpretation school at Karachi, 305
   German rail system, on, 226
   mission categories, 82–84
   photointerpretation, phases of, 83–85
   V-weapons, on, 216, 223
Photoreconnaissance
   by British, 5
   of Japan, 336
   OVERLORD demands for, 233–34
   role for Twelfth Air Force/MATAF, 189
   value in Mediterranean theater, 180
Piskounov, S. A., 391
Ploesti, Romania
   German oil refineries in, 191–92, 206, 210
Polifka, Karl L., 180
Port Moresby–Milne Bay, 263

495

Portal, Charles, 176, 353–54, 404
Post-Hostilities Intelligence Requirements Survey of the German Air Force, 372
Potsdam Conference, 384
Powell, Lewis, F., Jr., 69, 401
 photoreconnaissance, on, 80
 ULTRA information, on, 74–75, 77
Pratt, W. V., 22
Prince of Wales, 248
Princeton University, 152
Prisoners of war (POW)
 Japanese interrogations of, 294–96, 387
Prudential Insurance Company, 371
PURPLE (code) machine, 208, 250, 253

Quesada, Elwood R., 41, 69, 71, 351, 363–64, 375, 377–78, 390

Rabaul, Simpson Bay
 attacks on, 254, 265, 269, 273–74, 415
 importance to Japan, 272, 293
RABID intelligence, 108
Radar
 in B–29, 334
 intercept in Pacific war, 271
 limitations of, 367, 386
 sea-search, 317
 use by Japan, 335
Radar countermeasures (RCM) analyses, 328, 334
RAF. *See* Royal Air Force
Ramsey, DeWitt C., 46
Reed, Gerald E., 313
Repulse, 248
Research and Analysis Branch, OSS, 137
 interdiction report, Italy, 189
Research and Experiment (R.E.) Department (R.E.8), 138–39
Reserves, Air Corps
 in intelligence, 41
Richardson, A. T., 308
Rommel, Erwin, 167
 speculations on sources of Allied information, 165–66
Rood, Leslie L., 78
Roosevelt, Eliot, 87, 90–91
Roosevelt, Franklin D., 41, 50, 82, 395, 398
 ARCADIA conference, 111
 commissions USSBS, 371
 focus on German rather than Japanese threat, 400–401
 meets with and responds to Kenney, 267–68
 orders assault into North Africa, 157
 orders increased aircraft production, 38
 requests production requirements, 48
Root, Elihu, Jr., 152–53
Rostow, Walter, 213
Royal Air Force (RAF)
 Central Interpretation Unit (CIU), Medmenham, 5, 85–86, 88
 combined intelligence with, 4
 Eaker Plan and, 191
 Eighth Air Force personnel assigned to, 133, 403
 Intelligence School, 132
 photointerpretation training, 126–27
 quality of prewar information, 47, 50–51
 representation on air intelligence committee, 357
 strategic air operations and, 37
 Y-Service, 95, 133, 403
 Y-Service collection responsibility in India-Burma, 311
Royal Air Force Bengal Command, 305, 308
Royal Air Force Bomber Command
 attacks Peenemunde, 216
 attacks V-weapon sites, 222
 mapping needs of, 135
 urban area attacks by, 339
Royal Australian Air Force (RAAF)
 crash intelligence, 122
Royal Naval Intelligence Division (NID), 139
Runnalls, J.F.B., 302
Russian Far East Fleet, 400

Samford, John A., 368–69, 381
Saville, Gordon P., 40
Scanlon, Martin, 32, 43–46
Schneider, Max F., 48
Schuirman, R. E., 357
Schweinfurt, Germany, 201–3, 400, 408–9, 421–22
Schweppenburg, Geyer von, 410
Scientific Advisory Group, 373
Seventh Air Force, 324–28, 345
Sharp, A. C., 150
Sherman, L. C., 256–57
Sherr, Joe R., 250–51
Shigemitsu Namoru, 288
Shipbuilding
 reduction of Japanese, 331

Index

Shipping
  antisubmarine campaign effect on losses, 1943, 145
  campaign against Axis, 166–67
  Japanese, 271–72, 364
  stoppage of Japanese, 345–46
  ULTRA information on Axis, 164–67
Short, Walter C., 114
Sicily
  Allied attacks on, 168–69
  use of information for sorties against roads and railways, 174
  see also Operation HUSKY
Signal Intelligence Service, U.S. Army, 180
Signal Security Agency, 361
Signals intelligence (SIGINT), 57–58, 62
  American units in Mediterranean, 180
  Far East operations, 106–9
  forces, 98
  independent service units created by American tactical air forces, 98
  low-grade signal interception and application by, 94
  responsibilities divided between War and Navy departments, 102
  role during invasion of Sicily and Italy, 176
  value against GAF, 230–31
Sino-American Cooperative Organization (SACO), 316–17
Sixth Army, 281, 283, 287, 295
SKF (Swedish firm), 153
Slessor, John C., 46
Smith, Truman, 33, 35
Smith, Wilfred J., 313
Solomon Islands, 263
  defense of, 270
Sorenson, Edgar P., 7, 117, 122–24, 129, 152, 350, 360, 365–66
Sources of information
  A–2, 134–35
  COA, 153
  coast watchers, 276
  for OVERLORD, 226
  for STRANGLE, 188, 190
  on targets, 1945, 242–43
Southwest Pacific Area (SWPA), 107, 253
Soviet Army, 178
Soviet Union, 391–92
Spaatz, Carl A., 19, 92, 379–80, 414, 421
  aerial reconnaissance and antishipping campaign, 163
  campaign mission directive July 1946, 387
  commands USASTAF, 346
  commands USSTAF, 172, 178
  competition for German secrets, 374
  difficulties evaluating damage, 239
  directive on Eighth Air Force's mission, 140
  directs VIII Bomber Command against submarines, 142
  directs attack on German oil industry, 237–40
  directs or controls Eighth, Fifteenth, Ninth, 205
  establishes HQ NAAF, 161
  intelligence requirements of, 112
  jet production targeting, 244–45
  lessons of Mediterranean theater learned by, 406–7
  oil campaign, on, 213
  opposition to antisubmarine policy, 145
  persuades Eisenhower to bomb petroleum industry, 410
  photoreconnaissance and, 83, 89
  prewar air estimate by, 47
  readiness of air intelligence, on, 40
  strategic air forces' priorities, 1944, 205
  target priorities of, 155
  transportation system bombing, 412
  ULTRA access, 66
Spanish Civil War, 35–36
Special Intelligence Bulletin, 108
Special Operations Executive, British
  in CBI, 310
Special security officers (SSOs), 65–73
  covers of, 67
  recordkeeping by, 68
  role in air force organizations, 358
Speer, Albert, 147, 407–8, 410
Squadrons (numbered)
  1st Radio (Mobile), 361–62
  3d Radio, 362
  3d Radio Detachment 3 (Mobile), 98, 230
  5th Radio (Mobile), 311–12
  6th Radio Squadron, 363
  16th Reconnaissance, 180
  17th Reconnaissance, 87
  436th Bomb Squadron, 305
Stalin, Joseph, 171
Standard Oil, 31
Stark, Harold R., 53
Stearns, J. C., 380, 382

Stilwell, Joseph W., 298, 304, 320–21, 414, 417–18
Stimson, Henry L., 21, 50, 59, 64, 395
  and atomic bomb, 380, 383–86
  code breaking funding, 101
  forms Special Branch, 102
Stone, E. E., 8
Strategic Air Command
  nucleus of, 9
Strategic air attack concept, ACTS, 26–28
Stratemeyer, George E., 119, 123, 298, 308, 311–12, 315
Strong, George V., 40–42, 357
Strong, Kenneth, 37
Submarines, German
  attack policy of U.S., and outcomes, 142–46
  efficacy of Allied attacks on Japanese shipping, 284
  use against Japanese ships, 318
Sutherland, John R., 307
Sutherland, Richard K., 250, 256, 267, 415
Switzer, Byron R., 124

Tactical Air Intelligence Centre (TAIC), 312
Target analysis, Far East, 64–71
Target development and analysis of specific target data
  differences in American/British requirements, 136
Target selection
  ULTRA and, 74–75, 78
Taylor, Richard, 313
Taylor, Telford, 35, 64–66, 94, 401
Technical Air Intelligence Centre, New Delhi, 308
Technical intelligence
  early 1940s, 121–25
Tedder, Arthur, 160, 213, 412–13
Tenth Air Force, 298, 300–301
  China Air Task Force (CATF), 297–98, 301, 304
  combined into EAC, 308
  India Air Task Force (IATF), 297–98, 305
  intelligence available to, 305–6
  role against Japan, 112
Teramoto Kunachi, 281
Third Army, 66
Thirteenth Air Force
  activated in the Solomons, 256

  intelligence, 256–57
  reinforcements for, 268
  under navy control, 269
Thirteenth Air Task Force
  based in Admiralties, 279
  bombardment of Woleai, 282
Thorsheimer, 167
Tibbetts, Paul W., 345–46, 382
Timberlake, Patrick W., 30
Tizard, Henry, 62
Tizard Mission, 62
Togo Heihachiro, 400
Tokyo, Japan
  raids on, 342–43
Traffic analysis (TA), 58
Training
  air technical intelligence (ATI) course, 122
  Eighth Air Force personnel, in U.K., 132–33
  evolution of Air Intelligence School, 126–32
Transportation systems
  Allied successes against German, 411
  Burmese, 307
  German railways, 212–13, 241, 411–12
  Italian railways, 181–82, 187–88
Truk Atoll, 275
Truman, Harry S., 380, 383, 385
Tsuji Masanobu, 292
Tsunoda Koshiro, 287
Tunisia
  Allied failure to capture, 160
Twaddle, Harry L., 126
Twelfth Air Force, 78, 141, 349
  absorbed into NAAF, 161
  becomes tactical under MATAF, 178
  intelligence on Italian railways, 181–82, 187–88
  relationship with MATAF intelligence, 181
Twentieth Air Force, 333
  509th Composite and, 383
  bombing restricted before atomic attacks, 381–82
Twining, Nathan, 112, 178, 254, 256–57, 268
  becomes COMAIRSOLS, 272

ULTRA, 59–74
  British withhold information of, 3–4, 8
  Chennault's access to, 323
  civilian contributions to intelligence,

Index

398
clues of German offensive, 235–36
comprehensiveness on German army units, 182
contribution to successful campaign against oil industry, 411
crucial role in air war, North Africa, 163–69
discloses Japan's regional defense planning, 284
handled under air intelligence working agreement, 358
identifies *kamikaze*, 287
importance in American strategic air operations, 74–77
importance in last years of WWII, 173
indicates GAF losses, 208
information on German oil shortages, 239–40
information regarding GAF, 230
input for tactical air command, 79
intelligence-sharing agreement and, 350
Kenney's use of, 296
leads to deception around New Guinea coast, 281
limited access of A–2 to, 363
limited American clearance, in Mediterranean theater, 180, 181
limited role in damage assessment, 203, 208
locations of fuel and ammunition dumps, 234
policy level of, 189
reasons for success of, 406
relationship to Allied tactical air operations, 78–80
reliability on unit strength, 204
reveals Japanese plans to defend Kyushu, 384
reveals Japan's study of Allied air operations, 293
reveals location of panzer headquarters, 234
role of, 394
role in battle for Leyte, 288
role in Mediterranean theater, 182–83, 406
separation of Anglo-American intelligence regarding, 134
significant information on German movements, 410
strategic implications of information, 242

underutilization by air intelligence, 412–13
use by Australia, 108
use in Operation HUSKY, 174–75
use in Operation TORCH, 158
use in Pacific and CBI, 99–105
use against Japanese shipping, 317
usefulness in damage assessment, 139
value against GAF, 147
United Kingdom
  negative response to COA, 153
United States
  postwar strategic vulnerability of, 391–92
United States Army
  2d Signal Service Company, 107, 250, 252–53
  18th Photointerpretation Unit, 317
  32d Division, 263
  138th Signal Radio Intercept Company, 361
  837th Signal Service Detachment, 107
  849th SIGINT Company, 98, 180
  Air Service, 11
  interservice rivalries during WWII, 8
  Manhattan Engineer District, 380, 383
  Signal Intelligence Service, 51
United States Army Basic Field Manual, Military Intelligence, 49
United States Army Signal Corps' SIGINT Service (SIS), 101
  radio intercept at Fort Santiago, Manila, 250
United States Army Strategic Air Forces (USASTAF)
  creation of, 346
United States Board of Economic Warfare (BEW), 137–38
United States Joint Army-Navy Board, 51
United States Naval Group China, 259, 323
United States Navy
  Air Technical Section, 125
  air intelligence working agreement and, 357, 359
  breaking of Japanese codes by, 104
  claims to German secrets, 373
  crash intelligence by, 124
  defeat at Savo Island, 413
  exclusion from CB, 108
  Far East target identification work by, 368–69
  intelligence, 51

499

intelligence failures, Pearl Harbor, 113–15
intelligence operations in Manila, 247
Japanese code breaking, 59
Joint Intelligence Center, Pacific Ocean Area, relations with Army and mining by, 345
Office of Naval Intelligence (ONI), 30
presence in China, 312
quality of photography, 370–71
signal intelligence units (CAST and BELCONNEN), 250, 253
stages Yamamoto mission, 8
strategic offensive debates with, 22
withholding of SIGINT from air force, 257
United States Pacific Fleet, 51
United States Strategic Air Forces, Europe (USSTAF)
creation of, 172
information to assist targeting, 1945, 241–43
oil plan of, 212–13
United States Strategic Bombing Survey (USSBS), 371, 375–76, 387
planning for operations against GAF, 205
postwar analysis by, 90
Universities' contribution to intelligence, 402
University of Maryland, 127

Van Norden, Langdon, 67
Van Slyck, DeForest, 367–68
Vanaman, Arthur W., 34, 48
Vance, Reginald F., 252
Vandenberg, Hoyt, 69, 72, 232
Verville, Alfred, 19
Vincent, Clinton D., 319–20
Vuillemin, Joseph, 397

Walker, Kenneth, 48, 295
War Department
creates Army Air Forces Pacific Ocean Area (AAFPOA), 326–28
cryptanalysis by, 21
delineates intelligence responsibilities, 45–46
directs establishment of intelligence sections, 41
General Staff G–2, Army Intelligence, 3, 7–8
intelligence failures, Pearl Harbor, 113–15
mapping responsibilities, CBI, 305
TR 210–5, 22
Victory Program, AWPD–1, 3, 63
War plans
ACTS scenarios, 26–27
color coded, 21, 22
RAINBOW, 40, 48, 51
Washington Naval Disarmament Conference, 21
Washington Naval Treaty, 21
Wavell, Archibald P., 248, 415
Weapons
.50-caliber machine guns, 265
Weather
difficulty forecasting distant targets, 334
report interception, 97
reporting by Fifth Air Force, 261
Weaver, Walter R., 22, 123, 129
Webster, Charles, 156
Webster, Robert M., 26
Wedemeyer, Albert C., 320–21
Weekly Intelligence Report, 162
Western Desert Air Force, 168–69
Wewak airfields, 276–77, 281
Weyland, O. P., 69, 71
White, A. W., 370, 420
White, Thomas D., 30–31, 40, 43, 350–52, 398
on A–2/G–2 relationship, 360
named A–2, 357
struggle for an independent A–2, 360
Whitehead, Ennis, 258–59, 361, 415
prepares for Battle of the Bismarck Sea, 266, 416
receives regular reports of Japanese air activity, 275–76
use of intelligence with Kenney, 291
Wick, H. W., 365
Williams, C. G., 208
Williams, Jesse C., 313–14
Willoughby, Charles A., 108, 253, 384
complains of navy, 257
estimates troops on Los Negros, 278
Willoughby Bulletin, 108
Wilson, Donald, 26
Wilson, Hugh, 38
Wilson, R. B., 380
Wilson, Woodrow, 13
Wings (numbered)
8th Photographic Reconnaissance (Prov.), 82, 85, 89–90

Index

42d, 188
68th Composite, 318, 320
313th Bombardment, 345, 383
325th Reconnaissance, 90
see also Northwest African Photographic Reconnaissance Wing
Wireless Experimental Center, 105
Wise, S. C., 87
Wolfe, Kenneth B., 331, 336
World War I
　air intelligence in, 12–17
　use of aerial photography in, 81
Wright Field, Ohio, 31, 122, 125
Wurtsmith, Paul B., 261

XII Tactical Air Force, 69
XII Air Force Photo Center, 181

Y intelligence, 94–99
Y-Service
　of AAF, 361–64
　tracking of aircraft movement by, 175
　use in North Africa, 164
Yamamoto Isoroku, 247, 270–71
Yamashita Tomoyuki, 289, 292
Yardley, Herbert O., 21

Zuckerman, Solly, 184, 187, 213

www.ingramcontent.com/pod-product-compliance
Lightning Source LLC
Chambersburg PA
CBHW080049190426
43201CB00035B/2141